# Mastering™
## Windows® XP Professional

**Mark Minasi**

**with Quentin Docter and Faithe Wempen**

SYBEX®

San Francisco   London

Associate Publisher: Joel Fugazzotto

Acquisitions Editor: Elizabeth Peterson

Developmental Editor: Elizabeth Peterson

Production Editors: Rachel Gunn, Susan Berge

Technical Editors: Jim Kelly, Toby Skandier

Copyeditors: Rebecca Rider, Linda Recktenwald

Compositor: Maureen Forys, Happenstance Type-O-Rama

Proofreaders: Nancy Riddiough, Sunah Cherwin, James Brook

Indexer: Ted Laux

Book Designer: Maureen Forys, Happenstance Type-O-Rama; Judy Fung

Cover Designer: Design Site

Cover Illustration: Jack T. Myers, Design Site

Library of Congress Card Number: 2004113395

ISBN: 0-7821-4382-2

Manufactured in the United States of America

10 9 8 7 6 5 4 3 2 1

This book is dedicated to everyone who has ever taken one of my seminars. It's probably true that I've learned more over the years from my students than from anyone else.
—Mark Minasi

To Kara, Abbie, and Lauren.
—Quentin Docter

To Margaret, for the usual reasons.
—Faithe Wempen

# Acknowledgments

As you can tell by lifting this tome, a lot of work went into creating all these pages about the workings of Windows XP Professional.

First, I'd like to thank Quentin Docter and Faithe Wempen who revised and updated every chapter of this book.

I would be remiss if I didn't also thank those at Sybex who helped get this book out on time. Thanks go to Joel Fugazzotto, associate publisher, and Elizabeth Peterson, acquisitions and developmental editor, for helping get the book on the road and providing guidance throughout the process. Thanks to our copyeditors, Rebecca Rider and Linda Recktenwald, for making sure the manuscript was beautiful. Thanks also to the technical editors, James Kelly and Toby Skandier, for keeping a technical eye on the book at all times. Thanks to Rachel Gunn and Susan Berge, production editors, for keeping the book on schedule and making sure everything was in order, and to Maureen Forys, compositor, for making the pages look so good! Last, thanks go to the graphic artist, Tony Jonick, who contributed to the wonderful illustrations enhancing this book; the proofreaders, Nancy Riddiough and Sunah Cherwin; and the indexer, Ted Laux.

—*Mike Minasi*


As always, the Sybex crew has done an incredible job of getting this book ready to go. Special thanks goes out to Faithe Wempen, Elizabeth Hurley Peterson, Susan Berge, Rachel Gunn, Jim Kelly, Linda Recktenwald, and everyone else who contributed to make this project a success.

—*Quentin Docter*


Thanks to the great editorial and production team at Sybex for another job well done, to Quentin for his camaraderie in this endeavor, and to Mark for having the confidence in my work to allow me to be part of this book.

—*Faithe Wempen*

# Contents at a Glance

# Contents

# Introduction

What you have in your hands is a soup-to-nuts, beginner-to-expert, end-user-to-administrator handbook—the all-in-one guide to using and supporting Windows XP Professional, Microsoft's latest release in the NT family of operating systems.

This book is for you if you are upgrading from a previous version of Windows or if you're coming to the Windows world from another operating system. This book is also for you if you are new to networking or if you're thinking about setting up a network at home or in your business. In addition, this book is for you if you use a corporate client-server Windows 2000 or Windows Server 2003 network at the office. In other words, if you use Windows XP Professional in any environment, including a standalone system at home, you'll find here information you can use—all the way from installing Windows XP Professional to network-troubleshooting techniques.

## What Is Covered in This Book

This book is divided into eight parts, building in a logical order from setting up your system to configuring advanced features.

### Part 1: Installation and Setup

Chapter 1 is an overview of Windows XP Professional—what's new since the last incarnation, what makes it different from other operating systems and other versions of Windows (including what makes it different from Windows 9*x*), and what its main features are. Don't be misled if it seems there's a lot of jargon in this first chapter. I figured that power users who are already familiar with other operating systems will be looking to this chapter just to get an idea of what's different in Windows XP Professional; if you're not a power user on another system, you won't miss anything if you simply skim these comparisons.

In Chapter 2, I take up the topic of *installing* Windows XP Professional, on your own as well as for other users. This chapter discusses how to install Windows XP Professional in these three ways:

- ◆ As an upgrade to a previous version of Windows

- ◆ As a new installation on a computer that already has installed an operating system that you want to keep

- ◆ As a clean installation on a computer that doesn't have an operating system installed

I'll also show you how you can reduce the amount of work needed to install the system—by means of an automatic, "unattended" installation.

Chapter 3 shows you how to get started using the newly redesigned Desktop and Start menu. It also includes information about the radically different Help system, the Help and Support Center, and how to get remote assistance help from a colleague or coworker.

Chapter 4 shows you how to customize Windows XP so that it's specifically suited to your needs. You'll learn how to use the XP Control Panel to adjust your video settings and display, customize and snaz up your desktop, set systems sounds, and adjust your keyboard and mouse. Chapter 4 also shows you how to customize the Taskbar and Start menu so that you can work more efficiently. Readers with disabilities will want to read the section on using Windows XP's accessibility features.

Chapter 5 covers how to install, run, and remove programs, including how to set up an application for multiple users. You'll learn how to use Compatibility Mode to run non-native Windows XP applications, and you'll read about which types of programs you shouldn't install on Windows XP. Terminating an unresponsive application using Task Manager is also covered, as well as exchanging data between programs.

If you need to run Windows XP Professional on a portable computer, you'll definitely want to read Chapter 6. Topics cover using external monitors and PC cards, setting hardware profiles, managing battery usage, saving dial-up profiles for multiple locations, and troubleshooting. And no discussion of portables would be complete without coverage of file synchronization.

## Part 2: Managing Applications, Files, and Folders

Chapter 7 shows you how to work with and manage your files and folders. The chapter information includes searching, compressing, encrypting, and burning CD-ROMs.

Chapter 8 is all about printers, printing, and fonts. Step-by-step instruction is provided on installing and configuring local and remote printers, sharing a local printer, and managing a print queue. Fonts are tied closely to printers, so this chapter also shows you how to install and manage fonts. You'll also learn here how to use Microsoft Fax, a cousin to the printing features.

Chapter 9 covers installing and configuring specific types of hardware, how to assign and manage hardware resources, how to disable a device, and how to update hardware drivers. You'll also learn how to set up multiple monitors to your desktop system.

## Part 3: Digital Media

Chapter 10 concerns the latest version (version 10) of Windows Media Player, which you can use to play audio and video files, listen to Internet radio stations, and so on. Windows Media Player will be new to you if you were previously a user of Windows NT Workstation or Windows 2000 Professional. There have been several versions of Windows Media Player since Windows XP was originally released, but you can download all versions for free from Microsoft, so there's no reason not to upgrade.

Chapter 11 covers digital image management and Windows Movie Maker. You'll learn how Windows integrates with scanners and digital cameras and how it provides wizards for activities such as photo printing. Windows Movie Maker is a basic, few-frills digital video editor that you can use to put together simple movies.

## Part 4: The Internet and E-mail

The chapters in Part 4 cover how to use the communications tools included with Windows XP Professional.

Chapter 12 includes instructions for installing and configuring an Internet connection (including broadband connections) and for setting up Internet Connection Sharing. You'll also learn about the security enhancements to Internet Explorer that were introduced in Service Pack 2.

Chapter 13 covers all you need to know to use the Internet Explorer web browser.

Chapter 14 explains the communications programs: HyperTerminal, Windows Messenger, and Remote Desktop Sharing.

Chapter 15 is an overview of Outlook Express, the news and mail client that's included with Windows XP Professional.

## Part 5: Home Networking

This section of the book covers networking from a small-scale perspective. If you are new to networking, read this section before tackling the next one. Chapter 16 preps you for planning and setting up your Windows XP Professional network.

In Chapter 17, I show you how to set up and configure a Windows XP Professional peer-to-peer network. You'll learn how to create shares, attach to network resources, and utilize user and hardware profiles. Chapter 17 wraps up with a section on network troubleshooting.

Chapter 18 is brand-new to this edition of the book. It addresses wireless networking, a very hot topic today in both private and public arenas. You'll learn how to configure and secure wireless networks within Windows XP.

One of the ways that Windows XP Professional is radically different from every other operating system is that it is *secure*; in fact, Windows XP Professional has been certified by the U.S. government as meeting the requirements for C2-level security. Security is a great thing to have, for obvious reasons, but it can also cause problems—the first time you can't access a file on your own computer, you'll want to know why! Chapter 19 takes you through the details of security so that you can address problems quickly and directly.

## Part 6: Advanced Networking

Now we get into some of the networking topics that are applicable to larger-scale situations. Chapter 20 shows you how to connect Windows XP Professional machines to a domain, how to connect domain-based documents and printers, how to create user and hardware profiles, and how to troubleshoot your domain.

Chapter 21 addresses Windows Server 2003. While there's a whole 'nother book of things to be said on this topic (and in fact, I have written one!), this chapter will give you a basic overview of its capabilities.

Chapter 22 deals with the scenario of using your Windows XP Professional workstations over a non-Microsoft-based network. Microsoft has worked with Novell to provide Windows XP Professional users with Client Service for Novell NetWare tools to make it easy to operate over such systems. In Chapter 22, you'll learn the idiosyncrasies of those tools. In addition, Chapter 22 also covers working with two other major players in the networking space: Unix and Apple's Macintosh.

## Part 7: Network Administration

The chapters in Part 7 provide you with the tools and skills you need to work more efficiently and to keep your Windows XP Professional system and network in tip-top shape.

Chapter 23 shows you how to monitor and optimize your system using Windows XP Professional's administrative and diagnostic tools, including Disk Management, Event Viewer, and Task Manager.

In Chapter 24, I introduce you to Active Directory and show how it provides better, more flexible administration options and significant control to network administrators.

Chapter 25 explains how and when to use the Registry to change Windows applications and hardware settings. Also covered in Chapter 25 is the important topic of backing up and restoring the Registry.

Creating scripts that automate everyday tasks is explained in Chapter 26, as well as how to schedule your scripts to run at specific times.

Chapter 27 shows you how to prevent system crashes and other system disasters, how to restore a configuration, and how to recover lost data, among other topics.

Chapter 28 shows you how to use Windows XP Professional's security and monitoring tools to audit your security system. Apply what you learn in this chapter, and you'll be able to see if someone has logged on or off, changed security settings, created or modified users, or accessed system resources.

### Part 8: Advanced Topics

Chapter 29 is about virtual private networks (VPNs). A VPN is a tunnel through the Internet that connects your computer to a network. When you're on the road, you can dial up almost any ISP and set up a VPN session to your network over the Internet. If you're a road warrior, you shouldn't skip this chapter.

Chapter 30 discusses the Microsoft Management Console (MMC), an all-in-one administrative tool that can be set up to include everything you need to administer Windows XP Professional.

You'll learn how to configure and manage services—programs that run in the background to support basic activities—in Chapter 31.

Chapter 32 addresses the three basic services you can set up and configure with Internet Information Server (IIS): web service, FTP service, and SMTP service.

Chapter 33 looks at advanced troubleshooting principles and procedures. It also provides specific techniques for troubleshooting your Windows XP setup, printing, and error messages.

## Typesetting Conventions Followed in This Book

As much as I could, I attempted to be consistent throughout the book with the capitalization of menu commands and dialog-box options. All program-level filenames and command names appear in a `special` font to help distinguish them from the natural grammar of the sentence.

I've *italicized* terms for emphasis or as needed to avoid confusion. For example, terms being defined for the first time are in italic. Furthermore, when I'm presenting the syntax of a command (yes, system administrators will still occasionally be dealing with command-line entry), placeholders and variables will be represented in *italic*.

Finally, anything I instruct you to type into an entry field or command line will be shown in **boldface type.**

## Stay in Touch!

I hope you find the answers to all your Windows XP Professional questions here. In addition, please check out my web page for the latest information regarding Service Pack 2: www.minasi.com/sp2info/.

If you have questions I didn't cover, or if you have a comment on the book, or if I made a mistake, I'd love to hear from you. Just e-mail help@minasi.com with questions, comments, or suggestions for future editions. I try to answer all of the e-mail I get, but you can help me with that by doing a couple of things. First, please don't send me receipted mail. For various reasons that I won't go into here, I've set up my mail handler to automatically delete receipted mail. Sorry. Second, if you're asking for advice, please try to keep the problem statement to a few paragraphs. If it gets any more involved than that, then, well, we're sort of moving into the field of network consulting, which is partially how I make my living, so I'm afraid your request will be slotted to be dealt with *after* those of my contracted clients. As you've probably guessed by now, I *do* receive a lot of mail. Much of it is highly complimentary, and I am very thankful to all of you who have corresponded! I *will* try to reply to all mail I get—and thanks again for reading!

# Windows XP Multimedia

As computer processing, video, and sound capabilities have dramatically improved over the last several years, multimedia capabilities have become almost a given on any PC. It's assumed that any PC you buy today has some sort of sound support and a CD drive, for example. And many systems have much more than that—DVD burners, scanners, digital cameras, microphones, surround sound speaker systems, and so on.

This section provides a graphical look at many of the most popular multimedia activities that Windows XP supports, in three basic areas: Windows Media Player, digital imaging, and Windows Messenger. You'll find more comprehensive coverage of each of these topics later in the book.

## Contents

# WINDOWS MEDIA PLAYER 10

Windows XP originally came with Windows Media Player 8, but since then, two more versions have been released. The current version, 10, is available for free download through Windows Update or from Microsoft's website. Windows Media Player 10 is easier to use and more feature-rich than any previous version, offering such benefits as the following:

- Integrates with online stores for movies and CDs
- Easily acquires information about a CD or video from online databases
- Integrates Digital Rights Management (DRM) for playing protected content
- Easily rips tracks from audio CDs in either WMA or MP3 format
- Contains adjustable sampling rates for ripping
- Copies files to portable audio devices, including protected content where possible
- Includes a folder monitoring feature that automatically adds new tracks to the Library when they are copied to a monitored location
- Contains parental controls for limiting the DVDs that can be played on the PC to certain ratings

To start Windows Media Player, choose Start ➢ All Programs ➢ Windows Media Player. Or, if the Quick Launch toolbar appears on the Taskbar, click the Windows Media Player button there.

Another way to start Windows Media Player is to simply insert an audio CD or a DVD. Depending on the disc type and your settings, it either begins playing automatically or a box appears asking you what you want to do with it. From there, you can choose to play it in Windows Media Player.

# PLAYING AN AUDIO CD

Audio CDs play in Windows Media Player by
default (although you are free to set up some other
application as the default for them if you prefer).
When you insert an audio CD, Windows Media
Player opens and begins playing it automatically.
The Now Playing tab shows a track list and a visualization that moves with the music.

You can control virtually every aspect of the
playback experience, including both the sound
and the visual effect that accompanies it. Controls
for the sound include a graphic equalizer, Auto Volume Leveling, Play Speed adjustments, and SRS
WOW Effects. Controls for the visual display
include Visualizations and Color Chooser.

You can also adjust the player size. You can use
Windows Media Player in a regular application
window or switch to Skin mode where it is much
smaller. You can also choose from a variety of Skin
mode designs.

**To skip to the next or previous track:** Click the
Next or Previous button.

**To rewind a track slightly:** Drag the slider to
the left.

**To adjust the volume:** Drag the Volume slider.

**To mute the volume temporarily:** Click the Mute
button.

**To exclude a certain track:** Right-click the track
and choose Disable Selected Tracks. Re-enable a
disabled track by choosing Enable Selected Tracks.

**To change the play order for a track:** Right-click
the track and choose Move Up or Move Down.

# PLAYING AN AUDIO CD (continued)

**To use the Equalizer:** Click the Select Now Playing Options button, and then choose Enhancements ➢ Graphic Equalizer.

**To choose a different enhancement:** Click the right or left arrow button at the top of the Enhancements pane.

**To change the visualization:** Click the right or left arrow button at the top of the Visualization pane, or click the Select Now Playing Options button, then choose Visualizations, and then select a category and a specific visualization.

**To expand the visualization to fill the entire window:** Click the Maximize Video and Visualization Pane button.

**To return to regular viewing:** Click the Restore the Video and Visualization Pane button.

**To switch to Skin mode:** Choose View ➢ Skin Mode, or press Ctrl+2.

**To return to Full mode:** Click the Return to Full Mode button, or press Ctrl+1.

# PLAYING A DVD MOVIE

Windows Media Player 10 plays DVD movies as well as audio CDs, with the movie playing in the large center pane in place of the visualizations. It has most of the same controls as the full-featured PC-based DVD players and more features than the average home theatre DVD player.

If your PC will not play DVD movies in Windows Media Player, perhaps it lacks the needed MPEG-2 decoder. You need either a hardware or a software decoder. Some video cards have built-in MPEG decoding; on other systems, a software codec provides this functionality. Visit your PC's manufacturer's website to find out if the codec you need is available for download. To play a DVD movie, follow these steps.

**1.** Insert the DVD disc. If a dialog box appears asking what you want to do with it, click Play DVD Video Using Windows Media Player.

**2.** If the DVD does not start playing automatically, choose Play ➢ DVD, VCD, or CD Audio, and then click the name of the DVD.

**3.** You now have the following options:

**To watch the movie full screen on your monitor:** Click the View Full Screen button.

**To go back to the root menu:** choose View ➢ DVD Features ➢ Root Menu.

# ADDING AUDIO CLIPS TO THE LIBRARY

Windows Media Player can play not only music and video from CDs and DVDs but also digital audio and video clips you have downloaded from the Web, ripped from CDs, or acquired in other ways. This content is already in one of the recognized digital formats, such as WMA or MP3 for an audio clip or AVI or QT for a video clip.

You can open such clips on a one-time basis and play them in Windows Media Player, but it is much more efficient to add the clips to your Library, where you can access them easily in the future. Importing a clip to the Library does not create an additional copy of the clip; it merely creates a shortcut to it so that you can play it from its current location by clicking its name in the Library. From within Windows Media Player, you can view clip libraries in a single location that lets you access clips that are actually physically stored in many different folders and even on different drives.

## To add a single clip:

**1.** Choose File ➤ Add to Library ➤ Add File or Playlist.

**2.** Navigate to the folder containing the clip to add, select the clip, and click Open.

## To add many clips at once:

**1.** Choose File ➤ Add to Library ➤ By Searching Computer. In the dialog box that appears, open the Search On list and select a drive or special location to search.

# ADDING AUDIO CLIPS TO THE LIBRARY *(continued)*

**2.** (Optional) To confine the search to a certain folder within the chosen drive or location, click the Browse button to locate it.

**3.** (Optional) To add volume leveling as the clips are added, click the Advanced Options button to access the additional options in the dialog box. Then mark the Add Volume Leveling Values for All Files (Slow) check box. Click the Search button when you are finished setting options.

**4.** When the search has completed, click Close.

**5.** In the left pane, click All Music. The tracks in the Library appear in the center pane. To play one of them, double-click it. The track moves to the Now Playing list, and begins playing.

## RIPPING A MUSIC CD

To *rip* a CD is to copy its tracks to a PC in a digital audio format such as MP3 or WMA, so that you can play them without the CD being in the drive. It is legal to rip a CD for your own use, as long as you own the original CD, but it is not legal to share the ripped tracks with others by making copies of the disc or by posting them on the Internet.

Many people like to rip their CDs and then burn their own custom CDs comprised of their favorite tracks from multiple sources. See "Burning a Music CD" later to learn about the second half of this process.

**1.** Insert a music CD in your PC. Then click the Rip tab in Windows Media Player. A list of the tracks appears.

If any of these have been previously ripped to your library, Ripped to Library appears in the Rip Status column.

**2.** Clear the check box for any of the clips you do not want to rip. Then click Rip Music.

**3.** As the tracks are copied, their status changes to Ripped to Library. Tracks that have not yet been copied appear as Pending. When all tracks have a Ripped to Library status, you can remove the CD and play those tracks from the Library tab from this point on.

# BROWSING THE LIBRARY FOR CLIPS TO PLAY

The Library tab enables you to search and sort your digital audio and video files in a variety of ways. For example, you can view them by Album Artist or Contributing Artist. (What's the difference? For a one-artist album, there is none, but for a compilation, each song may have a different artist.) You can also view them by Composer, Album Name, Genre, Year Released, or the number of stars you have assigned the track in Windows Media Player's rating system. You can also see purchased music separately from non-purchased music (for example, if you use a for-pay download service through Windows Media Player).

**To browse by category:** Click a plus sign (+) in the left pane to expand a category. Within it, click plus signs next to specific entries to further expand them until the clips you want appear in the center pane.

**To play a single clip:** Double-click the clip to add it to the Now Playing List (at the right). It immediately begins playing.

**To play all the clips in the location shown:** Select all the clips in the center pane and click the Add to Now Playing List button.

Or click the first clip in the center pane, and then click the Play button at the bottom of the window. All the clips in that location are added to the Now Playing List automatically.

# USING THE NOW PLAYING LIST

New in Windows Media Player 10 is the Now Playing List on the Library tab, which you saw in the preceding section. You can add files to this list to queue them up for playing without creating a formal playlist.

The Now Playing List is not permanent; it is cleared when you close Windows Media Player or when you manually clear it. Therefore it is not a substitute for a real playlist (which is a saved list of tracks to play, explained in "Creating a Playlist" later). It merely provides a convenient staging area for playing clips on the spur of the moment.

Actually, several different lists can appear in the right pane of the Library, including the Now Playing List, the Burn List, and the Sync List. The Burn List is for assembling tracks for burning to CD, and the Sync List is for assembling tracks to copy to a portable player.

**To switch between the Now Playing, Burn, and Sync lists:** Click the button at the top of the right pane and choose the appropriate list from the menu that appears.

**To clear the list:** Click the button at the top of the right pane, and then choose Clear List.

**To save the Now Playing List as a formal playlist:** Click the button at the top of the right pane and choose Save Playlist As. Then type a name for the playlist and click Save.

# ASSIGNING RATINGS TO CLIPS

Windows Media Player assigns ratings (a number of stars from one to five) based on how often you play the tracks. An automatically rated track appears with pale blue stars. You can also manually assign ratings to tracks; the ratings you create result in stars that are bright yellow.

    Track ratings are useful for several reasons. You can sort any listing by the ratings so that you can locate your favorite tracks more easily. You can also take advantage of some of the automatic playlists that Windows Media Player creates based on ratings, as you will see in the next section.

**To change a clip's rating:** Point to the clip so that outlines of five stars appear. Then click the desired star to set the rating. For example, to give a clip a four-star rating, click the fourth star from the left. The stars change to bright yellow to indicate that the rating has been manually set.

**To set the rating for many clips at once:** Select the clips in the center pane. Either hold down Shift as you click the first and last clips in a contiguous group, or hold down Ctrl as you click individual clips. Then right-click the group and choose Rate, and then choose a number of stars.

**To browse rated tracks:** In the left pane, click the plus sign (+) next to Rated Tracks. Then click a number of stars to see only tracks that you have manually rated with that value.

# USING THE BUILT-IN PLAYLISTS

Another new feature in Windows Media Player 10 is the inclusion of several automatic playlists. There are several criteria by which a track might find itself a member of a certain auto playlist. For example, a track that has not been played since it was added to the library might appear on a "Fresh Tracks" list. Similarly, a track that has not yet received a manual rating might appear on a Music Tracks I Have Not Rated list.

Auto playlists are dynamic; their content changes as the situation in your Library changes. For example, if you make a change to a track that affects its membership in an automatic playlist (such as changing its rating), the playlist automatically updates itself.

**To view an auto playlist:** Scroll down the left pane, find Auto Playlists, and click the plus sign (+) to expand the list of playlists there. Then click a playlist to see its content in the center pane.

**To play an auto playlist and clear the existing Now Playlist List:** Right-click the playlist in the left pane and choose Play.

**To append an auto playlist to the end of the existing Now Playlist List:** Right-click the playlist in the left pane and choose Add to Playlist.

**To create a saved playlist based on the auto playlist:** Right-click the playlist in the left pane and choose Save as New Playlist. In the New Playlist box, type a name and click OK. The saved playlist appears in the My Playlists listing, covered in the next section.

# CREATING A PLAYLIST

You can create both manual and automatic playlists in Windows Media Player 10.

As you learned in the preceding section, an auto playlist is one that is based on certain criteria rather than on individually chosen tracks. For example, with an auto playlist, if you specify a certain artist as the criteria and then you rename a certain track so that it no longer appears to be by that artist, it no longer appears on that playlist.

A manual playlist is one that references specific tracks. Unlike the auto playlists from the preceding section, a manual playlist does not change if, for example, you change the rating or name of a track or play it more or less frequently. Manual playlists appear in the My Playlists section of the left pane.

### To create a manual playlist:

**1.** Click the button above the right pane and choose New List ➤ Playlist.

**2.** Select a group of clips and then click the Add Selection to Current List button, or double-click individual clips to add them.

**3.** Click the New Playlist button and choose Save Playlist As. In the Save As dialog box, type a name for the playlist and click Save.

## CREATING A PLAYLIST *(continued)*

### To create an automatic playlist:

**1.** Click the button above the right pane and choose New List ➤ Auto Playlist.

**2.** Under Music in My Library, choose Click Here to Add Criteria, and then choose the criterion by which the list should build. For example, you might want to build a list for a certain contributing artist.

**3.** Click <Click to Set> on the line with a funnel to its right that appears. Then choose a value from the list. (This list comes from the values for the music in your library.)

To add additional criteria, repeat steps 2 and 3.

**4.** (Optional) To include other types of clips besides music, click the <Click here to add criteria> text under And Also Include. For example, you can look for video clips.

If you want to add even more types of clips, repeat step 4.

# CREATING A PLAYLIST *(continued)*

**5.** (Optional) If you want to limit the playlist, click the <Click here to add criteria> text under And Apply the Following Restrictions to the Auto Playlist heading. Then choose a restriction. For example, you can choose to limit the number of items.

**6.** If you chose a restriction in step 5, choose <click to set> to specify the amount or quantity.

**7.** If you need to remove any criteria, click that line, and then click Remove. When you are ready, click OK.

When you click OK, the playlist is created and placed in the Auto Playlists listing in the left pane.

# CHANGING INFORMATION ABOUT A TRACK

If the tracks are ripped from a CD, they probably already contain correct information. However, if they came from online downloads, they might not have all the information filled in. This can result, for example, in the filename containing both the artist and the song title, and the Artist field being empty.

Information about a track is stored in two places: in the properties of the file itself, and in the Library in Windows Media Player. Changing the information for the file does not change it in Windows Media Player unless you delete and re-add the track or re-search for clips using the New Files and All Existing Files in Library option. Similarly, changing the information in the Library does not change the properties of the file, and if you delete and re-add that clip, any change you made to it in the Library is not retained.

## To change track information for the file:

1. Right-click the clip in the Library and choose Open Containing Folder. Windows Explorer opens the file location containing that particular clip.

2. Find the clip, right-click it, and choose Properties. A Properties dialog box opens for the clip.

3. Click the Summary tab. If the advanced properties do not appear (as shown here), click the Advanced >> button.

4. Click in the Value column to change a property, and edit the value there. Repeat this for each property you want to change, then click OK.

# CHANGING INFORMATION ABOUT A TRACK *(continued)*

## To change track information in Windows Media Player's Library:

**1.** Click the clip for which you want to edit information, and then either press F2 or right-click the clip and choose Edit. An insertion point appears in the song title.

**2.** Edit the song title if you need to, and then press Tab to move to the Artist column.

**3.** Edit the Artist column if you need to; then continue pressing Tab and editing each field as needed.

**4.** (Optional) To set other properties, right-click the clip and choose Advanced Tag Editor.

**5.** Fill in any additional information about the track on any of the tabs provided. You can use this information to search or sort tracks later if you want to. When you're finished, click OK.

# BURNING A MUSIC CD

Burning a CD means copying tracks to a writeable CD. It usually refers to making a CD in which the tracks are in CD Audio format and can be played on any CD player, not just a PC. However, it is also possible to burn a CD wherein the tracks are in WMA or MP3 format. Such a CD would be playable only in a PC or in a player that specifically supported those formats.

To burn a CD, you first create a burn list. This is like a playlist only its purpose is different. You can use any existing playlist for your burn list, or you can create a new one. Then you simply click a button and the tracks are copied to your writeable CD drive. To burn a CD, follow these steps.

**1.** On the Library tab, click the button above the right pane and choose Burn List.

**2.** Select a group of files in the center pane and then click the Add Selection to the Burn List button, or double-click any single file to move it to the Burn List. You can also right-click any existing playlist or category in the right pane and choose Add to Burn List.

**3.** Insert a blank CD-R disc in your drive, and then click the Burn tab. The Burn List appears at the left and the empty CD-R appears at the right. Click the Start Burn button. Then just wait for the burn to complete.

# COPYING TRACKS TO A PORTABLE PLAYER

A portable music player stores and plays music in MP3 or WMA format, not the CD Audio format of most audio CDs. It is able to store many more files per megabyte of space because it has the decoding capabilities to play the files as a computer would play them.

Most portable players use a USB interface to connect to the PC, so make sure that your player is connected and turned on before attempting to copy files to it. If it is low on batteries, use its AC adapter while it is interacting with the PC so that problems do not occur from losing power during the copy process.

Some earlier versions of Windows Media Player worked with only a select few models of players, but Version 10 should work with virtually any player being sold today. If you encounter problems with your player, choose Help ➢ Troubleshooting to go to a website where information about compatibility with specific players is available. To synchronize files with a portable player, follow these steps.

1. On the Library tab, click the button above the right pane and choose Sync List.

2. Select a group of files in the center pane and then click the Add Selection to the Sync List button, or double-click any single file to move it to the Sync List.

You can also right-click any existing playlist or category and choose Add to Sync List.

3. Click the Sync tab. The chosen files appear, in the left pane. If there are any files in the right pane, that's what's already on the device. You can delete these or leave them there.

4. Click the Start Sync button to copy the files to the portable device.

# LISTENING TO INTERNET RADIO

Broadband Internet users might find it amusing to listen to one of the thousands of radio broadcasts on the Internet. Most of these are free, although some require that you register at their website.

Some stations play directly within Windows Media Player, while others take you to their own websites where separate players launch. Windows Media Player does not make a distinction between them as you are searching for stations, so you will find a mix of both types.

Internet radio is a streaming medium, which means that each time you switch stations, there might be a pause while the stream downloads into your PC's buffer. Buffering is necessary to ensure that temporary slowdowns in Internet traffic do not interrupt the station's broadcast to your PC. To play an Internet radio station, follow these steps.

**1.** On the Guide tab, click the Radio Tuner hyperlink.

**2.** A list of stations and categories appears. Browse the listings, clicking any station. Details about it appear below its name.

**3.** Click the Play link, if present. (If the station has a Visit Website to Play link instead, click that and follow the instructions that appear.)

The station begins playing in Windows Media Player. Some have video content too.

**4.** You can stop the station from playing by clicking the Stop button, or you can try a different radio station by going back to the My Radio Web browser window.

# WORKING WITH DIGITAL IMAGES

Each version of Windows has gotten better and better at handling digital images. In Windows XP, you can not only import them from scanners and cameras, but you can also manipulate and print them.

## Acquiring an Image from a Scanner

To acquire an image from a scanner, follow these steps.

**1.** Choose Start ➤ All Programs ➤ Accessories ➤ Scanner and Camera Wizard.

**2.** At the opening screen click Next. Then choose the picture type you are going to scan.

Or, if you prefer, click the Custom button to open a dialog box where you can fine-tune the Brightness, Contrast, Resolution, and Picture Type settings. Then click OK to return.

## WORKING WITH DIGITAL IMAGES *(continued)*

**3.** Click the Preview button to see a preview of the image. The wizard attempts to crop it for you automatically, as shown here, but you can drag the square handles in the corners of the cropped area to enlarge or shrink the area you want scanned. Then click Next.

**4.** Fill in the name and location you want to use and choose a file format. Then click Next.

**5.** Wait for the picture to be scanned. When it is finished, a list of Other Options appears.

**6.** Click Next to accept the default option (Nothing. I'm Finished Working With These Pictures.)

**7.** Click Finish. Your scanned picture opens in Windows Explorer. From here you can change views (with the View menu) or use one of the hyperlinks in the bar to the left of the picture to print or view the picture or copy it to CD.

# TRANSFERRING FILES FROM A DIGITAL CAMERA

Most digital cameras can be used like regular removable drives. You can connect them to the PC and open a file management window to work with their contents as you would any drive. This is often the easiest way to work with a camera.

However, there is an alternative method as well. You can use the Scanner and Camera Wizard to transfer the pictures from the camera to your hard disk if you prefer. It might seem a little easier and less intimidating for a beginner, although it is more work than a simple, direct copy or move action. To acquire pictures from a digital camera, follow these steps.

**1.** When you connect your camera to your PC, a box appears asking what you want to do. Choose Copy Pictures to a Folder On My Computer....

The Scanner and Camera Wizard runs. Click Next to begin.

**2.** Clear the check marks from any of the photos on the camera that you do *not* want to transfer to your hard disk. Then click Next.

**3.** Type a name for the picture group. Choose a different location if desired, and mark the Delete Pictures... check box if desired.

**4.** Then click Next, wait for the pictures to be copied, then follow the prompts to finish up.

# PRINTING PHOTOS

The Photo Printing Wizard is useful for situations where you need to print a photo, but you don't have an application installed on the PC that opens that image type.

**1.** From a file management window where pictures are displayed, click Print Pictures.

**2.** At the opening screen of the wizard, click Next to begin.

Then select the picture(s) to print. You can print a single picture or any number of pictures in the current folder. Then click Next.

**3.** Select the desired printer, and if you want to change its properties, click the Printing Preferences button (then click OK to return here). Click Next.

**4.** Choose a layout for the print job. To print multiple copies of the same picture, increase the Number of Times to Use Each Picture. Click Next after making your selection, and the job is sent to the printer. Click Finish afterward to close the window.

# USING WINDOWS MESSENGER

Windows Messenger is a real-time chat program in which you can type back and forth with friends, send webcam video streams, and even use Voice over IP (VoIP) to have a voice chat. You can also share applications and send and receive files.

## Starting Up Windows Messenger

On some systems, Windows Messenger is configured to load automatically when the PC starts. If that's the case for you, you'll see a Windows Messenger icon in the notification area. Otherwise you need to start Windows Messenger manually. To use Windows Messenger, follow these steps.

1. Choose Start ➢ All Programs ➢ Windows Messenger. Unless it is set up to log you in automatically, you are prompted to log in with your .NET Passport ID. Do so.

   If you don't have a .NET Passport ID yet, click the Get a .NET Passport hyperlink.

2. After you have logged in, the list of any friends you have already set up appears. People who are available appear in green; people who are not available for chat appear in red.

   The next section explains how to add people to this list.

3. (Optional) To change whether Windows Messenger loads at startup, choose Tools ➢ Options and click the Preferences tab. Then mark or clear the Run Windows Messenger When Windows Starts check box, and click OK.

# ADDING CONTACTS TO YOUR LIST

In order to have a conversation with someone via Windows Messenger, you must set them up as a contact. You can set up contacts either by e-mail address or by .NET Passport sign-in name. The person you want to talk to must have a .NET Passport account.

**To add a contact by e-mail address or .NET Passport:**

1. Click the Add a Contact hyperlink in the Messenger window (or choose Tools ➢ Add a Contact).

2. Choose the By E-mail Address or Sign-In Name radio button and click Next.

3. Enter the e-mail address and click the Next button. Messenger searches for a matching user.

If it finds one, it displays a Success screen telling you that it has added the contact to your list. If Messenger doesn't find a match, it offers to send a message to the user inviting them to try Messenger. Take up this request if you like.

# ADDING CONTACTS TO YOUR LIST *(continued)*

**To add a contact by searching for them in the .NET directory:**

**1.** Click the Add a Contact hyperlink in the Messenger window (or choose Tools ➤ Add a Contact).

**2.** Select the Search for a Contact radio button, and click Next.

**3.** Enter the person's first name and last name. If you're sure of their country or region, specify that in the Country/Region drop-down list. Enter any other known information as well, like City and State, if the country you chose allows it. Then click Next.

**4.** Select the person from the Search Results screen that Messenger displays and click Next.

Messenger then walks you through the process of having the .NET service send an e-mail to the person to tell them how to install Messenger and contact you.

# STARTING A CONVERSATION

A conversation usually starts with text messaging. From there, you can determine whether both parties have the equipment needed for some other type of chat, such as voice or video.

A text conversation appears in its own window, and you have a separate conversation window for each person to whom you are speaking. You can invite multiple people to join the same conversation if you want, and in that case, they all appear in the same window and are all able to see one another's text.

**To chat with a Messenger user:** Double-click the user's entry on your list of contacts. A new Conversation window opens. Type a message and press Enter (or click Send).

**To accept a chat invitation:** The chat window appears on the invitee's screen in minimized form. Open the minimized window to participate in the conversation, and then type a message and press Enter (or click Send).

**To invite someone else to the same conversation:** Click the Invite Someone to This Conversation hyperlink. Then in the box that appears, click the name and click OK.

# STARTING A VOICE CONVERSATION

If both participants have functioning audio hardware, you can add voice to a Messenger conversation between two people. (You can't use voice in a conversation that has three or more people.)

If you haven't run the Audio and Video Tuning Wizard, Messenger runs it the first time you try to use voice chat. You must go through it (if only perfunctorily) to use the feature.

**1.** In an existing conversation, click the Start Talking heading in the right pane in the Conversation window. The heading changes to Stop Talking and sliders for Speaker and Microphone volumes appear.

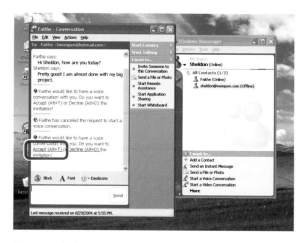

**2.** Wait for the other person to accept the voice conversation request.

**3.** Adjust the Speaker and Microphone volumes as needed once the chat gets underway. (It's tough to adjust those before this point because you don't know how loud things will be.)

To hang up the voice portion of the call, click the Stop Talking heading.

# STARTING A VIDEO CONVERSATION

If one or both participants have video hardware installed, you can add video to a Messenger conversation between two people. (As with voice, you can't use video in a conversation that has three or more people.)

With a video conversation, you have the option of using "picture-in-picture" whereby you see your own camera in a small window and the camera of your chat-mate in a larger window.

1. Make sure your webcam is functioning, and click the Start Camera heading in an existing chat window. The heading changes to Stop Camera and a window for the camera appears.

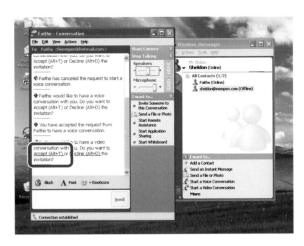

2. Wait for the other person to accept your invitation.

3. The camera image appears in the conversation window. To toggle your picture-in-picture on and off, click the Options button and choose Show My Video As Picture-in-Picture from the menu. To stop transmitting or receiving video, click the Stop Camera heading.

# SENDING AND RECEIVING FILES

Messenger provides an easy way to transfer files quickly to other Messenger users who are currently online.

## To send a file via Messenger:

1. During a conversation, choose File ≻ Send a File or Photo. Or from the Messenger window, choose File ≻ Send a File or Photo, and then choose a recipient from the dialog box and click OK.

2. Messenger displays the Send a File To dialog box. Navigate to the file, select it, and click the Open button.

   Messenger contacts the user, asking them if they want to accept or decline the file.

3. If the user accepts the file, Messenger displays a progress readout in the Conversation window.

   If the user does not accept the transfer, or if it fails, Messenger tells you that the user declined the file or the file could not be sent.

# SENDING AND RECEIVING FILES *(continued)*

## To receive a file that someone else is sending:

**1.** To accept the file, click the Accept link (or press Alt+T). To decline the file, click the Decline link (or press Alt+D).

**2.** If you choose to accept the file, Messenger displays a warning; click OK.

**3.** Messenger then transfers the file, stores it in the folder specified in the Preferences tab of the Options dialog box, and displays a link that you can click to open the file. You can click the link in the conversation window to open it.

**4.** You can also access the received file by choosing choose File ➢ Open Received Files.

# Part 1

# Installation and Setup

**In this section you will learn how to:**

- ◆ **Install Windows XP Professional**
- ◆ **Use the Desktop and Get Help**
- ◆ **Customize the Interface**
- ◆ **Install, Remove, and Run Programs**
- ◆ **Organize Programs and Documents**
- ◆ **Use Features Specific to Notebook PCs**

# Chapter 1

# Introducing Windows XP Professional

Since the advent of the personal computer, users have wanted three things in an operating system: power, stability, and usability. Windows XP Professional has all these and more in abundance. It features an indefatigable 32-bit architecture, complete with built-in networking and the capability to run almost every piece of Windows software on the market, as well as a new interface.

What does all this mean to the consumer, the person sitting at a desk 52 weeks a year who just wants to be a productive computer user? It means a lot. It means a fast, up-to-date operating system with a slew of advanced features that ensure the computer will almost never crash. It means an operating system that can host the emerging multitude of 32-bit software applications, some of which offer amazing facilities for professional audio and video recording, editing, and broadcasting. It means a new interface, which gives users tremendous control over how the system performs its tasks and how it maintains its connections to peripherals and to other computers.

In this chapter, I'll give you an overview of Windows XP Professional: what's new, what's different, and what's under the hood. I'll compare Windows XP Professional with its sibling, Windows XP Home, with its cousins Windows XP Media Center Edition and Windows XP Tablet Edition, and with previous versions of Windows. In later chapters, I'll expand on most of the topics I'll introduce in this chapter, but you'll find a lot here to whet your appetite.

- ◆ What is Windows XP Professional?

- ◆ What's new in Windows XP Professional?

- ◆ Should you upgrade to Windows XP Professional?

- ◆ How is Windows XP Professional different from other operating systems?

- ◆ What are the features of Windows XP Professional architecture?

## What Is Windows XP Professional?

In a nutshell: Windows XP Professional is the latest version of the Windows NT family of operating systems (which includes Windows 2000). Windows XP Professional comprises a feature set designed for business users, while its less powerful (and less expensive) sibling Windows XP Home offers features designed for home users.

If you've used Windows before, or if you're currently using Windows, you may wonder what the big deal is. The good news is that Windows XP *is* a big deal, especially if you've had less than satisfactory experiences with Windows in the past. Windows XP isn't the be-all and end-all of operating systems, but it's a great improvement on its predecessors.

As you probably know, in the past, Microsoft offered two main categories of Windows versions for 32-bit personal computers: the Windows 95 family and the Windows NT family. In the Windows 95 family were Windows 95 itself, naturally enough; Windows 98; Windows 98 Second Edition, which despite its unassuming name was a major upgrade to Windows 98; and Windows Millennium Edition, also known as Windows Me. In the Windows NT family were Windows NT versions 3.1, 3.5, 3.51, and 4, each of which came in a Workstation version and a Server version, and then Windows 2000, which came in a Professional version and several Server versions.

The Windows 95 family, widely referred to as Windows 9x in a brave attempt to simplify Microsoft's inconsistent nomenclature, offered impressive compatibility with older hardware ("legacy hardware," as it's sometimes politely termed) and software ("legacy software"), including full (or full-ish) DOS capabilities for running games and character-based applications. These versions of Windows kept their hardware demands to a reasonable minimum. They were aimed at the consumer market. When things went wrong (which happened regrettably often), they became unstable. And they crashed. Frequently.

Many of those people—both professionals and home users—who couldn't stand or afford to lose their work because of Windows 9x's frequent crashes migrated to Windows NT versions instead. (Others tried OS/2 while it lasted, then returned disconsolately to Windows. Others went to Linux and mostly stayed there.) NT, which stands for New Technology, had a completely different underpinning of code than Windows 9x. NT was designed for stability, and as a result, it crashed much less frequently than Windows 9x. Unfortunately, though, NT wasn't nearly as compatible as Windows 9x with legacy hardware and software. Most games and much audio and video software wouldn't run on NT, and it was picky about the hardware on which it would run. (Actually, this wasn't "unfortunate" at all—it was deliberate on Microsoft's part and probably wise. But the result was far from great for many users.)

So for the last half-dozen years, users have essentially had to decide between stability and compatibility. This led to a lot of unhappy users, some of whom couldn't run the software they wanted, and others who kept losing work or at least having to reboot their computers more than they should have had to.

The Windows 9x line culminated in Windows Me, which tacked some stability and restoration features on to the Windows 9x code base. NT culminated in Windows 2000 Professional, which featured increased compatibility with applications over NT (which wasn't saying all that much—many games still didn't run on Windows 2000 Professional), a smooth user interface, and usability enhancements.

Windows 2000 Professional was arguably the most stable operating system that Microsoft had produced until Windows XP came along. (Some old-timers reckoned Windows NT 3.51 was more stable.) But Windows 2000 Professional's stability came at a price: It had no interest in running any games or other demanding software that wouldn't conform to its stringent requirements. And while it was compatible with quite an impressive range of legacy hardware, many items still wouldn't work. Even up-to-date hardware could be problematic, especially if it connected via USB.

Since the late 1990s, Microsoft had been promising to deliver a consumer version of Windows that melded the stability of NT and the compatibility of Windows 9x. In Windows XP Home Edition, that version of Windows is finally here. According to Microsoft, Windows XP Professional is a strict superset of Home Edition, as well as of all the desktop clients that preceded Professional.

**NOTE**   Windows 2003 Server is a separate version of Windows, designed for use on servers. It does everything that Windows XP Professional does and adds a comprehensive set of tools for managing and administering a network. It is designed to run on a network file server or application server. Chapter 20, "Connecting to Domains," and 21, "Introduction to Server 2003," cover it.

# What's New in Windows XP Professional?

This section outlines the most striking and appealing new features in Windows XP, starting with installing and upgrading, moving through the user interface and visible features, and ending up with the features hidden under the hood.

Some of these new features fall into convenient categories, and this section presents them in those categories. Others don't; this section presents these features individually.

## The "Evil" Windows Product Activation

The notion behind this controversial new feature of Windows XP is really rather simple—to prevent piracy. In a nutshell, Windows Product Activation (WPA) ties each copy of Windows XP to a specific computer. Although activation is mandatory, it is anonymous. Your Product Key is coupled to a computer hardware ID that is nonunique and cannot be traced back to a specific computer.

WPA is not the same as product registration, and you can take care of it over the Internet or by phone. After installation, you are asked if you want to activate the product. If you don't do it then, you'll have a certain number of days to do so. If you still haven't activated your copy of Windows XP within that time, you'll be able to boot the system, but you won't be able to get beyond the opening screen until you activate.

**NOTE**   Corporate and academic users who purchase volume licenses for Windows XP don't have to worry about activation. Their versions of Windows XP don't include WPA.

## Easier Installation and Updating

Windows XP includes several features designed to make it easier to install and to keep up-to-date. These include Windows Update; the Files and Settings Transfer Wizard; more wizards for a variety of tasks; a wider selection of device drivers; simplified installation for multifunction devices; and an effective way to uninstall and revert to your previous version of Windows.

### WINDOWS UPDATE

The Automatic Updates feature runs periodically after setup and offers to download the latest patches, packages, and fixes and install them so that your copy of Windows is as up-to-date, secure, and compatible as possible. (You can also run Windows Update manually whenever you want.) When you install Service Pack 2 (SP2), or buy a PC with Windows XP SP2 already installed, the initial configuration routine offers to turn on automatic updating for you (highly recommended).

### FILES AND SETTINGS TRANSFER WIZARD

Making its debut in Windows XP is the Files and Settings Transfer Wizard, a feature that Windows users have been demanding for a good 10 years. The Files and Settings Transfer Wizard provides a way of transferring designated files and settings from one computer to another or from one installation of Windows to another on the same computer. You'll still need to reinstall all your programs on the new computer or new installation of Windows, but you can transfer your data and a good amount of information about your work environment easily.

If you're migrating from an old computer to a new computer, or if you're installing Windows XP as a dual-boot with an existing version of Windows, you can use the Files and Settings Transfer Wizard to clone your existing Desktop and files and transfer them to the new computer or new version of Windows.

### MORE WIZARDS TO MAKE TASKS EASIER

Windows XP includes a slew of wizards designed to walk you through complicated processes (and some that aren't so complicated). Perhaps most welcome are the improvements to the Network Setup Wizard, which provides effective configuration of simple networks and Internet Connection Sharing, and the Add Hardware Wizard. SP2 also adds a Wireless Network Setup Wizard that offers to configure WEP (Wired Equivalent Privacy) security for the network.

On the less useful front, Windows XP also includes wizards such as the Desktop Cleanup Wizard, which pops out periodically like the neighborhood dog and tries to persuade you to let it herd the stray icons on your Desktop into a folder where they'll be available but less obtrusive. If you refuse, it wags its tail and goes away for a while.

### MORE DEVICE DRIVERS

Windows XP comes complete with drivers for a large number of devices, including scanners, digital still cameras, digital video cameras, printers, and so on. So there's a better chance than with another version of Windows (say, Windows Me or Windows 2000) that when you plug in a new device, Windows XP will be able to load a driver for it and get it working without any fuss.

You'll probably want to take this improvement with a grain of salt. To enjoy the latest features and the best performance from a new device, you'll probably want to install the driver that comes with the device or (better) download the latest version from the manufacturer's website.

### SIMPLIFIED INSTALLATION FOR MULTIFUNCTION DEVICES

Apart from having more drivers (as described in the previous section), Windows XP makes it easier to install multifunction devices—for example, a multifunction printer/scanner/fax device (the kind that people sometimes call "hydra" machines), a PC card that combines a network interface card with a modem, or a sound board with extra features.

Previous versions of Windows tended to recognize the component pieces of multifunction devices separately in sequence. If you installed a hydra, Windows would recognize the printer and demand the installation software for it. Once that was done, Windows would recognize the fax and demand the software for *that*. After that, it would recognize the scanner and suggest you might want to install yet more software. Windows XP improves on this social ineptitude by recognizing multifunction devices as such the first time you introduce it to them, and so it demands the installation software only once.

### EFFECTIVE UNINSTALL BACK TO WINDOWS 98 AND WINDOWS ME

Windows XP Professional provides an effective uninstall feature for rolling back the Windows XP installation to your previous installation of Windows 98, Windows 98 Second Edition, and Windows Me. However, you can't revert to a previous installation of Windows NT 4 or Windows 2000 Professional.

## Effective Multiuser Capabilities

Windows XP provides far better multiuser capabilities than Windows 9*x* and requires an existing account and password in order to log on. Like NT and Windows 2000, Windows XP provides features for preventing one user from seeing another user's files. Windows XP keeps each user's files separate so that no user can see another user's files unless they have been shared deliberately.

Windows XP goes further than NT and Windows 2000, though, in that it lets multiple users be logged on at the same time, each with applications running. Only one user can be actually *using* the computer, or can be *active*, in Windows XP parlance, at any one time, but the other user sessions continue running in the background (*disconnected*, in Windows XP parlance). When you've finished with the computer for the time being, you can log off Windows, just as you did in previous versions. Logging off closes all the applications you were using and frees up the memory they took up. But if you stop using the computer only temporarily, you may prefer to "switch users," which leaves your applications running but lets someone else use the computer in the interim.

## Enhanced User Interface

Windows XP has a completely revamped user interface with a large number of visual enhancements and improved functionality. Some of the visual enhancements improve usability, while others are mere eye candy. But the overall effect is mostly easy to use and mostly looks good—and if you don't like the look, you can restore the "classic" Windows look with minimal effort.

The following sections discuss the main changes to the user interface.

### REDESIGNED START MENU

Windows XP sports a redesigned Start menu that's supposedly easier and quicker to use. Whether you find it so depends on your experience with the Start menu in Windows 9*x* and Windows 2000. But don't worry if you like the "classic" Start menu—you can restore it easily enough with a few clicks of the mouse.

The Start menu appears as a panel containing two columns (shown in Figure 1.1). The right-hand column remains the same unless you customize it. The lower part of the left-hand column automatically reconfigures itself to show your most used applications. You can pin an item to the Start menu to prevent it from moving and keep it available.

As you can see in the figure, the current user's name appears in a bar across the top of the Start menu, and the Log Off and Shut Down buttons appear at the bottom of the menu.

**FIGURE 1.1**
The redesigned Start menu contains a static column of choices on the right and a variable column of choices on the left.

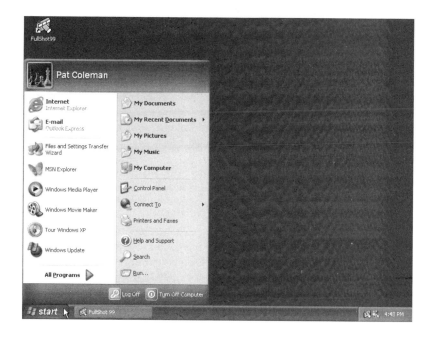

### REDESIGNED CONTROL PANEL

Windows XP also has a redesigned Control Panel (shown in Figure 1.2) that presents Control Panel as categories of items and actions you can take with them. The Security Center icon will appear only if you have installed SP2.

**FIGURE 1.2**

Control Panel divides its bevy of icons into categories. You can use the Classic view to see all the icons at once.

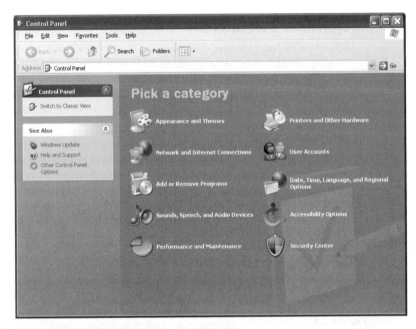

New users will likely find the Category view of Control Panel easy to use. Power users who are familiar with the regular manifestation of Control Panel in Windows 9x, Windows NT 4, and Windows 2000 will probably prefer to use the Classic view. (I know I do.) You can select it from the pane to the left of the main Control Panel window.

### EYE CANDY

To complement its highly graphical interface, Windows XP includes a dangerous amount of eye candy. Most people will like at least some of it. Some users will love it all. And no doubt, some people will claim to detest every pixel of it.

A prime example of eye candy is the My Pictures Slideshow screen saver, which lets you set up an automated (or mouse-controlled) slideshow of designated pictures instead of a regular screen saver. This feature seems destined to be widely popular.

Less assured of a rapturous welcome are the staggering amounts of adornment in the interface, such as shadows under the mouse pointer and under menus, the color gradient in the title bar of windows, and the effect of sliding icons, controls, and Taskbar buttons. This overbearing emphasis on graphics places heavy demands on your graphics board and processor, and if your computer's hardware tends to the lukewarm rather than hot, you may find the eye candy exacts an unacceptable performance penalty. Microsoft has had the sense to let you set performance options to balance the demands of appearance against your need for performance, so you can turn off the least necessary effects and speed up your computer. (Chapter 24, "Active Directory Essentials," discusses how to set performance options.)

## Taskbar Changes and Enhancements

Windows XP includes a number of tweaks to the Taskbar. These seem designed for beginners, so if you're an experienced Windows user, you may find some good and others bad. Fortunately, you can change the Taskbar's behavior back to how it was in previous versions of Windows.

### TASKBAR LOCKING

By default, the Taskbar is locked in Windows XP Professional. Presumably this is intended to prevent users from dragging their Taskbar to an inaccessible area at the edge of the screen. You can, however, easily unlock the Taskbar so that it can be resized or moved.

### TASKBAR SCROLLING

If you read the previous paragraph, you probably started raising objections: If the Taskbar is a fixed size, the buttons for the running applications must become tiny and useless as soon as you've got 10 or more applications running.

Two other changes come into play here, of which the first is Taskbar scrolling. When the Taskbar is locked, it keeps the buttons bigger than a minimum size. To accommodate the buttons, it increases the depth of the Taskbar, but displays only its top row. On the displayed portion of the Taskbar, it puts scroll buttons so that you can scroll the Taskbar up and down one row of buttons at a time.

### TASKBAR BUTTON GROUPING

The second change that makes Taskbar locking reasonable is Taskbar button grouping.

By default, Windows XP displays only one button per application on the Taskbar, whereas other versions of Windows displayed multiple buttons. For example, if you open nine Internet Explorer windows in Windows 98, it displays nine Internet Explorer buttons in the Taskbar. Having all these buttons can make it easy to find the window you want, but the buttons take up a lot of space (or each button on the Taskbar gets shrunk to a tiny size to fit them all in).

In Windows XP, if the application has multiple open windows, the Taskbar button displays the number of windows, the title of the current active window or last active window, and a drop-down arrow. To access one of the other open windows, click the Taskbar button. Windows displays a list of the windows by title. Select the window you want, and Windows displays it.

### NOTIFICATION AREA

By default, Windows XP Professional collapses the notification area (formerly known as the *system tray* or the *status area*) so that only the icons you've used most recently are displayed. You can choose which icons will always appear regardless of usage and which ones will be hidden when unused or always hidden.

## Better Audio and Video Features

Windows XP includes a slew of new features and improvements for audio and video. These include a new version of Windows Media Player, better features for grabbing and handling images from digital input devices such as scanners and cameras, and Windows Movie Maker, a modest video-editing application.

### WINDOWS MEDIA PLAYER

Front and center among the improved audio and video features of Windows XP is Windows Media Player. The original Windows XP came with Windows Media Player version 8, which was a great improvement over earlier versions. It combines a video and DVD player, a CD player, an Internet radio tuner, and a jukebox for playing and organizing digital-audio files such as Windows Media Audio (WMA) files and MP3 files. Windows Media Player comes with a number of visually interesting skins (graphical looks) that you can apply at will, and you can even create your own skins if you have the time and talent to invest. Later OEM releases of Windows XP came with version 9, and the latest is version 10 (available with the Windows XP Reloaded update and also available as a free download from Microsoft).

Windows Media Player versions 8 and higher are huge improvements over the 98-pound weakling version of Windows Media Player that shipped with all previous versions of Windows except Windows Me. (Me included Windows Media Player 7, which offered many of the features of version 8.) Windows Media Player can even burn audio CDs at the full speed of your CD-R or CD-RW drive. Chapter 10, "Media Player," explains Windows Media Player in detail.

### MY MUSIC FOLDER AND MY PICTURES FOLDER

Like several of its predecessors, Windows XP uses custom folders for music (the My Music folder) and pictures (the My Pictures folder). Again like its predecessors, it tries none too subtly to persuade you to save your music in these folders. But Windows XP goes further, in that it makes these folders much more useful than they were in earlier versions of Windows.

The My Music folder and the My Pictures folder present customized lists of actions you can take with music files and picture files. Some of these actions tend to the commercial—for example, the Order Prints Online link in the Picture Tasks list, and the Shop for Music Online link in the Music Tasks list. But others are solidly useful—for example, the Play All link in the Music Tasks list, which lets you play all the music in a folder without spelunking into it, or the View As a Slide Show link in the Picture Tasks list, which lets you set a whole folder of pictures running as a slide show with a single click.

Not surprisingly, the My Music folder works hand-in-hand (or is it glove?) with Windows Media Player. Windows Media Player is definitely happy for you to keep your music in the My Music folder, though it will let you keep it elsewhere as well. Better yet, Windows Media Player's features for cataloging music tracks are flexible enough to keep track of music files even when you move them from one folder to another.

The My Pictures folder works closely with Windows Image Acquisition, Image Preview, and Paint (all three of which are discussed in the next section). The folder includes a slideshow applet and a Filmstrip View, and it can publish your pictures to the Web.

**TIP** Filmstrip View can be used with any folder, not just My Pictures. Choose View ➤ Customize This Folder and choose the Photo Album template for the current folder to enable it.

### BETTER IMAGE ACQUISITION AND HANDLING

Windows XP provides strong features for capturing images from scanners, still cameras, and video cameras. It also provides better throughput for video streams, though unless you had a duplicate computer running an older version of Windows to use as a benchmark, you could be forgiven for failing to go into raptures over the improvement. Less cynically, the improvement in throughput is unquestionably a good thing, and on decent hardware, Windows XP delivers adequate to impressive video performance; but the chances of your confusing your PC with your GameCube remain poor. One of the central tools for image acquisition and handling is the Scanner and Camera Wizard. This wizard has a variety of duties, including transferring image files from still cameras and digital media (for example, CompactFlash cards and SmartMedia cards) to the computer. Most of its capabilities stay on the useful side of the esoteric. For example, you can scan multiple pages into a single image file, an ability that can come in handy in both home and business settings.

Windows XP provides some basic tools for handling still images. As mentioned, the My Pictures folder acts as a default repository for images and provides some basic image-handling abilities, such as rotating an image. The Image Preview feature lets you examine an image (and annotate a fax). And Paint, the basic image-manipulation and drawing package that's been included with Windows since Windows 3.*x*, has been beefed up as well. Paint can now open—and save—JPEG, GIF, TIFF, and PNG images as well as Windows bitmap (BMP) files, making it about five times as useful as before.

### WINDOWS MOVIE MAKER

Windows XP includes Windows Movie Maker, a basic package for capturing video, editing video and audio, and creating video files in the Windows Media format. You won't find yourself making the next *Timecode* or *Traffic* with Windows Movie Maker, but it's good enough for home-video editing. You can also create video slide shows with still images for those family occasions on rainy weekends or holidays. Service Pack 1 included a newer and more feature-rich version of Windows Movie Maker. See Chapter 11, "Digital Media and Movie Maker," for details about making movies.

## CD Burning

Windows XP comes with built-in CD-burning capabilities. You can burn CDs from an Explorer window with minimal effort. You can also burn CDs directly from Windows Media Player, which lets you easily create CDs containing music files, and work with packet-written CD-RWs as if they were normal disks.

## Compressed Folders

Windows XP has built-in support for compressed folders in both the ubiquitous ZIP format and the Microsoft Cabinet (CAB) format. You can create ZIP folders containing one or more files or folders. Better still, you can view the contents of a ZIP or CAB folder seamlessly in Explorer as if it were a regular folder. Just double-click either type of file to browse its contents.

**WARNING**    Sometimes you'll encounter problems if you try to run an executable file from a ZIP file, especially if it relies on support files to operate. You'll usually be able to open data files okay without extracting them, but you will probably want to copy or move an executable and its support files out of its ZIP file before running it.

## Search Companion

Windows XP includes Search Companion, an enhanced search feature for finding information both on your PC and in the wider world. You can use Search Companion to search for files, for computers or people online, or for information in Help and Support Center. Search Companion brokers the search requests that you enter and farms them out to the appropriate search mechanisms.

You can choose between having Search Companion appear in a straightforward and unexceptional window and having it manifest itself using an animated dog reminiscent of the Office Assistant.

### Easy Publishing to the Web

Windows XP makes it easier to publish files or folders to a website by using a web-hosting service. Windows XP includes a feature called Web Digital Authoring and Versioning (WebDAV for short) that lets you save information to the Web from any application rather than having to use the regular web-publishing protocols. You can set up a web server under My Network Places as a shortcut and then copy files directly to it.

### A Sane Implementation of Autoplay

If you've used Windows 9*x*, NT 4, or Windows 2000, you'll know all about the Autoplay feature and how it used to drive people crazy. You remember Autoplay—the moment you insert a CD, it starts playing the music from it or installing any software it contains. By default, Autoplay was enabled, so you had to switch it off (or override it by holding down the Shift key while closing the CD tray) to prevent it from occurring.

Windows XP includes a new version of Autoplay that's improved in several ways. First, you can customize it. Second, you can configure it to take different actions depending on what the CD (or other medium) contains. For example, you might want Windows to play your audio CDs automatically when you insert them (okay, you don't—but you *might*), or you might want Windows to display a slideshow automatically when you insert a CD containing nothing but pictures.

What's that about "other medium"? That's the third thing: In Windows XP, Autoplay works for CDs, DVDs, assorted flash cards (including CompactFlash, Memory Stick, and SmartMedia), PC Cards, ZIP and other removable disk drives, and FireWire hot-plug external drives.

### More Games

Windows XP includes more games than previous versions of Windows. Some of these are single-player games (for example, Spider Solitaire). Others are multiplayer games that you can play across the Internet via MSN's Zone.com website.

### Remote Desktop Connection

Windows XP Professional includes Remote Desktop Connection, a technology that lets you use your computer to access a remote computer (for example, your computer at the office) that's running Windows XP Professional. Once you've connected to the remote computer, you can control it as if you were sitting at it. This is one of the features that is available only in the Professional edition, not the Home edition.

### A More Useful Winkey

A what? "Winkey," pronounced "Win-key" rather than as the diminutive of "wink," is the Windows key on the keyboard—the key with the Windows logo. Most keyboards have one or two Winkeys, usually located next to the Alt or Ctrl keys.

Windows XP includes more functionality for the Winkey. You can still press the Winkey to open or close the Start menu, but you can also use it in a number of key combinations. For example, pressing Winkey+M issues a Minimize All command, and pressing Winkey+Shift+M issues an Undo Minimize All command.

For the full list of Winkey combinations, see Chapter 3, "Using the Desktop and Getting Help."

## Improvements for Portable Computers

Windows XP includes several improvements for portable computers.

First, Windows XP supports processor power control, which lets the computer make use of features in chips such as Intel's SpeedStep technology, in which the processor runs at full speed when the computer is plugged into the main power supply (or told that it's plugged in) but at a lower speed to save power when it's running on battery power (or told that it is).

Throttling back the processor like this reduces the computer's power usage a bit, improving battery life, but in most portables, the screen consumes far more power than the processor. Windows XP also targets the screen, providing a couple of features designed to reduce power use when the computer is running on battery power. First, Windows XP turns off the display when the user closes the computer's lid, on the basis that the user probably isn't looking at the display. Second, it runs the screen at a dimmer brightness when the computer is running off the battery. The cynical among you will point out that most sentient portables implement both these functions already in hardware. Still, it shouldn't do any harm to have Windows help out for the manufacturers who design their machines a little less carefully.

Windows XP also includes some other less obvious visual enhancements, such as support for ClearType, a Microsoft text-display technology that improves the look of fonts on LCD screens that have digital interfaces. With the popularity these days of desktop LCD monitors, this is a feature that can help not just notebook users but many desktop users as well.

## Faxing

Windows XP Professional contains a built-in fax client that's more than adequate for most home needs and many home office needs. You can send faxes from any application that supports printing and you can specify whether to print out incoming faxes automatically or store them in a folder. You can even configure different fax/modems to take different roles. For example, if you use faxes extensively, you might want to keep separate incoming and outgoing fax lines. You'll need a modem for each of the phone lines involved, but that's about as difficult as it gets. The fax service is not installed by default, but you can install it through Add or Remove Programs in the Control Panel. See Chapter 8, "Installing and Working with Printers and Fonts," for more information about it.

## More Help

Windows XP delivers more Help—and more different types of Help—than any other version of Windows. If you've searched fruitlessly for information in the past, you'll be aware that Windows' Help files have never exactly delivered the ultimate in user satisfaction. Digging information out of Help often felt so difficult that if you knew Windows well enough to find Help on the right topic, you could probably solve the problem without Help's assistance.

Windows XP takes a new approach to Help. There are Help files on your hard drive still, but they're integrated into an application called Help and Support Center. Help and Support Center not only works with the Help files but also with the Microsoft Knowledge Base (a database of support queries) and other online sources of information. For example, if you run a query within Help and Support Center to find information on hardware, it might return some information from local files, some information from the Microsoft website, and some information from hardware manufacturers' websites, all packaged into one window so that you can access them conveniently.

Help and Support Center also provides a gateway to other areas of support, including Microsoft Assisted Support and Support Communities, and to applications that you can use to get help from other users (such as Remote Assistance) and troubleshoot your computer (such as System Configuration Utility and System Restore).

The following sections discuss some of the Help and Support Center features.

### MICROSOFT ONLINE ASSISTED SUPPORT

Windows XP's Microsoft Online Assisted Support feature lets you automatically collect information on a problem you're having and submit it to Microsoft electronically. A Microsoft technician then sends a solution, which appears as a pop-up in your notification area. You can read the response in the Help and Support Center window and apply the wisdom it contains to fix the problem.

Microsoft Online Assisted Support is designed to bypass the problems inherent with tech support via phone call, namely: that it's difficult for the user to tell the Help technician what's wrong with their computer; that it's even harder for the technician to get a good idea of what's going wrong without knowing a fair bit of technical information about the computer; and that waiting on hold for tech support is nobody's idea of fun, especially if you're paying for any part of the privilege.

### SUPPORT COMMUNITIES

Instead of contacting a Microsoft technician via Microsoft Online Assisted Support, you can try to get support from one of the Windows Newsgroups, which are Microsoft-hosted newsgroups dedicated to Windows.

### REMOTE ASSISTANCE

Remote Assistance is an ingenious feature by which you can get assistance from a friend or other knowledgeable person remotely by computer.

Here's the brief version of how Remote Assistance works. You send out an invitation file via e-mail or via Windows Messenger instant messaging. Your helper receives the invitation and responds to it. Remote Assistance sets up a secure connection between their computer and yours, using a password to verify their identity. Your helper can then view your screen remotely and chat with you (via text chat and voice). If you trust your helper, you can even let them control your computer so that they can take actions directly.

### TOOLS SECTION

Help and Support Center includes a Tools section that gives you quick access to information about your computer (My Computer Information and Advanced System Information) and its configuration (System Configuration Utility), network diagnostic tools (Network Diagnostics), the System Restore feature, and more. In addition to the tools that Microsoft makes available in the Tools section, OEMs can add tools of their own, so you may also find custom tools provided by your computer manufacturer.

Many of the tools accessible through the Tools section are also accessible in other ways through the Windows interface. For example, Windows XP includes an improved version of Disk Defragmenter, which you can use to keep your hard disk from becoming fragmented (fragmentation decreases performance). You can run Disk Defragmenter from the Tools section, but you can also run it from the System Tools submenu of the Start menu (Choose Start ➤ All Programs ➤ Accessories ➤ System Tools ➤ Disk Defragmenter.); you can also schedule Disk Defragmenter to run automatically at convenient times.

### FIXING A PROBLEM TOOL

Help and Support Center includes an area called Fixing a Problem that contains a number of trouble-shooters for walking you through the steps of diagnosing and curing various common problems. Fixing a Problem isn't a panacea, but it's a good place to start, and it can save you a call to a guru or even a trip to your local computer shop.

### DEVICE DRIVER REFERRAL SITE

Help and Support Center contains a system for referring searches for drivers that don't come with Windows or with the hardware device. When you plug in a new hardware device, and Windows finds that it doesn't have a driver for it and you can't supply a driver, Windows invites you to send information about the hardware to Microsoft. Once you've sent the information, you can take a variety of actions depending on what information is available. For example, you might be able to view a list of compatible devices (if any), search for information on compatible devices or Knowledge Base articles about the hardware, or find a link to the vendor's website.

### OTHER HELP IMPROVEMENTS

Help and Support Center includes assorted other Help improvements that can save you time. For example, you can print out a whole chapter of Help information at once instead of having to slog through it screen by screen. And you can open multiple Help and Support Center windows at the same time. This makes it easier to pursue different avenues of exploration for the information you need. When you find useful information, you can create a favorite for it so that you can access it quickly again at need.

## Network Connectivity

Windows XP provides various improvements in network connectivity, from creating a home or office network to joining a computer to two separate networks. There are also great improvements in Internet connectivity, discussed in the next section.

### NETWORK SETUP WIZARD

The Network Setup Wizard simplifies the process of creating a network, sharing printers, Internet connections, and other resources, and configuring protocols and security. With SP2, there is also wizard-based functionality for configuring wireless networks and setting up Wireless Equivalent Privacy (WEP) security for them.

### ALTERNATIVE TCP/IP CONFIGURATION

Windows XP provides an alternative TCP/IP configuration that allows you to connect to a network that has a DHCP server and to a network that doesn't without changing your TCP/IP settings. For example, you might use a laptop at work (where the network has a DHCP server) and at home (where your network doesn't).

### NETWORK BRIDGING

Windows XP's network-bridging capability lets you use a computer with two or more network adapters to join two separate networks. You're perhaps unlikely to have two (or more) networks at home or in a small office—unless you have a wired network to which you've added a wireless component to provide roaming capabilities for some of the computers.

## Internet Connectivity and Web Browsing

Windows XP provides a number of enhanced features for Internet connectivity and web browsing, from favorites for Internet connections through to a new version of Internet Explorer.

### INTERNET CONNECTION FAVORITES

Windows XP lets you create favorites for your Internet connections. By using favorites, you can switch easily from one Internet connection to another. This is a great time-saver if you use multiple ISPs or (perhaps more likely) travel frequently and need to use different dial-up numbers from different locations.

### INTERNET CONNECTION SHARING AND INTERNET CONNECTION FIREWALL

Like Windows 98 Second Edition, Windows Me, and Windows 2000, Windows XP includes an Internet Connection Sharing (ICS) feature that lets you share an Internet connection on one computer with one or more networked computers. Windows XP's version of ICS has some tweaks, such as that you can disconnect the shared Internet connection from another PC if necessary—for example, if you need to use the phone line that the connection is using. Windows XP includes a Quality of Service Packet Scheduler that works to optimize the utilization of a shared Internet connection.

ICS is a great convenience, particularly if you have a high-speed connection such as a Digital Subscriber Line (DSL) or a cable modem—but it lays your network open to assault from the Internet. Some people may still prefer to share an Internet connection via a router instead of through Windows, but not all connections can be router-shared (for example, satellite broadband cannot).

Windows XP goes one better than its predecessors by including a personal firewall (called Internet Connection Firewall) to protect the Internet connection (whether shared or not). It is not enabled by default in the original Windows XP and Service Pack 1, but Service Pack 2 adds a Security Center and enables the firewall by default, as well as offers some customization options for the firewall. (The firewall in SP2 is actually a new and improved program, not just a new interface.)

### NEW VERSION OF INTERNET EXPLORER

Windows XP includes Internet Explorer 6, the latest version of Internet Explorer. Even if you feel you've already had it up to there with new versions of Internet Explorer, stifle your impatience, because Internet Explorer 6 offers a number of welcome innovations, including the following:

◆ You can save images, music, and videos more easily to your computer.

◆ The new Media bar makes it easier to listen to streaming audio directly in Internet Explorer.

◆ Internet Explorer provides better handling of cookies and digital certificates for securing information transfer and authenticating content.

◆ Internet Explorer can automatically resize an image you've displayed directly. If you've ever used Internet Explorer to open a digital photo and found it displayed bigger than your screen so that you could see only part of it, you may appreciate this feature. (But you'd be better off opening the photo in Paint in the first place.)

◆ Internet Explorer 6 has more integrated functionality for handling different file types. This won't strike you over the head; you'll simply find that more file types open without your being prodded to download and install extra components. For example, Internet Explorer 6 has built-in support for Macromedia Flash and Shockwave animations and support for Cascading Style Sheets Level 1 (CSS1). The net result is that more animations will play without your needing to add software, and documents formatted with cascading style sheets will be displayed as their authors intended. (They may still look horrible, but at least you'll know that they're meant to look that way.)

◆ Windows XP SP2 adds a pop-up blocker to Internet Explorer 6.

### MSN EXPLORER

Windows XP includes MSN Explorer, an Internet client dedicated to MSN. If you don't have an ISP, you may want to use MSN Explorer to connect to the Internet.

## Multiple Monitor Support—for Both Desktops and Laptops

Several versions of Windows have had multiple monitor support for desktops: By installing two or more graphics cards, each hooked up to a monitor, you can spread your Desktop across two or more monitors, giving you far more space to view multiple applications. Windows XP Professional includes multiple monitor support like its predecessors. Windows XP Professional also includes a new technology called DualView, which lets you hook up two monitors to a single graphics card that supports two interfaces. Relatively few AGP and PCI graphics cards support two VGA interfaces, but you'll find a number of cards with DVI outputs (for LCD panels) that have a regular VGA connection as well.

Most of the excitement here is for laptops, most of which have a connector for an external display as well as the internal connector for the built-in screen. Instead of using the external display to display the same image as the built-in screen, you can use DualView to make the external display an extension of your Desktop. This is a wonderful feature for laptop users who crave more screen space.

## Advanced Features

Just so you know, most of the new features I've described so far apply to both Windows XP Professional and Windows XP Home. Those that follow are specific to Professional.

### BACKUP AND AUTOMATED SYSTEM RECOVERY (ASR)

Windows XP Professional includes a Backup utility and an Automated System Recovery (ASR) feature that can be activated from bootup to restore a damaged system. The Backup utility comes on the Home Edition CD-ROM too (`Ntbackup.msi`), but it doesn't get installed by default, and it doesn't include ASR.

### OFFLINE FILES

Offline files let you cache (store) copies of files located on network drives on your local drive so that you can work with them when your computer is no longer connected to the network. Windows XP Professional can encrypt the Offline Files database to help keep the information in the files secure.

### REMOTE DESKTOP

Remote Desktop is a little confusing because of the terminology. The Remote Desktop component lets you make a computer available for remote control. The Remote Desktop Connection component lets you use a computer to access a remote computer that's running Remote Desktop. Both Professional and Home have Remote Desktop Connection. So you can use a computer running Home to access a computer running Professional, but not the other way around. If you need to be able to connect to your computer remotely via Remote Desktop Connection, you need Professional rather than Home.

### NETWORKING FEATURES

Windows XP Professional has many networking features, including the Simple Network Management Protocol (SNMP), the Client Services for NetWare, Simple TCP/IP Services, and the Multiple Roaming feature. If you need to connect to a NetWare server, or if you need to use roaming profiles, you'll need Windows XP Professional rather than Windows XP Home.

**NOTE**   One other thing—there is a 64-bit version of Windows XP Professional for the Intel Itanium processor.

### IMPROVED SYSPREP

SYSPREP is a tool used to prepare a system for drive imaging. It allows you to make a complete image of a hard drive and load it onto another system, thus facilitating the installation of the operating system on a large number of computers. In Windows XP Professional, SYSPREP has been modified so that you can more quickly and efficiently install the operating system on multiple computers. These modifications reduce startup and imaging time and minimize restarts.

## What's Hiding under the Hood?

The features mentioned so far catch the eye—some even on a cursory scan of the Windows XP Desktop and interface.

Less glamorous, but more important in the long run, are the enhancements hiding under Windows XP's hood. This section discusses the major enhancements that you probably *won't* see.

### PROTECTED MEMORY MANAGEMENT

Windows XP offers fully protected memory management. With protected memory management, Windows XP can handle memory errors with more aplomb. When an application tries to access memory that doesn't belong to it, Windows XP can close the application without affecting any other running application. You still lose any unsaved work in the guilty application, but all your other applications continue running.

While Windows XP is dealing with the misbehaving application, you can move the application's window so that it doesn't obstruct your view of any other applications you have open.

### SYSTEM FILE PROTECTION

Windows XP offers a feature called System File Protection that protects your system files from ill-advised actions on your part.

Windows XP tries to persuade you not to view the contents of folders that you probably shouldn't be messing with by refusing to show them to you until you demand it display them. You can then delete system files if you want (except for any file that's actively in use, which is locked automatically). But the next time that Windows boots, or if it catches the damage you've done before you reboot it, it replaces the files you deleted without notifying you.

### SYSTEM RESTORE

Windows XP offers a System Restore feature similar to but more effective than the System Restore feature in Windows Me. System Restore automatically creates restore points both periodically and each time you make a change to the system—for example, by installing an application or a driver. When one of your changes leads to an unwelcome result, such as your computer failing to boot, you can use System Restore to roll back the change to an earlier point at which the system was working properly.

### DEVICE DRIVER ROLLBACK

Device drivers have long been the bane of Windows—okay, *one* of the banes of Windows. By installing the wrong driver, or a buggy driver, you could render your computer useless until you reinstalled Windows (or turned in frustration to another operating system).

Windows XP tracks the drivers you install and lets you roll back the installation of the driver—in other words, you can revert to the driver you were using before.

Better yet, Windows XP stores details of the previous driver in what's called the Last Known Good Configuration—the configuration used the last time the computer seemed to be running okay. This means that if installing a new driver prevents your computer from booting as normal, you can boot into Safe Mode and use the Last Known Good Configuration to restore the previous driver.

### COMPATIBILITY WITH WINDOWS 9x APPLICATIONS

Windows XP aims to be able to run all applications that would run on Windows 9x, Windows NT, and Windows 2000. As you'll know if you've struggled to run a Windows 9x application on NT or Windows 2000, this is quite a challenge. NT-based operating systems (including Windows XP) handle memory and hardware access in a different way than Windows 9x operating systems. These differences mean that applications designed for Windows 9x often won't run satisfactorily on NT and Windows 2000.

Being able to run these legacy applications is a big feature of Windows XP—but because Microsoft has implemented this feature very successfully, it remains hidden most of the time. Usually, you can simply install a legacy application and run it without complications. Behind the scenes, Windows XP may be running the application in its Compatibility mode or applying one of its new AppFixes to the application (to prevent it from detecting the wrong operating system and from causing problems such as referencing memory once it's been freed up), but you often won't know about it. You may need to specifically run some applications in Compatibility Mode, and you may see Windows Update automatically downloading new information for AppFixes to keep your copy of Windows up-to-date, but most of the time your old applications will simply work—which of course is the way it should be.

## Should You Upgrade to Windows XP Professional?

Whether you should upgrade to Windows XP Professional depends on your needs, how well your current version of Windows is fulfilling them, and whether your hardware is up to the test. The decision is wholly yours (of course), but the following sections offer some suggestions, depending on where you're coming from.

## Windows 9x

If you're using one of the versions of Windows 9x—Windows 95, Windows 98, Windows 98 Second Edition, or Windows Me—the main attractions of Windows XP Professional are much greater stability, the enhanced user interface, the extra features that Windows XP includes, and security. You can use an Upgrade version of XP, as long as you either install over the top of it or, if you are doing a clean install, have your original product CD handy to insert as verification of past ownership when prompted.

Exactly which extra features Windows XP includes depends—obviously enough—on which version of Windows 9x you have. Not surprisingly, later versions of Windows 9x offer more features than earlier versions. For example, the ICS feature debuted in Windows 98 Second Edition, so ICS might be a reason to upgrade to Windows XP if you have Windows 95 or Windows 98 (first edition), but not if you have Windows 98 Second Edition or Windows Me. (The Internet Connection Firewall feature, however, is new.) Likewise, Windows Me includes Windows Media Player 7, a version that greatly improved on the earlier, anemic versions of Windows Media Player, but it isn't as capable as Windows Media Player 8, the version included in Windows XP. From Windows Me, the new version of Windows Media Player provides only a modest incitement to upgrade, whereas from earlier versions of Windows 9x, it provides much more encouragement—assuming you're interested in multimedia, that is.

Whichever version of Windows 9x you're using, you'll need to make sure that your hardware is up to scratch for Windows XP. Very generally speaking, if your computer is capable of running Windows 98 or Windows Me at a decent clip, it should be able to run Windows XP without much trouble (though you might need to add memory). You'll find details of Windows XP's hardware requirements in Chapter 2, "Installing Windows XP Professional."

## Windows 3.1

If you're still using Windows 3.1 and DOS as your main operating system, Windows XP Professional represents a considerable upgrade. There are two major considerations in taking this step:

◆ First, unless you've installed Windows 3.1 on a modern system (as you might have done for backward compatibility with ancient applications), you'll almost certainly need to get a new PC to run Windows XP.

◆ Second, if you will need to continue running DOS applications and 16-bit Windows applications (rather than upgrading to 32-bit applications that provide similar functionality), check to make sure that these applications are compatible with Windows XP before upgrading. As mentioned earlier, Windows XP runs older 32-bit Windows applications quite impressively, but it has problems with some 16-bit applications.

## Windows 2000 Professional

If you're currently using Windows 2000 Professional and are happy with it, stick with it for the time being. The "natural" upgrade path from Windows 2000 Professional is to Windows XP Professional, but make this upgrade only after carefully evaluating the benefits that Windows XP Professional will provide. If Windows 2000 Professional is currently fulfilling all your computing needs, stick with it.

## Windows XP Home Edition

As its name suggests (and is designed to suggest), Windows XP Professional is geared toward use in a "professional" setting—for example, in an office or in a corporate setting. That doesn't mean you can't use it at home if you want, just that it has features designed for use in office and corporate settings. For example, it's designed to connect to Windows 2000 servers running Active Directory, and it has features for being managed remotely by administrators.

Home-to-Professional is a minor upgrade, and not worth the money for most people. Peruse the section earlier in this chapter comparing the features between these two, and decide whether or not any of those features are worth the $100 or more. Professional Edition will not make your PC run any better of faster—it's purely a features thing.

# How Is Windows XP Professional Different from Other Operating Systems?

I've discussed the differences and advantages of Windows 2000 Professional compared with Windows 95/98, but how does it stack up against other popular operating systems?

## Windows XP Professional Compared with UNIX

Of all the operating systems under discussion here, UNIX is probably the most similar to Windows XP Professional in terms of architecture. There are many different flavors of UNIX, however. Each flavor has a different user interface, and not all of them are graphical. As a group, UNIX operating systems are 32-bit, secure, and capable of running on Intel, RISC, and DEC Alpha processors.

UNIX is mostly a server operating system (OS) these days; it is not very popular as a client OS anymore. In the past, artists and designers have used high-end UNIX -based workstations to create special effects for films. Windows XP Professional, however, supports high-end 3-D protocols such as Raydream. Running Windows XP Professional on a high-powered $x86$ processor will give you equal processing power to those UNIX workstations, with the added punch of Windows XP Professional, for a fraction of the price. And running Windows XP Professional on a high-end Pentium IV processor will pretty much leave every other workstation in the dust.

## Windows XP Professional Compared with Linux

Linux is a freely distributed 32-bit OS, a variant of UNIX. Many shells are available that add a friendly graphical face to Linux, making it more accessible to the average end-user than standard UNIX, but with all of UNIX's stability.

A large segment of the Linux fan base is the "anti-Microsoft" crowd that sees Microsoft's industry dominance as a very bad thing and wants to counteract it in any way they can. They love Linux because of the philosophy behind it—free and constantly being collaboratively improved. There's something to be said for that. But me, I'm not political. I just want to run some applications.

In the end, the main reason for owning a computer is to run applications, right? So it's important to choose an OS that runs the applications you need. Some business software companies have released versions of their applications that run on Linux, but the majority of applications still run only on Windows XP. I am not going to disparage Linux here, partly because I think it's a great OS and partly because I'm somewhat afraid of all those rabid Linux enthusiasts out there. However, I will say this: not all of the applications I need to run will work on a Linux system.

### Windows XP Professional Compared with the Macintosh OS

Like Windows XP Professional, the Macintosh OS is a 32-bit environment with built-in networking capabilities. Despite its well-known and intuitive interface, the Macintosh OS lacks many of the powerful features found in Windows XP Professional. Object linking and embedding (OLE), MAPI, and TAPI are all unfamiliar to Apple users. The Mac OS supports only a limited sort of cooperative multitasking, and you can switch between programs only with the mouse; there's no equivalent to the mighty Alt+Tab key combination in Windows. There is also a relatively limited amount of software available to the Macintosh market as compared with the Windows market, and the Mac OS runs only on Mac hardware.

## What Are the Features of Windows XP Professional Architecture?

I've already discussed some of the Windows XP Professional architecture. In this section, I'll analyze it a little more closely to see what makes Windows XP Professional tick and why it is different from other operating systems.

From a programmer's perspective, Windows XP Professional is divided into two layers. These are actually two separate operating modes. The *kernel mode* is where Windows XP Professional performs its internal tasks and controls interaction between programs and the operating system, and between programs themselves. It is generally protected from end users fiddling with it. The *user mode*, which is usually described as sitting above the kernel mode because it is closer to the end user, is where your applications run. The area is considered nonprotected because you have access to it through your applications.

### Kernel Mode

Nothing happens in the Windows XP Professional universe without the operating system knowing about it and giving its blessing. The kernel is the core of Windows XP Professional. It acts as a "gofer" between the operating system and the computer's processor. As such, it is responsible for scheduling all the operating system's interactions with your computer. The kernel also manages all the interrelationships between the different kernel mode operations. It does this by means of *threads*. A thread is a series of instructions that are attached to a command that is executed by a program. Threads include memory addresses, scheduling for the amount of time the process will take, and anything else that describes the process.

The kernel mode is divided into three subsections: the Hardware Abstraction Layer (HAL), the kernel, and Executive Services. Executive Services is subdivided further into its own component parts; more on those parts shortly.

#### THE HAL AND THE KERNEL

The HAL controls the interaction between the kernel and the system hardware. One of the design goals of Windows XP Professional was the capability to be easily ported from one type of computer to another. To this end, the HAL *abstracts* the hardware from the kernel so that the kernel does not need to know what type of hardware is installed in the computer. This extends to running multiple processors in your computer. Windows XP Professional is one of the only PC-based operating systems that can take advantage of symmetric multiprocessing. The abstraction provided by the HAL gives Windows XP Professional greater stability.

Because of the abstraction provided by the HAL, software that attempts to directly access the hardware is not permitted to run. The HAL, working with the kernel, stops those programs dead in their tracks. For performance reasons, many DOS programs—particularly games—use direct hardware access. Programs written for Windows XP Professional don't need to worry about how to access the hardware; they just ask the operating system for support, and Windows XP Professional takes care of the rest.

Windows XP Professional does have some communication that bypasses the HAL and goes directly to the hardware. In each of these cases, the communication is between the Executive Services and the individual drivers for hardware devices such as the video card and network card. But the concept of hardware abstraction is still maintained.

### EXECUTIVE SERVICES

Executive Services is a set of separate components that complete the underpinnings of the Windows XP Professional kernel mode. Each Executive Service controls a specific function. The following is a brief overview of each of those functions.

#### *I/O Manager*

I/O Manager handles all communication between your applications and your hard disk. Additionally, it manages drivers for different file formats (FAT, NTFS) and keeps the Windows XP Professional kernel informed of the hard drive's status. I/O Manager also manages network cards and modems. In short, this manager controls any device that delivers data to or from the computer. Its components are illustrated in Figure 1.3.

**FIGURE 1.3**
I/O Manager is built to simultaneously control multiple devices and drivers.

I/O Manager is divided into the following sections:

**Cache Manager**   Monitors your use of disk cache and disk pages.

**File systems**   Manages the file systems you have installed on your computer.

**Network drivers**   Controls your network cards and network protocols.

**Device drivers**   Manages the hardware you have in your computer. This includes everything from your hard drive(s) and modem to your keyboard and mouse.

### Object Manager

Object Manager manages all the system objects that are used by Windows XP Professional. An object is a piece of data used by the operating system to create system events. Objects are acted upon by processes. Every object has a handle (yes, that's the technical term) that a process connects to in order to complete its job. The Object Manager is extensible, meaning that it can be expanded and added to as new object types are developed.

### Security Reference Monitor

Security Reference Monitor is the "watchdog" for Windows XP Professional. Security Reference Monitor assigns security tokens and authenticates users each time they execute a task.

### Process Manager

Process Manager is the complement to Object Manager. Process Manager manages the creation and deletion of processes. A *process* is a set of threads combined with a memory address and the necessary objects needed to complete a system task. The Process Manager works in conjunction with the Security Reference Monitor to ensure that every process is assigned a security token.

### Local Procedure Call Facility

Local Procedure Call facility acts as a negotiator between user mode and kernel mode. From an internal standpoint, Windows XP Professional uses a client-server model to administer itself. Just as Windows XP Professional connects to a server and requests services from it, the Windows XP Professional user mode requests services from the Windows XP Professional kernel mode. Those requests are handled by local procedure calls. Local procedure calls are also used in standard client-server networks.

### Virtual Memory Manager

Virtual Memory Manager oversees how Windows XP Professional uses virtual memory. To increase the amount of usable memory space, Windows XP Professional uses hard-disk space as memory when it runs out of memory (which can happen fairly quickly with some high-powered programs). The disk memory is known as *virtual* memory.

### Win32K and GDI

The Win32K and Graphics Device Interface (GDI) are the graphics subsystem of Windows XP Professional. The graphics functions in earlier versions of Windows NT were provided by the Win32 subsystem in user mode. Microsoft moved the graphics subsystem into Executive Services for version 4 to give the graphics functions a performance boost. In fact, this resulted in the single greatest increase in the apparent speed of Windows NT 4.

## User Mode

In the Windows XP Professional user mode, each of your programs runs in a separate memory space, an arrangement that protects each program from the others in case one should crash. This is true for 32-bit and 16-bit programs, both Windows and DOS.

The user mode is divided into subsystems. Each subsystem handles a different type of application and can report directly to the kernel mode. The subsystems are described briefly in Table 1.1.

**TABLE 1.1:** User Mode Subsystems

| SUBSYSTEM | DESCRIPTION |
| --- | --- |
| Win32 | Administers 32-bit and 16-bit Windows programs. |
| OS/2 | Administers character-based OS/2 programs. |
| POSIX | Administers POSIX programs, which are Unix hybrids that can be run on any POSIX-compliant system, including Windows XP Professional. They are written to a series of application programming interfaces (APIs) that are platform independent. They control interaction with system components such as hard drives and memory. |
| Security | Administers system security and manages security tokens, monitors, and passwords. The user mode portion of the Security subsystem runs only during a user logon. |

In addition to the subsystems noted in Table 1.1, user mode may also contain VDMs (video display metafiles). A VDM simulates a computer running MS-DOS 5, with 16MB of RAM and conventional, expanded, and extended memory. As stated earlier in this chapter, this simulation makes it possible to run MS-DOS programs on Windows XP Professional. It also enables you to run 16-bit Windows applications by simulating Windows 3.1 running on that MS-DOS computer with 16MB of memory. By default, Windows XP Professional starts all 16-bit Windows applications in the same Win16 on Win32 or *WOW* environment. This simulates exactly the environment the programs were written to operate in under Windows 3.1. However, Windows XP Professional gives you the ability to start the application in a separate memory space, which creates another WOW for each 16-bit Windows application.

Remember that the WOW environment imitates Windows 3.1 so well that it even hangs just like the old Windows did! That means that if one of your 16-bit Windows applications crashes, it will take all the other 16-bit applications with it—unless you have chosen to start them in their own memory spaces, in which case the other 16-bit programs will keep running without a problem.

**TIP** If a 16-bit application crashes, it will also crash any other program running in the same memory space. If this happens, you can stop the WOW by using Task Manager and restart the 16-bit program. All 32-bit applications will be unaffected by the crash and continue to run normally.

## Summary

This chapter has discussed what you need to know about Windows XP Professional in order to decide whether to upgrade to it or stay with your current version of Windows.

CHAPTER 1

# Chapter 2

# Installing Windows XP Professional

This chapter discusses how to install Windows XP Professional in each of the three ways in which you may want to install it: as an upgrade to Windows 9*x*, Windows NT, or Windows 2000 Professional; as a new installation on a computer that already has installed an operating system that you want to keep; and as a clean installation on a computer that doesn't have an operating system installed (or a computer whose operating system you want to wipe).

At the end of the chapter, you'll find a discussion of how to perform an unattended installation, which can be useful if you need to install the same operating system multiple times.

- ◆ Preparing for installation

- ◆ Upgrading Windows 9*x* or Windows 2000 Professional to Windows XP

- ◆ Performing an installation of Windows XP Professional

- ◆ Using the Files and Settings Transfer Wizard to transfer files and settings

- ◆ Uninstalling Windows XP Professional and reverting to Windows 9*x*

- ◆ Removing your old version of Windows

- ◆ Keeping Windows updated

- ◆ Automating the installation of Windows XP

## The Order of Business

Here's the order of business for installing Windows XP successfully:

1. First, make sure that your computer will be able to run Windows XP Professional. Start by comparing your system specifications with the minimum requirements, and see if you need to upgrade any components.

2. Then, assuming your computer has an operating system loaded already, insert the Windows XP CD in your computer and run the Windows Upgrade Advisor.

3. If you want to perform a clean installation of Windows XP rather than an upgrade, but you want your new installation to pick up your current settings and some of your files, run the Files and Settings Transfer Wizard to save the settings from your current version of Windows and then boot from the Windows XP CD to start the installation.

4. Then perform the upgrade, new installation, or clean installation.

5. If you ran the Files and Settings Transfer Wizard, run it again to apply your files and settings.

## Will Your Computer Be Able to Run Windows XP Professional?

First, make sure that your computer will be able to run Windows XP Professional. The following sections discuss the main requirements.

### Processor

Windows XP requires a minimum of a Pentium II processor running at 233MHz. But realistically, you'll want a 600MHz or faster processor for the kind of performance you'll need in a business setting.

If you don't know what processor your computer has, watch the information that comes up as it boots. This will give you at least the processor speed, though it may give an incorrect classification of the chip. For example, some systems classify Celeron chips as Pentium III chips. (Mid-range Celeron chips *are* in fact cut-down Pentium III chips, but your system should really know the difference.)

### RAM

Windows XP requires a minimum of 64MB of RAM to install and run. This too is an absolute minimum and delivers poor performance unless your processor is extremely fast (in which case the lack of RAM cannibalizes processor performance). For a single user running one or two tasks at a time, 128MB is enough. For multiple concurrent users (with Fast User Switching) or for running several large applications at once, get 256MB or more RAM. (At this writing, 256MB RAM modules are selling for prices as low as $45, so upgrading your RAM is relatively painless.)

**NOTE**    Windows XP Professional can access a maximum of 4GB of RAM.

If you don't know how much RAM your computer has, watch the count of RAM when you boot. If the number is in kilobytes, divide by 1024 to get the number in megabytes. Alternatively, click Start, right-click My Computer, and choose Properties from the shortcut menu. Windows displays the System Properties dialog box open at the General tab. The amount of RAM is reported at the bottom.

---

**GET PLENTY OF RAM**

Everyone knows that you need plenty of RAM to run Windows. That's true—up to a point. But most people still have too little RAM on their computers.

Windows XP Professional will run—well, more like stagger along—on 64MB RAM. If the computer has a fast processor, and if you don't use any large applications or large files, performance may be tolerable. But the hard disk will be kept busy as Windows continually uses virtual memory to store the information that won't fit in the RAM.

If you're buying a new computer, you'll be much better off saving a little money on the processor and putting it into RAM. Unless you're running the latest 3-D games or performing terrain mapping or other advanced imaging, you'll notice little benefit from having a few hundred extra megahertz of CPU on your computer. But another 128MB (better, another 256MB or even 512MB or 1GB) of RAM will make a huge difference on a system with just about any processor. For an existing PC, the slower and older your CPU, the more dramatic a difference more RAM will make in performance.

### Free Disk Space

Windows XP Professional requires approximately 650MB of free disk space to install on a 2GB hard drive. If you're installing over a network, you'll need more free space. In addition, there has to be room for your paging file (by default, 1.5 times the amount of RAM in your computer) and for your hibernation file (the same size as the amount of RAM) if your computer supports hibernation. On top of that, you'll need space for any applications you want to install and any files you want to create.

In practice, it's a good idea to have at least 1GB of free space on the drive on which you install Windows XP, plus space for your applications and files. To see how much space is free on a drive, right-click the drive in an Explorer window and choose Properties from the shortcut menu. The General tab of the resulting Properties dialog box for the drive shows how much free space it has. Hard disks are so inexpensive these days, and so easy to install, that there is little reason to try to hobble along with a full hard disk.

### SVGA-Capable Video Adapter and Monitor

Your video adapter and monitor need to be capable of SVGA resolution (800×600 pixels) with 256 or more colors. This is the minimum display resolution permitted, unlike in earlier Windows versions. (Safe Mode still runs in standard VGA, and you can configure individual apps to switch to that mode with Compatibility Mode, but it's not for regular use.) Beyond that, just about any PCI or AGP video adapter should work (drivers permitting, of course), as should any CRT or LCD monitor.

### CD Drive or DVD Drive

You need a CD drive or DVD drive, or access to one or the other, to install Windows XP. If the drive is on another computer, you can install across a network or copy the files to your local drive and run them from there. You can also do diskless network installs in a corporate environment.

## Checking System Compatibility

To check whether Windows XP thinks your computer will be able to run it, run the Windows Upgrade Advisor program by following these steps:

1. Insert the Windows XP CD. If your computer doesn't automatically start running the CD, open an Explorer window, navigate to the CD, and double-click the `setup.exe` program.

2. On the opening screen, click the Check System Compatibility link. Setup offers the choices Check My System Automatically and Visit the Compatibility Web Site.

3. Click the Check My System Automatically link.

4. If an Internet connection is available, Setup runs Dynamic Update to download any new files that may help with the installation. It then runs the Windows Upgrade Advisor program and displays the Upgrade Report screen of the Microsoft Windows Upgrade Advisor. Figure 2.1 shows an example of an upgrade report.

5. If your computer seems to be fit for Windows XP, the report tells you that the check found no incompatibilities or problems. Any problems are listed in the list box in summary form. Click the Full Details button to view the details (broken up into categories such as Blocking Issues, Warnings, and Helpful Information) and advice on what to do about the problems. (Click the

resulting Summary button to return to the summary view.) Click the Save As button to save the information to file, or click the Print button to print a copy of it.

**6.** Click the Finish button. Windows closes the Microsoft Windows Upgrade Advisor.

**FIGURE 2.1**

Use the Microsoft Windows Upgrade Advisor to check whether your computer will be able to run Windows XP.

Follow the Upgrade Advisor's advice to get your computer ready for upgrading to Windows XP. In particular, you need to take care of any blocking issues that the Advisor has identified. An example of a blocking issue is not having enough disk space to install Windows XP. You might need to remove some existing files or reconfigure your partitions (for example, by using a tool such as Partition-Magic), in order to resolve such an issue.

## Choosing an Installation Method

Once you've decided to install Windows XP, your next decision is how to install Windows XP Professional on your computer. You can install Windows XP in three ways:

**Upgrade**    If you have Windows 9x, Windows NT 4 Workstation (including service packs), Windows 2000 Professional (including service packs), or Windows XP Home Edition, you can perform an upgrade, essentially overwriting the previous version of Windows with Windows XP Professional. Upgrading like this transfers all your files, settings, and applications to Windows XP, so (in theory) you can pick up your work or play straight away in Windows XP where you left off. If you're upgrading from XP Home to Professional, upgrading simply adds more features; it doesn't change anything system-wise.

**New installation**    A new installation installs Windows XP on a new disk or a separate partition. You can use the Files and Settings Transfer Wizard to copy your files and settings from your previous version of Windows to Windows XP.

**Clean installation**    You can install Windows XP from scratch on your computer, deleting the previous copy that was there rather than upgrading it. Again, you can use the Files and Settings Transfer Wizard to copy your files and settings from your previous version of Windows to Windows XP. You'll need to install all the applications you want to use after you install Windows XP.

Which type of installation to perform can be a tricky decision. The longer you've been running Windows on this computer since installing it, the stronger the arguments are for both an upgrade and a clean installation:

◆ By now, you've probably installed all the applications you need and got them working together. By upgrading, you can transition your whole work environment to Windows XP, so that your Desktop, Start menu, and folder structure retain their current settings and your applications all work as before.

◆ Then again, you probably have applications that you no longer use, or applications that no longer work. (Techies call this a "dirty system.") By performing a clean install, you can strip your system down to only the software you need. It'll take longer, but the result may be better. Similarly, your data folders could probably do with some cleaning out and archiving.

If you need to install a new hard drive as your main hard drive, you'll need to perform a clean install. (The exception is if you use a hard-drive cloning or migration package such as DriveImage or Ghost. These packages are often used for upgrading the hard drives in laptops, where the lack of expansion room forces you to replace the current hard drive rather than add a drive, but some of them work for desktops as well.)

## Preparing for Installation

Once you've established that your computer should be able to run Windows XP, prepare for installation by taking those of the following steps that are applicable to the type of installation you're planning (upgrade, new installation, or clean installation).

### Back Up All Your Data Files

For safety, back up all your data files shortly before installation, using your usual backup medium.

### Write Down Internet Connection Information

If you're planning a new installation or a clean installation rather than an upgrade, and you use a dial-up Internet connection, write down the information you need to create the connection: your ISP account username, your password, your ISP's phone number, and your ISP's primary DNS server and secondary DNS server. You might also want to write down the information for connecting to your mail server(s).

### Plug In and Switch On All Hardware

Make sure that all the hardware you intend to use with the computer is attached to it and powered on. For example, if you'll use a printer and scanner with the computer, make sure these devices are attached to the computer and powered on, so that Setup can detect them if it's smart enough.

**WARNING**  Make sure your hardware configuration is exactly the way you want it before activating Windows XP. Activation creates a code based on the installed hardware that locks that copy of XP to that hardware, so if you make a lot of hardware changes to the system later, you might need to re-activate (by calling Microsoft). I'll explain activation in more detail later in this chapter.

## Use the Files and Settings Transfer Wizard to Transfer Settings

Windows XP includes a wizard for transferring files and settings from one computer or operating system to another. You don't need to use this wizard, which is called the Files and Settings Transfer Wizard, if you're upgrading Windows 9x to Windows XP, because Windows automatically transfers all your settings when you perform an upgrade. But the wizard can save you a great deal of time when you want to transfer files and settings either to a new computer that's running Windows XP or to a new installation of Windows XP on the same computer on which you've kept your previous installation of Windows as a dual-boot. For example, if you choose to test Windows XP on a new partition before committing yourself to it, you can use the Files and Settings Transfer Wizard to transfer your work environment to the new partition so that you can use your regular settings and files.

Before you use the Files and Settings Transfer Wizard, make sure you've connected any network drive you want to use, or that you have a removable disk or recordable CD ready. To transfer files and settings, you'll need plenty of storage. You can save settings files to a floppy drive, but most data files will be too big.

To use the Files and Settings Transfer Wizard, follow these steps:

1. Insert the Windows XP CD. If your computer doesn't automatically start running the CD, open an Explorer window, navigate to the CD, and double-click the `setup.exe` program. Windows displays the Welcome to Microsoft Windows XP screen.

2. Click the Perform Additional Tasks link.

3. On the next screen, click the Transfer Files and Settings link. Setup starts the Files and Settings Transfer Wizard.

4. Click the Next button. If this computer is running Windows XP, the wizard displays the Which Computer Is This? screen. If it does, select the Old Computer option button and click the Next button. (If this computer isn't running Windows XP, the wizard knows it's the old computer.) The wizard then displays the Select a Transfer Method screen (shown in Figure 2.2).

5. Select the Direct Cable option button, the Home or Small Office Network option button (if it's available), the Floppy Drive or Other Removable Media option button, or the Other option button as appropriate. The Other option button lets you use the Browse button and the resulting Browse for Folder dialog box or the Folder or Drive text box to specify a removable drive or a network drive.

**FIGURE 2.2**
On the Select a Transfer Method screen of the Files and Settings Transfer Wizard, specify how you want to transfer files and settings from the old computer to the new computer.

**6.** Click the Next button. The wizard displays the What Do You Want to Transfer? screen (shown in Figure 2.3).

**7.** In the What Do You Want to Transfer? list, select the Settings Only option button, the Files Only option button, or the Both Files and Settings option button as appropriate. The list box on the right side of the dialog box lists the types of settings and files that will be affected.

**8.** If you want to customize the list of settings, files, or both, select the Let Me Select a Custom List of Files and Settings When I Click Next check box. Customizing the list of files lets you specify particular folders for transfer. By default, the wizard transfers the Desktop folder, the Fonts folder, the My Documents folder, the My Pictures folder, the Shared Desktop folder, and the Shared Documents folder.

**9.** Click the Next button. If you selected to customize, the wizard displays the Select Custom Files and Settings screen (shown in Figure 2.4).

**FIGURE 2.3**

On the What Do You Want to Transfer? screen of the Files and Settings Transfer Wizard, specify which settings and files you want to transfer to the new computer (or to Windows XP).

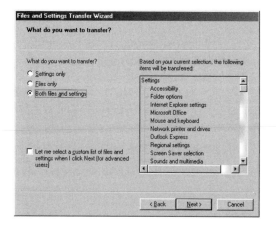

**FIGURE 2.4**

On the Select Custom Files and Settings screen of the Files and Settings Transfer Wizard, choose the files and settings to transfer.

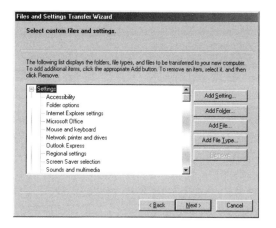

10. Select the files and settings to transfer:

♦ To add a setting, click the Add Setting button. The wizard displays the Add a Setting dialog box. Select the setting or settings in the list box and click the OK button. The wizard closes the Add a Setting dialog box and adds the setting or settings to the list.

♦ To add a folder, click the Add Folder button. The wizard displays the Browse for Folder dialog box. Select the folder and click the OK button. The wizard closes the Browse for Folder dialog box and adds the folder to the list.

♦ To add a file, click the Add File button. The wizard displays the Add a File dialog box (a common Open dialog box in disguise). Select the file and click the Open button. The wizard closes the Add a File dialog box and adds the file to the list.

♦ To add a file type, click the Add File Type button. The wizard displays the Add a File Type dialog box (shown in Figure 2.5). Select the file type in the Registered File Types list box; if it's not listed there, enter its extension in the Other text box. Then click the OK button. The wizard closes the Add a File Type dialog box and adds the file type to the list.

♦ To remove a setting, folder, file, or file type, select it in the list box and click the Remove button.

**FIGURE 2.5**

Use the Add a File Type dialog box to add a file type to the list of file types to transfer.

11. Click the Next button. The wizard may display the Install Programs on Your New Computer screen, suggesting some programs that you may want to install on your new computer (or new installation of Windows) before transferring settings. If so, note these suggestions.

12. The wizard then displays the Collection in Progress screen (shown in Figure 2.6) while it collects your files and settings. It then displays the Completing the Collection Phase screen.

13. Click the Finish button. The wizard closes itself.

For details of how to apply your saved files and settings to your new installation of Windows, see "Applying Your Files and Settings" later in this chapter.

## Stop Any Antivirus Software or Disk Utilities

Stop any antivirus software or disk utilities before running the Windows installation, because the installation process needs direct access to your hardware and the antivirus software might see that access as an attack and prevent it.

**FIGURE 2.6**
The wizard collects
the files.

## Upgrading to Windows XP

When you upgrade, the installation procedure copies the settings from your current version of Windows and applies them to the installation of Windows XP. If the installation doesn't work correctly, or if you find Windows XP doesn't suit you, you can uninstall it and revert to your previous installation of Windows unless you are upgrading from Windows NT or Windows 2000 Professional.

To perform an upgrade, follow these steps:

1.  Insert the CD in a CD drive or DVD drive. If Autoplay is enabled on your computer, Windows displays the introductory screen (shown in Figure 2.7). If not, open an Explorer window and double-click the CD. This should trigger the Autoplay action. If it doesn't, double-click the `setup.exe` file on the CD to run it.

**FIGURE 2.7**
To start the upgrade,
select the Install Windows XP link.

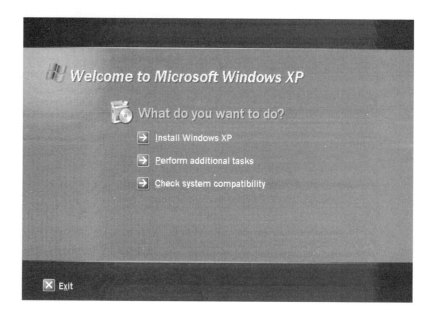

2. Click the Install Windows XP link. Setup displays the Welcome to Windows Setup screen (shown in Figure 2.8).

**FIGURE 2.8**
On the Welcome to Windows Setup screen, choose the Upgrade item in the Installation Type drop-down list.

3. In the Installation Type drop-down list, choose the Upgrade item.

4. Click the Next button. Setup displays the License Agreement screen. Read it.

5. If you agree to the license, select the I Accept This Agreement option button and click the Next button. (If you don't agree to the license, Setup exits.) Setup displays the Your Product Key screen.

6. Enter your product key and click the Next button. Setup displays the Upgrade Report screen (shown in Figure 2.9).

**FIGURE 2.9**
On the Upgrade Report screen of Setup, choose the type of upgrade report you want for this computer.

7. Choose the type of upgrade report you want by selecting the Show Me Hardware Issues Only option button, the Show Me the Full Report option button, or the Do Not Show Me the Report option button.

**8.** Click the Next button. Setup displays the Get Updated Setup Files screen (shown in Figure 2.10), which lets you choose whether to use Dynamic Update to download any new Setup files that Microsoft may have released since your copy of Windows XP was pressed.

**FIGURE 2.10**
On the Get Updated Setup Files screen of Setup, choose whether to let Dynamic Update download the latest Setup files.

**9.** To download any available files, leave the Yes, Download the Updated Setup Files option button selected, as it is by default. To skip Dynamic Update, select the No, Skip This Step and Continue Installing Windows option button.

**NOTE**    You can download any updated files by using Windows Update after you finish installing Windows XP. The only advantage to Dynamic Update comes if the new files are needed for any of the hardware on your computer during installation.

**10.** Click the Next button. If you chose to use Dynamic Update, Setup contacts the Microsoft website and downloads any relevant files. Setup then starts analyzing your computer for possible problems in upgrading to Windows XP.

◆   If you don't have enough space to install Windows XP, you'll see a Windows XP Setup dialog box such as that shown in Figure 2.11 warning you of the problem. Click the Quit Setup button, retire disconsolately from the fray, and return when you've made more space available.

**FIGURE 2.11**
Setup warns you if you don't have enough space available to install Windows XP.

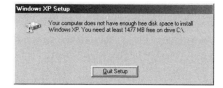

**11.** If you have any incompatible hardware or software, Setup displays the Upgrade Report screen (of which Figure 2.12 shows a sample). You can click the Full Report button to view the details of the hardware and software, click the Save As button to save the information to file, or click the Print button to print a copy of it. If you don't select one of these options, Setup displays the

Windows XP Setup dialog box, which warns you that some devices on your computer may not work with Windows XP and offers you a View Report button, a Continue button, and a Quit Setup button. Click the Continue button if you want to continue.

**FIGURE 2.12**

The Upgrade Report screen of Setup summarizes any potential hardware and software upgrade problems you may face.

12. Click the Next button. Setup continues running the setup routine, reboots your computer, and takes the installation all the way to the Welcome to Microsoft Windows screen. Skip ahead to "The Installation Paths Converge" later in the chapter.

## Performing a New Installation of Windows XP

To perform a new installation of Windows XP (without upgrading your current version of Windows), follow these steps:

1. Insert the CD in a CD drive or DVD drive. If Autoplay is enabled on your computer, Windows displays the introductory screen (shown in Figure 2.13). If not, open an Explorer window and double-click the CD. This should trigger the Autoplay action. If it doesn't, double-click the `setup.exe` file on the CD to run it.

2. Click the Install Windows XP link. Setup displays the Welcome to Windows Setup screen (shown in Figure 2.14).

3. In the Installation Type drop-down list, choose the New Installation item.

4. Click the Next button. Setup displays the License Agreement screen. Read it.

5. If you agree to the license, select the I Accept This Agreement option button and click the Next button. (If you don't agree to the license, Setup exits.) Setup displays the Your Product Key screen.

6. Enter your product key and click the Next button. Setup displays the Setup Options screen (shown in Figure 2.15). From this screen, you can choose language options, installation options, and accessibility options.

7. To change the language used, select the language in the Select the Primary Language and Region You Want to Use drop-down list. If you want to install support for East Asian languages, select the Install Support for East Asian Languages check box.

**FIGURE 2.13**

To start installing, select the Install Windows XP link.

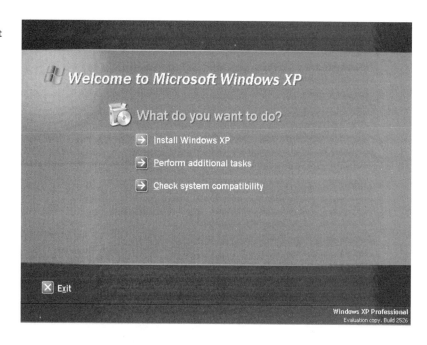

**FIGURE 2.14**

On the Welcome to Windows Setup screen, choose the New Installation item in the Installation Type drop-down list.

8. To set the advanced options, which let you control the installation folder and specify that you want to select the installation partition, click the Advanced Options button on the Setup Options screen. Setup displays the Advanced Options dialog box (shown in Figure 2.16), which offers the following options:

   ◆ The Copy Installation Files from This Folder text box lists the path from which you ran the Setup program (or it ran itself). Usually, you won't need to change this path, but you can if necessary.

**FIGURE 2.15**
When you perform a new installation, Setup displays the Setup Options screen, on which you can choose advanced options and accessibility options.

**FIGURE 2.16**
In the Advanced Options dialog box, you can specify the installation folder and tell Setup that you want to choose the installation partition.

◆ The To This Folder on My Hard Drive text box shows the location to which Setup is planning to install Windows XP: your current Windows folder. If you don't want Windows XP to overwrite your current version of Windows, choose a different folder. For example, you may want to create a dual-boot setup so that you can compare Windows XP to your current version of Windows without yet removing the latter from your computer.

◆ The Copy All Installation Files from the Setup CD check box enables you to force Setup to copy all its files to the hard drive rather than leaving them on the CD. Use this option when installing Windows XP from a CD that will not be available after Setup reboots the computer. For example, when installing Windows XP on a laptop computer using an external CD drive (such as a parallel-port drive, a USB drive, or a PC Card–connected drive), you'll probably need to copy all setup files to the hard drive because the CD drive will not be available from the reboot until Setup is complete. You may also need to use this option if your CD drive will not read the Windows XP CD reliably during the setup routine after the reboot. (This shouldn't happen, but it does. After the reboot, Setup uses a different CD driver that apparently disagrees with some CD drives.) By default, this check box is cleared unless you're installing from a network drive, in which case it's not available (as in Figure 2.16).

◆ The I Want to Choose the Install Drive Letter and Partition During Setup check box lets you tell Setup to display the partitioning screen so that you can specify the partition on which to install Windows XP. If you're performing a new installation of Windows XP, you don't need to select this check box, because Setup automatically displays the partitioning screen so that you can specify where to install Windows XP.

9. Click the OK button. Setup closes the Advanced Options dialog box.

10. During Setup, Windows XP offers two accessibility options, Magnifier and Narrator. Magnifier is designed for people with limited but viable vision and displays an enlarged version of the selected portion of the screen. Narrator is designed for the blind and those with more limited vision. It reads the contents of the screen aloud. To use these options, click the Accessibility Options button on the Setup Options screen. Setup displays the Accessibility Options dialog box (shown in Figure 2.17). Select the Use Microsoft Magnifier During Setup check box or the Use Microsoft Narrator During Setup check box as appropriate. Then click the OK button. Setup closes the Accessibility Options dialog box and applies your choices.

**FIGURE 2.17**

Setup offers Magnifier and Narrator accessibility options for those with impaired vision.

11. Once you've finished choosing special options, click the Next button on the Setup Options screen. Setup displays the Get Updated Setup Files screen (shown in Figure 2.18), which lets you choose whether to use Dynamic Update to download any new Setup files that Microsoft may have released since your copy of Windows XP was pressed.

12. To download any available files, leave the Yes, Download the Updated Setup Files option button selected, as it is by default. To skip Dynamic Update, select the No, Skip This Step and Continue Installing Windows option button.

**FIGURE 2.18**

On the Get Updated Setup Files screen of Setup, choose whether to let Dynamic Update download the latest Setup files.

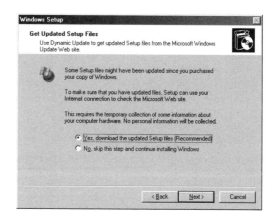

13. Click the Next button. If you chose to use Dynamic Update, Setup contacts the Microsoft website and downloads any relevant files. Setup then continues running the setup routine, reboots your computer, and displays the partitioning screen. Go to the "Choosing a Hard Disk Partition" section in the "Performing a Clean Install of Windows XP" section, a little later in this chapter.

---

**WHY IS THE FOLDER CALLED "I386"?**

If you're looking at the Advanced Options dialog box, the Copy Installation Files from This Folder text box is probably listing a path that ends in i386. What's this all about?

i386 stands for Intel 386. The 386, as you'll remember if you've been computing for a while, was Intel's hottest processor at the end of the 1980s. But it's also the descriptor for the entire family of chips that has continued through the 486 chips and Pentium chips (renamed from 586, which wasn't trademarkable) to the Pentium 4 chips of today.

But why is i386 there? Why is the folder not called something intuitive like "Files"? It's because NT was originally written to be processor independent so that it could run on various types of processors without major rebuilding.

The early versions of NT ran on Intel chips, Alpha chips, MIPS chips, and PowerPC chips. The installation CD came with a separate folder for each of these. Over the years (or, more correctly, over the versions of NT), Microsoft gradually dropped support for processors other than the Intel 386 family. But the i386 folder survives as a holdover of the old days.

---

# Performing a Clean Install of Windows XP

To perform a clean installation of Windows XP, put the Windows XP CD in your CD-ROM drive or DVD drive and boot from it. (You may have to change the boot settings in your computer's BIOS to boot from the CD.) Windows Setup automatically launches itself.

First, Setup displays the Welcome to Setup screen. From here, press the Enter key to start the installation. (Press the F3 key if you've reached this stage by mistake and need to quit.) Setup displays the partitioning screen.

## Choosing a Hard Disk Partition

The partitioning screen lets you create and delete partitions as well as specify the installation partition. The screen lists the current partitions on the disk, their label, their type (for example, NTFS for an NTFS partition, FAT32 for a FAT partition, and Raw for a new, unformatted partition), their size, and the amount of space free on each. Any unpartitioned space is listed as such. Any space you've deliberately left unpartitioned will of course be free, but there will often be a few megabytes of unpartitioned space left over after you've tried to allocate all the space on the disk.

To choose an existing partition for the installation, use the up and down arrows to move the highlight to it. Then press the Enter key.

To create a new partition, select some unpartitioned space and press the C key. Setup displays a Details screen. Specify the size of the partition in megabytes and press the Enter key.

If you want to install Windows XP and use up the full amount of unpartitioned space, you don't need to explicitly create a partition first. Just select the Unpartitioned Space item and press the Enter key to start the installation.

To delete an existing partition, select it in the list and press the D key. Setup displays a screen confirming the action. Press the L key. If the partition is a system partition, Setup displays a more extensive warning. And if the partition is the partition on which Setup has installed its temporary files for carrying out the installation of Windows, Setup refuses to delete the partition.

Once you've chosen a partition, Setup proceeds. If the partition is a new partition, Setup offers you the choice of formatting it with NTFS or with FAT. For each, there's the option of a quick format. A full format includes a scan of the disk for bad sectors; a quick format skips this scan. Unless you're in a tearing hurry and have checked the disk recently for bad sectors, go with the full format.

**NOTE**    If you choose to install Windows XP on a partition that already contains another operating system, Setup displays a screen warning you that this may cause problems. Press the C key if you're prepared to continue. Press the Esc key to return to the partitioning screen and select another partition.

### Converting the Partition to NTFS

If you're installing Windows XP on an existing partition that uses FAT, Setup offers you the option of converting the installation partition to NTFS. Think seriously about doing so, because NTFS is one of the major improvements in Windows XP Professional over Windows 9x.

NTFS offers two compelling advantages over FAT. First, NTFS has security features (including auditing and file-level permissions), while FAT does not. And second, NTFS keeps a log of activities so that it can restore the disk to order after a hardware or power failure; FAT simply loses your data instead.

**WARNING**    If you are creating a dual-boot configuration with a version of Windows 9x, be aware that NTFS can access FAT partitions but Windows 9x cannot access NTFS partitions. If this doesn't matter to you, go ahead and convert the partition to NTFS.

Next, you see the license agreement. Read it and press the F8 key if you agree and want to proceed. Press the Esc key to cancel installation.

### Choosing Regional and Language Options

After this, Setup entertains itself for a few minutes as it performs part of the installation. Next, you see the Regional and Language Options screen. From here, you can change the computer's standards and formats setting so that it displays numbers, currencies, and dates in the appropriate formats for the country or user. You can also change the default keyboard layout.

To change the standards and formats setting, click the Customize button. Setup displays the Regional and Language Options dialog box with the Region Options tab foremost, as shown in Figure 2.19. In the Standards and Formats group box, select the language and locale you want to use. The text boxes in the Samples area show samples of a number, a currency, a time, a short date, and a long date for that language and locale. (You can change these by clicking the Customize button and working in the Customize Regional Options dialog box.) In the Location drop-down list, select your geographical location so that Windows knows which part of the world you're in when its services try to present you with local information. Click the OK button. Setup closes the Regional and Language Options dialog box.

**FIGURE 2.19**
On the Region Options tab of the Regional and Language Options dialog box, specify the standards and formats setting to use and tell Windows your location.

To change the keyboard layout, click the Details button. Setup displays the Text Services and Input Languages dialog box (shown in Figure 2.20). Select the language in the Default Input Language drop-down list. To add an input language, click the Add button and use the resulting Add Input Language dialog box to specify the input language and keyboard layout. For example, if you use the Dvorak layout for your keyboard, set it as the default keyboard layout. Then click the OK button. Setup closes the Text Services and Input Languages dialog box.

Click the Next button to continue the setup process.

**FIGURE 2.20**
Use the Text Services and Input Languages dialog box to change your default input language.

### Entering Your Name and Organization

Next, Setup displays the Personalize Your Software screen, which demands your name and your organization's name. Enter these with due care and consideration, as they get deeply buried within the Windows Registry. (Chapter 25 discusses how to change them if you get them wrong.) You have to enter some text in the Name text box, but you can leave the Organization text box empty if you want.

Click the Next button to proceed.

### Entering Your Product Key

Next, for a clean installation (but not for a new installation), Setup displays the Your Product Key screen. Enter the 25-character product key (it should be on a yellow sticker on the back of the folder or CD box your Windows CD came in) and click the Next button to proceed.

**TIP**   If there's any risk of your misplacing your product key, write it on the Windows CD using a permanent pen such as a Sharpie.

### Entering the Computer Name

Next, Windows Setup displays the What's Your Computer's Name? screen. By default, Setup suggests a complex and unmemorizable name that starts with the first part of the first name you entered in the previous dialog box. Change this name to something descriptive that you'll be able to remember and associate easily with this computer. The name can be a maximum of 63 characters, but you'd do well to keep it shorter than this to make it manageable. Names of more than 15 characters will be visible to other computers only via TCP/IP; via other network protocols, they won't be visible.

Click the Next button once again.

### Entering the Modem Dialing Information

Next, if the computer has a modem that Setup was able to detect, Setup displays the Modem Dialing Information screen. Specify your country or region (for example, United States of America), your area code (which is compulsory), any number you dial to get an outside line, and whether the phone system uses tone dialing or pulse dialing. Then click the Next button to proceed.

### Checking the Date and Time

Next, Setup displays the Date and Time Settings screen. Check the date, time, and time zone, and select or clear the Automatically Adjust Clock for Daylight Saving Changes check box as appropriate. Then click the Next button.

### Specifying Networking Settings

Next, Setup installs some networking components and attempts to detect any network cards installed in your computer. Setup then displays the Networking Settings screen, which offers you the choice of Typical Settings or Custom Settings.

The Typical Settings option installs the Client for Microsoft Networks, the QoS Packet Scheduler, File and Print Sharing for Microsoft Networks, and TCP/IP with automatic addressing. You can install other services after Setup completes (or remove these services), of course, but usually you'll be better off choosing the Custom Settings option and specifying suitable settings as described in the rest of this section.

If you select the Custom Settings option button and click the Next button, Windows Setup displays the Networking Components screen.

You can adjust the default settings by adding other services, uninstalling the default services, or choosing not to apply the selected services to this network adapter. When you remove a service, you make it unavailable to any of the network or dial-up adapters on your computer. So if you need to install a service but not use it for your primary network connection, let Setup install it, but clear its check box on the Networking Components screen.

### UNINSTALLING A SERVICE

To uninstall one of the services, select it and click the Uninstall button. Setup displays a confirmation message box warning you that uninstalling the component removes it from all network connections. Click the Yes button if you want to remove the service.

### ADDING A SERVICE

To add other services to the default services, follow these steps:

1. Click the Install button. Setup displays the Select Network Component Type dialog box.

2. Select the type of component you want to add—Client, Service, or Protocol—and click the Add button. Setup displays the Select Network Client dialog box, the Select Network Service dialog box, or the Select Network Protocol dialog box, as appropriate.

3. Select the client, service, or protocol in the list box. To add an unlisted client, service, or protocol that you have on disk, click the Have Disk button and use the resulting Install from Disk dialog box to identify the file.

4. Click the OK button. Windows Setup installs the client, service, or protocol and closes the Select Network Component Type dialog box.

### CONFIGURING TCP/IP

Some of the network components have parameters you can configure. Of these, the key component is TCP/IP, the Internet protocol suite. Windows does a pretty good job of setting up TCP/IP for automatic detection of an IP address, and that's the way to go if you will be sharing an Internet connection with Internet Connection Sharing (ICS) on this system (or using a shared ICS connection on it) or if you will be connecting to a DHCP server.

If you need to manually specify an IP address and/or a DNS server, follow these steps:

1. Select the Internet Protocol (TCP/IP) item in the list box on the Networking Components tab.

2. Click the Properties button to open the Internet Protocol (TCP/IP) Properties dialog box.

3. On the General tab, select the Use the Following IP Address option button.

4. Enter the IP address in the IP Address text box (for example, **192.168.0.11**).

5. Enter the subnet mask in the Subnet Mask text box (for example, **255.255.255.0**). Setup automatically enters a suggested subnet mask appropriate to the IP address you enter, but you may need to change it.

6. Enter the IP address of the default gateway in the Default Gateway text box.

7.  Select the Use the Following DNS Server Addresses option button.

8.  Enter the IP address of your primary DNS server in the Preferred DNS Server text box.

9.  Enter the IP address of your secondary DNS server (if you have one) in the Alternate DNS Server text box.

10. Click the OK button. Setup closes the Internet Protocol (TCP/IP) Properties dialog box and applies your settings.

**NOTE**   If necessary, you can also set advanced TCP/IP settings by clicking the Advanced button on the General tab of the Internet Protocol (TCP/IP) dialog box and working in the resulting Advanced TCP/IP Settings dialog box.

Click the Next button to proceed with the installation. You've now chosen all the custom options.

### CHANGING DISPLAY SETTINGS

If Setup detects that your screen has a recommended resolution (for example, if it is an LCD panel) or if it detects that you are using the 640×480 screen resolution, Setup displays the Display Settings dialog box, which announces that Windows will automatically adjust your screen resolution to improve the appearance of visual elements. Click the OK button. Windows adjusts the resolution and displays a Monitor Settings dialog box asking if you want to keep the change. Click the OK button if you do. If not, click the Cancel button or (if the screen isn't legible after the change) wait 30 seconds, after which Windows restores the previous screen resolution.

## The Installation Paths Converge

The installation paths converge at the Welcome to Microsoft Windows screen, at which point Setup starts playing active elevator music while an animated help logo struts its stuff. Click the Next button to move along.

### Setting Up Your Internet Connection

Setup then tries to get you connected to the Internet. It tests any detected network adapter to see if it can find an Internet connection. If it detects an Internet connection, Setup displays the How Will This Computer Connect to the Internet? screen, which offers three options: the Telephone Modem option button, the Digital Subscriber Line (DSL) or Cable Modem option button, and the Local Area Network (LAN) option button.

   Select the appropriate option button. If you don't want to configure an Internet connection at the moment—for example, you don't have your ISP or network information—click the Skip button.

   The following sections describe what happens when you select each of these options.

### TELEPHONE MODEM

If your computer connects with a telephone modem, select the Telephone Modem option button, then click the Next button. Setup displays the Ready to Activate Windows? screen.

   After the step of activating Windows (or your turning down the invitation to do so), Setup displays the Do You Want to Set Up Internet Access Now? screen. Select the Yes, Help Me Connect to the Internet option button or the No, Not at This Time option button as appropriate.

If you choose the Yes option button, Setup displays the Let's Get on the Internet screen. This offers three choices: the Get Online with MSN option button, the Use My Existing Internet Account with Another Service Provider (ISP) option button, and the Create a New Internet Account After I Finish Setting Up Windows option button. Select the appropriate option button and click the Next button to proceed.

If you choose Get Online with MSN and click Next, you'll see the Ready to Get an Internet Account? screen, which tells you that Setup will make a call to sign you up for an Internet account. Click Next to dial in to MSN. When you're connected, follow the instructions on the screen to set up an account.

If you choose to use your existing Internet account, Setup displays the Do You Want Help Finding an Internet Service Provider? screen. If you don't have your connection information available, click the Yes, I Need Help Finding Information about My Account option, and click Next. Setup dials the Microsoft Referral Service to locate an ISP in your area. If you do have your connection information available, click the No, I Have My Username, Password, and My ISP's Name and Phone Number Handy option, and click Next. Windows displays the Set Up Your Internet Account screen.

Enter your username, password, and ISP phone number. By default, Windows selects the Obtain IP Automatically (DHCP) check box and the Obtain DNS Automatically check box. If you need to specify a static IP address rather than have the IP address be assigned automatically, clear the Obtain IP Automatically (DHCP) check box and enter the IP address in the Static IP Address text box. Similarly, if your ISP does not supply DNS information automatically, clear the Obtain DNS Automatically check box and enter the IP addresses of the primary and secondary DNS servers in the Preferred DNS text box and the Alternate DNS text box.

When you click the Next button, Setup displays a Congratulations screen telling you that you can connect to the Internet using your phone line. Bear in mind that this isn't necessarily true—you've entered the information, but Windows hasn't checked that it works.

### DIGITAL SUBSCRIBER LINE (DSL) OR CABLE MODEM

If your computer connects with a DSL or cable modem, select the Digital Subscriber Line (DSL) or Cable Modem option button, then click the Next button. Setup displays the Do You Use a Username and Password to Connect to the Internet? screen. Select the Yes, I Use a Username and Password to Connect option button or the No, This Computer Is Always Connected to the Internet option button as appropriate. Click the Next button to display the Do You Use a Username and Password to Connect to the Internet? screen. If you select the Yes, I Use a Username and Password to Connect option and then click Next, you'll see the Let's Set Up Your Internet Account screen. Enter your username, password, and the name of your ISP and click Next. Setup displays the Ready to Activate Windows? screen.

If you select the No, This Computer Is Always Connected to the Internet option and click Next, you'll see the Setting Up a High Speed Connection screen.

If your network is set up to automatically supply an IP address and Domain Name System (DNS) information, this screen is easy: Select the Obtain IP Automatically check box and the Obtain DNS Automatically check box, and you're all set. If your network isn't set up to deliver the goods, leave these check boxes cleared and enter your static IP address, your subnet mask, and your default gateway in the left stack of text boxes; your primary DNS server's IP address in the Preferred DNS text box; and your secondary DNS server's IP address (if you have one) in the Alternate DNS text box.

Click the Next button to proceed. Setup displays the Ready to Activate Windows? screen.

### LOCAL AREA NETWORK (LAN)

If your computer connects through a LAN, select the Local Area Network (LAN) option button, then click the Next button. Setup displays the Setting Up a High Speed Connection screen.

If your network is set up to automatically supply an IP address and DNS information, this screen is easy: Select the Obtain IP Automatically check box and the Obtain DNS Automatically check box, and you're all set. If your network isn't set up to deliver the goods, leave these check boxes cleared and enter your static IP address, your subnet mask, and your default gateway in the left stack of text boxes; your primary DNS server's IP address in the Preferred DNS text box; and your secondary DNS server's IP address (if you have one) in the Alternate DNS text box.

Click the Next button to proceed. Setup displays the Ready to Activate Windows? screen.

## Creating User Accounts

Next, Setup displays the Who Will Use This Computer? screen, which provides an easy way of setting up accounts for one to five users. This screen contains five text boxes. The first is named Your Name; the rest are numbered 2nd User through 5th User.

**NOTE**  When you're upgrading from Windows 9x, Setup creates an account for the username under which you upgraded if you yourself forget to do so.

Enter the names of the users in the text boxes. Each name can be up to 20 characters long, and each must be unique. Names cannot use the characters " * + , / : ; < = > ? [ ] \ or |, and no name can consist of all spaces, all periods, or a combination of the two.

Click the Next button. Setup displays the Thank You! screen telling you you're ready to start using Windows.

Click the Finish button. Setup completes a few odds and ends, and then displays the Welcome screen for you to log in.

## Activating Windows

When Windows starts, you'll see a message about activating Windows in the lower right of your Desktop.

Activation is a one-time procedure that you need to perform within a certain number of days of installing Windows. If you don't activate Windows, it stops working after 30 days. The activation procedure is intended to reduce software piracy. A side effect is to increase the annoyance of legitimate software users.

Activating Windows now is convenient because you get the activation out of the way once and for all. But I recommend you wait until you're sure that all your hardware works before activating Windows. This needn't take long, and it's much better than needing to get your activation revoked because you need to install Windows on another computer instead. If you don't activate Windows now, it reminds you every few days, so the chances of your forgetting are slim to none.

Activation is a little creepy, even though it doesn't involve supplying any personal information. Windows creates what it calls "a unique hardware configuration that represents the configuration of the PC at the time of activation."

The Windows Product Activation Privacy Statement reassures you that "Windows can detect and tolerate minor changes to your PC configuration" and that only a complete overhaul will need reactivation. But you have to wonder: if you upgrade, say, the BIOS, the processor, and the network card, how will Microsoft be able to tell that it's the same computer? The magic number for "how many hardware changes can you make without reactivating?" seems to be somewhere between two and four, depending on how integral the changed components are to the system. For example, a new motherboard would count more than a USB flash drive.

If you want to activate Windows now, click the icon in the message box. You'll see the Let's Activate Windows screen. You can activate Windows over the Internet or by phone. Click the appropriate option and click Next. If you want to wait to activate Windows, you can do so later by choosing Start ➤ All Programs ➤ Activate Windows.

### REGISTERING WINDOWS

During activation, you're heavily encouraged to register your copy of Windows XP with Microsoft.

If you've already registered on Microsoft's website, your Windows registration information gets merged into your current information. If you haven't registered, Microsoft creates a new profile for you with a personal information number (PIN) and adds the PIN to your hard drive in a cookie file. When you then visit the Microsoft website, it prompts you to create a Registration ID (not usually acronymed to RID). You can keep a profile with personal information—and you can opt out of the communications that Microsoft and the other companies it "occasionally" allows to offer its customers information will bombard you with.

## Applying Your Files and Settings

To apply the files and settings you saved by using the Files and Settings Transfer Wizard to your new installation of Windows, take the following steps:

1. Choose Start ➤ All Programs ➤ Accessories ➤ System Tools ➤ Files and Settings Transfer Wizard.

2. Click the Next button. The wizard displays the Which Computer Is This? screen.

3. Select the New Computer option button.

4. Click the Next button. The wizard displays the Do You Have a Windows XP CD? screen, which offers to create a wizard disk that you can use to collect the information from your old computer.

5. Select the I Don't Need the Wizard Disk. I Have Already Collected My Files and Settings from My Old Computer option button.

6. Click the Next button. The wizard displays the Where Are the Files and Settings? screen (shown in Figure 2.21).

7. Select the Direct Cable option button, the Floppy Drive or Other Removable Media option button, or the Other option button as appropriate.

   ◆ If you select the Floppy Drive or Other Removable Media option button, select the drive in the drop-down list.

   ◆ If you select the Other option button, use the text box and (if necessary) the Browse button and the resulting Browse for Folder dialog box to specify the location of the files and settings.

8. Click the Next button. The wizard displays the Transfer in Progress screen (shown in Figure 2.22) as it transfers the files and settings.

**FIGURE 2.21**

On the Where Are the Files and Settings? screen of the Files and Settings Transfer Wizard, tell the wizard where you saved the files and settings.

**FIGURE 2.22**

The Files and Settings Transfer Wizard transfers the files and settings.

9. If the wizard displays a dialog box that tells you that you need to log off for the settings to take effect and invites you to log off now, choose the Yes button. The wizard logs you off and finishes applying the settings.

10. Log back in, and your files and settings are available.

## Uninstalling Windows XP and Reverting to a Previous Version of Windows

If you upgraded from Windows Me or Windows 98 to Windows XP, you can uninstall Windows XP and revert to your previous version of Windows if necessary. To do so, take the following steps:

1. Choose Start ➢ Control Panel. Windows displays Control Panel.

2. Click the Add or Remove Programs link. Windows displays the Add or Remove Programs window with the Add or Remove Programs page foremost.

3. Select the Windows XP Uninstall item. Windows displays its details, including a Change/Remove button.

4. Click the Change/Remove button. Windows displays the Uninstall Windows XP dialog box (shown in Figure 2.23).

**FIGURE 2.23**
In the Uninstall Windows XP dialog box, choose whether to uninstall Windows XP or to remove the backup of your old version of Windows.

5. Select the Uninstall Windows XP option button.

6. Click the Continue button. Windows displays a confirmation dialog box checking that you're absolutely sure.

7. Click the Yes button. Windows closes, runs the uninstall procedure, and automatically restarts your computer with your previous version of Windows.

**WARNING** You cannot revert to a previous installation of Windows NT 4 Workstation or Windows 2000 Professional.

## Removing Your Old Version of Windows

If you decide to stick with Windows XP after upgrading to it, you can reclaim the space taken up by the backup of your old version of Windows. To do so, follow the first four steps in the previous section but then select the Remove the Backup of My Previous Operating System option button in the Uninstall Windows XP dialog box. Click the Continue button, confirm your choice, and Windows deletes the backup of your previous operating system.

## Keeping Windows Updated

Windows XP includes a feature called Windows Update that's designed to keep Windows up-to-date by automatically downloading Windows updates, such as patches and fixes for security holes, and offering to install them. If you need to run old applications that have compatibility problems, Windows Update may be of particular interest because it also includes new fixes for applications to run on Windows XP.

You should know several things about Windows Update before you find it springing into action: how it works, how to configure it, and what to do when an update presents itself.

### When Windows Update Runs

By default Windows Update runs automatically, but only when an Administrator user is logged in. (Microsoft assumes that you don't want Limited users—let alone guests—to install or refuse updates.) If multiple Administrator users are logged on to the computer at the same time, Windows Update runs for only one of them.

Shortly after Windows has first been installed, an icon appears in the system tray with a balloon offering to help configure automatic updates. If you click that balloon a box appears where you can choose to allow Windows Update to download the updates automatically or not. I highly recommend it. With Service Pack 2 (SP2), the Security Center prompts you to configure automatic updates.

You can also run Windows Update manually by choosing Start ➢ All Programs ➢ Windows Update. (If you prefer to run Windows Update manually, you may also want to turn off automatic updating. Read on.)

Windows Update's default setting is to automatically download updates when they're available (and an Administrator user is logged on) and then invite the Administrator to install them. You can change this default behavior, as described in the next section.

Here's what happens:

1. Windows Update decides it's time to run (or an Administrator runs it manually).

2. Windows Update goes online and checks which updates are available and then compares the list to those that have already been applied to the computer and those that have been offered to the computer but refused by an Administrator.

3. If update files are available, Windows Update downloads them in the background, using bandwidth-throttling technology to make sure it doesn't prevent you from using your Internet connection by grabbing all bandwidth when you need it. ("Bandwidth-throttling" means that Windows Update throttles back the amount of bandwidth the download is taking up, not that it throttles your bandwidth.) If you're not using your Internet connection, Windows Update downloads the update files as fast as possible.

4. Once the update files are downloaded, Windows Update notifies you (assuming you're an Administrator) that they're available and invites you to install them.

## Configuring Windows Update

To configure Windows Update, follow these steps:

1. Press ⊞+Break. Windows displays the System Properties dialog box. (Alternatively, click the Start button to display the Start menu, then right-click the My Computer item and choose Properties from the shortcut menu.)

2. Click the Automatic Updates tab (shown in Figure 2.24).

3. In the Notification Settings section, choose one of the three option buttons:

   **Download the Updates Automatically and Notify Me When They Are Ready to Be Installed**   The default, this setting is convenient if you want to use automatic updating and you have a fast Internet connection.

   **Notify Me Before Downloading Any Updates and Notify Me Again Before Installing Them on My Computer**   Use this setting if you want to use automatic updating but you want to be aware of when Windows Update is downloading updates. You might want to know this because your Internet connection isn't fast enough to support your surfing (or downloading MP3s) at the same time as Windows is trying to squeeze a large update through it, or because you don't like unexplained activity across your Internet connection.

**Turn Off Automatic Updating. I Want to Update My Computer Manually**   Select this option button if you prefer to control not only when Windows Update downloads and installs updates but when it checks for them—or if you don't want to use Windows Update at all.

4. If you have previously declined updates that Windows has offered you, you can click the Restore Declined Updates button in the Previous Updates section to make them available again. (Until you've declined an update, the Restore Declined Updates button is unavailable.)

5. Click the OK button. Windows closes the System Properties dialog box.

**FIGURE 2.24**

You can configure Windows Update on the Automatic Updates tab of the System Properties dialog box.

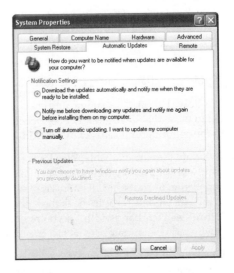

## Running Windows Update Manually

If you don't want to wait for Windows Update to run automatically on schedule, or if you don't like to have your computer calling Microsoft secretly in the wee hours of dark and stormy nights, you can run Windows Update manually. You can do so either from the Start menu (Start ➤ All Programs ➤ Windows Update) or from the Help and Support Center window.

## Summary

This chapter has discussed how to install Windows as a clean install, an upgrade to your current version of Windows, or as an entirely new installation. You've also learned how to use the Windows Update feature to keep your copy of Windows updated, compatible, and secure.

# Chapter 3

# Using the Desktop and Getting Help

In the first part of this chapter, I'll discuss how to get started with Windows XP Professional. I'll cover how to log on and log off; how to switch from one user session to another; and how to exit Windows. I'll also discuss how you can find out who else is logged on to the computer when you're working at it; how you can get an idea of which programs the other users are running; and how you can log off another user (or all other users) in order to reclaim the resources they're using.

In the second part of this chapter, I'll discuss how to find the help you need to use Windows XP most effectively. XP includes a greater amount of help than previous versions of Windows and presents that help in a new interface, the Help and Support Center program. I'll describe how to use Help and Support Center and the various areas it offers. I'll also mention other resources that you may need to turn to when you run into less tractable problems.

- ◆ Logging on and off
- ◆ Using the Desktop and the Start menu
- ◆ Switching users
- ◆ Seeing what other users are doing
- ◆ Using the Winkey
- ◆ Shutting down Windows
- ◆ Using the Help and Support Center
- ◆ Using Remote Assistance
- ◆ Using the troubleshooters
- ◆ Finding help on the Internet

**NOTE**  Before we start, here's something you need to know. Windows XP Professional supports three types of users: Computer Administrator users, Limited users, and the Guest user. By default, all named users are set up as Computer Administrator users, which gives them full authority to configure and customize the computer. Limited users, which you create manually, can perform only minimal configuration and customization. The Guest user, an account that's created automatically by Windows, can perform no configuration or customization. In the first part of this chapter, I'll assume you're logging on as a Computer Administrator user, because that's most likely to be the case. Chapter 19 discusses how to create and manage user accounts.

## Logging On and Logging Off

Logging on and off in Windows XP work differently from previous versions of Windows. Logging on and off could hardly be easier, but it's important to understand what happens when you do so, and how logging on and off differ from switching users.

In earlier versions of Windows, only one user at a time could be logged on to a computer running Windows. For a second user to log on, the first user needed to log off. Logging off involved closing all the open programs and files: either the user could close the programs and files manually before logging off, or Windows would close them automatically when the user issued the Log Off command (and confirmed that they wanted to log off).

Once all the programs and files were closed and all network and Internet connections were closed as well, Windows displayed the Log On to Windows dialog box or the Enter Network Password dialog box, depending on whether the computer was attached to a network. Another user could then log on to Windows, run programs, open files, establish network and Internet connections, and so on.

---

### FAST USER SWITCHING, PERFORMANCE, AND FILE INTEGRITY

Having multiple users logged on to Windows at the same time affects performance because each user who's logged on takes up some of the computer's memory. Having a user logged on takes up relatively little memory, but each program that the user has running, and each file that they have open, adds to the amount being used.

Windows XP needs a minimum of 64MB of RAM to run at an acceptable speed. For each light user, reckon another 32MB of RAM; for each moderate user, 64MB; and for each heavy user, 128MB. If you have 256MB of RAM, you should be able to have two or three users logged on and running several programs each without running short of memory.

Having multiple users logged on at once can also affect file integrity. For example, what happens when two users try to change the same file at the same time? The short answer is: It depends.

Some programs are smart enough to realize that someone else has a copy of the file open. For example, if you try to open in Word 2003 the same document that another user has open, Word displays the File in Use dialog box to warn you that the document is locked for editing and to offer you ways to work with the document (open a read-only copy; create a local copy and merge your changes later; or receive notification when the original copy is available).

Other programs aren't smart enough to spot the problem. For example, WordPad (Windows XP's built-in word processing program) lets you open a document that another user has open, change it, and save the changes. The other user can then save *their* changes to the same file, so it can end up with some of the changes you've made and some that the other user has made. And this is assuming that only two users are editing the document at the same time. For all WordPad knows, half the people in Delaware could be editing the document at the same time and wiping out each other's changes.

If your computer has a modest amount of RAM—say, 64MB, 96MB, or 128MB—or if you're having problems with users opening files at the same time, turn off the Fast User Switching feature. Choose Start ➢ Control Panel to open Control Panel, click the User Accounts link to open the User Account screen, click the Change the Way Users Log On or Off link, clear the Use Fast User Switching check box, and then click Apply Options. When you turn off Fast User Switching, only one user can be logged on to the computer at any given time, and that user must log off before another user can log on. This reduces the amount of memory needed and avoids most problems with shared files.

In Windows XP, multiple users can be logged on at the same time, though of course only one user can actually be using the computer. Each of those users who is logged on can have programs running and files open. Windows XP lets you switch quickly between users without closing the programs and files.

Only one user can be *active*—actually using the computer—at any time. (Given that most computers have only one keyboard, mouse, and monitor, this may seem too obvious to mention—but things are very different in UNIX and Linux, in which multiple users can be actively using the same computer at the same time, some locally and some remotely.) A user who is logged on but not active is said to be *disconnected*.

This means that, for example, Jane and Jack can keep their programs open while Ross is using the computer. When Jane logs back on (in the process disconnecting Ross, who perhaps stepped away for a cup of coffee), Windows resumes her session from where she left off, displaying the programs she had running and the files she had open. Windows reestablishes any of Jane's persistent network connections, including any Internet connection that's set to connect automatically.

Being able to leave multiple users up and running is great—up to a point. But it has serious implications for performance and file integrity. The following sections discuss these considerations briefly.

## Logging On

Let's assume for the moment that you are working with a standalone or workgroup PC. To start using Windows, log on from the Welcome screen. Figure 3.1 shows an example of the Welcome screen, which displays a list of the users who have accounts set up on the computer. Any programs a user has running appear listed under the username, together with the number of e-mail messages waiting for them. If a user is logged on but has no programs running, the Welcome screen displays *Logged on* beneath their name.

**FIGURE 3.1**
The Welcome screen lists the users with accounts on this computer, any tasks the user has running, and any unread e-mail messages they have.

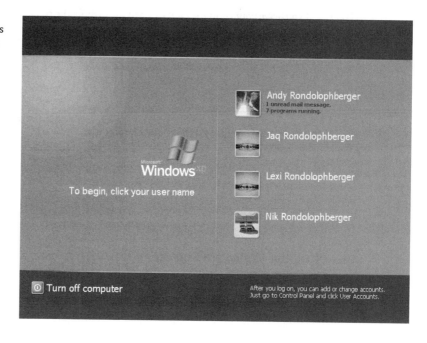

By default, user accounts are set up without passwords, so you log on by clicking the username under which you want to log on. (If an administrator has set up Windows to require passwords, you'll need to enter the password for the account as well.)

When it accepts your logon, Windows displays your Desktop with its current settings. (The section "Using the Desktop and Start Menu" a little later in this chapter discusses the basics of the Desktop and Start menu.)

The first time you log on, Windows creates your folders and sets up program shortcuts for you—so the logon process takes a minute or two. Subsequent logons are much quicker.

If your Windows XP Professional computer is connected to a domain, when you power on the computer, it will boot to a Windows Log On screen. You'll need to press Ctrl+Alt+Del to get to the Log On to Windows dialog box. You must supply a valid username and password that has domain access privileges. If you do not have this information, contact your domain administrator. Passwords are required for network access; you cannot have an account that has a blank password.

Before clicking OK, check that the Log On To entry has your domain name listed. If it does not, use the drop-down arrow and select your domain name. If the Log On To entry does not appear, click the Options button. Click OK, and you will log on to the domain. You can only access information in the domain to which you have privileges.

## Logging Off

The counterpart to logging on is (unsurprisingly) logging off. When you log off, Windows closes all the programs and files you've been using. If the files contain unsaved changes, Windows prompts you to save them.

To log off, display the Start menu by clicking the Start button, and click the Log Off button. Windows displays the Log Off Windows dialog box (shown in Figure 3.2). Click the Log Off button to log off.

**NOTE** If you leave your computer unattended for a while, the screen saver usually kicks in—unless you have something open that prevents the screen saver from starting (or you've disabled the screen saver). For example, a dialog box open on-screen usually prevents the screen saver from starting. The default setting is for the screen saver to start after 10 minutes and to display the Welcome screen. The screen saver gives you some protection against prying eyes (particularly if you're using passwords for logging on), but it also makes it harder to see who's doing what on the computer.

**FIGURE 3.2**
The Log Off Windows dialog box lets you log off, cancel the command, or switch to another user.

## Disabling the Welcome Screen

You can turn off the Welcome screen so that a normal username-and-password logon box appears at startup, as it did in Windows 2000 (and as it does if you're logging in to a domain). Disabling the Welcome screen has a side effect of disabling Fast User Switching (although you can also disable Fast User Switching while keeping the Welcome screen if you prefer).

**TIP** If you do not want Windows to display any logon prompt at all, but simply load the Desktop, you must delete all users except one from the Users applet in the Control Panel, remove the password from it, and disable the Guest account. When there is only one user, and no password specified, that user is logged on automatically at startup.

To disable the Welcome screen (or enable it again after it has been disabled), follow these steps:

1. Choose Start ➢ Control Panel to open Control Panel, and then click the User Accounts link to open the User Accounts screen.

2. Click the Change the Way Users Log On or Off link to open the Select Logon and Logoff Options screen.

3. Click the Use the Welcome Screen check box to turn it off or on. If you are turning it on, you can click the Use Fast User Switching check box to turn that option off or on.

4. Click Apply Options. Close all open windows, and then restart your system.

**FIGURE 3.3**

The components of the Windows Desktop

## Using the Desktop and Start Menu

Once you've logged on successfully, Windows displays the Desktop. Figure 3.3 shows what the Desktop looks like the first time you start Windows and start a couple of programs. Because you can customize the Desktop extensively, your Desktop might not look anything like the Desktop shown in the figure: the wallpaper might be different; the Taskbar could be located at a different side of the screen; or various toolbars might be displayed. About the only unchanging thing about the Desktop is the Start menu button—but even this might not be displayed if someone has chosen to hide the Taskbar (of which the Start button is a part).

We'll examine the Desktop in more detail in the forthcoming chapters, but these are the basic actions for navigating it:

◆ The Desktop contains one or more shortcuts to items. Usually, there's an icon for the Recycle Bin, if nothing else. Double-click an icon to run the program associated with it.

◆ The Start menu provides access to the full range of programs and features currently installed on Windows. Click the Start button to display the Start menu. Choose one of the items that appears on it, or click the All Programs button to display a cascading menu containing further items.

◆ The Taskbar gives you quick access to each program that's currently running. The Taskbar displays a button for each active program window. To display that window in front of all other windows, click its button. To minimize the program, click its Taskbar button again.

◆ The notification area contains items that are useful to have displayed all the time (such as the clock, which is displayed by default), together with information and alerts (which are displayed at appropriate times).

◆ The Desktop background is a graphic that you can change at will.

## Using the Winkey

As I mentioned in Chapter 1, Windows XP provides a number of keyboard combinations for the Winkey, the key (or keys) with the Windows logo on the keyboard. If you're comfortable leaving your hands on the keyboard, these combinations are doubly convenient, because not only can you avoid reaching for the mouse, but you can also display with a single keystroke a number of windows and dialog boxes that lie several commands deep in the Windows interface.

Table 3.1 lists the Winkey combinations.

**TABLE 3.1:**     Winkey Combinations

| WINKEY COMBINATION | WHAT IT DOES |
| --- | --- |
| Winkey | Toggles the display of the Start menu |
| Winkey+Break | Displays the System Properties dialog box |
| Winkey+Tab | Moves the focus to the next button in the Taskbar |
| Winkey+Shift+Tab | Moves the focus to the previous button in the Taskbar |

**TABLE 3.1:** Winkey Combinations *(CONTINUED)*

| WINKEY COMBINATION | WHAT IT DOES |
|---|---|
| Winkey+B | Moves the focus to the notification area |
| Winkey+D | Displays the Desktop |
| Winkey+E | Opens an Explorer window showing My Computer |
| Winkey+F | Opens a Search Results window and activates Search Companion |
| Winkey+Ctrl+F | Opens a Search Results window, activates Search Companion, and starts a Search for Computer |
| Winkey+F1 | Opens a Help and Support Center window |
| Winkey+M | Issues a Minimize All Windows command |
| Winkey+Shift+M | Issues an Undo Minimize All command |
| Winkey+R | Displays the Run dialog box |
| Winkey+U | Displays Utility Manager |
| Winkey+L | Locks the computer |

# Managing Multiple Users

When multiple users share a single PC, a special set of challenges arises. How will their data be kept separate? How can more than one user log on at a time? How can you tell who is logged in and what they are doing? The following sections address some of these concerns.

### USING THE CONNECT COMMAND TO SWITCH USERS QUICKLY

Switching users as described above is easy but takes a few clicks. There's a quicker way of switching—by using Task Manager as follows:

1. Right-click open space in the Taskbar and choose Task Manager from the shortcut menu. Windows opens Task Manager.

2. Click the Users tab (shown in Figure 3.4, later in this chapter).

3. Right-click the user that you want to connect as and choose Connect from the shortcut menu. If the user's account has a password, Windows displays the Connect Password Required dialog box. When you enter the password correctly (or if the account has no password), Windows disconnects your session and connects you as the user you selected.

Note that this works only if Fast User Switching is enabled; otherwise there won't be a Users tab.

### Switching to Another User

As you saw in Figure 3.2, the Log Off Windows dialog box also contains a button called Switch User. When you click the Switch User button, Windows keeps your programs running (instead of closing them, as it does when you log out) and displays the Welcome screen so that you can log on as another user or (more likely) other users can log on as themselves.

### Locking the Computer

To leave your current session running but display the Welcome screen quickly, press Winkey+L. (If you're not using the Welcome screen, Windows displays the Log On to Windows dialog box instead.)

**NOTE**  If you're connected to a domain, pressing Winkey+L locks the computer.

Microsoft calls this action *locking* the computer, though the term is neither accurate nor helpful with Windows XP's default settings. The computer isn't locked in any useful sense unless all user accounts are protected with effective passwords.

However, if you turn off the Welcome screen and Fast User Switching, Windows manages a semblance of locking. When the current user disconnects their session, Windows displays a blank background topped by the Unlock Computer dialog box, which tells the user that the computer is in use, that it has been locked, and that only the current user or an administrator can unlock it. If you've applied passwords, this is true; if you haven't, anyone can click the OK button in the Unlock Computer dialog box to unlock the computer and log on as the current user.

### Checking Which User Is Currently Active

If you're in any doubt as to which user is currently active, display the Start menu (by clicking the Start button or pressing the Winkey) and check the username displayed at the top.

### Seeing Who Else Is Logged On to the Computer

As you saw in Figure 3.1, the Welcome screen displays details of each user logged on to the computer and the number of programs they're running. But if you don't want to display the Welcome screen (and disconnect your session by doing so), you can find out which other users are logged in by using Task Manager as follows:

1. Right-click the Taskbar and choose Task Manager from the shortcut menu. Windows displays Task Manager.

2. Click the Users tab (shown in Figure 3.4), which lists the users and their status.

**NOTE**  Limited users and the Guest user can't see which other users are logged on or which processes they're running. As a result, Limited users and the Guest user can't switch directly to another user's session by using Task Manager, though they can disconnect their own session or log themselves off by using Task Manager.

**FIGURE 3.4**

The Users tab of Task Manager shows you which other users are logged on to the computer. You can send them messages, switch to their sessions, or log them off forcibly.

## Seeing Which Programs the Other Users Are Running

It's not easy to see exactly which programs the other users of the computer are running unless you know the names of the executable files for the programs, but you can get an idea by using the Processes tab of Task Manager. This tab also shows you how much memory each program is using, which helps you establish whether—or why—your computer is running short of memory.

Follow these steps to start Task Manager and display its Processes tab:

1. Right-click the Taskbar and choose Task Manager from the shortcut menu to open Task Manager.

2. Click the Processes tab, which lists the processes you're running.

3. Select the Show Processes from All Users check box. (This check box is cleared by default.) Task Manager adds to the list all the processes that the other users are running as well. Figure 3.5 shows an example of the Processes tab. You can sort the list of processes by any column by clicking the column heading. In the figure, the processes are sorted by the User Name column so that it's easy to see which process belongs to which user.

As you can see in the figure, three of the Rondolophbergers are running programs, and between them, they're using quite a chunk of memory: the Commit Charge counter in the lower-right corner of the Processes tab shows that 172932K (about 169MB) out of 633656K (about 619MB) of memory has been used up. In the list, you can see some of the principal offenders: copies of WINWORD.EXE (Microsoft Word) that Andy and Jaq are running (24,624K and 18,148K, respectively), several instances of explorer.exe, and some programs with unpronounceable names such as devldr32.exe and wpabaln.exe.

Some of the other names are readily identifiable. For example, wmplayer.exe is the executable for Windows Media Player, as you'd expect, and taskmgr.exe is the executable for Task Manager. You don't need to memorize the mapping of each executable filename to its program, but if you look at Task Manager now and then, you'll learn to scan the list of processes and see which is running. This will help you decide whether you should go ahead and log another user off Windows (as described in the next section) or whether doing so will trash their work and ruin their life.

**FIGURE 3.5**
Use the Processes tab of
Task Manager to see
which programs the oth-
er users are running.

While you're looking at Task Manager, there are a couple of other things you might as well know. First, you can also see in the figure that it's not just the Rondolophbergers who are using memory like there was no tomorrow—Windows also has a number of processes open on its own account. The LOCAL SERVICE account is running `svchost.exe` (service host), as is the NETWORK SERVICE account. The SYSTEM account is running a dozen or more processes, of which you can see only the top few in the figure. Of these, the first, the System Idle Process, is consuming 91 percent of the processor cycles. (This is actually good news. When the System Idle Process is taking up most of the processor cycles like this, the computer is idling along—goofing off until the user does something that presses it into action.)

### WHICH NAME CORRESPONDS TO WHICH PROGRAM?

To find out which program corresponds to each executable file, display the Applications tab of Task Manager. Right-click a program and choose Go to Process from the shortcut menu. Task Manager displays the Processes tab and selects the process for that program.

That's easy enough—but there are many more processes running than programs. Try closing all the programs listed on the Applications tab of Task Manager, and you'll see that there's still a goodly list of processes left. Try stopping any obvious services that you can temporarily dispense with, and see if an associated process disappears. For instance, try closing your Internet connection or stopping your PC Cards. Did either of those actions lose you a process? Then you have an idea of what that process does.

If you're desperate to find out which function or service an executable runs, try searching for the executable. The folder that contains the executable may give you a clue as to the program, or there may be a comment on the executable that reveals its purpose. Then again, the executable may prove to be one of the mysterious system files stored in the Windows folder or the Windows\System32 folder. If the latter is the case, figure it's something unknowable and leave it alone.

Second, you may have noticed that the numbers in the Mem Usage column don't add up to anything like the 172932K listed as being committed (even though you can't see the whole column). That's because that committed figure is both physical memory (RAM) used and virtual memory (hard disk space being used to simulate more RAM). If you want to see how much virtual memory each process is taking up, follow these steps:

1. In Task Manager, choose View ≻ Select Columns to open the Select Columns dialog box (shown in Figure 3.6).

**FIGURE 3.6**
Use the Select Columns dialog box to add further columns of information to Task Manager's Processes tab.

2. Select the Virtual Memory Size check box.

   ◆ Also select the check boxes for any other information you want to see in Task Manager. Many of the items here are somewhat arcane, but you might want to look at CPU Time or Peak Memory Usage.

3. Click the OK button. Task Manager closes the Select Columns dialog box and adds the columns you chose to the Processes tab.

Figure 3.7 shows the Processes tab of Task Manager with the Virtual Memory Size column added and the processes sorted by that column. Notice that the two copies of Word have very heavy memory usage indeed (when you add the Mem Usage column and the VM Size column). svchost.exe also shows itself as a heavyweight, using a little over 11MB of virtual memory in addition to its 10MB of RAM.

## Logging Another User Off

If necessary, any Computer Administrator user can log another user off the computer.

Logging someone else off isn't usually a great idea, because although you can use Task Manager to see which processes they're running (as described in the previous section), you can't see whether they have any unsaved work in them. If you don't use passwords to log on to Windows, it's much better to log on as the other user and close the programs and documents manually. Then log off (as the other user) and log back on as yourself. If you do use passwords, you'll need to know the other user's password to log on as them, which kinda defeats the point of having passwords in the first place.

CHAPTER 3

**FIGURE 3.7**
If you want to see virtual memory usage, add the Virtual Memory Size (VM Size) column to the Processes tab in Task Manager.

That said, you may need to log another user off if they are running enough programs to affect the computer's performance or if they have open a single-user program or a document that you need to use. If you do so, you may want to send them a message as described in the next section so that they know what's happened.

To log another user off, follow these steps:

1. Right-click the Taskbar and choose Task Manager from the shortcut menu to display Task Manager.

2. Click the Users tab (shown in Figure 3.8).

**FIGURE 3.8**
From the Users tab of Windows Task Manager, you can log another user off the computer.

3. Select the user and click the Logoff button. (Alternatively, right-click the user and choose Log Off from the shortcut menu.) Windows displays the Windows Task Manager dialog box (shown in Figure 3.9), asking if you want to log the selected user off.

**FIGURE 3.9**
You can log another user off the computer—but be aware that doing so will cost them any unsaved work.

4. Click the Yes button. The other user's session is toast—as is any unsaved work they had open.

## Sending a Message to Another User

You can send a message to another user logged in to this computer. Because the other user can't be using the computer at the same time as you, this feature is not useful for real-time communication—it's not exactly instant messaging—but it can be useful for making sure a family member or a colleague gets a message the next time they use the computer. (For example, you might ask them not to shut down the computer because you're still using it.) It's also useful for notifying another user that you've had to terminate a program that they were using.

To send a message to another user, follow these steps:

1. Right-click the Taskbar and choose Task Manager from the shortcut menu to display Windows Task Manager.

2. Click the Users tab.

3. Right-click the user and choose Send Message from the shortcut menu. Windows displays the Send Message dialog box (shown in Figure 3.10).

**FIGURE 3.10**
Use the Send Message dialog box to send a message to another user logged on to this computer.

4. Enter the message title in the Message Title text box and the message in the Message text box.

   ◆ To start a new line, press Ctrl+Enter. (Pressing the Enter key on its own registers a click on the OK button, sending the message.)

   ◆ To type a tab, press Ctrl+Tab. (Pressing the Tab key on its own moves the focus to the next control.)

5. Click the OK button to send the message.

The next time the user logs on to Windows, they receive the message as a screen pop-up. Figure 3.11 shows an example.

## Shutting Down Windows

You can shut down Windows in several ways:

◆ By clicking the Turn Off Computer button at the bottom of the default Start menu or by choosing Start ➢ Turn Off Computer from the classic Start menu. (If you're connected to a domain, Turn Off Computer becomes Shut Down.)

◆ By clicking the Turn Off Computer button on the Welcome screen and then clicking the Turn Off button on the Turn Off Computer screen (shown in Figure 3.12).

**FIGURE 3.12**
To turn off the computer, click the Turn Off button on the Turn Off Computer screen.

◆ By choosing Shut Down ➢ Turn Off from Windows Task Manager.

◆ By pressing Alt+F4 with the Desktop active and then clicking the Turn Off button on the Turn Off Computer screen.

---

**POWERING DOWN YOUR COMPUTER WHEN WINDOWS HAS CRASHED**

If Windows won't shut down because it has crashed, you'll need to shut it down the hard way. To do so, press the power button on the computer. On ACPI-compliant computers, you may need to hold the power button down for four seconds or more to shut the system down—short presses of the power button may have no effect.

On some computers, a short press of the power button may make Windows display the Turn Off Computer screen so that you can specify whether to hibernate, turn off the computer, or restart it. Under normal circumstances, catching the power signal like this is pretty smart, helping to dissuade users from powering down the computer without exiting Windows first. But if Windows has crashed, you won't be able to do anything from the Turn Off Computer screen.

From the Turn Off Computer screen, you can also click the Stand By or Hibernate button to make your computer hibernate or stand by, or the Restart button to restart the computer and Windows. If your computer doesn't support hibernation or standby, the Hibernate or Standby button doesn't appear on the Turn Off Computer screen. Chapter 6 discusses standby and hibernation modes in more detail, including how to enable them on the Turn Off Computer screen.

## Help and Support Center

Help and Support Center is the latest in Microsoft's efforts to provide help resources powerful enough to silence the ringing of the phones on its costly support lines. Windows XP's Help and Support Center builds on the improvements introduced in the Help and Support Center in Windows Me, which introduced a web-style interface to replace the old-style Help-file interface in earlier versions of Windows, by integrating many more external resources. For example, you can now search the Microsoft Knowledge Base, an online database of questions and answers, directly from Help and Support Center instead of having to access it separately by using Internet Explorer. And many hardware manufacturers are now providing product-support information that's accessible through Help and Support Center.

### Starting Help and Support Center

Choose Start ➤ Help and Support to open Help and Support Center at the Home page. You should see something like Figure 3.13, except that it will contain some updated information. (Your hardware manufacturer may also have customized Help and Support Center by adding content to it or by adapting its interface.)

**FIGURE 3.13**
The Home page in Help and Support Center provides links to the many different areas of Help and Support Center.

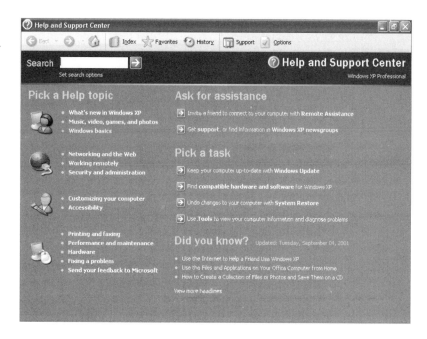

CHAPTER 3

As you can see in Figure 3.13, the Help and Support Center window has a toolbar (at the top, starting with the Back button) for primary navigation rather than a menu bar. This toolbar is called the *navigation bar*. Below the navigation bar appears the Search bar. The help topics vary somewhat depending on the service pack installed, and the Did You Know? section changes frequently by drawing the latest information from Microsoft's website. They also vary depending on any customization provided by the PC manufacturer. (For example, Dell and HP both customize the Help system.)

**TIP** You can open multiple Help and Support Center windows at once, which can help when you're searching for different pieces of help information or navigating different routes searching for the same piece of information.

## Finding Your Way around Help and Support Center

Help and Support Center has access to a large amount of information in Help files that Windows installs on your hard drive, together with troubleshooters for stepping you through the process of finding solutions to common problems and links for running Windows programs (such as Remote Assistance and the System Configuration Utility) that may help you solve or eliminate problems. But Help and Support Center's strongest feature is that it also provides a gateway to information resources on the Web and Internet.

Because of the amount of information and resources that Help and Support Center offers, you may find that it takes you a while to get the hang of navigating around it. This section highlights the main ways of finding the information you need: searching, browsing, using the History feature, and using the Index.

### SEARCHING FOR HELP

If you don't see an immediately appropriate link on the Help and Support Center Home page, the easiest way to find information on a particular topic is to search for it.

To search, enter the search term or terms in the Search text box and click the Start Searching button or press Enter. Help and Support Center displays the Search Results pane on the left side and adds a toolbar containing four buttons (Add to Favorites, Change View, Print, and Locate in Contents) under the right side of the Search bar.

The Search Results list box breaks up the results into three categories:

**Suggested Topics** Suggested topics are keyword matches—one or more of your search terms match a keyword in each of these topics. These topics are further broken up into subcategories such as Pick a Task and Overviews, Articles, and Tutorials.

**Full-Text Search Matches** Full-text matches are topics that contain one or more of your search terms in the body text of the help topic rather than in the keywords.

**Microsoft Knowledge Base** These results are from the Microsoft Knowledge Base (see the next sidebar). Use them to glean extra or extraneous information beyond that offered by the topics listed in the Suggested Topics and Full-Text Search Matches lists.

To display a category, click its heading. Then click a search result to display it in the right pane, as in the example in Figure 3.14. By default, Windows highlights the word or words you searched for, as in the figure. If there are one or two instances, this can be a help, but if there are many instances, this highlighting appears as more of a defacement than an enhancement. But you can get rid of it, as described after the sidebar.

**FIGURE 3.14**
Click a search result in
the Search Results pane
to display the page in the
right pane.

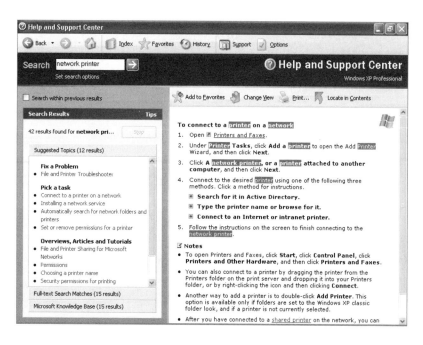

**NOTE**  You can also start searching for help from Search Companion by clicking the Information in
Help and Support Center link. There's no advantage to starting to search this way unless you happen
to have Search Companion displayed when you want help.

### SETTING SEARCH OPTIONS

Help and Support Center lets you specify how you want it to search. To set search options, take the
following steps:

1. Click the Options button on the navigation bar. Help and Support Center displays the Options
   screen.

2. In the Options list in the left pane, click the Set Search Options link. Help and Support Center
   displays the Set Search Options screen (shown in Figure 3.15).

3. In the Return Up to *NN* Results per Provider text box, enter the number of search results you
   want Help and Support Center to get at once from each source of help. The default setting is
   15, but you may want to increase this number if you find that 15 doesn't give you the information you need. The disadvantage to returning more search results is that it takes longer to
   download those that come across your Internet connection.

4. Clear the Turn On Search Highlight check box if you don't want Help and Support Center to
   highlight your search terms in each result it displays.

5. If you don't want to use the Suggested Topics category, clear the Suggested Topics check box.
   (Usually, this category is well worth using, but in some circumstances you might want to set
   up Help and Support Center to search only the Knowledge Base.)

**FIGURE 3.15**
Choose search options on the Set Search Options screen in Help and Support Center.

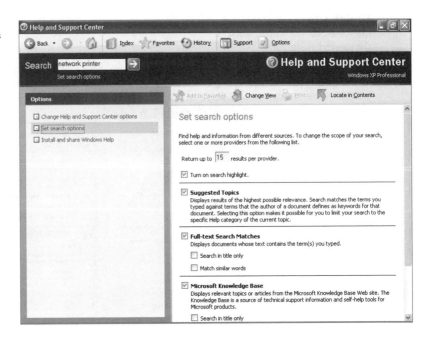

6. If you don't want to use full-text searching, clear the Full-Text Search Matches check box. If you do use full-text searching, you can refine it by selecting the Search in Title Only check box to limit full-text searches to the titles of documents instead of including their body text, or the Match Similar Words check box to have full-text searching include matches with words it thinks are similar to (instead of identical to) your search terms.

7. Clear the Microsoft Knowledge Base check box if you don't want to search the Knowledge Base. You might want to avoid searching the Knowledge Base if you find its suggestions too esoteric or if you're working offline. If you continue to search the Knowledge Base, you can set the following search options to target the results:

◆ In the Select a Product or Topic drop-down list, select the product or topic to search for.

◆ In the Search For drop-down list, choose the search method you want by selecting the All of the Words item, the Any of the Words item, the The Exact Phrase item, or the The Boolean Phrase item. (A *Boolean phrase* is one that uses terms such as AND, OR, or NOT—for example, "Internet NOT Explorer" to search for documents that contain *Internet* but do not contain *Explorer*.)

◆ Select the Search in Title Only check box if you want to limit searches to the titles of documents instead of including their body text.

## MAKING THE MOST OF THE MICROSOFT KNOWLEDGE BASE

The Microsoft Knowledge Base is an online repository of knowledge and wisdom accumulated by Microsoft about its products. Given that the Knowledge Base is one of the main tools that Microsoft's support engineers use for troubleshooting customer problems with Windows, it's a great resource for searching for solutions to problems that Windows' local help resources don't know about.

The disadvantage to the Knowledge Base, and perhaps the reason it's not more heavily emphasized in Microsoft's battery of help solutions, is the way it's arranged and the necessarily scattershot nature of its coverage. The Knowledge Base consists of a large number of answers that Microsoft's support engineers and other experts have written to questions that frustrated users and developers have submitted. The answers vary greatly in length, depending on the complexity of the problem and user level, ranging from beginner topics to super-advanced (developer-level) topics. Coverage is patchy, because the questions tend to be answered only when they're not covered in the Help files and other more accessible resources. This is why the Help and Support Center Search Results pane presents the Microsoft Knowledge Base list after the Suggested Topics list and the Full-Text Search Matches list: the Knowledge Base's offerings may be helpful, but they may equally well be completely irrelevant to your needs.

Each article is identified by an Article ID number, which consists of a six-digit number (for example, 201950). Previously Microsoft had a Q in front of each article number but has recently dropped that convention.

Each article has a title that describes the problem it covers, information on which products and versions it covers, a summary that you can scan to get an idea of the contents, and the full text of the article. Beyond this, each article is tagged with keywords describing the main areas of its content. By searching for keywords, you can avoid passing references to words you might have included in the search, thus producing a more focused set of results.

For power use, you may get better results by searching the Knowledge Base directly by using Internet Explorer or another browser, because the Knowledge Base's web interface offers extra options that Help and Support Center does not, such as searching for what's new in the last few days on a particular product and being able to display either titles and excerpts from hits found or just titles. To search the Knowledge Base directly, point your browser at `search.support.microsoft.com/kb/c.asp`.

If you know the number of a particular query, enter it in the Search text box. For example, if you read newsgroups on Microsoft-related subjects, you'll often see references to particular queries (or, more accurately, to the *answers* to particular queries) mentioned as the place to find a fix for a given problem.

You can also use the Article ID to retrieve the article by e-mail by sending a message to `mshelp@microsoft.com` with the Article ID number in the Subject line.

If you don't know the Article ID but think you can locate it by searching article titles, you can get an index of Knowledge Base articles by e-mail by sending a message to `mshelp@microsoft.com` with the word "Index" in the Subject line.

### SETTING HELP AND SUPPORT CENTER OPTIONS

While you're setting search options, your eye will probably be caught by the Change Help and Support Center Options link in the Options pane on the Set Search Options screen. These are the options you can set:

**Show Favorites on the Navigation Bar check box**   Leave this check box selected (as it is by default) to have Help and Support Center display the Favorites button on the toolbar. Clear this check box to remove the Favorites button.

**Show History on the Navigation Bar check box**   Leave this check box selected (as it is by default) to have Help and Support Center display the History button on the toolbar. Clear this check box to remove the History button.

**Font Size Used for Help Content list**   Select the Small option button, the Medium option button, or the Large option button to set a font size you find comfortable.

**Options for Icons in the Navigation Bar list**   Specify whether Help and Support Center should display text on the navigation bar buttons by selecting the Show All Text Labels option button, the Show Only Default Text Labels option button, or the Do Not Show Text Labels option button.

## Browsing for Help

As you saw in Figure 3.13, Help and Support Center provides a list of a dozen or so *help topics* on the left side of its Home page. You can browse any of these help topics by clicking its link. Figure 3.16 shows an example of a help topic. Click one of the links in the topic area to display the links or information available.

**FIGURE 3.16**
Follow the links in the
Pick a Help Topic list to
reach help topic areas.

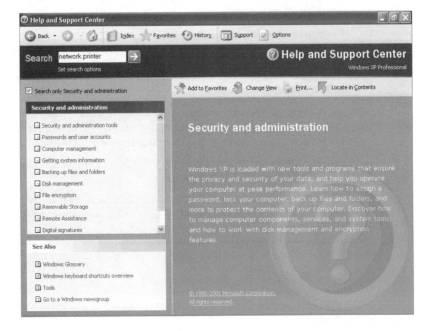

Similarly, Help and Support Center provides a list of key support topics on the right side of its Home page. The Ask for Assistance list provides links to Remote Assistance, Support (from Microsoft), and Windows XP Newsgroups. The Pick a Task list includes links to tools such as Windows Update and System Restore, the Tools area of Help and Support Center for help-specific tools, and Help and Support Center's features for finding XP-compatible hardware and software.

### SUPPORT PAGE

The Support page (shown in Figure 3.17 with Remote Assistance information displayed) offers a variety of support tools, some of the items that actually provide support (such as Remote Assistance—accessed via the Ask a Friend to Help link—and Microsoft Online Support) and some that are just links to Windows utilities (such as My Computer Information and System Configuration Utility).

**FIGURE 3.17**
The Support area contains tools and links to Windows utilities.

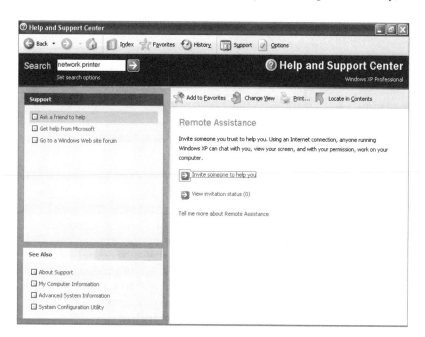

### WINDOWS UPDATE PAGE

The Windows Update page provides an alternative method of accessing Windows Update. (You can also access Windows Update from the Start menu.)

### COMPATIBLE HARDWARE AND SOFTWARE PAGE

Depending on the service pack installed, the Compatible Hardware and Software for Windows XP link (in the Pick a Task section) either opens a Search for Hardware and Software by Name pane, as in Figure 3.18, or opens a web browser window that displays the Windows Catalog.

**FIGURE 3.18**
Use the Compatible
Hardware and Software
page to search for com-
patibility information
for a specific product.

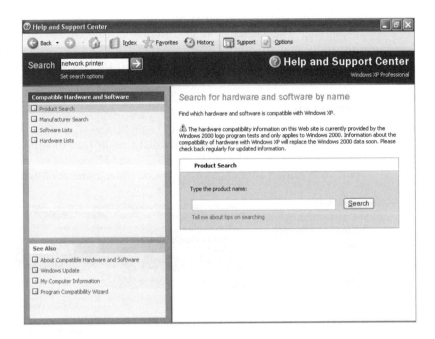

## TOOLS PAGE

To access the Tools page, in Help and Support Center, click the Use Tools to View Your Computer Information and Diagnose Problems in the Pick a Task section. The Tools page (shown in Figure 3.19 with the Advanced System Information screen displayed) contains the Tools Center, which provides access to a number of tools for configuring and troubleshooting Windows. You'll notice that some of these tools have already popped up on other Help and Support Center pages you've seen so far. This illustrates the large number of redundant paths deliberately built into Help and Support Center to make it easier for you to find the information and tools you need to solve a problem.

## Creating and Using Favorites in Help

You can create favorites in Help and Support Center so that you can access pages of information quickly whenever you need to.

To add the current page to your favorites, click the Add to Favorites button. Help and Support Center adds the favorite to your Favorites list and displays a message box telling you that it is doing so.

To access a favorite, click the Favorites button on the toolbar. Help and Support Center displays the Favorites pane. Select the favorite you want to display and click the Display button.

To rename a favorite, click it in the Favorites pane, and then click the Rename button. Help and Support Center displays an edit box around the favorite's name. Type the new name and press the Enter key.

To delete a favorite, select it in the Favorites pane and click the Remove button.

**FIGURE 3.19**
The Tools page provides links to a large handful of system tools.

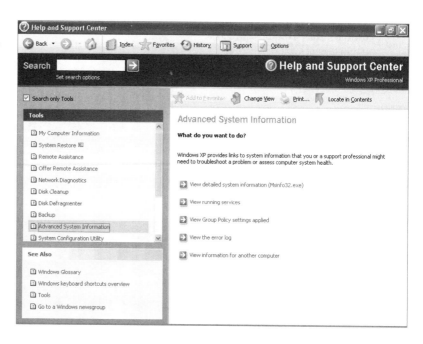

## Using Views

Designed to display a serious amount of information and options at the same time, the Help and Support Center window can threaten visual overload or simply swamp a small screen. To help you retain your sanity and your screen estate, the Help and Support Center window has a reduced view as well.

Click the Change View button to toggle between the full Help and Support Center window (including the left navigation pane, the Search bar, and the toolbar) and the reduced window, which contains only the content page.

## Navigating with Help History

You can navigate backward and forward in the chain of pages you've browsed by using the Back button and Forward button on the toolbar. If you want to see the history of where you've been, click the History button. Help and Support Center displays the History pane (shown in Figure 3.20). Click the topic you want to access.

## Printing Help Information

To print the current topic, click the Print button, and then click the Print button in the Print dialog box that Help and Support Center displays.

Instead of printing just an individual screen at a time, you can print a whole section of help by selecting the Print All Linked Documents check box on the Options tab of the Print dialog box. You can also select the Print Table of Links check box if you want to print a table of linked pages.

CHAPTER 3

FIGURE 3.20
Use the History pane to return to topics you've visited recently.

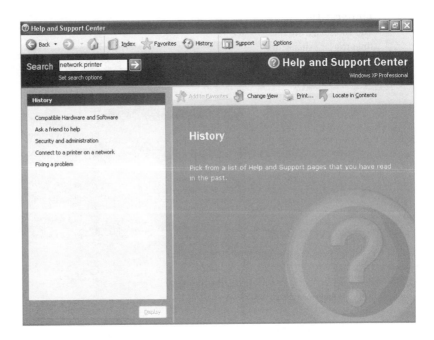

## Using Remote Assistance

Remote Assistance lets you permit a designated helper to connect to your computer, see what's going on, and help you out of trouble. The helper—a friend or an administrator; whomever you choose—can control the computer directly if you give them permission, or you can simply chat with them and apply such of their advice as you deem fit.

To use Remote Assistance, both your computer and your helper's must be running Windows XP. You send an invitation via e-mail or via Windows Messenger, or save it as a file (for example, to a network location designated for Remote Assistance request files, or on a floppy or CD that you then pop in the snail mail). When your helper responds, you decide whether to accept their help.

Each of the three methods of requesting Remote Assistance has its advantages and disadvantages. An e-mail invitation lets you include details of the Windows problem with which you need help—but you don't know when the recipient will check their e-mail. A Windows Messenger invitation will be received immediately (because you can't send an invitation to someone who isn't online), but you can't include details of the problem. A file invitation, like an e-mail invitation, lets you include details of the problem, but you have no idea of when you'll receive a response to it (if ever).

On the other end of the wire, you can offer Help via Remote Assistance. All you need is for someone to send you an invitation.

### Security Considerations

Like all remote-control technologies, Remote Assistance has serious security implications that you need to consider before using it.

If you give another person control of your computer, they can take actions almost as freely as if they were seated in front of the computer. You can watch these actions, and you can take back control of the computer at any time, but you may already be too late: it takes less than a second to delete a key file, and little longer to plant a virus or other form of malware.

Even if you *don't* give your helper control and instead simply chat, keep your wits about you when deciding which of their suggestions to implement. Malicious or ill-informed suggestions can do plenty of damage if you apply them without thinking. Never take any actions that could compromise your security or destroy your data. Above all, treat any incoming files with the greatest of suspicion and virus-check them using an up-to-date antivirus program before using them.

One particular problem is that you can't tell that the person at the other computer is who they claim to be. For this reason alone, you should always protect your Remote Assistance connections with a strong password known only to the person from whom you're requesting help. That way, if someone else is at their computer or has identity-jacked them, they won't be able to respond to the Remote Assistance invitation you send.

## Enabling Remote Assistance

Remote Assistance is enabled by default. To find out if Remote Assistance is enabled on your computer, follow these steps:

1. Display the System Properties dialog box (for example, by pressing Winkey+Break or clicking the System link on the Performance and Maintenance screen of Control Panel).

2. Click the Remote tab:

3. Check the status of the Allow Remote Assistance Invitations to Be Sent from This Computer check box. If this check box isn't selected, select it.

4. Click the OK button. Windows closes the System Properties dialog box.

## Setting Limits for Remote Assistance

To set limits for Remote Assistance:

1. In the Remote Assistance section of the Remote tab, click the Advanced button to open the Remote Assistance Settings dialog box:

2. In the Remote Control section, clear the Allow This Computer to Be Controlled Remotely check box if you don't want your helpers to be able to control the computer. (This check box is selected by default.) Even when this check box is selected, you need to approve each request for control of the PC manually.

3. In the Invitations section, use the two drop-down lists to specify an expiration limit for Remote Assistance invitations that your computer sends out. The default setting is 30 days; you might want to shorten this period considerably for security.

4. Click the OK button. Windows closes the Remote Assistance Settings dialog box, returning you to the System Properties dialog box.

5. Click the OK button. Windows closes the System Properties dialog box.

You're now ready to start sending out invitations for Remote Assistance.

## Sending a Remote Assistance Invitation via E-mail

To send a Remote Assistance invitation as an e-mail message via your existing e-mail account, follow these steps:

1. Choose Start ➤ All Programs ➤ Remote Assistance. Windows opens a Help and Support Center window to the Remote Assistance topic.

2. Click the Invite Someone to Help You link. Help and Support Center displays the Pick How You Want to Contact Your Assistant screen of Remote Assistance (shown in Figure 3.21).

   ◆ The first time you go through these steps, Help and Support Center displays a screen bearing Important Notes. If you want to skip this page in the future, leave the Don't Show This Page Again check box selected (as it is by default) and click the Continue button.

3. In the Or Use E-mail area, enter your putative assistant's e-mail address in the Type an E-mail Address text box. Either type in the address or click the Address Book button and use Address Book to specify the address.

4. Click the Invite This Person link. Help and Support Center displays the Provide Contact Information screen (shown in Figure 3.22).

**FIGURE 3.21**

On the Pick How You Want to Contact Your Assistant screen of Remote Assistance, specify which type of Remote Assistance invitation to send.

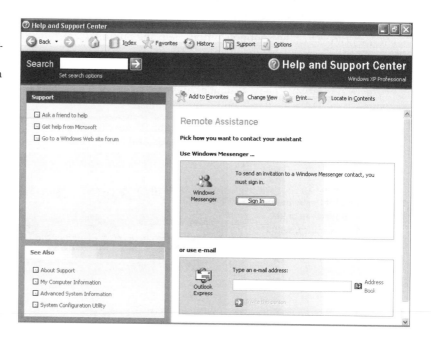

**FIGURE 3.22**

On the Provide Contact Information screen of Remote Assistance, check your name and enter a message detailing the problem you're having.

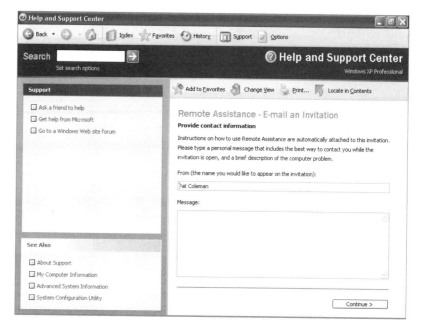

5. Change the name in the From text box if you want.

6. In the Message text box, enter a description of the problem and any blandishments necessary to get the help you want.

7. Click the Continue button. Help and Support Center displays the Set the Invitation to Expire screen (shown in Figure 3.23).

8. In the Set the Invitation to Expire area, specify the time limit for the recipient to accept the invitation. Choose a number in the first drop-down list and a time period—Minutes, Hours, or Days—in the second drop-down list.

9. To set a password, make sure the Require the Recipient to Use a Password check box is selected, and then enter the password in the Type Password text box and the Confirm Password text box.

**FIGURE 3.23**
On the Set the Invitation to Expire screen of Remote Assistance, set the expiration period for the invitation and enter a password.

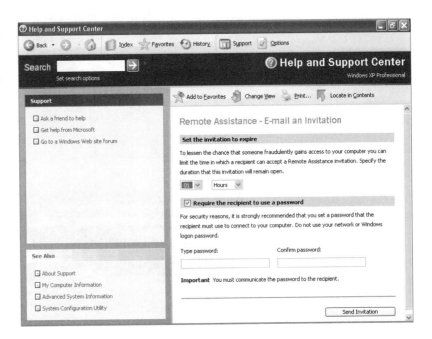

10. Click the Send Invitation button. Help and Support Center creates a file named rcBuddy .MsRcIncident containing the invitation and sends it via your default e-mail client with a message explaining how to use it. Help and Support Center then displays a screen telling you that the invitation has been sent successfully.

◆ If Help and Support Center can't send the file—for example, if your ISP's mail server is down—it invites you to save the file and send it manually.

◆ If you've set Outlook Express to warn you if other programs attempt to send mail in your name, Outlook Express will display an Outlook Express dialog box, warning you that a program (Help and Support Center) is trying to send a message. Click the Send button.

#### SENDING AN INVITATION VIA WINDOWS MESSENGER

To send an invitation via your existing Messenger account, follow these steps:

1. Start Messenger as usual, or activate it from the notification area.

2. Choose Tools ➢ Ask for Remote Assistance and choose either a contact name or the Other item from the submenu.

    ◆ If you choose Other, Messenger displays the Send an Invitation dialog box. Enter the person's e-mail address in the text box and click the OK button.

    ◆ You can also send an invitation to an existing contact by right-clicking them in the Online list and choosing Ask for Remote Assistance from the shortcut menu.

3. Messenger opens an Instant Message window with the specified user and displays a note saying that you've invited the user to start Remote Assistance.

    ◆ To cancel the invitation, click the Cancel link in the Instant Message window, or press Alt+Q.

4. Wait for a response, then proceed as described in "Receiving Remote Assistance," later in this chapter.

#### SAVING AN INVITATION AS A FILE

Saving an invitation as a file works in essentially the same way as sending an invitation as an e-mail message, except that instead of specifying an e-mail address, you click the Save Invitation As a File link, create the invitation, and then specify a filename and location in the Save File dialog box. For example, your company might designate a network folder as a drop-box for Remote Assistance requests. Administrators would then examine the contents of the folder and respond to the requests accordingly. Alternatively, you could save the file to a floppy disk or other mobile medium and mail it to a helper.

## Viewing the Status of Your Invitations

To view the status of the Remote Assistance invitations you've sent (or saved), display the Remote Assistance screen in Help and Support Center.

Click the View Invitation Status link. Windows displays the View or Change Your Invitation screen of Remote Assistance. Figure 3.24 shows an example.

From here, you can view the details of an invitation by clicking the Details button, kill off an open invitation by clicking the Expire button, resend an invitation by clicking the Resend button, or delete an invitation by clicking the Delete button.

## Receiving Remote Assistance

The following sections describe what happens when you receive a response to your Remote Assistance request.

#### E-MAIL INVITATION

When a helper responds to an e-mail invitation, Windows displays a Remote Assistance dialog box such as that shown in Figure 3.25, telling you that the person has accepted the invitation and asking if you want to let them view your screen and chat with you. Click the Yes button to start the Remote Assistance session.

**FIGURE 3.24**
Viewing the status of invitations you've sent

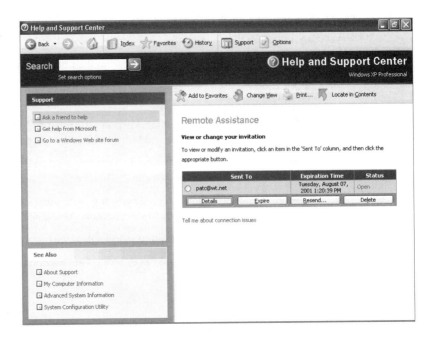

**FIGURE 3.25**
Remote Assistance dialog box indicating an accepted invitation

**NOTE** If you don't take any action for a few minutes, Windows assumes you're not in the market for Remote Assistance and times out the connection.

### WINDOWS MESSENGER INVITATION

When an invitee responds to a Messenger request for Remote Assistance, Windows displays a Remote Assistance dialog box such as that shown in Figure 3.25.

### FILE INVITATION

When a helper responds to a Remote Assistance request saved in a file, Windows displays a Remote Assistance window telling you that the person has accepted the invitation and asking if you want to let them view your screen and chat with you. Click the Yes button to start the Remote Assistance session.

### RECEIVING ASSISTANCE

Once the Remote Assistance session is established, Remote Assistance displays the Remote Assistance window shown in Figure 3.26, which provides a chat pane and control buttons.

**FIGURE 3.26**
During a Remote Assistance session, this Remote Assistance window provides a chat pane and control buttons.

### Chatting with Your Helper

To chat with your helper, Type a message in the Message Entry text box and press the Enter key or click the Send button to send it.

To start voice transmission, click the Start Talking button. Your helper then sees a dialog box asking if they want to use a voice connection. If they click the Yes button, Remote Assistance establishes the voice connection. Talk as usual, and then click the Stop Talking button when you want to stop using the voice connection.

**NOTE**   The first time you use the talk feature, Remote Assistance runs the Audio and Video Tuning Wizard if you haven't run it before.

To choose voice settings, click the Settings button. Windows displays a Remote Assistance Settings dialog box. Choose the Standard Quality option button or the High Quality option button as appropriate. Alternatively, click the Audio Tuning Wizard button (if it's available) to run the Audio and Video Tuning Wizard to optimize your speaker and microphone settings. Close the Remote Assistance Settings dialog box when you've finished.

### Giving Your Helper Control of Your Computer

If your helper requests control of your computer, Windows displays the Remote Assistance dialog box (shown in Figure 3.27). Click the Yes button or the No button as appropriate.

You can regain control by pressing the Esc key, by pressing Alt+C, or by clicking the Stop Control button.

### Disconnecting Your Helper

To disconnect your helper, click the Disconnect button. Remote Assistance closes the connection and restores your Desktop to its full complement of colors (if you chose to optimize performance for your helper).

**FIGURE 3.27**
When your helper
requests control of the
computer, decide
whether you trust them
or not.

When your helper disconnects themselves, Windows displays a Remote Assistance dialog box telling you so. Click the OK button to close this dialog box, then close the Help and Support Center window.

## Responding to a Remote Assistance Invitation

This section discusses how to respond to a Remote Assistance invitation that someone sends you. As you'd expect, the specifics vary depending on whether it's an e-mail invitation, a Messenger invitation, or a file invitation.

### E-MAIL INVITATION

When someone sends you a Remote Assistance invitation via e-mail, you receive an e-mail message with the subject line YOU HAVE RECEIVED A REMOTE ASSISTANCE INVITATION FROM and the username. The message comes with explanatory text augmenting whatever message text the requester entered, and an attached file with a name such as rcBuddy.MsRcIncident.

Open the file by double-clicking it. Alternatively, in Outlook Express, click the Attachment icon, select the file from the drop-down menu, select the Open It button in the Open Attachment Warning dialog box, and click the OK button. Windows displays a Remote Assistance window such as that shown in Figure 3.28, giving the details of the Remote Assistance invitation: who it's from, and when it expires.

Enter the password (if the window is displaying a Password text box) and click the Yes button to start the help session. Windows tries to contact the remote computer.

**FIGURE 3.28**
Double-click the file
you receive to open
the Remote Assistance
invitation.

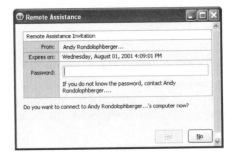

### WINDOWS MESSENGER INVITATION

When someone sends you a Remote Assistance invitation via Messenger, you see a Conversation window such as that shown in Figure 3.29. Click the Accept link (or press Alt+T) to accept it or click the Decline link (or press Alt+D) to decline it.

**FIGURE 3.29**

Receiving a Remote Assistance invitation in Messenger

If the user chose to specify a password, you'll need to enter it in a Help and Support Center window after the user accepts the incoming Remote Assistance connection.

### FILE INVITATION

If you find a file invitation waiting for you or receive one on a physical medium, double-click the file to open it. The rest of the procedure is the same as for an e-mail invitation, discussed in the section before last.

### PROVIDING REMOTE ASSISTANCE

If Windows is able to contact the remote computer, and if the user accepts the Remote Assistance connection, Windows displays the Remote Assistance window, which features a chat pane, a view panel that shows the user's Desktop, and assorted command buttons.

#### Chatting with the User

To chat with the user via text, click the Show Chat button to display the chat pane if it's not currently displayed. Type a message in the Message Entry text box and press the Enter key or click the Send button to send it.

To hide the chat pane so that you can see more of the remote screen, click the Hide button.

To chat via voice, click the Start Talking button. Remote Assistance displays a dialog box asking the person at the other end whether they want to use voice. If they click the Yes button, Remote Assistance activates the audio hardware. Click the Stop Talking button to stop using voice to chat.

CHAPTER 3

### Scaling the Display

You can scale the remote display to fit the area available on your screen by clicking the Scale to Window button, and restore it to its actual size by clicking the Actual Size button. Depending on the resolution you and the remote user have set, scaling the display may make the fonts illegible, but viewing the whole screen at once may make it easier for you to see what's happening on the computer than viewing only a partial screen and having to scroll to its outer reaches.

### Taking Control of the Remote Computer

To request control of the remote computer, click the Take Control button. Windows displays a Remote Assistance dialog box on the remote screen asking the user if they want to give you control. If they click the Yes button, you get a Remote Assistance dialog box telling you so. When you dismiss this dialog box, you have control of the computer and can take any action with it as if you were working directly on it. To release control, click the Release Control button or press the Esc key.

**WARNING**  Avoid pressing the Esc key when taking keyboard actions on the remote computer. Even combinations that use the Esc key will release control.

### Transferring Files to and from the Remote Computer

To transfer a file to the remote computer, click the Send a File button. Windows displays a Remote Assistance dialog box. Use the Browse button to locate the file, and then click the Send File button to send it. The remote user then gets to decide whether to keep the file and in which folder to save it. (If you have control of the computer, you can make these decisions.)

To transfer a file from the remote computer to your computer, have the user click the Send a File button in their Remote Assistance window. Alternatively, if you have control of the computer, you can do this yourself.

### Disconnecting from the Remote Computer

To disconnect from the remote computer, click the Disconnect button. Then close the Remote Assistance Services window manually. Unless you expect you'll need to reconnect to the remote computer to help the user further during the time remaining before the Remote Assistance invitation expires, delete the invitation file before you forget.

If the person you're helping disconnects the connection, Windows displays a Remote Assistance dialog box telling you so.

## Microsoft Online Support (Get Help from Microsoft)

Microsoft Online Support lets you automatically collect information on a problem you're having and submit it to Microsoft electronically. A Microsoft technician then sends a solution, which appears as a pop-up in your notification area. You can read the response in the Help and Support Center window and apply the wisdom it contains to fix the problem.

Microsoft Online Support lets you avoid both long waits on hold and the difficulty of explaining complex problems and system configuration over the phone.

To use Microsoft Online Support, you need a Microsoft Passport or a Hotmail account. If you don't have one, Help and Support Center walks you through the process of getting one.

To connect to Microsoft Online Support, click the Get Help from Microsoft link in the Support pane and follow through the steps the Help and Support Center presents. For obvious reasons, your computer needs a working Internet connection to use this feature.

## Windows Newsgroups (Go to a Windows Web Site Forum)

The Windows Newsgroups are an assortment of Windows-related online newsgroups that you can access through a web-based front end. Though these newsgroups are run under the auspices of Microsoft, they suffer to some extent from the problems of noise and irrelevance that characterize public newsgroups. (See Chapter 15 for a discussion of newsgroups and how to use Outlook Express to access them.)

To access the Windows Newsgroups, take the following steps:

1. Display the Support page of Help and Support Center.

2. In the Support pane, click the Go to a Windows Web Site Forum link. Help and Support Center displays the Windows Newsgroups screen.

3. Click the Go to Windows Newsgroups link. Help and Support Center activates or launches Internet Explorer (or your default browser) and displays the Windows XP Newsgroups home page, which lists the newsgroups.

4. Click one of the newsgroup links. Internet Explorer activates or launches Outlook Express (or your default newsreader) and opens that newsgroup in it.

## Using the Troubleshooters

Windows XP includes a number of *troubleshooters* for troubleshooting common problems with hardware and software configuration. Help and Support Center provides a central starting point for running these tools, though Windows also offers you the chance to run the appropriate troubleshooter when it detects that you've run into a configuration problem.

To run one of the troubleshooters, follow these steps:

1. From the Help and Support Center Home page, click the Fixing a Problem link. Help and Support Center displays the Fixing a Problem screen.

2. In the Fixing a Problem list, click a link to display a list of troubleshooters for that problem.

3. Click a Troubleshooter, and then follow the onscreen instructions. Figure 3.30 shows the Printing Troubleshooter.

## Finding Help on the Internet and Web

If you can't find the information you need through Help and Support Center, try the Internet and the Web.

### Help on the Web

With earlier versions of Windows, the first port of call when looking for help on the Web was the Microsoft website, which offered all sorts of resources from the latest patches and drivers to the Knowledge Base. But now that Help and Support Center both seamlessly searches the Microsoft

CHAPTER 3

website and provides links to some hardware and software manufacturers' offerings, and Windows Update can automatically download and prompt you to install updates and patches to Windows, there's less reason to access the Microsoft website manually unless you need, say, the extra search capabilities that the Knowledge Base website offers.

**FIGURE 3.30**
Windows XP includes troubleshooters that attempt to walk you through the steps of solving a problem.

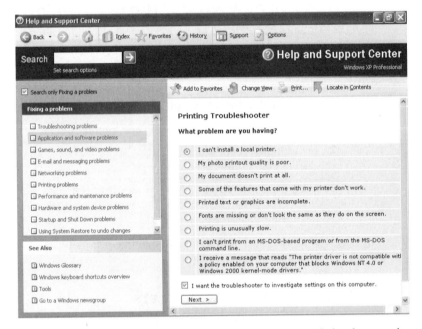

To find information from hardware and software manufacturers not partnered closely enough with Microsoft to rate inclusion in Help and Support Center's repertoire, to download the latest drivers, or to find other sources of information, the Web can be either more or less valuable, depending on your luck and your persistence in searching.

Chapter 13 discusses how to surf the Web with Internet Explorer.

### Help in Newsgroups

Another good source of information and help are the many computer-related public newsgroups (such as the comp.sys hierarchy) and the Microsoft public newsgroups (in the microsoft.public hierarchy).

Chapter 15 discusses how to use Outlook Express to read news.

## Summary

This chapter has covered a lot of ground, but now you have the information you need to navigate the Desktop and to get help when you run into a problem. Help and Support Center gives you access to much more information than previous versions of Windows did, and it's easy to make using it your first step when trying to solve a problem.

# Chapter 4

# Customizing the Interface

Windows XP can be customized in an amazing number of ways. You can move, resize, tweak, or change the color of just about everything. In this chapter, you'll learn about some of the most important interface adjustments you can make for usability, convenience, and just plain old personal preference.

This chapter covers the following topics:

◆   Working with the XP Control Panel

◆   Changing the date and time

◆   Adjusting video settings

◆   Customizing Windows XP display

◆   Customizing the desktop

◆   Customizing the Taskbar

◆   Setting Start menu options

◆   Adjusting the keyboard and mouse

◆   Choosing system sounds

◆   Using Accessibility options

## Working with the XP Control Panel

To open Control Panel, simply click Start ➤ Control Panel.

**TIP**   In previous versions of Windows there was a Control Panel icon in the My Computer window, but it doesn't appear there in XP by default. If you want an icon for Control Panel to appear there, open My Computer and choose Tools ➤ Folder Options. On the View tab, mark the Show Control Panel in My Computer check box.

In previous versions of Windows, the number of icons in Control Panel had gotten rather large, so Windows XP organizes them into categories rather than simply showing all the icons at once. This new view, called Category view, is the default view in Control Panel. See Figure 4.1.

If you would prefer the traditional Control Panel layout, you can click the Switch to Classic View hyperlink to switch to it, as in Figure 4.2. The icons on your Control Panel might be different than the ones shown in Figure 4.2, as some third-party applications add icons here.

**FIGURE 4.1**
Control Panel in
Category view

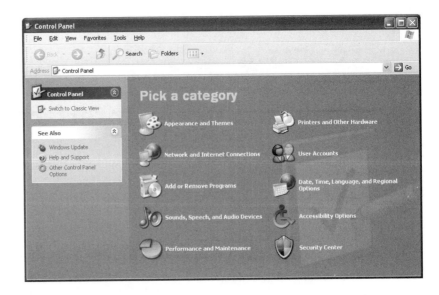

**FIGURE 4.2**
Control Panel in
Classic view

This book uses Category view in its figures and steps, but experienced users will probably prefer Classic view because it involves fewer mouse clicks and because the category in which an item resides is not always obvious.

If there are any items that don't have a category assigned (such as applets added by some third-party program), you can access them from Category view by clicking Other Control Panel Options in the Explorer bar, or by switching to Classic view.

**TIP**  Sometimes adding new hardware or software to your PC will add Control Panel applets. If the Setup program that placed the applet in Control Panel was written prior to Windows XP, it will not assign the applet to a category. You'll need to view Control Panel in Classic view to have access to that icon. If you would like for that icon to be assigned to a category, use the Registry Editor (see Chapter 25) to alter the *DWORD* value for the applet in the HKEY_LOCAL_MACHINE\SOFTWARE\ Microsoft\Windows\CurrentVersion\Control Panel\Extended Properties\{305CA226- D286-468e-B848-2B2E8E697B74}  2 section of the Registry. If the applet appears on the list there, change its current *DWORD* value (probably 0) to that of an existing applet that is already in the category in which you want to place it. You can also do this to change the category of any applet on the list, not just third-party applets.

## Changing the Date and Time

The system clock in your PC keeps track of the date and time; you can set the date and time through your BIOS setup program. You can also set it from within Windows for the same effect. Double-click the clock in the notification area, or go through Date and Time in Control Panel. See Figure 4.3.

**FIGURE 4.3**
You can adjust the date and time from within Windows XP.

**TIP**  Point at the clock in the notification area to see today's date.

On the Time Zone tab, you can select your time zone. It's just a simple drop-down list with all the zones in the world.

One problem many people have had with PC clocks over the years is their tendency to lose time. To combat this problem, Windows XP introduces a new feature that automatically synchronizes the system clock with a time server on the Internet. It's turned on by default, and updates your system clock periodically. You can turn it off, or update it immediately, in the Internet Time tab shown in Figure 4.4.

**NOTE**  When you update the time online, it relies on the Time Zone setting you have selected to know how to adjust the server's time to fit the correct time in your zone. The server is not necessarily in the same time zone as you, after all! That's why the Time Zone setting in the Time Zone tab is important.

Here are a couple of useful Registry tweaks for working with the Internet Time feature.

CHAPTER 4

**FIGURE 4.4**
Choose whether to update time automatically, and which time server to use.

By default, Windows checks the time against the time server once a week (that's every 604,800 seconds). If you want to use some other interval, go to HKEY_LOCAL_MACHINE\SYSTEM\ControlSet001\Services \W32Time\TimeProviders\NtpClient and set the decimal value of the *SpecialPolInterval* key to some other value in seconds. There are 86,400 seconds in a day, just FYI.

There are only two servers available by default time.windows.com and time.nist.gov. To add more, just add them in the registry key HKEY_LOCAL_MACHINE\SOFTWARE\Microsoft\Windows\CurrentVersion\DateTime\Servers. Not sure what other time servers are available? Check out www.eecis.udel.edu/~mills/ntp/clock1.htm.

---

**ADDING MULTIPLE TIME SERVERS AT ONCE**

One easy way to add a lot of time servers to the Registry at once is to create a REG file containing them in Notepad. For example, you could create the following text file in Notepad and save it as timesrvr.reg (or whatever name you want, as long as it has a .reg extension):

```
Windows Registry Editor Version 5.00[HKEY_LOCAL_MACHINE\SOFTWARE\Microsoft\Windows\
CurrentVersion\DateTime\Servers]@="1""1"="time.windows.com""2"="time.nist.gov""3"=
"clock.isc.org""4"="timekeeper.isi.edu"
```

You can keep going ad infinitum with the list, giving each time server you want to add a consecutive number. Then save your work and close Notepad. Locate the file in Windows Explorer, right-click it, and choose Merge.

---

## Adjusting Video Settings

Video settings are the settings and options for both your video card and monitor and their drivers that affect overall display appearance in Windows. These are separate from the color schemes, fonts, and other appearance features you might choose (covered later in this chapter). The following sections review some important information about video.

## Installing Video and Monitor Drivers

Windows XP is fairly good at detecting the video card during Setup, so the correct video drivers should already be installed. (It's somewhat less adept at detecting monitors.) You can check by doing the following:

1. Right-click the desktop and choose Properties.

2. On the Settings tab, notice the video card and monitor names that appear under the Display heading. If these match your actual hardware, Windows has accurately detected them. See Figure 4.5.

If either is incorrect, see the following sections to change them.

**FIGURE 4.5**
The Settings tab reports what video card and monitor Windows thinks you have.

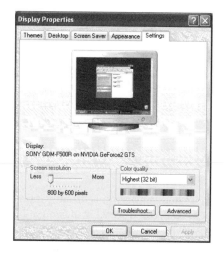

### UPDATING THE VIDEO CARD DRIVER

Having the right video card driver is important because the driver tells Windows what display resolutions, color depths, refresh rates, and other performance settings should be available. If Windows cannot detect your video card type, it will install a driver for a standard VGA card, which will limit the display options to 640×480 and 16 colors. In addition, the standard VGA video driver does not support power management, so you will not be able to use features like Suspend or Hibernate (see Chapter 9).

An outdated or corrupted video driver can also be a problem, although there is not a simple test to look for this. If you suspect a video driver problem, your best bet is to go to the card manufacturer's website and download a driver designed specifically for Windows XP and for your exact model of card.

To install a video driver, do the following:

1. Right-click the desktop and choose Properties; then click the Settings tab.

2. Click the Advanced button. This opens a Properties box for your video card and monitor.

3. Click the Adapter tab, and then click the Properties button. This opens a separate Properties box just for the video card.

CHAPTER 4

**4.** Click the Driver tab, and then click the Update Driver button. The Hardware Update Wizard runs.

**5.** If you see a message asking whether Windows Update can search for updated drivers on the Internet, click No, not this time, Yes, this time only or Yes, now and every time I connect a device. (This prompt was added with Service Pack 2.) Then click Next.

**6.** Click Install from a List or Specific Location, and then click Next.

**7.** If Windows already knows the video card name, choose Search for the Best Driver in These Locations and then make sure the location of the updated driver is included in the search locations. Then click Next and go on to step 7.

Or, if Windows does not currently report the correct video card, choose Don't Search, and then click Next. You'll see a list of compatible hardware with only one item on it.

If you have a specific driver you want to use, click Have Disk and point to the desired driver. If you don't, clear the Show Compatible Hardware check box to see a larger list of models.

**8.** Continue working through the Wizard to install your chosen driver. (It's fairly self-explanatory from this point on.)

**UPDATING THE MONITOR DRIVER**

The procedure for updating the monitor driver is very similar to that for a video card. Monitor drivers are very simple; they're basically just INF files that tell Windows what the monitor's capabilities are (resolution, refresh rate, and so on). They don't actually do anything much within Windows. So if Windows reports that your monitor is standard VGA when in fact it's something better, the worst thing that happens is that you're limited to a lower refresh rate than you would normally be.

**TIP** Most high-end monitors come with their own setup disk containing the INF files needed to set them up in Windows. However, since most people keep a monitor much longer than they do a PC, you will likely run into some fairly old monitors out there with unsigned drivers. That just means that the drivers have not been certified to work with Windows XP. For some devices this is a big deal, but the monitor driver does so little in terms of close interaction with Windows XP that it doesn't matter in this case. So if you see a dire warning about not using an unsigned driver, feel free to bypass it with a shrug.

To let Windows know you have a different monitor than the one currently chosen:

1. Right-click the desktop and choose Properties, and then click the Settings tab.

2. Click the Advanced button, and then choose the Monitor tab.

3. Click the Properties button, and then choose the Driver tab.

4. Click the Update Driver button. The Hardware Update Wizard runs.

5. If you see a message asking whether Windows Update can search for updated drivers on the Internet, click No, not this time, Yes, this time only or Yes, now and every time I connect a device. (This prompt was added with Service Pack 2.) Then click Next.

6. Click Install from a List or Specific Location, and click Next.

7. Click Don't Search, and then click Next.

8. Clear the Show Compatible Hardware check box. Then locate the monitor make and model on the list, as in Figure 4.6, or click Have Disk to use your own driver on disk.

9. Continue working through the Wizard to its finish.

**FIGURE 4.6**
Select your monitor's
correct make and model
from the list.

## Setting Resolution, Color Depth, and Refresh Rate

If you are not familiar with the terms resolution, color depth, and refresh rate, review the following information before you get started changing those settings in Windows.

*Resolution* refers to the number of unique pixels that make up the display. It's expressed in two numbers: width and height. For example, standard VGA is 640×480.

Windows XP no longer runs in 640×480 resolution except in Safe Mode; the minimum it supports is 800×600 unless a video driver is loaded that supports only standard VGA. From there the resolution can go up to whatever the maximum is that the video card and monitor can both support. On a high-end monitor, this could be as high as 2048×1536 or more. The higher the resolution, the smaller icons, windows, and text will appear on the screen. The video card has a maximum resolution it can support, and so does the monitor. The overall maximum resolution for the system is the one that both can agree on.

**NOTE**   Why does everything on-screen get smaller as the resolution goes up? It's because each item—an icon, for example—is a fixed number of pixels in size. When you switch to a higher resolution, that number of pixels takes up less space on-screen in proportion to the total screen area.

*Color depth* refers to the number of digital bits needed to accurately describe the color of each pixel. For example, in 4-bit color, there are 4 binary digits to work with, from 0000 to 1111. There are a total of 16 combinations of 0s and 1s in 4 digits, so 4-bit color supports 16 colors. Standard VGA is 4-bit color. Windows XP supports only the much higher color depths (again, except for in Safe Mode), such as 16-bit and 32-bit. Color depth is an issue only for the video card; most monitors can support any color depth.

*Refresh rate* is the speed at which the monitor is able to refresh each pixel of the display. As soon as the monitor's electron gun hits a pixel, it immediately begins to decay, so each pixel must be refreshed many times a second. Refresh rates are expressed in Hertz (Hz). At low refresh rates, such as 65Hz, the monitor appears to flicker because the pixel light is decaying faster than the monitor is refreshing it. At high refresh rates (85Hz or above), flicker is not noticeable. Refresh rate is primarily an issue for the monitor; most video cards can support any refresh rate that the monitor is capable of. The maximum refresh rate for a monitor goes down as the screen resolution goes up; a monitor that supports 120MHz at 800×600 might support only 85MHz at 2048×1536.

The amount of memory on the video card determines the resolutions and color depths you can use. Windows automatically detects the RAM installed on your video card and adjusts its available settings accordingly. To calculate how much video RAM a particular resolution and color depth combination will require, use this formula:

Width × Height × Number of bits ÷ 8

Dividing by 8 converts bits into bytes. So, for example, 1024×768 resolution with 32-bit color depth would be 1024×768×32÷8, or 3,145,728 bytes (approximately 3.1MB).

Since most video cards come with at least 16MB of RAM these days, you really don't need to worry about having a video card with a huge amount of memory on it unless you have an extra-large monitor that you plan to run in some very high resolution. And even then you don't need a monster video card with 64MB of RAM on it. For example, my high-end Sony 21-inch monitor goes up to 2048×1536. At 32-bit color, it would require only about 12.6MB of video RAM.

### Changing the Resolution and Color Depth

After all that theoretical build-up, changing the resolution and color depth is really simple:

1. Right-click the desktop and choose Properties.

2. Click the Settings tab.

3. Drag the Screen Resolution slider to the right or left to adjust the resolution.

4. Open the Color Quality drop-down list and choose a color depth.

5. Click OK.

**TIP**  As I mentioned earlier, the lowest resolutions and color depths are not available in Windows XP by ordinary means. However, there's a way to get to them. From the Settings tab shown in the previous image, click Advanced; then go to the Adapter tab and click the List All Modes button. Select the video mode you want (each is a unique combination of refresh rate, color depth, and resolution).

### Changing the Refresh Rate

As noted earlier, the refresh rate is more of a function of the monitor since it depends on the physical ability of the monitor's electron guns to keep up with the pixel refreshing. Therefore, as you would expect, you adjust it in the monitor properties:

1. Right-click the desktop and choose Properties.

2. Click the Settings tab, and then click the Advanced button.

3. Click the Monitor tab.

CHAPTER 4

**4.** Open the Screen Refresh Rate drop-down list and select a refresh rate. Or, if there is an Optimal setting available, choose that to select the highest refresh rate that the monitor and video card can collectively support in the current screen resolution.

**5.** Click OK. If you see a message asking if you want to keep the current settings, click Yes. You will see this only the first time that you choose a particular setting.

**6.** Click OK again to close the Properties box.

**TIP**    With refresh rate, higher is better; but do not exceed the maximum for your monitor, or damage to the monitor could result. This is where having the correct driver loaded for your exact model of monitor is handy; the driver knows your monitor's capabilities. If you don't have the right driver for your monitor and are using a driver for some other model instead, look up your monitor's capabilities on the manufacturer's website to be sure. A refresh rate of 85Hz is supported by most monitors and results in a decent display. Refresh rate is an issue primarily with CRTs.

## Setting Monitor Controls

Most monitors today have external controls for adjusting the size and positioning of the image. These adjustments can help you remove a black ring from around the outside of the picture and help you center the picture precisely. The positioning is sometimes called *phase*. Each monitor is different, so check the manual that came with yours.

You might have controls on your monitor for adjusting other factors, such as the straightness of the sides. Some monitor images bow out at the middle; some constrict at the middle. This adjustment is called *pincushioning*. Another adjustment you might be able to make is to tilt the entire image to the left or right slightly.

Many good-quality monitors also have controls for convergence. *Convergence* refers to the alignment of each red, green, and blue pixel. Display a pure white page in Windows (such as a blank word-processing document); if you notice a red, green, or blue tint, making a convergence adjustment may correct it.

## Troubleshooting Video Problems

If you still have display problems after ensuring that the right drivers are loaded and compatible resolution, color depth, and refresh rate settings have been chosen, try the Display Troubleshooter feature:

1. Right-click the desktop and choose Properties. Then click the Settings tab.

2. Click the Troubleshoot button. The Video Display Troubleshooter starts.

3. Work through the troubleshooter by answering the questions and trying the fixes suggested. See Figure 4.7.

**FIGURE 4.7**
Try the Video Display Troubleshooter if you need further help with video drivers or settings.

If you are having problems only with a specific program, the Video Display Troubleshooter may be able to offer some suggestions. You might also try the DirectX Diagnostic Tool, for troubleshooting problems related to DirectX technology (which is used in many of the most popular games today). To run it, choose Start ➢ Run and type **dxdiag**; then click OK. With Service Pack 2, you will see a box asking whether you want Windows to check to see if your drivers are digitally signed. This is a good idea, so click Yes to do that.

Figure 4.8 shows the DirectX Diagnostic tool's Display tab, which may be helpful for display-related problems. Yours may look different (for different monitors).

# Customizing the Windows XP Display

Now we get into the "fun" display settings, the ones that affect the color choices, backgrounds, shapes, icons, and so on. Some of these settings will be old hat to experienced Windows users, but others are welcome surprises new to Windows XP.

**FIGURE 4.8**

For problems with a game, the DirectX Diagnostic Tool may be helpful.

## Working with Themes

A *theme* is a collection of settings with complementary colors, icons, sounds, background, and so on. Rather than changing each individual aspect of the appearance separately, you can apply a theme to make a group of selections that work well together.

Themes were part of the Plus Pack for Windows 95 released back in the mid 1990s. They came standard with Windows 98 and Me. Now in Windows XP, the Themes feature is alive and well, but there are only two to choose from: Windows XP and Windows Classic. You can get more themes by buying the Plus Pack for Windows XP, or get free themes from www.themexp.org. (You will want to make sure you have a pop-up blocker running before visiting this site, however. IE includes a built-in pop-up blocker as of Service Pack 2.)

The Windows XP theme is the default. The Windows Classic theme sets Windows' appearance to resemble Windows 2000. If you (or users you support) are more comfortable in Windows 2000, you might want to set up that theme as a transition helper.

To select a theme, follow these steps:

1. Right-click the desktop and choose Properties; then click the Themes tab.

2. Open the Theme drop-down list and choose the theme you want.

3. Click OK.

Applying a theme changes many different settings at once. In the next several sections, you will learn how to change many of these settings manually. After you have made your selections of these settings, you might want to return to the Themes tab and save your set of settings under a new theme name. To do so, from the Themes tab, click the Save As button.

**NOTE**    Changing to the Windows Classic theme does not affect the Start menu; it remains in the new Windows XP two-column layout. If you want to change the Start menu so it looks more like the Windows 2000 Start menu, do so from the Start menu's Properties. See "Setting Start Menu Options" later in the chapter for details.

## Customizing the Desktop

The next few sections show you how to set individual appearance attributes for the desktop. Most of these are set automatically when you apply a theme, but you can also adjust them individually.

### BACKGROUND

The *background* is the image (or solid color) that appears as the desktop surface. In some previous versions of Windows it was called wallpaper.

You can use a variety of formats of graphics, including bitmap (.bmp or .dib), GIF (.gif), JPEG (.jpg or .jpeg), and PNG (.png). You can also use any HTML file, even though it's not necessarily a graphic; if you do that, the hyperlinks on the Web page remain active, and you can use them as shortcuts to your favorite Web locations.

If you do not choose a background image, the desktop will appear in whatever solid color you specify. The solid color is actually there all the time, even when a background picture obscures it; if you use a small picture, you will see the background color around the edges.

To select a background, complete the following steps:

1. Right-click the desktop and choose Properties; then click the Desktop tab.

2. Select a background image from the Background list. If the image you want doesn't appear on the list, use Browse to locate it.

3. Set a position for the image from the Position drop-down list. Stretch enlarges the image to fill the whole desktop. Center places one normal-size copy in the middle. Tile repeats the image as needed to fill the desktop.

CHAPTER 4

4. Choose a color from the Color list. This color appears behind the image if the image does not fill the desktop, or if you choose None for the image.

5. Click OK.

### CHANGING DESKTOP ICONS AND PROPERTIES

If you used previous versions of Windows, you probably remember that there were several system icons on the desktop, for things such as My Computer, My Documents, and so on. Windows XP has only one system icon on the desktop: Recycle Bin. If you miss those old-style icons, you can reinstate them. You can also change their appearance.

1. Right-click the desktop and choose Properties; then click the Desktop tab.

2. Click the Customize Desktop button. This opens the Desktop Items dialog box.

3. In the Desktop Items section, mark the check box for any icons you want to appear on the desktop.

4. Optionally, to change the look for an icon, select its picture in the middle section of the dialog box and then click Change Icon. The Change Icon dialog box opens.

5. Select a different icon for that item and click OK.

**TIP** You can click Browse to pick up an icon from a different source; you aren't limited to the ones shown initially in the Change Icon dialog box.

6. Click OK.

### CLEANING UP THE DESKTOP

Over time, you may end up with a clutter of icons on your desktop that were placed there by programs you install or shortcuts you create yourself for various purposes. To organize and tidy up this clutter, use the Desktop Cleanup Wizard.

From the General tab of the Desktop Items dialog box, click the Clean Desktop Now button to start the Desktop Cleanup Wizard.

This Wizard presents a list of the shortcuts on the desktop with a check box next to each one (see Figure 4.9). Clear the check box for any that you want to remain on the desktop; all others will be moved to a new folder on the desktop called Unused Desktop Shortcuts.

**FIGURE 4.9**

Clean up the desktop.

### USING WEB CONTENT ON THE DESKTOP

Back when Windows 98 was first introduced, desktop Web content was heavily hyped. Microsoft thought it was going to be the biggest thing ever. But as it turned out, most people don't find it all that useful, so the feature has faded into obscurity. It's still around, however, and you can still play with it.

Here's the basic idea: you can make your desktop "active" and place items on it that get automatically updated from the Web whenever you are connected to the Internet. These items can include normal Web pages as well as special mini-applications such as stock tickers and weather maps.

**TIP**　You can also place an HTML file on the desktop as a background image, as you learned earlier in the chapter.

To turn on Web content on the desktop, get back to the Desktop Items dialog box (right-click the desktop, choose Properties, click Desktop, click Customize Desktop) and select the Web tab. This tab lists any Web content that you have already set up. See Figure 4.10. To turn on an item, mark its check box.

You will probably want to add some items. To add one, click the New button to open the New Desktop Item dialog box, shown in Figure 4.11. Enter the URL for a Web page or other item to use, or click the Visit Gallery button if you want to peruse the items that Microsoft provides free of charge. (It's a pretty cool side trip; give it a try.)

**FIGURE 4.10**
Turn on Web content for
the desktop.

**FIGURE 4.11**
Enter the URL for the
Web item to display on
the desktop, or click Visit
Gallery.

If you choose Visit Gallery, a Web page opens in Internet Explorer offering various mini Web applications for your desktop. Select one and follow the prompts to install it.

Each desktop Web item is synchronized with the Web according to a specified schedule. You can go with the default schedule for an item, or you can click the Properties button for it (on the Web tab) to customize its settings.

You can also set properties directly from the desktop for an item. For example, Figure 4.12 shows a weather map on the desktop. When you point to a desktop control, a thin gray title bar appears on it, with a down-pointing arrow on the left end. Click that arrow for a menu from which you can manage that item. Using that same title bar, you can turn the item off (with the Close button at the right end).

## Working with Screen Savers

Screen savers are another once-hot feature that has fallen by the wayside. Put simply, people have gotten bored with seeing images dance across their screens. The practical need for screen savers has also diminished. Originally they were designed to keep images from burning into a monitor when a PC sat idle for a long time, but with today's monitors, burn-in is not an issue, so screen savers are just for decoration and amusement.

**FIGURE 4.12**
Click the arrow to
display a menu for the
desktop item.

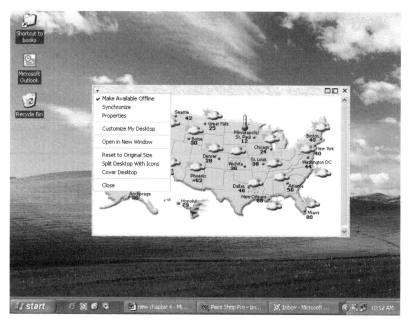

Using a screen saver can provide a small amount of local security, because you can set it to return to the Welcome screen when resuming out of the screen saver display. If you have set up a password for yourself for logging in on the Welcome screen, that password must be retyped to regain entry. This can prevent casual passers-by from tampering with the system.

To set up a screen saver:

1. Right-click the desktop and choose Properties; then click the Screen Saver tab.

2. Select a screen saver from the Screen Saver drop-down list. If you want to preview it, click the Preview button.

3. Enter a number in the Wait box for the number of minutes that should elapse before the screen saver starts.

4. If you want to return to the Welcome screen when resuming after the screen saver, mark the On Resume, Display Welcome Screen (or On Resume, Password Protect) check box.

5. Optionally, click the Settings button if you want to change any of the settings for the chosen screen saver. The box that appears is different for each screen saver because each has different options.

6. When finished, click OK.

## Changing Color and Appearance Options

Windows users have always loved having the ability to express themselves through color choices, and Windows XP offers a full array of settings in this area.

Right-click the desktop and choose Properties; then click the Appearance tab. See Figure 4.13.

**FIGURE 4.13**
Choose appearance options such as color here.

From here you have three choices to make:

◆ **Windows and buttons**: Your choices are Windows XP Style or Windows Classic Style. The latter makes Windows look like earlier versions.

**TIP** If you want more choices for window and button styles, check out a program called Window-Blinds at www.windowblinds.net.

◆ **Color Scheme**: If you chose Windows XP Style in the Windows and Buttons drop-down list, there are only a few choices here: Default (blue), Olive Green, or Silver. If you chose Windows Classic Style in the Windows and Buttons drop-down list, however, you get a huge array of color scheme choices here, as in earlier Windows versions.

◆ **Font Size**: Your choices are Normal, Large, and Extra Large.

**TIP** Some people like to set the display resolution fairly high, so that everything is really small on-screen, and then use Large or Extra Large font size to make the text more readable. This can result in some odd but harmless display quirks in some programs, such as in cases where the dialog box size is fixed and the large-size text overflows it.

But wait—there's more. Click the Effects button for an Effects dialog box where you can turn on/off various visual effects, as in Figure 4.14. Generally speaking, the more of these you can turn off, the better the video performance you'll get.

We're not done yet. Back on the Appearance tab, click the Advanced button to open the Advanced Appearance dialog box. Here's where you can customize the chosen color scheme, item by item, as in earlier Windows versions. (This works only for Windows Classic Style windows and buttons.) For example, you could choose Active Title Bar from the Item list, and then select a color, size, and font for it, as shown in Figure 4.15.

**NOTE** You can't save your custom color schemes in Windows XP, although you could in earlier Windows versions.

**FIGURE 4.14**
Choose which visual
effects you want in
Windows.

**FIGURE 4.15**
You can customize each
aspect of a color scheme.

# Customizing the Taskbar

The Taskbar is your gateway to all sorts of programs and windows, both those that are already running and those that you can run. In the following sections you'll learn how to control its appearance and functionality.

## Setting Taskbar Options

To set Taskbar options, right-click the Taskbar and choose Properties; then click the Taskbar tab. See Figure 4.16.

In the Taskbar Appearance section of the Taskbar tab, you have the following options:

**Lock the Taskbar**   The Taskbar is locked at its current position by default so that a user cannot move it to another location. Another way to access this same setting is to right-click the Taskbar and click Lock the Taskbar to toggle it on/off.

**TIP**   Another way to lock or unlock the Taskbar is to right-click the Taskbar and choose Lock the Taskbar from the shortcut menu.

CHAPTER 4

**FIGURE 4.16**
The Taskbar and Start
Menu Properties dialog
box

**Auto-Hide the Taskbar** Hides the Taskbar until you move your mouse pointer to where the Taskbar is hidden. Auto-hiding the Taskbar is useful if you have limited screen space or if you just don't like the look of the Taskbar.

**Keep the Taskbar on Top of Other Windows** Keeps the Taskbar visible at all times. This is the default setting. (Screen saver programs ignore this setting, however, as they cover the entire screen.)

**Group Similar Taskbar Buttons** Groups together buttons for files opened by the same program. This is a new feature in Windows XP and is on by default.

If you unlock the Taskbar, you can then drag it to one of the other sides of the screen; it need not be on the bottom.

You can also make the Taskbar appear in multiple rows. (Unlock it first.) This is useful if you keep a lot of windows open at once and you would like to be able to see them more easily from the Taskbar. To do so, position the mouse pointer over the top edge of the Taskbar and drag upward. Figure 4.17 shows the Taskbar with two rows.

**FIGURE 4.17**
A Taskbar with two rows

## Working with Taskbar Toolbars

In Windows 98 and Windows 2000, a Quick Launch toolbar appeared by default next to the Start button. This toolbar is still available in Windows XP but it is turned off by default. To display it, first make sure the Taskbar is unlocked. Then right-click the Taskbar and choose Toolbars ➢ Quick Launch. There are other toolbars you can choose the same way as well, but Quick Launch is the most useful. Figure 4.18 shows the Quick Launch toolbar.

**FIGURE 4.18**

The Quick Launch tool-
bar is displayed.

You can customize the Quick Launch toolbar (or any other Taskbar toolbar) by dragging shortcuts directly onto it and dropping them there. To remove an icon from a toolbar, right-click it and choose Delete.

Here are some things you can do to a toolbar:

◆ Add icons to it by dragging shortcuts onto it from the desktop or Start menu.

◆ Delete icons by right-clicking them and choosing Delete.

◆ Resize it by dragging the dotted "handle." If you don't see any dots at the left end of a toolbar, the Lock the Taskbar setting is probably turned on.

◆ Drag it into the center of the screen to make it a floating toolbar, in its own window.

◆ Drag it to a different side of the screen to dock it there as its own separate bar.

You can also make your own toolbars, although not out of thin air. First you create a folder; then you right-click the Taskbar and choose Toolbars ➤ New Toolbar to make that folder into a toolbar. Then any files you put into that folder will appear as shortcuts on the toolbar.

## Customizing the Notification Area

The notification area, also called the system tray, is at the far right of the Taskbar and displays icons for programs and tasks that are running in the background. These might include drivers or managers for devices such as a PDA interface or satellite Internet service.

To control which programs load at startup, see Chapter 5. If you just want to control which icons appear in the notification area, however, you can right-click the Taskbar and choose Customize Notifications. Then set notification options in the Customize Notifications dialog box. See Figure 4.19.

When some icons are hidden in the notification area, a left-pointing arrow appears to the left of the area; you can click that arrow to see the hidden icons. Click it again to hide them again.

**FIGURE 4.19**

You can specify which
icons appear in the noti-
fication area and which
are hidden.

CHAPTER 4

## Setting Start Menu Options

The Start menu's options are found in the same Taskbar and Start Menu Properties dialog box as the previous section covered, but on the Start Menu tab.

Windows XP has a new look for the Start menu, but you can revert to the old-style ("Classic") Start menu if you prefer it. Each has its own separate set of customization options. To switch between them:

1. Right-click the Start button and choose Properties.

2. Click Start Menu or Classic Start Menu, whichever you prefer. See Figure 4.20.

Then, to customize the appearance of the Start menu you chose, click the Customize button beside it.

**FIGURE 4.20**
The Start Menu tab

**NOTE**   This chapter's coverage of the Start menu focuses on its overall appearance and settings; in Chapter 5 you will learn how to add, remove, and arrange shortcuts on the Start menu for the programs you want to run.

## Customizing the Windows XP Start Menu

Clicking the Customize button for the regular (that is, the Windows XP) Start menu brings up the Customize Start Menu dialog box, containing two tabs.

In the General tab, you can:

◆ Choose an icon size for programs. This controls the icons on the Start menu only.

◆ Set the number of programs to appear on the Start menu. This controls the area on the left side of the Start menu, where recently or frequently used program shortcuts appear. The higher this setting, the taller the Start menu will be.

◆ Choose whether to have an Internet and/or e-mail link in the top left section of the Start menu, and if so, which programs they should represent.

In the Advanced tab, you can:

◆ Choose whether submenus should open automatically when you pause on them with the mouse. If you turn this off, you must click each submenu level to open it.

◆ Choose whether to highlight newly installed programs. This is on by default and makes newly installed programs and their submenus a different color.

◆ Choose and customize Start menu items. This is a list of various items that can appear on the Start menu if you like, such as the Favorites menu. Some of them have additional options, such as displaying them as a link versus a menu. The Control Panel in Figure 4.21 is like that, for example.

**FIGURE 4.21**
Choose what will appear on the Start menu and in what way.

**TIP**  When you install a new program, it doesn't find its place in the alphabetical Start menu hierarchy right away; it hangs out at the bottom for awhile. If you're using the Classic Start menu, you can re-alphabetize it manually by right-clicking the Taskbar and choosing Properties, clicking the Customizing button next to Classic Start Menu, and clicking the Sort button. There is no equivalent button if you use the Windows XP style of Start menu, however. To have Windows always alphabetize the list, remove the permissions from the Registry key that controls the sort order for the Start menu. To do so, in the Registry Editor, go to HKEY_CURRENT_USER\Software\Microsoft\ Windows\CurrentVersion\Explorer\MenuOrder. Then choose Edit, Permissions, and click the Advanced button. Deselect Inherit from Parent, and then click Copy in the Security dialog box. Then click OK and clear the Full Control entry from your account and all security groups you are a member of. Leave only Read permission.

## Customizing the Classic Start Menu

The Classic Start menu has customization options similar to those for earlier versions of Windows. See Figure 4.22.

CHAPTER 4

**FIGURE 4.22**
Set options for the Classic Start menu here.

The Add, Remove, and Advanced buttons enable you to add, remove, and arrange content on the Start menu. You'll learn more about changing the Start menu content in Chapter 5.

The Sort button re-sorts the Start menu content in alphabetical order. When you install a new program, it appears at the bottom of the menu at first; this Sort feature places it in its rightful alphabetical location.

The Clear button erases the historical usage records for the Start menu; it clears the My Documents menu and also the Personalized Menus feature if you are using it.

The Personalized Menus feature is available only when you use the Classic Start menu. It keeps track of which programs you use the most and displays them first on the Start menu; after a few seconds' pause or when you click the down-pointing arrow at the bottom of the Start menu (present when the feature is on), the complete list appears. To turn Personalized Menus on/off, mark or clear its check box in the Advanced Start Menu Options section.

Speaking of that section, there are many other fine-tune settings you can adjust for the Start menu there. Some of these options are "Display" this or that; mark such a check box to add a certain special-purpose folder or utility to the Start menu. Others are "Expand" something; turn these on to make certain features display as a submenu rather than opening a window when you select them.

## Adjusting the Keyboard and Mouse

Your mouse should work automatically in Windows XP Professional, with no special drivers or adjustments. However, the default settings are not optimal for everyone; some people prefer a faster or slower mouse pointer, greater or lesser sensitivity, or for the buttons to be switched for left-hand operation.

The adjustments for both keyboard and mouse are made through Control Panel. (If you're using Category view, you'll find them in the Printers and Other Hardware category.)

### Keyboard Properties

The keyboard properties are rather simple. They let you adjust these features:

◆ **Repeat delay**: the amount of time between holding down a key and the key starting to repeat (that is, repeatedly type the character quickly on-screen).

◆ **Repeat rate**: the speed at which repeating occurs once it begins.

◆ **Cursor blink rate**: the speed at which the insertion point (vertical line) flashes in a text-editing program.

## Mouse Properties

There are a surprising number of adjustments possible for the average mouse. You can control what the buttons do, how fast the pointer moves across the screen, what that pointer looks like, and whether any special features are applied to its movement. Table 4.1 lists the mouse adjustments you can make.

**TABLE 4.1:**     Mouse Properties

| TAB | SETTING | PURPOSE |
| --- | --- | --- |
| Buttons | Switch primary and secondary buttons | Useful for left-handed people to enable the index finger to control the primary button. |
| | Double-click speed | Adjusts the sensitivity for double-clicks. Useful for users who have a difficult time double-clicking fast enough. |
| | ClickLock | Makes the mouse button into an on/off toggle. Useful for people who have mobility problems that hinder normal dragging. |
| Pointers | Scheme | Enables you to select a predefined set of mouse pointers. |
| | Customize | Enables you to select a specific image for an individual pointer in a scheme. |
| Pointer Options | Select a pointer speed | Controls the distance the pointer moves on-screen when you move the mouse. |
| | Enhanced pointer precision | Enables more precise control of the pointer through little enhancements such as assisted deceleration. |
| | Snap to | Automatically moves the mouse pointer to the default option in a dialog box. |
| | Display pointer trails | Turns on a trail for the mouse pointer to make it easier to see, especially for people with vision impairment. |
| | Hide pointer while typing | Makes the mouse pointer vanish while you are working in a text editing application, so you don't get it confused with the insertion point. |
| | Show location of pointer when Ctrl key is pressed | Just what the name says. Useful for people who "lose" the pointer on-screen due to visual impairment. |

CHAPTER 4

**TABLE 4.1:**  Mouse Properties *(CONTINUED)*

| TAB | SETTING | PURPOSE |
|---|---|---|
| **Wheel** | Scrolling | Controls how much the display scrolls for every notch movement of the wheel (if present). |
| **Hardware** | Troubleshoot | Helps troubleshoot mouse problems. |
| | Properties | Displays properties for the mouse device installed. |

## Choosing System Sounds

If you have a sound card and speakers, you hear sounds when certain system events occur, such as Windows startup and shutdown, an error message, and so on. You can change these sounds individually, or you can apply an entirely different sound scheme.

To do so, go to Control Panel and choose Sounds, Speech, and Audio Devices ➢ Change the Sound Scheme. (Or, in Classic view, double-click Sounds and Audio Devices.) Then pick a scheme from the Sound Scheme drop-down list on the Sounds tab or click an individual sound on the Program Events list and assign a sound to it from the Sounds list or with the Browse button. See Figure 4.23. To play a sound, click the button that looks like a right-pointing arrow.

## Using Accessibility Options

Accessibility features in Windows XP help people with hearing, vision, or mobility impairments to use their PCs more easily. There's an Accessibility Wizard that sets up several of the settings automatically based on questions you answer; you can also set up each of the settings manually.

**FIGURE 4.23**
Select different system sounds.

There are other display settings that aren't specifically classifiable as Accessibility features, but are nevertheless useful for people with vision impairments. For example, in the Display Properties, you can choose Large or Extra Large font size on the Appearance tab, and you can click the Advanced button (still on the Appearance tab) to specify a color and size for an individual screen element.

**TIP** The CompTIA A+ Certification Operating Systems Technologies exam contains some questions about accessibility in Windows, so you may wish to familiarize yourself with the accessibility features if you plan on taking that exam.

## Using the Accessibility Wizard

Running the Accessibility Wizard is a great way to gain a general familiarity with the accessibility capabilities of Windows XP; it's also a useful tool for an end user who wants to set up accessibility without learning about every setting individually.

To run it, choose Start ➤ All Programs ➤ Accessories ➤ Accessibility ➤ Accessibility Wizard. Then click Next and work through the Wizard, answering its questions, to configure your system. The Wizard will then enable the needed features to carry out your wishes.

**TIP** You can also run the Accessibility Wizard through Control Panel. From Category view, choose Accessibility Options. Then choose Configure Windows to work for your vision, mobility, and hearing needs.

For example, in Figure 4.24, you're asked about the size of type you can read. If you choose Use Large Window Titles and Menus, it will switch to the Large setting for fonts (which you learned to do manually earlier in this chapter, in the Display Properties). If you choose Use Microsoft Magnifier, the Magnifier feature will be turned on. (More about it later in this chapter.)

## Accessibility Options in Control Panel

The Accessibility Options dialog box, accessible from Control Panel, contains dozens of features you can turn on to help with vision, hearing, or mobility limitations. Check out the following sections that apply to your situation.

**FIGURE 4.24**
The Accessibility Wizard helps you find the right size of on-screen type for your vision ability.

### FOR VISUALLY IMPAIRED USERS

Here are some settings that people who have difficulty seeing the default Windows display might appreciate. All of these are in the Display tab (Figure 4.25):

◆ Turn on a high-contrast display theme by marking the Use High Contrast check box. You can then click the Settings button to select a high-contrast color scheme that includes large fonts. Note that these are Windows Classic color schemes, and if you choose one, the button and window style will change to Windows Classic. Once you enable High Contrast, you can toggle it on/off by pressing Alt+Left Shift+Print Screen.

**NOTE**  Turning on High Contrast in the Accessibility Options is different from simply selecting a high-contrast or large-font color scheme in the regular Display Properties. When you turn it on via Accessibility Options, the on/off toggle with Alt+Left Shift+Print Screen is available, whereas normally it would not be.

◆ Adjust the cursor blink rate to blink faster or slower—whatever is best for you to be able to see it.

◆ Drag the Width slider to make the cursor wider so it's easier to see.

**FIGURE 4.25**
Make adjustments in the Display tab to help compensate for visual impairment.

Vision-impaired users may also be interested in the Magnifier program, which magnifies a section of the screen, and/or the Narrator program, which reads the text in dialog boxes aloud. These are covered later in this chapter, in their own separate sections, because they are applications rather than Control Panel options.

### FOR DEAF OR HEARING-IMPAIRED USERS

In most programs, deaf or hearing-impaired users should have no problem with the default Windows settings. That's because Windows is primarily a visual operating system, and the sound cues are of minimal importance. However, such users might miss out on the warning beep that accompanies an error message or the system sound that alerts the user to incoming mail or some other event.

Here are some features that might be of interest to users with a hearing disability. Both are in the Sound tab (Figure 4.26):

♦ Turn on SoundSentry to generate a visual cue on-screen when a system sound plays. You can then choose what you want this visual cue to be, such as flashing the desktop or the active window.

♦ Turn on ShowSounds to turn on captioning for any programs that support it. When used in a supported program, this works somewhat like closed captioning on a television.

**FIGURE 4.26**
Make adjustments in the Sound tab to help compensate for hearing impairment.

### FOR MOBILITY-IMPAIRED USERS

Windows XP contains many adjustments for people who have difficulty performing common keyboard and/or mouse activities.

In real-world usage, the biggest help is Windows' ability to accept alternative input devices called SerialKey devices. These attach to the PC's serial port (most models; newer ones may be USB) and are specifically designed to help mobility-impaired people. You can turn on access to a SerialKey device, and set up which port it uses, on the General tab.

There are also numerous features that assume you're using the standard keyboard or mouse but make them work in a non-standard way.

If you have trouble using a standard keyboard, try some of these options, all of which are in the Keyboard tab (Figure 4.27):

♦ Turn on StickyKeys to make the Shift, Ctrl, Alt, and Windows logo keys into on/off toggles by pressing them twice in succession. You can also turn this feature on/off at any time without going through Accessibility Options by pressing the Shift key five times in a row. Click Settings to adjust the properties for the StickyKeys feature.

♦ Turn on FilterKeys to have Windows ignore brief or repeated keystrokes. This is useful for someone who might have a hard time zeroing in on a single key and releasing it quickly. Another way to turn on this feature is to hold down the Shift key for 8 seconds. Click Settings to adjust the feature's properties.

◆ Turn on ToggleKeys if you want a sound to play when the Caps Lock, Num Lock, or Scroll Lock key is pressed. This is useful for someone who might accidentally press one of those keys and turn on the Lock toggle without realizing it.

**FIGURE 4.27**
Make adjustments in the Keyboard tab to enable features helpful for users with limited mobility or dexterity.

If you have trouble using a mouse but can successfully use a keyboard, you might want to turn on the MouseKeys feature on the Mouse tab. This enables you to move the pointer on-screen with the arrow keys on the keyboard. To turn this feature on you can also press Alt+Left Shift+Num Lock.

If you can use a mouse but not a keyboard, you might be interested in the On-Screen Keyboard application, discussed later in this chapter.

### FOR ALL USERS

No matter which accessibility options you choose, you will probably want to take control of the general configuration settings for them so they don't become obtrusive or a nuisance. Check out these settings in the General tab (Figure 4.28):

◆ **Automatic Reset**: You can disable all accessibility features after a certain interval of idle time; this is useful if a person with disabilities shares a computer with someone who does not need or want any of the accessibility features.

◆ **Give Warning Message When Turning a Feature On**: This makes sure that nobody turns on an accessibility option accidentally.

◆ **Make a Sound When Turning a Feature On or Off**: This plays a sound whenever the status of an option changes.

◆ **Apply All Settings to Logon Desktop**: This applies the chosen accessibility options so that the same preferences will be loaded again the next time Windows restarts.

◆ **Apply All Settings to Defaults for New Users**: This makes the chosen accessibility options the default for any new user profiles you might later create.

**FIGURE 4.28**
The General tab provides settings that affect all accessibility options.

## Using Magnifier

The Magnifier application can be very useful for people who are not totally blind but have some degree of visual impairment. It magnifies in a special panel at the top of the screen whatever portion of the screen the mouse pointer passes over. To turn it on, choose Start ➤ All Programs ➤ Accessories ➤ Accessibility ➤ Magnifier.

As long as Magnifier is running, a Magnifier Settings dialog box appears, as shown in Figure 4.29. You can minimize it and keep Magnifier open; however, if you click Exit in that box, the entire Magnifier program will terminate.

**FIGURE 4.29**
Magnifier focuses in on the current location of the mouse pointer.

## Running Narrator

Narrator is useful for people who have a hard time reading text in dialog boxes. When enabled, it reads the text in the active dialog box or window. To turn it on, choose Start ➤ All Programs ➤ Accessories ➤ Accessibility ➤ Narrator.

When you turn on Narrator, a dialog box describing it appears. Read the info, and then click OK to clear it; a Narrator window appears containing options for narration. You must leave this window open for Narrator to continue to work, but you can minimize it. See Figure 4.30.

**FIGURE 4.30**
Narrator reads the content of the active window aloud.

You can then switch to any other program, and it will attempt to read whatever text appears in it. It works in Microsoft Word, for example, and can read the letters that you type as you type them.

## Using the On-Screen Keyboard

The On-Screen Keyboard is an application that displays a facsimile of a keyboard in a window onscreen. You can click the letters you want to type. This might be useful for someone who can use a mouse but cannot type on a keyboard. To turn it on, choose Start ➤ All Programs ➤ Accessories ➤ Accessibility ➤ On-Screen Keyboard. When you're finished with it, close its window. Figure 4.31 shows it in action.

**FIGURE 4.31**
The On-Screen Keyboard lets you simulate a keyboard by using the mouse.

## Using Utility Manager

The Utility Manager is a one-stop shop for controlling the three applications you just learned about: the Magnifier, the Narrator, and the On-Screen Keyboard. You can open it by pressing Winkey+U or by selecting it from the Start menu (Start ➤ All Programs ➤ Accessories ➤ Accessibility ➤ Utility Manager).

The Utility Manager is very handy because it can be accessed quickly with a shortcut key combination so you don't have to wade through multiple levels of the Start menu to turn on an accessibility application. Figure 4.32 shows its interface. Just select the application and click Start or Stop.

**FIGURE 4.32**
The Utility Manager makes it easier to turn accessibility programs on/off.

## Summary

In this jam-packed chapter, you learned how to customize the Windows interface—how it looks, how it sounds, and how it behaves. You also learned about some of the Accessibility features in Windows XP Professional. In the next chapter, we'll take a look at installing and running applications. You'll not only find out how to add and remove programs, but also how to make old programs work well under Windows XP and how to control what programs run automatically.

# Chapter 5

# Installing, Running, and Managing Applications

However wonderful the features built into Windows XP—and some of them *are* pretty wonderful; some less so; see the rest of the book for details—they're not the be-all and end-all of computing. The programs bundled with Windows XP let you perform a few basic tasks, from creating simple documents, to playing music and video, to creating simple video movies of your own. But sooner or later, you're going to want to install a third-party program and run it so that you can carry on with your business and your life.

On the assumption that this is probably going to happen sooner rather than later, this chapter discusses how to install, configure, remove, and run programs—and how to shut them down when they fail to respond to conventional stimuli.

This chapter uses various programs as examples, ranging from the latest (and supposedly greatest) programs specially designed for Windows XP, to Windows 9x programs, to DOS programs that are still only just starting to suspect that graphical environments exist. The odds are overwhelmingly against these programs being those you want to use with your copy of Windows XP, but these programs provide examples of many of the issues you'll encounter with installing, running, and removing programs.

This chapter covers:

- ◆ Multiuser considerations
- ◆ Installing and removing programs
- ◆ Adding and removing Windows components
- ◆ Running programs
- ◆ Dealing with unresponsive programs
- ◆ Program compatibility issues
- ◆ Sharing data between applications
- ◆ Organizing the Start menu

**NOTE**    If you performed an in-place upgrade of your previous version of Windows to Windows XP, the installation processes should have configured all your programs for use already, so you shouldn't need to reinstall them. However, if you have old programs that you find don't run properly on Windows XP, you may need to run them in Compatibility Mode. If so, turn to the section "Running Programs in Compatibility Mode" later in this chapter.

# Multiuser Considerations

As you saw earlier in the book, Windows XP offers strong multiuser capabilities. From the start, Windows XP encourages you to set up your computer for multiple users, allowing each their own custom settings. And multiple users can be logged on to the computer at the same time (though only one user can be active). Some users can be running programs in the background (as it were) while the current user is working away unaware of them.

Windows XP's multiuser capabilities raise some issues for programs and files, as discussed in the next section.

## Who Can Install Programs?

Windows XP Professional supports three types of user accounts: Computer Administrator, Limited, and Guest. Only Computer Administrator users can install and remove programs. Limited users and the Guest user cannot install or remove programs. (You'll learn how to set up user accounts and control their type in Chapter 19.)

If a Limited user or the Guest user tries to install a program, Windows displays the Install Program As Other User dialog box (shown in Figure 5.1), telling them that they'll need administrator rights to do so. The user must specify a valid Computer Administrator username in the User Name text box and the appropriate password in the Password text box in order to proceed with administrative privileges.

If the user tries to continue with the installation without supplying Computer Administrator credentials, they usually run into an error message and abrupt termination of the setup routine.

## To Whom Is the Program Available?

In some operating systems, you can install a program for some users but not for others. In contrast, by default, Windows XP Professional makes any program you install available to all users of the computer—provided that the program's setup routine does things in the right way. For example, if you install Office XP or 2003, the setup routine automatically creates shortcuts for all users to use the programs, so the next time any user logs on, they'll have a swath of new programs that they can use from the Start menu.

Of course, Microsoft Office knows all about Windows XP, because they're both Microsoft products and they're roughly the same vintage. Eudora Pro 4.2, on the other hand, is several years old and hasn't heard of Windows XP. But it installs fine and is available to all users after installation because its setup routine was (presumably) constructed along Microsoft's guidelines.

If the program's setup routine is deficient, you may need to install the program to an explicitly shared location or create shortcuts for it manually. For example, if you install Lotus SmartSuite Millennium Edition on Windows XP by using its setup routine, the user who installs SmartSuite gets the full set of shortcuts for it (plus a slew of shortcuts clogging the notification area (a.k.a. system tray), plus the indescribably wretched SmartCenter program launcher and general menace). Other users get none of these—except for shortcuts to Net-It Now! Starter Edition, the little-known web-publishing companion software that was included with SmartSuite. This isn't useful, helpful, or even amusing.

**FIGURE 5.1**

To install or uninstall a program, you need to have Computer Administrator rights. If you don't, Windows stops you in your tracks with a warning such as this one.

**TIP**  Windows expects all programs to be installed into the Program Files folder. Putting them there seems to help make them available for all users, though it's not a guarantee of success. Putting them in another folder is usually not a good idea, though if you need to make small programs easily accessible to all users, you might be tempted to put them in the Documents and Settings\All Users folder.

## What Happens When Multiple Users Open the Same File at the Same Time?

Problems arise with some programs when different users have the same file open. For example, multiple users can open the same WordPad file at the same time, and each can save their changes into (or through) the other's changes. The result is pretty horrible.

Of course, some files are *designed* to be accessed by multiple users at the same time. For example, most database files are designed so that they can routinely be accessed by dozens, hundreds, or even thousands of users at the same time. However, the program prevents any *record* from being accessed by more than one user at a time. Some database programs prevent users from accessing records adjacent to any record being accessed by another user to avoid the problems that can occur when records are added to or deleted from the database—either of these actions changes the numbering of records. But as long as each user is (virtually) cordoned off from all other users in the recordset, all is well. Similarly, Excel lets you explicitly share workbooks with other users.

At the risk of generalizing absurdly, more complex (or perhaps more sentient) programs use some form of locking mechanism so that they can tell when another user has a file open. This locking mechanism can consist of flags on the file in question, but often it's implemented as a separate file that's created when the file is opened and is deleted when the file is safely closed. You can see this easily enough with Word, which creates a locking file in the same folder as the document you've opened (or just saved, in the case of a new document) *and* sets a flag on the document. The locking file replaces the first two characters of the file's name with the characters ~$, so that a document named Penguins.doc would generate a locking file named ~$enguins.doc. (Before you ask what happens with two-character filenames—if the file's name is six characters or fewer, Word *adds* the ~$ to the beginning of the filename. Seven characters, it replaces the first character. Eight characters, it replaces the first two.) If you open the locking file in a text editor (such as Notepad), you'll see that it contains the name of the current user (several times over, with variations in the spacing), some extended characters, and a variety of spaces.

**NOTE**  Word's locking files are hidden, so you won't see them in Explorer or in common dialog boxes unless you've selected the Show Hidden Files and Folders option button in the Advanced Settings list box in the View tab of the Folder Options dialog box (choose Tools ➤ Folder Options) in Explorer.

When you go to open a file, Word takes a quick look through the folder that contains the file to see if there's a locking file for it. If there is, it displays the File in Use dialog box to let you know about the problem and offer you options for proceeding. When you close the file that was open, Word deletes the locking file. But if you delete the locking file while the file is open, Word still knows that the file is open because the flag is still set on the file, locking file or no.

As you might imagine, any program that doesn't use a locking mechanism so that it can tell when its files are open is going to have problems with multiple users accessing the same file. Very generally speaking, the less complex the program, the less likely it is to check that a file is open, and the more likely you are to have a problem with multiple users opening a file at the same time.

This problem also arises with files that can be opened with two or more different programs that are available on the computer. For example, if you use WordPad to open a Word document, it opens the document without any locking. You can then open the same document in Word while it's still open in WordPad. Word then locks the document, and you won't be able to save changes to the original file from WordPad.

## What Happens When Multiple Users Run the Same Program at the Same Time?

By and large, having two or more users open the same document file at the same time (in the same program or in different programs) is more of a problem than having two or more users run the same program at the same time.

The brief answer to this question is as follows:

◆ Some programs are designed to be used by multiple users simultaneously, so they don't cause problems.

◆ Some programs are too dumb to notice that they're being used by multiple users at once, so each session is happy enough. Some of these programs are designed to run multiple instances for any given user anyway, so they're in good shape to run multiple instances for multiple users.

◆ Some programs notice there's a problem with multiple sessions and deal with it gracefully.

◆ Some programs notice there's a problem and sulk conspicuously.

With most programs, the problem comes not with the executable files and libraries (DLLs) but with the settings files. Windows XP handles the executables and libraries, running each in a separate memory space and segregating each user's programs from all other users' programs. But if a program is designed to use a central settings file rather than to implement a separate settings file for each user, the settings file can cause problems. If the program locks the settings file when the first user runs it (the program), the settings file won't be available when the second user runs the program. The same goes if the settings information is stored in a central location in the Registry.

Perhaps the easiest way around this, is to use a separate settings file for each user or to keep separate Registry entries. As you'd imagine, that's what the Microsoft Office programs do. For example, if you're familiar with Word, you probably know that it stores a lot of information in the global template, which is saved in the file `Normal.dot`. The global template is always loaded when you're running Word, so Word maintains a separate global template for each user. This way, it avoids problems when users in separate sessions of the same installation of Word change their settings at the same time.

Problems also arise when separate instances of a program try to use the same hardware resources on the computer at the same time—for example, the COM ports, the audio output, or the microphone input—or the same set of data files.

How a program handles a problem gracefully depends on what the program does and what the problem is. In a program that can manage only one instance running on the computer at the same time, when you start a new instance in another user session, you'll typically see a warning dialog box that lets you choose to either cancel running the new instance of the program or forcibly terminate the other user's session of the program.

As you'd expect, some programs are smarter than others. In particular, it shouldn't come as a shattering surprise to learn that current Microsoft programs are much more aware of Windows XP's multiuser functionality than earlier Microsoft programs or programs from other software companies.

For example, Windows Media Player lets you switch users while you're still playing music or video or copying a CD. The music (or video) continues to run even while the Welcome screen is displayed. If you then log back on as the same user, Windows Media Player simply keeps going without interruption. Only when you log on as another user does Windows Media Player stop playing the music or video (or copying the CD). And—perhaps more important—it exits the instance that was playing or copying for the other user, freeing up the sound and video circuitry together with whatever system resources it was using. (Before you ask—Windows Media Player quits when you switch to another user even if it wasn't playing.)

**TIP** If you're experiencing problems with programs that can't run multiple instances successfully at the same time, or with shared documents being opened by multiple users at once, turn off Fast User Switching, as discussed in Chapter 3. All these problems should disappear in a quick puff of logic.

## Installing a Program

You have probably already installed programs, so you don't need a full-blown explanation of it. Most programs these days come on CD-ROM, and if you have Autoplay enabled for your CD-ROM drive, the Setup program usually starts automatically when you insert the CD. If it doesn't, you can browse the CD's content, locate the `setup.exe` file, and double-click it to start the ball rolling.

**TIP** If you get an error when installing a program from a CD that started Setup using Autoplay, try opening My Computer, right-clicking the CD-ROM drive, and choosing Explore. This lets you browse the CD's content. (Double-clicking won't work in this case; it'll just relaunch the Autoplay.) Perhaps you can find a file on the CD that will run the Setup program correctly; sometimes the bug is with the `Autorun.inf` file rather than with the Setup program itself.

You can also use the Add or Remove Programs applet in Control Panel. This method is advantageous if there is no `setup.exe` file in the root folder of the setup disk, because it locates the Setup program automatically, even if it's not named `setup.exe`. However, since it takes longer to get the ball rolling this way, advanced users seldom employ this method. To do so:

1. From Control Panel, choose Add or Remove Programs.

2. Click Add New Programs.

3. Insert the setup disk for the program in your PC; then click the CD or Floppy button and follow the prompts.

What happens when you run the Setup program depends on the whims of the setup routine's programmers or (more commonly) on which of the two commonly used Windows installers they used—InstallShield or WISE. Suffice it to say that the usual steps for installing a program include agreeing to its license agreement, choosing which of the program's components to install, selecting a Start Menu folder (often still called a Program Group, in an embarrassing hangover from Windows 3.*x* days), and twiddling your thumbs (or fetching a fresh cup of wheat grass). For some programs, you'll have to reboot as well.

## Installing and Running Multiple Versions of the Same Application

In previous versions of Windows, any program that you wanted to run needed to be installed on that operating system, even if you dual-booted two different operating systems. For example, if you dual-booted Windows 2000 Professional and Windows 98 and had Office 2000 installed on the Windows 98 partition, you still had to install Office on the Windows 2000 Professional partition in order to run it.

No longer. Now if you dual-boot, for example, Windows XP Professional and Windows 98, and have Office 2000 installed on the Windows 98 partition, you can access that program while running Windows XP Professional. In some cases, the program will appear on the All Programs menu in Windows XP Professional. If it does not, you can locate its executable file in an Explorer-type window and double-click its shortcut to start the program.

## Making Programs Run at Startup

If you want a program to start every time you log on to Windows, place a shortcut to it in your Startup folder. Starting programs automatically like this can save you a few seconds each time you start Windows if you always need to use the same programs.

Your Startup folder is the `Documents and Settings\`*Username*`\Start Menu\Programs\Startup` folder. Navigating to this folder usually takes nearly as long as placing in it the shortcuts you want.

**TIP**  To make a program start automatically each time any user of your computer logs on to Windows, place a shortcut to the program in the Startup folder for All Users. As you'd guess, this folder is the `Documents and Settings\All Users\Start Menu\Programs\Startup` folder.

To prevent a program from running at startup, obviously enough, you remove its shortcut from the Startup folder.

Some programs run automatically at startup even though they don't appear in the Startup folder. Some of them run for a good reason, such as applications that start certain Windows services. Others are optional. If you think you can tell the difference, try using the System Configuration Editor (type **msconfig** from the Run command) to disable certain items from loading at startup. See Figure 5.2. Simply deselect the check box in the Startup tab for whatever you want to disable the next time Windows starts. When you do so, Selective Startup in the General tab automatically becomes selected. If undesirable results occur, return to the System Configuration Editor (in Safe mode if need be) and reselect that item, or to reselect all items, go to the General tab and choose Normal Startup.

If you decide you want to permanently prevent that item from loading at startup, you can edit the Registry to make that so. Go to `HKEY_LOCAL_MACHINE\SOFTWARE\Microsoft\Windows\CurrentVersion\RUN` and `HKEY_CURRENT_USER\SOFTWARE\Microsoft\Windows\CurrentVersion\RUN` and delete any unwanted items.

**TIP**  Surfing the Internet, you can accumulate adware and spyware that loads automatically at startup. Before you go manually stripping this stuff out of your Registry, first try some more graceful and thorough uninstall methods, such as removing them from the Add or Remove Programs applet in Control Panel and running a spyware removal tool such as Spybot Search & Destroy (`www.safer-networking.org`). See the next section for more information about program removal.

**FIGURE 5.2**

You can use the System Configuration Utility (msconfig) to selectively disable certain items that load at startup.

## Removing a Program

You should always remove a program through its Uninstall routine or through Windows' Add or Remove Programs applet in Control Panel. This keeps your Registry tidy by deleting references in it to that program; it also deletes any files in the %SystemRoot% folder and any other non-program-specific folders that were used only for that program. If you try to delete a program by removing its folder from the hard disk and deleting its shortcuts from the Start menu and Desktop, you might not have removed all the pieces.

To remove a program, follow these steps:

1.  From Control Panel, choose Add or Remove Programs. If the Change or Remove Programs page of the window isn't displayed, click its button.

2.  In the Currently Installed Programs list box, select the entry for the program you want to remove. The Add or Remove Programs window displays information about the program—its size (the amount of space it's taking up on disk), a rough description of how often you've used it over the last 30 days (Frequently, Occasionally, or Rarely), and the date you used it last—together with a Change/Remove button (or separate Change and Remove buttons, depending on the program). Figure 5.3 shows these details.

3.  Click the Change/Remove button (or the Remove button, if they're separate). Windows checks to see if other users are using the computer (because they might be using the program that you're about to remove).

4.  If any other user is logged on, Windows displays a Warning dialog box. At this point, you can click the Switch User button to display the Welcome screen, then log on as each user from there and log them off. But usually you'll find it easier to use the Users tab of Task Manager to either switch to the other users or simply log them off. When you're ready, click the Continue button if the Warning dialog box is still displayed. (If it's not, click the Change/Remove button in the Add or Remove Programs dialog box instead.)

**TIP** If you have a lot of programs installed, use the Sort By drop-down list to sort the programs. You can sort by Name, Size, Frequency of Use, and Date Last Used. Obviously enough, the Name category is useful for finding programs by name. The Size category is good for determining which programs are hogging disk space when you need to free some up in a hurry. And the Frequency of Use category and Date Last Used category are useful for rooting out the programs you installed on a whim and have used hardly at all.

**NOTE** If you have Service Pack 2 (SP2) installed, a Show Updates check box appears at the top of the Add or Remove Programs listing, as in Figure 5.3. By default it is not marked, and any removable Windows updates are hidden on the list. (In general, you would not want to remove a Windows update, since it was installed for a reason.) If you ever need to remove one, mark the check box to make the installed updates appear. If you do not have SP2, all updates appear on the list and you cannot hide them.

**FIGURE 5.3**
Click the Change or Remove Programs button on the Add or Remove Programs dialog box to uninstall a 32-bit program.

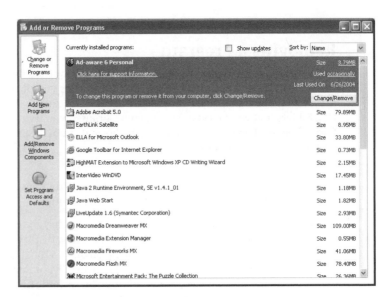

Once you've cleared the Warning hurdle, Windows invokes the uninstall routine for the program. The next steps vary depending on the program (or on its programmers or the tool they chose), but in most cases, you either specify which parts of the program to uninstall (if the program contains discrete components) or simply confirm that you want to get rid of the program.

If the uninstall routine tells you that it was unable to remove some parts of the program that you've asked to uninstall completely, it usually lets you know which parts are left. This is often caused by someone having previously tried to remove the application manually. For example, unInstallShield provides a Details button that you can click to display a dialog box such as that shown in Figure 5.4. In this case, it's easy enough to delete these folders manually by using Explorer.

**TIP** If a program still shows up on the Installed Programs list after you have removed it, you can remove it from the list by going to HKEY_LOCAL_MACHINE\SOFTWARE\Microsoft\Windows\ CurrentVersion\Uninstall in the Registry and deleting the key for that program.

**FIGURE 5.4**

If unInstallShield can't remove all the components of a program, it provides details in the Details dialog box.

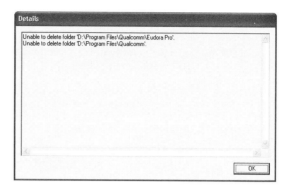

---

## REMOVING 16-BIT WINDOWS PROGRAMS AND DOS PROGRAMS

Windows' Add or Remove Programs feature tracks all 32-bit programs installed on the computer, and it's able to track many 16-bit programs as well. But some 16-bit Windows programs and most DOS programs don't show up in the Add or Remove Programs dialog box, so you can't remove them that way.

The preferred way of removing a program that doesn't show up in the Add or Remove Programs window is to run its uninstall routine manually. Some Windows programs add a shortcut to their uninstall routine to the program folder (or, in Windows XP, to the Start menu) that contains their other shortcuts. If there's no shortcut, you'll need to dig through the folder that contains the program to see if it has one. The file might be an EXE file, but it might also be a BAT (batch) file.

If the program doesn't have an uninstall routine, you'll need to remove it manually. (If you've only just installed the program, you *could* use the System Restore feature to return your system to its state before you installed the program—but usually you'll have made other changes to your computer since installing the program. Chapter 27 discusses how to use System Restore.) This usually means deleting the folder (or folders) that contains the program and removing any references to it that you can find.

There are two problems with removing a program manually like this. First, you don't necessarily know where the program has put all its files. This is usually more of a problem with Windows programs, which (following Microsoft's own recommendations) often put shared files into the Windows folder or one of its subfolders, than with DOS programs (which probably don't know that the Windows folder exists, and certainly don't care about it even if they do know). So if you simply delete the folder or folders the program created, it may leave detritus in other folders. (This is why uninstall routines exist, of course.)

The second problem is that the program may also have added commands to configuration files of their era (such as autoexec.bat or win.ini) that will cause errors when you've deleted its files. You'll need to discover these additions manually (usually when you get an error message) and delete them or comment them out manually. Because Windows XP uses these configuration files only for compatibility, these errors are likely to cause you annoyance rather than grief—unlike in the old days, when a command for a missing program could make Windows 3.1 refuse to load.

## Adding and Removing Windows Components

Many of the accessory programs that come with Windows XP are optional. You can remove them if disk space is tight or if you simply don't want them taking up space on your Start menu.

Here are the steps to add or remove Windows accessories and other optional components:

1. In Control Panel, choose Add or Remove Programs.

2. Click the Add/Remove Windows Components button. A window appears showing various individual components and component categories. See Figure 5.5.

**FIGURE 5.5**
Select an item or category to add or remove.

3. Place or remove the check mark next to an item to install or remove it. Some of the items on the list are for single features, such as MSN Explorer; others are for entire categories. If you choose a category, you can then click the Details button to see a list of accessories in that category, and then select each one individually. For some categories there are multiple levels; for example, opening the Accessories and Utilities category produces two subcategories: Accessories and Games.

4. After you have made all your selections, click OK. If prompted for the Windows XP CD-ROM, insert it and click OK to continue.

**TIP** Don't want to keep the Windows XP CD-ROM handy? If you copy the contents of its i386 folder to your hard disk (create a folder for it there), you can then browse to that folder whenever a Setup program such as Add/Remove Windows Components asks for access to the Windows XP CD-ROM. The downside—it takes up some space on your disk (a couple hundred megabytes).

Depending on what you're installing, you might be asked to restart the PC at the end of the procedure; do so if needed. When Windows reboots, any items you added will be available, and any items you removed will not.

## Setting Program Access and Defaults

If you have Service Pack 1 (SP1) or higher installed, there's an extra icon in the Add or Remove Programs window: Set Program Access and Defaults. (There is a shortcut for it at the top of the All Pro-

## REMOVING HIDDEN WINDOWS COMPONENTS

You might be disappointed when you look at the Accessories category of things you can add or remove—not all of the accessories on the Start menu's Accessories submenu appear here. Many of them are actually removable, but by default, Windows hides them from the Add/Remove Windows Components screen. Windows Messenger is one example.

However, there's a great little tweak that will make Windows Messenger, and many other "hidden removal" programs, available for removal. Here's what to do:

1. In Notepad, open the text file `sysoc.inf`, which is located in your `Windows\Inf` folder.

2. Notice there's a Components section, and under it, lines for various applets. Windows Messenger's name is `msmsgs`, for example. Find the line for the program you want to remove. For example:

   ```
   msmsgs=msgrocm.dll,OcEntry,msmsgs.inf, hide, 7
   ```

3. Edit the line to remove the word *hide* and the comma and space preceding it. For example, if you are using Windows Messenger, the line might look like this after you edit it:

   ```
   msmsgs=msgrocm.dll,OcEntry,msmsgs.inf,,7
   ```

4. Close Notepad, saving the changes.

5. Now go to Add or Remove Programs in Control Panel and click Add/Remove Windows Components. The previously hidden program should now be available for removal.

grams menu too.) This utility provides quick access to a variety of default settings, such as the default web browser, e-mail utility, media player, and so on. Yes, all those options are individually changeable in different places in Windows, but this provides sort of a one-stop shopping experience for them.

Click the Set Program Access and Defaults icon as shown in Figure 5.3, and you'll see a list of three options: Microsoft Windows, Non-Microsoft, and Custom.

Click Microsoft Windows to expand the list of Microsoft components. You may be surprised to find that you won't find many (or any) items you can customize here. Wait a minute, aren't we supposed to be able to customize things here? Yes, but not from this category. Try the Custom category. As you can see in Figure 5.6, there are many customizable settings under Custom, including the default web browser and default media player.

# Running Programs

In Windows, you can start a program in any of several ways. If you've used a previous version of Windows, you'll probably be familiar with these ways. They break down into two categories: starting a program directly by opening it, and starting a program indirectly by opening a file whose file type is associated with the program.

You can start a program directly in any of the following ways:

◆ Click its shortcut on the Start menu.

◆ Double-click a shortcut on the Desktop or in an Explorer window. (Chapter 7 discusses how to create shortcuts wherever you want.)

**FIGURE 5.6**
Access to some program
defaults is available here.

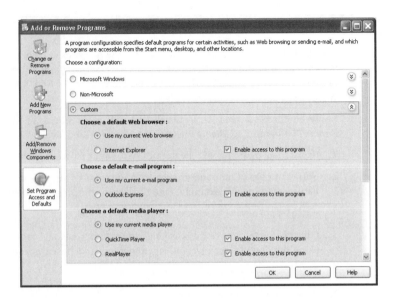

- Click a shortcut on the Quick Launch toolbar or another Desktop toolbar. (Chapter 4 discusses the Desktop toolbars and how to customize them.)

- Choose Start ➢ Run. Windows displays the Run dialog box. Enter the name of the program in the Open text box (either by typing or by clicking the Browse button), using the resulting Browse dialog box to identify the file, and clicking the Open button. Then click the OK button.

**NOTE**   Using the Run dialog box seems a clumsy way of running a program, but it's useful for running Windows utilities for which Windows doesn't provide a Start menu entry (for example, the Registry Editor, discussed in Chapter 25, and the System Configuration Utility, MSCONFIG) and for running programs for which you don't want to create a shortcut but whose path and filename you can type (or otherwise enter) without undue effort.

- Double-click the icon or listing for the program in an Explorer window (or on the Desktop). You can also use the Search Companion (Start ➢ Search) to locate the program you want to run.

Almost all setup routines create shortcuts to their programs automatically. Usually, the setup routine puts a shortcut on the Start menu or in a subfolder of the Start menu. Some setup routines place a shortcut directly on the Desktop; some consult you first, others don't. Some setup routines offer to also put a shortcut in the Quick Launch toolbar and/or notification area; other setup routines do so without consulting you.

An icon in the Quick Launch toolbar is simply an alternative shortcut to one on the desktop; an icon in the notification area indicates that some portion of the program is already running. You can right-click an icon in the notification area to see a menu of choices for dealing with that running program. If there's a Properties, Setup, Options, or some similar command, it might open a dialog box in which you can prevent the program from loading automatically at startup. You can also use MSCONFIG to prevent it from loading at startup.

# Dealing with Unresponsive Programs

Programs run pretty well on Windows XP—but not all programs run well all the time. Sooner or later, a program will hang or crash on you.

When this happens, first make sure the program hasn't got an open dialog box that you can't see. When you're working with multiple programs, you can easily get an open dialog box stuck behind another open window. If the dialog box is application modal, it prevents you from doing anything else in the program until you dismiss it. (Dialog boxes can also be *system modal*, in which case they prevent you from doing anything else on your computer until you deal with them.)

Minimize all other open windows and see if the dialog box appears. If not, you'll probably have the program that's not responding still displayed on your screen, probably with only some parts of the window correctly drawn. For example, typically the areas of the program that were covered by other programs or windows will not be redrawn (or not redrawn correctly).

**TIP**   To quickly minimize all open windows, click the Show Desktop button on the Quick Launch toolbar (if present) or right-click an empty area of the Taskbar and choose Minimize All Windows from the shortcut menu.

Next, try using Alt+Tab to switch to the program and bring it out from behind any dialog box that's hiding. Chances are that this won't work either, but it's worth a try. If the dialog box appears, deal with it as usual, and the program should come back to life.

If that didn't work, try using Task Manager to switch to the program:

1. Right-click an empty area of the Taskbar and choose Task Manager from the shortcut menu. Windows displays Task Manager. Or, if you can't get to the Taskbar, press Ctrl+Alt+Delete and then click the Task Manager button.

2. If the Applications tab isn't displayed, click it. The Applications tab (shown in Figure 5.7) lists each running program and its status. The status can be either Running (all is well with the program, as far as Windows is concerned) or Not Responding (Windows believes that the program is not responding to conventional stimuli).

**FIGURE 5.7**

The Applications tab of Task Manager lists all running programs and their status: Running or Not Responding.

3. Select the program that's not responding.

4. Click the Switch To button. Task Manager attempts to switch to it, and minimizes itself in the process.

If that didn't work either, it's probably time to kill the program. Take the following steps:

1. Restore Task Manager by clicking its button on the Taskbar.

2. Decide whether the program has hung or crashed. (See the nearby sidebar "'Not Responding' Status Isn't Always Terminal" for advice on determining whether the program is still viable.)

3. Select the task in the Task list.

4. Click the End Task button. Windows displays the End Program dialog box (shown in Figure 5.8). The box looks a little different with SP2 installed, but it contains the same information.

5. Click the End Now button. Windows terminates the program and frees up the memory it contained.

**FIGURE 5.8**
To terminate the program, click the End Now button in the End Program dialog box.

If killing the program like this doesn't work, you have several options. Here they are, in descending order of preference:

◆ Close all other programs that are responding. Then log off Windows. Doing this should shut down any programs you're running.

◆ If you can't close the program and can't log off Windows, but Task Manager is still working (apart from not being able to kill the program), use Task Manager to switch to another user, then log off the user session with the crashed program.

◆ At this point, you're pretty much out of options. Reach for the Reset button on your computer. When Windows restarts, check the disk for errors. (See Chapter 27.)

## Program Compatibility Issues

If you've used any of the versions of Windows NT, or if you've used Windows 2000, you'll know that program compatibility has been a major issue for the NT code base. In order to make NT stable and crash proof, the designers made heavy sacrifices in compatibility. Many Windows 9x programs flat out wouldn't run on NT. Games and other programs that tried to access hardware directly were particularly problematic: Windows 9x lets a program access hardware directly, whereas NT's Hardware Abstraction Layer (HAL) forces all hardware requests to be brokered by the operating system.

## "Not Responding" Status Isn't Always Terminal

When you see a program listed as having Not Responding status in the Programs tab of Task Manager, you may be tempted to kill it off right away. But you'd do better to stay your hand for a minute or two. Why? Because Not Responding status doesn't necessarily mean that a program has hung or crashed:

◆ First, Not Responding may mean nothing more than that program is responding more slowly than Windows expects; if you give it a few seconds, or perhaps a few minutes, it may start responding normally again. If your computer seems unresponsive overall, back off, and give it a few minutes to sort itself out.

◆ Second (and often related to the first point), Not Responding may mean that Windows is struggling to allocate enough memory to the program; this often causes the program to run slowly. Task Manager is a little harsh in this respect—it's Windows' fault that the program isn't responding, but Task Manager points the finger at the program.

◆ Third, VBA-enabled programs (for example, Microsoft Word and Microsoft PowerPoint) are often listed as Not Responding when they're running a VBA routine or macro. In this case, Not Responding means only that VBA temporarily has control over the program. When VBA releases control of the program—in other words, when the routine ends—Task Manager lists the program as Responding again. (If the program shouldn't be running a macro, try pressing Ctrl+Break to stop it.)

In Windows 2000 Professional, Microsoft greatly increased the number of programs that would run on the NT code base—but some Windows 9x programs still wouldn't run, and many DOS-based games wouldn't run either. Direct hardware access was still a problem, because the HAL was still there. Briefly, if the program could run in protected mode, letting the HAL handle the communications with the hardware, it would usually run, though it might run a bit more slowly than on other versions of Windows (or on DOS). If the program insisted on trying to communicate with the hardware directly, HAL gave it grief. (Fill in your own *2001* joke here: "I'm sorry, Doom, I'm afraid I can't do that," and so on.)

On this front, Windows XP brings very welcome news: XP is able to run most 32-bit Windows programs without problems. It can also run many 16-bit Windows programs. And it can run a number of DOS programs. Most of this happens transparently: You install the program by running its setup routine or installation routine as usual; you run the program as usual; and that's that. Behind the scenes, Windows XP provides more flexibility in providing the program with the type of environment it needs. On the surface, all is serene.

That's for many programs—perhaps most programs. But some programs don't run properly like this. For some, you need to explicitly use Windows XP's Compatibility Mode to fool the program into thinking that it's running on the version of Windows that it expects. Windows XP then mimics the environment of that version of Windows for that program, sustaining the illusion that things are to the program's liking. For example, if a program expects Windows 95 and won't run without it, Compatibility Mode tells the program that it's running on Windows 95 and tries to prevent it from finding out the truth. Usually the program then runs fine, though you may notice some loss of performance as Windows XP soft-soaps the program to keep it happy.

**NOTE**   If you're familiar with the Mac, you might be wondering how Windows XP's Compatibility Mode compares with Mac OS X and its Classic technology for running programs that won't run on OS X. Basically, there are similarities between Compatibility Mode and Classic, but Compatibility Mode is both less gruesome conceptually and far lighter on the memory. Classic essentially loads a hefty chunk of System 9.1 (on top of OS X, which isn't exactly svelte itself) and uses it to run the program, whereas Windows XP essentially dupes the program into a false sense of security by giving it the cues it expects. This duping requires a bit more memory and system resources, but nothing like the overhead that the Mac needs to run a program in Classic mode. But then Windows XP is less of a drastic change from its predecessors than OS X, which is essentially mutated UNIX with a GUI interface.

Once you've set up Compatibility Mode for a program, that program runs in Compatibility Mode each time, so you shouldn't need to tweak it any further unless some of its features misbehave. (However, you might need to enable Compatibility Mode for the application's Setup program and then again for its executable after it is installed.)

Compatibility Mode is very impressive, and it's great when it works. But some ancient programs (particularly DOS programs) may never work, even with Compatibility Mode. In these cases, your choices of course of action are approximately (a) give up on the program, (b) dual-boot your system with the version of Windows with which the program was last known to work, or (c) use emulation software such as VMware to run on top of Windows XP. Create a session of the version of Windows with which the program works.

## Programs You Shouldn't Even *Try* to Run on Windows XP

No matter how impressive Windows XP's compatibility with programs designed for earlier versions of Windows (or for DOS), there are some types of programs you should never try to run on Windows XP. These include the following:

**Operating systems**   Obviously, you can't install DOS, an earlier version of Windows, or another operating system or operating environment on top of Windows XP—at least, not without using some kind of PC-emulation software (such as VMware). If you need to run something from a DOS-like command prompt, open a command prompt window from within Windows (Choose Run from the Start menu and type **cmd**.)

**Old antivirus programs**   Antivirus programs designed for previous versions of Windows, including Windows 2000 Professional, don't know how to deal with Windows XP. You may be able to update the program. More likely, you'll need to get a whole new version.

**WARNING**   Attempting to install some of these antivirus programs may crash your Windows XP computer.

**Old troubleshooting and cleanup utilities**   Most troubleshooting and cleanup utilities designed for earlier versions of Windows will give XP nothing but grief. So will disk utilities (for example, Norton Utilities) designed for earlier versions. As with the antivirus programs, these utilities don't know how Windows XP works—in fact, most of them assume that Windows works in a completely different way. So despite Windows XP's ability to restore your system after bad software goes on the rampage, it's a mistake to let old troubleshooting and cleanup utilities loose on your system in the first place. Where you still need the added functionality to supplement Windows XP's capabilities, invest in a new utility specifically designed for Windows XP.

## 16-BIT PROGRAMS AND 32-BIT PROGRAMS

Okay, time out. What *is* a 16-bit program, and what's a 32-bit program? Where does the number of bits come from, and what does it mean?

A layperson's answer to the first question might be that 16-bit programs are programs designed to run on 16-bit versions of Windows (for example, Windows 3.1) and 32-bit programs are programs designed to run on 32-bit versions of Windows (Windows 9x, Windows NT, Windows 2000, and Windows XP).

Actually, it's not quite that simple. To get a fraction more technical, 16-bit programs are written to the Win16 application programming interface (API) and 32-bit programs are written to the Win32 API. The APIs are sets of rules that tell programmers how they can access the functionality that an operating system exposes to them and how a program should behave so that it gets along with the operating system and other programs running on it.

Normally, 32-bit programs *are* written for 32-bit operating systems, and 16-bit programs *are* (or, you might hope, *were*) written for 16-bit operating systems (which have largely gone the way of the dodo). But by using the Win32's extensions—a 32-bit operating system extension that sat on top of the 16-bit Windows 3.1 operating environment (which in turn sat on top of the 16-bit DOS operating system)—you could run a 32-bit program on Windows 3.1. So some 32-bit programs were written for a 16-bit operating system. (Well, sort of.) And because 32-bit operating systems can normally run 16-bit programs, many 16-bit programs are used to this day, running more or less happily in virtual machines on 32-bit operating systems.

The 32-bit operating system may have to perform a process called *thunking*, essentially gearing down to run a 16-bit program. Thunking typically involves some overhead and a slight loss of performance. But if the 16-bit program ran at an acceptable speed on Windows 3.1 with, say, a 486 processor, it should run at a decent speed on even a modest Celeron or Duron processor, even with any thunking needed.

Just as 32 valves are better than 16 (for making a satisfactory engine growl if not for reaching the speed limit ahead of that pickup in the next lane at the traffic signal), 32 bits are better than 16. The advantage of 32 bits is that you can move more information at once—*much* more information. Thirty-two bits can represent a range of more than 4 billion integer values (4,294,967,296, to be precise), whereas 16 bits can represent only 65,536 integer values. Sixty-four bits can represent correspondingly more than 32 bits, and 64-bit PC operating systems are on their way. In fact, Windows XP Professional and Windows 2003 Server both have 64-bit versions for the 64-bit Itanium processor from Intel.

That still hasn't answered the second question: Where does the number of bits come from, and what does it mean? The *bit-ness* of a program essentially comes from the word size of the computer it's running on. The *word size* is the biggest number that the computer can handle in one operation. Those fire-breathing speed demons of the mid 1980s, 286 systems, used a 16-bit word size, enabling them to handle much more data at once than the (exhaust-breathing) 8-bit systems that preceded them. Then, 386 systems upped the ante to a 32-bit word size, at which it stayed for several generations of chips: even Pentium IV and Athlon systems use 32-bit words. The Itanium processor has a 64-bit word size, enabling it to handle impressively large chunks of data in a single operation.

When you're installing programs on Windows XP, you seldom need to worry about how many bits they're going to use, because Windows XP handles any necessary transitions between 32-bit and 16-bit code seamlessly. You *do* sometimes have to worry about *where* you install older programs so that all users of the computer can use them—but more on this a little later in this chapter.

Some potential offenders are smart enough to figure out the problem and quit on their own. Figure 5.9 shows the Incorrect Operating System dialog box that an old version of Network Associates' VirusScan displays if you try to install it on Windows XP without using Compatibility Mode.

**FIGURE 5.9**

This old version of VirusScan is smart enough to refuse to be installed on Windows XP.

## Running Programs in Compatibility Mode

Compatibility Mode lets you tell Windows XP to emulate Windows 95, Windows 98, Windows NT 4, or Windows 2000 so that a program thinks it's running on the operating system it knows and likes.

**TIP**    Often you will need to run the program's setup utility in Compatibility Mode. Then run the program itself in Compatibility Mode after installation.

Windows XP comes with the Microsoft AppCompat database of compatibility problems known about programs. AppCompat is automatically updated by Windows Update, which gives you another incentive to accept Windows Update's offers to download every update available—at least until your computer's hardware and all your software are working as perfectly as you could wish.

**NOTE**    You can set Compatibility Mode only on files on local drives. You can't set Compatibility Mode on a program located on a network drive, on a CD drive or other removable drive, or on a floppy drive. But you can create a shortcut on a local drive to a program located elsewhere, and then specify Compatibility Mode for the shortcut.

Windows provides two ways of setting up a program to run in Compatibility Mode. The first way is formal and cumbersome, but it lets you test whether the Compatibility Mode you chose works for the program. The second way is much quicker, but you run the risk of getting a program comprehensively hung if Compatibility Mode doesn't work.

### THE FORMAL WAY OF SETTING COMPATIBILITY MODE

Here's the formal way to run a program in Compatibility Mode:

1. Choose Start ➤ All Programs ➤ Accessories ➤ Program Compatibility Wizard. Windows displays a Help and Support Center window and starts the Program Compatibility Wizard in it.

2. Read the information and cautions on the Welcome to the Program Compatibility Wizard screen and click the Next button. Windows displays the How Do You Want to Locate the Program That You Would Like to Run with Compatibility Settings? screen (shown in Figure 5.10).

**FIGURE 5.10**

Choose how to select the program you want to run in Compatibility Mode.

3. Use one of the following three ways to locate the program:

◆ To set Compatibility Mode for a program that's already installed, select the I Want to Choose from a List of Programs option button and click the Next button. The wizard scans your hard drive and displays a list of programs (Figure 5.11 shows an example). Select the program and click the Next button.

**FIGURE 5.11**

Select a program from the list that the Program Compatibility Wizard assembles.

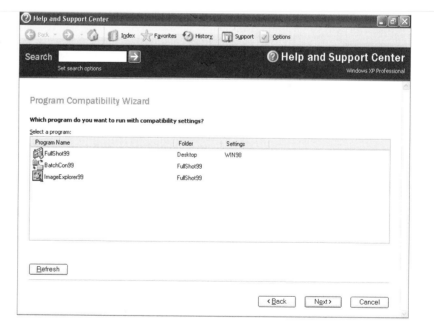

◆ To set Compatibility Mode for a program you're installing from CD, insert the CD, select the I Want to Use the Program in the CD-ROM Drive option button, and click the Next button.

◆ To set Compatibility Mode for a program that isn't installed and whose installation medium isn't on CD, or if you're just feeling ornery, select the I Want to Locate the Program Manually option button and click the Next button. The wizard displays the Which Program Do You Want to Run with Compatibility Settings? screen (shown in Figure 5.12). Enter the path in the text box, either by typing or by clicking the Browse button and using the resulting Please Select Application dialog box (a common Open dialog box) to select the program. Click the Next button.

**FIGURE 5.12**

If necessary, or if you prefer, you can identify the program manually on the Which Program Do You Want to Run with Compatibility Settings? screen of the Program Compatibility Wizard.

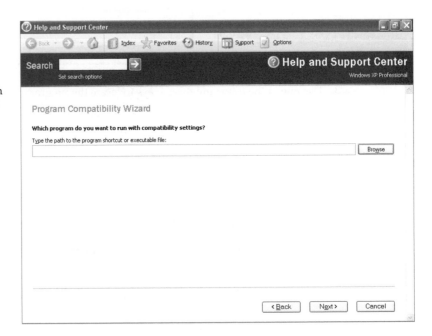

The wizard displays the Select a Compatibility Mode for the Program screen (shown in Figure 5.13).

4. Select the option button for the operating system you think the program needs: Windows 95, Windows NT 4 (Service Pack 5), Windows 98/Windows Me, or Windows 2000.

5. Click the Next button. The wizard displays the Select Display Settings for the Program screen (shown in Figure 5.14).

6. If you know the program needs display limitations, select the 256 Colors check box, the 640×480 Screen Resolution check box, or the Disable Visual Themes check box.

For most programs, you don't need to select any of these display limitations.

**FIGURE 5.13**

On the Select a Compatibility Mode for the Program screen of the Program Compatibility Wizard, select the Compatibility Mode you want to use.

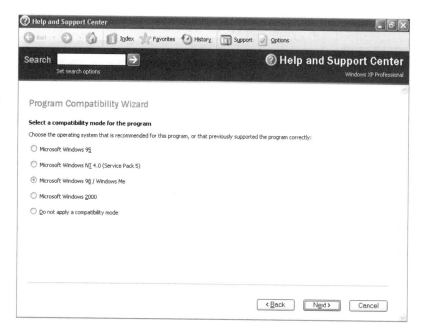

**FIGURE 5.14**

On the Select Display Settings for the Program screen of the Program Compatibility Wizard, you can apply limitations to the display settings used for the program.

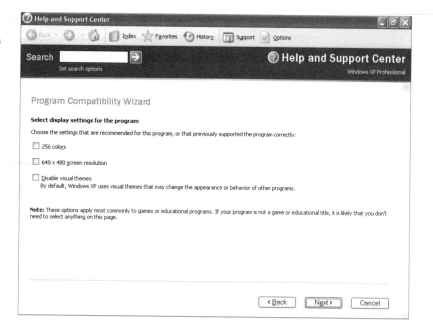

**7.** Click the Next button. The wizard displays the Test Your Compatibility Settings screen (shown in Figure 5.15).

**FIGURE 5.15**
On the Test Your Compatibility Settings screen of the Program Compatibility Wizard, check through the settings you've chosen, and then click the Next button to test them.

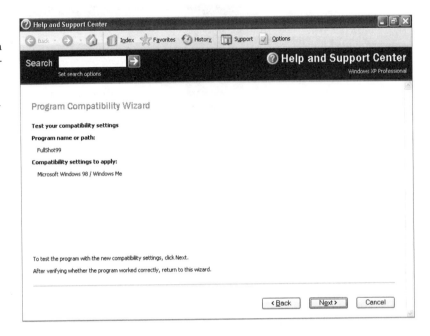

**8.** Check the settings you've chosen, and then click the Next button. The wizard launches the program with the compatibility settings you specified and displays the Did the Program Work Correctly? screen (shown in Figure 5.16).

**9.** Choose the appropriate option button:

♦ If the program ran okay, select the Yes, Set This Program to Always Use These Compatibility Settings option button. The wizard displays the Program Compatibility Data screen (shown in Figure 5.17), on which you can choose whether to send Microsoft information on the program, the settings you chose, and whether they solved the problem.

♦ If the program didn't run correctly, but you want to try other settings, select the No, Try Different Compatibility Settings option button. Click the Next button. The wizard returns to the Select a Compatibility Mode for the Program screen. Return to step 5 and try again.

♦ When no compatibility settings seem to work, select the No, I Am Finished Trying Compatibility Settings option button. Click the Next button. The wizard displays the Program Compatibility Data screen (discussed previously). In this case, you have more incentive for sending Microsoft information, as it may help them fix the problem with this program in the future.

**FIGURE 5.16**

On the Did the Program Work Correctly? screen, tell the Program Compatibility Wizard whether the program launched correctly with the computer settings.

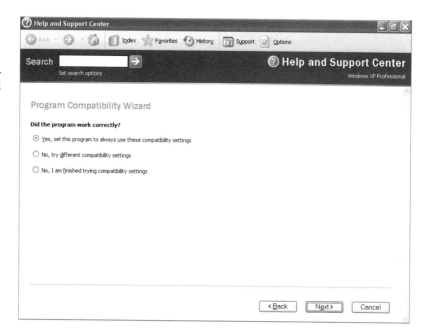

**FIGURE 5.17**

On the Program Compatibility Data screen of the Program Compatibility Wizard, you can choose whether to send Microsoft information on a program that you couldn't get to work.

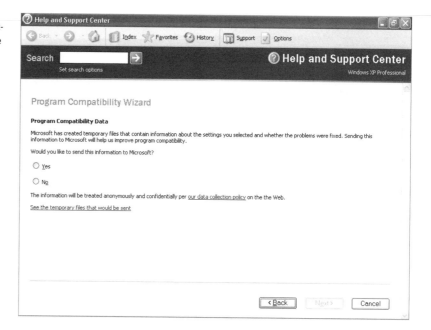

10. Choose the Yes button or the No button as appropriate.

11. Click the Next button. If you chose the Yes button, the wizard sends the compatibility data. Either way, it displays the Completing the Program Compatibility Wizard screen.

12. Click the Finish button. The wizard closes itself.

You remember that old version of VirusScan from earlier in the chapter that didn't want to install on Windows XP? It was happy to install in Compatibility Mode for Windows 95—but parts of it wouldn't run on Windows XP (see Figure 5.18).

**FIGURE 5.18**
VirusScan decided it really didn't like Windows XP after all.

### THE QUICK WAY OF SETTING COMPATIBILITY MODE

The quick way of setting Compatibility Mode is as follows:

1. Right-click the shortcut for the program and select Properties from the shortcut menu. Windows displays the Properties dialog box for the shortcut.

2. Click the Compatibility tab, which is shown in Figure 5.19.

3. Select the Run This Program in Compatibility Mode For check box if it's not already selected.

4. In the drop-down list, select the mode you want to use.

**FIGURE 5.19**
You can also choose Compatibility Mode settings in the Compatibility tab of the Properties dialog box for the shortcut.

5. In the Display Settings section, select the Run in 256 Colors check box, the Run in 640×480 Screen Resolution check box, or the Disable Visual Themes check box as necessary. (Again, for most programs, you won't need to set these options.)

6. Click the OK button. Windows applies your choice and closes the Properties dialog box.

This method of specifying Compatibility Mode settings has the advantage that you can specify different Compatibility Mode settings for different shortcuts for the same program or even for the shortcuts to different documents of the same file type.

**TIP** If you want to use Compatibility Mode for a shortcut that points directly to a file on CD-ROM, you won't be able to access the Compatibility tab for the shortcut while there is a CD in the drive. Remove it, and then open the properties for the shortcut. Then you can replace the CD in the drive before you run the program to test the settings.

### EVEN WITH COMPATIBILITY MODE, SOME PROGRAMS DON'T WORK

Some programs plain don't work even when you use Compatibility Mode. For example, Lotus SmartSuite 96 won't install on Windows XP, even if you try to run it from the CD or copy its files to a local drive and use Compatibility Mode. When you run the SmartSuite 96 installation routine on Windows XP, you get to specify the program folder and the type of installation (typical, minimal, custom). Then the installation crashes with the Output message box shown in Figure 5.20. This message box mentions an overflow (trying to put more information in a memory register than will fit), but beyond that, it tells you next to nothing useful.

**FIGURE 5.20**
The Lotus SmartSuite 96 installation routine crashes with an Output CNTR+318 Overflow message box.

After this message box, the program terminates. If you're feeling determined, and you lather, rinse, and repeat, exactly the same thing happens again.

## Exchanging Data Between Programs

Ever since the early versions of Windows, one of its great advantages has been its ability to transfer data between programs via its Clipboard.

The Clipboard can transfer data of different types that would not normally be compatible with one another. For example, suppose you are writing a letter in a simple word processor such as WordPad that does not support the import of very many types of graphics. You have a graphic in some odd format that you want to include; it will open in a Windows-based drawing program, but not in WordPad. You can copy the graphic to the Clipboard in the drawing program, and then paste it into WordPad, bypassing the whole import/export hassle entirely.

But wait—there's more. In addition to the simple copy (or cut) and paste of the Clipboard, you can also maintain links between the original material and the copy. That's object linking and embedding (OLE).

CHAPTER 5

## Clipboard Basics

You're probably already familiar with basic Clipboard operation. Almost all Windows programs have an Edit menu containing commands for Cut, Copy, and Paste. These commands place and retrieve things on the Clipboard. There may be several shortcuts for these commands, depending on the program. Here are the most common ones:

◆ Cut: Ctrl+X or the Cut button on the toolbar

◆ Copy: Ctrl+C or the Copy button

◆ Paste: Ctrl+V or the Paste button

The Clipboard is not designed to be permanent storage. It holds only one clip at a time, so when you cut or copy something else, whatever was there before is erased. (In Microsoft Office 2000 or Office XP you have an expanded Clipboard available, which is discussed in the next section.) If you want to store something from the Clipboard for later use, check out the Clipboard Viewer, discussed later in this chapter.

**TIP**   You can capture all or part of a screen image to the Clipboard, and then paste it into a graphics program such as Paint to save it. To do so, press Shift+Print Screen for the entire screen or Alt+Print Screen for the active window.

## For Microsoft Office Users: The Enhanced Microsoft Office Clipboard

In Microsoft Office 2000, an enhanced clipboard called Office Clipboard was introduced that enabled you to copy multiple selections to the Clipboard without losing whatever content was already there. Office XP and 2003 expanded on this idea to enable even more clips at a time (up to 24). Figure 5.21 shows the Office Clipboard in Microsoft Word XP.

**FIGURE 5.21**
The enhanced Office Clipboard in Microsoft Word XP

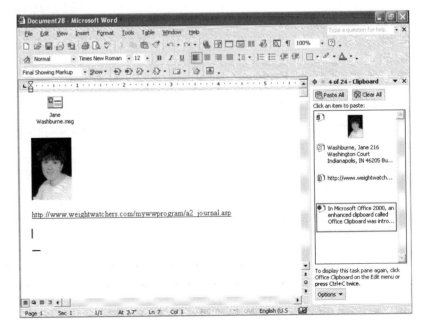

When you use the Office Clipboard, the last item you place on it also appears in the Windows XP Clipboard, so the two Clipboards are related. The Copy, Cut, and Paste commands in all applications, including Office applications, apply to the most recently used clip as well. The only difference is that in the Office Clipboard, when you replace the Windows XP Clipboard contents with something else, instead of that old content being deleted, it simply moves down one slot on the Office Clipboard. When the Office Clipboard fills up completely, the oldest items start scrolling off. Like the Windows Clipboard, the Office Clipboard is cleared when you exit Windows.

As long as an Office application is open, the Office Clipboard is available, and whatever you copy or cut to the regular Clipboard appears there. However, when it comes to pasting from the Clipboard, you can paste the full range of clips only into Office applications; in any other application you are limited to whatever is currently on the regular Windows Clipboard.

## Using the ClipBook Viewer

If you ever forget what's on the Clipboard, you can bring up the ClipBook Viewer by running the program `clipbrd.exe` with the Run command. If you find yourself doing that often, you might want to create a shortcut to it on the Desktop or Start menu.

The ClipBook Viewer program comes in handy in a variety of other ways as well. If you're on a network, you can use it to connect to a ClipBook on a remote PC, to share clips with others. You can also use it to save Clipboard contents to a file, and then open that file whenever you want to reuse that content on the Clipboard. This is sort of like the Office Clipboard in that it enables you to retain multiple clips. However, it has some important differences. The clips stored in the ClipBook Viewer are permanently held in saved files (at least until you choose to delete them), so shutting off the PC does not affect them. Also, to paste from the ClipBook Viewer, you must enter the ClipBook Viewer program and copy a saved clip to the Windows XP Clipboard first. Figure 5.22 shows the ClipBook Viewer with the current Windows Clipboard content showing.

**TIP**   Don't panic if the image shown in ClipBook Viewer is not as high quality as the clip you copied to the Clipboard, or if the image appears distorted. The ClipBook Viewer is simply not as adept at displaying all file types to best advantage as other programs. Rest assured that when you save the clip and then open it later from ClipBook Viewer, it will retain all its original quality.

**FIGURE 5.22**
The ClipBook Viewer lets you save and manage Clipboard content.

## Object Linking and Embedding

Object linking and embedding (OLE) could be the subject of an entire chapter by itself; it's a very rich technology for creating links between original data and copies of it, or between original data and the program in which it was created. We'll try to keep the discussion succinct here, however, focusing on the facts that an end user would need to know.

**NOTE**   You may have heard of Dynamic Data Exchange (DDE) an older version of the same basic technology as OLE. It was used in Windows versions prior to 3.1, and some 16-bit programs still employ it as opposed to OLE. Windows XP includes a DDE driver called NetDDE that helps applications that require DDE to interface with those that use OLE.

When you share data between applications with the Clipboard (either the standard Windows version or the Office Clipboard), the resulting pasted copy is static. When the original from which it came changes, the copy does not change. In addition, the pasted copy becomes part of the destination document (or whatever data file type it is), and no connection is maintained between that pasted item and the program from which it came.

There are two main features in OLE: linking and embedding. *Linking* refers to creating a link between the original data file and the new location, so that when the original changes, the pasted copy changes too. *Embedding* refers to creating a link between the pasted data and the application in which it was created so that you can double-click the pasted data to reopen it in its native application for further editing.

Not all programs support OLE, and those that do support it may access it in slightly different ways. Most Microsoft Office applications support it through two separate commands: Edit ➢ Paste Special and Insert ➢ Object.

### OLE WITH THE PASTE SPECIAL COMMAND

The Paste Special method is useful when you want to embed a fragment of data from some other program. Embedding works whether or not the data has been saved in that other program; Linking requires that it be saved (since the link must refer to a specific filename). To link or embed with Paste Special:

1. Copy the data to the Clipboard normally in its native program.

2. Switch to the program into which you want to paste it, and choose Edit ➢ Paste Special. The Paste Special dialog box appears.

3. If you want to embed only, leave Paste selected. If you want to link, choose Paste Link. See Figure 5.23.

**FIGURE 5.23**
Pasting content with
Paste Special

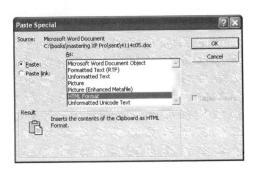

4. Select the type of object you want it to be pasted as. If you want embedding, make sure you choose a type that ends with the word "object" such as Microsoft Word Document Object in Figure 5.23.

**TIP**   It is possible to do regular pasting with the Paste Special dialog box. If you choose Paste rather than Paste Link, and then do not choose an object type that supports embedding, the net result will be the same as if you had used the regular Paste command. You might occasionally want to do such a thing if you wanted it pasted as a particular non-embeddable data type other than the default one.

5. Click OK. Your new link or embedded object is created.

### OLE WITH THE INSERT OBJECT COMMAND

The Insert Object method is useful when you want to insert the entire file, not just a fragment of it. You can also use Insert Object to create a new embedded object within a document of any type for which you have an installed Windows application. For example, suppose you want a drawing in a Word document but you find Word's drawing tools too rudimentary. You could embed a Paint Shop Pro drawing in the document and have access to all of Paint Shop Pro's graphics tools from within Word.

To insert an existing object:

1. Start in the application and document into which you want to insert the object. Then choose Insert ➤ Object.

2. Click the Create from File tab.

3. Type the path to the file, or browse for it with Browse.

4. If you want it to be linked, mark the Link to File check box. (Embedding happens automatically this way, whether you choose linking or not.) See Figure 5.24.

**FIGURE 5.24**
Inserting an existing file with Insert Object

5. If you want the object to appear as a clickable icon in the document, rather than in its native format, mark the Display as Icon check box.

**TIP**   You probably won't want to use Display as Icon in most cases; most people want embedded/ linked content to appear seamless with the rest of the file. An exception might be if you are embedding a large graphic file that takes a long time to draw on-screen, and you didn't want it to always be visible while you are editing the rest of the document.

**6.** Click OK. The file is inserted.

If you want to create a new embedded object, you won't be able to link it, of course, since it won't exist outside of the host document. To create a new embedded object:

**1.** Start in the application and document into which you want to insert the object. Then choose Insert ➢ Object.

**2.** Click the Create New tab if it is not already on top. Then select the program with which you want to associate the new object. See Figure 5.25.

**FIGURE 5.25**
Creating a new embedded object

**3.** If you want the object to appear as a clickable icon in the document, rather than in its native format, mark the Display as Icon check box.

**4.** Click OK. The application opens, and you can create your new object.

What happens at this point depends on the application. If it is fully compatible with the host application, its menus and tools may appear directly in the same window as the host application. If that happens, you can click away from the embedded object to return to the host application at any time; it's seamlessly saved.

Some applications do not support full integration, so they appear in their own separate window for you to create the object. In such programs, there will be a special command on the File menu that isn't normally present, such as Exit and Return to [application]. Choose it to go back to the host application.

### EDITING AN EMBEDDED OBJECT

Any time you want to edit an embedded object, just double-click it. It will reopen in the application with which it is associated.

### MANAGING LINKED OBJECTS

Most OLE-enabled applications have a link manager built into them. Microsoft Word is like that; to manage the links in a document, choose Edit ➢ Links. This opens a Links dialog box, as shown in Figure 5.26.

**FIGURE 5.26**

Managing links in Microsoft Office XP; other programs may have a different-looking dialog box.

Links are updated automatically by default whenever the file is opened or closed. You can change to Manual updating from the Links dialog box. You can also break a link, terminating the connection to the original so that the copy is no longer updated when the original changes. You can also change the source of the link. This might be useful if you have moved the original file to another folder, for example, and need for the link to point to the new location.

## Organizing the Start Menu

In Chapter 4, you learned about customizing the way the Start menu works in general; you can also customize it by selecting which shortcuts appear on it and in what positions.

The Windows XP Start menu has several sections containing program shortcuts, pointed out in Figure 5.27:

◆ The pinned shortcuts area, at top left, shows Internet and E-mail shortcuts by default. You can add shortcuts here for whatever programs you like as well.

◆ The frequently used programs list, at bottom left, contains shortcuts for the programs you use most often or have used most recently. This list is managed automatically by Windows; you cannot edit it manually.

◆ The All Programs menu, accessible when you click All Programs, lists folders and shortcuts for all installed programs. You can add and remove shortcuts from here freely, as well as create and remove folders and rearrange items.

**FIGURE 5.27**

Shortcuts appear on the
Start menu in several
places.

Notice in Figure 5.27 at the top of the All Programs menu is a special area containing four short-cuts. When you use the Classic Start menu, there is a section at the top of the top-level Start menu that is much like the pinned shortcuts area on the XP Start menu. Some programs released prior to Windows XP will place shortcuts for themselves there; Windows itself also places a few shortcuts there as well. There's nothing sacred about that area; you can move programs into and out of that area freely.

## Editing Pinned Shortcuts

To add a shortcut to the pinned shortcuts area, drag-and-drop it directly onto the Start button without opening the Start menu. Or, drag it onto the Start menu and pause a moment, waiting for the Start menu to appear, and then drag it into the exact spot you want.

To remove the Internet or E-mail shortcut, or to change what program either one of those points to, right-click the Start button and choose Properties; then click Customize. Clear the check marks next to Internet and/or E-mail to get rid of them completely, or select other programs to be represented by them from their respective drop-down lists. See Figure 5.28.

To remove a pinned shortcut other than Internet or E-mail, right-click it and choose Delete.

## Editing the All Programs List

The All Programs list is really just a set of folders nested within one another, so you can edit the structure of the All Programs menu by adding, moving, and/or deleting shortcuts and folders within it. For easy access to it, right-click the Start button and choose Open for a My Computer-like Window, or Explore for a Windows Explorer-like Window. Then work with it as you would any other file-management window.

**FIGURE 5.28**
Change the Internet and/or E-mail shortcuts in the pinned shortcut area.

One quirk with Windows XP is that the Start menu structure for all users of the PC is stored separately from that for the current user. When the Start menu actually displays, the two are combined into one Start menu, but you edit them separately. This enables any user to customize the Start menu, even if they do not have the needed permissions to change the settings for the PC as a whole. When you right-click the Start button and choose Open or Explore, you get the version for the current user. If you want to edit the version for all users, right-click and choose Open All Users or Explore All Users instead. Figure 5.29 shows the Programs menu for All Users being explored.

**NOTE**   If you are new to file management, you may want to refer to Chapter 7 for some help.

**FIGURE 5.29**
The contents of the All Programs menu for All Users in Windows Explorer.

CHAPTER 5

Another way to edit the All Programs menu is to use drag-and-drop. This method has several advantages. For one, it is quicker. For another, it works with the Start menu structure as an integrated whole, so you don't need to worry whether the shortcut you want to work with is part of the current user or All Users configuration. With drag-and-drop, you can:

◆ Drag a shortcut from the Desktop or a file-management window into the menu system. To do so, drag it to the Start menu and pause, holding the mouse button down, until the Start menu opens. Then pause on All Programs; then continue your way through until the desired location is displayed.

◆ Drag an item from one folder to another on the menu. To make a folder open, drag the item to it and pause, still holding the mouse button down; the folder will open after a few seconds.

◆ Delete an item from the menu by right-clicking it and choosing Delete.

## Summary

This chapter has discussed how to install programs, how to run them—using Compatibility Mode if necessary—and how to remove them when you tire of them. It's also touched on the types of programs you shouldn't even try to install on Windows XP, and it's shown you how to use Task Manager to kill a program that's crashed. Finally, you learned how to exchange data between programs and how to edit the Start menu's content.

# Chapter 6

# Using Windows XP Professional on Notebook PCs

Windows XP includes many features designed to make life easier for notebook PC users. Some of these features work on all PCs but are especially applicable to portables; other features don't even appear when you install Windows XP on a desktop PC. In this chapter, we'll look at some Windows features that people who own notebook computers can use to make their computing experience more trouble-free.

- ◆ How notebook PCs are physically different
- ◆ Using built-in and external monitors
- ◆ Working with PC cards
- ◆ Working with hardware profiles
- ◆ Monitoring and optimizing battery usage
- ◆ Establishing dial-up connections from multiple locations
- ◆ Synchronizing files with other PCs
- ◆ Troubleshooting problems with notebook PCs

## How Notebook PCs Are Physically Different

Besides the obvious of "everything's smaller," notebook PCs have a few important differences from desktop PCs. Here's a quick rundown:

- ◆ **Fn key**: In addition to the normal keys on a keyboard, most laptops have a key labeled Fn. This is an additional system key, much like Control and Alt. You use it in conjunction with the function keys (F1 through F12) and sometimes with other keys as well to issue special laptop-specific commands. Figure 6.1 shows several function keys on a notebook PC; notice that they have additional writing on them that shows what they do when combined with the Fn key.

- ◆ **LCD screens**: Notebooks have built-in LCD monitors; most can also accept an external monitor through a built-in VGA output jack. An Fn key combination switches between the two monitors when an external one is plugged in.

**FIGURE 6.1**

Some function keys have extra functionality when combined with the Fn key. For example, the F7 key here turns down screen brightness.

**TIP** Near the end of Chapter 8, you learned about an XP feature called ClearType that can make text on an LCD monitor appear sharper. You will probably want to turn it on for your notebook PC's monitor.

◆ **Docking station connector**: Most notebooks have a connector on the back for plugging into a docking station.

◆ **Mouse alternative**: You can connect an external mouse via PS/2 port or serial port, but most notebook PCs have a built-in mouse alternative. One older style of mouse alternative is called a pointing stick. (Toshiba calls theirs an Accupoint.) A newer mouse alternative, found on most laptops sold today, is a touchpad (sometimes called a glidepad).

◆ **PC card slots**: Since laptops do not have expansion slots in the motherboard the way that desktop PCs do, they need a way of accepting expansion cards. The modern standard for this is *CardBus*, which is the 32-bit version of the PC Card specification, also known by its standards organization's name, PCMCIA (Personal Computer Memory Card International Association). Like USB, PC Cards are hot pluggable.

**NOTE** You might hear the terms PC Card and CardBus used interchangeably (I even do this myself, out of habit). In this chapter, I use the term PC Card to mean any PC Card, and CardBus to specifically refer to the 32-bit ones.

◆ **Battery**: In addition to using an AC adapter to feed power to your portable computer, you can choose to run your system with an internal battery. The most common substances used in computer battery packs are Nickel Cadmium (NiCad), Nickel Metal Hydride (NiMH), and Lithium Ion (LIon).

These physical features are discussed in more detail later in the chapter, in sections that pertain to them.

## Using Built-In and External Monitors

Most notebook PCs have an external VGA graphics port, and you can switch between using it and using the built-in LCD display by pressing the Fn key in combination with one of the function keys. On my Compaq Presario laptop it is Fn+F3, for example. Pressing that combo toggles between LCD only, external only, and both on at once.

If your notebook supports it, you can also use the DualView feature in Windows XP to extend the desktop across both monitors. Normally when you enable both monitors at once, both show the same thing, but with DualView, each can show separate content. Microsoft has certified that the following notebook graphic adapters will work with DualView:

- S3 Savage MX
- Trident 3D
- Trident XP

Others may work as well, either by default or with an update from the graphic adapter manufacturer.

**TIP**   If you have the ATI Rage Mobility video adapter in your notebook PC, in theory, it *should* be able to support DualView, but it doesn't work with the Rage Mobility driver that ships with Windows XP. By the time you read this, an updated driver may be available through your notebook's manufacturer. Unfortunately ATI does not have a generic Rage Mobility driver available at their website.

DualView is almost exactly like the multiple monitors feature you will learn about in Chapter 8 except for the name, and except that on a laptop, the primary monitor is always the built-in one; an attached external monitor is always the secondary one.

Not all laptops support the DualView feature. To determine whether yours does, and to try it out if possible, hook up an external monitor to the laptop and enable both displays (with an Fn key combination). They should both show the exact same thing. That part should work even if the video chipset does not support DualView.

Then do the following:

1. Right-click the desktop and choose Properties; then click the Settings tab. If your PC supports DualView, there will be two separate monitor icons there. If not, there will be only one.

2. If there are two, click the one for the external monitor, and then click Extend My Windows Desktop onto This Monitor.

3. Click OK. The desktop is now stretched out over both monitors rather than them both showing the same thing.

## Working with PC Cards

As mentioned at the beginning of this chapter, notebook PCs use PC Card slots as their primary means of accepting expansion devices. PC Card technology predates USB; today many USB devices are available that take the place of PC Card devices.

PC cards use software known as *socket services* and *card services*. Socket services are similar to device drivers; they handle the interaction between the PC and the card. Card services handle high-level functions and control the transfer of information from the card's memory to the CPU.

Windows XP handles the interface between all types of PC card devices behind the scenes, resulting in hot-pluggable functionality. You can insert a PC Card device at any time, and Windows will automatically detect it, as you will see in Chapter 9 when we discuss adding hardware.

When you remove a PC Card from the system, you are supposed to use the Safely Remove Hardware utility to shut it down first. (You will also learn about this in Chapter 9.) However, if you forget and simply remove the card, it'll probably be okay. Using the Safely Remove Hardware feature simply ensures that all the device's activities complete normally rather than being aborted in midstream.

When one or more hot-pluggable devices are attached to the PC, an icon appears in the notification area for them. You can click this icon to see the attached devices, and then click the one you want to choose to shut down for safe removal. See Figure 6.2.

**FIGURE 6.2**
You can stop a PC card or USB device from the notification area by clicking the Safely Remove Hardware icon.

You can also double-click the Safely Remove Hardware icon in the notification area to open a dialog box showing the installed hot-pluggable devices and stop one from there. See Figure 6.3.

**FIGURE 6.3**
Double-click the icon to see the Safely Remove Hardware dialog box.

**TIP**  See the troubleshooting section at the end of this chapter if you are having problems getting a particular PC Card device to work under Windows XP.

## Working with Hardware Profiles

Hardware profiles enable you to have different devices enabled/disabled at different times. This can be useful on any PC, but it is especially so on a notebook PC because you can have different profiles for different usage situations.

For example, suppose you have a built-in network card in your laptop. When you start up the PC, Windows takes about one minute longer than usual to boot when you aren't connected to a LAN because the adapter has to search for a LAN and time out before it can continue. You might want to create a hardware profile called No LAN and choose it when you start up while away from the office.

If you have a docking station for your notebook PC, you can also set up separate profiles for docked versus undocked configurations. That way when it's docked, you can take advantage of any extra devices in the docking station such as drives or PCI cards. When it's undocked, the PC will know not to waste time trying to connect to those devices.

**NOTE**   When you have more than one hardware profile set up, you'll see an extra boot menu when you start Windows XP that asks you to select which profile you want. When you delete all hardware profiles except one, that boot menu goes away.

To create a hardware profile:

1. Right-click My Computer (on the Start menu) and choose Properties; then click the Hardware tab.
2. Click the Hardware Profiles button. The Hardware Profiles box appears.

3. Click Copy to copy the current profile. Type a name for the new profile and click OK.
4. Click the Properties button. A Properties box for the new profile opens.

5. If this is a portable computer, mark the This Is a Portable Computer check box and choose an option button to define the docked/undocked state that this profile will represent.

6. If you want this profile to appear on that aforementioned menu at startup so that you can select a profile, mark the Always Include This Profile As an Option When Windows Starts check box. Then click OK to close the Properties box.

7. Back in the Hardware Profiles box, select an option in the When Windows Starts section. You can have the startup menu stay on-screen indefinitely until a profile has been selected, or you can specify an amount of time that it should wait before going with the default profile.

8. Click OK. Then reboot the PC and select the new hardware profile.

9. Disable any devices in Device Manager that you won't want to be available in that profile. (See Chapter 9.)

10. If you don't want to continue working in this profile now, restart the PC again and choose your original profile.

## Monitoring and Optimizing Battery Usage

Windows XP has several features for helping you make the most of your notebook battery's charge. You don't want the screen going blank every minute that you pause to gather your thoughts, but neither do you want it to remain on using power for a long time if you get called away unexpectedly. Windows XP lets you adjust the settings to come up with your own best compromise between usability and battery life.

Power management is available on both notebooks and desktops, but it's more important on notebooks. In addition, on laptops the controls are more complex, offering separate settings for each profile for when the PC is plugged into AC power versus running on batteries.

**NOTE** There are two standards for power management in PCs: Advanced Power Management (APM) and Advanced Configuration and Power Interface (ACPI). ACPI is the more modern one, and it works the most smoothly with Windows XP. If you have an older notebook PC, you might investigate whether a BIOS update is available that would switch it over from APM to ACPI. (Of course, if your computer is old enough that it still has an APM-supported BIOS, it's probably not going to run Windows XP very well in the first place.)

To configure power management, open the Power Options Properties dialog box as follows:

1. Right-click the desktop and choose Properties from the shortcut menu. Windows displays the Display Properties dialog box.

2. Click the Screen Saver tab.

3. Click the Power button to open the Power Options Properties dialog box.

### Choosing a Power Scheme

First, choose a power scheme and adjust it as necessary:

1. Display the Power Options Properties dialog box as discussed in the previous section, and click the Power Schemes tab if it is not already on top. See Figure 6.4.

If you do not have a System Hibernates row as in Figure 6.4, you do not yet have hibernation enabled (on the Hibernate tab).

**FIGURE 6.4**
Choose basic power-management options in the Power Schemes tab of the Power Options Properties dialog box.

**NOTE**   Figure 6.4 shows the Power Schemes tab for a notebook PC. A laptop PC will have only a single column, rather than separate columns for Plugged In and Running on Batteries. Other tabs vary as well depending on the PC type. A notebook PC will have Alarms and Power Meter tabs; a desktop PC will have a UPS tab.

2. In the Power Schemes drop-down list, select the power scheme that best describes your computer's role. These are simply sets of settings to begin with; you can customize any of them.

3. Change any of the settings for the chosen power scheme as needed, for both Plugged In and Running on Batteries.

4. Click the Apply button to apply the power scheme to your computer, or click OK to apply the changes and close the dialog box.

**NOTE**   If you adjust the settings for a power scheme, you can save your custom power scheme by clicking the Save As button and specifying a name for the scheme in the Save Scheme dialog box that Windows displays.

## Setting Power Alarms

An alarm situation occurs when the remaining battery life drops below a certain percentage. In the Alarms tab (Figure 6.5) you can choose what will happen when the battery life crosses two thresholds: Low Battery and Critical Battery. You define for yourself each of these thresholds and the activity that should occur at each.

For example, you might want a warning to appear on-screen when the battery becomes low, and you might define "low" as having 15 percent of its charge left. You might want the PC to go into Hibernate mode when battery life is critical, and you might define "critical" as having 5 percent left.

**FIGURE 6.5**
Specify the power
thresholds for low and
critical battery alarms.

To set the alarm action for a threshold, click the Alarm Action button and choose an action from the dialog box that appears. See Figure 6.6. From here, you can choose whether an alarm should sound, whether a message should display, and what action will occur, if any, when the alarm goes off. You can have the system go into Standby or Hibernate modes, for example, or you could run some external program.

**FIGURE 6.6**
Specify what should hap-
pen when an alarm is
triggered.

## Working with the Power Meter

In the Power Meter tab, use the check box to show the details for each battery. This is an issue only on systems with multiple batteries installed at once. You also can see in this tab how much battery power is left and whether it is currently charging. See Figure 6.7.

By default on a laptop, a Power Meter icon appears in the notification area, showing an electrical plug when the PC is running on AC power and showing a battery when it's on battery power. You can double-click that icon at any time to see a Power Meter dialog box telling how much power is left. See Figure 6.8.

**FIGURE 6.7**
View the remaining battery life in the Power Meter tab.

**FIGURE 6.8**
This dialog box appears when you double-click the Power indicator in the notification area.

**NOTE** Notice in Figure 6.8 the Always Show Icon on the Taskbar check box. If you deselect it, the icon in the notification area will go away. To get it back, mark the Always Show Icon on the Taskbar check box in the Advanced tab of the Power Options dialog box, covered in the next section.

## Choosing Advanced Power Options

The Advanced tab of the Power Options Properties dialog box (shown in Figure 6.9) offers various advanced power-management options. Which of these options you see depends on the hardware configuration of your computer.

**Always Show Icon on the Taskbar check box** Select this check box to display a power icon in the notification area or not.

**Prompt for Password When Computer Resumes from Standby check box** Select this check box if you want Windows to make you enter your password when you wake the computer from a standby state.

**FIGURE 6.9**
If necessary, choose further power-management options in the Advanced tab of the Power Options Properties dialog box.

**When I Close the Lid of My Portable Computer drop-down list**    In this drop-down list, select the action you want Windows to take when you close the lid while Windows is running. The options are Do Nothing, Stand By, or Hibernate. This option appears only on portable computers (as you might expect).

**When I Press the Power Button on My Computer drop-down list**    In this drop-down list, select the action you want Windows to take when you press the Power button on your computer when Windows is running. The options are Do Nothing, Ask Me What to Do, Sleep, Hibernate, and Shut Down.

**When I Press the Sleep Button on My Computer drop-down list**    In this drop-down list, select the action you want Windows to take when you press the Sleep button on your computer. As for the Power button, the options are Do Nothing, Ask Me What to Do, Sleep, Hibernate, and Shut Down.

## Enabling and Disabling Hibernation

First, let's review the difference between Standby and Hibernate. *Standby* places the computer in a low power consumption state. It turns off the display, the drives, the fan—everything possible short of shutting down the PC. Only the memory continues to receive power, to save its contents. Standby can make a battery last a long time—days, even—but it eventually does run down and you lose everything in memory.

*Hibernation*, on the other hand, copies the content of memory to the hard disk, and then shuts everything down. When you resume from Hibernate, the memory content is transferred back into memory and the system resumes where it left off. With Hibernate, the computer can be shut off for days, weeks, or more, and will resume exactly in the same state regardless of battery power left.

The more RAM you have, the longer it takes for your computer to enter hibernation and to emerge from it again. But using hibernation is usually substantially faster than shutting down the computer and restarting it, especially as hibernation allows you to keep your programs and documents open, so that you can restart your work where you left off.

To enable hibernation, select the Enable Hibernation check box in the Hibernate tab of the Power Options Properties dialog box (shown in Figure 6.10).

**FIGURE 6.10**
Use the Hibernate tab to enable and disable hibernation.

To place the PC in a Standby or Hibernate state, you can:

◆ Choose them as actions in the Advanced tab (Figure 6.9) in the Power Buttons section.

◆ Choose them as Alarm Actions in the Alarms tab.

◆ Choose Start ➢ Turn Off Computer and then click the Stand By button, or press the Shift key to make the Stand By button turn to a Hibernate button and then click it.

To wake up the PC after entering Standby, press any key. To wake up the PC after entering Hibernate, press the PC's Power button.

**TIP**   If you have trouble waking the PC up after placing it in Standby or Hibernate, or you get errors or lockups going into or out of those modes, see "Troubleshooting Power Management Problems" later in the chapter.

## Using Multiple Dialing Locations

People who travel between cities with a notebook PC often need to connect to the Internet using different dialing settings depending on where they are. For example, in one location you might need to dial a 1 before the number; in another location a 1 plus the area code; in still another it's a local call; and so on.

To make it easier to remember the appropriate settings for each location, Windows XP offers Dialing Rules. Set them up through Control Panel:

1. From Control Panel, open the Phone and Modem Options applet. (The first time you do this, you are prompted for Location Information such as your area code; enter it and click OK.)

2. In the Dialing Rules tab, click New to open a New Location dialog box.

3. Enter all the details about the location you are setting up, as shown in Figure 6.11. Make sure you hit all three tabs: General, Area Code Rules, and Calling Card. The Calling Card tab is useful if you need to punch in the numbers for your calling card or credit card before each call from a certain location.

**4.** Click OK. Now you have a new location.

To use your new location, select it from the Dialing Rules tab.

**FIGURE 6.11**
Set up a new dialing location for every city from
which you make dial-up
connections and need
different settings.

# Synchronizing Files with Other PCs

Many people use the "low tech" way of exchanging files between PCs—they copy them onto a floppy for transfer. And there's nothing wrong with that. Others hook the notebook PC into the LAN and copy files over the network. Still another method along those same lines is Direct Cable Connection, a way of creating an impromptu network on PCs that don't have network interface cards.

**TIP** To set up a direct cable connection, you could connect the PCs via parallel or serial cable and then run the New Connection Wizard (Start ➤ All Programs ➤ Accessories ➤ Communications ➤ New Connection Wizard) on each PC. Choose Set Up an Advanced Connection on both PCs. Then on one of them, choose Accept Incoming Connections, and on the other, choose Connect Directly to Another Computer. Then finish working through the wizard to set it up. You can also connect directly via other types of connection this way, including modem and infrared.

However, each of those methods has a fundamental problem: What if the copy on the desktop PC or network location has changed too? How do you manage synchronization when it's possible that neither copy is in its original state? To solve this problem, Windows XP offers two different features: Offline Files and Briefcase.

## Working with Offline Files

The Offline Files feature is useful if you need access to files and folders that are not always available 24/7, such as files on a network that periodically goes down for maintenance or files on a desktop PC

CHAPTER 6

that you want to access while you are traveling with your laptop. It's designed to be an improvement over the Briefcase feature from previous Windows versions.

**TIP**   The Briefcase feature is still available in Windows XP, and is discussed later in this chapter, because Briefcase offers one feature that Offline Files does not: it enables synchronization and transfer via floppy or other removable disk. The Offline Files feature works only with a network.

Offline Files is available only in Windows XP Professional, not Windows XP Home Edition. However, only the computer that needs to maintain and synchronize the offline file access needs Windows XP Professional; the computer where the originals are maintained can be running any operating system.

**NOTE**   Don't confuse the Offline Files feature with the ability in Windows Explorer to cache websites for offline reading by subscribing to them. That capability is covered in Chapter 13.

### TURNING OFF FAST USER SWITCHING

To use Offline Files, you must first turn off the Fast User Switching feature in Windows XP.

1. In Control Panel, open up User Accounts.

2. Click Change the Way Users Log On or Off.

3. Deselect the Use Fast User Switching check box, and then click Apply Options. Then close Control Panel.

### CONFIGURING THE OFFLINE FILES FEATURE

Now you are ready to set up the Offline Files feature.

1. From any Explorer window, choose Tools ➤ Folder Options.

2. Click the Offline Files tab and mark the Enable Offline Files check box. See Figure 6.12.

**FIGURE 6.12**
Set configuration options for Offline Files.

**3.** Change any synchronization settings. They're described in Table 6.1. Many of these can also be set through the Offline Files Wizard that runs when you select offline files, so you don't have to pay close attention to them now.

**4.** Click OK to apply the new setting.

**TABLE 6.1:** Offline Files Settings

| SETTING | PURPOSE/NOTES |
| --- | --- |
| Synchronize All Offline Files When Logging On | If the source is available when you log on, it will be checked for updates and your locally cached copies will be updated as needed. |
| Synchronize All Offline Files Before Logging Off | Same as above, except it occurs when you shut down Windows or log off. |
| Display a Reminder Every | Specifies the interval at which a notification will appear when you are not connected to the network. |
| Create an Offline Files Shortcut on the Desktop | Places a desktop shortcut through which you can easily manage your offline files. |
| Encrypt Offline Files to Secure Data | Allows EFS encryption for the offline files, as discussed earlier in this chapter. |
| Amount of Disk Space to Use for Temporary Offline Files | Limits the amount of space that offline files can occupy, as a percentage of the total drive space. |

You can return to the Offline Files tab at any time to delete offline files (Delete Files button), view offline files (View Files button), or configure the behavior for when a connection to another PC is lost (Advanced button).

#### SELECTING FILES AND FOLDERS TO BE AVAILABLE OFFLINE

Next, you select certain networked files and folders to be cached to your local hard drive. To do so, follow these steps:

**1.** Locate a file or folder in My Network Places that you want to cache.

**2.** Right-click it and choose Make Available Offline.

**NOTE** If you have made files or folders available online before, and if there are no subfolders in the folder you chose, you are finished at step 2.

**3.** The first time you do this procedure, the Offline Files Wizard runs. Work through it, setting any configuration options desired. These configuration options are a subset of the ones that you saw in Table 6.1.

4. If you selected a folder that contains subfolders, a dialog box appears. Choose whether you want to include the subfolders and click OK.

## WORKING OFFLINE

When Offline Files is enabled, the files/folders you have set up appear as if they were online even when they are not actually available. You access them in the same way you normally do—for example, through My Network Places or via shortcuts to them. If they are available via a network, you get the "live" copy; if they are not available, you get the cached, offline copy. An icon appears in the notification area to let you know you are working offline.

## SYNCHRONIZING

When you have network access once again after having worked offline, you must synchronize your cached copies with the online originals. If you have set the configuration options to synchronize automatically at logon and/or logoff, this process is automatic.

You can also manually synchronize by choosing Start ≻ All Programs ≻ Accessories ≻ Synchronize. This opens the Items to Synchronize dialog box, shown in Figure 6.13. Clear the check boxes for any resources you don't want to synchronize, and click the Synchronize button.

What happens when you synchronize? It depends on what changes have been made. If your copy has changed but the original has not, the original is updated with your changes. If vice versa (your copy has not changed, the original changed), then your copy is updated with the original's changes. If both have changed, a dialog box appears asking what you want to do. You can keep your copy, keep the original as is, or keep both under different names.

**FIGURE 6.13**

Synchronizing files manually with the Synchronize command.

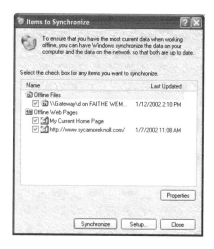

## Using Briefcase

Offline Files works only if you have a network connection between the two PCs. If you must rely on transferring files via removable disk (such as a floppy or rewritable CD-ROM), you might be interested in the Briefcase feature instead.

With Briefcase, you create Briefcase folders on both PCs—the PC containing the originals (probably the desktop PC; in this chapter I'll call it the *main PC*) and the PC on which you will temporarily work with the original files (probably the notebook PC; in this chapter I'll call it the *secondary PC*). Then you synchronize the Briefcase files with one another initially, and then again later when you are ready to return any changes you've made to the original PC.

### CREATING A NEW BRIEFCASE FILE

To use Briefcase, you need to have a Briefcase icon on each of the PCs (both the desktop and the notebook). If there isn't already a Briefcase icon on your desktop, you can put one there by right-clicking the desktop and choosing New ➤ Briefcase. You can create a Briefcase anywhere, not just on the desktop, but most people prefer to store it there for convenience.

**NOTE**   The Briefcase will have the name New Briefcase; you can change its name the same as any other icon (press F2 and type a new name).

### COPYING FILES TO A BRIEFCASE

The procedure for copying files to a Briefcase depends on whether you plan on using a floppy disk or a network connection. In reality, if you are going to use a network connection, you're better off using the Offline Files feature instead. However, I'll explain both methods in this chapter.

#### Copying Files to My Briefcase for Floppy Transfer

Let's start with the steps necessary for copying files from My Briefcase to a disk.

1. Start on the main PC. Open a file management window and drag the files you want onto the Briefcase icon on the desktop. This copies those files to the Briefcase folder. You can double-click the Briefcase icon to open the folder and confirm that they are there if desired.

**NOTE**   The first time you use a Briefcase folder, the Welcome to Windows Briefcase window opens. Read what it has to say, then click Finish.

2. Insert a blank floppy disk (or other removable disk). Then drag the Briefcase icon from the desktop onto that drive's icon in My Computer. The entire Briefcase is moved there.

3. Take that disk to the secondary PC, and open that drive in My Computer there. Drag the Briefcase folder onto the desktop there.

Now the Briefcase is on the secondary PC's desktop, and you can open the Briefcase folder and work with the files from there.

### Copying Files to My Briefcase for Network Transfer

Now that we've copied files from My Briefcase to a disk, let's try copying files from My Briefcase onto a network.

1. Make sure both PCs are logged onto the network and that file sharing is enabled on the main PC.

2. Start on the secondary PC. Open My Network Places and navigate to the files you want to copy.

3. Drag the files from My Network Places and drop them on the Briefcase icon on the desktop. If desired, you can double-click the Briefcase icon to open the folder window and confirm that the files are there.

Now you can work with the files directly from the Briefcase folder on the secondary PC's desktop.

### SYNCHRONIZING BRIEFCASE FILES

When you synchronize files, you overwrite the originals with updated versions from the Briefcase. You can update all the files or only selected ones—your choice.

To see which files in the Briefcase need updating, view the Briefcase window in Details view. The Status column tells which files have changed. See Figure 6.14.

**FIGURE 6.14**
Use Details view to see which files have changed in the Briefcase.

Even if none have changed on the secondary PC, you might still want to synchronize if there is any chance that the originals have changed on the main PC, and if you want to continue to have the most recent versions on the secondary PC.

Once again, the procedures for synchronizing are different depending on whether you are using the floppy disk or network transfer method.

### Synchronizing with Floppy Disk Transfer

Now that you've learned to synchronize Briefcase files, let's try synching them up during a disk transfer.

1. Copy the Briefcase folder from the secondary PC's desktop to a floppy disk, and take that floppy disk to the main PC.

2. Display the floppy disk's content on the main PC, and drag the Briefcase icon onto the desktop there.

3. Double-click the Briefcase icon on the main PC desktop, opening the Briefcase window.

4. To update all files, choose Briefcase ➤ Update All. Or, to update only certain files, select them and choose Briefcase ➤ Update Selection.

5. A report appears. Make sure it lists the actions you want to perform. If you need to change the action for an item, right-click it and choose a different action. See Figure 6.15.

6. Click Update.

**FIGURE 6.15**
Confirm the update for
each changed file.

### Synchronizing with Network Transfer

Now let's try synching up with a network:

1. Make sure both PCs are connected to the network.

2. On the secondary PC, double-click the Briefcase icon, opening its window.

3. To update all files, choose Briefcase ➤ Update All. Or, to update only certain files, select them and choose Briefcase ➤ Update Selection.

4. A report appears (Figure 6.15). Make sure it lists the actions you want to perform. If you need to change the action for an item, right-click it and choose a different action.

5. Click Update.

## Troubleshooting Notebook PC Problems

We'll finish up this chapter by looking at some of the more common problems people experience with notebook PCs in particular, and some possible solutions.

### Problems with PC Cards under Windows XP

Windows XP supports most PC Card devices, including very old 16-bit cards designed to work with the ISA (which is short for *Industry Standard Architecture*) interface. These cards are sometimes referred to as R2 cards. You might find that such a device doesn't work under Windows XP, and you see a message like this in Device Manager:

```
This device is either not present, not working properly,
or does not have all the drivers installed. (Code 10)
Try upgrading the device drivers for this device.
```

If this is your predicament, it's probably because the card doesn't support IRQ sharing and there aren't enough free IRQs. To get around this, you can edit the Registry to disable ISA to PCI routing for PCMCIA devices.

To do so, open the Registry Editor, and go to KEY_LOCAL_MACHINE\System\CurrentControlSet\ Services\PCMCIA\Parameters. Choose Edit ➢ Add Value and add a value with the name of **DisableIsaToPciRouting**. Set the type to DWORD and the value to 1. Then reboot.

After you have done the above, you can install 16-bit PC Cards on computers that are low on ISA interrupts by using a shared-PCI interrupt.

If that doesn't work, perhaps the underlying problem is a different one. If you see the black/yellow exclamation point symbol next to the device in Device Manager, perhaps the PC Card device has its configuration information in common memory instead of attribute memory (where the Card information structure and configuration registers are mapped). The Pcmcia.sys driver in Windows XP does not recognize such devices, and because of this, it does not allocate resources to the device.

If you think this may be the problem for your situation, contact Microsoft technical support for a fix. A patch is available, but it's intended only to correct this specific problem and is not freely available on the Internet. Explain your problem and ask for the updated version of Pcmcia.sys.

**NOTE**   There are a few PCMCIA network interface cards that Windows XP does not work with no matter what you try. If you are having trouble with a NIC under Windows XP, the following Knowledge Base article may be helpful: http://support.microsoft.com/directory/ article.asp?ID=KB;EN-US;q315275.

## Problems with a Wheel-Style PS/2 Mouse

If you plug a PS/2 wheel mouse into the notebook's PS/2 port, the mouse pointer may jump around on-screen when using that mouse, but the touchpad built into the notebook makes the mouse work fine. Wheel mouse devices may be incompatible with some laptops because the wheel mouse transmits in 4-byte packets, while the touchpad transmits in 3-byte packets. If the notebook PC does not detect that there are two different pointing devices in use, each sending data in different format, it may misinterpret the data sent from the PS/2 port, causing erratic mouse pointer movement.

To fix this problem, create a hardware profile that disables the touchpad, leaving only the PS/2 mouse. (See the section on hardware profiles earlier in the chapter.)

## Power Management Problems

One of the biggest complaints I hear from laptop users is that the power management tools don't work correctly. The main problem is that most notebook PCs come with some sort of operating system–independent power-management tool built into the BIOS. Windows itself also has power management tools, and the two often conflict. Another common problem is a non-ACPI-compliant video driver. Many people don't realize it, but Standby and Hibernate work closely with the video card, and if the video driver isn't up for the challenge, problems will ensue.

### CAN'T WAKE THE PC UP AFTER PLACING IT IN STANDBY OR HIBERNATE

This is a really scary problem. After placing the PC in Standby or Hibernate, it refuses to resume. Pressing the power button has no effect; pounding your head on the keyboard is in vain.

In the short term, here are some ways to regain control of the PC:

◆ Be a little patient. Some PCs take up to 30 seconds to wake up.

◆ Look for a Suspend or Hibernate key. Some laptops have special keys or buttons for one or both, but the user might not have noticed them if he normally uses some other wake-up method.

◆ Try pressing and holding the PC's power button for 5 seconds or more. On a PC that is configured to suspend or Hibernate with a press of the power button, holding down the Power button will usually reset and reboot.

◆ Look in the PC's documentation for a key combination that might wake it up. Most laptops have an Fn key that you can press in conjunction with other keys to control laptop-specific features.

◆ As a last resort, remove all batteries, wait a few minutes, and then replace the batteries.

After you successfully restart the PC, you need to look for the underlying problem, which is generally a disagreement either between the power management features of the BIOS and those of Windows XP, or between power management and the video card.

To begin troubleshooting, first make sure you have the most recent version of the video driver installed. Download the latest from the manufacturer's website and install it. It never hurts, and outdated video drivers have been known to cause power management problems in some systems.

A conflict between the BIOS power management and Windows XP's power management is the most common cause of wake-up failure. Experiment with different settings in the BIOS to see if any can solve the problem. For example, one scenario under which a PC might not wake up is if APM is enabled in the Power Options in Control Panel and the BIOS is configured to suspend the computer and its time-out value is less than the value configured in the Alarms tab in Windows. To correct this, you would set the BIOS time-out higher than the Windows time-out.

If tweaking the BIOS and Windows power settings doesn't help, try visiting the PC manufacturer's website to see whether a BIOS update might be available. There are known issues with some PCs regarding failure to resume from Standby; these are corrected by updating the BIOS.

Remember, there are two power management standards that your BIOS can support: APM and ACPI. ACPI is the more recent and more sophisticated; a BIOS upgrade can add ACPI support to the computer and can potentially clear up compatibility problems between APM and your hardware or Windows. If you can't upgrade from APM to ACPI in your BIOS, try disabling APM entirely in the BIOS if you continue having wake-up problems.

**NOTE**  There's an APM diagnosis tool, apmstat.exe, on the Windows XP CD-ROM in the Support/ Tools folder in the Support.cab archive file. Extract it and then run it with the -v switch (for Verbose) to get more data.

If you can't solve the problem from the BIOS, try it from the other side: from Windows. Experiment with Windows Power Management settings to see whether any of them make a difference.

Remember also that you don't necessarily have to use the Windows interface for Standby or Hibernate if your BIOS has direct support for it. On one laptop I worked on, for example, the client finally had to forgo the Windows Power Management and use the Hibernate feature built into the BIOS by pressing the PC's power button.

### LOCKUP WHEN ENTERING STANDBY OR HIBERNATION

The symptoms: when you attempt to place the computer in either Standby or Hibernate through Windows XP, the computer locks up, either with a black screen and flashing cursor in the corner or with the Windows desktop locked up.

This is usually a video adapter problem. Try a different video card driver, making sure you have the latest one from the manufacturer's website. If the problem occurs only when using Hibernate (not Standby), you might simply have to resort to not using Hibernate on that computer.

It can also result from a COM port being open on some laptops. If you have an open connection through a COM port, such as to a modem or handheld device, close it before entering Standby.

### LOCKUP OR ERRORS WHEN RESUMING AFTER HIBERNATION

In this scenario, after resuming from Hibernate, Windows XP doesn't work right. For example, the Start menu might not work anymore, the screen might be totally black, or you might get blue-screen errors.

This is a known bug when using the generic VGA video driver that comes with the OS with a PCI or AGP video card. The generic VGA video driver doesn't support hibernation. You might also see this error with other video drivers too, especially on cheap laptops that use off-brand video drivers not supporting APM or ACPI, or a video driver not designed specifically for your video card and for Windows XP.

If possible, switch to a newer video driver or one designed specifically for the video card. If not, you won't be able to use Hibernate on this PC; go into Power Options in Control Panel and turn off hibernation support.

**TIP** If you need to know how to contact your video adapter manufacturer, check the following lists: A through K—http://support.microsoft.com/support/kb/articles/Q65/4/16.ASP; L through P—http://support.microsoft.com/support/kb/articles/Q60/7/81.ASP; Q through Z—http://support.microsoft.com/support/kb/articles/Q60/7/82.ASP.

### A PROGRAM OR DEVICE PREVENTS STANDBY

Perhaps you try to use Standby but you get an error message instead that goes something like this:

```
The device driver for the device name is preventing
the machine from entering Standby or Hibernation.
Please close all applications and try again.
If the problem persists, you may need to update
the driver.
```

You close all open programs, but the message still persists.

Some programs or devices, particularly those with outdated drivers or that are not ACPI compliant, can cause this error to occur. You need to determine the root of the problem and then disable the program or device before standing by.

**TIP** Look for a file called nohiber.txt in the Windows folder; if present, it will give you clues about what device is preventing Hibernation or Standby.

You can also try looking for the errant device on your own. For example, some models of Epson USB printers have been known to prevent a PC from entering Standby, as well as several models of multifunction devices, particularly those that listen for incoming faxes. Try disconnecting all USB devices and removing all PC cards as part of your troubleshooting process. If that doesn't work, try disabling all USB devices in Device Manager if they do not automatically disappear from Device Manager when disconnected.

Also investigate whether you have any built-in device disabled; this can sometimes cause Standby problems. For example, there are known issues with Intel network cards interfering with Standby when they have been disabled in Device Manager.

A few devices have no workaround and cannot coexist with Standby or Hibernate. Some versions of the Tseng Labs ET-4000 video adapter are like that. On such computers you cannot use Windows-based Standby or Hibernate; you might try the OS-independent BIOS power management if available.

## Summary

In this chapter you learned about the hardware, features, and issues involved in working with Windows XP on a notebook computer. In the next chapter, we'll look at file management—not only the obvious stuff like moving and copying files, but also the techie goodies like NTFS encryption and compression.

# Part 2

# Managing Applications, Files, and Folders

**In this section you will learn how to:**

- ◆ **Organize Your Files and Folders**
- ◆ **Burn CDs**
- ◆ **Install and Manage Local Printers**
- ◆ **Work with Fonts**
- ◆ **Set Up Fax Services**
- ◆ **Use Hot-Pluggable Devices**

# Chapter 7

# Managing Files and Folders

At some point, almost all users are called upon to work with files, even if it's just to copy an important document to a floppy disk or unzip a compressed archive. For those who understand how files and folders are organized on a disk, file management is not that difficult, but the learning curve can be fairly steep for beginners.

This chapter offers something for both beginning and advanced users. Beginners will want to start with the basics of Windows Explorer; advanced users will likely skip ahead to the sections that cover more advanced operations, such as burning CDs and working with NTFS features.

This chapter covers:

◆ Using Explorer

◆ Organizing your files and folders

◆ Understanding the multiuser environment

◆ Customizing the Explorer interface

◆ Setting file and folder properties

◆ Searching for files and folders

◆ Working with compressed files and folders

◆ Using Encrypting File System (EFS)

◆ Creating CDs

## Using Explorer

Windows Explorer, often just called Explorer, is the formal name for the file-management window from which you can perform operations on files, like moving, copying, deleting, renaming, and so on. If you're a relative newcomer to Windows, the following sections explain some basics of working with files in Windows Explorer for your benefit.

### Opening vs. Exploring

One thing you'll notice right away when you use Explorer is a difference between *opening* a Desktop object and *exploring* a Desktop object. Figures 7.1 and 7.2 show the difference. When you open the My Computer window, for example, you'll see its contents in the pane on the right and an Explorer bar on the left. However, if you right-click My Computer and choose Explore from the shortcut menu, or if you click the Folders button in the My Computer window, a Folders bar appears on the left. You can use the Folders bar to navigate between locations easily.

If you already know where you want to go, that is, the location of the file or object you want to access, Open is the way to go. But, as the name suggests, Explorer functions best when you want to "explore" the computer for the file or application you want to use.

**FIGURE 7.1**

Opening My Computer

**TIP**   To switch quickly from the "opening" view to the "exploring" view and vice versa, simply click the Folders button on the toolbar.

**TIP**   You can also open Windows Explorer with the Folders pane showing by choosing Start ➢ All Programs ➢ Accessories ➢ Windows Explorer. This opens up the window to your My Documents folder. If you'd like, you can have it open up somewhere else by right-clicking the Windows Explorer item on the menu, choosing Properties, and then specifying a different location in the Start In box.

## Branches

It's easy to think of Windows Explorer as the filing system of Windows XP Professional. It may be more accurate, though, to describe it as a *window* to the filing system of Windows XP Professional. The views in Windows Explorer depict an upside down tree with its root being My Computer. It branches down from there showing the various connected drives and other resources. When you open Explorer, you'll notice two panes: on the left is a view of the tree structure of your system; on the right is a group of icons and names representing all the main branches or resources of your computer.

Each item that appears in Explorer is considered an object. Every object has its own properties, many of which you can modify to suit your needs, regardless of whether you're working with a file, a folder, a program, or a network computer. Although Explorer is often thought of as a method to view or locate objects, you could just as easily think of it as the glue that holds this diverse environment together.

**FIGURE 7.2**

Exploring My Computer

## Views

You can arrange objects in Explorer in many ways, all of which are called *views*. The View menu not only controls how objects in the right Explorer pane appear, but also how Explorer itself can be configured to work best for you.

The left and right panes are controlled separately. The left pane's content depends on what you have selected:

◆ If neither Folders nor Search is selected, an Explorer pane appears (as in Figure 7.1). If the window is narrow, however, the Explorer pane disappears. (Try this yourself; resize a window to be very narrow and watch the Explorer pane vanish.)

◆ If the Folders button is selected on the toolbar, the Folders pane appears (as in Figure 7.2).

◆ If the Search button is selected on the toolbar, the Search pane appears.

The right pane shows the content of the currently selected location. There are several views available for the right pane, including Tiles, Icons, Thumbnails, List, and Details. There is also a sixth view, Filmstrip, available for some folders.

Tiles is the default view for My Computer, and Figures 7.1 and 7.2 show this view. In Tiles view, the names of the icons appear to the left of the icons.

Icons view (see Figure 7.3) makes the icons slightly smaller and places their names beneath them rather than off to the side.

**FIGURE 7.3**
Icons view

Thumbnails view (see Figure 7.4) is particularly useful for sorting through graphic files. With this view, the graphic files are displayed as miniatures that you can sort through quickly to find just the picture you need. Icons for folders contain mini-thumbnails of the first several graphics within them (if any). If a file is not a graphic, it appears with its regular icon in large size, as with the `att1.wav` file in Figure 7.4.

**FIGURE 7.4**
Thumbnails view

Another view is available for graphic files, Filmstrip, shown in Figure 7.5. In Filmstrip view, select a thumbnail from the filmstrip at the bottom of the screen to display it in a larger size. You can then use the tools in the middle of the screen to move forward and backward through the filmstrip and to rotate a graphic. Filmstrip view is not available for every folder—only the ones that Windows recognizes as containing graphics. See "Customizing an Individual Folder" later in this chapter to learn how to apply a template to a folder so that Windows will make the Filmstrip view available to that folder.

**FIGURE 7.5**

Filmstrip view

List view (see Figure 7.6) shows tiny icons for each item, with the names to the right, and the listing appears in columns. Folders appear first, arranged alphabetically along the left side of the pane, and then the rest of the files appear, also arranged alphabetically.

Details view (see Figure 7.7) moves all the icons to the left-most column and uses the other columns for file/object information. This information includes the file type (which is determined by how the file is associated), the size of the file, and the date the file was last modified or saved. If you can't see all these columns, move the horizontal scroll bar to the right.

## Reordering Files

What if you can't remember the name of a file you need, but you do remember the date it was created? Or what if you know which application created the file and what the file extension is? With Explorer, you can arrange the items in the right pane so that they are sorted or organized by name, size, date, or file type. You can then see at a glance what is and isn't inside the folder.

**FIGURE 7.6**
List view

**FIGURE 7.7**
Details view

To rearrange the order of your files in Explorer's right pane, choose View ➤ Arrange Icons By, and then select an option from the submenu. Name is self-explanatory; size refers to the size of the file in bytes, kilobytes, or megabytes, whichever is appropriate. Type refers to the three-character extension at the end of the filename (for example, the files for this book have the .doc extension); and Modified refers to the date. You can also display a Date Picture Taken column and a Dimensions column for digital photos.

**TIP**   When you're working in Details view, you can click a column heading to sort by that column. For example, you could sort by the Size column or the Date Modified. Click a column heading again to shift between an ascending and descending sort.

You can also set the View using the Views button on the toolbar, and you can arrange the icons by right-clicking anywhere in the right pane, clicking Arrange Icons By, and selecting an order from the submenu.

**TIP**   Select Auto Arrange if you want the listing to always arrange automatically. Otherwise, sometimes when you create a new file or folder, it will initially appear at the bottom of the list (until you refresh the display by pressing F5 or until you close and reopen the window).

## Working with Shortcut Menus

Right-clicking objects throughout the Windows XP Professional interface displays a shortcut menu that contains options pertaining to the objects at hand. The same options are typically available from the main menus but are more conveniently reached with the right-click.

Which commands appear on a shortcut menu depends on such factors as the current folder's location, the current file or folder type, user privileges, and which programs are installed on your computer. Figure 7.8 shows a typical shortcut menu for a document file.

**FIGURE 7.8**

A shortcut menu for a document file

Some of the commands shown in Figure 7.8 were added by third-party applications, so you won't necessarily see them on your PC. For example, Scan for Viruses was added by Norton Antivirus Corporate Edition, and TextPad was added by a text editor I use, TextPad.

Of these commands, most are equivalent to what you'd find on the application's File or Edit menu. Choosing Properties, which usually appears at the bottom of a shortcut menu, generally takes you to the object's Properties dialog box.

Here are a couple of the most notable ones from Figure 7.8:

◆   **Open and Open With.** The Open command opens a data file in whatever application is set to be the default for its file extension. The Open With command opens a submenu of all the programs that could potentially open that file, so you can choose. This is useful when you want to open a file using a different application but not change the association for all files of that type.

♦ **Send To.** This command opens a submenu of various locations where you might want to send a copy of the file. All your removable disks are included here, plus My Documents, Mail Recipient, Desktop, and Compressed (zipped) Folder. The latter points to Windows XP's built-in support for the ZIP file format. To create a ZIP file, select a group of files, right-click the group, and choose Send To ➤ Compressed (zipped) Folder.

The shortcut menu for a folder is very different. When you right-click the white background in a folder's file listing, you get a shortcut menu like the one in Figure 7.9. I won't go into what each of these commands does right now because most of them are addressed throughout the remainder of this chapter.

**FIGURE 7.9**
A shortcut menu
for a folder

## Organizing Your Files and Folders

Working with files and folders might be old familiar territory for you, and if so, feel free to skip this section. But if you don't have the firmest of grasps on skills like creating, deleting, renaming, and so on, stick with me here.

### Creating New Folders

To create a new folder in Explorer, follow these steps:

1. Choose where you want to create a new folder. You can create a folder on the Desktop, at the root of a hard drive or a floppy drive, or inside another folder.

2. In Explorer, choose New ➤ Folder, or right-click the drive or folder in which you want to create the folder (or the background in the currently displayed folder) and choose New ➤ Folder from the shortcut menu. To create a folder on the Desktop, right-click an empty area, and choose New ➤ Folder from the shortcut menu.

3. The folder is created with the default name New Folder. By default, the name is highlighted. To give a new name to the folder, type it now. You can always rename a folder by selecting it and choosing File ➢ Rename or by pressing F2 or right-clicking the folder and choosing Rename from the shortcut menu. (I'll discuss renaming in detail later in this chapter.)

## Moving Items

You can move files and folders anywhere on your computer or over the network as long as you have permission to do so. To move a file or folder, follow these steps:

1. Select the file or folder you want to move. To select more than one object, hold down Ctrl while you click each one. If the objects constitute an uninterrupted group, hold down Shift while you click the first object and the last.

2. Choose Edit ➢ Cut (or press Ctrl+X).

3. Select the destination, and choose Edit ➢ Paste (or press Ctrl+V).

You can also drag items from one place to another:

◆ Drag from the right Explorer pane to the left.

◆ Drag from either Explorer pane to another Explorer or Explorer-type window.

◆ Drag from either Explorer pane to the Desktop. (Optionally, if you hold down the right mouse button while you drag, you can create a shortcut or shortcuts on the Desktop for the object or objects you are dragging.)

◆ Drag from the Desktop to an Explorer folder.

**TIP**    If you drag a folder from the right Explorer pane to the left on a *different* drive, Windows XP Professional defaults to copying the file instead of moving it. (As long as you are dragging the object to the same drive, Windows XP Professional moves the file or folder by default.) If you don't want Windows XP Professional to copy the file, hold down the Shift key while you drag the object to another drive. That way it will be moved rather than copied.

## Copying Items

You can also copy files and folders anywhere on your computer or the network as long as you have permission to do so. To copy a file or folder, follow these steps:

1. Select the file or folder you are going to copy. To select more than one object, hold down Ctrl while you click each object. To select objects that constitute an uninterrupted group, hold down Shift, click the first object, and then click the last object.

2. Choose Edit ➢ Copy (or press Ctrl+C).

3. Select the destination, and choose Edit ➢ Paste (or press Ctrl+V).

You can also drag the items from one place to another, as described in the previous section, with one difference: to ensure that the objects you are dragging are copied and not moved, hold down the Ctrl key while you are dragging.

**TIP** If you drag a folder from the right Explorer pane to the left on the same drive, Windows XP Professional defaults to moving the file instead of copying it. (As long as you are dragging the object to a different drive, Windows XP Professional copies the file or folder by default.) If you don't want Windows XP Professional to move the file, hold down the Ctrl key while you drag the object to another drive. It will be copied, not moved.

## Saving Files and Folders to the Desktop

You can keep files on your Desktop for quick and easy access. To store files and folders on the Desktop, do one of the following:

- Drag a file from Explorer to the Desktop.

- If you are saving the file from within an application, select Desktop (it's at the very top of your local drive hierarchy) in the application's Save As dialog box.

When you right-click a file, drag it, and then release the button, you'll see a shortcut menu with the following options:

**Copy Here**  Copies the file to the new location.

**Move Here**  Moves the file to the new location.

**Create Shortcut(s) Here**  Creates a shortcut to the file at the new location. As I've discussed, a shortcut is a pointer to the real file or folder and can be stored anywhere on your computer.

**Cancel**  Cancels the operation.

**TIP** If you are new to Windows XP Professional or are confused about when to use Ctrl or Shift when moving or copying files, the safest thing to do is to drag the file with the right mouse button. This way, you are always presented with a choice of whether to move or copy the file.

## Renaming Files and Folders

You can quickly and easily rename files and folders. Because Windows XP Professional keeps track of file associations, you don't have to worry about including the three-character file extensions.

**WARNING** The sentence above is true only if you have not turned off the Hide Extensions for Known File Types setting in Folder Options. When a file's extension is hidden, it is not involved in the renaming process. However, for a file that does show the extension on-screen, you must retype the extension when renaming the file. Don't type an extension if the extensions are hidden, or you will end up with a double extension on the file—one hidden, one showing. For example, Mytext.doc will become Mytext.doc.doc.

To rename a file or folder, follow these steps:

1. In Explorer, select the file or folder you want to rename.

2. Choose File ➢ Rename, or right-click the file and choose Rename from the shortcut menu.

3. When only the name of the file (the text associated with the icon) becomes highlighted, do one of the following:

   ♦ If you want to simply replace the entire name, start typing the new name; the old name disappears the moment you start typing.

   ♦ If you want to make only a correction or two to the existing name, use the arrow keys to move to specific characters within the existing name. The highlight disappears the moment you start moving within the name, enabling you to insert or delete specific characters without deleting the entire name.

4. To accept the name, press Enter or click outside the name area. If you make a mistake, press Escape.

**TIP** You can also rename files and folders with two single-clicks (but don't click so fast that Windows XP Professional interprets it as a double-click) on the name of the object so that it is highlighted. Then follow steps 3 and 4.

## Deleting Files and Folders

If you decide that you don't want a file or a folder, you can easily delete it. By default, the file is not actually deleted when you tell Windows XP Professional to delete it: instead, it is compressed and sent to the Recycle Bin folder. A file in the Recycle Bin hasn't been removed from your hard drive, only placed on inactive duty, so to speak. (You can periodically delete items within the Recycle Bin to *actually* remove them entirely, or you can empty the Recycle Bin to delete everything in it.)

The Recycle Bin is a good intermediate place to keep files you're pretty sure you want to delete, because if you change your mind after "deleting" them to the Recycle Bin, you can always open the Recycle Bin and resurrect the object. Mutter your apologies for treating the item so shabbily, and it's ready for use once more.

**TIP** If you're the kind of person who hates being pestered by second thoughts, and you'd prefer to avoid the nice little safeguard of the Recycle Bin, you can *really* delete an item by selecting it and pressing Shift+Delete.

**TIP** You can turn off the Recycle Bin so that no deleted files go there at all. Just right-click the Recycle Bin icon and choose Properties; then mark the Do Not Move Files to the Recycle Bin check box in the General tab.

### SENDING ITEMS TO THE RECYCLE BIN

You can send a file or a folder to the Recycle Bin in several ways:

   ♦ Select the item, and then press the Delete key.

   ♦ Select the item, and then choose File ➢ Delete.

   ♦ Right-click the file or folder, and then choose Delete from the shortcut menu.

   ♦ Select the item, and then drag and drop it on the Recycle Bin icon.

### EMPTYING THE RECYCLE BIN

By default, the size of the Recycle Bin folder is set at 10 percent of your hard drive. If you have more than one hard drive, or if you have a dual-partitioned drive, you will have a Recycle Bin folder for each drive, and the size of the folder is set at 10 percent for each drive. For example, if drive C is 3.44GB, the Recycle Bin folder is 353MB; and if drive D is 6.09MB, its Recycle Bin folder is 624MB.

When the Recycle Bin folder is full, Windows XP Professional automatically deletes enough items, starting with the oldest, to accommodate whatever you are currently sending to it. When an item is removed from the Recycle Bin, it is gone forever.

To better control the Recycle Bin and maintain its intended functionality (which is to provide second chances), you can periodically empty it manually. You can delete all the items it contains or only selected items.

◆ To delete selected items, double-click the Recycle Bin to open the Recycle Bin folder. Now delete items as you would in Explorer.

◆ To totally empty the Recycle Bin, right-click its icon, and choose Empty Recycle Bin from the shortcut menu.

**WARNING**   When a file is deleted in Windows XP Professional, it is *really* deleted. Other operating systems such as MS-DOS or Windows 9x delete only the first byte from a file and mark the space as available. Windows XP Professional is much more thorough because of its secure nature. When you delete a file in Windows XP Professional, all the bytes in the file are set to a zero value. This is like reformatting the space where the file was so that it can be reclaimed.

### RESTORING ITEMS FROM THE RECYCLE BIN

To restore items from the Recycle Bin you can do one of the following:

◆ Open the Recycle Bin folder, select an item, and drag it to the folder of your choice.

◆ Open the Recycle Bin, select the item you want to restore, and click Restore This Item in the Recycle Bin Tasks bar. The item is restored to its original location.

## Understanding the Multiuser Environment

From the ground up, Windows XP Professional is designed as a multiuser-networking environment. Because security is so integral to the way that Windows XP Professional operates, it is possible for two or more users to use the same workstation without stepping on each other's toes. That is, one user can log in and do the work they want to do without necessarily knowing who else has access to the computer or without having access to another user's files.

When a user logs on to a Windows XP Professional workstation, the operating system assigns that user a security token. The Windows XP Security Manager portion of the Executive Services manages security tokens. Each time that user attempts to do something in Windows XP Professional, be it open a file, send e-mail, or change the way the Desktop looks, the Security Manager checks that person's token to see if they have the rights and permissions to perform the task they've requested. See Chapter 19 for a more thorough discussion of security.

As a result of the token-based security system, Windows XP Professional administers multiuser environments logically. User profile information is stored in the user's folder in the Documents and

Settings folder on the drive where Windows XP Professional is installed. Inside the Documents and Settings folder is a folder for each user that logs in to a workstation, and inside each user's folder is a set of folders that customize the Windows XP Professional environment for that user.

Following is a list and a description of some of the folders commonly found inside each user's folder.

**NOTE**    Some of these folders are hidden folders. To display hidden folders, choose Tools ➤ Folder Options to open the Folder Options dialog box. Select the View tab, and then in the Advanced Settings list, click Show Hidden Files and Folders.

**Cookies**    Contains any cookies that you may have stored from websites. Cookies are a small bit of text information that enables a website to customize its appearance just for you.

**Desktop**    Contains any files that a user stores on the Desktop. This does not include the Recycle Bin.

**Favorites**    Stores your favorite programs, files, and websites. You can add files to this folder and delete files from it as you would with any other folder.

**Local Settings**    Contains a portion of the user-specific information of the Registry, as well as some personal settings for your History, Temporary Internet Files, and a system Temp folder.

*Your User Name*'s **Documents**    Keeps files that you don't want any other users to access, even though the users may share other aspects of your workstation. The My Documents folder is empty by default, except for subfolders Your User Name Pictures, Your User Name Music, and Your User Name Videos. Your Pictures folder is the default location for storing your picture files, your Music folder is the default location for storing music files, and your Videos folder is the default location for storing movie files.

**NetHood**    This folder contains some cached information that normally appears in My Network Places. This is where you will store the browse list for your local network and any persistent network connections.

**PrintHood**    Stores the mappings for any network printers you have installed. Network printers are actually part of the user profile and are not part of the overall system configuration.

**My Recent Documents**    Stores files and folders you have accessed recently.

**Send To**    Stores customizations to your Send To menu.

**Start Menu**    Stores configurations and customizations you have made to your Start menu. For example, it shows all the shortcuts you have added to your Start menu.

**Templates**    This folder stores the system templates for various applications that can be installed on Windows XP Professional.

## Customizing the Explorer Interface

There are many ways to change the way the Explorer window looks and acts. In the following sections, I'll outline some of the most important ones.

## Setting Folder Options

The Folder Options dialog box is a rich source for customizing the Explorer interface. Changes made there affect all Explorer windows, regardless of what drive or folder's content appears there. To access it, choose Tools ➢ Folder Options.

In the General tab (shown in Figure 7.10), you can:

◆ Turn off the Common Tasks pane to the left of the file listing by choosing Use Windows Classic folders.

◆ Choose to open each folder in a separate window, instead of the default of having the next-chosen location replace the preceding one.

◆ Choose to have Windows (the Explorer window and the Desktop) work more like a web page, wherein you single-click to activate something and point at it to select it.

**FIGURE 7.10**
Folder options apply to all Explorer windows.

**NOTE**   When Windows 98 was in beta testing, the default was this single-click-to-activate behavior, but it drove most people crazy because it was so different from what they were used to. Therefore, in the final version, and in all versions since, the double-click-to-select method has been the default and this single-click one has been just an alternative.

In the View tab, you can:

◆ Set a particular View option to apply to all folder listings. By default, when you change the View setting, it applies to that folder only.

◆ Select or deselect a wide variety of Advanced Settings for how files should be displayed. Table 7.1 lists the complete set.

The File Types tab, covered later in the chapter, lets you change file associations for an extension. The Offline Files tab, covered in Chapter 6, lets you cache copies of files available through a connection that may only be available sporadically.

**TABLE 7.1:**      Advanced Settings in the View Tab of the Folder Options Dialog Box

| SETTING | PURPOSE/NOTES |
| --- | --- |
| Automatically search for network folders and printers. | On by default. Allows Windows to requery the network periodically to see whether any new resources are available. |
| Display file size information in folder tips. | On by default. Includes file size in the ScreenTip that appears when you hover the mouse pointer over a file. |
| Display simple folder view in Explorer's folder list. | On by default. Collapses any branches open in the folder list when you move to a different branch of the folder tree. |
| Display the content of system folders. | Off by default. Displays a warning when you try to view a system folder; you must click the warning to continue. |
| Display the full path in the address bar. | Off by default. Shows the full path rather than just the folder's name. |
| Display the full path in the title bar. | Off by default. Same as above but for title bar. |
| Do not cache thumbnails. | Off by default. When viewing a folder in Thumbnail view, thumbnail images of the content are created. Turn this option on to save them so that they need not be regenerated each time you view that folder, saving a little time. |
| Hidden files and folders. | By default set to Do Not Show Hidden Files and Folders. Power Users generally change this to Show Hidden Files and Folders so that hidden items appear in file listings (but ghosted, to distinguish them from normal files). |
| Hide extensions for known file types. | On by default. Power Users generally turn this off so that all file extensions appear. |
| Hide protected operating system files. | On by default. Excludes files with the System attribute from file listings. |
| Launch folder windows in a separate process. | Off by default. Launches each folder window in a separate memory space, increasing stability but decreasing performance. |
| Managing pairs of web pages and folders. | Specifies how Windows should treat web page files that have associated folders in a file management window. |
| Remember each folder's view settings. | On by default. Opens each folder to the same View setting as was previously selected for it. |
| Restore previous folder windows at logon. | On by default. When Windows shuts down with open folder windows, they are redisplayed when Windows restarts. |
| Show Control Panel in My Computer. | Off by default. In previous Windows versions, this was on by default. Adds a Control Panel icon to My Computer. |

CHAPTER 7

**TABLE 7.1:** Advanced Settings in the View Tab of the Folder Options Dialog Box *(CONTINUED)*

| SETTING | PURPOSE/NOTES |
|---|---|
| Show encrypted or compressed NTFS files in color. | On by default. Changes the text color for any files that use NTFS compression or NTFS encryption (covered later in this chapter). |
| Show pop-up description for folder and desktop items. | On by default. Displays a pop-up ScreenTip when you hover over an item. |
| Use simple file sharing. | On by default. Limits the capability to assign complex permissions to files and folders in the interest of simplicity. This option is available only in XP Professional, not XP Home Edition, because simple file sharing is turned on permanently in Home Edition. |

## Customizing an Individual Folder

In addition to the global settings, you can also specify settings for each folder. As you have already seen, by default, Windows remembers your choice of View setting for each folder individually. You can also do the following to further customize the folder:

1. Choose View ➢ Customize This Folder. A Properties box for the folder appears.

2. Click the Customize tab and then choose a different folder type from the Use This Folder Type As a Template list if desired. See Figure 7.11. For example, if the folder will be holding pictures, you might choose that. The folder type template sets several default options appropriate for that content type, including a view.

3. If you want a picture thumbnail to appear for the folder in Thumbnails view, click the Choose Picture button and add one.

**FIGURE 7.11**
Properties for the current folder affect how it appears in Explorer.

**4.** If you want a different icon to appear for the folder whenever icons are shown, click the Change Icon button and select an icon.

**5.** Click OK when finished.

### Customizing the Toolbar

You might want to add, remove, or rearrange the buttons on the toolbar in Explorer. Changes you make apply to Explorer in general, not just to the current folder.

To customize the Explorer toolbar, follow these steps:

**1.** Choose View ➤ Toolbars ➤ Customize to open the Customize Toolbar dialog box:

**2.** To add a button, select it from the list on the left and click Add.

**3.** To remove a button, select it from the list on the right and click Remove.

**4.** To change the order of the buttons on the toolbar, click the Move Up or Move Down button until the arrangement is to your liking.

**5.** Click the drop-down lists to take a look at text and icon options.

**6.** When you're finished, click Close.

## Setting File and Folder Properties

Right-click any file or folder and choose Properties to display its Properties box. Files typically have two tabs in their Properties: General and Summary. Some types of data files, such as Word documents, may also have a Custom tab.

The General tab lists information about the file and lets you turn on/off three attributes for the file:

◆ Read-only prevents the file from being modified or deleted.

◆ Hidden excludes the file from file listings (unless the Show Hidden Files and Folders option is chosen in Folder Options).

◆ Archive marks the file as having been changed since the last time a backup operation turned off the archive attribute. (This check box is present only on FAT and FAT32 volumes; for what happens on an NTFS volume, see the following description.)

On NTFS volumes, the General tab has an Advanced button, which you can use to set NTFS options such as encryption and compression. When you click the Advanced button, you can then mark the Folder Is Ready for Archiving check box to turn the Archive attribute on/off.

The Summary tab contains a variety of text boxes into which you can enter information about the file for classification purposes. Not all files have this tab in their Properties box.

For folders, the Properties box contains a General tab, the same as with files, but also a Customize tab (which you saw in "Customizing an Individual Folder" earlier in the chapter) and a Sharing tab for setting up network sharing permission for the folder. You'll learn about networking features in Part 3 of this book.

## Searching for Files and Folders

The Search Companion feature in Windows XP is built into Explorer. You can turn it on from any Explorer window by clicking the Search button in the toolbar. You can also start it up by choosing Start ≻ Search.

By default, an animated character called the Search Companion appears in the Search pane, guiding you through a search operation. See Figure 7.12.

**FIGURE 7.12**

The Search Companion, shown here with an animated character

Just follow the prompts to build a set of search criteria. The All Files and Folders option will be the most familiar choice for experienced users; it offers up a wide array of search criteria. In addition to filename, file content, and location to specify, there are three other categories, as shown in Figure 7.13: When Was It Modified?, What Size Is It?, and More Advanced Options. Each of these has a down arrow next to it; clicking that arrow will expand the full range of options for that choice.

The other choices, such as Pictures, Music, or Video, automatically filter for certain file extensions. With each of these other choices, you can click a Use Advanced Options hyperlink to use the full array of search criteria available with All Files and Folders.

The Search feature allows the use of wildcards, just like in MS-DOS file specifications. Use ? for a single character or * for any number of characters. For example, to find all files that end in .doc or .dot, you might use *.do?.

When you click the Search button, the search begins, and the found files and folders appear in the right-hand pane. See Figure 7.14. The list appears in Detail view by default, so you can compare the locations, sizes, dates modified, and so on. You can work with this list of found items the same as with any other file listing.

**FIGURE 7.13**
The All Files and Folders search enables searching based on many possible criteria.

**FIGURE 7.14**
The results of a search for *.do?

# Working with Compressed Files and Folders

There are two kinds of compressed files and folders available in Windows XP. You can use Zip compression to create compressed archives of multiple files in a single ZIP file that Windows XP can work with as if it were a folder; you can also compress files with NTFS compression if you are using the NTFS file system on the drive. The following sections look at these compression features.

## Using Zip Compression

If you have limited disk space on your computer or on your network, or if you often need to transfer files over the Internet and have a slow connection, you have probably used a compression utility. Windows XP Professional includes its own version of a compression utility called WinZip, a popular program that has been widely distributed in stand-alone versions for many years.

When you compress, or "zip," a file or a folder in Windows XP Professional, that file or folder can be uncompressed, or "unzipped," by almost any other compression utility. In addition, Windows treats ZIP files like folders, so you can open and browse them just like you would a normal folder.

A compressed folder has a zipper on it.

Compressing a file or a folder is fast and easy. You simply right-click the file or folder in an Explorer-type window, choose Send To on the shortcut menu, and click Compressed Folder on the submenu. A compressed copy of the file or folder is placed in the folder that contains the original file. The filename is the same as that of the original file or folder, but with a `.zip` extension. If you selected more than one file or folder for zipping into a single ZIP file, the ZIP file will bear the name of the last file or folder in the selected group.

Once a ZIP file exists, you can open it in Explorer and compress other files or folders by simply dragging them to the compressed folder. When you then move the file or folder out of the compressed folder, it is uncompressed.

You can also compress files in Windows applications, and in Chapter 15, we'll look at how to do so in Outlook Express.

**WARNING**   Even though a ZIP file appears to be a normal folder when opened in Explorer, it has limitations. For example, if a Setup program and its helper files are contained in a ZIP file, the Setup program probably won't run correctly from its ZIP file location; you will likely need to extract the contents of the ZIP file to a real folder on your hard disk before you can run it. And if you open a document from a ZIP file, it will be read-only and you'll need to save it under a different name.

## Using NTFS Compression

As you learned way back in Chapter 1, the NTFS file system has many advantages over FAT32 under Windows XP. One of these is the capability of compressing a folder to save disk space. Retrieving files from a compressed folder takes slightly longer than a normal folder; other than that the compression is totally invisible. You might want to compress folders that you don't use frequently if disk space is an issue. NTFS compression does not compress as dramatically as Zip-type compression, but is less obtrusive.

On an NTFS drive, files and folders have an Advanced button in the General tab of their properties box. It's your gateway to the NTFS properties for the item:

1. From the file or folder Properties box, click the General tab.

2. Click the Advanced button. The Advanced Attributes dialog box opens (Figure 7.15).

**FIGURE 7.15**
Set NTFS compression here.

3. Mark the Compress Contents to Save Disk Space check box to compress the item, and then click OK.

4. Choose Apply Changes to This Folder Only, or choose Apply Changes to This Folder, Subfolders, and Files. Then click OK.

NTFS compressed folders and files appear with their names in blue rather than black to differentiate them from normal ones. To decompress them, follow the same steps but clear the check box.

When you move or copy a compressed file or folder onto a non-NTFS drive, it is automatically uncompressed. Here are some additional rules:

◆ Any new files/folders created in a compressed folder become compressed.

◆ Any files/folders copied into a compressed folder become compressed.

◆ Any files/folders moved from another NTFS drive into a compressed folder become compressed.

◆ Any files/folders moved from another location on the same NTFS drive into a compressed folder retain the compression settings from the original location.

◆ Any compressed files/folders moved into an uncompressed location on the same NTFS drive remain compressed.

◆ Any compressed files/folders moved into an uncompressed location on a different NTFS drive become uncompressed.

**TIP**    NTFS compression and NTFS encryption (covered in the following section) are mutually exclusive; you can use one or the other but not both. If you need NTFS compression, consider using some other method of protection such as network security; if you need NTFS encryption, consider some other method of compression such as Zip compression.

## Using Encrypting File System (EFS)

You might have noticed in Figure 7.15 that NTFS encryption is also available, in addition to compression. This encryption is sometimes referred to as Encrypting File System, or EFS. It is not available in Windows XP Home Edition; instead the option appears grayed out.

EFS encryption is different from network permissions because it deals with security on a local level. It's based on the logged-in user on the machine. When the user who encrypted the folder or file is logged in, it's transparent, but when anyone else is logged in, the file or folder is inaccessible. This is handy when multiple users share a PC and must work with sensitive data.

**NOTE**  Encryption is not limited to local machines only; there is also encryption between a web browser and a server using Secure Socket Layers and encryption between computers on virtual private networks (VPNs) and e-mail. However, this chapter will limit the discussion to local EFS.

It works like this: EFS encryption uses the logged-in user's public key to generate a file-encryption key that the encrypted file or folder must pass through in order to be accessed. When you are logged in as the same user who did the encrypting, Windows automatically accesses the needed keys, but when anyone else is logged in, there is a different public key in use, so the decryption doesn't happen.

## Backing Up Your Certificates

Before you start using NTFS encryption, you should make a backup copy of the certificates needed to access encrypted files, and store them on a removable disk. There is virtually no way to hack into an encrypted file if you lose the needed certificates/keys.

The first time you use NTFS encryption, Windows generates your personal encryption certificate. This certificate includes a public key and a private key. Windows can also create another certificate, for a designated recovery agent, which will also permit access to the user's encrypted files. You'll want to back up these two certificates separately. The personal encryption certificate should be stored in a safe location that you can personally access; the recovery agent certificate should be given to your system administrator.

To back up your personal encryption certificate:

1. Make sure you are logged in using the user account for which you want to back up the certificate.

2. Display the Internet Options dialog box, either from Control Panel or from Internet Explorer (Tools ➤ Internet Options).

3. In the Content tab, click the Certificates button to open the Certificates dialog box.

4. In the Personal tab, select the certificate that shows Encrypting File System in the Certificate Intended Purposes area. See Figure 7.16.

**WARNING**  If you do not have a certificate listed on the Personal tab, you have no encrypted files or folders. Go ahead and encrypt one file just for the purpose of creating the certificate, and then come back here to continue.

5. Click Export. The Certificate Export Wizard starts.

6. Click Next, and then click Yes, Export the Private Key and click Next again.

7. Click Next to accept the defaults on the next screen.

8. When prompted for a password, make one up and enter it/confirm it. Then click Next.

**FIGURE 7.16**
Manage certificates, including backing them up, from here.

9. Enter a path and name for the exported file. You might want to export to a floppy, for example. You do not need to type a file extension, because a `.pfx` extension will be automatically appended. Then click Next.

10. Click Finish. A box appears telling you it was a success; click OK.

## Encrypting and Decrypting

Windows allows you to encrypt both folders and files, but most experts recommend that you encrypt only folders. Any files you place in an encrypted folder become encrypted while they are there, but if you move them out of the folder they become decrypted. However, if you encrypt an individual file, it remains encrypted no matter where you move it.

**TIP** Some programs generate temporary files as they operate that store parts of your data file. Even though you may be storing the data file in an encrypted folder, these temp files are not encrypted because they are stored someplace else—for example, in `C:\Windows\Temp` or some other location. If you can determine where the program stores its temporary working files, you might want to encrypt that folder for added security.

To encrypt a folder:

1. From the folder's Properties, click Advanced in the General tab.

2. Mark the Encrypt contents to secure data check box. Refer back to Figure 7.15.

3. Click OK, and then OK again. The folder's name turns green to indicate it is encrypted.

When you encrypt a file, rather than a folder, you are asked whether you also want to encrypt the parent folder of the file; you don't get a prompt like that when encrypting a folder.

To decrypt, repeat the process but clear the Encrypt Contents to Secure Data check box. Obviously, you must do this while logged in with the same user account as you used to encrypt. A dialog box asks whether you want to decrypt only the folder or the folder and its contents. If you choose to decrypt the contents too, it will only decrypt the files for which the current user account has valid certificates. When moving or copying, the following rules apply:

♦ If you move or copy an unencrypted file into an encrypted folder, it becomes encrypted.

♦ If you move or copy a file from an encrypted folder into an unencrypted folder, encryption is removed.

♦ If you have encrypted a file itself (not just the folder in which it resides), it retains its encryption no matter where it is moved or copied.

♦ If you try to move an encrypted file or folder to a non-NTFS drive, encryption is removed.

♦ If you delete an encrypted file or folder to the Recycle Bin, it remains encrypted in the Recycle Bin.

**WARNING**    Beginners can get themselves into a fair amount of trouble by using EFS encryption without really understanding it, so don't experiment with EFS on important files, and don't use EFS unless you are confident that you understand its risks and limitations.

## Sharing Encrypted Files with Other Local Users

This is a brand-new feature in Windows XP; in Windows 2000, EFS-encrypted files were accessible locally only to the user who encrypted them.

You can set up sharing for individual encrypted files only; you can't do it for folders or multiple files at once. ("Encrypted files" here includes both files that have been individually encrypted and files that are encrypted because they reside in an encrypted folder.)

**NOTE**    This sharing does not have anything to do with sharing files and folders via network. EFS is for local access only. If you want to share an encrypted file or folder via network, place it in your Shared Documents folder or set up its network sharing permission as explained in Chapter 19.

To share an encrypted file:

1. Right-click the file and choose Properties.

2. In the General tab, click Advanced. Then, in the Advanced Attributes dialog box, click Details.

3. In the Encryption Details box, click Add. The Select User dialog box appears.

4. Select the user that you want to have access, and click OK.

**NOTE**    Only other local users of this PC who have an EFS certificate appear here. If the person you want to designate does not appear, have him or her log in to the local PC and encrypt a file or folder.

## Transferring Encrypted Files to Another PC

To work with an encrypted file on another PC, you must export your personal encryption certificate on the original PC and then import it on the other one.

1. Back up your personal encryption certificate using the steps in "Backing Up Your Certificates" earlier in this section.

2. On the computer that is to receive the certificate, open the Internet Options dialog box (Tools ➢ Internet Options from within IE) and display the Content tab.

3. Click the Certificates button, and then click Import. The Certificate Import Wizard runs. Click Next to Continue.

4. Browse to locate the exported certificate, which has a `.pfx` extension. Then click Next.

5. Enter the password you assigned when you exported it, and then click Next.

6. Click Place All Certificates in the Following Store. Then click Browse to open the Select Certificate Store dialog box, choose Personal, and click OK.

7. Click Next, and then click Finish.

## Setting File Associations

File extensions are the primary way in which Windows determines what program to use to open a particular data file. For example, Microsoft Word opens DOC files, Paint opens BMP files, Notepad opens TXT files, and so on. The extension also signals the file's format, so a program that can open more than one type of file knows how to treat that particular file.

Sometimes when you install a new application, it commandeers a particular file extension without asking permission. For example, you might install a graphics-editing program that takes the `.bmp` extension away from Paint and assigns it to itself.

To change a file extension association:

1. From an Explorer window, choose Tools ➢ Folder Options and click the File Types tab.

2. Find and select the extension you want to change. See Figure 7.17.

3. Click the Change button. The Open With dialog box opens.

**FIGURE 7.17**
Manage file extensions and their associated applications here.

4. Select another program with which to associate the extension. Recommended programs appear at the top of the list. See Figure 7.18. Then click OK.

5. Click Close to close the Folder Options dialog box.

## Creating CDs

The recordable CD is without doubt the most cost-effective backup and transfer medium available. If you bought your computer recently, it may have come with a recordable CD drive, and you'll be interested to know that Windows XP includes CD-writing (also known as "burning") capability.

Burning CDs from Explorer is an easy, three-step process:

1. Copy the files to the storage area.

2. Check the files in the storage area to make sure that they're the right files and that there aren't too many of them.

3. Write the files to CD.

### Copying the Files to the Storage Area

The first step in burning files (or folders) to CD is to copy them to the storage area. You can do so in several ways, of which these three are usually the easiest:

◆ Select the files in an Explorer window or in a common dialog box. Then right-click in the selection and choose Send To ➤ CD Drive from the shortcut menu. (Alternatively, choose File ➤ Send To ➤ CD Drive.) This technique is the most convenient when you're working in Explorer or in a common dialog box.

◆ Drag the files and drop them on the CD drive in an Explorer window or on a shortcut to the CD. For example, you could keep a shortcut to the CD on your Desktop so that you could quickly drag files and folders to it. This technique is good for copying to CD files or folders that you keep on your Desktop.

♦ Open an Explorer window to the storage area, and then drag files to it and drop them there. This technique is mostly useful for adding files when you're checking the contents of the storage area. When you insert a blank CD in your CD drive, Windows displays a CD Drive dialog box offering to open a folder to the writable CD folder.

When you take one of these actions, Windows copies the files to the storage area and displays a notification area pop-up telling you that you have files waiting to be written to the CD.

Either click the pop-up or (if it has disappeared) open a My Computer window and double-click the icon for the CD drive. Windows opens an Explorer window showing the storage area, which appears as a list called Files Ready to Be Written to the CD. (For a CD-RW that already contains files, the storage area also contains a list of Files Currently on the CD.) Figure 7.19 shows an example of the storage area. As you can see in the figure, Windows displays a downward-pointing arrow on the icon for each file or folder to indicate that it's a temporary file destined to be burned to CD and then disposed of.

While Windows copies the files, the CD drive will appear to be busy, but it won't actually be writing any information to CD yet.

**FIGURE 7.19**

The storage area holds the copies of files to be copied to the CD. The downward-pointing arrow on each file icon and folder icon indicates that the item is temporary and will be deleted after being burned to CD.

### CHECKING THE FILES IN THE STORAGE AREA

Once you've copied to the storage area all the files that you want to burn to the CD, activate the window that Explorer opened to the storage area and check that the files are all there, that you don't want to remove any of them, and that there aren't too many to fit on the CD. (If you closed the window showing the storage area, you can display the storage area again by opening an Explorer window to My Computer and double-clicking the icon for the CD drive.)

**NOTE**    By default, the storage area is located in the Local Settings\Application Data\Microsoft\ CD Burning\ folder under the folder for your account in the Documents and Settings\ folder.

To check the size of files in the storage area, select them all (for example, by choosing Edit ➤ Select All), and then right-click and choose Properties from the shortcut menu. Windows displays the Properties dialog box for the files. Check the Size readout in the General tab.

## Writing the Files to CD

Once you've looked at the files in the storage area and are satisfied all is well, start the process of writing the files to CD. Take the following steps:

1. Click the Write These Files to CD link in the CD Writing Tasks list. Windows starts the CD Writing Wizard, which displays its first screen (shown in Figure 7.20).

**FIGURE 7.20**
On the first screen of the CD Writing Wizard, specify the name for the CD and choose whether the wizard should close itself when the CD is finished.

2. Enter the name for the CD in the CD Name text box. CD names can be a maximum of 16 characters.

3. If you want the wizard to close itself when the CD is finished, select the Close the Wizard After the Files Have Been Written check box. If you select this check box, you won't have the option of creating another CD containing the same files because the wizard automatically clears the storage area.

4. Click the Next button. The CD Writing Wizard displays the screen shown in Figure 7.21 as it burns the CD. The burning goes through three stages: Adding Data to the CD Image, Writing the Data Files to the CD, and Performing Final Steps to Make the CD Ready to Use.

**NOTE**  If the PC seems to be locked up during the CD burning process, wait. Sometimes the mouse will stop responding while a CD is being written. This is normal.

5. When the wizard has finished burning the CD, it displays the Completing the CD Writing Wizard screen (shown in Figure 7.22) and ejects the CD.

6. If you want to create another CD containing the same files, select the Yes, Write These Files to Another CD check box.

**FIGURE 7.21**

The CD Writing Wizard shows you its progress in burning the CD.

**FIGURE 7.22**

The CD Writing Wizard displays the Completing the CD Writing Wizard screen when it has finished creating the CD.

7. Click the Finish button. The wizard closes itself and deletes the files from the storage area unless you selected the Yes, Write These Files to Another CD check box.

## When Things Go Wrong Writing the CD

If you try to write more files to a CD than will fit on it, the CD Writing Wizard displays the Cannot Complete the CD Writing Wizard screen (shown in Figure 7.23). You can remove some files from the storage area, then select the Retry Writing the Files to CD Now option button, and click the Finish button if you want to try to fix the problem while the CD is open; but, in most cases, you'll do best to leave the Close the Wizard without Writing the Files option button selected and click the Finish button. Then you can return to the storage area, fix the problem, and restart the writing process.

The CD Writing Wizard may also warn you that there was an error in the recording process, and that the disc may no longer be usable. This is the other reason that people like the term "burning" for recording CDs—when things go wrong, you get burned and the disc is toast. In this case, you'll probably want to try writing the files to another CD.

**FIGURE 7.23**
The CD Writing Wizard displays the Cannot Complete the CD Writing Wizard screen to warn you that the files won't fit on the CD.

When you've finished creating the CD, test it immediately (preferably on a different computer) by opening an Explorer window to its contents and opening some of the files. Make sure all is well with the CD before archiving it or sending it on its way.

**TIP**   If the CD you create won't read or play properly, it may have suffered recording errors. Try reducing the burning speed by using the Select a Recording Speed drop-down list in the Recording tab of the Properties dialog box for the drive.

### Clearing the Storage Area

If you end up deciding not to create the CD after all, clear the storage area by deleting the files in it. To do so, click the Delete Temporary Files link in the Tasks list. Windows displays the Confirm Delete dialog box (shown in Figure 7.24) to make sure you know the files haven't yet been written to CD. Click the Yes button. Windows deletes the files and removes the Files to Add to the CD heading from the Explorer window.

**FIGURE 7.24**
Windows displays the Confirm Delete dialog box to make sure you want to delete all the files from the storage area.

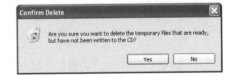

## Summary

In this chapter, you learned how Windows XP handles files and folders, and how to manage them on your own system. You not only reviewed the basics of moving, copying, deleting, and so on, but also learned about searching, compression, encryption, and the Offline Files feature. You also learned how to use Windows XP's built-in capability for burning CD-ROMs.

In the next chapter, we'll discuss printers and fonts. The two topics are integrally tied together, since the main purpose of a font is as a formatting device for printouts. Even if you have been using printers and fonts for a long time, you might want to review this chapter to pick up some additional pointers and timesaving tips.

# Chapter 8

# Installing and Working with Printers and Fonts

Windows XP makes printing seem so easy that it's easy to overlook the printing subsystem. You simply issue a Print command in an application, select a printer, and out comes your hard copy. But if you need to step beyond the daily end-user routine and install or configure printers, you might need a little help. It's not always obvious what settings are best for network versus local printers, for PostScript versus Printer Control Language (PCL) operating modes, and any number of other operating details.

In this chapter, you'll learn how to install and configure printers and how to manage Windows fonts. This chapter covers the following topics:

- How Windows XP handles printing
- Installing local printers
- Sharing a local printer
- Installing remote printers
- Working with printer properties
- Managing a print queue
- Creating and using separator pages
- Installing and managing fonts
- Changing the display font

## How Windows XP Handles Printing

If you're interested in the theory behind Windows XP printing, check out the following explanation; if you just want to learn the practical stuff, feel free to skip it.

Let's start with a bit of pre-Windows history (yes, back in the dark ages—that is, the 1980s). The MS-DOS applications each interacted directly with the printer through its own proprietary driver. The PC needed a separate driver for each printer and each application. Applications typically came with at least one disk full of printer drivers, covering the bases for dozens of the most popular models, but someone with a less popular printer could be out of luck unless that printer happened to emulate one of the more popular ones. Some of the less popular printers came with driver disks for the most popular applications, so you could sometimes acquire the needed driver from that end of the equation instead of from the application side. Still, acquiring the correct driver for each application and each printer was often a dicey proposition.

Then there was the waiting. Most applications did not include a print spooler, so when you issued the Print command, you had to wait until the print job was finished printing before you could resume using the application. And remember, printers printed much more slowly back then, so a big print job could tie up your whole system long enough for you to take a very leisurely coffee break.

Not only did the application need a printer driver, but it also needed font files. Most printers had only one or two typefaces built in; if you wanted anything else, the application had to send font files to the printer before a print job. There was a separate font file for each combination of size, typeface, and attribute. So, for example, 16-point bold Helvetica was a separate file from 16-point italic Helvetica or 14-point bold Helvetica. These font files took up space on the hard disk, and if you were going to print a document containing many fonts, the printing was delayed while the fonts were transferred to the printer's memory. To compound matters further, if you had two printers, you had to have a separate set of font files for each of them in some applications. Programs like Ventura Publisher would generate the needed font files during setup, and if you got a new printer, you needed to rerun the setup to generate a new set of fonts for it.

**NOTE**    Back in this era, add-on cartridges for some laser printers were popular; you could plug a cartridge in to add several typefaces to the printer that some applications could then use in addition to the software fonts (aka soft fonts).

Then thankfully, along came Windows. Starting around version 3.*x*, Windows began solving the problem of needing a different driver for each application by taking over the printing process itself. All Windows-based applications that needed to print sent their requests to the Windows printing subsystem. Since the applications did not interact with the printer, you did not need a separate printer driver for each one. All you needed was a Windows driver for each of your printers.

Windows used (and still uses) the term *printer* to mean a printer driver, because to Windows, the terms are synonymous. Windows interacts with the printer driver, and the printer driver then interacts with the printer. So when you set the properties for a printer, you are actually setting up the behavior of the driver and not the printer itself. You can have multiple drivers installed for a single physical printer, each set up for a different behavior. For example, you might have one driver set up to use separator pages between print jobs and another one set up not to do so. Windows would consider each of these separate printers, and it would look from an application's Print dialog box as though you had two printers installed on the same port.

The printer driver tells Windows a variety of things about the printer, including what its paper handling capabilities are, how much RAM is has installed, and what *Page Description Language (PDL)* it speaks. There are several PDLs popular today; two of the most popular are PCL (by Hewlett-Packard) and PostScript (by Adobe).

**TIP**    Almost all laser printers support either PCL or PostScript, so if you don't have the exact driver you need for a laser printer, you can usually hobble through using a driver for some other laser printer that uses the same version of PCL or PostScript.

Having Windows handle the printing rather than the individual application also frees up the application for continued work more quickly after you issue the Print command. The application quickly prints the entire job to the Windows *print spooler*, basically a holding tank for print jobs. Then Windows spoon-feeds the print job to the printer as the printer can accommodate it.

Remember that the other big hassle with MS-DOS printing was the need for separate font files for each typeface, size, and attribute combination. Starting with Windows 3.1, Windows began offering generic, scaleable typefaces called *TrueType*. These font files have several advantages:

◆ A TrueType font file contains an outline of each letter, rather than a fixed size, so a single font file can produce any size of text.

◆ TrueType fonts work with the Windows printing subsystem, so they work with any Windows application.

◆ TrueType fonts work with almost any printer, so you need only one set of TrueType fonts no matter what printers you have.

Windows XP continues to support TrueType, but introduces an improved variant of it called OpenType. The improvements are behind the scenes and not significant for an end user, but you need to be aware of the two different names because when you start working with fonts (later in this chapter), you'll see two different icons for them.

## Installing Local Printers

A *local printer* is one that is directly attached to your PC. It could be attached through a parallel, serial, USB, infrared, or some other port type. With a local printer, you have complete control; you can install and remove drivers for it, share it, control the permissions for the sharing, and so on. (In contrast, you might not always be able to have your way completely with a network printer, discussed later in this chapter.) The following sections explain how to install and share a local printer.

### Installing a Local Printer Driver

Most printers these days come with a setup disk of their own. Running the Setup program on the disk installs the needed Windows drivers. If you have such a disk available, you should use it because some Setup programs install a proprietary print spooler for the printer. For example, many of the Epson ink jet printers have their own spooler. If you install the printer manually using the Add Printer Wizard described next, you will miss out on any special utilities such as that.

If you do not have a setup disk for the printer, or if the Setup program will not run under Windows XP, the next most preferable path is to download a setup utility from the printer manufacturer's website. (Actually, this is not a bad idea even if you do have a setup disk already, because the setup disk might have been created prior to Windows XP's introduction and might not have XP-specific drivers on it, or a newer version of the XP driver might be available.)

If no setup files are available from the printer manufacturer, you can try the Add Printer Wizard in Windows. Windows XP provides drivers for hundreds of different printers, so it's possible that it includes a driver for your printer.

**NOTE**　If no Windows XP driver is available for your model, try the Windows 2000 driver. If no 2000 driver is available, try the one for NT 4.0. Still no luck? Check the printer's manual to find out whether it emulates any other printers; perhaps Windows XP includes a driver for one of them. You might also be able to kludge through with a driver for a similar model by the same manufacturer. For example, all the Lexmark Optra S models are basically the same except for their speeds and feature sets, so you could print with a different driver using the default settings even if you couldn't reliably set printing properties.

In earlier versions of Windows, there used to be an Add Printer icon in the Printers folder, but not in Windows XP; instead there's an Add a Printer link in the Printer Tasks bar.

To add a local printer with the Add Printer Wizard:

1. Choose Start ≻ Printers and Faxes. Or, if that command does not appear on the Start menu, open the Control Panel, and from Classic view, choose Printers and Faxes.

**TIP**  If you would like Printers and Faxes to appear on the Start menu, right-click an empty area of the Start menu and choose Properties. On the Start Menu tab, make sure Start Menu is selected, and then click Customize. In the Customize Start Menu dialog box, click the Advanced tab, and then scroll down through the list of options there and place a check mark next to Printers and Faxes. Click OK twice to close the open dialog boxes.

2. Click the Add a Printer link in the Printer Tasks bar.

3. The Add Printer Wizard runs; click Next to continue.

4. Click Local Printer Attached to This Computer.

5. If you want Windows to try to detect the printer, leave the Automatically Detect and Install My Plug and Play Printer check box marked. Otherwise clear it.

6. Turn the printer's power on (if it is not already on) if you want Windows to detect it, and then click Next.

   At this point, if Windows finds the printer, a bubble pops up in the notification area and the wizard reports that the printer has been installed and offers to print a test page.

**NOTE**   If Windows doesn't find the printer, see the next section, "Installing Multiple Drivers for the Same Printer." Even though you don't actually want multiple drivers in this case, you'll see in that section how to set up a printer without Plug and Play.

7. Click Yes, and then click Next to print the test page; then click Finish.

8. A box pops up asking whether the test page printed okay; click OK if it did, or click Trouble-shoot if it did not; then work through the Printing Troubleshooter.

## Installing Multiple Drivers for the Same Printer

As I mentioned earlier, one of the advantages in Windows printing is that Windows can accept multiple drivers for a single physical printer. You can use this capability for any number of purposes, such as:

◆ Installing both a PCL and a PostScript driver for a printer that is capable of using either PDL. Sometimes having two separate PDLs can be a boon when troubleshooting a problem; for example, the printer might run out of memory when printing a large graphic using one PDL but manage to print the page using another.

◆ Using different printer properties for certain jobs. For example, you might have one driver set up by default to pull from a paper tray containing letterhead stationery and another driver set up by default to pull plain paper from a different tray.

◆ Turning off the print spooler for one driver while leaving the other one to use the Windows print spooler.

◆ Setting one printer driver to Landscape by default and another one to Portrait so that you don't have to switch between the two orientations in the application in which you're printing.

Setting up a second driver for an already-installed printer is just like setting it up initially except you don't allow Windows to detect the printer automatically:

1. Perform steps 1–4 of the preceding section's steps for setting up a new local printer.

2. Make sure the Automatically Detect and Install My Plug and Play Printer check box is *not* marked, and click Next.

CHAPTER 8

**3.** Choose the port to which the printer is connected, and click Next.

**NOTE** The Create a New Port option is useful chiefly for setting up a TCP/IP printer connection; you'll see it in use later in this chapter in the section "Installing a Printer on a TCP/IP Port."

**4.** Select the printer from the list of manufacturers and models provided. (Or, if it isn't listed, click Have Disk and point to a location where a driver can be found.) Then click Next.

**NOTE** Clicking the Windows Update button connects to Microsoft's website and brings up a list of any updated drivers that have been released since Windows XP came out. Superficially it looks like nothing has changed in the dialog box, but scroll through and you'll notice that it's now a much shorter list—just the updated ones. To go back to the original list after clicking Windows Update, click Back to go back to the previous screen and then click Next to go forward again.

**5.** In the Printer Name box, type a name for the printer driver icon. You'll need to give it a different name from any already-installed drivers.

**6.** Choose Yes or No to set this printer as the default one or not. Then click Next.

7. If you want to set the printer up for sharing now, click Share Name and then type a name by which it should be shared. Then click Next. Or, if you want to skip sharing for now and set it up later, just click Next and skip to step 9.

**NOTE** If you use a share name of more than eight characters, or containing any spaces, it might not be accessible from MS-DOS programs. You'll see a warning to that effect if you enter such a name.

8. If you chose to share the printer, you're prompted for Location and Comment text. Enter these descriptors if you wish, and then click Next.

9. Click Yes to print a test page or No to skip it; then click Next.

10. Click Finish. You might be prompted for the Windows XP CD-ROM, or not, depending on what driver you chose and whether it was already installed.

When you finish up, you'll have a second driver for the printer in your Printers folder. It will also appear in any applications you print from (at least, any applications that let you specify which printer you want to use).

## Sharing a Local Printer

You saw in the preceding section how the Add Printer Wizard can set up printer sharing for you as part of the printer driver installation. (That's an option only if you don't have Windows detect the Plug and Play printer.) But you can also set up sharing manually.

**NOTE** Some printers have built-in network cards so that you can attach them directly to a network hub; no particular PC has local control over these printers. You can print to one of these using its IP address. Other printers are not network-capable by themselves, but you can hook them up to a print server that manages their network connection. (Wireless print server boxes are very reasonably priced these days, and enable you to place a printer anywhere—not just near a PC.) Then there's the shared local printer. When you share a local printer, you give other network users permission to access it, and when they do use it, the request goes through your own local copy of Windows. If the printer is heavily used, you might notice the drain on your system resources while the print jobs are spooled off to the printer. That's why on busy networks, it is preferable to have printers networked through a print server or their own network address.

To share one of your local printers, do the following:

1. Right-click the printer in the Printers and Faxes folder and choose Sharing.

2. Enable the Share This Printer option button, and enter a share name for it (or accept the default name).

3. Click OK.

Pretty simple, eh? But see the following section to gain some control over the specifics of the sharing.

## Setting Permissions for a Shared Printer

The simple Sharing tab shown in the preceding section might lead you to believe that no options are available for controlling how your printer is shared. However, that's not the case.

First, you can control when the shared printer is available to others in the Advanced tab. You can specify certain times of day when the printer should be available, and you can assign a priority to the print jobs coming in from other people. For example, if you set the priority to 2, and your own print jobs have the default priority of 1, your own jobs will print first, and then anyone else's. See Figure 8.1.

You can set the permissions for the printer—that is, which users can use it and what they can do to it—in the Security tab. See Figure 8.2.

**TIP**   If you don't have the Security tab in your printer's Properties box, it's probably because Simple File Sharing is turned on. (It's on by default in Windows XP installations.) To turn it off, from any Explorer window choose Tools ➤ Folder Options. In the View tab, scroll down to the bottom of the Advanced Settings list and deselect Use Simple File Sharing.

For each listed user or group, you can assign permissions to Print, Manage Printers, and Manage Documents. You'll learn more about users and groups in Chapter 19, but let's look at the printing-specific permissions here:

**Print**   Can send documents to the printer's queue.

**Manage Printers**   Can view the print queue and can pause and resume it.

**Manage Documents**   Can view the print queue and can pause, resume, or delete print jobs in it.

**FIGURE 8.1**
Control when others can
use your printer and
what priority should
be assigned to their
print jobs

**FIGURE 8.2**
You can assign different
permissions for the
printer to different
users and groups.

You'll learn about working with print queues later in this chapter, but when you get there, keep in mind that the actions explained there can be performed only with the needed permissions to do so.

As with other network resources, you can also click the Advanced button to fine-tune the permission settings, but this is probably beyond the scope of what you want to get into right now. When you learn about advanced permissions in Chapter 19, you might want to come back here and explore the printer's permissions further.

## Installing Multiple OS Support for a Shared Local Printer

When others share your local printer, as long as they have Windows XP installed on their PCs, everything works fine. But if they are running some other version of Windows, it's a no-go.

To circumvent this problem, users wanting to access your printer must install a printer driver for that printer on their own PCs, in a version appropriate for their operating systems. For example,

Windows 98 users would need a Windows 98 driver for your printer. If they happen to have the needed driver on a disk at their local workstation, they can use it when they set up the printer. However, most people don't keep printer driver disks lying around for printers they don't own, so the likelihood of this is slim.

As a courtesy to users who might want to print to your local printer over the network, you can pre-install the needed drivers for various operating systems. Then when the person sets up your printer, the needed drivers will be copied from your PC to theirs as part of the setup process.

To add these drivers, click the Additional Drivers button in the Sharing tab of the printer properties. This opens an Additional Drivers dialog box (see Figure 8.3). Place a check mark next to the drivers you want to install and click OK.

**FIGURE 8.3**
You might want to provide drivers for other operating systems as a courtesy to other network users.

A dialog box will then appear, prompting for the location of the needed driver. If you have a setup CD-ROM for the printer, you might find the driver there; otherwise you can download it from the manufacturer's website. Point the dialog box to the needed location with Browse, and then click OK to continue. See Figure 8.4.

**FIGURE 8.4**
You must have the driver available for each operating system that you wish to support, and you must tell Windows where to find it.

## Installing Remote Printers

A *remote* printer is one that is not connected to your PC directly. It could be connected to another individual's PC on the network, connected directly to the network itself, or accessible through the Internet via TCP/IP.

## Setting Up a Remote Printer

Before you can print to a remote printer, you must install a driver for it on your local PC. That's actually a good thing, because then you can set your own properties for the printer and not have to rely on someone else's settings for it. For example, perhaps you always print your documents in Landscape orientation, but the printer owner always prints in Portrait. Since you maintain your own copy of the driver, you can have your own default Landscape setting without manually making the change every time.

To install a remote printer, do the following:

1. From the Printers and Faxes folder, click the Add a Printer link. The Add Printer Wizard starts; click Next.

2. Click the A Network Printer, or A Printer Attached to Another Computer option button. Then click Next.

3. If you have an address for the printer already, enter it. It could be a network path (such as \\server\printer) or a URL. If you don't know the address, choose Browse for a Printer, and then click Next and locate it.

**NOTE**   If you have an IP address for the printer (a set of four numbers like 198.157.281.2), set up the printer as a local printer and choose the Add Port option to add a TCP/IP port. This is covered in the next section of the chapter.

4. If you see a security warning about installing a driver on your PC, click Yes to continue.

**5.** If the PC to which the printer is connected is running a different operating system than Windows XP, you might see the following message.

If you see that message, click OK.

**6.** A list of printer manufacturers and models will then appear. If the printer is listed, select it to install the Windows XP driver for it. If it isn't, click Have Disk and then point it to a driver on CD-ROM or downloaded driver.

**7.** Choose Yes or No to make this printer the default or not; then click Next, and then Finish. The needed drivers are copied to your PC, and the printer is set up.

## Installing a Printer on a TCP/IP Port

If a network-capable printer is connected directly to the network rather than to a print server or some other PC, its built-in network card will have its own unique TCP/IP address. You can use that address to set up the printer.

To do so, start out with the Add Printer Wizard as if it were a local printer, but don't let Windows automatically detect the printer. Then when asked about the printer port, choose Create a New Port, and then choose Standard TCP/IP Port from the list. See Figure 8.5.

When you click Next after doing this, a whole new wizard runs: the Add Standard TCP/IP Printer Port Wizard. Follow along with its prompts to install the printer.

**FIGURE 8.5**
You can print to a printer using its IP address by setting it up as a local printer on a TCP/IP port.

### Installing a Printer Through a UNIX Host

If your network includes UNIX-based computers, you can print through the network to a printer attached to them, or to network-capable printers on a UNIX network, but you have to do a couple of setup things first:

1. Through Add/Remove Windows Components, install Print Services for UNIX. (It's under Other Network File and Print Services.)

2. Run the Add Printer Wizard and start setting up a new local printer, but do not automatically detect.

3. Then when asked about the port to use, create a new LPR port.

4. Enter the IP address for that printer's host in the Name or Address of Server Providing LPD box.

5. In the Name of Printer or Print Queue on That Server box, enter the name of the printer as it is known by the host device.

6. Click OK.

7. Complete the wizard normally.

## Managing Installed Printers

From the Printers and Faxes window you can view the installed printer drivers. The printer icons are different depending on the printer's status:

 A local printer's icon is a regular printer.

 A remote printer's icon has a cable beneath it, indicating that it's on the network.

The default printer's icon has a check mark on it.

 A shared local printer has a hand underneath it.

A fax driver (such as for Microsoft Fax) has a fax machine icon.

### Removing a Printer Driver

To remove a printer driver, select it and press Delete, just like any other file or folder in Explorer.

Depending on the printer, you might see a message stating that some files were used only by that driver and asking whether you want to delete them. If you never plan on reinstalling this printer, answer Yes. If you think you might reinstall it, choose No; that way you might not need to reinsert the Windows XP or printer CD-ROM when you reinstall.

### Working with Printer Properties

Through a printer's properties, you can adjust almost every aspect of the way it works, from the print quality to the paper feed. To set properties for a printer, right-click it and choose Properties.

The properties for a printer vary widely depending on the printer model. Because the printer manufacturer supplies the printer drivers, there is no real standardization in the options they include or in the layout of the various tabs. However, there are at least a few settings that are available for all printers, regardless of model. The following sections outline some of the broad categories of settings that you might find in the properties for various types of printers.

### GENERAL PROPERTIES

All printers have a General tab. In it, you can change the printer driver's name, enter comments about the printer, and print a test page. See Figure 8.6.

**FIGURE 8.6**
The General tab helps
you identify the printer.

From the General tab you can also click the Printing Preferences button to open the Printing Preferences dialog box for the printer. The content of this dialog box will vary depending on the printer model; Figure 8.7 shows it for my laser printer.

**FIGURE 8.7**
Printing Preferences
set basic operational
parameters such as
page orientation.

## PORTS PROPERTIES

In the Ports tab you can select which port a printer uses. On the surface, this seems simple enough: one printer, one port. But if you mark the Enable Printer Pooling check box at the bottom of this tab (see Figure 8.8), you can then choose multiple ports for a single printer driver. This enables you to put multiple identical printers on different ports and have print jobs sent to whichever one happens to be free through a single print driver and print queue.

**FIGURE 8.8**
In the Ports tab, you can select ports to be associated with the selected printer driver.

Clicking a port and then clicking the Configure Port button brings up a dialog box with options for that type of port. With a parallel port, there is only one option: Transmission Retry. However, with a serial (COM) port you can set the communication settings (such as bits per second, parity, stop bits, and so on).

## ADVANCED PROPERTIES

In the Advanced tab (Figure 8.9) are a variety of special-purpose settings. You saw earlier about the availability hours, when sharing was discussed. Some of the other options here are:

**Spooling**   By default, a printer uses the Windows print spooler, but you can choose to print directly to the printer instead. If you do that, the application might slow down or lock up entirely while the job prints.

**Hold Mismatched Documents**   When this is on, the driver checks the document to be printed to make sure it can be successfully printed on the printer (correct page size, etc.). If not, it holds it in the queue.

**Print Spooled Documents First**   There's a delay between when a document begins being transferred from the application to the print spool. If you have the Spooling setting set so that the document will not start printing until the last page is spooled, the printer will sit idle waiting, even if other documents of a lower priority are completely spooled and waiting. If you mark this check box, however, those lower priority documents will be able to "cut in line" to allow more efficient usage.

CHAPTER 8

**Keep Printed Documents**   If you turn this on, items in the print spool will not be deleted after they are printed; they'll just go into an inactive status there. This enables you to resubmit the same print job from the spool without having to reprint it in the application.

**Enable Advanced Printing Features**   When this is on, any special options the printer is capable of, such as booklet printing, page order, and pages per sheet, will be available.

**FIGURE 8.9**
Advanced properties for the printer control special situations

### DEVICE SETTINGS

Most printer drivers have a Device Settings tab, but the content of it varies dramatically from printer to printer. These are generally the same settings that you can control from the LED panel on the printer itself, but they are accessible through the printer driver for convenience. Figure 8.10 shows one for a PostScript/PCL laser printer.

**FIGURE 8.10**
Device Settings are specific to the printer model.

### COLOR MANAGEMENT

For color printers only, a Color Management tab may appear, enabling you to select a color profile. A color profile is a configuration file that specifies color fine-tuning for a particular source. This is handy if you are trying to match the colors on-screen more closely with the actual output from the printer, so it's more of a "what you see is what you get" affair. If the printer is shared, the Color Management properties are not usually alterable from the remote PCs using the shared printer, although the settings can be viewed from there.

### UTILITIES

Found primarily in ink jet printer drivers, the Utilities tab offers shortcuts to self-tests, head-cleaning routines, and other utility programs built into the printer. Most of these can also be run by pressing buttons on the printer itself or by running a separate utility application for the printer; they're provided in the driver for convenience.

## Managing the Printing Process

Once a print job leaves the application, it's at the mercy of the print spooler (aka the *print queue*), a holding area where print jobs wait to be printed. The bottleneck here is the printer's speed and available memory. The more memory a printer has, the more print jobs can be stacked up in it waiting for the printer's hardware to catch up. The less memory a printer has, the more it relies on the print queue in Windows to hold the excess incoming data.

### Managing a Print Queue

To open a print queue, double-click the printer in the Printers and Faxes window. Another way is to double-click the printer icon appears in the notification area when a print queue is active (that is, when it contains something to be printed). Figure 8.11 shows a print queue with several print jobs.

**FIGURE 8.11**

A printer's queue shows what print jobs have been submitted and are waiting to be printed.

You can control two things from the print queue: the queue itself and individual print jobs within it. As you learned earlier in the chapter, you can grant permissions for these activities separately when assigning sharing permissions to other users.

The overall print queue is controlled from the Printer menu. Some of the important commands there are:

**Pause Printing**   Freezes the print queue but leaves all print jobs intact.

**Cancel All Documents**   Clears the entire queue.

**Use Printer Offline**   Pauses the connection between the printer and the queue. The queue stops sending data to the printer temporarily, but the queue itself continues accepting incoming documents.

There are several other commands on the Printer menu, but they're all commands you've already seen in this chapter, such as Sharing and Properties.

Individual print jobs are controlled from the Document menu. The important commands here:

**Pause**  Pauses the print job. If the job is currently printing, it also pauses the printer. If the job is waiting to be printed, it makes other non-paused jobs able to pass the paused job in the queue. So if you submit a big print job and then a small one and decide you want the small one to print first, you can pause the big one.

**Resume**  Resumes a paused print job.

**Cancel**  Cancels the print job.

Occasionally a document might get "stuck" in the print queue. It can't print, and you can't delete it. To fix this, you must stop and restart the Print Spooler service from the Computer Management console (in Administrative Tools in Control Panel). You'll find the print spooler under Services there. Right-click the service and choose Stop, and then right-click it and choose Start (see Figure 8.12).

**FIGURE 8.12**
Stop and restart the Print Spooler from the Services window.

## Taking a Printer Out of Service with Pending Print Jobs

Suppose you have a printer with lots of jobs waiting in its queue and the printer has a blowout that requires you to take it out of service. What happens to all those print jobs? You don't want them to be lost, so you must transfer them to another printer.

To do so, open the print queue for the broken printer, and choose Printer ➢ Properties. In the Ports tab, click the port to which the other printer is assigned and then click OK. You can do this to redirect to any printer on the same print server.

If you need to redirect to a printer on a different print server, you must add a port for it. Click Add Port, click Local Port, and then click New Port. Then enter the name of the other print server and shared printer in this format: **\\*print_server*\*share_name***.

## Using Separator Pages

A separator page is an extra page that prints before each document. It identifies who printed it, the date and time, and so on. On a printer that many users share, this can be a valuable tool for determining to whom a print job belongs, even though it wastes a certain amount of paper.

A separator page also can have another purpose—it can send a printer-specific hexadecimal code to the printer. This is useful for activities such as switching the printer between PCL and PostScript modes.

Separator pages are text files with a `.sep` extension. Windows XP includes four separator page designs:

**`Sysprint.sep`**   Switches to PostScript and prints a separator page with the account name, job number, date, and time.

**`PCL.sep`**   Switches to PCL and prints a separator page with the account name, job number, date, and time.

**`Pscript.sep`**   Switches to PostScript but does not print a separator page.

**`Sysprtj.sep`**   Same as `Sysprint.sep` but uses Japanese fonts if available.

### SELECTING A SEPARATOR PAGE

To select a separator page to use with a certain printer, do the following:

1. Open the Properties for the printer and go to the Advanced tab.
2. Click the Separator Page button. The Separator Page dialog box opens.
3. Type the path to the separator page, or click Browse to locate it.

4. Click OK.

### DESIGNING YOUR OWN SEPARATOR PAGE

You can design your own separator pages by creating text files in Notepad and saving them with a `.sep` extension. You can modify one of the existing `.sep` files or start fresh.

At the top of the file, type one single character on a line by itself. The SEP files that come with Windows XP use the backslash (\) for this but you can use @ or some other character if you prefer. This defines the character that will precede all subsequent commands—the escape character. From there, just start typing your codes. Table 8.1 lists the codes you can use for separator pages. Table 8.1 shows a \ as the escape character.

Make sure that \E is the final code of the file. Then save it with a `.sep` extension in the `%systemroot%/system32` folder.

**TABLE 8.1:**     Separator Page Codes

| PAGE CODE | DESCRIPTION |
|---|---|
| \N | Name of the user who is printing. |
| \I | Job number. |
| \D | Date. |
| \T | Time. |
| \L *message* | Prints a message. Type your message in place of *message*. For example, \L Acme Corporation would print the name "Acme Corporation" on the page. It prints everything that follows the \L code until the next \ is found or until it runs out of page width. (Messages won't wrap to multiple lines automatically.) |
| \F *pathname* | Prints the content of the specified file. Type your file path and name in place of *pathname*. |
| \H*nn* | Sends a hexadecimal instruction to the printer. Type the hex code in place of *nn*. |
| \W*nnn* | Specifies the maximum width of the separator page, in characters. The default is 80; the maximum is 256. Type the width in place of *nnn*. |
| \B\S | Prints in single-width block letters. |
| \B\M | Prints in double-width block letters. |
| \U | Turns off block-letter printing. |
| \\*n* | Skips a number of lines (0 through 9). Type the number of lines in place of *n*. |
| \E | Ejects the page from the printer. |

## Setting Print Server Properties

So far, you have learned about setting properties for individual printers, but you can also make global printing settings that affect all the installed printers. To do so, right-click an empty area of the Printers and Faxes window and choose Server Properties. This opens the Print Server Properties dialog box. This dialog box has four tabs:

**Forms**    This is a master list of the available forms that can be assigned to the various paper trays in the Device Settings tab for an individual printer. You can add new forms here.

**Ports**    This is the same as the Ports tab in an individual printer's properties.

**Drivers**    This tab tells what drivers have been installed for which operating systems. For example, if you have added drivers for additional operating systems for some of your shared printers, you'll see them listed here. You can add and remove drivers from here.

**Advanced**    Here you'll find an assortment of check boxes and other controls for fine-tuning the printing subsystem on your PC. Table 8.2 lists the options here.

**TIP**  The Spool folder you set in the Advanced tab applies to all printers. If you want to specify a different spool folder location for a specific printer, you must do so by editing the Registry. Go to `HKEY_LOCAL_MACHINE\Software\Microsoft\WindowsNT\CurrentVersion\Print\Printers\printer` key, and change the SpoolDirectory to the desired location.

**WARNING**  If you want users to be able to receive notifications when their print jobs are complete, you must start the Alerter service using the Services snap-in in Computer Management. Alerter does not start automatically by default.

**TABLE 8.2:**       Advanced Print Server Properties

| SETTING | PURPOSE |
| --- | --- |
| Spool Folder | Specifies where the print queue's file will be stored. |
| Log Spooler Error Events | Creates a log file containing any error messages generated. Error messages would include things like Out of Paper. |
| Log Spooler Warning Events | Creates a log file containing any warning messages generated. Warnings might include things like Toner Low. |
| Log Spooler Information Events | Creates a log file containing information messages generated. You would not normally want to log these; they're things like Print Job Completed. |
| Beep on Errors of Remote Documents | Signals the print server to beep when errors occur. |
| Show Informational Notifications for Local Printers | Makes pop-up bubble messages appear in the notification area for routine events associated with local printers. |
| Show Informational Notifications for Network Printers | Makes pop-up bubble messages appear for routine events associated with network printers. |
| Notify When Remote Documents Are Printed | Displays a message when you print to a network printer to let you know the print job has finished. This might be useful if you want to go pick up a printout but don't want to get there too early and have to wait for it to complete. |
| Notify Computer, Not User, When Remote Documents Are Printed | Normally the user gets the message with the "Notify with Remote Documents Are Printed" setting; if you log on as another user, you won't get the message. But if you mark this check box, the message will go to the computer regardless of who is logged on. |

## Managing Fonts

Whenever you produce anything containing text, you select a font to specify the style of lettering. As you learned earlier in the chapter, Windows versions 3.1 and higher have included a type of font file called TrueType. TrueType revolutionized the desktop publishing industry by providing the average end user with a huge assortment of cheap, scaleable fonts. Windows XP includes support for True-Type fonts, but the fonts that come with Windows XP are of a new type called OpenType.

**NOTE**    The term *font* has a somewhat ambiguous meaning. Some people claim it refers to the style of lettering only and is synonymous with typeface. Other people claim a font is a particular typeface at a particular size with a particular set of attributes applied (bold, italic). Usage has been inconsistent over the years in the computer industry, and Windows itself is inconsistent in terminology. In this chapter, I'll use the term font to be synonymous with typeface.

The Fonts window in Windows XP, accessible through Control Panel, shows all the installed TrueType and OpenType fonts (as well as a few other types of special-purpose fonts that are neither).

### Installing Fonts

Most of the fonts you'll acquire will come as part of an application. For example, when you install Microsoft Office XP, the Setup program automatically installs dozens of fonts in Windows. Even when you buy a CD-ROM full of fonts in a computer store, it usually comes with a Setup program for browsing the fonts and choosing the ones you want.

If the font source does not include any installation utility, you can install the fonts from within Windows' Fonts window by doing the following:

1. From Control Panel, click Appearance and Themes, and then in the sidebar area, click Fonts. That's the only way to get to the Fonts applet in Category view; if you're using Classic view, you can simply double-click the Fonts icon.

2. In the Fonts window, choose File ➢ Install New Font.

3. Navigate to the drive and folder where the new font is located. If there are a lot of fonts in that location, it may take a minute for the list to populate. Click the Network button if you need to map a network drive to locate the fonts.

**4.** Select the font you want. To select multiple fonts, hold down the Ctrl key as you click each one, or hold down Shift to select a block.

**NOTE** If you clear the Copy Fonts to Fonts Folder check box, it will save the space on your hard disk by using the fonts from their source location. However, if that source location is ever unavailable, the fonts that are there will be unavailable as well.

**5.** Click OK to install the fonts.

**TIP** You can also drag and drop font files into the Fonts folder instead of going through the process just described.

## Managing Your Font Collection

From the Fonts window, shown in Figure 8.13, you can browse the installed fonts, remove any that you don't want, and see previews of the fonts.

**FIGURE 8.13**
Browse the installed
Windows fonts here.

Here are some activities you can perform on fonts:

◆ To see a preview of a font, double-click its icon; when done looking at it, click Close. See Figure 8.14.

◆ To remove a font, delete its icon from the Fonts folder.

◆ To hide variations of the same font, choose View ➢ Hide Variations. This hides any fonts that are exactly like some other font except for being bold or italic.

◆ To sort the fonts by similarity to a chosen font, choose View ➢ List Fonts by Similarity. Then open the List Fonts by Similarity To drop-down list and choose one of the fonts. The other fonts will appear in order from most to least similar to it. This is a great way to trim your font collection by eliminating any identical or virtually identical fonts that have different names. See Figure 8.15.

**FIGURE 8.14**
A preview of the
selected font

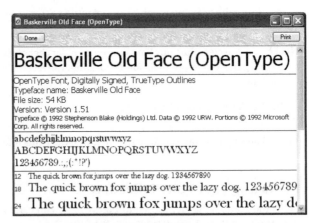

**FIGURE 8.15**
Listing fonts by similarity helps identify duplicates with different names.

## Using Other Types of Fonts

Most people think of TrueType or OpenType fonts only when they hear the term *font*, but there are in fact many different kinds of fonts that Windows applications can use.

### TYPE 1 FONTS

These are scaleable soft fonts (that is, fonts contained in software) designed for use with PostScript printers. Type 1 is an Adobe technology that predates TrueType and is still in use today in commercial printing operations.

You install Type 1 fonts the same way you install OpenType or TrueType fonts, as explained earlier in the chapter.

### NON-SCALEABLE FONTS

Windows supports several types of fonts that come in fixed sizes, rather than being scaleable. There are two main types:

**Vector fonts**   These are soft fonts designed for use on plotters. Windows XP comes with three vector fonts: Roman, Modern, and Script. These are non-scaleable; they come in a fixed few sizes.

**Raster fonts**   These are soft fonts stored in sets of bitmap images, with one size of lettering per raster file. They're non-scaleable. Before TrueType, almost all PC fonts were of this type.

Both can be installed using the same procedure outlined in "Installing New Fonts" earlier in the chapter.

If you have raster (PCL) printer fonts on a disk and you want to install them into the printer's memory, you would install them from the printer's properties. To do so, go to the Device Settings tab in the printer's Properties box and double-click External Fonts. Then specify the location from which you want to import the fonts. See Figure 8.16. These fonts would be available only for this printer, of course.

**FIGURE 8.16**

Install raster fonts for a printer.

### PRINTER-RESIDENT FONTS

Some printers have a number of built-in fonts. Some are scaleable (notably PostScript fonts in a Post-Script printer); others are in a few fixed sizes. They are automatically available in applications but do not show up in the Fonts window. For example, in Figure 8.17, which shows Microsoft Word, notice that some of the fonts have a printer icon next to them; these are printer-resident fonts.

The fonts may be stored in the printer itself, or in an add-on cartridge that plugs into a printer. Back in the early days of Hewlett-Packard LaserJet printers, cartridge fonts were very popular. Today, however, you will seldom see them.

The printer driver knows about any printer-resident fonts automatically, but you may need to tell the printer driver about any cartridges you have installed. If your printer supports cartridges, there will be an Installed Font Cartridges option in the printer's Device Settings tab in its properties. Click it and then select which slot the cartridge is plugged into to make Windows XP recognize the cartridge.

**FIGURE 8.17**
Printer-resident fonts appear in your font list within an application.

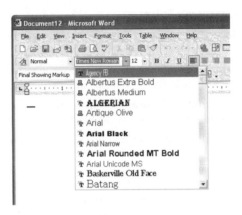

## Working with the Font Substitution Table

When a printer has its own resident fonts, you can choose to have them override certain soft fonts that an application might call for in a printout. This makes printing quicker because the soft font does not need to be sent to the printer prior to the print job. The table establishing the rules for which fonts should be substituted, and for what, is the *font substitution table*. Mostly you will find it available on laser printers; ink jet printers typically don't have resident fonts.

To work with the font substitution table, open the printer's Properties box and go to the Device Settings tab. Then locate the Font Substitutions listing, and click the plus sign next to it, expanding the font list. See Figure 8.18.

This font list consists of all the soft fonts in the Fonts folder in Windows. Click one of them and a drop-down list appears containing all the resident fonts in the printer. Choose one of them, and then whenever a document calls for the chosen soft font, the printer's own font will be used instead.

**FIGURE 8.18**
You can substitute printer-resident fonts for soft fonts selectively.

## Selecting a Different Display Font

There are two kinds of fonts in Windows XP: printer fonts and display fonts. So far we have been talking only about the printer fonts. Each printer font has a corresponding display font that is used for displaying the font on-screen when you use it in an application (and also when you preview it in the Fonts window).

To change the font used in Windows title bars, dialog boxes, and so on, do the following:

1. Right-click the Desktop and choose Properties.

2. In the Appearance tab, click the Advanced button.

3. Select one of the screen elements that contains text, such as Active Title Bar.

4. Open the Font drop-down list and select a different font to use for that element. Change the size, too, if desired, from the Size list.

5. Repeat steps 3 and 4 to change other screen elements if desired; then click OK.

## Enabling ClearType for the Display Font

Windows XP comes with a new feature called ClearType that can help with poor on-screen text appearance on LCD monitors. You should not turn it on unless you have an LCD monitor because it can actually make the fonts appear worse on a regular CRT monitor. To turn it on, do the following:

1. Right-click the Desktop and choose Properties.

2. Display the Appearance tab, and then click the Effects button.

3. Mark the Use the Following Method to Smooth Edges of Screen Fonts check box.

4. Choose ClearType from the list, and click OK twice.

## Faxing in Windows XP

Windows XP comes with a Microsoft Fax module that will serve adequately as a simple PC-based fax utility, so you don't have to buy a separate program like WinFax PRO just to send and receive the occasional page or two. I'm bringing it up here in this chapter because Windows tends to lump printing and faxing into the same category. (Witness the name of the Control Panel applet: Printers and Faxes.)

**WARNING**  You can install Microsoft Fax without having a modem installed in the PC, but you can't use it to send and receive faxes.

### Installing Microsoft Fax

Microsoft Fax is not installed by default; add it in with Add/Remove Windows Components through the Control Panel:

1. From the Control Panel, open Add or Remove Programs.

2. Click Add/Remove Windows Components.

3. Place a check mark next to Fax Services (see Figure 8.19) and click Next.

4. Follow the prompts to complete the installation.

**FIGURE 8.19**
Install faxing as a Windows option.

Once the Microsoft Fax service is installed, three new components appear in the menu system (Start ➢ All Programs ➢ Accessories ➢ Communications ➢ Fax): Fax Console, Fax Cover Page Editor, and Send a Fax. A fax driver also appears in the Printers and Faxes folder.

**TIP**  You can quickly fax from any application that prints simply by printing to the fax driver instead of to one of the installed printers.

### Working with the Fax Console

The Fax Console is the core application for Microsoft Fax. The first time you run it (Start ➢ All Programs ➢ Accessories ➢ Communications ➢ Fax ➢ Fax Console), the Fax Configuration Wizard runs. Work through it, entering your contact information when prompted, as in Figure 8.20. If you ever need to change this information in the future, from within the Fax Console choose Tools ➤ Configure Fax.

**FIGURE 8.20**
Configure the Fax Console by providing your contact information to append to outgoing faxes.

The Fax Console is a fax management window where you can see your incoming and outgoing faxes. It's a lot like Microsoft Outlook is for e-mail, except it's for faxes. Figure 8.21 shows it. Of course, once you've sent and received some faxes, there will be some content there, not just a blank as shown.

**FIGURE 8.21**
The Fax Console provides access to sent and received faxes. (There aren't any here yet.)

## Sending a Fax

To send a fax, you must have a fax-capable modem, of course, and it must be set up in the Printers and Faxes folder as a print device. (Windows did this automatically when you installed the faxing capability from Add/Remove Windows Components.)

There are two ways to send a fax. You can use the Send Fax Wizard that's part of the faxing module, or you can print to the fax driver as you would a printer from within any application to fax a document from that application.

### SENDING A STANDALONE FAX

A standalone fax is appropriate when you just want to send a quick cover page with a message on it. To start the wizard, you can either choose Start ➤ All Programs ➤ Accessories ➤ Communications ➤ Fax ➤ Send a Fax, or you can open up the Fax Console window and choose File ➤ Send a Fax (or click the New Fax button on its toolbar).

When prompted for a recipient, enter the name and fax number and then click the Add button. You can send the same fax to multiple recipients. You can also pull from the Address Book by clicking the Address Book button. See Figure 8.22.

**FIGURE 8.22**

When preparing a fax to send, specify the recipient's name and contact information.

**TIP** If the country and area code choices are unavailable, mark the Use Dialing Rules check box to enable them.

When you are prompted for a cover page, choose one of the designs provided. Your sender information is automatically added to the cover page. (You can click the Sender Information button to change it.) On this same screen you also enter the subject line for your cover page and type any text that you want to appear on it. See Figure 8.23.

**FIGURE 8.23**

Choose a cover page design and edit your sender information if desired.

### FAXING FROM AN APPLICATION

Faxing from an application is appropriate when you need to fax more pages than just a cover page. For example, you can fax from Word to send an entire Word document or any portion of it.

To fax from an application, begin printing normally in that application, but choose Microsoft Fax as the printer in the application's Print dialog box. The Send Fax Wizard runs, and from that point, the process is the same described as in the preceding section.

## Receiving a Fax

When the Microsoft Fax service is installed, it adds a service that runs all the time, listening for the phone to ring. When it does, an icon pops up in the notification area letting you know. You can click that icon to answer the call with the fax driver, or ignore it to decline. From the Fax Console, you can choose Tools ➤ Fax Monitor to open a window that shows the monitoring system. Once the fax is received, it appears in the Fax Console and you can double-click it to view it.

The Fax Console program does not make it obvious how to configure it to automatically receive faxes. That's because that setting is more properly associated with the modem, not the application. It is possible for a system to have several modems that work with a single Fax Console, all with different settings.

Here's how to change the receive mode for a modem to Automatic:

1. Open the Printers and Faxes folder from the Control Panel. Right-click the Microsoft Fax driver and choose Properties.

2. Click the Devices tab, and then click the Properties button. The Properties dialog box for the modem opens.

3. Click the Receive tab and then choose Automatic in the Answer Mode section. See Figure 8.24.

   (Optional) While you're here, explore the other properties available for the modem's fax settings.

4. Click OK to close all open dialog boxes.

**FIGURE 8.24**
Configure the fax modem's settings for answering automatically (or not).

## Creating a Cover Page

Are you finding the cover pages provided by Windows XP Professional a little dull? They just don't seem to reflect your sense of taste and style? Maybe you want something a little flashier? In this section, you will learn how to create a new custom cover page. Follow these steps:

1. In the Printers and Faxes folder, double-click the Fax icon to open the Fax Console.

2. Choose Tools ➢ Personal Cover Pages to open the Personal Cover Pages dialog box:

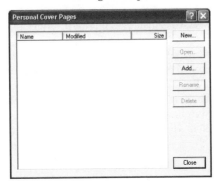

3. Click New to open the Fax Cover Page Editor:

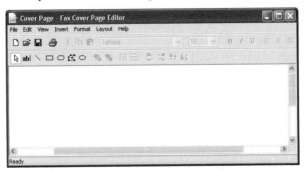

4. Click OK to close the Tips dialog box. The Tips are worth reading through if you are new to Fax and editing cover pages, but we'll pass on them for now.

The Cover Page Editor is now ready to work with a blank document already loaded for use. The Cover Page Editor looks like a simple word processor, such as WordPad, at first glance. But if you browse through the menus and toolbars a little, you'll soon discover that the editor is more akin to a desktop publishing program. The Cover Page Editor is more concerned with placement of fields on the page and the overall layout and appearance of the page than with entering text. Let's take a closer look at some of the capabilities of this editor.

## The Basics of Cover Pages

Every cover page needs certain bits of information: the name of the recipient, the fax number of the recipient, the name and phone number of the sender, and so on. Let's start our exploration of the Cover Page Editor with a look at adding these basic fields, and then we'll move on to some of the more advanced features.

First, let's make it easier to place the fields evenly on the page by turning on grid view: choose View ➢ Grid Lines. You'll see something similar to the following:

The Insert menu contains commands that place the common fields on your cover page. The fields are dropped into the center of the page, and you will need to drag them to their final destination. The fields are divided into three groups:

◆ Recipient

◆ Sender

◆ Message

The Recipient menu contains fields for the person's name and fax number. You will most likely want to include these in your cover page unless you're certain that the recipient is the only person at that number.

The Sender menu has a few more options. You can mix and match until you find the balance that's right for you. A good minimum might be to include your name and number, though your company name, office location, and department also might be useful.

The Message menu has only four options:

◆ Note

◆ Subject

◆ Date/Time Sent

◆ Number of Pages

At a minimum, include a Subject field and a Date/Time Sent field. Most cover pages include all four of these options as standard practice. Again, you'll have to decide what works best for you.

After you insert the fields that you want to include, you can drag them anywhere you want. In Figure 8.25, you can see that the Subject fields are highlighted with drag handles at the corners. These handles signify that you can move the fields by clicking anywhere in them and dragging them to a new position. You can also use the handles to resize the fields.

**FIGURE 8.25**

You can easily move any of the fields on your cover page.

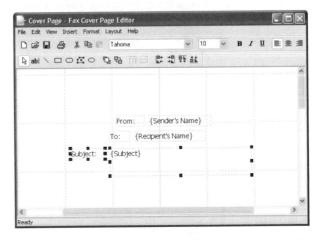

To select multiple fields, click somewhere near the outermost field in the group, and then, holding the mouse button down, drag the cursor until you've selected all the fields in the group. When you let go of the mouse button, all those fields will be selected, and you can move them as a unit.

## Advanced Cover Page Editing

Well, now you can create a simple cover page that contains all the necessary information. But just having the basic information is, yawn, so dull. You need to spice it up a bit with some graphics.

You can use the tools on the Drawing toolbar to add some visual interest to your cover page. The shapes and text buttons are much like those in the Paint program included with Windows XP Professional, but the Fax Cover Page Editor also includes some tools such as Send to Back and Send to Front that make it simple to create some great layered looks.

Here are the buttons you'll be using in the Fax Cover Page Editor:

| | | |
|---|---|---|
| ↖ | **Select** | The standard arrow cursor that you can use to select and move items on the page. |
| ab| | **Text** | Changes the cursor to a crosshair style and lets you draw a box in which to place text. |
| ╲ | **Line** | Draws lines of different types based on the Format settings. |
| ▢ | **Rectangle** | Draws a simple rectangular shape. If you configure the fill settings before drawing, the rectangle can be filled or colored. |

| | Rounded Rectangle | Draws a rectangle that has rounded corners. |
|---|---|---|
| | Polygon | Draws, well, *polygons*. That may not be too clear, but each time you click your mouse button you will define a vertex of a polygon. When you are satisfied with the shape, double-click the last "corner" to stop drawing. |
| | Ellipse | Draws circles or ovals. |
| | Send to Front | Moves the selected field or object to the front of the picture or to the top of the stack of images. |
| | Send to Back | Sends the selected object to the back of the picture. |
| | Space Across | Evenly spaces the selected objects across the page horizontally. |
| | Space Down | Evenly distributes the selected objects vertically on the page. |
| | Align Left | Aligns the selected objects with the left of the page. |
| | Align Right | Aligns the selected objects with the right side of the page. |
| | Align Top | Aligns the selected objects with the top of the page. |
| | Align Bottom | Aligns the selected objects with the bottom of the page. |

Using these tools, you can create very complex or very simple cover pages. When you have finished your work of art, be sure to save it so that it will be available in the future.

## Summary

This chapter has covered printing and font management. You learned how to set up local and network printers, and how to fine-tune their operation using their Properties. You also learned to manage a print queue, to install and remove fonts, and to change the display font in Windows. In the next chapter, you'll learn how to install and configure hardware devices.

# Chapter 9

# Installing and Configuring Hardware

Windows XP makes it easier than ever to install and configure new hardware. Its full support of Plug and Play, USB, FireWire, and other technologies makes for effortless installation of most new hardware. And for those situations where Plug and Play doesn't work quite right, Windows XP includes several utilities for helping identify and correct the problem.

- ◆ How hardware interacts with Windows XP
- ◆ Using hot-pluggable devices
- ◆ Using the hardware wizards
- ◆ Disabling a device
- ◆ Uninstalling a device
- ◆ Adding some specific hardware items

## How Hardware Interacts with Windows XP

Let's start out this chapter with a little background information about Windows XP's support for hardware devices.

### Device Drivers

Each device—whether it's a modem, a sound card, a printer, or whatever—speaks its own language. In order for Windows to communicate with a device, a *device driver* for it needs to be installed. A device driver is a program that translates between Windows and the actual piece of hardware. Most device drivers also include user-adjustable settings that you can use to fine-tune the device's behavior, as you saw in Chapter 8 with printer drivers.

The driver files themselves usually have a .sys extension, but there may be helper files associated with them that use other extensions. For example, there might be a file with a .dll extension (Dynamic Link Library), an .hlp extension (a Help file for the device), a .cpl extension (for Control Panel access to the device's properties), an .htm extension (a web document) containing help information, and others.

**NOTE**  The drivers that come with Windows are stored in the file Driver.cab on the Windows XP CD or in the %Systemroot%\Driver Cache\i386 folder on your hard disk.

For almost a decade now, nearly all hardware manufactured has included support for a standard called *Plug and Play* in Windows. It enables Windows to detect the hardware automatically and install the correct driver for it from its own internal database of drivers. Windows XP includes thousands of drivers for popular hardware items. If the correct driver is not available through Windows XP itself, it prompts you to insert the disk provided by the device manufacturer and copies the needed driver from that location to your hard drive. From then on, each time Windows starts up, the driver for that device loads automatically.

### DRIVER SIGNING

One reason that earlier versions of Windows could become unstable was because of an outdated or corrupted device driver. This was a problem because not all device manufacturers produced error-free drivers and because sometimes, different devices used driver files of the same name that would overwrite one another when you installed a new device. To combat this problem, Microsoft came up with a way of attaching a digital signature to a device driver to certify that it is capable of working with Windows XP and has not been modified since its creation. Drivers that live up to this standard are known as *signed drivers*. When you install a new device, Windows will prefer a signed driver to an unsigned one. If only an unsigned driver is available, you'll see a warning before Windows installs it.

Should you install an unsigned driver? It's a gamble. An unsigned driver could cause system instability, including lockups and blue-screen error messages. On the other hand, the unsigned driver might work just fine. You never know. Try searching the device manufacturer's website for a signed driver first; if you can't find one, back up your Windows configuration with System Restore before installing the unsigned driver.

**TIP**   The default security setting for driver signing is to warn you but allow you to install an unsigned driver if you confirm the warning. If you want some other setting, such as to always allow unsigned drivers without a warning or never allow them, open the System Properties (by right-clicking My Computer or going through Control Panel) and, in the Hardware tab, click the Driver Signing button. This opens a dialog box where you can adjust that setting.

In a few cases, a certain driver may be known to cause problems in Windows XP. If you try to install such a driver, a feature called Windows Driver Protection will kick in and refuse to allow you to install it. Windows XP comes with a database listing the prohibited drivers, and when you use Windows Update, this database gets updated from Microsoft.

### INF FILES

When Windows searches for a driver for a device, it isn't looking directly for the driver file(s); instead it's looking for an information file (`.inf` extension). This is a text file that tells what driver files should be used for the device and what settings for it should be entered into the Registry. Figure 9.1 shows an INF file for an IDE controller card, for example.

For some devices, the INF file is actually all there is to the driver. For example, if you have a driver disk for a monitor, chances are that there aren't any real "drivers" for that monitor; there's just an INF file that describes the monitor to the Registry for the purposes of defining the maximum resolution and refresh rate that should be allowed.

**FIGURE 9.1**
This INF file tells Windows how to install the drivers for an IDE controller card.

```
; ULTRA.INF
; Copyright 2000 Promise Technology, Inc.

[Version]
CatalogFile=Ultra.cat
signature="$CHICAGO$"
Class=SCSIAdapter
ClassGUID={4D36E97B-E325-11CE-BFC1-08002BE10318}
Provider=%PROMISE%
DriverVer=02/19/2001, 1.60 Build 36

;Class Install
[ClassInstall32.NT]
Addreg=SCSIReg

[SCSIReg]
HKR,,,,%SCSIClassName%
HKR,,Installer32,,"SysSetup.Dll,ScsiClassInstaller"
HKR,,Icon,,"-10"
HKR,,LegacyInfOption,,"SCSI"

[DestinationDirs]
DefaultDestDir = 12 ; DIRID_DRIVERS
MoveMiniPort.NT = 12;

[ControlFlags]

[Manufacturer]
%Promise%=Promise

[Promise]
%PCI\VEN_105A&DEV_4D30&SUBSYS_4D33105A.DeviceDesc%=ultra100PCI,PCI\VEN_105A&DEV_4D30&SUBSYS
[ultra100PCI.NT]
CopyFiles=MoveMiniPort.NT
```

### DRIVER VERSIONS

Windows XP works best when all device drivers are written specifically for Windows XP. However, if such a driver is not available for a critical piece of hardware, you may be forced to try a driver written for an earlier version of Windows.

Since Windows XP is based on Windows 2000, the Windows 2000 driver, if available, is your best bet. If that's not available, try the Windows NT 4 driver. Drivers written for Windows 9x or Windows Me will probably not work in Windows XP because the operating systems are too different.

## System Resources

Each device requires system resources. These resources can include a range of I/O addresses, an interrupt request (IRQ) line, and/or a direct memory access (DMA) channel. Or, to be more precise, the controller through which the device is attached requires the resources. For example, even though you might have two hard disks on an IDE bus, that IDE bus takes up only one set of system resources. Another example: you might have six SCSI or USB devices chained together on a single interface, but that interface would use only one resource.

### IRQs

When the CPU communicates with a device, the CPU must initiate the conversation. The device must signal to the CPU, "Hey, I need to talk to you!" and that's the purpose of IRQs. A device has an assigned IRQ, and whenever it needs attention, it places a message on that bus. The CPU receives it and initiates a conversation. On most systems there are 16 IRQs, numbered 0 through 15, but over half of them are preassigned to system devices such as the keyboard, system clock, and built-in IDE controllers.

CHAPTER 9

**NOTE**   On chipsets that use an Advanced Programmable Interrupt Controller (APIC), more than 16 IRQs might be listed in use in Device Manager. You can find a somewhat dated (2001), but still valuable article about the APIC at www.microsoft.com/whdc/system/sysperf/IO-APIC.mspx. This article is part of a larger site at Microsoft called Hardware and Driver Central, directly accessible at www.microsoft.com/whdc/default.mspx, which contains many useful articles about hardware resource allocation in Windows.

When you install a new piece of hardware, an IRQ must be assigned to its controller.

Some devices have a built-in controller that requires the IRQ. An internal modem would fit that description, for example. Other devices share a controller with others—for example, a SCSI device shares a SCSI interface card with up to six other devices, and a USB device can share a USB root hub. Therefore it's advantageous to choose USB or SCSI devices when they are available.

So what happens if all the IRQs are taken? It depends on the device. If it's an Industry Standard Architecture (ISA) device, there's not much you can do, because all ISA devices require their own separate IRQ. However, ISA is virtually obsolete, so you probably won't find yourself working on systems with a lot of ISA devices. If it's a Peripheral Connect Interface (PCI) device, there should not be a problem because PCI devices can automatically share IRQs. Windows will assign multiple PCI devices to the same IRQ, and no conflict will occur.

### I/O ADDRESSES

In addition to the IRQ, the device must have a meeting area for its conversations with the CPU. This assigned area for the device is its I/O address. This is a section of the PC's memory set aside for that device's use. Some devices have a range of memory addresses. Memory addresses are expressed in hexadecimal, so you might have a range like DF68–DF6F. Some devices might have multiple ranges. Since there is more memory to go around than there are IRQs, I/O address conflicts are rare.

### DMA CHANNELS

Some devices have a way of working directly with memory, circumventing the CPU, for faster performance. This is called direct memory access (DMA), and in order to do it, the device must have a DMA channel assigned to it. This is most common for keyboards and sound cards. Some IDE devices can also use DMA. Each device that uses DMA must have a unique DMA address (0 through 5).

### HOW RESOURCES ARE ASSIGNED

Plug and Play also manages the system resource assignments for the devices, ensuring that there are no conflicts. When Windows starts up, it makes a list of the available system resources and then doles them out to devices, trying for a "best fit" so that all devices have what they need.

Devices that are not Plug and Play compatible typically have jumpers on them for manually setting resource assignments. If your system includes one or more such devices, you should make a note of their manually set assignments and then make sure that Windows uses those same assignments in Device Manager (covered later in this chapter).

## What Happens When You Install a Device in Windows?

When Windows automatically detects a new device, or when you run the Setup program for a device or install it with Add New hardware, a number of things happen:

◆  Registry entries are made for the new device.

- If the device requires any drivers, they are copied to your hard drive.

- If the device requires any system resources, Windows claims them on behalf of the device so they won't be assigned to anything else.

Depending on the device, you may see some or all of these tangible signs of the device being installed:

- The device appears in the Device Manager listing.

- A New Hardware bubble appears briefly in the notification area.

- An icon for controlling the new device appears in Control Panel. Some Windows-only modems do this.

- An icon for controlling the new device appears in My Computer. Some digital cameras do this, but only when the camera is physically connected to the PC.

**NOTE**   If a device's Setup program does add a Control Panel applet, you'll find it only in Classic view, not Category view.

## Using Hot-Pluggable Devices

Hardware devices that use USB, FireWire, and PC Card connections are *hot pluggable*—you can plug in and unplug the device while Windows is running, without any adverse effects. Windows automatically loads and unloads drivers for hot-pluggable devices as needed. Serial ATA hard disks are also hot pluggable, although you would not commonly connect or disconnect one while the system was running.

**NOTE**   Limited users and Guest users can install hot-pluggable devices. This is good because it enables someone to sit down at a computer and connect a flash memory device, for example. However, only Computer Administrator users or users with administrative privileges can install devices that are not hot pluggable.

When you plug in a hot-pluggable device for the first time, Windows displays a pop-up message in the notification area to let you know that it has noticed the device. Windows then automatically looks for a driver to let Windows and the device communicate with each other. It first checks in its capacious driver cache, which contains a wide variety of preinstalled drivers. If it draws a blank there, and if your computer is connected to the Internet, it checks the Windows Update site for a driver for the device; if it finds a driver, it downloads it and installs it. If Windows is able to find a suitable driver in either the driver cache or Windows Update, it unpacks and installs the driver, displaying a pop-up message identifying the device as it does so.

When the driver is installed and working, Windows displays a pop-up message telling you that the hardware is ready to use.

If Windows can't find a driver for the device, it starts the Found New Hardware Wizard, so that you can supply the driver for the device manually. I'll discuss how to use the Found New Hardware Wizard in just a minute.

Removing a USB device or FireWire device is as simple as unplugging it. Windows notices that you've removed the device and unloads its driver. Any data transfers that were in progress are aborted.

CHAPTER 9

If the device is one through which you are transferring important data, such as an external drive, you might want to use the Safely Remove Hardware feature to ensure that all transfers have completed before you unplug the device. To do so, double-click the Safely Remove Hardware icon in the notification area. The Safely Remove Hardware dialog box opens. Select the device you are going to unplug and click Stop. Then, when a message appears that the device has been stopped, you can click Close and then unplug the device.

When you plug a hot-pluggable device in again, Windows notices it and loads the driver without displaying any pop-up message.

## Using the Hardware Wizards

For devices that aren't hot pluggable, or for hot-pluggable devices for which Windows can't find a suitable driver, you use Windows' two hardware wizards, the Found New Hardware Wizard and the Add Hardware Wizard.

When Windows discovers some hardware for which it can't find a suitable driver, it starts the Found New Hardware Wizard. Figure 9.2 shows this wizard's first screen.

**FIGURE 9.2**
The first screen of the Found New Hardware Wizard

As you can see in the figure, the wizard lists the type of hardware it has found—in this case, the Multimedia Controller. If the wizard can't identify the type of hardware, it displays *Unknown Device*. The What Do You Want the Wizard to Do? list gives you two options:

**Install the Software Automatically**  Select this option button (which is usually selected by default) if you want the wizard to have a go at installing the software needed for the hardware. This is usually a good option: the wizard often manages to set up the hardware, and if it doesn't, you can easily return to this stage and try the second option. Click the Next button. The wizard searches for the software and installs it automatically.

**Install from a List or Specific Location**  Select this option button if you want to specify a particular driver for the hardware. Then follow the procedure described in the next section.

If the Found New Hardware Wizard *doesn't* find the driver it needs, it displays the Cannot Install This Hardware screen (shown in Figure 9.3).

**FIGURE 9.3**

The Found New Hard-
ware Wizard displays the
Cannot Install This Hard-
ware screen if it can't
find the software needed
for the device. Click the
Back button if you want
to return to the start of
the wizard so that you
can try the procedure
manually.

At this point, you have three choices:

◆ If you want to give up on installing the software for this hardware completely (or at least for the foreseeable future), make sure the Don't Prompt Me Again to Install This Software check box is selected. Then click the Finish button. The wizard closes itself and makes a note not to find this piece of hardware again.

◆ If you want to give up on installing the software for the time being, clear the Don't Prompt Me Again to Install This Software check box. Then click the Finish button. Each time you restart Windows (or run the Add New Hardware Wizard), the Found New Hardware Wizard will offer to install the hardware. These offers get old fast, but you may sometimes want to leave the installation of hardware for a day or two while you dig out the driver disk or download a new driver.

◆ To try to identify the necessary software yourself, click the Back button to return to the start of the wizard. Then follow the steps in the next section.

## Installing a Driver from a Specific Location

To install a driver from a specific location, take the following steps:

1. On the first screen of the Found New Hardware Wizard (Figure 9.2), select the Install from a List or Specific Location option button.

2. Click the Next button. The Found New Hardware Wizard displays the Please Choose Your Search and Installation Options screen.

3. Choose whether to let the wizard search for a driver or to specify a specific driver:

◆ To let the wizard search, leave the Search for the Best Driver in These Locations option button selected. Then select the Search Removable Media (Floppy, CD-ROM) check box if you want the wizard to search your floppy and CD-ROM drives. (Insert a floppy or CD at this point if appropriate.) Alternatively, or additionally, select the Include This Location in the

CHAPTER 9

Search check box and use the text box, drop-down list, or Browse button to specify the location to search.

◆ To specify a driver yourself, select the Don't Search. I Will Choose the Driver to Install option button.

**4.** Click the Next button.

◆ If you choose to search for a driver, the wizard searches for one, installs it (if it finds one), and displays the Completing the Found New Hardware Wizard screen.

◆ If you choose to specify a driver, the wizard displays the Hardware Type screen (shown in Figure 9.4).

**FIGURE 9.4**
On the Hardware Type screen of the Found New Hardware Wizard, choose the type of hardware you're installing.

**5.** In the Common Hardware Types list box, select the type of hardware you're installing. The list is extensive, but if the device doesn't fit any of the descriptions, select the Show All Devices item.

**TIP** If you're installing a driver from a floppy or a CD, it's not crucial that you get the Hardware Type right. The function of this screen is to display the appropriate list of manufacturers and devices on the Select the Device Driver You Want to Install for This Hardware screen of the wizard.

**6.** Click the Next button. The Found New Hardware Wizard displays the Select the Device Driver You Want to Install for This Hardware screen. Figure 9.5 shows this screen with all devices shown.

**7.** If Windows has a driver for the device, you can select it by selecting the manufacturer in the Manufacturers list box and the device in the Models list box. But usually the Found New Hardware Wizard will have identified the driver if Windows has it already, so you'll be visiting this screen of the wizard only if you need to install a driver that Windows *doesn't* have. Click the Have Disk button. Windows displays the Install from Disk dialog box.

**FIGURE 9.5**
On the Select the Device Driver You Want to Install for This Hardware screen, select the manufacturer and device, or click the Have Disk button to identify the driver by its file.

8. If you have the driver on a floppy or a CD, insert it in the appropriate drive and select the drive in the Copy Manufacturer's Files From drop-down list. If you have the driver on a local drive or network drive, click the Browse button, use the resulting Locate File dialog box (a common Open dialog box) to locate the driver file, and click the Open button to enter its name and path in the Copy Manufacturer's Files From text box.

9. Click the OK button. The wizard displays the Select the Device Driver You Want to Install for This Hardware screen (shown in Figure 9.6) again, this time with the name of the hardware model or models identified by the driver.

**FIGURE 9.6**
When you specify the driver to use, the wizard displays the Select the Device Driver You Want to Install for This Hardware screen.

10. Select the driver and click the Next button. If Windows doesn't think the driver is correct for the device, it displays the Update Driver Warning dialog box, warning you that the hardware may not work and that your computer might become unstable or stop working. Click the Yes button if you're sure you want to install this driver. Otherwise, click the No button and select another driver.

CHAPTER 9

**NOTE** If the wizard can't find hardware information in the location you specified, it displays the Select Device message box telling you that the location you specified doesn't contain information about your hardware. The wizard then displays the Install from Disk dialog box again so that you can specify a different location for the file. If you get to this stage, you're probably stuck. You can click the Cancel button to close the Install from Disk dialog box and return to the Select the Device Driver You Want to Install for This Hardware screen so that you can select a built-in driver, but that's about it. Click the Cancel button to cancel the wizard.

**11.** The wizard checks to make sure that the driver you're installing has passed the Windows Logo testing to verify its compatibility with Windows XP. This is basically the same thing as driver signing, explained earlier in the chapter. If the driver has passed Windows Logo testing, all is well; if it hasn't passed, the wizard displays a warning box warning you of the problem and strongly discouraging you from installing the driver. If you're sure the driver is okay, click the Continue Anyway button. If you have any doubts about the driver, click the STOP Installation button.

**12.** If Windows finds no problem with the driver, it installs it and displays the Completing the Found New Hardware Wizard screen.

**13.** Click the Finish button. Once the wizard closes, the hardware is ready for use.

If the Found New Hardware Wizard is unable to install the device, it displays the Cannot Install This Hardware screen telling you what the problem was.

**NOTE** Help and Support Center contains a system for referring searches for drivers that don't come with Windows or with the hardware device. When you plug in a new hardware device and Windows finds that it doesn't have a driver for it and you can't supply a driver, Windows invites you to send information about the hardware to Microsoft. Once you've sent the information, you can take a variety of actions depending on what information is available. For example, you might be able to view a list of compatible devices (if any), search for information on compatible devices or Knowledge Base articles about the hardware, or find a link to the vendor's website.

## Running the Add Hardware Wizard

If Windows doesn't find the new hardware you want to install, run the Add Hardware Wizard so that you can add the hardware manually. As you'll see, there's considerable overlap between the Add Hardware Wizard and the Found New Hardware Wizard, so don't be surprised if some of the steps in this list duplicate those in the previous section.

To run the Add Hardware Wizard, follow these steps:

**1.** Choose Start ➢ Control Panel. Windows displays Control Panel.

**2.** Click the Printers and Other Hardware link. Windows displays the Printers and Other Hardware screen.

**3.** Click the Add Hardware link in the See Also pane. Windows starts the Add Hardware Wizard, which displays the Welcome to the Add Hardware Wizard screen.

**4.** Click the Next button. The wizard searches for new hardware.

5. You might be prompted at this point to choose Yes, I Have Already Connected the Hardware, or No I Have Not Added the Hardware Yet. Make the appropriate selection and click Next.

6. The wizard then displays a list with the heading The Following Hardware Is Already Installed on Your Computer (shown in Figure 9.7). If the device you want to install is listed in the Installed Hardware list box, select it. If it's not, select the Add a New Hardware Device item in the list box—the last item in the list.

**FIGURE 9.7**

On the The Following Hardware Is Already Installed on Your Computer screen of the Add Hardware Wizard, select the Add a New Hardware Device item.

**NOTE** If the Add Hardware Wizard doesn't find any hardware it didn't already know about, it displays the Is the Hardware Connected? screen, which asks whether you've already connected the hardware to the computer. Select the Yes, I Have Already Connected the Hardware option button or the No, I Have Not Added the Hardware Yet option button as appropriate. If you select the Yes, I Have Already Connected the Hardware option button, the wizard displays the The Following Hardware Is Already Installed on Your Computer screen. If you select the No, I Have Not Added the Hardware Yet option button, the wizard displays the Cannot Continue the Add Hardware Wizard screen, which offers to turn off the computer for you so that you can connect the hardware and try the Add Hardware Wizard again.

7. Click the Next button. The wizard displays the The Wizard Can Help You Install Other Hardware screen (shown in Figure 9.8), offering to search for the hardware.

8. Select the Install the Hardware That I Manually Select from a List (Advanced) option button.

9. Click the Next button. The wizard displays the From the List Below, Select the Type of Hardware You Are Installing screen.

10. In the Common Hardware Types list box, select the type of hardware you're installing. Again, if the device doesn't fit any of the descriptions, select the Show All Devices item.

11. Click the Next button. If you choose the Show All Devices item, the wizard displays the Select the Device Driver You Want to Install for This Hardware screen (shown in Figure 9.9). If you choose a specific type of hardware, the wizard leads you off on a byway of options appropriate to that type of hardware.

CHAPTER 9

**FIGURE 9.8**
The Add Hardware Wizard offers to search for the hardware, but usually you'll do better to select it manually.

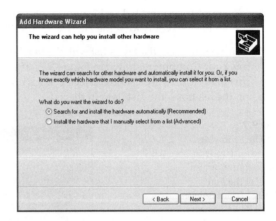

12. If Windows has a driver for the device, select it by selecting the manufacturer in the Manufacturers list box and the device in the Models list box. If you have a new driver, click the Have Disk button and use the resulting Install from Disk dialog box to specify the location of the driver.

13. Click the Next button. The wizard displays the The Wizard Is Ready to Install Your Hardware screen, listing the hardware that's lined up for installation.

**FIGURE 9.9**
On the Select the Device Driver You Want to Install for This Hardware screen of the Add Hardware Wizard, select the device driver.

14. Click the Next button. The wizard installs the hardware and displays the Completing the Add Hardware Wizard screen.

15. Click the Finish button. The Add Hardware Wizard closes itself. The hardware should be ready for use.

## Disabling a Device

If you want to stop using a device temporarily, you can disable it. For example, you might want to disable a device that you think is making Windows unstable as a troubleshooting strategy. Or you might want to create multiple hardware profiles (covered in Chapter 6) and disable certain devices in certain profiles.

To disable a device, open Device Manager by clicking Start, right-clicking My Computer to open the System Properties dialog box, clicking the Hardware tab, and then clicking the Device Driver button. Right-click the device, and then choose Disable from the shortcut menu. Windows displays a confirmation message box such as that shown in Figure 9.10. Click the Yes button. Windows closes the message box and disables the device.

**FIGURE 9.10**
Windows displays a confirmation message box when you instruct it to disable a device.

## Uninstalling a Device

If you want to stop using a device permanently and want to remove it from your computer, uninstall it first. To do so, right-click the device in Device Manager and choose Uninstall from the shortcut menu. Windows displays the Confirm Device Removal dialog box. Click the OK button. Windows closes the dialog box and uninstalls the device.

Uninstalling a device from Device Manager without physically removing it from the PC may result in Windows redetecting it and reinstalling it the next time you start up (or the next time you refresh the listing in Device Manager). Perhaps that's what you want, if you were removing it only so that you could reinstall it as a troubleshooting technique. But more likely, you really don't want it to appear, even though you plan to leave it physically connected. In a case like that, you would be better off disabling it (see the preceding section), since then it won't come back automatically.

**NOTE**   You can also uninstall a device by clicking the Uninstall button on the Driver tab of its Properties dialog box; this is covered in the next section.

## Working with Device Properties

Device drivers have properties, just like any other files. The properties for the device driver determine how the device behaves, so it's important to know how to set them. In the following sections, I'll explain some basics that apply to any type of device, and then we'll look at configuring some specific device types.

### Viewing Device Properties

Some device types have their own applet in Control Panel, through which you can see all of the installed devices of that type and work with their properties. Modems are like that, for example.

However, you can also work with the Device Manager, which lists all devices of all types. Most people find this the most expedient way to check on multiple device types. To display Device Manager (shown in Figure 9.11), do the following:

1. Right-click My Computer and choose Properties.

2. Click the Hardware tab, and then click the Device Manager button.

Click a plus (+) sign to open a category. In Figure 9.11, the Network Adapters category is open. Then double-click a device to see its properties (or click it once and then click the Properties button in the toolbar).

**FIGURE 9.11**
Device Manager displays all installed hardware in a single location.

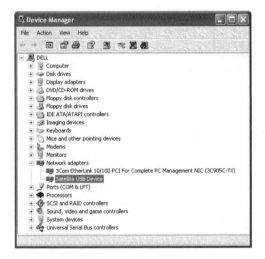

## Viewing and Changing Drivers

You can work with a device's drivers in the Drivers tab of its Properties box. Figure 9.12 shows the Drivers tab for a satellite USB device, for example.

From the Drivers tab, you can choose:

◆ Driver Details to see exactly what files are being used for the device.

◆ Update Driver to start the Hardware Update Wizard. It's like the Add New Hardware Wizard except it searches for better drivers for an existing device.

◆ Roll Back Driver to revert to a previously used driver after using Update Driver.

◆ Uninstall to completely remove the device's drivers.

**FIGURE 9.12**
View, change, or remove drivers here.

## Viewing and Changing Resource Assignments

Plug and Play automatically assigns resources to a device. In earlier versions of Windows, Plug and Play technology was not fully reliable, so it was a rather common occurrence to need to adjust the resource allocations manually. However, in Windows XP, Plug and Play works well nearly every time; in fact, with an ACPI-compliant system, it can be rather difficult to find a resource it will let you modify. That's because ACPI takes control of most of your Plug and Play devices and runs its own show.

If No Conflicts appears in the Conflicting device list, the current resource assignments are okay. If, on the other hand, you see one or more conflicting devices listed there, you might want to try to resolve the conflict by assigning different resources either to this device or to one of the conflicting ones.

**FIGURE 9.13**
View resource assignments here, and change them if there are conflicts.

**NOTE**    If the Use Automatic Settings check box is available, as it is in Figure 9.13, you will be able to try manual resource assignments for the device. In Windows XP, however, for the vast majority of devices, this check box will not be available, and you will not be able to manually change resources.

If a device is working okay, you should not change its resource assignments. Windows XP works best when you allow Plug and Play to handle all resource allocations automatically.

If you do need to change resources, do the following:

1. Deselect the Use Automatic Settings check box in the device's Resources tab. The other controls in the dialog box become available.

2. Open the Setting Based On drop-down list and choose a different configuration. Keep trying configurations until you find one that reports No Conflicts in the Conflicting Devices list.

**TIP**    If you cannot find one that reports No Conflicts, you can try setting an individual resource manually. To do so, select it from the Resource Settings area and then click Change Setting. For most devices, you won't be allowed to do this; you'll see an error message. However, some devices do allow this, and if it's possible, it's one possible way around an otherwise irresolvable resource conflict.

3. Click OK to close the device's properties.

**TIP**    Here's a little-known tweak for all you hard-core techies out there. For more control over manual resource assignments in Windows XP, set the ACPI driver to Standard PC instead of its default of ACPI PC. To do so, view the properties for ACPI in Device Manager (in the Computer category). Go to the Driver tab and choose Update Driver. Then choose Install from a List or Specific Location, and then choose Don't Search. In the list that appears, select Standard PC and then complete the wizard. Warning: power management features like Standby and Hibernate will no longer work, and you will probably need to reinstall the drivers for some of your devices.

## Configuring a Modem

If your modem is Plug and Play (and it probably is if you acquired your computer within the last decade), Windows XP Professional will recognize and install it automatically. If not, you can use the Add Hardware Wizard as described earlier in the chapter.

**NOTE** Windows XP uses a universal modem driver called Unimodem. Unimodem is the software interface between all your computer's 32--bit Windows-compatible communications applications (including the ones that use TAPI) and your modem or other communications hardware. It includes integrated control for port selection, modem initialization, speed, file transfer protocols, and terminal emulation. Because Unimodem handles the modem configuration, you only have to specify setup parameters once.

After you install your modem, all your TAPI-aware communications programs will use the same configuration settings. When you change them in one application, those changes carry across to all the others.

To change the modem's properties, open up Phone and Modem Options in Control Panel. (It's in the Printers and Other Hardware category if you're using Category view.) Then in the Modems tab, select the modem you want to work with and click Properties. Figure 9.14 displays the Properties dialog box for an MDP 7800-U modem.

**FIGURE 9.14**

Use this Properties dialog box to change your modem configuration.

Here are some highlights of the modem properties you can set.
In the Modem tab:

**Speaker Volume**   This controls the internal speaker in the modem. It does not affect the sound coming through your speakers.

**Maximum Port Speed**   Leave this at the default in most cases. You might reduce it if your modem is having connection problems at higher speeds and you want to limit its speed for greater reliability.

**Dial Control**   Normally you want the modem to detect a dial tone before dialing; deselect this check box if you don't.

On the Diagnostics tab:

**Query Modem** Click this button if you aren't sure whether the modem is installed correctly. This utility sends some test codes to the modem and shows the modem's response. This is handy because the modem does not have to be connected to a phone line for the test to work. See Figure 9.15.

**FIGURE 9.15**
The Diagnostics tab of the Modem Properties dialog box lets you test your modem configuration and set logging options.

In the Advanced tab (Figure 9.16):

**Extra initialization settings** You can enter AT commands here if the modem requires any special codes to be sent to it before it dials. For example, some programs like AOL send special initialization strings to the modem, and they can sometimes cause the modem to drop the carrier or have other problems. You could type **&FI** in this box to tell the modem to use its built-in factory settings instead of the initialization string that a particular program sends.

**NOTE** AT commands, also known as Hayes commands, are codes that tell the modem how to operate. AT is short for "Attention" because the first two letters of a command are always AT to get the device's attention. They used to be a lot more common in the days before PPP and TCP/IP Internet connections. To find out more about AT commands, see www.modems.com/general/extendat.html.

**WARNING** You should exercise some caution here, though, and consult the documentation for your modem to verify the actions of the command before using it. If the command isn't right for your modem, using it could cause some real damage.

**Advanced Port Settings** This opens a dialog box (see Figure 9.17) where you can turn off/on FIFO buffers (First In, First Out), adjust the size of the Receive and Transmit buffers, and specify which COM port the modem uses. By default, the buffers are on and set to the highest settings. Turn them down or off to troubleshoot connection problems.

**Change Default Preferences** This opens a dialog box (Figure 9.18) in which you can set disconnect-when-idle settings and adjust some other low-level modem properties such as compression and flow control.

**FIGURE 9.16**
The Advanced tab of
the Modem Properties
dialog box

**FIGURE 9.17**
The Advanced Settings
dialog box

**FIGURE 9.18**
The Default Preferences
dialog box

## Configuring a CD Drive

Windows should detect new CD-ROM drives automatically without having to install any drivers for them. This includes most DVD and CD-RW drives too.

Depending on the model of DVD or CD-ROM drive, Windows may be able to work with it directly with no special software, or you may need to install the software that came with the device to enable its DVD or CD-RW functionality. However, all CD-ROM type drives should at least work as a generic CD-ROM drive with no extra setup.

There are two different Properties dialog boxes for a CD or DVD drive. One is accessible from Device Manager, and the other from My Computer.

### CONFIGURING A CD DRIVE FROM DEVICE MANAGER

From Device Manager, double-click the drive to display a Properties dialog box that controls its driver and some of the base-level settings. For example, as you can see in Figure 9.19, it has a Properties tab where you can change these settings:

**CD Player Volume slider**   Drag the slider to set the volume you want the CD player to deliver when playing audio CDs. This setting controls the output of the CD drive. You can control the output volume from your sound card by using Volume Control.

**Enable Digital CD Audio for This CD-ROM Device check box**   Select this check box if you want to use digital output rather than analog output from the CD drive for audio CDs. Digital output typically gives you higher audio quality, especially when you're copying audio CDs to your hard drive. Most newer CD-ROM drives and just about all DVD drives support digital output, but some older CD-ROM drives don't. If digital output doesn't work for you, clear this check box to return to analog output. Enabling digital output makes it possible to play an audio CD on a drive that does not have an audio patch cable running from the drive to the sound card inside the case.

**FIGURE 9.19**
On the Properties tab of the Properties dialog box for a CD-ROM drive, you can set the CD's volume and specify whether to use digital CD audio.

**TIP**  By default, CD-ROM drives are set to AutoPlay. That means any CDs play automatically if they have an `Autorun.inf` file on them. To turn off AutoPlay, run the command `GPEDIT.MSC` at the Run prompt. Then navigate to `Computer Configuration\Administrative Templates\System` and set the Turn Off Autoplay option to Enabled. This Group Policy Editor program is a good place to make other tweaks too; look around while you're there. Actually, there is an easier way to change a drive's AutoPlay setting. Just open up My Computer, right-click the CD drive, and choose Properties. A different Properties dialog box appears for the drive than the one shown in Figure 9.19, and it has an AutoPlay tab where you can control AutoPlay behavior for the drive.

---

### DVD ENCODING REGIONS

In case you've managed to avoid the question of DVD encoding regions: as far as DVDs are concerned, the world is divided into eight regions, or locales:

◆  Region 1 is the United States, Canada, and U.S. Territories.

◆  Region 2 is Europe, Japan, South Africa, and the Middle East.

◆  Region 3 is Southeast Asia, East Asia, and Hong Kong.

◆  Region 4 is Australia, New Zealand, the Pacific Islands, South America, Central America, Mexico, and the Caribbean.

◆  Region 5 is Eastern Europe, Mongolia, North Korea, the Indian subcontinent, and Africa.

◆  Region 6 is China.

◆  Region 7 is "reserved" (for off-world use, perhaps).

◆  Region 8 is for international vessels such as airplanes and cruise ships.

DVD players are encoded to play only DVDs for their region. Almost all DVDs are encoded for the region in which they're intended to be sold. (There are also all-region DVDs that will play in any region.) So to play a DVD, you need a player with a matching region code.

Most consumer-electronics DVD players are coded for one region only. Some players—typically more expensive ones—can play discs for two, more, or all regions. Other players can be *chipped*—modified—to play DVDs with different regional encoding or even to play any regional encoding.

PC DVD drives are a little more flexible. With most drives, you can switch regions a certain number of times before the drive goes into a locked state in which you can no longer change the region. The DVD Region tab of the Properties dialog box for the DVD drive displays the number of times you can change the region again. Use them sparingly.

Why do DVDs have regional encoding anyway? In theory, it's to let the movie studios control the release of the movie in different countries. For example, U.S.-made movies are usually released in the United States several months before they're released in Europe, and DVDs and videos of the movie are often released in the United States while the movie is still running in Europe. Regional encoding prevents most of the Europeans from viewing the movie on DVD until it's released with Region 2 encoding.

In practice, regional encoding also enables the distributors to charge different prices for DVDs in different countries without being undercut by imported DVDs from the least expensive regions. For example, at this writing, DVDs in Region 2 are substantially more expensive than those in Region 1, and the European Union is investigating whether this constitutes price-fixing.

The Properties dialog box for a DVD drive through Device Manager also contains a DVD Region tab, which displays the DVD encoding region currently set for the DVD player. To change the region, select the country you want in the list box and click the OK button.

### CONFIGURING A CD DRIVE FROM MY COMPUTER

In My Computer, you can right-click a CD drive and choose Properties to see a very different Properties dialog box. Some of its settings and information apply to the individual disc that happens to be inserted at the moment; others are for the drive itself. Here's a quick rundown:

**General** Shows the space usage on the individual disc, if one is inserted.

**Sharing** Enables you to share the drive on the network.

**Settings** Describes the status and specifications for the drive, such as its maximum read and write speeds, its name, and its firmware revision.

**Hardware** Shows a list of all local drives (not just this one). You can click on one and click Properties for more information about it.

**AutoPlay** Here you can specify what should happen when a disc is inserted. You can choose to be prompted every time, or choose a default action. See Figure 9.20.

**FIGURE 9.20**
This Properties box for a CD drive is accessible from My Computer, rather than Device Manager.

There might be other tabs here too, depending on the drive and on what software is installed. For example, since I have Roxio Easy CD Creator installed, I've got a DirectCD 5.0 Options tab in Figure 9.20.

## Configuring a Removable Drive

The first time you plug in a removable drive or a local drive and Windows finds pictures or audio files on it, Windows displays the Removable Disk dialog box or Local Drive dialog box to let you specify whether you want to set a default action to take with files of this type. Figure 9.21 shows an example of the Removable Disk dialog box for a CompactFlash card in a PC Card adapter. The CompactFlash card contains picture files, so the Removable Disk dialog box contains actions that Windows can take with picture files: Print the Pictures, View a Slideshow of the Images, Copy Pictures to a Folder on My Computer, Open Folder to View Files, or Take No Action. If this seems familiar, it's because it's basically the same as Figure 9.20. The options are different because it's a specific drive type, whereas in Figure 9.20 they were generic because no disc was inserted.

**FIGURE 9.21**

In the Local Disk dialog box or Removable Disk dialog box (shown here), you can specify which action you want Windows to take for a particular file type when you add a local disk or removable disk.

Select the action you want to take. If you want Windows to take this action for every disk you add that contains this type of file, select the Always Do the Selected Action check box. Then click the OK button. Windows closes the Local Disk dialog box or Removable Disk dialog box and takes the action you specified.

## Configuring a Video Card

When you install a new video card, Windows may detect it on startup and display the Found New Hardware Wizard so that you can install the correct driver for it. Other times, you may have to change the video driver manually by using the Hardware Update Wizard.

After installing the driver for the new video card, you usually need to restart Windows. When you log back in, Windows displays the Display Properties dialog box so that you can test and apply the screen resolution and color quality you want. See Chapter 4 for a discussion of how to choose a suitable screen resolution and color depth.

If you're seeing corrupt images on your monitor, or if the mouse pointer doesn't respond properly to conventional stimuli, or if DirectX isn't working, you may need to change the graphics hardware acceleration on your computer or disable write combining.

**NOTE**    Write combining is a method of shunting more information from the video card to the monitor at once. It can cause screen corruption by providing the monitor with more information than it can handle.

To do so, take the following steps:

1. Right-click open space on the Desktop and choose Properties from the shortcut menu to open the Display Properties dialog box.

2. Click the Settings tab.

3. Click the Advanced button to open the Monitor and Graphics Card Properties dialog box.

4.  Click the Troubleshoot tab, which is shown in Figure 9.22.

5.  Move the Hardware Acceleration slider one notch at a time from Full (or wherever you find it) toward None until the problems disappear. At each setting, click the Apply button, and check your computer to see the effect of the change.

6.  Alternatively, or additionally, try clearing the Enable Write Combining check box to prevent screen corruption. Click the Apply button and see the effect of the change.

7.  When the screen seems to be behaving as it should, click the OK button. Windows closes the Monitor and Graphics Card Properties dialog box, returning you to the Display Properties dialog box.

8.  Click the OK button. Windows closes the Display Properties dialog box.

**FIGURE 9.22**

If you see corrupt images on the screen, try reducing hardware acceleration or disabling write combining on the Troubleshoot tab of the Monitor and Graphics Card Properties dialog box.

## Viewing USB Hub Usage

USB hubs can support multiple devices. Each of these devices appears in Device Manager separately, but with no Resources tab since the device uses no system resources directly. The hub itself also appears there.

In Device Manager you may see several devices listed in the USB category. The ones associated with the motherboard (or add-on USB controller card) will have a Resources tab; it's the only one that directly draws resources. In Figure 9.23 that would be the Intel entries.

If you view its Properties, you find an Advanced tab that lists System Reserved as the only user of the device.

You'll also see a USB Root Hub entry, which is the system interface for the above-mentioned controller. It draws no resources directly. On some systems, any USB devices that are directly plugged into the USB ports on the PC appear in this device's Power tab. On others, the General Purpose USB Hub appears on its list and then the devices plugged directly into the PC's USB ports are in turn on the Power tab for the General Purpose USB Hub.

**FIGURE 9.23**
The Universal Serial Bus
Controllers section of
Device Manager shows
the USB management
devices.

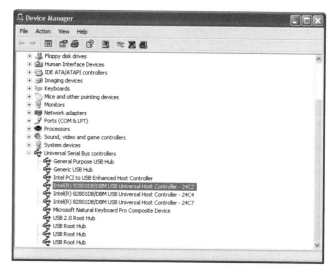

If you have any expansion hubs connected to the root hub, they also appear in Device Manager. In Figure 9.23 that would be the Generic USB Hub entry, representing a USB hub that's built into the base of my monitor. In its properties is a Power tab that lists the USB devices connected to it. See Figure 9.24.

**FIGURE 9.24**
View a USB hub's Power
tab to see what devices
use it.

If you have problems with USB devices, the first thing to check is the Power tab for the hub into which it is plugged. If there are many USB devices chained together coming through this hub, there may not be enough power to support them all; this Power tab can tell you how much power is available and how much is used. In Figure 9.24 there is only one device, but a single USB port can support up to 127 devices, provided they have enough power.

You would typically run into problems with power in situations where you are plugging in a device to an unpowered hub—such as the USB expansion port on a keyboard—and where the device being connected does not have its own power source and needs to draw a substantial amount of power. One example might be a USB Webcam. In such a case, Windows will throw up a warning that the device is underpowered, and you would need to connect it to one of the USB ports directly on the system unit instead.

## Using Multiple Monitors

Windows XP Professional lets you attach multiple monitors to your computer to increase the amount of Desktop space available to you. This feature can make both work and play much easier—but it can also lead you to loading your desk with more monitors than it can comfortably provide a footing for.

This discussion of using multiple monitors concerns only desktop computers to which you can add one or more extra graphics cards. But Windows XP also includes a feature called DualView that lets you use multiple monitors with portable computers and graphics cards with multiple outputs. Mentioned in Chapter 6, DualView works exactly the same way except with notebook PCs with both a built-in LCD screen and an external VGA port.

**WARNING**    Setting up multiple monitors can be a tricky and frustrating business. With some combinations of motherboards and graphics cards, you need to install the graphics cards in the right sequence in order to get them to work. Others work fine immediately. Others never work. Before you try to implement multiple monitors, check the Hardware Compatibility List (HCL) at the Microsoft website, www.microsoft.com, for details of the graphics cards that are known to work in multiple-monitor configurations with Windows XP.

To use multiple monitors, you need to make sure that your graphics cards work together (some graphics cards don't) and that your computer's motherboard supports multiple monitors (some motherboards don't). In most cases, you'll want to use an AGP graphics card (or one of the new PCI Express cards in a system that supports that) and one or more regular PCI graphics cards; two or more regular PCI graphics cards without an AGP or PCI Express card can provide a satisfactory solution as well. Many of the newer video cards have two inputs: one analog (VGA) and one digital (DVI.) so you can connect one CRT and one LCD (provided it has a digital input port) to a single video card.

The monitors, by contrast, don't need to know about each other—each gets its own input, so each can believe it's the only monitor in town if it wants to. So any monitors should do. You can mix CRTs and LCDs freely on a system, as long as you have the right ports to which to connect them.

**NOTE**    In the 1990s, large monitors were so expensive that it was much cheaper to buy two, three, or even four small monitors than one large one. That's now changed, at least with cathode-ray tube monitors (LCD monitors are still relatively expensive, at least when you're thinking about buying several of them.) There's no reason why you shouldn't have a monster monitor and a couple of satellite monitors if you want—or even two or more monsters...

To set up multiple monitors, power down your computer and insert the new graphics card. (You *can* install multiple graphics cards and monitors at a time, but unless you're very lucky and everything works, you'll be looking at some doubly confusing troubleshooting.) Connect the second monitor, and then power everything on. Don't be surprised if the bootup display appears on the second monitor rather than your primary one. After you log in to Windows, it should discover the new hardware, which will trigger a Found New Hardware notification-area pop-up followed by the Found

New Hardware Wizard. If Windows seems not to have noticed the new hardware, run the Add Hardware Wizard manually to add the graphics card and monitor.

Next, display the Settings tab of the Display Properties dialog box. For each monitor you want to use (hint: all of them), select the monitor and then select the Extend My Windows Desktop onto This Monitor. Once you've done that, let Windows know where the monitors are positioned in relation to each other by dragging the monitor icons into their relative positions. If you get confused as to which monitor is which, click the Identify button to have Windows flash up the number of each monitor on the monitor. Then set the screen resolution, color depth, and refresh rate for each monitor as usual.

Once you close the Display Properties dialog box, you should have a substantially enlarged Desktop. By default, the Taskbar appears on your primary monitor (the one that shows the boot sequence), but you can drag it to any of the other monitors as you see fit.

Maximizing a window maximizes it for the monitor it's currently (or mostly) on. You can extend a "normal" window across two or more monitors by dragging its window border to the appropriate size.

# Configuring Windows to Use an Uninterruptible Power Supply

One of the great benefits of a laptop computer is that its battery protects it from data loss when a power outage occurs. To get similar protection in a desktop computer, you need to attach a separate device—an uninterruptible power supply (UPS).

## What Is a UPS?

A UPS is essentially a large battery of above-average intelligence that sits between your computer and the electricity supply and ensures a steady power stream to your computer to protect it from blackouts, brownouts, and surges. Different UPSes do this in two different ways.

The simpler way is for the device to monitor power fluctuations and kick in when the power supply falls outside acceptable thresholds. Technically, this type of device is called a *standby power supply* (SPS) rather than a UPS, but you'll often hear SPSes described as UPSes.

The more complicated—and better—way is for the device to feed power to the computer continuously, charging itself when the power supply is running within acceptable parameters. This device is technically a UPS. This way of supplying power is better because the UPS delivers conditioned power to the computer all the time, protecting it better from fluctuations and avoiding the critical moment of changeover from main power to battery power that can be a drawback with an SPS.

## Choosing a UPS

If you're looking for a UPS, keep these features in mind:

**Operating system support**   Make sure the UPS is designed for use with Windows XP. With operating system support and an appropriate system management port (discussed next), the UPS can warn Windows XP when the electricity supply has failed. Windows can then shut itself down automatically if the computer is unattended. (More on this in a moment.)

**System management port**   Make sure the UPS has an appropriate system management port for your computer. Many UPSes use a serial port connection. Others use a USB connection.

**NOTE**   If you don't plan on connecting the PC and the UPS, you don't need to worry about a system management port or operating system support. Some people simply ignore their UPS's capability of communicating with the PC and treat it like a dumb battery backup.

**Indicators for line voltage and battery power**  The UPS should have one indicator to indicate when the incoming power to the UPS is okay and another indicator to indicate when the devices attached to the UPS are running on battery power. (Many UPSes also sound an alarm when battery power is being used.)

**Multiple power outlets**  Make sure the UPS has enough outlets for all the devices you want to plug into it directly.

**Enough power and battery life**  Before buying the UPS, work out how much power and battery life you need it to have. Make a list of the computers and devices you'll need to have plugged into the UPS, and then use a power-supply template such as that on the American Power Conversion Corp. website (`www.apc.com`) to calculate the number of volt-amps (VA) you'll need to keep the equipment running. (You can simply add up the voltages listed on the equipment, but be aware that the power-supply rating on your computer equipment shows the maximum power rather than typical power usage.) Then decide the amount of time you'll need to shut down the computers once the power alarm goes off. Generally speaking, the more power and battery life you need, the more the UPS will cost. If you just want a few minutes to allow you to shut down Windows under control (or to have Windows shut itself down), a modest and inexpensive UPS may fit the bill.

**TIP**  Unless you're convinced that you'll need to print during a power outage, don't plan to plug your printer into your UPS. Printers are power hogs. Laser printers are such power hogs that they can kill a UPS.

## Installing a UPS

Power down your computer, unplug the computer power source from the wall, and plug it into the UPS. (You might also need to connect a serial or USB cable from the UPS to the computer). Now, bring up the computer again, log on to Windows, and display the UPS tab of the Power Options Properties dialog box (shown in Figure 9.25).

**FIGURE 9.25**
The UPS tab of the Power Options Properties dialog box

To let Windows know about your UPS, take these steps:

1. Click the Select button to open the UPS Selection dialog box (shown here with American Power Conversion chosen in the Select Manufacturer drop-down list).

2. In the Select Manufacturer drop-down list, choose the manufacturer of your UPS. If the manufacturer isn't listed, choose the Generic item.

3. If the manufacturer was listed, specify the model of UPS in the Select Model list box, and select the port in the On Port drop-down list. Click the Finish button. Windows closes the UPS Selection dialog box, returning you to the Power Options Properties dialog box.

4. If the manufacturer wasn't listed, select the Custom item in the Select Model list box. Then click the Next button. Windows displays the UPS Interface Configuration dialog box. Consult your documentation, and then choose settings for Power Fail/On Battery, Low Battery, and UPS Shutdown as appropriate. Then click the Finish button. Windows closes the UPS Interface Configuration dialog box, returning you to the Power Options Properties dialog box.

CHAPTER 9

**5.** In the Power Options Properties dialog box, click the Configure button. Windows displays the UPS Configuration dialog box.

**6.** Select or clear the Enable All Notifications check box as appropriate. Adjust the value in the Seconds between Power Failure and First Notification text box and the Seconds between Subsequent Power Failure Notifications text box to suit your needs. For example, if your electricity supply suffers from mini-outages of a few seconds each, you might choose to increase the Seconds between Power Failure and First Notification setting to a value such as 20 or 30 seconds so that the UPS raises the alarm only for a more serious outage than usual.

**7.** In the Critical Alarm group box, specify what actions Windows should take when the UPS sends Windows a critical alarm, warning Windows that the UPS is almost out of battery power.

**Minutes on Battery before Critical Alarm check box and text box**   Select this check box if you want Windows to sound an alarm after the specified number of minutes running on battery power.

**When the Alarm Occurs, Run This Program check box and text box**   If you want Windows to run a program when an alarm occurs, select this check box and specify the program in the text box. For example, you might want to run a custom shutdown utility or use a program to send a warning to users of connected computers.

**Instruct the Computer To drop-down list**   In this drop-down list, choose Shut Down or Hibernate as appropriate.

**Turn Off the UPS check box**   Leave this check box selected (as it is by default) to have Windows turn off the UPS (and stop the alarm).

**8.** Click the OK button. Windows closes the UPS Configuration dialog box.

**9.** Click the Apply button. Windows applies your UPS settings. The Status section shows status information on your UPS, and the Details section shows the UPS's type.

**10.** Click the OK button.

## Summary

This chapter has discussed how to add and support new hardware items in Windows XP Professional. You can use this information when you're having trouble with a device and need to reconfigure it as well as when you get ready to install a new monitor, a DVD drive, or some other hardware device.

In the next chapter, you'll learn about Windows Media Player 10, the latest and greatest version of Microsoft's music and video player.

# Part 3

# XP Digital Media

**In this section you will learn how to:**

◆ Play digital music and video clips with Windows Media Player
◆ Play audio CDs and DVDs
◆ Listen to Internet radio
◆ Record sounds with Sound Recorder
◆ Manage digital photographic images
◆ Create movies with Windows Movie Maker

# Chapter 10

# Windows Media Player

This chapter discusses how to use Windows Media Player, the powerful multimedia player incorporated in Windows XP. A vast improvement on its predecessor of the same name, Windows Media Player not only provides features for enjoying audio and video, but it also supports ripping (that is, copying CD tracks to your hard disk) and burning (making audio CDs from digital audio files). It also covers sound volume control and the Sound Recorder. In this chapter, you'll learn about

- Configuring Windows Media Player
- Playing music in Windows Media Player
- Understanding digital rights management
- Copying a CD to your hard disk
- Tuning in to Internet radio
- Backing up and restoring digital licenses
- Using Volume Control to control output and input
- Recording and converting sounds with Sound Recorder

## Introducing Windows Media Player

Windows Media Player is a multipurpose player that plays music, video clips, DVD movies, and Internet radio. It rips, burns, and copies files to portable digital players. In short, it does virtually everything that most people would want a media player to do.

Windows XP originally came with Windows Media Player 8, but since then two more versions have been released: 9 and 10. You can download an update to the latest version from Microsoft, and I highly recommend that you do so. (Just choose Tools ➤ Check for Updates in your current version.) In this chapter, I'll cover only the latest version as of this writing—version 10. Version 10 is a dramatic improvement over earlier versions, incorporating features that users have been clamoring for, and it also arranges features differently in the hierarchy. For example, Internet radio no longer warrants its own tab; now it's blended in with the online Guide. I'll point out some of the other differences throughout this chapter as we go along.

Start Windows Media Player by choosing Start ➤ All Programs ➤ Windows Media Player. Or, if you have the Quick Launch toolbar displayed, click the Windows Media Player icon there.

Versions 8 and 9 of Windows Media Player always started on the Media Guide page, which is essentially a browser window that displays the latest news from the WindowsMedia.com website.

The trouble with that, though, was that if you had a slow Internet connection or none at all, it took awhile for that fact to become apparent to the application. In the meantime, you were stuck drumming your fingers until it decided to release you. So now in Version 10, it starts up on whatever tab it was on the last time you closed it.

Figure 10.1 shows Windows Media Player in its Full mode, with a track playing. Notice the player controls at the bottom of the window (Play, Pause, and all the usual stuff) and the tabs across the top for accessing different sections in the application (Burn, Rip, and so on). Also notice the right pane, which is a Now Playing list of tracks I've queued up for my listening pleasure.

**FIGURE 10.1**

Windows Media Player 10, shown here in Full mode, rivals many of the best standalone media player applications available today.

As you can see in Figure 10.1, Full mode takes up a serious chunk of a small screen, even when Windows Media Player isn't maximized and the menu bar and window frame are hidden. For sustained use, you might prefer Skin mode, shown in Figure 10.2. (Ctrl+1 takes you to Skin mode; Ctrl+2 takes you back to Full mode. You can also use menu commands or right-click menus.)

**FIGURE 10.2**

In Skin mode, Windows Media Player occupies a more reasonable amount of your screen.

## Using the Guide

The Guide tab (which was Media Guide in versions prior to 10) is essentially a web page (www
.windowsmedia.com/mediaguide) with lots of hyperlinks to audio and video clips available online.
If you have a fast Internet connection, it can be a fun browse, sort of like reading the Entertainment
section of your local newspaper but with sound and video (see Figure 10.3). If your tastes don't run to
the mainstream, check out the Artists A-Z link on this tab and look up your favorites independently.

**FIGURE 10.3**

The Guide tab presents a
constantly changing as-
sortment of hyperlinks
to downloadable media
content.

In Version 10, the Internet Radio feature is also accessed from the Guide tab. I'll tell you more
about Internet Radio later in the chapter.

## Working with Player Controls

The player controls at the bottom of the Windows Media Player window are the same as on a cassette
deck or audio CD player—you've got your standard Play, Pause, and Stop buttons, plus buttons for
skipping forward and back among tracks. The slider bar above them can be dragged to rewind or fast
forward within the current track (see Figure 10.4).

**FIGURE 10.4**

The player controls are
similar to those found on
a home stereo system.

# Working with Audio and Video Clips

One of the most common uses for Windows Media Player is to play audio or video clips you have stored on your hard drive. These could come from Internet sites, from audio CDs you have "ripped" (more on that later), or from other sources.

## Cataloging Media Files on Your PC

Media Player can store a list of all the media clips on your PC and display the list in the Library tab for easy selection and playback. If you click the Library tab before you have done an initial search, it prompts you to search for files. You can also manually initiate the search by doing the following:

1. Choose Tools ➢ Search for Media Files or press the F3 key.

2. In the Add to Library by Searching Computer dialog box, specify which drives (and if necessary, which folders) to search, and choose any advanced search options needed. (Click the Advanced Options button to expand the dialog box.)

Here are the two advanced options:

**Add Files Previously Deleted from Library**   When you delete a file from the library, you don't delete it from the hard disk—just from the listing. Therefore, it could be redetected and re-added later, provided you mark this check box.

**Add Volume Leveling Values for All Files (Slow)**   Tracks from commercially produced CDs usually have a consistent volume level, but tracks from other source might vary in their volume level. Mark this check box if you want Windows Media Player to correct volume levels for clips being added to the Library list. It makes the process take a lot longer, though.

3. Click the Search button to start the search. The search takes a few minutes. Windows Media Player lists the files it found on the Media Library page.

4. Click Close when the search is completed.

**WARNING**    The Media Library is shared with all other users of the computer, including the Guest user. Don't put anything in your Media Library that you don't want other users to see or hear.

**TIP**    In addition to searching for clips, you can also add individual clips. To do so, choose File ➢ Add to Library ➢ Add File or Playlist. Then browse to locate the file and click Open.

## Playing Audio and Video Clips

Once you've let Windows Media Player discover the tracks that you have on your computer and list them in the Media Library, you can play any track by navigating to it and double-clicking it (or by selecting it and clicking the Play button). You can select multiple clips and then click the Add Selection to Now Playing List button as well.

On the Library tab, the rightmost pane lists the files queued up for playing. This is the Now Playing list (or at least it is by default).

Click the Now Playing List button to open a menu from which you can clear the playlist, start a new playlist to save, and more. See Figure 10.5.

**FIGURE 10.5**
The Now Playing List button has a menu associated with it.

## Choosing Visualizations

When it's playing audio, Windows Media Player shows visualizations (graphical displays) on the Now Playing page.

To toggle a visualization to full screen, press Alt+Enter or choose View ➢ Full Screen. Press the Esc key (or Alt+Enter again) to toggle off full screen.

To change the visualization, choose View ➢ Visualizations and make a choice from one of the category menus.

You can also set options for visualizations by choosing Tools ➢ Options and clicking the Plug-Ins tab, and then clicking Visualization (see Figure 10.6). You can add and remove visualization collections here, and for some collections, you can click the Properties button to display settings you can adjust for it.

CHAPTER 10

**FIGURE 10.6**
Choose a visualization collection on the Plug-Ins tab of the Options dialog box.

## Adjusting Video Quality Settings

If your digital video playback in Windows Media Player is unsatisfactory, you can try making adjustments to the Video Acceleration setting. These are for both digital video and DVDs (which you'll learn about later in this chapter).

Choose Tools ➤ Options, and on the Performance tab, drag the Video Acceleration slider to change the overall setting or click the Advanced button to open a Video Acceleration Settings dialog box with more than enough fine-tuning tweaks to please almost anybody. See Figure 10.7.

**FIGURE 10.7**
Adjust video playback settings.

The Digital Video (DV) slider (which, as its name suggests, works only for digital video, not for analog video) kicks in when you expand the Windows Media Player window to a larger size than the original video and Windows Media Player needs to stretch the video to fit. The Large setting allows Windows Media Player to interpolate (add) pixels that are not in the original video in order to stretch the picture. The Small setting keeps the video more faithful to the original. For best results, experiment with this setting.

Another setting you might need is the Display Full-Screen Controls check box. Actually, there are two of these: one in the Digital Video section and one in the DVD section.

If you have both hardware and software DVD decoders installed, you'll be able to choose the Hardware option button or the Software option button in the Preferred Decoder area.

## Displaying Other Lists

The Now Playing list is not the only thing that can potentially appear in the right pane of the Library tab. You can change it to a Burn List (that is, files you've chosen to burn to CD), a Sync List (files you've chosen for synchronizing with a portable player), or a Play List (described in the preceding section). To choose among those options, click the down arrow on the Now Playing List button at the top of the right pane, and then choose from the menu, as in Figure 10.5. (The button changes name when you make a different selection.)

## Creating Playlists

Playing audio files from disk is easy enough, but you can make it even easier by creating playlists of the audio files you like to play together. It is like a Now Playing list (as in the preceding section) except that you save it for later replaying.

To create a new playlist, follow these steps:

1. Click the Now Playing List button on the Library page and choose New List ➢ Playlist. The right pane changes to the new playlist, and the button name changes to New Playlist.

2. Drag-and-drop files into the playlist from the file listing (middle pane).

3. Click the New Playlist button and choose Save Playlist As. The Save As dialog box opens.

4. Type a name for the playlist and click Save. It'll be saved in the My Documents\My Music\My Playlists folder (unless you change that location).

To play a playlist, scroll down to the bottom of the folder tree (left pane) and locate the playlist under Playlists. Click it to select it, and then click Play. To delete a playlist, right-click it and choose Delete.

**TIP**   Use File ➢ Add to Library ➢ Add File or Playlist to import playlists from other users or other PCs.

## Customizing the Now Playing Pane

As you are playing a clip, the Now Playing tab can display a variety of things, depending on the settings you choose.

First, choose which screen elements should be present during the playback from the View ➢ Now Playing Options menu. Figure 10.8 points them out.

**Title**   Name of the clip.

**Media Information**   A picture of the CD or album cover, if available (downloaded from the Internet)

**Playlist**   The list of tracks that are queued to be played. (I'll explain later in the chapter how to work with this queue.)

**Resize Bars**   The thin gray lines between the various panes, which can be dragged to resize the panes in proportion to one another.

**FIGURE 10.8**

Turn screen elements on/off for the Now Playing tab from the View ➤ Now Playing Options menu.

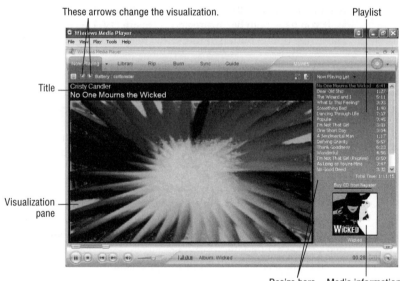

These arrows change the visualization.

Playlist

Title

Visualization pane

Resize bars   Media information

## Using Player Enhancements

The Enhancements pane (Figure 10.9) is an optional pane in the Now Playing view that provides access to various special-purpose functionalities such as color correction (for video clips) or a graphic equalizer (for audio clips, and video with audio included).

To view the Enhancements pane, from the Now Playing tab, choose View ➤ Enhancements and then pick the desired set of controls.

Of these enhancements, the most popular is the graphic equalizer. It's a minimalist utility in that, although it comes with a number of preset equalizations and allows you to adjust 10 bands of frequency to your taste, it does not let you save your custom equalizations or load equalizations automatically with tracks.

The graphic equalizer is straightforward to use. Figure 10.10 points out the various controls available for the equalizer.

You can display the other enhancements by selecting them from the View menu, or by clicking the left and right arrow buttons on the Enhancements pane to cycle among them. They include the following:

**Color Chooser**   Lets you control the colors used in the Windows Media Player window.

**FIGURE 10.9**

The Enhancements pane offers features such as a graphic equalizer.

**FIGURE 10.10**

Use the graphic equalizer to enhance audio playback.

**Cross-Fading and Auto Volume Leveling**   Enables you to turn volume leveling and cross-fading on/off. Cross-fading has a slider for overlap between tracks, so you can eliminate the "dead air" between the tracks.

**Media Link for E-mail**   This is pretty cool. You can mark a section of a track (beginning and end points) to be sent to someone via e-mail.

**Play Speed Settings**   Drag the slider to move the track speed up or slow down—without changing the pitch.

**Quiet Mode**   Lets you set up volume adjustment that minimizes the difference between the loud and the quiet parts of a track so that you don't have to crank up the volume to hear the quiet parts, only to have your ears blasted when the loud parts come on.

**SRS WOW Effects**   Contains sliders where you can adjust the TruBass and WOW special effects. You can also optimize for standard speakers, large speakers, or headphones.

**Video Settings**   Drag sliders here for Hue, Saturation, Brightness, and Contrast when playing video clips.

CHAPTER 10

## Editing MP3 and WMA Tags

Windows Media Audio (WMA) files and MP3 files include a *tag*—a virtual container with slots for a number of pieces of information such as the artist's name, the track name, the album name, the genre, and so on. By using these tags, not only can you keep your music clearly identified, but you can also sort the tracks by any of the pieces of information. For example, you could sort tracks by artist or by album.

To edit the tag on an MP3 file, follow these steps:

1. In an Explorer window (*not* in Windows Media Player), right-click the file and choose Properties from the shortcut menu. Windows displays the Properties dialog box for the file.

**TIP** Not sure where the clip is actually stored on your hard disk? Right-click it in Windows Media Player and choose Open Containing Folder.

2. Click the Summary tab, and then click the Advanced button (if present).

3. Edit the tag information as appropriate by clicking the current value. It changes to an editable text box. You can change any field that has a pen on its icon. You can't change fields such as Duration, Bitrate, and License.

4. Click the OK button. Windows applies the changes to the track's tag and closes the Properties dialog box for the file.

You can also change some details for the clips from within Windows Media Player, but it doesn't change the actual file—just its representation in the application. For example, you could change the artist's name in Windows Media Player, but it would still be set to the original artist's name in the file's Properties, and if you deleted it from the Windows Media Player library and re-added it, the old name would come back.

To change the details for a clip from within Windows Media Player, select the clip on the Library tab, and then right-click it and choose Edit. You can then click any displayed field for the clip and edit the text there.

## Rating Your Library Entries

Each track in your library starts out with a default rating of three stars. You can change this to reflect your enjoyment of a particular track. This information can then be used with some of the automatic playlists generated by the program, such as playlists that consist only of tracks with a certain number of stars or higher.

To change a track's number of stars, simply click the highest star to assign to it from the Library's center window. For example, to give it two stars, click the second star. The maximum rating is five stars. Tracks you have rated have gold stars; auto-rated tracks have pale blue ones.

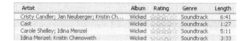

## Setting Media Library Options

Choose Tools ➢ Options and click the Library tab to adjust library settings, as in Figure 10.11.

**FIGURE 10.11**
Set your preferences for the Library.

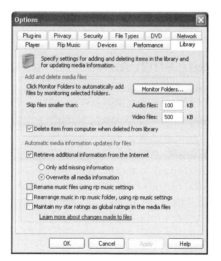

Here are some of the adjustments you can make on the Library tab:

**Monitor Folders**   Click this button to specify folders to monitor. When media content changes in a monitored folder, the information in the Library is automatically updated. Confine this to the folders that contain most of your music; monitoring the entire hard disk can impair performance.

**Skip Files Smaller Than**   Use these settings to omit very short media clips from the library. This is particularly useful if you have a lot of games installed that have sound clips associated with them, so you don't end up with those sound effects in your Library after searching your hard disk for clips.

**Delete Item from Computer When Deleted from Library**   Mark this check box if you want a clip's associated file to be deleted when removed from the Library. If you use this feature, be careful not to let it delete sound files for other programs (like the aforementioned games) just because you don't want them in your Library.

**Retrieve Additional Information from the Internet**   When this is selected, Windows Media Player will automatically connect to the Internet and try to find any missing information about the clip from online databases. For example, it can download album cover art to display on the Now Playing tab.

**Rename Music Files Using Rip Music Settings**   Later in the chapter, when I tell you about ripping, I'll explain how you can control the file naming conventions on the Rip Music tab of this same Options dialog box we're looking at now. Marking this check box here will enforce that naming convention on other files as well.

**Rearrange Music in Rip Music Folder...**   Same deal here. Marking this check box will enable clips to be rearranged based on your Rip Music settings.

**Maintain My Star Ratings...**   Marking this check box will store your star ratings with the clips themselves.

## Working with Audio CDs and DVD Movies

In addition to playing stored audio and video clips, Windows Media Player can also read media content directly from audio CDs and DVDs. You can also transfer the content of an audio CD to your hard disk, in full or in part, for later playback when you don't have the CD handy.

### Playing a CD

Unless you turn off Autoplay, Windows Media Player automatically starts playing an audio CD you insert in your CD drive. Use the player controls at the bottom of the window, or double-click a certain track in the Now Playing list to jump to that track. Right-click a track and choose Disable Selected Tracks if there's one you want to skip.

### Retrieving CD Data

If your computer is connected to the Internet, Windows Media Player attempts to retrieve the CD information by submitting the CD's ID number to the WindowsMedia.com database of information. (According to Microsoft, Windows Media Player doesn't submit any information about you other than the Globally Unique Identifier [GUID] and your IP address, which is required to get the information about the CD back to your computer.)

If Windows Media Player doesn't automatically display the track names, or if it shows them as Unknown Artist—Unknown Album, you'll need to retrieve them manually. Click the Find Album Info hyperlink below the playlist on the Now Playing tab's window, and Windows Media Player leads you through a search for the artist and album, as in Figure 10.12, or enables you to enter information for a custom-created CD.

**FIGURE 10.12**
Search for information about the CD in the online database.

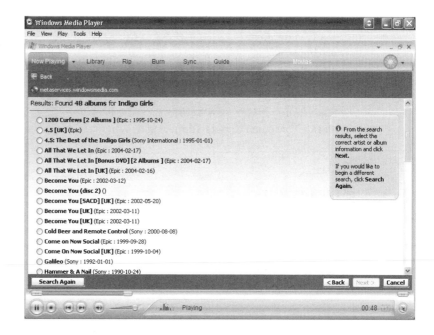

**TIP**   In the past, the WindowsMedia.com database wasn't very complete, but it is getting better all the time. If it can't find a certain CD, you might try CDDB, the online database of CD information (www.cddb.org). The CDDB is widely used by MP3 rippers and contains impressively accurate information for a very wide range of CDs. CDDB works in the same way as WindowsMedia.com: it uses the unique identifying code that each commercially released audio CD contains. By submitting this code, a program can download the CD information: artist name, CD name, and track titles. Most rippers handle this process automatically when you insert a CD. Part of CDDB's wide coverage of CDs is because it receives many entries from its users. If a CD you try to look up in CDDB doesn't have an entry, you can submit one. Many MP3 rippers have a built-in mechanism for submitting entries to CDDB.

## Copying (Ripping) a CD

Windows Media Player enables you to extract the audio data from the CD (a process normally called *ripping*) and encode it to a compressed digital format that can be played on the PC or on a portable digital player.

**CONFIGURING RIP SETTINGS**

As you probably know, CD-quality audio files are huge, taking up about 9MB per minute. (This is why about 74 minutes of audio fits on a 650MB CD.) Ripped files are much smaller than that. How small? It depends on the format and bit rate you choose.

Windows Media Player 10 can rip in either WMA or MP3 format. If you choose WMA format, you can further choose between Standard, Variable Bit Rate, or Lossless WMA. (Audiophiles might have a preference.) This is a change from earlier versions of Windows Media Player, which required a third-party codec to be installed in order to rip to MP3 format. Table 10.1 details the differences between the available choices of rip format. MP3 is a very compact and popular format, but its bit rate is limited. WMA offers several choices, from very compact (Variable Bit Rate at the lowest quality setting) to very high fidelity (Lossless). Let your inner audiophile decide.

**TABLE 10.1:** Media Formats Supported in Windows Media Player 10

| FORMAT | BIT RATE | SPACE REQUIRED FOR AN AVERAGE CD |
|---|---|---|
| MPEG Layer 3 (MP3) | 128Kbps to 320 Kbps | 57 to 144MB |
| Windows Media Audio (WMA) | 48Kbps to 192 Kbps (you choose) | 22 to 86MB |
| Windows Media Audio (Variable Bit Rate) | 40Kbps to 355Kbps (you choose a range) | 18 to 155MB |
| Windows Media Audio (Lossless) | 470Kbps to 840Kbps (whatever the CD is recorded at; no choice) | 206 to 411MB |

Once you've made up your mind in what format you want to rip, choose Tools ➢ Options, click the Rip Music tab, and make your selection in the Rip Settings area (see Figure 10.13). First choose a format and then drag the Audio Quality slider to the left or right to specify a bit rate.

**FIGURE 10.13**
Specify the format and bit rate for the rip.

While you're here in the Options dialog box (Figure 10.13), go ahead and make your other selections for rip settings:

◆ **Click the Change button** to browse for a different location in which to store the ripped tracks. The default is My Documents\My Music.

◆ **Click the File Name button** to specify how the files should be named. Some people like more or less information in the filename; it's up to you. Use the Move Up and Move Down buttons to reorder the information (see Figure 10.14).

---

**WHAT CAN YOU LEGALLY DO WITH DIGITAL AUDIO?**

If you're going to enjoy digital audio, you need to know what you can and cannot do with it. Here's what you can legally do:

◆ Listen to streaming audio from a website or an Internet radio station, even if the site or person streaming the audio is doing so illegally.

◆ Record audio from a medium you own (for example, a CD) to a different medium (for example, a cassette) so that you can listen to it at a different time or in a different place.

◆ Download a digital file that contains copyrighted material from a website or FTP site provided that the copyright holder has granted the distributor permission to distribute it.

◆ Download a digital file from a computer via P2P technology (for example, Napster, audioGnome, or Gnutella) provided that the copyright holder has granted the distributor permission to distribute it.

◆ Create digital-audio files (for example, WMA files or MP3 files) of tracks on CDs you own for your personal use.

◆ Distribute a digital-audio file to which you hold the copyright or for whose distribution the copyright holder has granted you permission.

◆ Download (or copy) MP3 files or other supported digital-audio files to portable audio devices (such as the Diamond Rio or the Creative Labs Nomad).

◆ Broadcast licensed audio across the Internet.

Here are some of the key things that you *cannot* legally do with audio:

◆ Download a digital-audio file that contains copyrighted material if the copyright holder has not granted the distributor permission to distribute it.

◆ Distribute a digital-audio file that contains copyrighted material if the copyright holder has not granted you permission to distribute it.

◆ Lend a friend a CD so they can create digital-audio files from it.

◆ Borrow a CD from a friend and create digital-audio files from it.

◆ Upload digital-audio files from a portable audio player that supports music uploading, such as the I-Jam or the eGo, to another computer. (In this scenario, you're essentially using the portable player to copy the files from one computer to another.)

CHAPTER 10

**FIGURE 10.14**
Choose the details about
the track to be included
in the filename.

**NOTE**    The first time you go to rip a CD with Windows Media Player, it displays a notice asking
whether you want to protect your content from "unauthorized use." If you choose Yes, Windows
Media Player will not allow the ripped track to play on any computer other than this one. If you
choose Do Not Protect Content, you'll be able to use the files you copy on other PCs. See the "What
Can You Legally Do with Digital Audio" sidebar for more information about copyright restrictions
on content.

### RIPPING AUDIO CD TRACKS

To copy a CD, follow these steps:

1. Insert the CD in your PC. If it starts playing, stop it.

2. Click the Rip tab in Windows Media Player.

3. If you want to exclude any tracks, clear their check boxes (see Figure 10.15).

4. Click the Rip Music button. Then just wait for it to finish.

## Burning CDs

Ripping and burning—what violent metaphors we seem to have come up with for working with
audio content on a PC. Some of this probably stems from how difficult it used to be "back in the day"
to copy audio content between formats. After struggling with the software of yesteryear, a lot of users
were probably ready to rip and burn anything they could get their hands on. But no more. In Windows Media Player 10, it's easy to make audio CDs.

**TIP**    Before you decide for sure that you want an audio CD, consider this. An audio CD holds only
about 70 minutes of music. On the other hand, a data disk containing MP3 or WMA files hold hours
and hours of music. More and more CD players these days support digital-audio formats, including
many car stereos, so check to see if the player for which you are creating the CD will support that. If
so, you can do yourself a favor and make your disc a data disc, and receive many times the capacity
out of the same little blank disc.

**FIGURE 10.15**

Select the desired tracks (or rather, deselect the undesired ones) and then click Rip Music.

Windows Media Player creates audio CDs by running the tracks through a two-phase process. First it converts each track to CDA format (CD-Audio); then it burns them to the CD blank. It takes about twice as long to create an audio CD as a data CD because of the extra step of file conversion.

### CREATING A BURN LIST

To make a compilation CD out of the tracks in your Library, follow these steps:

1. Click the Library tab.

2. Click the Now Playing button and choose Burn List. The button's name changes to Burn List.

3. Drag and drop files to the burn list (showing in the right pane in Figure 10.16), or select them and click the Add Selection to Burn List button.

4. Click the Burn tab. The chosen files appear in the left pane.

5. Insert a blank CD-R in your writeable CD drive and wait for it to be recognized in the left pane.

6. Check the Status column in the left pane. If you have chosen more clips than will fit, some of them at the bottom of the list will report Will Not Fit. Right-click a clip and choose Remove from List until all the clips report "Ready to Burn." See Figure 10.17.

CHAPTER 10

**FIGURE 10.16**
Build your burn list with files from your Library.

**FIGURE 10.17**
Check the Status column to make sure the clips you chose will fit on the inserted blank.

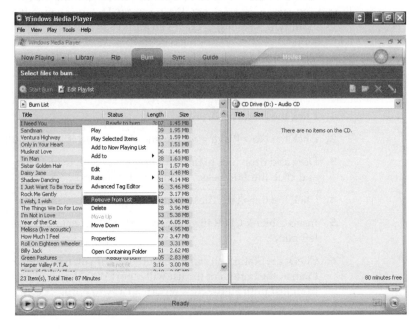

**7.** When you are satisfied with your burn list, click the Start Burn button. Then just wait for the CD to be created. Try not to use your PC for anything else while it is burning the CD (to avoid buffer underrun errors as much as possible).

**WARNING**    A buffer underrun error occurs when the CD is ready for more data but the PC isn't sending it fast enough. This used to be a huge problem, but now most CD drives have buffers built-in that help with this problem, and some software solutions are available as well. Still, it doesn't hurt to be cautious about overtaxing the CPU while the PC is trying to burn a CD, just to be on the safe side. It's better than wasting a blank.

## Playing a DVD

Once you've installed a DVD drive and a DVD player, you can play a DVD by putting it in the drive and choosing Play ➢ DVD, VCD, or CD Audio. Windows Media Player uses the standard Play controls for DVDs and displays a list of the DVD chapters in the playlist area. The Enhancements menu I mentioned earlier in the chapter is also available (see Figure 10.18).

**NOTE**    VCD stands for Video CD. It is a format for storing video on a CD that would normally be stored on a DVD. It was popular before DVD writing became so ubiquitous.

**FIGURE 10.18**
You can use Windows Media Player to play DVDs.

In order for a DVD drive to play DVD movies, you must have the appropriate codec installed for DVD video encoding. In earlier days, this was usually a piece of hardware because of the processor-intensive nature of the decoding process, but on modern systems, it is usually software since systems have gotten powerful enough that the burden is not so burdensome. If you get an error message when you try to play a DVD movie but you can read data DVDs, your system probably lacks the needed codec. Lots of companies would like to sell you a codec; see www.microsoft.com/windows/windows-media for vendors that Microsoft recommends.

**TIP**   If you have done a clean Windows install and have deleted everything that came on your PC originally and you now find that you don't seem to have the right codec, it was probably lost in the reinstall. Check the discs that came with the PC; perhaps there is a DVD player application that will serve. Once a DVD player application installs the needed codec, you might be able to play DVDs through Windows Media Player (so you will not necessarily have to use the player you just installed if you preferred Windows Media Player to it.)

To make the most of your DVDs, you'll probably want to view them full-screen. To do so, choose View ➢ Full Screen or press Alt+Enter. Windows Media Player switches to full-screen view. You can display pop-up controls on screen by moving the mouse. These disappear after a few seconds when you stop moving the mouse.

To display DVD controls (such as Root Menu, Title Menu, and Update DVD Information), choose View ➢ DVD Features.

Choose Tools ➢ Options to set properties for the DVD player feature. The DVD tab offers these options (see Figure 10.19):

**FIGURE 10.19**
You can choose parental control and language settings on the DVD tab of the Options dialog box.

**Parental Control**   To implement parental control on DVDs played on the computer, select the Parental Control check box and use the Select a Rating drop-down list to specify the rating to apply.

**Language Settings**   Click Defaults to set the default language for audio, captions, and DVD titles.

**Advanced Settings**   Click the Advanced button to set audio modes, such as choosing between regular stereo and Dolby Surround Sound. The options here depend on your sound card(s) and speakers.

# Tuning into Internet Radio

Windows Media Player provides good features for tuning into Internet radio—radio broadcast across the Web via streaming audio servers such as SHOUTcast, icecast, or RealAudio.

As of version 10, Windows Media Player has relegated Internet radio to the Guide tab; it no longer has its own tab. No matter. It does somewhat make sense, given that you need to be connected to the Internet to work with it, just as you need to be connected to the Internet to see the Guide.

To listen to Internet radio, take these steps:

1. Click the Guide tab.

2. Click the Radio Tuner hyperlink. A list of featured stations appears.

3. If you see a station that interests you on the Featured Stations list, click it to display its details. See Figure 10.20.

4. Depending on the station, there will either be a Play link or a Visit Web Site to Play link. If you have a Play link, click it and the station will begin playing in Windows Media Player; if you have a Visit Web Site to Play link, a website will appear with instructions for playing that station.

**FIGURE 10.20**
Use Windows Media Player's Radio Tuner page to listen to radio stations broadcasting across the Internet.

## Searching for a Radio Station

From the Radio Tuner controls in Figure 10.20, you can click one of the categories to browse for stations in that category. Alternatively, click the Find More Stations link and use the screen shown in Figure 10.21 to search by keyword or zip code.

**FIGURE 10.21**
You can browse for a radio station by genre or search by keyword or zip code.

You can also perform an advanced search. To do so, click the Use Advanced Search link to display the Advanced Search controls (shown in Figure 10.22). Specify whichever criteria you want—Genre, Language, Country, State (in the U.S. only), Speed, Band (AM, FM, or the Net), Keyword, Call Sign, or Frequency—and click the Search button to locate stations that match.

**FIGURE 10.22**
Use the Advanced Search panel to use multiple criteria in your search for a radio station.

### Creating and Editing Presets

You can edit your presets by changing the My Stations list as you need. You cannot change the Featured Stations list.

To add a station to your My Stations list, expand its heading and click its Add to My Stations link.

To remove a station from your My Stations list, expand its heading in the My Stations list and choose Remove from My Stations.

## Applying Skins

You can apply *skins* (custom graphical looks) to Windows Media Player to change its appearance in Skin mode. Windows Media Player comes with a selection of skins built in. To apply a skin, select View ➤ Skin Chooser. Select a skin in the list box to see how it looks. When you find one you like, click the Apply Skin button to apply it. You can also apply a skin quickly by double-clicking its file in an Explorer window or on your Desktop.

To download extra skins, click the More Skins button on the Skin Chooser page. Windows Media Player opens a browser window of the appropriate page of the WindowsMedia.com website, which maintains a gallery of skins, some created by Microsoft and others by users. (You'll also find skins in online software archives such as CNET's Download.com, but WindowsMedia.com is a good place to start.)

When you download a skin package, Windows displays the Windows Media Download dialog box. From this, you can click the View Now button to display the skin or the Close button to dismiss the dialog box.

**NOTE**    Windows Media Player skins can have the file type Windows Media Player Skin File and the .wms extension, but you'll usually find them compressed into files of the Windows Media Player Skin Package file type. These have the .wmz extension.

To delete a skin from Windows Media Player, select it in the list box and click the Delete button; then click the Yes button in the Confirm Skin Delete dialog box that Windows Media Player displays.

You can create your own custom skins for Windows Media Player. To do so, download the Windows Media Player Software Development Kit from the Microsoft website and follow the tutorials on the Microsoft Developer Network (MSDN; msdn.microsoft.com/workshop/imedia/windowsmedia/wmpskins.asp). When you've created a skin, store it in the Program Files\Windows Media Player\Skins folder, and Windows Media Player will automatically list it on the Skin Chooser page.

## Working with Content Licenses

Being able to store audio and video in digital format on a PC, play them back easily, and even transfer them via the Internet or removable media is great for consumers of audio and video content. But it can be much less than great for creators of audio and video content: These computer capabilities pose a severe threat to their livelihoods by compromising their copyrighted works and robbing them of sales.

In the past, audio and video works have largely been distributed on physical media, such as CDs, cassettes, LPs, video cassettes, and DVDs. The tangible nature and physical presence of such media generally makes it clear when a theft has occurred: physical media can't walk out of stores by themselves. Making unauthorized copies of a work distributed on a physical medium such as a videotape involves cost (for the media, for the copies, and for any duplicating equipment needed), time (typically real-time copying), and effort. Distributing those copies involves further cost, time, and effort. And the illegality of such pirated works is widely known (and recognized, if not exactly appreciated): most consumers are aware that it's illegal to distribute (let alone sell) copies of copyrighted works. Besides, copies of works on analog media (such as videotape or audiotape) are lower fidelity than the originals, so the unauthenticity of late-generation copies is clear.

By contrast, any work stored in a digital medium accessible by a PC can be copied in seconds at almost zero cost, and the copies are perfect every time. These perfect copies can be distributed via the Internet, again at negligible cost. And they can be distributed in quantities and over distances unthinkable for physical media. For example, if someone buys a CD in Sioux Falls, makes MP3 files of its tracks, and makes them available on a file-sharing service such as gnutellaNet or Freenet, anyone with Internet connectivity anywhere in the world—from Vladivostok to Tierra del Fuego, from Juneau to Java—can download them and then distribute them further.

At this writing, there are several technologies intended to protect the rights of content creators (and their authorized distributors) while allowing consumers to use the content. For example, most DVDs use an encryption system called Content Scrambling System (CSS), which requires an encryption key in order to be decoded. CSS keys were licensed and tightly controlled by the DVD-Copy Control Association (DVD-CCA)—tightly controlled, that is, until Norwegian hackers in the LiVid (Linux Video group) created a utility called DeCSS by reverse engineering some unencrypted code they discovered in a sloppily constructed software DVD player. Now that DeCSS is widely available, CSS-encrypted content can be deciphered by anyone who has the code.

Perhaps the most promising of the technologies designed to protect content is the digital license. A digital license is encrypted information that links a particular copy of a downloaded work to a particular computer or individual. For example, in the current model of digital licenses for audio, if you download a track that uses a digital license, you buy or are otherwise granted a license to play the track on the computer on which you downloaded it. If you transfer the track to another computer, it won't play, because the computer lacks the necessary license information.

So far, so good. But in order to be viable enough to become widely accepted, digital licenses need not only to be easy and intuitive to use but also compatible with both generally used technology and with the prevailing laws. For example, the First Sale Doctrine laid out in the Copyright Act allows consumers to sell or give a copy they've legitimately acquired of a copyrighted work to another person. Any copyright-protection technology that prevents consumers from doing this effectively (for example, because any subsequent recipient would not be able to view or listen to the work because it was locked by encryption and a nontransferable license to the first purchaser's computer) would be open to heavy-duty legal challenges.

Leaving aside such details for the moment, digital licenses are now being used to secure some copyrighted content. Windows Media Player adopts a two-pronged approach to digital licenses for audio content: it supports digital licenses for both tracks you buy and download and tracks you copy from CD. Windows Media Player automatically issues a license for each track you copy from a CD (unless you set it to copy tracks without licensing them).

Windows Media Player lets you choose whether to use digital licenses or whether to be free, easy, and possibly illegal. As long as you use those tracks on the PC with which you created them, there's no problem with using licenses. But if you want to be able to play the tracks from another computer, you've got a problem, because the license ties the associated digital media file to the PC for which the license is issued: you'll need to acquire a new license or transfer a license from the original computer. Similarly, you may not be able to download a copy of a licensed track to a portable player without licensing gymnastics.

Simply *playing* a track from another computer should be fine, legally, because it's the same file that you created from the CD. So should be moving the track to another computer that belongs to you and using it on that computer. Only if you create an illegal copy of the track—and particularly if you distribute it—should there be a problem. More on this later in the chapter, but you can see that the implementation of digital licenses tends to be problematic, partly because of the nature of the beast and partly because of the assumption of those who implemented the technology that anything unlicensed will tend to be licentious. There's no good reason for using digital licenses for the tracks you copy from CD unless you can't trust yourself (or other users of your computer) not to take illegal actions with them.

If you choose to use digital licenses for the tracks you copy from CD and the tracks you purchase and download (or download for free), you need to back up your licenses in case you lose them and need to restore them. If your computer crashes, if you reinstall Windows, or if you install another operating system, you'll need to restore your licenses in order to be able to use the tracks.

License files are small, so you can store a good number of them on a floppy disk. If you're not good at keeping your floppy disks in order, or if you want to protect them against local or natural disasters, back them up to an Internet drive instead.

## Backing Up Your Licenses

To back up your licenses, follow these steps:

1. Choose Tools ➤ Manage Licenses. Windows Media Player displays the Manage Licenses dialog box:

2. Check the folder indicated in the Location text box. If necessary, click the Browse button and use the resulting Browse for Folder dialog box to specify a different folder.

**TIP**  For safety, keep the backup on a removable medium, or make a copy of it on an online drive.

3. Click the Back Up Now button. Windows Media Player closes the first Manage Licenses dialog box, copies the licenses, and displays a Transfer Complete message. Click OK to close it.

## Restoring Your Licenses

To restore your licenses from backup, follow these steps:

1. Choose Tools ➤ Manage Licenses. Windows Media Player displays the Manage Licenses dialog box.

2. Click the Restore Now button. Windows Media Player warns you that the restoration needs Internet access and that Windows Media Player will send your GUID to a Microsoft service.

3. Click the OK button. Windows Media Player contacts the Microsoft site for authorization. If it receives authorization, Windows Media Player copies the licenses and displays a message to let you know the operation has succeeded. Click OK to close it.

# Working with Portable Devices

Windows Media Player can help you copy audio files to a portable digital audio device. Earlier versions of Windows Media Player treated a portable device the same as a writeable CD, but in Windows Media Player 10, a special tab, Synchronize, is designed for use specifically with portable devices.

**TIP**  Most portable devices come with effective software for loading tracks and playlists onto them. Because this software is specifically designed for the portable device, it may offer enhancements that Windows Media Player does not. However, some portable device software packages cannot rip, encode, and load to the portable device in one move, as Windows Media Player can with some of the players it supports.

## Creating the Sync List

Creating a Sync list is the same as the process for creating a playlist or a Burn list. To do so, follow these steps:

1. Click the Library tab.

2. If you do not see a Sync List button in the top right, click the button you do see there (probably Now Playing or Burn List) and choose Sync List from the menu that appears.

3. Drag and drop files into the right pane, or select files in the center pane and click the Add to Sync List button.

You can create the Sync list at any time, either before or after you connect your portable device.

## Making Media Player Recognize Your Device

Media Player will automatically recognize a wide variety of portable devices, so this may not be an issue for you. When you plug in your portable device (usually to a USB port), go to the Sync tab and press F5 to refresh the device list. Then open the drop-down list over the right pane to see whether your device is listed. If it is, select it and you're ready to go.

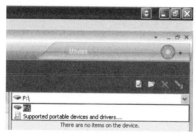

If it doesn't appear on that list, try the following steps to make it noticed:

1. Choose Tools ➢ Options and click the Devices tab. Currently installed devices for media input and output appear on the list.

2. Click the Add button. Windows Media Player opens an Internet Explorer window to the WindowsMedia.com site, which maintains a list of compatible devices and links to the software you can download to make the devices agree with Windows Media Player.

3. Scroll down the web page to the list of compatible devices and click the hyperlink for the device you have. Then follow the instructions to download a driver or an update that will enable the device to work with Windows Media Player.

## Copying Audio Files to a Portable Player

To copy files to a portable player, follow these steps:

1. Make a Sync list as described earlier. (You can also use any existing playlist or category, if it happens to match what you want to sync.)

2. Click the Sync tab.

3. (Optional) Click the Display Properties and Settings icon above the right pane, opening the Properties box for your portable player. Then change any of its settings as desired and click OK.

4. In the left pane, the Sync list should already appear, as in Figure 10.23. If it does not, open the drop-down list at the top and choose Playlist to Copy.

**NOTE**    The status for each item will be Ready to Copy. If you select more clips than will fit, some clips will report May Not Fit as the status; deselect clips until none of them display this message.

**5.** Click the Start Sync button. The clips are copied to the portable device.

**FIGURE 10.23**
Synchronize a portable device with a sync list.

When you are tired of those clips and want to delete them from the portable device, you can either use the controls on the device itself or do it through Windows Media Player. To delete through Media Player, simply display the contents of the device on the Copy to CD or Device tab and press the Delete key.

## Synchronizing Playlists Automatically

New in Windows Media Player 10, you can set up the portable device to be automatically synchronized every time it is connected. For example, you could create a playlist called My Portable and place the tracks in it that you want to copy there. Then set it up for automatic synchronization, and whenever you connect your portable, Windows Media Player will add, delete, and update tracks on the portable to match the current content of that playlist.

Here's how:

**1.** Make sure the playlists exist that you want to set up. You can use automatically generated playlists such as Favorites or Fresh Tracks that Windows Media Player 10 creates, or you can create your own custom playlists.

**2.** Click the Sync tab, click the Set Up Sync hyperlink. The Device Setup dialog box opens.

**3.** Click Synchronize Device Automatically. Then mark the check boxes next to the playlists you want to include.

**4.** Click OK. The sync begins automatically.

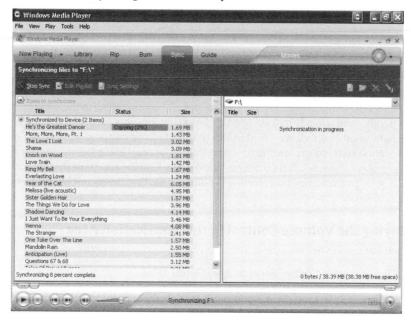

**WARNING**   Keep in mind the capacity of your device and don't over-choose. If you select more than will fit, it will copy from the top down on the list. Use the up and down arrow buttons at the bottom of the list to reorder playlists if needed.

When it's finished, you see a status report in the left pane, indicating which clips were synchronized and which did not fit.

# Setting Output Volume and Recording Volume

As you saw earlier in the chapter, you can adjust the output volume by moving the Volume slider in Windows Media Player. If you prefer, you can put a Volume control in the notification area so that it's always handy even when Windows Media Player or your other favorite noisemaker is minimized or hidden behind other windows. (And in fact, it might already appear there in the notification area.)

This section starts by explaining how that volume control gets placed into the notification area, in case yours is not there yet. It then covers the Volume Control program that Windows provides for controlling output volume and recording volume, adjusting the sound balance, choosing input and output, and so on.

## Displaying the Volume Control in the Notification Area

For immediate access to a volume control, you can put one in the notification area. Follow these steps:

1. Choose Start ➢ Control Panel to open Control Panel.

2. From Category View, click the Sounds, Speech, and Audio Devices link and then click Sounds and Audio Devices. Or from Classic view, double-click Sounds and Audio Devices.

**3.** Mark the Place Volume Icon in the Taskbar check box if it is not already marked.

**4.** Click the OK button. Windows closes the Sounds and Audio Devices Properties dialog box and displays the Volume control in the notification area.

**TIP**  By default, Windows applies its default notification-area behavior to the Volume control: Hide When Inactive. You'll probably want to change the Volume control's behavior to Always Show so that it's always available.

## Setting Playback Volume Levels

To set the volume, single-click the Volume control. Windows displays a pop-up panel bearing a Volume slider and a Mute check box. Drag the slider up and down to set the volume. Windows emits a Ding chord when you release the slider so that you can hear the approximate loudness of that volume. Click anywhere other than the pop-up panel to make the panel disappear.

When you mute the sound by selecting the Mute check box on the pop-up panel, Windows displays a red circle and bar beside the Volume control as a visual reminder.

You can double-click the Volume control, or right-click it and choose Open Volume Control from the shortcut menu, to display the Play Control dialog box. Then drag the sliders for various types of playback devices to control them individually.

You can change the devices that each have their own sliders here. To do so, choose Options ➢ Properties and then select or deselect check boxes for the available playback devices.

## Setting Recording Volume Levels

Notice that the sliders shown in the preceding section are for playback devices. If you want to set volumes for recording devices, choose Options ➢ Properties, click the Recording option button, then select or deselect check boxes for the available recording devices and click OK.

## Setting Speaker Balance

To set speaker balance on the signal output by your sound card (as opposed to setting it via your amplifier), display the Sounds and Audio Devices Properties dialog box (from the Control Panel) and on the Volume tab, click the Speaker Volume button. Then drag the sliders individually from left and right.

## Setting Advanced Audio Properties

Beyond the speaker balance settings, Windows also offers advanced audio settings. You can specify your speaker layout, the degree of hardware acceleration to use on audio playback, and the sample rate conversion quality to use.

CHAPTER 10

To choose advanced audio settings, click the Advanced button in the Speaker Settings section on the Volume tab of the Sounds and Audio Devices Properties dialog box. Windows displays the Advanced Audio Properties dialog box.

The Speakers tab of the Advanced Audio Properties dialog box (shown in Figure 10.24) contains only one setting: the Speaker Setup drop-down list. Choose the appropriate option for your speakers or headphones. Your choices range from Desktop Stereo Speakers through to 7.1 Surround Sound Speakers (seven satellites and a subwoofer).

**FIGURE 10.24**

Specify your speaker set-up on the Speakers tab of the Advanced Audio Properties dialog box.

The Performance tab of the Advanced Audio Properties dialog box (shown in Figure 10.25) contains two settings:

**Hardware Acceleration**   Drag this slider to set the amount of hardware acceleration you want to use. On most computers, it's best to start with full acceleration and decrease it only if your computer exhibits audio problems.

**Sample Rate Conversion Quality**   Drag this slider to choose a balance between audio quality and CPU usage. Windows starts you off with a setting of Good. Try improving this and reduce it only if your computer's performance suffers.

Click the OK button. Windows closes the Advanced Audio Properties dialog box.

## Recording Audio Files with Sound Recorder

If you need to create some simple WAV files, use Sound Recorder, which comes with Windows. Sound Recorder is a simple program with some severe limitations. The worst limitation is that its maximum file length is a mere 60 seconds, so while it's fine for recording sound effects, short memos, and so on, it's no good for, say, recording a song of even modest length.

You can also use Sound Recorder for converting WAV files to some other formats, including MP3. But Sound Recorder is limited in this, too, offering only bit rates of 56Kbps and lower for MP3 files.

**FIGURE 10.25**

Choose audio performance settings on the Performance tab of the Advanced Audio Properties dialog box.

## Starting Sound Recorder

To start Sound Recorder, choose Start ➤ All Programs ➤ Accessories ➤ Entertainment ➤ Sound Recorder. Figure 10.26 shows Sound Recorder.

**FIGURE 10.26**

Sound Recorder is useful for recording WAV files.

## Recording a Sound File with Sound Recorder

To record a sound file with Sound Recorder:

1. Use Record Control to select the input you want to use. Choose appropriate volume and balance settings.

2. If you currently have a file open in Sound Recorder, choose File ➤ New. Sound Recorder closes the current file, prompting you to save it if it contains unsaved changes, and opens a new file.

3. Get the input ready. For example, bring your microphone within kissing distance of your mouth or throat, or feed in a signal through the Line-In jack.

4. Click the Record button.

5. Start the input.

6. Click the Stop button to stop recording. (Sound Recorder automatically stops recording after 60 seconds.)

7. Save the file by choosing File ➤ Save and specifying the name and path in the Save As dialog box.

Once you've recorded a sound, you can take assorted self-explanatory actions with it:

◆ Click the Play button to play back the file.

◆ Drag the slider to move to a specific position in the file.

◆ To add to the end of a sound file you've created, or to record over part of it and add to the end of it, position the slider at the end or at the position at which you want to start recording over its current contents. Then click the Record button.

◆ To truncate the file, place the slider in the appropriate position and choose Edit ➢ Delete before Current Position or Edit ➢ Delete after Current Position as appropriate.

◆ Apply one of the effects by using the Effects menu: Increase Volume (by 25 percent), Decrease Volume, Increase Speed (by 100 percent), Decrease Speed, Add Echo, and Reverse.

**TIP** Because Sound Recorder doesn't offer an Undo feature, it's a good idea to save the sound file before adding to a file or applying an effect. If you don't like the result, you can then close the file without saving changes.

## Converting a File to Another Format

To convert a WAV file to another format, follow these steps:

1. Open the WAV file.

2. Choose File ➢ Save As. Sound Recorder displays the Save As dialog box.

3. Click the Change button at the bottom of the Save As dialog box. Sound Recorder displays the Sound Selection dialog box (shown in Figure 10.27).

**FIGURE 10.27**
Use the Sound Selection dialog box to specify the format of the sound file when converting a WAV file to another format.

4. Choose the format in the Format drop-down list.

5. Choose any applicable attributes (for example, the bit rate) in the Attributes drop-down list.

6. Click the OK button. Sound Recorder closes the Sound Selection dialog box and returns you to the Save As dialog box.

7. Specify the filename as usual in the Save As dialog box.

8. Click the Save button. Sound Recorder closes the Save As dialog box, converts the file to the specified format, and saves it under the name you chose.

## Summary

This chapter has concentrated on audio and video, discussing how to make the most of Windows Media Player for listening to CDs, copying CDs to your hard disk, and tuning into Internet radio. You've also seen the assorted ways of controlling the volume that Windows outputs and how to record sounds with Sound Recorder, the distressingly limited tool that Windows provides for the purpose. In the next chapter, we'll turn our attention to the visual portion of multimedia, and look at Windows Movie Maker and the image handling features of Windows XP.

# Chapter 11

# Digital Media and Movie Maker

In the preceding lesson, I showed you how Windows Media Player helps manage sound and video files, but what about still graphics, like the ones you acquire from scanners and cameras? In this chapter, we'll look at how Windows interacts with graphic files. We will also explore the Windows Movie Maker application, which enables you to build your own graphic and video presentations.

- ◆ Understanding image formats

- ◆ Acquiring images from a scanner or digital camera

- ◆ Viewing images in Windows Explorer

- ◆ Making prints of digital pictures

- ◆ Using Windows Movie Maker

## Acquiring Images

Image files come from various sources, including Internet downloads, e-mail attachments, digital cameras, and scanners. If you're getting an image file that someone else has already digitized—like your Aunt Velda's photos of downtown Ketchikan that she e-mailed to you from the cruise ship—then the format and resolution have already been predetermined. When you digitize pictures on your own, however, you get to make some choices.

### Understanding Image Formats

Why are there so many image formats, anyway? Here are my theories:

- ◆ Because different formats are suitable for different uses

- ◆ Because people who work with graphics a lot are always looking for ways to improve on the weaknesses of whatever format they are stuck using

- ◆ Because there are lots of companies that want to make big bucks by inventing the perfect image format

Don't laugh—these are real. There are tons of image formats, and each one was created for one of these reasons.

You don't need to know the intricate details of every image format out there, but you should know the basics of a half-dozen of the most popular ones so that you can make good choices about what format is appropriate for what job.

When evaluating an image format, here are some questions you should ask:

**Size**   How large is the size of the file compared to the same image saved in some other format? If you are planning to use the file for Web use, you should know that using small files provides a great advantage. You can decrease file size by applying compression to the file.

**Compression type**   Is the file type compressible? If so, does it use lossless compression (compression with no loss of quality) or lossy compression (compression that sacrifices image quality somewhat)? For Web and on-screen use, a lossy compression format is fine, but for print, you'll want something that is either lossless or uncompressed.

**Compatibility**   Is it a well-known format that many applications support? A graphic file seldom stands alone; you need an image viewer to look at it, and it usually gets put into an application to accompany some text. The best graphic format in the world is no good if the application you use doesn't support it.

**Color Depth**   Does the format have any limitations on the number of colors you can use? For example, GIF has a 256-color limitation, making it unsuitable for photography.

**Special Features**   Does the format support any special features that most other formats do not? For example, does it support 48-bit color definition? Does it support animation? (For example, GIF and PNG can store several versions of a graphic in the same file and then alternate between them for a crude animation effect.) Does it support alpha channels for transparency?

Table 11.1 evaluates some of the most popular image formats based on these criteria.

Besides the image's format, the other consideration is its resolution—the number of pixels vertically and horizontally that make up the image.

**TABLE 11.1:**   Image File Formats

|  | **TIF** | **JPG** | **GIF** | **PNG** | **BMP** |
|---|---|---|---|---|---|
| Size | Large | Small | Small | Small | Large |
| Compression | Lossless | Lossy | Lossless | Lossless | None |
| Compatibility | Excellent | Excellent | Good | Good | Good |
| Max. Color Depth | 48-bit | 24-bit | 8-bit | 48-bit | 24-bit |
| Special | alpha channel support |  | Can be animated | alpha channel support |  |
| Notes | Widely considered the best format for high-resolution print publications | Widely considered the best format for web page use | Proprietary compression algorithm | Improved version of GIF | Native format for Windows graphics |

The "correct" resolution for a picture is almost entirely usage dependent. To avoid loss of image quality, you want to make sure that there will be enough pixels to display or print the image at the size you want.

For example, suppose you take a picture with your digital camera in a 1024×768 image mode. (Most cameras do better than that today, but let's go with a conservative example.) Now you want to display it on a web page. Computer monitors display at 96 dots per inch (dpi), so you could display this image at a huge size on a web page without losing one iota of quality. In fact, 1024×768 is probably too big for optimal Web use, because it will take longer than necessary to download.

Now let's say you want to print that picture on a 1200dpi color printer, and you want a regular-sized photo print (6" × 4"). At 1200dpi, the native size for that picture would be less than 1" wide (1024 pixels), so to print it at 6" wide, you would need to enlarge it sixfold. Since those extra five pixels between the actual ones don't exist, your software would need to create them by averaging the values of the surrounding pixels resulting in a blurry mess.

The moral of the story: consider the context in which you'll be using an image and resize it if you need to. Use an image-editing program such as Adobe Photoshop or Jasc's Paint Shop Pro to cut the resolution to fit the needs of the project. Unfortunately, you can't do much to increase the resolution of a picture, so try to capture or scan images in a higher resolution than you think you will need, and then preserve that high-res original for later repurposing.

## Transferring Images from a Digital Camera

When you connect a digital camera to the PC, a box pops up, as in Figure 11.1. Your choices may vary depending on what applications are installed. You might also see a proprietary screen instead of this one if you have some special application installed for photo handling (such as the one that came with your camera, for example).

You have several options to choose here, including the Picture and Fax Viewer, the Photo Printing Wizard, or the Microsoft Scanner and Camera Wizard. You can also choose Open Folder to View Files.

All those wizards are great, but I most often stick with the basics and choose Open Folder to View Files. This opens the camera's storage as a removable disk, much like a flash RAM drive. You can then just drag and drop the pictures onto your hard disk or desktop. It opens it in Filmstrip view (as in Figure 11.2), but you can change to any other view from the View menu, as you would any other file listing. Later in this chapter, in the Viewing Images section, I'll cover the Picture and Fax Viewer and the Photo Printing Wizard.

**FIGURE 11.1**
Choices offered when connecting a digital camera

**FIGURE 11.2**
Open the camera like any other folder.

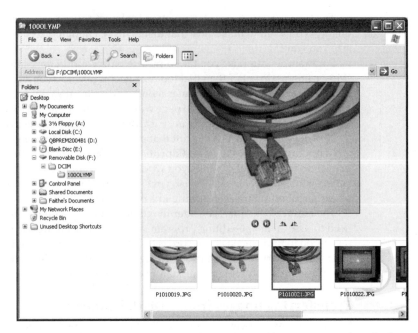

In the interests of completeness, let's look at the Microsoft Scanner and Camera Wizard method too:

1. After connecting the camera, choose Copy Pictures to a Folder On My Computer (see Figure 11.1). The Scanner and Camera Wizard runs.

2. Click Next to begin, and then clear the check marks from any of the photos on the camera that you do *not* want to transfer to your hard disk.

3. Click Next. Then type a name for the picture group. This will become a prefix for the filenames. For example, if you enter **Hardware** here, the files will be named Hardware 001, Hardware 002, and so on.

4. Choose a location in which the pictures will be placed. (The default is My Pictures.)

5. (Optional) Mark the Delete Pictures from My Device After Copying Them check box.

6. Click Next and then wait for the pictures to be copied to your hard disk.

7. Leave the default option selected (Nothing. I'm Finished Working With These Pictures.) and click Next, and then Finish.

Notice that you had no choice in the steps of the preceding exercise for either resolution or file format. That's because the camera already made those decisions for you when you took the pictures. If you want to change those settings, you need to do so in the camera itself. (Time to drag out its manual.)

## Acquiring Images from a Scanner

When you snap a photo with a digital camera, you are digitizing the image right then and there. Any later relationship you have with the PC is strictly on a transfer basis, as you just saw.

On the other hand, with a scanner, you are digitizing the image *during* the interaction between the PC and the scanner, so you have much more control over the process. You can choose both the resolution and the image file format.

**WARNING**    Not all scanners work equally well with Windows XP. Check the Hardware Compatibility List (www.microsoft.com/hcl) for the specific models that are guaranteed to be compatible. If you have a model that is not compatible, it will still work, but you'll need to use its own image acquisition driver rather than the Windows XP one. The Scanner and Camera Wizard will probably not work with it.

Many applications have a hook to the scanner built into them, so you can acquire the image and place it directly into that application. Most Microsoft Office XP and 2003 applications are like that, as are many image editing programs such as Paint Shop Pro and Photoshop. Check the documentation for the individual application to figure out how to access it. In Office applications, the command is Insert ➤ Picture ➤ From Scanner or Camera. In this chapter, however, I'll show you the stand-alone method, separate from any particular application.

To scan an image on a Windows XP compatible scanner, follow these steps:

1. Choose Start ➤ All Programs ➤ Accessories ➤ Scanner and Camera Wizard.

2. At the opening screen, click Next. Then choose the picture type you are going to scan:

Or, if you prefer, click the Custom Settings button to open a dialog box in which you can fine-tune the Brightness, Contrast, Resolution, and Picture Type settings. The Resolution setting is the key item here; for example, you can increase the resolution for a scan that is destined for a print publication.

3. Click the Preview button to see a preview of the image. The wizard will attempt to crop it for you automatically, as shown below, but you can drag the square handles in the corners of the cropped area to enlarge or shrink the area to be scanned.

4. Click Next, fill in the name and location you want to use, and then choose a file format. Note that the name you provide will be a group name for a folder, not the individual picture name. (You cannot control the individual picture name from here.)

5. Click Next, and wait for the picture to be scanned. When it is finished, a list of Other Options appears.

6. Click Next to accept the default option (Nothing. I'm Finished Working With These Pictures.).

7. Click Finish. Your scanned picture opens in Windows Explorer, in Filmstrip view. See the next section for more information about working with pictures.

## Viewing Images

Windows XP tries to be very user-friendly when it comes to pictures, to the point where, to a hardcore techie, it can be downright insulting. There's a special utility for doing everything from looking at a picture to printing a copy of it. Still, you can't really fault Microsoft for catering to the largest segment of the Windows XP audience.

### Thumbnail and Filmstrip Views

From the View menu, there are two views that show previews of image files: Thumbnails and Filmstrip. Thumbnails view shows small versions of each of the image files (Figure 11.3).

Filmstrip view shows the same type of thumbnails along the bottom, but devotes most of the window to a preview pane that displays whatever file is currently selected (Figure 11.4).

### Enabling Filmstrip View in a Folder

You might have noticed that some folders have Filmstrip as one of the view options and other don't. The key is the template applied to the folder. The Photo Album template enables the graphics-browsing capabilities for the folder.

**FIGURE 11.3**
Thumbnails View shows all pictures at equal size.

**FIGURE 11.4**
Filmstrip view shows the selected picture in a large size.

Take these steps to apply the Photo Album template to a folder:

1. From Windows Explorer, click the folder, and then choose View ≻ Customize This Folder.

2. The Properties dialog box for the folder appears with the Customize tab on top. From here, open the Use This Folder Type as a Template drop-down list and choose Photo Album.

3. (Optional) To make one of the pictures the folder icon (that is, the picture that appears on the folder in file listings), click the Choose Picture button, select one of the pictures, and click OK.

4. (Optional) To apply this template to subfolders within this folder, mark the Also Apply This Template to All Subfolders check box.

5. Click OK.

While you were doing the preceding steps, you might have noticed that there are other templates available for other types of content, such as music and video. You also might have noticed that there was a Pictures template that we didn't select. Both the Pictures and the Photo Album template allow you access to Filmstrip view, but the difference is that Pictures opens the folder in Thumbnails view by default, whereas Photo Album opens it in Filmstrip view by default.

## Viewing a Picture Slide Show

Many of my non-techie friends (yes, I have non-techie friends) seem to be really enamored with showing pictures on their monitors and televisions in full-screen mode, like the PC was a slide projector of yore. Personally, I do not understand the appeal of this.

Nevertheless, there is a feature in Windows XP that allows you to do this. While viewing a folder containing pictures that's set up with the Photo Album or Pictures template (described in the preceding section), you will notice a Picture Tasks pane to the left. From here, you can click View as a Slide Show to display the current folder's pictures full screen, one by one. Just click to go to the next one or press Back Space or the left arrow to go backward.

## Working with the Windows Picture and Fax Viewer

The Picture and Fax Viewer utility enables you to view your pictures, rotate them, print them, and do other common tasks. It's a poor substitute for a real image editing utility because you can't make changes to the picture, but it comes free with Windows and will serve if you are working on a PC with no other image-editing capabilities.

When you double-click a picture file, it will open in whatever image editor is your default. If you don't have some other image editor installed, it opens in the Microsoft Picture and Fax Viewer. You can force it to open in that utility by right-clicking the picture and choosing Open With ➢ Windows Picture and Fax Viewer, which is shown in Figure 11.5. The buttons along the bottom have various picture-management purposes; point at one to see its name, or click one if you are feeling adventurous.

**FIGURE 11.5**

A picture open in the Windows Picture and Fax Viewer

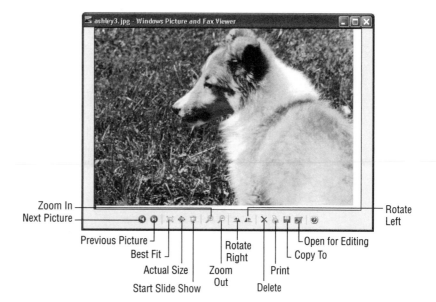

Zoom In
Next Picture
Previous Picture
Best Fit
Actual Size
Start Slide Show
Zoom Out
Rotate Right
Print
Delete
Copy To
Open for Editing
Rotate Left

## Printing Photos

The Photo Printing Wizard is useful for situations where you need to print a photo but you don't have an application installed on the PC that will open that image type. To activate it, choose Print from any file management window where you're working with photos (such as in Figure 11.5).

Then just work through the wizard:

1. At the opening screen of the wizard, click Next to begin.

2. Select the picture(s) to print. You can print a single picture or any number of pictures in the current folder. Then click Next.

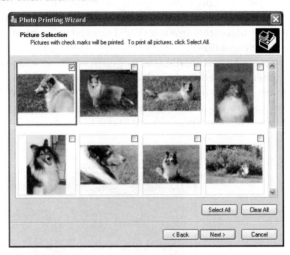

3. Select the desired printer, and if you want to change its properties, click the Printing Preferences button (then click OK to return here). Click Next.

4. Choose a layout for the print job. To print multiple copies of the same picture, increase the Number of Times to Use Each Picture. Click Next after making your selection.

**TIP**   Step 4 is the reason I use this wizard. It's pretty cool how you can choose different layouts and numbers of prints per page—kind of like printing your own school portraits.

**5.** Click Next. The print job is sent to the printer. Click Finish afterward to close the wizard window.

## Setting a Picture as a Windows Background

The easy way to set a picture as a Windows wallpaper background is to right-click it and choose Set as Desktop Background. Or, if the picture is in a folder that uses the Pictures or Photo Album template, click the picture and then click in the left pane on the Set as Desktop Background hyperlink.

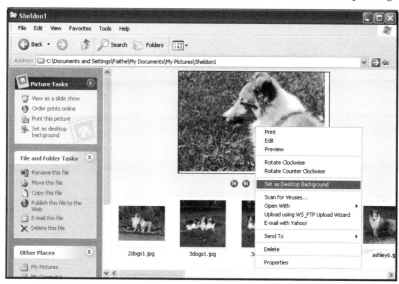

You can also open up the Display properties (right-click the Desktop and choose Properties) and choose a picture from the Desktop tab. This method has the advantage of enabling you to choose None to turn off the wallpaper feature entirely. You can also choose a Position (Stretch, Center, or Tile).

## Using Windows Movie Maker

Windows Movie Maker is a tool for combining different kinds of media clips into "movies" that you can share with others via disk, Web, or e-mail. You could combine home video footage from a video camera with voice-over narrative, a musical soundtrack, still photos, and other media types into a single movie file that can be played on any PC with a player that supports the Microsoft movie (.mov) format.

**NOTE**    If you want to use footage from a video camera, you need a way of getting it into the PC. If it's a digital video camera, that's simple—just hook it up to the PC via whatever interface type it uses. (Most digital video cameras use a FireWire port, which you might need to add on a PCI expansion card.) If it's an analog camera, or you want to transfer from videotape with a VCR, you need a video interface device to convert from analog to digital format.

Here's the big picture for creating a movie:

1. Create one or more collections. *Collections* are organizational folders for content, and they are not specific to a particular movie project. Once you import a clip, it can be used again and again in different movies.

2. Import or record the content for the movie into the collection(s).

3. Start a new movie project, and place the media clips into it.

4. Add a soundtrack or voice narration if desired.

5. Save your project.

6. Export your project to a movie file. You cannot edit a movie file; that's why you save the project first, in case you need to make changes to the movie. You can make the changes to the project and then re-export.

The following sections look at these steps in more detail. Start up Windows Movie Maker (Start ➢ All Programs ➢ Accessories ➢ Windows Movie Maker) and then proceed through these sections.

**NOTE**    There have been several versions of Windows Movie Maker. This chapter covers the most recent version at this writing—Version 5.1, the one that comes with Service Pack 2. You can download the newest version through Windows Update for free.

## Creating Collections

Collections are organized beneath a master folder called My Collections. It's a lot like the folder tree in Windows Explorer. Here's what to do to create a collection:

1. Click the collection you want the new one to appear under. To place it at the top level organizationally, click Collections in the folder tree.

2. Click the New Collection Folder button on the toolbar or choose Tools ➢ New Collection Folder.

3. Type a name for the collection and press Enter.

You might want a collection for video clips, another for still photos, one for sound files, and so on. Figure 11.6 shows several collections ready for use. You can have multiple levels in the folder hierarchy; that's the point of clicking the parent collection in step 1.

**FIGURE 11.6**
Set up your collections for storing incoming clips.

## Importing Content

The easiest way to get content into a collection is to import existing content from your hard disk. To do so, follow these steps:

1. Select the collection into which you want to import.

2. Choose File ➢ Import Into Collections. The Import File dialog box opens.

3. Locate and select the file you want to import; then click Import to import it. You can import sounds, videos, and/or still images.

You can drag clips between collections if you find that you imported it into the wrong folder; it's just like working with files in Windows Explorer.

**TIP**   You can't import CD audio directly from a CD, but you can use Windows Media Player to convert it to WMA or MP3 format and then import that file from disk.

## Recording Content

If you have a digital video camera that can be used while attached to the PC, a microphone, or some other input device, you can record new content directly into Movie Maker.

### RECORDING VIDEO CONTENT

You can directly record video content only if you have a supported video device—for example, a digital video camera that can record while it is hooked up to the PC, or another brand of analog-to-digital converter such as Dazzle.

Assuming you do have a supported device, here's how to record with it:

1. Make sure the device is connected to the PC and that your PC recognizes it. You may need to go through the Add Hardware Wizard, as described in Chapter 9.

2. Choose File ➢ Capture Video.

3. The Video Capture Wizard dialog box opens. Select the desired camera (if there is more than one).

4. Choose the audio input device from the Audio Device list. Adjust the audio input level by dragging its slider up/down.

**5.** Choose an audio input source from the Audio Input Source list. This is usually a microphone.

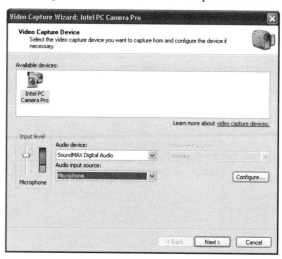

**6.** Make any other adjustments you desire. Click the Configure button to see the available settings for your video equipment.

**7.** Click Next. Then enter a filename for the captured video and specify a location in which it should be saved.

**8.** Click Next. A screen appears where you can adjust the recording quality.

9. Leave the Best Quality for Playback on My Computer option selected, and click Next.

10. The Capture Video screen appears. Adjust any settings here as desired, and then click Start Capture.

**NOTE** If you use Create Clips, it breaks the video into separate clips whenever it detects a different frame (such as when you turn the camera on/off or turn off the Pause feature). Otherwise it records a single, long video clip.

11. When you are done recording, click Stop Capture.

12. Repeat steps 10 and 11 to capture more clips if desired. When you are done, click Finish.

If you marked Create Clips, it creates a separate folder containing the multiple clips. If you didn't, it creates a single file with the name you specified.

## Creating a Movie Project

Now you're ready to create the movie project. Remember that the clips in collections are available to all movie projects; your collections are entirely separate from any particular project.

When Windows Movie Maker starts, it starts a blank movie project. You can go with this one or create a new one with the File ➤ New Project command.

### ADDING VISUAL CONTENT TO A PROJECT

Simply start dragging visual content (video or still photos) from collections into the project area at the bottom of the window in the order that you want it to appear in the movie.

There are two project views. Storyboard view is the default; it's the one that looks like a filmstrip. Each clip takes up an equal amount of space in Storyboard view, regardless of its actual length. You can work only with visual clips in Storyboard view; there is no audio track displayed. See Figure 11.7.

**FIGURE 11.7**
Storyboard view shows
visual clips only.

Timeline view shows each visual clip's size according to the amount of time it will remain on-screen. In Timeline view, you see a soundtrack line below the visual clips, indicating what sounds will play as each visual image appears. See Figure 11.8.

**FIGURE 11.8**
Timeline view shows
both sound and picture
and spaces them out in
their actual proportions.

To switch between them, click the Show Timeline or Show Storyboard button.

### ADDING A SOUNDTRACK OR NARRATION

To add a soundtrack, you need to be in Timeline view. Then drag any sound clip onto the timeline. At this point, you can drag it to the left or right to adjust its position in the movie.

You will probably want to wait to record narration at the last minute, after you have finalized the order and duration of each clip. To record narration, follow these steps:

1. Make sure your microphone is plugged in to the Mic port on your sound card.

2. Switch to Timeline view and click the Record Narration button (it looks like a microphone). Or you can choose Tools ➤ Narrate Timeline.

3. The Narrate Timeline controls appear in the upper pane. Drag the microphone volume slider up or down as needed.

4. Click Start Narration. Your movie displays in the Preview pane. Speak into the microphone to narrate as the movie progresses.

5. Click Stop Narration. A Save Windows Media File box appears.

6. Enter a filename and click Save. The track is saved in WAV format, just like files you create in Sound Recorder.

**TIP**   If you have added other audio to the movie, you might find that the narration has taken its place, forcing it to move farther to the right on the timeline. Drag them so they overlap to make both play at once.

### ADDING VIDEO EFFECTS AND TRANSITIONS

New in this latest version of Windows Movie Maker is the ability to add special effects, somewhat like in Microsoft PowerPoint.

You can add video effects and video transitions. Video effects apply to the entire clip; video transitions occur as the clip is first appearing.

To apply an effect or transition, follow these steps:

1. On the Collections list, click Video Effects or Video Transitions. A list of available effects appears in the center pane.

**TIP**   To see more of the effects listed in that center pane at once, choose View ➢ Details.

2. Drag and drop one of the effects onto a clip in the timeline or filmstrip.

**PREVIEWING THE MOVIE**

To preview the movie, click the Play button under the preview pane. If you want to view it full screen, click the Full Screen button under the preview pane.

## Exporting a Project to a Movie File

When the movie is exactly the way you want it, save your work on the project (File ➢ Save Project). Then export the movie by doing the following:

1. Choose File ➢ Save Movie File.

2. Choose the location for the movie to be saved. You can save to your hard disk, to the Web, to a recordable CD, to e-mail, or to an attached digital video camera. Then click Next.

3. Enter a name for the movie file and choose a location. Your choices here will depend on your choice from step 2. Then click Next.

4. Accept the default quality setting and click Next.

5. Wait for the movie file to be saved.

6. You're asked whether you want to watch the movie now. Click Yes to play it in Windows Media Player or click No to return to Windows Movie Maker.

## Summary

In this chapter, we looked at image file management and Windows Movie Maker. You learned how to acquire images from scanners and cameras and how to work with them in Windows and incorporate them into Windows Movie Maker files. In Chapter 12, we'll switch gears a bit and start looking at online functionality, starting with the Internet itself.

# Part 4

# The Internet and E-mail

**In this section you will learn how to:**

◆ Connect to the Internet
◆ Use Internet Explorer
◆ Use Communications Programs Such as Messenger, NetMeeting, and Remote Desktop Connection
◆ Use Outlook Express

# Chapter 12

# Connecting to the Internet

Will Rogers once explained that the telephone is like a very big dog: when you pulled on its tail in New York, the dog would bark in Los Angeles. Radio, he said, works exactly the same way, but without the dog. In Windows XP Professional, communications functions are integrated into the operating system. Maybe Will Rogers would have said that the dog is now using a keyboard and an Internet connection.

Communications capability has been part of DOS and Windows since the earliest IBM PCs. Windows XP Professional includes an extensive set of communications tools that enable you to exchange electronic mail with other computers, browse the Internet, and use your computer to control telephone calls. In this chapter, I'll discuss the following:

◆ Using the Internet Connection Wizard

◆ Connecting to the Internet with a dial-up modem

◆ Connecting to the Internet with a cable modem

◆ Connecting to the Internet with DSL

◆ Connecting to the Internet with Satellite

◆ Sharing an Internet connection

◆ Troubleshooting Internet connections

You can find more specific information about communications applications in the remaining chapters of this part of the book:

◆ Chapter 13 covers the Internet Explorer web browser.

◆ Chapter 14 covers Windows Messenger, NetMeeting, and Remote Desktop Connection.

◆ Chapter 15 covers Outlook Express, the Windows XP Professional control center for messaging components and news.

**NOTE**   For the latest information on Service Pack 2, please check out my website: www.minasi .com/sp2info/

## Types of Internet Connections

The most common way to connect to the Internet used to be through a dial-up modem, but that is all changing. People are increasingly finding better, faster ways to gain Internet access. We'll look at some of them in this chapter, along with the traditional dial-up modem.

High-speed Internet connectivity is also known as *broadband*. In theory, connecting through a broadband device can be as much as 1,000 times faster than connecting through a 56Kbps modem. Though only a gleam in our collective browsing and e-mailing eyes in the very recent past, broadband connections are now proliferating. And as you will see in the following sections, they are affordable and, with Windows XP Professional, extremely easy to install and get up and running.

## Connecting to the Internet with an Analog Modem

During installation of Windows XP Professional, you were given an opportunity to configure an Internet connection. If you didn't do so then, you can do so at any later time using the New Connection Wizard, which walks you through the steps. You can use this wizard to set up a broadband connection as well as an analog modem connection, to connect to your office computer system from a location outside the office, or to set up a local area network (LAN).

**NOTE** Chapter 9 covers the installation and configuration of a modem driver.

If you have a connection that requires you to log on, you'll need your username and password. If you are connecting through an analog modem, you need an account with an Internet Service Provider (ISP), your username and password, and the phone number to dial in to your ISP. To start the New Connection Wizard, click Start ➤ All Programs ➤ Accessories ➤ Communications ➤ New Connection Wizard.

To create a new dial-up (modem) connection, follow these steps:

1. At the welcome screen, click Next to open the Network Connection Type screen:

**2.** Click the Connect to the Internet option, and then click Next to open the Getting Ready screen. You can choose from one of these actions:

◆ If you don't have an ISP already, click the first option, and then click Next. In the next screen, you can choose to set up an account with MSN Explorer or to select from a list of other ISPs. If you choose MSN Explorer, a wizard will guide you through the steps to getting set up.

◆ If you have an installation CD from an ISP such as America Online, select the Use the CD I Got from an ISP option, and click Next. Click Finish to close the New Connection Wizard, insert the CD, and follow the on-screen instructions.

◆ If you already have an account with an ISP and have its phone number, your username, and your password, click the Set Up My Connection Manually option, and click Next to open the Internet Connection screen:

**3.** Click the Connect Using a Dial-up Modem option, and then click Next to open the Connection Name screen.

4. In the ISP Name box, enter a name and then click Next to open the Phone Number to Dial screen.

5. Enter the phone number (and area code if necessary), specify whether the modem needs to dial 1 before dialing the phone number, and click Next to open the Internet Account Information screen:

6. Enter your username and password, and enter your password again to confirm it. Leave the two check boxes at the bottom of the screen selected if you want to do the following:

◆ Allow anyone who uses your computer to connect to the Internet using this account and password.

◆ Make the current connection the default.

Clear a check box to disable either of these options. When you've made your selections, click Next to open the final screen of the wizard.

7. If the summary of your choices is correct, click Finish to close the wizard. If you want to change anything, click Back to find that screen or screens and make the changes. If you want quick access to this connection, click the Add a Shortcut to This Connection to My Desktop check box before you click Finish.

## Connecting to the Internet with a Cable Modem

It's amazing how much times have changed. Less than five years ago, everyone wanted the latest and greatest in computer hardware—the fastest processors, the best video, the biggest hard drives. Nowadays, if you offer someone a choice between a computer with all the best hardware on the market or an average computer with a really fast Internet connection, 9 out of 10 people would choose the computer with the Internet connection.

Internet bandwidth is king, and there is no sign that things will change in the near future. So, what can you do when you decide it's time to upgrade from your 56K modem to something a bit faster? One option is to sign up for Internet access over the same cable that brings TV into your home—provided it is offered in your area.

**THE TELEPHONY INTERFACE**

Whenever you work with an Internet connection that involves dial-up, you work with TAPI(Telephony Application Programming Interface). TAPI is a set of software hooks to applications that control the way your computer interacts with the telephone network. TAPI is an internal part of Windows XP Professional rather than a specific application program—it provides a standard way for software developers to access communications ports and devices, such as modems and telephone sets, to control data, fax, and voice calls. Using TAPI, an application can place an outgoing call, answer an incoming call, and hang up when the call is complete. TAPI also supports features such as hold, call transfer, voice mail, and conference calls. TAPI-compliant applications work with conventional telephone lines, Private Branch Exchange (PBX), and Centrex systems; these applications also work with specialized services such as cellular and ISDN.

End users don't usually work directly with TAPI. The closest you'll get is when you set up dialing locations, as you learned in Chapter 6. When you create a set of rules for dialing from a particular location, such as dialing a number for an outside line, you are communicating your preferences to TAPI.

## Cable Internet Access—How Does It Work?

A cable modem has at least two (and maybe more) interfaces on it. The first is a standard F port connector, a coaxial cable connector that is similar to the one on the back of a television or a VCR. Your cable service is connected to that port. The second interface is a 10Base-T (Ethernet) connector or USB connector, which connects your cable modem to your computer. If it's an Ethernet connector it uses an RJ-45 plug, which looks like a wider-than-normal telephone plug. If it's a USB connector, it connects to any USB port on your PC.

Once your cable modem is up and running, data comes down to your system on a special channel on your cable signal and, unlike an analog modem, it is always on.

## How Fast Is It?

Being the techie that I am, I like absolutes. I like to know exactly how things work and exactly how fast something will run. So I did a bit of research to find out how fast cable modem service actually is. What I learned is that you can't find out.

When determining how fast a cable modem will actually run, you must consider a number of factors. Some factors (but not all) are out of the control of the cable ISPs, so their common answer—if you really press them on it—will be "it depends." Of course, this doesn't prevent them from bragging that their service is up to 1,000 times faster than a 33.6 modem. In theory, it is.

Let's take a look at that theory. On a typical cable modem installation, a 6MHz analog carrier channel is dedicated to carrying downstream data from the Internet to your computer. Now, the way all the bits and bytes are put together over a cable modem yields a throughput of 36MB on a 6MHz carrier channel. So, in theory, 36,000,000bps is 1,000 times greater than 33,600bps.

Ah, but a few factors get in the way. First, let's start with your computer. A cable modem either connects to the PC via a 10BaseT or a USB connector. The former is called a "10"Base-T connection because the maximum throughput it will support is 10,000,000bps (10Mbps). That's a bit less than 36Mbps—about 73 percent less. So much for the claim of being 1,000 times faster. If it's a USB 1.1 connection, it's limited to 12Mbps. USB 2.0 is better—with an upper limit of 480Mbps—but both the cable modem and the PC's USB port have to support it.

That's not the only possible bottleneck. The signal that is coming down the 6MHz carrier channel and into your computer is mixed in with other signals headed to other nearby computers. Your cable Internet traffic is traveling across the same cable that connects all the other homes and apartments in your neighborhood. Now, in theory, that cable can carry the entire 36Mbps of signal into your area. But how many users does it take to completely saturate that connection to your neighborhood? Four computers using 9Mbps each? What about 40 users running 900,000Kbps each? What about 400 users running 90Kbps (less than two 56K modems) each? Each combination would saturate the cable signal for your neighborhood and—believe it or not—it is not uncommon for between 500 and 2,000 cable TV subscribers to all be running on the same cable (that is, running into the same cable "head-end" or "node"). Hopefully, not all of them are subscribing to cable Internet access as well. If they are, and if everyone is using their cable modems, your connectivity might not be much better than that of two 56K modems, but I admit I'm stretching things a bit to make a point. Simply put, the best neighbor to have is one who doesn't even have a computer.

There is also the potential for a bottleneck from your cable company out to the Internet itself. Now, in all fairness, this is a bottleneck point for any ISP—whether you have dial-up, DSL, a cable modem, or whatever. Just as airlines make their money by selling more seats on a plane than they actually have, ISPs make money by selling more bandwidth than they actually have. They wouldn't be able to survive if they didn't.

A close companion who has a cable modem was able to confirm my speed rating of "it depends." In his particular scenario, he was able to see average throughputs of 256Kbps to 512Kbps, with his best connection being about 1.3Mbps—roughly the speed of a T1 connection. So, cable modems are definitely faster, but don't buy into the hype about their being 1,000 times faster than a regular modem.

## Cable Internet Access—Advantages and Disadvantages

A number of advantages and disadvantages are associated with cable modem service in comparison with typical analog modems. I've outlined a few of the positives and negatives for you.

### ADVANTAGES OF CABLE MODEM INTERNET ACCESS

Here are the advantages:

**Always on**   Full-time dedicated Internet access—you'll definitely appreciate this once you have it.

**High-speed**   Despite the possible bottlenecks I discussed earlier, 99 times out of 100, cable modems will give you far better speed and reliability than analog modems. Once you get connected, you'll never be willing to move somewhere that *doesn't* have high-speed access.

**One less phone line required**   If you had a dedicated second phone line installed in your house for computer access, you can drop that phone line. This should save you $10–$30 per month, which can offset the cost of the cable modem service.

**Affordable**   In comparison with other high-speed Internet access options, cable modems are one of the most affordable.

### DISADVANTAGES OF CABLE MODEM INTERNET ACCESS

Here are the disadvantages:

**Privacy**   Since all systems in a "neighborhood" of cable Internet subscribers use the same connection to send and receive data, someone may be able to intercept your traffic and analyze it—a security risk. I have even seen cases where shared network folders showed up as available on their neighbors' PCs under 9x versions of Windows.

**Few choices**   Unlike phone companies and Internet service providers, cable companies are more or less a monopoly here in the United States. You usually won't be able to choose from multiple cable Internet providers; you'll have to take whatever is available in your neighborhood.

## Getting Hooked Up

Okay, so let's assume you've decided to take the plunge and get hooked up to the Internet with a cable modem. Here's what you might go through, from start to finish.

### QUESTIONS TO ASK YOUR PROVIDER

You should definitely ask your cable provider a number of questions before getting hooked up. You might not get answers to all of them, but I would want any provider to be able to answer at least some of the following questions to my satisfaction:

- How can you ensure that my neighbors won't be able to intercept my data and read it?

- Will I receive a public IP address? If so, will it be fixed or dynamic? (Fixed IP addresses are better if you need to access your computer remotely or if you plan on setting up a web server of your own; dynamic IP addresses are better from a security point of view.)

- How fast can I expect it to be? Can you guarantee a certain level of service? (By all means, e-mail me if you get any provider to actually guarantee a certain level of bandwidth—I'd like to hear about them!)

- Are there any speed restrictions on my uplink speed? (*Uplink* refers to data sent from your computer to the Internet. Uploading a large e-mail message, videoconferencing, or transferring a large file to someone are all affected by slow uplink speeds.)

- Are there any restrictions on the type of services I can run on my computer? For example, can I run my own web server? If so, is there a traffic limit, above which I have to pay extra?

### SERVICE DELIVERY

Once you've talked with your provider and agreed to purchase the service, they will set up a time to send an installer out to your location. Now, I don't have cable modem Internet access, but I would expect the service to be just about as prompt as my regular cable service (meaning: not very prompt). Once they're at your location, they will work with the cables a bit and hook up their cable to a box—the cable modem.

Once the box is hooked up, it is time to hook the computer up. If your computer already has an Ethernet adapter in it, they will most likely connect the cable modem to the Ethernet adapter. If your system doesn't have an Ethernet adapter, they should add one to your computer for you (make sure that you have your original Windows XP Professional software handy, just in case they need it). Or they might install a USB model of cable modem instead.

### Configuring Your Connection

All that remains is to tell Windows XP Professional about your connection, and you do that with the New Connection Wizard. Follow these steps:

1. Choose Start ➢ All Programs ➢ Accessories ➢ Communications ➢ New Connection Wizard to open the wizard at the welcome screen.

**TIP** You can also get to the New Connection Wizard from the Network Connections window; click the Create a New Connection hyperlink in the Network Tasks pane there.

2. In the Welcome screen, click Next to open the Network Connection Type screen.

3. Click the Connect to the Internet option, and then click Next to open the Getting Ready screen.

4. Click the Set Up My Connection Manually option, and then click Next to open the Internet Connection screen.

If your connection doesn't require you to log on, click the Connect Using a Broadband Connection That Is Always On option, click Next, and then click Finish. If you have to supply a username and a password to log on, follow these steps:

1. Click the Connect Using a Broadband Connection That Requires a User Name and Password option, and then click Next to open the Connection Name screen.

2. Enter a name in the ISP Name box, and click Next to open the Internet Account Information screen.

3. Enter your username and password, and then retype your password to confirm it. Leave the three check boxes at the bottom of the screen selected if you want to do the following:

   ◆ Allow anyone who uses your computer to connect to the Internet using this account and password.

   ◆ Make the current connection the default.

   ◆ Enable Internet Connection Firewall.

   Clear a check box to disable any of these options. When you've made your selections, click Next to open the final screen of the wizard.

4. If the summary of your choices is correct, click Finish to close the wizard. If you want to change anything, click Back to find that screen or screens and make the changes. If you want quick access to this connection, click the Add a Shortcut to This Connection to My Desktop check box before you click Finish.

## Connecting to the Internet with DSL

Another popular high-speed Internet option is Digital Subscriber Line (DSL) service. DSL typically comes in two varieties: Asymmetric DSL (ADSL) and Symmetric DSL (SDSL). Since the two technologies move data in a similar manner, you may also see these commonly referred to as xDSL.

Asymmetric DSL is called asymmetric because the uplink and downlink speeds are different, with more of the speed usually being allocated to the downlink (what you use to download content from the Internet). With Symmetric DSL, the same amount of bandwidth is available in both directions—up and down.

## DSL—How Does It Work?

DSL uses the existing copper phone lines already in your house to send a high-speed data signal. Your plain old telephone service (POTS) typically uses a low frequency range for all the types of signals you're accustomed to: voice, fax, and data. DSL operates on the same line—at the same time—by using a higher (inaudible) set of frequencies to transmit data. Since the DSL signal is operating in a different frequency range, you can still use your phone, fax machine, or even a dial-up modem at the same time you are using your DSL service to access the Internet.

When you have a DSL modem installed in your home, the device will have at least two or three interfaces on it. The first will be a standard RJ-11 phone connector that you're probably very familiar with. Your phone line will be connected to that port.

The second interface on your DSL modem will either be a 10Base-T connector (also known as an RJ45) or a USB connector. Either can connect your DSL modem to your computer. If you have a 10Base-T model, your computer will need a 10Base-T port on the back of it in order to connect the two. If your computer does not have a 10Base-T port, your DSL provider will probably install one for you. If you have a USB model, all you need is a spare USB port.

The third port that you might have on the back of your DSL modem is another RJ-11 jack—this is for connecting your phone to the DSL modem.

## How Fast Is It?

Unlike cable modems, DSL service usually has very defined levels of service associated with it, from 1.5 all the way up to 9Mbps. A speed of 1.5Mbps is the same as a T1 Internet access line, the same type of line that many businesses use for their Internet access needs, and it's probably more than enough for the average individual user.

**NOTE**    A T1 line is a long-distance circuit that provides 24 channels of 64Kbps each, giving you a total bandwidth of 1.544Mbps.

You will usually have at least a few providers to choose from. Compare the speed offerings from all the providers able to service your neighborhood and choose what is best for you.

Depending on how your provider's network is configured, the potential for a bottleneck exists from your DSL provider out to the Internet itself. Remember, this is a bottleneck point for any ISP, whether you have dial-up, DSL, a cable modem, or whatever. As I mentioned earlier, ISPs make their money by selling more bandwidth than they actually have, in the expectation that not everyone will use it at once.

Having DSL myself, I can tell you that—in my case—it has lived up to its service speed. I've been able to verify a full 1.1Mbps worth of connectivity on my service, which is exactly what I paid for. Being able to download Windows service packs in five minutes instead of four hours is a definite advantage in my line of business.

## DSL—Advantages and Disadvantages

A number of advantages and disadvantages are associated with DSL service in comparison with typical analog modems. I've outlined a few of the positives and negatives for you.

CHAPTER 12

### ADVANTAGES OF DSL SERVICE

Here are the advantages:

**Always on**    Full-time dedicated Internet access—once you've had it, you'll never want to go back.

**High-speed**    Once you get connected, you'll never be willing to move somewhere that doesn't have high-speed access.

**One less phone line needed**    If you had a dedicated second phone line installed in your house for computer access, you can drop that phone line because you can still use your DSL line as a voice line—even when you are on the Internet. This should save you $10–$30 per month, which can off-set the cost of the DSL service.

### DISADVANTAGES OF DSL SERVICE

Here is the major disadvantage:

**Limited service area**    Due to technical limitations, your location must be within three miles (some providers say anywhere from 12,000 to 20,000 feet) of the phone company's DSL-capable switching location. And that distance is based on the length of cabling between you and the phone company's office, not the "as the crow flies" distance. So, even if you live two miles from a DSL-capable switching location, you won't be able to get DSL if there are more than three miles of cable between you and the switch.

## Getting Hooked Up

Okay, so let's assume you've decided to take the plunge and get hooked up to the Internet through DSL. Let's take a look at what you might go through, from start to finish.

### QUESTIONS TO ASK YOUR PROVIDER

Before ordering service, you should probably ask any prospective provider a few questions. Although this isn't a complete list of items you may need to consider, it's a good start.

◆   Will I receive a public IP address? If so, will it be fixed or dynamic? (Fixed IP addresses are better if you need to access your computer remotely or set up a web server; dynamic IP addresses are better from a security point of view.)

◆   Do you guarantee the level of service that I am purchasing?

◆   Are there any speed restrictions on my uplink speed? (*Uplink* refers to data sent from your computer to the Internet—uploading a large e-mail, videoconferencing, or transferring a large file to someone are all affected by slow uplink speeds.)

◆   Are there any restrictions on the type of services I can run on my computer?

### SERVICE DELIVERY

Once you've decided on a provider and agreed to a level of service, your provider will set up a time to send an installer out to your location (or, in some areas, they can send you a kit to install the DSL modem yourself—although you should have more technical knowledge than the average casual Internet user does if you're going to do this). Once they're at your location, they may have to work with your phone lines a bit before hooking up your DSL modem.

Once the DSL modem is hooked up, it is time to hook up the computer. If your computer already has an Ethernet adapter, the installer will most likely connect the DSL modem to the Ethernet adapter. If your system doesn't have an Ethernet adapter, they should add one to your computer for you (make sure that you have your original Windows XP Professional software handy, just in case they need it).

You may or may not need to run the New Connection Wizard to set up your connection. Your ISP will most likely give you set-up instructions. If you do need to run the New Connection Wizard, follow the steps I gave you earlier in the "Connecting to the Internet with a Cable Modem" section.

# Connecting to the Internet with Satellite

Cable and DSL are the preferred methods of broadband connection, but if you live in an area where neither is available, then what? Satellite Internet access may be the answer for you.

## Satellite: How Does It Work?

Originally, satellite Internet was a one-way service. Over the last several years, the one-way systems have become obsolete, replaced by two-way systems. You might still occasionally see a one-way system.

One-way satellite Internet uses a satellite dish for downloads, but uploads are handled with a regular 56Kbps dial-up modem. Therefore, you need to have two Internet connections—one for the satellite and one dial-up. They must both be active at once for you to surf the Web. The satellite is available all the time, but the dial-up you must connect and disconnect with a dial-up connection. You can use your own dial-up ISP or contract ISP service for the modem through the satellite provider.

Two-way satellite is a much newer technology; it uses a different type of satellite dish, and handles both uploading and downloading through it. Two separate cables run from the satellite dish—one to a Transmit box and one to a Receive box. (Some newer models combine both functionalities into a single physical box.) These boxes hook to one another and then connect to your PC via a USB port. The end result—a connection nearly as good in speed and reliability to that of cable or DSL that doesn't require the use of a phone line. As with ADSL, upload speeds are slower than download speeds; you can expect about 128Kbps uploading and between 300Kbps and 600Kbps downloading, on the average.

## Satellite: Advantages and Disadvantages

The main advantage of satellite Internet over dial-up is speed. Downloads happen at up to 1Mbps, and since you spend much more of your time downloading than uploading, this results in greater Internet productivity.

Two-way satellite is obviously better than one way because of the higher speed in uploading, and also because you don't need to tie up a phone line or contract with a dial-up ISP. Two-way satellite is also always on, with no per-hour charges.

There are no advantages for satellite over DSL and cable other than broader availability. Satellite is slower, less reliable, and more expensive than either of those.

All satellite Internet systems have the disadvantage of needing to buy and install a satellite dish. The two-way satellite dish must be professionally installed (by FCC mandate) because of its transmitting capability, and installation will cost $200 or more. The hardware for a two-way satellite connection will run $500 or more.

Satellite Internet also cannot be shared via router with other PCs in your home or office, unlike cable and DSL. You can share a satellite connection through Internet Connection Sharing, but you can't hook the satellite cable directly into a router.

Setup for satellite Internet on the PC is also a bit more involved. With cable and DSL, you simply plug in the cable and it works; with satellite you must run through a configuration and registration process using an analog modem. You must redo this setup if you ever need to reinstall Windows or if you get a new PC.

In addition, weather conditions can cause problems with satellite service. Heavy rain or snow can cause the service to stop responding, and I have also observed problems on bright and sunny days due to sunspots. There's not much you can do other than wait for it to start working again.

**WARNING**   Some people have also run into problems using satellite Internet on a dual-boot system. For example, if you dual-boot with Windows 98 and Windows XP, and you configure the satellite in Windows XP, when you boot to Windows 98 it won't work. So you rerun the Setup program in Windows 98, and it starts working, but then when you go back to Windows XP, it doesn't work anymore and you have to run Setup there again. This is because when you connect to do the configuration, it dynamically assigns you an IP address. You keep that IP address as long as that copy of Windows is installed, but if you run the Setup on a different Windows version, it asks for another IP address and locks your user ID onto it instead.

### Satellite: Getting Hooked Up

Currently only a few companies are offering satellite Internet service. The largest is Direcway (www.direcway.com). You can place an order for service online, and they will ship your hardware to a professional installer in your area who will come to your home and do the installation. (The dish will need a clear view of the southern sky.) Other ISPs subcontract from Direcway to offer service, such as Earthlink. If you go with a subcontractor provider, they handle all your tech support requests but pass along the hardware-related ones to Direcway for resolution.

Depending on the installer you get, they may do the PC setup for you, or you may need to do it yourself. You'll receive a CD-ROM containing the Setup program; it is fairly self-explanatory. You will need an analog modem to complete it; you might need to borrow one if you don't have one, just for this one usage.

## Protecting Your System with a Firewall

A *firewall* is a security system that deters would-be mischief makers from accessing your computer system through the Internet. No matter what type of Internet connection you use, you'll want to be sure that the Windows Firewall is enabled. (It's called Internet Connection Firewall, or ICF, in Service Pack 1 and below, but in this chapter I'll call all versions Windows Firewall for simplicity's sake.) Windows Firewall is included with Windows XP Professional. In Service Pack 2, it is enabled by default, even if you have an analog modem connection. In earlier versions, it might or might not already be enabled for all connections.

To make sure Windows Firewall is enabled, follow these steps:

1. Click Start ➢ Connect To ➢ Show All Connections to open the Network Connections folder.

2. Right-click your connection, and choose Properties from the shortcut menu to open the Properties dialog box for your connection.

3. Click the Advanced tab.

4. Depending on which Service Pack you have, you will take one of the following actions to proceed:

◆ If you have Service Pack 1 or below, make sure that the Internet Connection Firewall check box is checked, and then click OK.

After clicking OK, you can skip the rest of the steps in this exercise.

◆ On the other hand, if you have Service Pack 2 installed, you'll need to click the Settings button on the Advanced tab. Doing so will display the Windows Firewall dialog box. (You can also access this dialog box directly from the Control Panel.)

The rest of the steps in this exercise are only necessary if you have Service Pack 2.

1. Make sure that the On option button is selected.

**2.** (Optional) If you want to exclude certain services from firewalling (for example, if they don't function properly otherwise), display the Exceptions tab and mark or clear check boxes here as needed. You can also click Add Program or Add Port to create more items for the list.

You might find adding a port useful if you want to allow access through the firewall on a certain TCP or UDP port. You need to specify a port number. You can also specify a scope to limit access to a certain range of IP addresses or to your local subnet.

**3.** (Optional) Click the Advanced tab and configure any of the advanced firewall settings the way you want them. Most of these are best left at their defaults, but if you have a specific situation you are troubleshooting, it might help to make a change or two here. For example, you can configure security logging if you suspect intruders are attempting to connect, and you can fine-tune what you'll allow for the Internet Control Message Protocol (ICMP).

**4.** Click OK to accept the settings.

If you have a larger network or a corporate network, you'll need a more sophisticated firewall. You might start by asking the advice of your ISP. You can also find a wealth of information, vendors, consultants, and so forth on the Internet by searching on "firewall." A good jumping-off place is www.firewall.com.

**TIP** Check out the Microsoft Internet Security Advisor check at www.microsoft.com/technet/mpsa/start.asp to see how vulnerable to hacking your local PC and network are. You can get the same service with the Shields Up tool available from www.grc.com.

## Using the Network Setup Wizard to Share an Internet Connection

As you may know, Windows XP lets you share your Internet connection with other computers on your network. Logically enough, the feature that lets you do this is called *Internet Connection Sharing*, which gets abbreviated to ICS.

ICS can be a great way of saving time and money: instead of needing a modem and a phone line (or a DSL or cable modem) for each computer that needs Internet connectivity, you can get by with one modem and one phone line(or the equivalent). ICS is particularly good if you have a fast Internet connection such as a DSL or a cable modem that provides enough bandwidth for several computers under normal circumstances. (If someone's perpetually trying to watch streaming video, all bets are off.)

This is all good—provided your Internet connection is fast enough. It goes without saying that ICS doesn't speed up your existing Internet connection. If your connection is slow with one person using it, it'll be glacial once you've connected the whole household or office through it.

## Set Up the Computer That Will Share the Connection

Start with the computer that will share the Internet connection. First set up your Internet connection, and then use the Network Setup Wizard to configure the computer by taking the following steps:

1. Choose Start ≻ All Programs ≻ Accessories ≻ Communications ≻ Network Setup Wizard to start Network Setup Wizard.

2. At the Welcome screen, click the Next button. The wizard displays the Before You Continue screen, which tells you to plug in your devices, turn on all the computers and devices, and connect to the Internet.

3. Click the Next button. The wizard displays the Select a Connection Method screen:

4. Make sure the This Computer Connects Directly to the Internet. The Other Computers on My Network Connect to the Internet through This Computer. option button is selected.

5. Click the Next button. The wizard displays the Select Your Internet Connection screen:

**6.** In the Connections list box, select your Internet connection. In this example, you have several connections to choose from. Windows has preselected the correct one, however.

**7.** Click the Next button. If multiple connections remain after the Internet one has been selected, you are prompted to choose from among them for your private connection (that is, the one that connects to your LAN).

**8.** Make your selection of private network (if prompted), and click Next. The wizard displays the Give This Computer a Description and Name screen:

**9.** Enter the description for your computer in the Computer Description text box. This description is for your benefit and that of other users of the network, so make it concise and descriptive.

**10.** In the Computer Name text box, enter the name for your computer. Typically, for dial-up connections and DSL connections, you can choose more or less any name that suits you (within Windows' naming conventions). For cable-modem connections, you may have to use a name designated by your ISP.

**11.** Click the Next button. The wizard displays the Name Your Network screen:

**12.** In the Workgroup Name text box, enter a name for the network. It's best to use a unique name rather than the default name, MSHome, in case your network or Internet connection puts you on the same network loop as your neighbors.

**13.** Click the Next button. If you have Service Pack 2 installed, you will next be asked about file and printer sharing. Choose to turn it on or off as desired.

**14.** Click the Next button. The wizard displays the Ready to Apply Network Settings screen. Confirm your settings here.

**15.** Click the Next button. The wizard starts configuring the home network. While it works, it displays the Please Wait screen.

**16.** When the wizard has finished configuring the computer, it displays the You're Almost Done screen, which offers to create a network setup disk for use on non-XP computers connecting to the same computer:

**17.** If you want to create a network setup disk, select Create a Network Setup Disk and, when the wizard displays the Insert the Disk You Want to Use screen, follow these steps:

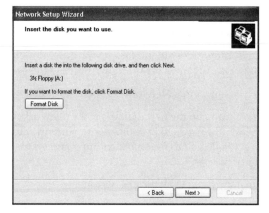

**A.** Insert a floppy disk in the floppy drive.

**B.** If you need to format the floppy disk, click the Format Disk button.

**C.** Use the resulting Format 3 $^1/_2$ Floppy dialog box to format the disk as usual.

**D.** Then click the Close button. Windows closes the dialog box.

**E.** Click the Next button. Windows copies files to the floppy and then displays the To Run the Wizard with the Network Setup Disk screen, which contains instructions for using the disk.

**F.** Click the Next button.

Otherwise, select the Just Finish the Wizard; I Don't Need to Run the Wizard on Other Computers option. (Selecting the Use the Network Setup Disk I Already Have option or the Use My Windows XP CD option displays a screen of instructions for using the network setup disk or the CD.)

**18.** Click the Next button.

**19.** The wizard displays the Completing the Network Setup Wizard screen, which provides links to Help and Support Center topics on sharing files and folders.

**20.** Click the Finish button. The Network Setup Wizard closes itself.

## Setting Up a Client Computer

Next, set up the first of your client computers. Make sure the Internet connection is still open on the computer you set up to share it, and then take the following steps:

**1.** Start the Network Setup Wizard.

If you are working on an XP computer:

**A.** Choose Start ➤ All Programs ➤ Accessories ➤ Communications ➤ Network Setup Wizard. The wizard displays the Welcome to the Network Setup Wizard screen.

If you are working on a computer that is running an earlier version of Windows:

**A.** Put the network setup disk you made earlier into the floppy drive.

**B.** Open an Explorer window to the floppy drive and double-click the file named NETSETUP (or NETSETUP.EXE, if you've set Windows to show file extensions).

The wizard displays three Network Setup Wizard dialog boxes in sequence.

**C.** Click the Yes button on the first dialog box the Network Setup Wizard displays. This tells you that the wizard needs to install network support files on your computer. Then a second dialog box tells you to remove the floppy and warns you that it will prompt you to restart your computer.

**D.** Remove the floppy and click the OK button.

**E.** Click the Yes button to restart your computer on the third dialog box.

After the restart, the wizard displays the Welcome to the Network Setup Wizard screen.

**2.** Click the Next button. The wizard displays the Before You Continue screen prompting you to confirm physical connectivity first.

**3.** Click the Next button. The wizard displays the Do You Want to Use the Shared Connection? screen:

**4.** If the wizard has identified the right connection, leave the Yes, Use the Existing Shared Connection for This Computer's Internet Access option selected. If not, select the No, Let Me Choose Another Way to Connect to the Internet option.

**5.** Click the Next button. At this point, you might move through any of several prompts that appear in various special circumstances:

- If you chose the No option in step 4, Windows displays the Select a Connection Method screen. From here, make sure the This Computer Connects to the Internet through Another Computer on My Network or through a Residential Gateway option button is selected and click Next.

- If your computer has more than one Internet connection, you will be prompted to choose one. By default, the wizard selects the Determine the Appropriate Connections for Me option. If you leave this option selected, the wizard guesses which Internet connection you want to use. If you prefer to choose the connection yourself, select the Let Me Choose the Connections to My Network option.

- If your computer has multiple connections to be bridged, the Select the Connections to Bridge screen appears. Select the check boxes for the connections you want to bridge. Clear the check box for any direct Internet connection.

**6.** When you (finally) arrive at the Give This Computer a Name and Description screen, enter the description and name for the computer. Because this computer isn't connecting to the Internet directly, you should be free to use any name you want for it even if your ISP requires you to use a specific name for the computer that's directly connected.

**7.** Click the Next button. The wizard displays the Name Your Network screen, shown earlier in this chapter.

**8.** In the Workgroup Name text box, enter the name you chose earlier for the network.

**9.** Click the Next button. The wizard displays the Ready to Apply Network Settings screen.

CHAPTER 12

10. Click the Next button. The wizard displays the Please Wait screen while it configures the computer. It then displays the You're Almost Done screen, shown earlier in this chapter.

11. Select the Just Finish the Wizard; I Don't Need to Run the Wizard on Other Computers option.

12. Click the Next button. The wizard displays the Completing the Network Setup Wizard screen.

13. Click the Finish button. The wizard closes itself and displays the System Settings Change dialog box telling you that you need to restart your computer before the new settings will take effect.

14. Click the Yes button if you want to restart your computer immediately. Click the No button if you want to close some programs and then restart your computer manually.

## What ICS Does

In networking terms, ICS combines several elements: a proxy server, a router, and a DHCP server. As such, it's relatively simple—but it comes free with Windows, and it's easy to set up and use.

ICS uses Network Address Translation (NAT), which is also known as *IP masquerading* (particularly in the Linux world). In NAT, the host (in this case, ICS) acts as an intermediary between the client (the PC connected to the network) and the server (the Internet server that is supplying information).

In NAT, the identity of the client submitting a request is hidden: instead, the request appears to come from the host. This can be good and bad. NAT gives you more freedom in the IP addresses you assign within the network. For example, you can use nonroutable internal IP addresses to make sure that incoming packets can reach a computer only through the router. But if someone on your network takes some illegal or offensive action (for example, posting libelous comments or downloading, uh, *unsuitable* material), the culprit will appear to be the host rather than the individual concerned. (If you had multiple IP addresses, only the specific IP address involved would appear to be guilty.)

## NAT Improvements in Windows XP

The nonroutable IP addresses lead us (indirectly, sure, but that's what happens when you're routing requests) to something that's been more of a problem with NAT in the past: computers not being able to communicate with each other across *two* NAT routers.

That might sound complicated, but it really isn't. You see, what usually happens with NAT is that one of the computers inside the network originates the conversation with a computer on the Internet. For example, consider Figure 12.1. This shows two simple home networks, unimaginatively named West Network and East Network. Each network contains a computer that's connected to the Internet (West 1 and East 1) and running NAT so that it can provide Internet connectivity to the two other computers in its network (West 2, West 3, East 2, and East 3). In the middle of the figure is the Internet, represented by its traditional cloud of uncertainty. And right below the cloud (quite coincidentally) is the Sybex Web server, represented by a computer the size of a walk-in freezer.

**FIGURE 12.1**

Two networks using NAT to connect internal computers to the Internet

**West Network**

West 1
NAT router
External IP address: 206.13.99.12
Internal IP address: 192.168.0.1

**East Network**

East 1
NAT router
External IP address: 204.202.111.112
Internal IP address: 192.168.0.1

Internet

Hub

Hub

Sybex web server

West 2
Internal IP address:
192.168.0.24

West 3
Internal IP address:
192.168.0.25

East 2
Internal IP address:
192.168.0.69

East 3
Internal IP address:
192.168.0.99

So far, so good. Now, here's the problem that used to occur with NAT. The computers that connect through the NAT boxes have only internal IP addresses. That means they can originate a conversation with a computer on the Internet, but they can't take part in a conversation originated from beyond their NAT box. For example, West 2 can access the Sybex web server with no problem. It sends its request to the NAT router on West 1, which says the binary equivalent of "ah, an address on the Internet" and shunts the request out through its external connection. The Sybex web server responds to the request and sends back a response to West 1. The NAT router intercepts this response, matches it to the outgoing request, says "ah, it's for West 2" (again in binary), and passes the data on to West 2. And so it continues: West 2 (and the other internal computers) can access Internet sites provided that it starts the conversation.

But if West 3 wants to start a conversation with East 2, it can't, because it can't see East 2 through the NAT router on East 1. It can get as far as East 1, because that computer has an external IP address. But the computers beyond the NAT router are hidden from view. So you can't access them for a quick Deathmatch, for videoconferencing, for chat—well, for anything. And with NAT routers becoming widely implemented, thanks to the rapid spread of broadband availability, that inability to start a conversation quickly becomes a problem. At one end of the connection, the activity has to take place on the computer running the NAT router rather than on the "inside" machine you want to use.

The good news is that Windows XP fixes this problem, letting you communicate across two NAT routers, from one inside machine to another inside machine. This is quite clever, because both the server (the NAT router) and the client (the inside machine) need to understand what's going on and work together. Some of the software has to be reworked in order to make the connection work, but you'll find that many things work.

**ALTERNATIVES TO INTERNET CONNECTION SHARING**

The preceding description probably makes ICS sound pretty good. And it is—up to a point. But it has two significant limitations:

◆ First, you need to keep the ICS computer running all the time so that it can handle the Internet connection and the sharing.

◆ Second, because of the way ICS is set up, you can share only one Internet connection at the same time on the same network by using ICS. To share two Internet connections, you'll need to set one up manually for sharing via another technology. (Alternatively, you can create two separate networks with an ICS connection in each, but doing so is usually much more work than setting up a second shared connection manually, because those two networks won't be able to talk to each other directly without ICS conflicts.) You can also use unshared Internet connections alongside your shared connections without any problems.

There are better alternatives—*much* better alternatives—to using ICS. Unfortunately, almost all of them want you to pay for them and put some more effort into implementing them than ICS takes. But they're worth a quick mention here in case you're interested.

Depending on your ISP, you may be able to get multiple IP addresses for your broadband connection without paying more for them. Other ISPs consider supplying multiple IP addresses to involve a different category of service than supplying a single IP address and charge accordingly. For example, some ISPs charge around $40 a month for "residential" DSL service (which gives you just one IP address) and $100–$200 for "business" DSL service (which gives you multiple IP addresses—usually between 5 and 20). Apart from the IP addresses and the fistful of dollars, the distinctions between the residential and business services tend to be detectable only under sustained scrutiny through an electron microscope.

If you want the residential service but need to be able to connect multiple computers through your single IP address connection, get a cable router or DSL router designed for this purpose. All these routers have NAT built in, and most can run DHCP as well, which means that you don't need to keep one computer running the whole time to handle DHCP and NAT so that other computers can access the Internet. Some routers have firewalls built in as well, which you can use instead of or in addition to Windows XP's Internet Connection Firewall (ICF) or Windows Firewall.

Some models are designed to connect to a network switch or hub and have two ports: an internal port for connecting to the switch or hub and an external port for connecting to the cable modem or DSL splitter. Others have hubs or switches built in, so if you haven't yet bought the hub or switch for your network, you can solve all your connectivity needs with a single box.

## Configuring ICS Manually

To configure ICS manually, take the following steps:

1. Choose Start ➢ Connect To ➢ Show All Connections to open the Network Connections window.

2. Right-click the dial-up connection for which you want to implement ICS and choose Properties from the shortcut menu to open the Properties dialog box for the connection.

3. Click the Advanced tab. It looks different on a PC that has an Internet connection to be shared than it does on one that doesn't:

4. Select the Allow Other Network Users to Connect through This Computer's Internet Connection check box.

5. Choose the connection used for your LAN from the Home Networking Connection box. This box might not be present depending on the service pack of Windows XP and whether you have multiple connections from which to choose.

6. If this is a dial-up connection you are sharing, and you want other computers to be able to cause ICS to start up the network connection when it's not running, make sure the Establish a Dial-up Connection Whenever a Computer on My Network Attempts to Access the Internet check box is selected. Clear this check box if you want only the computer with the connection to be able to start the connection. This option does not appear for network-type connections (as in the preceding figure).

7. If you want users of the other computers on the network to be able to control the Internet connection, make sure the Allow Other Network Users to Control or Disable the Shared Internet Connection check box is selected. Clear this check box if you don't want them to be able to manipulate the Internet connection directly.

8. If you want to use Windows Firewall on this connection, enable it as described earlier in the chapter.

**TIP**  Unless you're using a separate firewall or you've established that Windows Firewall interferes with an Internet program that you must run, it's a good idea to use Windows Firewall on your Internet connection.

9. Click the OK button. Windows closes the Properties dialog box for the connection, changes the IP address of your network adapter to the static IP address 192.168.0.1, and starts telling the other computers to get their IP addresses from it (if there's no other DHCP server on the network).

**NOTE** If you have another computer on the network using the 192.168.0.1 IP address, Windows gives you an angry message telling you to change that IP address before it will let you implement ICS on this computer. You're likely to be using this IP address only if you've previously set up ICS on another computer or the stars have decided you're due for a bad-horoscope day. If the other computer is running ICS, display the Properties dialog box for its shared connection and clear the Allow Other Network Users to Connect through This Computer's Internet Connection check box; then click the OK button. If the other computer isn't running ICS but has the 192.168.0.1 IP address set manually, either set a different address manually or switch to automatic addressing.

At this point, ICS should be up and running. The shared connection appears with a palm-upward hand on its icon to indicate that it's shared. If it's your default connection, the icon has a white check mark in a black circle. And if you're using Windows Firewall, the connection has a lock icon in its upper-right quadrant.

## Specifying Which Programs and Services Can Use the Shared Connection

Next, if you want, you can specify which programs and services can use the shared connection. This can be useful if you need to manage the shared connection or make sure that only authorized programs are run via it. You may not want to do this, but simply let any program that wants Internet connectivity via the shared connection have it.

To specify which programs and services can use the shared connection, take the following steps:

1. Display the Advanced tab of the Properties dialog box for the network connection in question.

2. Click the Settings button at the bottom of the tab. Windows displays the Advanced Settings dialog box:

3. In the Services list, select the services running on your network that you want Internet users to be able to access. By default, none of these services are accessible from outside the network—you need to turn them on explicitly.

♦ You can add a service by clicking the Add button and working in the Service Settings dialog box (shown in Figure 12.2). Enter the description of the service, the name or IP address of the computer hosting the service, and the port number and port type (TCP or UDP) of the service; then click OK. Windows closes the Service Settings dialog box and adds the service to the Services list box.

**FIGURE 12.2**

If necessary, you can use the Service Settings dialog box to add a service for sharing.

◆ You can change one of the listed services by selecting it, clicking the Edit button, and working in the resulting Service Settings dialog box.

**4.** If you have a Security Logging tab, click it. (You won't have this under Service Pack 2; instead you set security logging through the Windows Firewall dialog box discussed earlier in the chapter.)

**5.** Select the Log Dropped Packets check box if you want to log dropped data packets. Select the Log Successful Connections check box if you want to log successful inbound and outbound connections (for example, to see which Internet sites the computers on your network are connecting to and which computers are connecting to your network from the Internet).

**6.** In the Log File Options section, use the Name text box (and if necessary the Browse button and its resulting Browse dialog box) to specify where to store the log file. If you want, use the Size Limit text box to change the size limit for the security log file. The default setting is 4096KB—

in other words, 4MB—which is enough for a large number of successful connections and a few dropped packets.

7.  If you have an ICMP tab, click it. (Again, you won't have this under Service Pack 2; instead you'll configure this through Windows Firewall.)

8.  Select the check boxes for the ICMP (Internet Control Message Protocol) options you want to use. When you select an item in the list box, Windows displays information about it in the Description text box. These options control how the computers on your network respond to incoming requests for information. For example, the Allow Incoming Echo Request check box controls whether the computers respond to Ping packets sent to them. (Usually, it's best not to respond to Ping packets, because it tells other people—including crackers—that there's a computer at that IP address. But if you're trying to establish that your network is alive from a remote location, echoing Ping requests becomes very valuable.)

9.  Click the OK button. Windows closes the Advanced Settings dialog box, returning you to the Properties dialog box for the connection.

10. Click the OK button. Windows closes the Properties dialog box.

11. If the connection is open when you close the Properties dialog box, Windows displays the Network Connections dialog box warning you that some changes may not take effect until the next time you start the connection. Click OK.

### Setting the IP Addresses of Connected Computers

If your Windows computers are set to get IP addresses via DHCP, they should automatically get IP addresses from ICS within a few minutes after you implement ICS. If you're configuring IP addresses manually, you'll need to set each computer to an IP address in the 192.168.0.2 to 192.168.0.254 range.

### Turning Off ICS

To turn off ICS on the host computer, clear the Allow Other Network Users to Connect through This Computer's Internet Connection check box on the Advanced tab of the Properties dialog box for the connection, and then click OK. Windows closes the Properties dialog box and changes your computer's IP address from using 192.168.0.1 to obtaining an IP address automatically.

If you have a DHCP server on your network, Windows grabs an IP address from it on the next go-around of network polling. If Windows doesn't find a DHCP server (which will be the case if ICS was handling DHCP for you before you turned it off), Windows falls back on its alternate TCP/IP configuration, which uses Automatic Private IP Addressing (APIPA) to automatically assign an IP address in the range 169.254.0.1 to 169.254.255.254.

## Using a Shared Internet Connection

Depending on how a shared Internet connection is configured, you can use it in much the same way as you use a regular Internet connection on your computer.

The shared connection appears under the Internet Gateway heading in the Network Connections window with a flashy icon.

To tell Windows to display an icon in the notification area when the connection is connected, take the following steps:

1. Right-click the connection and choose Properties from the shortcut menu to open the Properties dialog box for the connection.

2. Select the Show Icon in Notification Area When Connected check box.

3. Click the OK button. Windows closes the Properties dialog box and applies the setting.

If the connection is configured to start automatically on demand, you can start the connection by starting a program that attempts to access the Internet. For example, if you start Internet Explorer or Outlook Express, ICS automatically starts the connection.

If the connection is configured to let you control it, you can start it manually by double-clicking its entry on the Network Connections screen, and you can disconnect the connection by right-clicking its notification-area icon and choosing Disconnect from the shortcut menu.

## Troubleshooting Internet Connectivity Problems

The following sections provide some solutions for common problems with connecting to the Internet.

### Dial-Up Modem Problems

Here are some issues you might encounter with an analog modem:

**No dial tone**    Make sure the phone line is connected to the Line port on the modem and to the wall outlet. Try plugging a telephone into that jack to confirm that it's working.

**Lots of static on the line/slow connection speeds**    Make sure the phone line is plugged into the Line port on the modem, not the Phone port. It makes a big difference on some modems; on others, none at all. Also make sure you are using a good-quality phone cable, that it isn't overly long (say, over 15 feet), and that it isn't next to any cables or devices emitting electromagnetic interference. Finally, have the phone company run a line quality check on your phone line to make sure there is not undue static interference.

**Modem won't dial**    Check the modem through Phone and Modem Options in Control Panel, as you learned to do in Chapter 9. In the Modems tab, click Properties, and then click the Diagnostics tab; then click Query Modem.

**Modem leaves phone off the hook**    Remove and reinstall the driver for the modem. See Chapter 9.

**Frequent disconnects**    Try a different access number if there is more than one in your area. Also, you might contact your ISP to see whether there are any special modem settings you need to make in order for the connection to be more reliable. Remember from Chapter 9 that you can add extra initialization AT commands to a modem's Properties.

## Cable/DSL Problems

Here are some problems you might face with a cable or DSL connection:

**Blinking lights on cable or DSL box**    If there are no always-on lights on the box but just one or two blinking ones, the connection is not being made from the box to the Internet. Try turning off or unplugging the box, waiting a few seconds, and then turning it on again. Sometimes temporary network outages prevent access and there's nothing you can do about it, so try again in an hour or so. It won't help you after the fact, but if you can catch the cable or DSL box when it's working right, notice which lights are on and which are blinking. Then you'll know what's "normal" for that device.

**After reinstalling Windows, no access**    If the lights on the cable or DSL box indicate it's functioning correctly but you can't get a web page to come up, the problem is between the box and your PC. You probably don't have the right settings in Windows. Check the IP address for TCP/IP to make sure you are using the assigned IP address (if you have one assigned), and check the computer name in the Computer Name tab of the System Properties dialog box. Some cable or DSL connections require you to use a certain computer name.

## Satellite Problems

Here are some problems you may encounter with satellite Internet service:

**After upgrading or reinstalling Windows, no access**    You may need to rerun the Setup program. If you use the Direcway system, you can run WebSetup (Start ➤ All Programs ➤ DIRECWAY ➤ WebSetup) to reconfigure the settings without having to completely reinstall everything.

**Loss of satellite signal**    If you use Direcway, you can double-click the DW icon in the notification area to open a status box for the connection. If the connection strength is poor (under 50 percent), make sure nobody has bumped your dish out of alignment. Signal strength tends to degrade in rainy or snowy weather. You may need to go out and brush the snow off the dish. (Don't use your hand; use a broom or similar tool.)

# Summary

This chapter covered how to install and configure modem and broadband connections to the Internet. It also gave you step-by-step instructions for implementing Internet Connection Sharing by using the Network Setup Wizard and by setting up this configuration manually.

In the next chapter, you'll learn how to configure and use Internet Explorer to surf the Web.

# Chapter 13

# Web Browsing with Internet Explorer

Obviously, the most important thing about Internet Explorer (IE) is not the program itself but all the resources you can access using it. And, to be completely honest about it, Internet Explorer is so easy to use that you hardly need a how-to book, a manual, or even this chapter. If you know how to open any Windows XP Professional program, you know how to open Internet Explorer, and you can start browsing immediately by simply clicking links.

Thus, in this chapter, I'm going to move briskly through the tasks you most commonly perform with Internet Explorer. As I proceed, I'll point out some new features of version 6 and show you how to expand on what comes naturally.

- ◆ Starting Internet Explorer
- ◆ Touring Internet Explorer
- ◆ Moving around the Web
- ◆ Finding exactly what you want on the Internet
- ◆ Customizing Internet Explorer

## Starting Internet Explorer

When you first start Internet Explorer after installing Windows XP Professional, you'll see the start page shown in Figure 13.1. (The content of the page changes daily, so yours will look different.)
You can start Internet Explorer by doing any of the following:

- ◆ Choose Start ➢ Internet Explorer.
- ◆ Choose Start ➢ All Programs ➢ Internet Explorer.
- ◆ Click the Internet Explorer icon in the Quick Launch toolbar (if displayed).
- ◆ Double-click the icon for a web page from a file management window or from the Desktop.
- ◆ Click a hyperlink in an e-mail message, document, or some other data file.

**FIGURE 13.1**

You can retain the page at www.msn.com as your start page or select any other page that suits your fancy or interests.

**TIP**  If you use both Internet Explorer and some other browser, such as Netscape Navigator, when you start up Internet Explorer, if it is not set as the default browser, you'll see a dialog box offering to "fix" the problem. Clear the Always Perform This Check with Starting Internet Explorer check box to prevent it from doing this in the future. You can also control this preference from the Internet Options dialog box's Programs tab. That'll take care of it from the IE side. If you want to also take care of it from Netscape, choose Edit ➤ Preferences in Netscape, expand the Advanced category, and choose Desktop Integration. In the File Types box, you can select file types you want to associate with Netscape. If .htm and .html are not associated with Netscape, Netscape won't think it's the default browser. You can also change file associations from any Windows Explorer window as you learned in Chapter 6.

## Moving around the Web

You probably already use Internet Explorer (or some other web browser) nearly every day, so we won't dwell on the basics of web surfing here, other than to run down this quick list of skills:

◆ To open the page represented by a hyperlink, click the hyperlink.

◆ To go to a specific URL, type it in the Address box.

**NOTE**  Internet Explorer assumes that when you enter a URL in the Address bar, you want to go to a web page or some other HTML document. Therefore, whether you enter http://www.sybex.com or www.sybex.com, you'll reach the Sybex website. If you want to access another type of resource, such as an FTP archive, a Telnet host, or a Gopher server, you'll need to enter the full URL, for example, ftp://ftp.archive.edu for the FTP site at archive.edu.

♦ To open a web page saved locally, use the File ➢ Open command.

♦ To return to a URL you have visited recently, open the Address box's drop-down list and choose it.

♦ To return to a site you have visited in the last several days, click the History button on the toolbar and select it from the History pane (covered in more detail later in this chapter).

♦ To go to a URL you have saved on your Favorites list, open the Favorites menu and select it, or click the Favorites button on the toolbar and then select the address from the Favorites pane (also covered in more detail later).

♦ To return to the page you last viewed, click Back. To go back multiple steps, open the drop-down list on the Back button and choose the step in which you are interested.

♦ After having used Back, click Forward to go forward again to the page you started from when you clicked Back. The Forward button has a drop-down list, too, for multiple hops at once.

**TIP**  If you want to edit only part of an address that's already displayed in the Address bar, place the cursor in the Address bar, hold down Ctrl, and press the right or left arrow to jump forward or backward to the next separator character (\\ \ . ? - or +).

---

### A LOOK BEHIND THE SCENES: VIEWING HTML PAGES

HTML is the abbreviation for Hypertext Markup Language, the language that is used to create web pages. HTML uses tags to tell the browser how to display the page on the screen. Tags are enclosed in angle brackets, and most come in pairs. For example, the <H1> tag defines a first-level heading, like this:

<H1>This is a level 1 heading.</H1>

An HTML file is really just a plain text file that can be created with a text editor such as Notepad or with a program such as Microsoft FrontPage. To view the HTML behind any page you open in Internet Explorer, choose View ➢ Source. The file is displayed in Notepad and looks similar to the following:

To return to Internet Explorer and the page displayed in the browser, click the Close button in Notepad.

If you're interested in learning more about HTML and creating web pages, check out the following Sybex titles: *Mastering FrontPage 2002 Premium Edition* and *Mastering HTML and XHTML*.

## Working with the Links Bar

One way to keep track of links that you follow and want to revisit is to add them to the Links bar. When you first install Windows XP Professional, the Links bar contains the following:

◆ Customize Links, which takes you to a Microsoft page that gives you information on how to add, remove, and rearrange items on the Links bar

◆ Free Hotmail, which takes you to a page where you can sign up for a Hotmail e-mail account

◆ Windows, which takes you to the Microsoft Windows site

◆ Windows Media, which takes you to WindowsMedia.com

◆ Windows Marketplace (in some installations), which takes you to the Windows Catalog site, where you can peruse Microsoft products for sale

The Links bar is locked into place by default, with only its name appearing at the right end of the Address bar. You must click the double arrow on it to display its contents. See Figure 13.2.

**FIGURE 13.2**
To view the Links bar's hidden content, click the double arrow.

If you would prefer to have it take up a whole row by itself, or at least a little more room to the right, first unlock it by choosing View ➢ Toolbars ➢ Lock the Toolbars to remove the check mark from that command. Then drag the word *Links* to the left, right, up, or down.

To add a link to the Links bar, simply drag it from the web page to the Links bar. (You can then rename it if the name is too long by right-clicking and choosing Rename.) To remove a link, right-click it and choose Delete from the shortcut menu. To rearrange items on the Links bar, click the item and then drag it to a new location.

To turn off the Links bar altogether, choose View ➢ Toolbars ➢ Links to remove the check mark from next to its name.

**TIP**  You can put a link to any file on the Links bar, not just a web page. If you maintain a log file where you store interesting information you come across on the Web, for example, you could put a link to that text file there.

## Keeping Track of Your Favorite Sites

If you add lots of links to the Links bar, it can get really crowded. You might find that you need a more sophisticated method of keeping track of your favorite sites, and the Favorites list is just the thing. To open it, click the Favorites button on the Standard toolbar, or choose Favorites from the menu bar. Figure 13.3 shows the screen you'll see if you click the Favorites button, and Figure 13.4 shows the Favorites menu.

**FIGURE 13.3**
Click the Favorites button to open the Favorites bar.

**FIGURE 13.4**
Choose the Favorites menu to see this drop-down list.

# Adding a Site to Your Favorites List

To add a site to your Favorites list, follow these steps:

1. Go to the site you want to add.

2. Click Favorites to open the Favorites bar, or open the Favorites menu.

3. Click Add (on the Favorites bar) or Add to Favorites (on the Favorites menu) to open the Add Favorite dialog box:

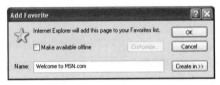

4. In the Add Favorites dialog box, Internet Explorer provides a name for this Favorite site. To give the site another name in your Favorites list, replace the default name with the name you want.

5. If you want to place this page in your top-level Favorites menu, click OK.

   If you want to add the item to an existing Favorites folder, click Create In and select a folder, and then click OK.

   If you want to create a new folder for this item, click New Folder, enter a name for the folder, and click OK. Then click OK again to save into that new folder.

**NOTE**  On some web pages, you will see a suggestion that you "bookmark" this page. Netscape and some other web browsers refer to a list of sites that you want to revisit as a *bookmark list* rather than as a Favorites list. If you want to use a Netscape bookmark list in IE, from Netscape, choose Bookmarks ➢ Manage Bookmarks, and then choose File ➢ Export Bookmarks from the window that appears.

You can also add items to your Favorites list in some other ways:

◆ Right-click a link, and choose Add to Favorites from the shortcut menu.

◆ Right-click the current page outside a link, and choose Add to Favorites from the shortcut menu.

◆ Drag and drop a link on a web page to the Favorites button on the Standard toolbar or to the Favorites bar if displayed.

◆ Press Ctrl+D. This places the item at the top level of the Favorites organizational tree, using the full name of the page.

## Maintaining Your Favorites List

You'll find out soon enough that your Favorites list will grow quickly, and before too long, it will become out of date. To keep your list manageable, you need to do some periodic housekeeping, weeding out what you don't want and rearranging or retitling what you do keep so that it is meaningful.

Deleting a site from your Favorites list is simple: open the Favorites bar or Favorites menu, right-click it in the list, and choose Delete from the shortcut menu. You might, however, want to get in the habit of following the link before you right-click—just in case the site is more important than you remembered and you want to keep it in the list.

To move an item to another place in the list or to another folder, simply click and drag it. To rename an item, right-click it and choose Rename from the shortcut menu. Type the new name and press Enter.

You can also do all of this management and more from the Organize Favorites dialog box, shown in Figure 13.5. From here you can rename, delete, move, and so on, plus create new folders.

**TIP**  If your Favorites list gets very long, it may be difficult to wade through. One way to reduce its size is to turn on the Personalized Favorites Menu option. This hides favorites that have not recently been used, much like the personalized menus feature in Office XP. Choose Tools ➢ Internet Options, click Advanced, and mark the Enable Personalized Favorites Menu check box.

**FIGURE 13.5**
Organize your list of favorites.

## Working with the History List

Yet another way to keep track of where you've been and to quickly revisit sites of interest is the History list. To display it, click the History button on the Standard toolbar. You'll open the History bar, which will look similar to that in Figure 13.6. Simply click a link to go to that page. Click a folder to see pages in that site that have links in the History list.

**NOTE**  To specify how many days you want to keep links in the History list, choose Tools ➢ Internet Options, and in the General tab change the number in the Days to Keep Pages in History box. You can also clear the history list from there by clicking Clear History.

**FIGURE 13.6**
You can use the History bar to see where you went today and in previous days and weeks.

You can display the items in the History list by date, by site, by most visited, and by the order in which you visited them. Click the View down arrow to choose an order. If you want to search for something on the History list, click Search, enter a word or a phrase, and click Search Now.

To delete an item from the History list, right-click it, and choose Delete from the shortcut menu. To clear the History list completely, click the Clear History button in the General tab of the Internet Options dialog box.

**NOTE**    The original version of IE 6 came with a Media bar that you could use to listen to music and play videos from within IE. Lots of people found it annoying, though, especially for video playback because the video would be so tiny. As of Service Pack 2 (SP2), it's no longer a part of IE.

## Accessing E-mail and Newsgroups from Internet Explorer

To read your e-mail as you're exploring the Internet, you can quickly open your Inbox in Outlook Express (or Outlook, or whatever your default e-mail program is) by clicking the Mail button on the Standard toolbar and choosing Read Mail. To check a newsgroup, click the Mail button, and choose Read News. To compose an e-mail message, click the Mail button, and choose New Message to open the New Message window. See Figure 13.7.

**FIGURE 13.7**
Click the Mail button for
a menu of mail-related
options.

**TIP**   Using Outlook Express is one way of reading e-mail and newsgroups; there are other ways too. There are web-based servers that you can use for e-mail, for example, such as Hotmail. If you have such an e-mail account, you can access it by displaying the web page for that service (such as www.hotmail.com). Depending on your ISP, you may be able to use some other web interface for reading your e-mail. You can also read and post to newsgroups via a web interface. One of the most famous web interfaces for newsgroups was Dejanews, which has since been bought by Google and renamed Google Groups (http://groups.google.com). You will learn more about e-mail and newsgroups in Chapter 14.

## Sending a Link or Page via E-mail

When you find a web page that someone else you know might enjoy, you can e-mail its link to them. To send a link, follow these steps:

1. Open the page.

2. Click the Mail button, and choose Send a Link. The New Message window opens with the link in the body of the message and the site title in the Subject and Attach lines. (You can also choose File ➤ Send ➤ Link by Email to do the same thing.)

3. Address your message, compose your message, and click Send.

If your recipient is connected to the Internet and has a web browser, they merely need to click the link in the message to open that page.

Some e-mail programs block the sending and/or receipt of e-mail links sent in this manner. If the recipient can't read it, or if you can't send it this way, try sending the page itself. To send the page itself, follow the same steps but choose Send Page (or Send Page by Email). The current page you are viewing will appear in the body of the message.

**WARNING**   Before you willy-nilly include web pages in your e-mail, be sure that your recipient's e-mail program can handle HTML messages. For more information about e-mail and HTML, see Chapter 15.

## Saving and Printing Web Pages

If you always want to see the most current version of a web page, you probably want to place a link to it on the Links bar or the Favorites bar. However, in some cases, you'll want to save it to your local hard drive or to a drive on your network. For example, I recently wanted easy access to a rather long

U.S. government document. In this case, the document had been written and distributed over the Internet and was not going to change. It was what it was, so I saved it to my local network so that I could get to it quickly without being connected to the Internet.

### SAVING THE CURRENT PAGE

To save the current page, follow these steps:

**1.** Choose File ➢ Save As to open the Save Web Page dialog box:

**2.** Select a folder in which to save the page, and in the File Name box enter a name if you want something different from that which Internet Explorer proposes.

**3.** In the Save As Type drop-down box, select the format in which you want the page saved.

**4.** Click Save.

You can also save a web page without opening it if its link is displayed. Follow these steps:

**1.** Right-click the link, and choose Save Target As from the shortcut menu. You'll see a dialog box that shows you that the page is being downloaded.

**2.** In the Save As dialog box, select a folder, and specify a filename.

**3.** Click Save.

### SAVING PORTIONS OF A PAGE

You can also save only a portion of text from a web page or an image. To save a portion of text to use in another document, select the text, and then press Ctrl+C. Open the other document, place the insertion point where you want the text, and press Ctrl+V.

### SAVING AN IMAGE

To save an image, follow these steps:

1. Right-click the image, and choose Save Picture As from the shortcut menu to open the Save Picture dialog box.

2. Select a folder, a filename, and a type, and click Save.

To save an image as wallpaper, right-click the image and choose Set As Background from the shortcut menu. To specify how you want the wallpaper displayed, right-click the image on the Desktop, choose Properties to open the Display Properties dialog box. Click the Desktop tab, and select an option in the Position drop-down box.

### PRINTING THE CURRENT PAGE

If you want to quickly print the current page, simply click the Print button on the Standard toolbar. If, however, you want more control over what's printed and how, choose File ➢ Print to open the Print dialog box.

For the most part, this is your standard Windows Print dialog box. (For details about printers and printing in Windows XP Professional, see Chapter 8.) The difference is the Options tab, which you can use to specify how frames and links are printed; it is shown in Figure 13.8.

**FIGURE 13.8**
The Print dialog box,
open at the Options tab

Here are the specifics:

◆ Select the As Laid Out on Screen option in the Print Frames section to print the web page exactly as it is displayed on your screen.

◆ Select the Only the Selected Frame option to print only a frame you have previously selected. (To select a frame, click inside it in an empty space—in other words, not on a link.) If you are not sure which frame is selected, use File ➢ Print Preview.

◆ Select the All Frames Individually option if you want to print each frame on a separate sheet of paper.

◆ Select the Print All Linked Documents option if you want to print the pages that are linked to the current page as well. (Be sure you really want to do this; you could need lots of paper.)

◆ Select the Print Table of Links option if you want to print a table that lists the links for the page at the end of the document.

When you have all your options selected, click the Print button on any tab to print the document. To print the target of any link, right-click the link, and choose Print Target from the shortcut menu to open the Print dialog box.

**TIP**    By default, Windows does not print the background colors and background images of web pages. First, the printed output could be illegible, and, second, unless you have a rather powerful printer, spooling and printing could be really slow. If, for whatever reason, you want or need to print the background, choose Tools ➤ Internet Options to open the Internet Options dialog box. Click the Advanced tab, scroll down to the Printing section in the Settings list, check the Print Background Colors and Images check box, and click OK.

### PRINTING YOUR FAVORITES LIST

There is no way to directly print the favorites list in Internet Explorer, but you can do so indirectly like this:

1. Export it to a file (File ➤ Import and Export and use the wizard).

2. Open that file in Internet Explorer (File ➤ Open).

3. Choose File ➤ Print, and in the Options tab, choose Print Table of Links.

## Working with Offline Favorites

If you want to view web pages when you aren't connected to the Internet, and their age is not important, you can simply save them to your local hard drive.

If you need to always have the most up-to-date version available, you can choose to "work offline." This uses the online version of the page whenever possible, and the offline version whenever the online version is unavailable.

To make the current page available for offline viewing, follow these steps:

1. Right-click in an empty spot on the page, and choose Add to Favorites to open the Add Favorite dialog box.

2. Click the Make Available Offline check box.

3. If you want to view only certain content offline, click the Customize button to start the Offline Favorite Wizard. Otherwise click OK and you're done.

If you are using the Offline Favorite Wizard, follow these steps:

1. From the Offline Favorite Wizard's introductory screen, click Next.

2. If you want the pages that link to the current page to also be available offline, choose Yes, and then set a number of levels deep. Then click Next.

**WARNING** The more levels you choose, the longer it will take to synchronize and the more space it will take up on your hard disk. To limit the amount of disk space a particular item and its associated pages can consume, after you complete the wizard, display the favorite's Properties and in the Download tab, mark the Limit Hard-disk Usage for This Page To check box and specify a limit in kilobytes.

3. Choose when to synchronize. You can choose manual synchronization only or choose to create a new schedule. Then click Next.

4. If you chose to create a new schedule, choose a certain number of days for an interval and an update time. Then click Next.

5. If the site requires a password, choose Yes and enter the username and password to use. Otherwise leave No marked. Then click Finish.

To view pages offline rather than using the online versions, choose File ➢ Work Offline. To return to online pages, repeat.

CHAPTER 13

**TIP**    If you want to take a current favorite and make it available offline, you can select it in the Organize Favorites dialog box and then mark the Make Available Offline check box. This bypasses the wizard and makes it available with default settings. Click the Properties button to fine-tune those settings if desired.

If you choose manual updating only, you must choose Tools ➤ Synchronize to update it. Otherwise the updates occur automatically at the interval you specify. When you choose Tools ➤ Synchronize, the Items to Synchronize dialog box appears; you can choose from it which items to synchronize. See Figure 13.9.

**FIGURE 13.9**

When you synchronize with the Synchronize command, you can choose which pages to update.

## Finding Exactly What You Want on the Internet

The serendipitous experience of clicking and following hyperlinks may suffice while you're polishing off your lunch of tuna sandwich and chips or filling the occasional lazy, rainy afternoon, but most of the time when you connect to the Internet, you have something specific in mind that you want to do or find. Regardless of what you're looking for—information about a topic, an e-mail or mailing address, a business, a web page, and so on—the way to find it is to use a search service. *Search service* is a relatively new term for what we referred to in the past as a search engine, a program that can search a file, a database, or the Internet for keywords and retrieve documents in which those keywords are found.

Examples of search services that you may have used include Yahoo!, AltaVista, Google, and HotBot Advanced. To search with one of these services, you go to the site (for example, www.yahoo.com); optionally, select a category, enter a keyword or phrase, and click Search (or some similar button). You can also access search services within Internet Explorer. Let's do a simple search to see how this works.

### PERFORMING A SIMPLE SEARCH

You can simply go directly to the website of a search service and follow the prompts there, or you can use the Search feature built into Internet Explorer 6. To do the latter, follow these steps:

1. In Internet Explorer, click the Search button on the Standard toolbar to open the Search Companion bar:

2. Enter a term or a question in the text box, and click Search.

You'll see the results of your search in the pane on the right, as shown in Figure 13.10. You can either click a link on the left to refine your search or click one of the found pages in the right pane to go to that page.

### EXPANDING A SEARCH

As you can see in Figure 13.10, the Search Companion bar now presents you with options for expanding or refining your search. Click a link to take your search further. By default, MSN Search is your search service. If you'd like to search using other search services, click the Automatically Send Your Search to Other Search Engines link, and then select a search service from those displayed, or click the Send Search to More Search Engines link to display still other search services.

**TIP**   Click the vertical scroll bar to view all the options in the Search Companion bar.

To modify how the Search Companion bar works, click Start a New Search, and then click the Change Preferences link to open the How Do You Want to Use Search Companion? list shown in Figure 13.11. Click a link that corresponds to how you want to search. If you are presented with more options, follow the on-screen instructions.

CHAPTER 13

**FIGURE 13.10**
The results of a search in
Internet Explorer

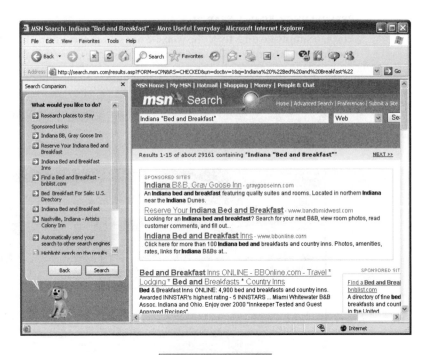

**FIGURE 13.11**
Setting your search
preferences

**TIP** You can also do a fast search from the Address bar. Simply enter your search term or phrase and press Enter.

### OTHER WAYS TO SEARCH

Here are two other ways to search the Web that don't involve the Search Companion:

◆ Type a search string directly into the Address bar. IE passes your search along to the default search engine (probably MSN) and displays the results.

◆ Display the website of one of the major search engines on the Internet, such as Google, Ask Jeeves, Excite, WebCrawler, and so on, and use the search tools on that page.

# Downloading Files

Sometimes when you click on a hyperlink, it doesn't take you to another web page; instead it starts a file download, as in Figure 13.12. (The version here is from SP2; it looks slightly different for earlier versions, and has an Open button instead of a Run button.)

**FIGURE 13.12**
When a hyperlink points to a downloadable file, this box appears.

If you choose Run (or Open), the file is downloaded to a temporary folder and run from there. This is useful if you are downloading a setup program but you don't need to retain that setup program after you run it.

If you choose Save, it prompts you for a folder in which to save the file, but it does not run it. When the download is finished, you'll see a box like the one in Figure 13.13. From there you can choose Run (or Open) to run the program or Open Folder to open the folder into which it was saved.

**FIGURE 13.13**
You'll see this box when the download is finished.

With SP2 installed, IE might block the download if it is not from a trusted site. You'll see a thin horizontal bar across the top of the window reporting that it has blocked it. You can click that bar to allow the download to go through.

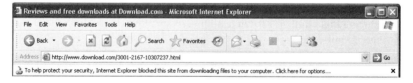

# Customizing Internet Explorer

In Windows XP Professional, you can view or change the configuration options relating to Internet Explorer in two ways:

◆ Use Internet Options in Control Panel.

◆ Choose Tools ➢ Internet Options from within Internet Explorer.

Regardless of which you choose, you open the same dialog box. However, if you open it from Control Panel, it is called Internet Properties, and if you open it from within Internet Explorer, it is called Internet Options. In both cases, the contents of the dialog boxes are identical. In this section, we'll use Internet Explorer. (To open the Internet Properties dialog box, choose Start ➢ Control Panel ➢ Network and Internet Connections ➢ Internet Options.)

The Internet Options dialog box has seven tabs, and in the next few sections, I'll review the most important configuration choices you can make on each of these tabs. I'll start with the General tab.

## Configuring the General Tab

The General tab, which is shown in Figure 13.14, contains these groups of settings:

**Home Page** Lets you choose which web page opens each time you connect to the Internet. A home page is the first web page you see when you start Internet Explorer. Click Use Current to make the current page your home page (if you are online to the Internet), click Use Default to return to the default setting, and click Use Blank to start each Internet session with a blank screen. To use a different web page as your home page, type the URL in the Address box.

**Temporary Internet Files** Lets you manage those web pages that are stored on your hard disk for fast offline access. If these files are occupying too much hard disk space, click the Delete Files button or the Delete Cookies button to remove them. (I'll discuss cookies in detail later in this chapter.) To control how these files are stored on your hard disk, click Settings to open the Settings dialog box. Click the option that applies to when you want Internet Explorer to check for newer versions of these stored web pages. You can use the slider to specify how much hard disk space is given over to these temporary Internet files. Click Move Folder if you want to use a different folder to hold your temporary Internet files; you must remember to restart your computer after making this change so that the new folder is used in place of the default. Click View Files to open a Windows Explorer window listing all the web and graphics files in the folder, or click View Objects to open an Explorer window listing all the other web-related files such as ActiveX controls and Java-related files.

**History** Contains a list of the links you have visited so that you can return to them quickly and easily using the History button on the Internet Explorer toolbar. You can specify the number of days you want to keep pages in the History folder; if you are running low on hard disk space, consider reducing this number. To delete all the information currently in the History folder, click the Clear History button.

**Colors button** Opens the Colors dialog box in which you can choose which colors are used as background, links, and text on those web pages for which the original author did not specify colors. By default, the Use Windows Colors option is selected.

**TIP** You can always change the Windows colors. In Control Panel, click Display, and then select the Appearance tab.

**FIGURE 13.14**

The General tab in the Internet Options dialog box

**Fonts button**   Opens the Fonts dialog box in which you can specify the font style and text size to use on those web pages for which the original author did not make a specification.

**Languages button**   Opens the Language Preference dialog box in which you can choose the character set to use on those web pages that offer content in more than one language. English is rapidly becoming the most common language in use on the Internet, so you may not use this option often.

**Accessibility button**   Opens the Accessibility dialog box in which you can choose how certain information is displayed in Internet Explorer, including font styles, colors, and text size. You can also specify that your own style sheet is used.

## Looking at the Security Tab

When you are connected to the Internet, you immediately have a couple of concerns that are not at issue otherwise: security and privacy. Security concerns involve protecting your computer from unsafe software. Privacy concerns involve protecting your personally identifiable information. To configure the security settings in Internet Explorer, you click the Security tab in the Internet Options dialog box, which we'll look at in this section. To configure privacy settings, you use the Privacy tab, which we'll look at in the next section.

The Security tab, which is shown in Figure 13.15, lets you specify the overall security level for each of four zones. Each zone has its own default security restrictions that tell Internet Explorer how to manage dynamic web page content such as ActiveX controls and Java applets. The zones are as follows:

**Internet**   Sites you visit that are not in one of the other categories; default security is set to Medium.

**Local Intranet**   Sites you can access on your corporate intranet; default security is set to Medium-Low.

**Trusted Sites**   Websites that you are confident will not send you potentially damaging content; default security is set to Low.

**Restricted Sites**   Sites that you visit but do not trust; default security is set to High.

**FIGURE 13.15**

The Security tab in the Internet Options dialog box

To change the current security level of a zone, select the zone, click the Default Level button, and then move the slider to the new security level you want to use:

**High**   Excludes any content capable of damaging your system. Cookies are disabled, and so some websites will not work as you might expect. This is the most secure setting.

**Medium**   Opens a warning dialog box in Internet Explorer before running ActiveX or Java applets on your system. This is a moderately secure setting that is good for everyday use and is selected by default.

**Medium-Low**   Same as Medium but without the prompts.

**Low**   Does not issue any warning but runs the ActiveX or Java applet automatically. This is the least secure setting.

Click the Custom Level button to create your own settings in the Security Settings dialog box, which is shown in Figure 13.16. You can individually configure how you want to manage certain categories, such as ActiveX controls and plug-ins, Java applets, scripting, file and font downloads, and user authentication.

**FIGURE 13.16**

The Security Settings dialog box

## Using the Privacy Tab

When you visit a site on the Internet, that site can store information about you in a file that resides on your computer. This file, called a cookie, might contain your name, your e-mail address, any other personal information you supply, and any preferences you established when visiting the site. When you revisit the site, it accesses the cookie in order to personalize the site for your visit. For example, you might get a message that welcomes you by name.

Once a site saves a cookie on your computer, only that website can access the cookie; it is not available to other websites. In addition, the website that created the cookie cannot access any other information that is stored on your computer.

### TYPES OF COOKIES

Using the settings on the Privacy tab in the Internet Options dialog box, you can choose to allow all websites to store cookies on your computer, to allow only some sites to do so, or to allow none to do so. Before we look at these settings, though, it is helpful to understand the types of cookies:

**Persistent cookies**   Are stored on your computer and remain there after you close Internet Explorer. You saw earlier in this chapter how to delete cookies using the options in the Temporary Internet Files section in the General tab of the Internet Options dialog box.

**Temporary cookies**   Are stored on your computer only as long as you have Internet Explorer open. When you close Internet Explorer, these cookies are deleted.

**First-party cookies**   Originate on or are sent to the website you are currently visiting.

**Third-party cookies**   Originate on or are sent to a website that you are not currently viewing. For example, a site that is advertising on the site you are currently viewing might create a cookie to track your Internet usage for marketing purposes.

**Unsatisfactory cookies**   Allow access to your personal information that can be used without your knowledge or consent.

### ESTABLISHING COOKIE PREFERENCES

In the Privacy tab, which is shown in Figure 13.17, you use the slider in the Settings section to specify how you will deal with cookies in the Internet zone. You have the following choices:

◆   Block All Cookies does exactly that. No website is allowed to store a cookie on your computer, and any existing cookies that are stored will not be able to be read by the sites that created them.

◆   High blocks all cookies from websites that don't have a compact privacy policy and blocks cookies that collect personal information without you knowledge or consent.

**NOTE**   A *compact privacy policy* is a statement in condensed computer-readable form about how a site handles personal information.

◆   Medium High blocks the following:

  ◆   Third-party cookies from sites that do not have a compact privacy policy

  ◆   Third-party cookies from sites that use personal information without your knowledge or consent

  ◆   First-party cookies from sites that use personal information without your knowledge or consent

◆ Medium, the default setting, blocks third-party cookies from sites that do not have a compact privacy policy and from sites that use personal information without your knowledge or consent. This setting restricts first-party cookies that use personal information without your knowledge or consent.

◆ Low restricts third-party cookies from sites that do not have a compact privacy policy and from sites that use personal information without your knowledge or consent.

◆ Accept All Cookies does exactly that. All cookies from all sites are accepted and stored on your computer, and any cookies that are already on your computer can be accessed by the websites that created them.

**FIGURE 13.17**

The Privacy tab in the Internet Options dialog box

When you use the slider bar to set your preferences, you establish a sort of one-size-fits-all rule that applies to all websites that you visit. You can use the other options in the Privacy tab to take a more granular approach and override the settings established using the slider bar.

To apply custom settings that you have stored in a file on your computer, click the Import button to open the Privacy Import dialog box, which is simply an Open dialog box in disguise and works the same as an Open dialog box.

To choose to Accept, Block, or Prompt for first-party and third-party cookies, click the Advanced button to open the Advanced Privacy Settings dialog box:

Click the Override Automatic Cookie Handling check box, and then select the options that you want. If you want to allow session cookies, click that check box, and then click OK.

To establish privacy settings for individual websites, click the Sites button (or the Edit button, if you are using Service Pack 1 or earlier) in the Web Sites section to open the Per Site Privacy Actions dialog box:

In the Address of Web Site box, type the complete URL for the site you want to allow or block, and then click Block or Allow. The site's domain name and your chosen setting will appear in the Managed Web Sites list. Use the Remove or Remove All button to delete a site from the list.

**TIP**    To back up your cookies, use the Import/Export Wizard (File ➤ Import and Export.)

### CONFIGURING THE POP-UP BLOCKER

One of the benefits of upgrading to SP2 is the pop-up blocker built into Internet Explorer. You can configure it on the Privacy tab by clicking the Settings button at the bottom of the dialog box (Figure 13.17). From the Pop-Up Blocker Settings dialog box, you can enter specific sites that should not be blocked, set other options, and set whether a sound should be played when a pop-up is blocked.

CHAPTER 13

You can also control pop-up blocking on a case-by-case basis as you are surfing the Web. When a pop-up is blocked, a bar appears across the top of the window letting you know. You can click that bar to open a menu containing your choices for that site:

If you choose Always Allow Pop-Ups from This Site, the site will be added to the list of allowed sites.

## Using the Content Tab

The Content tab, which is shown in Figure 13.18, contains settings you can use to restrict access to sites and specify how you want to manage digital certificates:

**Content Advisor**   Lets you control access to certain sites on the Internet and is particularly useful if children have access to the computer. Click Enable to open the Content Advisor dialog box. Use the tabs in this dialog box to establish the level of content you will allow users to view:

    **Ratings**   Lets you use a set of ratings developed by the Recreational Software Advisory Council (RSAC) for language, nudity, sex, and violence. Select one of these categories, and then adjust the slider to specify the level of content you will allow.

    **Approved Sites**   Lets you create lists of sites that are always viewable or always restricted regardless of how they are rated.

    **General**   Specifies whether people using this computer can view material that has not been rated; users may see some objectionable material if the website has not used the RSAC rating system. You can also opt to have the Supervisor enter a password so that users can view web pages that may contain objectionable material. You can click the Create Password button to create or change the Supervisor password; remember that you have to know the current Supervisor password before you can change it.

    **Advanced**   Lets you look at or modify the list of organizations providing ratings services.

**Certificates**   Lets you manage digital certificates used with certain client authentication servers. When you visit a site that has a secure connection, you can choose to verify that site's certificate. Such certificates are stored in a cache until you reboot your computer. To remove these certificates manually, click the Clear SSL State button. (SSL is an abbreviation for Secure Sockets Layer.) Click Certificates to view the personal digital certificates installed on this system, or click Publishers to designate a particular software publisher as a trustworthy publisher. This means that Windows XP Professional applications can download, install, and use software from these agencies without asking for your permission first.

**Personal Information**   Lets you look at or change the settings for Windows AutoComplete and your own personal profile. Click AutoComplete to change the way that this feature works within Windows XP Professional, or click My Profile to create an Address Book entry for yourself that represents your profile or to select an existing Address Book entry to represent your profile. You can then send this information to any websites that request information about you when you visit their site.

**FIGURE 13.18**

The Content tab in
the Internet Options
dialog box

## Setting Up the Connections Tab

The Connections tab, which is shown in Figure 13.19, allows you to specify how your system connects to the Internet. Click the Setup button to run the New Connection Wizard and set up a connection to an Internet Service Provider. (See Chapter 12 for complete details on this.) If you use a modem, click the Settings button to open the My ISP Settings dialog box, where you can specify all aspects of the phone connection to your ISP.

**FIGURE 13.19**

The Connections tab
in the Internet Options
dialog box

CHAPTER 13

## Looking at the Programs Tab

The Programs tab, which is shown in Figure 13.20, lets you set your default program choices for HTML editor, e-mail, newsgroup reader, Internet call, calendar, and contact list. Finally, you can specify that Internet Explorer check to see if it is configured as the default browser on your system each time it starts running.

A new feature as of SP2 is the ability to manage add-ons. Click the Manage Add-Ons button in Figure 13.20, or choose Tools ➢ Manage Add-Ons. In the Manage Add-Ons dialog box, open the Show list and choose Add-Ons Currently Loaded in Internet Explorer, as in Figure 13.21. From there you can decide to disable certain add-ons or even remove them completely. Very handy! This feature also provides a way of getting rid of adware add-ons that you might have stumbled into at some point, like redirecting Search bars.

**FIGURE 13.20**

The Programs tab in the Internet Options dialog box

**FIGURE 13.21**

With SP2 installed, you can manage IE add-ons.

### Configuring the Advanced Tab

The Advanced tab, which is shown in Figure 13.22, lets you look at or change a number of settings that control much of Internet Explorer's behavior, including accessibility, browsing, multimedia, security, printing, and searching, and how HTTP 1.1 settings are interpreted. Click a check box to turn an option on; clear the check box to turn the option off.

Changes you make here stay in effect until you change them again, until you download an automatic configuration file, or until you click the Restore Defaults button, which returns the settings in the Advanced tab to their original values.

**FIGURE 13.22**

The Advanced tab in the Internet Options dialog box

# Customizing the Internet Explorer Toolbar

When you unlock the toolbars in Internet Explorer (View ➢ Toolbars ➢ Lock the Toolbars to toggle it on/off), each becomes movable. You can drag it around by its *handle* (the dotted area at its left edge).

You can also customize the Standard toolbar, adding buttons for features you use frequently and removing buttons for features you don't use. To do so, follow these steps:

1.  Choose View ➢ Toolbars ➢ Customize. The Customize Toolbar dialog box opens.

2. To remove a button, click it in the Current Toolbar Buttons list and click Remove. To add a button, click it in the Available Toolbar Buttons list and click Add.

3. To rearrange buttons, click one in the Current Toolbar Buttons list and then click Move Up or Move Down.

4. To control the associated text for each icon, open the Text Options list and select a setting.

5. To control the size of the icons, open the Icon Options list and choose a size.

6. Click OK when you are finished.

**NOTE**   The Reset button returns the Standard toolbar to its default configuration. However, if you have installed any add-on programs that add their own buttons to the toolbar, such as an antivirus program or a conduit for a PDA, it remains even after you click Reset.

## Changing Text Size

In addition to the many customizations you have already learned about, you can control how a web page appears by using commands on the View menu.

One of the handiest ones for people with limited vision is the ability to change the font size for web page content. To do so, choose View ➢ Text Size and then choose Larger or Largest. This works with all web pages that have been formatted with standard HTML tags and are not encoded to use a particular font size. Figure 13.23 shows a web page set to Largest.

If you have a mouse with a wheel on it, you can use the wheel to change the text size too. Hold down the Ctrl key as you roll the wheel. Rolling forward decreases the text size; rolling backward increases it.

**FIGURE 13.23**
This web page is being viewed with the text size set to Largest.

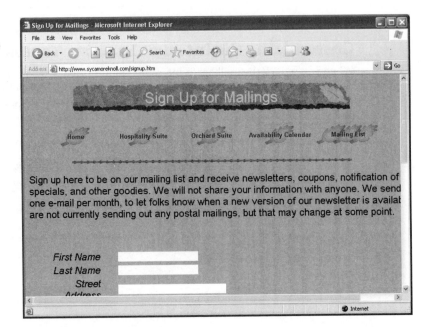

# MSN Explorer

Windows XP comes with an alternative to Internet Explorer known as MSN Explorer. It's a custom version of IE for use primarily with the MSN Internet service, but you can use it as your only browser if you prefer it, no matter which ISP you use. It's a "friendlier" interface than IE, and perhaps more suitable for beginners, but serious techies will probably not want to bother with it.

As you can see in Figure 13.24, MSN Explorer is basically just an alternate version of Internet Explorer with larger buttons and closer ties to Microsoft-affiliated web content such as Hotmail. It's meant to be a competitor to true online communities such as AOL.

**FIGURE 13.24**

MSN Explorer is an alternative way to surf the Web, well suited for beginners.

Take these steps to set up MSN Explorer to work with your existing Internet connection:

1. Choose Start ➢ All Programs ➢ MSN Explorer.

   The first time you do, you'll see a question asking whether you want to get on the Internet and write e-mail through the Start menu using MSN Explorer. Answer No unless you want it to replace the program assignments at the top of the Start menu with MSN Explorer for both web and e-mail.

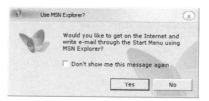

2. The first time you run MSN Explorer, a wizard will walk you through its setup. Work through it until you come to the question Do You Want MSN Internet Access? (If you have a customized

version that came preinstalled, it might look a little different, such as with the DellNet version shown here.) Then make sure you answer No, I Already Have Internet Access.

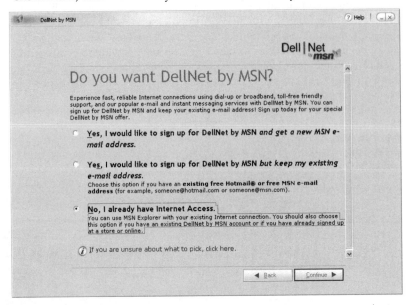

**3.** Continue through the wizard until it asks about your e-mail address. To use MSN Explorer, you must have a Hotmail or MSN e-mail address. If you don't have one, you'll need to sign up for one in order to use MSN Explorer; you can do that through the wizard.

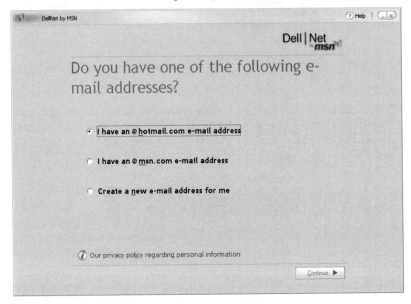

4. Finish working through the wizard. Eventually a Welcome window for MSN Explorer will appear.

5. From here, just start clicking things to figure out how MSN Explorer works, or click Take the Tour if you want more help.

**TIP** When you close the MSN Explorer window, it remains active; to really close it completely you must right-click its icon in the notification area and choose Exit MSN Explorer.

# Using Built-In Internet Utilities

Windows XP Professional includes several standard Internet utilities. These programs are, in most cases, functionally identical to the same programs or commands found on pretty much every flavor of UNIX. Although most people are not going to use these nearly as often as they will their web browsers, I describe each in the following sections so that you at least know what they are. It is useful to acquaint yourself, for example, with FTP—if you are ever on a Windows XP Professional system that for some reason does not have a web browser, knowing how to use FTP to transfer files enables you to connect to Spry, Netscape, or Microsoft and download a browser.

Following this brief rundown of each of the tools, we will look at other Internet applications you can download via the Internet. Note that with each of the following programs, you can get help by typing the program name at the command prompt followed by **-?** (hyphen, question mark).

To open any of the following utilities, you type a command at a command prompt. To open a command prompt window, do one of the following:

♦ Choose Start ➤ Run, and in the Open text box, type the command (the name of the utility).

♦ Choose Start ➤ All Programs ➤ Accessories ➤ Command Prompt.

## Address Resolution Display and Control

The Address Resolution Protocol (ARP) program is used to display and/or modify entries in the Internet-to-Ethernet (or Token Ring) address translation tables that are used by the Address Resolution Protocol. Various command-line switches are documented in the -? option. To use ARP, type **arp** at the command prompt.

## File Transfer Protocol (FTP)

FTP is the standard TCP/IP file transfer protocol used for moving text and binary files between computers on the Internet. If you have an account on a distant computer on the Internet, you can use FTP to download files from the other computer to your PC and to upload files from your PC to the host. In addition, there are tens of thousands of *anonymous* FTP archives all over the Internet that accept logins from anybody who wants copies of their files.

**TIP** You can do FTP from Internet Explorer; you don't necessarily have to use the command prompt for it. Just type the FTP address in the Address bar, as in `ftp.mysite.com`. However, the FTP capabilities in IE are rather limited. If you do a lot of FTP transferring, consider a stand alone FTP application.

The Windows XP Professional FTP program (and the others mentioned here) can be found in the `Winnt\System32` folder, which is included in your search path. Therefore, you don't have to specify the path when you enter an FTP command. To connect to an FTP server, follow these steps:

**1.** At a command prompt, type the following, and then press Enter:

   `FTP <host name>`

**2.** Windows XP Professional displays the `ftp>` prompt:

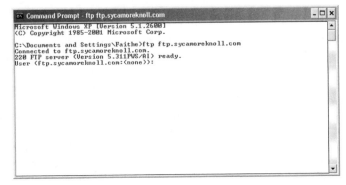

**3.** After FTP connects to the server, the server asks for your username and password. If you're connecting to an anonymous FTP server, type **anonymous** as your username, and type your e-mail address as your password or leave the password field blank and press Enter. For your password, use the standard *name@address.domain* format.

Most FTP servers use the same system of directories and subdirectories that you may be familiar with from DOS and Windows. To see the contents of the current directory, type **dir** or **ls** at the `ftp>` prompt.

If the FTP server is in UNIX mode, a *d* as the first letter in a listing indicates that the item in that line is a directory. If a dash is the first character, the item is a file. The name of the file or directory is at the extreme right. See Chapter 28 for more info regarding UNIX mode.

Use the command **cd** *name* (typing the name of the subdirectory in place of *name*) to move to a subdirectory.

Use the command **cd ..** to move to the next higher level. (Press the spacebar after you enter the *d* and before you type the first period.)

When you download a file from an FTP server, you must specify that it is either an ASCII text file or a binary file. As a general rule, binary files that you can read on a PC have a DOS file extension (rather than TXT for a text file or PS for a Postscript print file), but you really can't be certain. ASCII text files may or may not have a file extension.

When you initially connect to an FTP server, you're in ASCII mode. Before you try to transfer a binary file, you have to change modes. To switch to binary mode, use the command **binary**. To switch back to ASCII mode, use the command **ascii**. The host acknowledges your mode-change command.

To download a file from the server, use the command **get** *filename* (typing the name of the file in place of *filename*). If you want to store the file on your PC with a different name, use the command **get** *filename newname* (typing the file you want to get in place of *filename* and the name you want to store the file under in place of *newname*). When the file transfer is complete, the host sends you another message.

When you are finished with your FTP session, type **disconnect** to break the connection to the server. You can connect to another host by typing the new server's address.

To close the FTP utility, type the command **quit**.

**TIP**   One handy use for the command-line FTP client is automating file transfers. Because FTP accepts scripts (via the -s:*filename* switch), you can easily create a script (which is just a text file of FTP commands) to log on to an FTP server, switch to a particular directory, transfer a long listing of files in one or both directions, and then log off. You can even set this to occur at a given time of day by using the Windows XP Professional at command. (For details on using the at  command, type **help at** from any command prompt.)

## Finger

The finger program can be used to retrieve user-supplied information about a user (or host computer). Unfortunately, many users do not have a finger file for others to retrieve and view (or even know about creating one), and some host computers do not provide finger services, so your mileage will vary. On the other hand, some universities and institutions do use finger services, and on these you can find some useful (or at least interesting) information. To use finger, type **finger** *auser@someplace.com*. Enter a valid username or at least a host name, press Enter, and you may get a listing of information.

## Ping

Ping is a useful diagnostic utility that tests your ability to connect your computer to another device through the Internet by sending an echo request and displaying the number of milliseconds required to receive a reply. Whenever you need to diagnose your Internet connection problems, pinging a known host computer is a good first test.

To set up a Ping test, follow these steps:

1. At a command prompt, type **ping** *destination*. Use the domain name or the IP address of the host you want to test in place of *destination*. If you do not get a response when using the domain name of the destination, try the IP address of the destination instead.

2. Ping sends four sets of Internet Control Message Protocol (ICMP) echo packets to the host you specify and displays the amount of time it took to receive each reply, as shown here:

*CHAPTER 13* (vertical margin text)

The important part of the Ping display is the time</>nnnms section of the Reply lines. Ping's capability to connect to the distant host tells you that your connection to the Internet is working properly; the number of milliseconds can tell you if you have an efficient connection to this particular host (anything less than about 500ms is usually acceptable).

## Protocol Statistics (*netstat*)

Use the netstat command to display a list of currently active Internet connections. At the command prompt, type **netstat**. A list of connections similar to the ones in the following illustration appears:

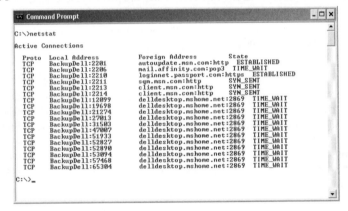

A netstat report includes the following information:

**Proto**   Shows the networking protocol in use for each active connection. For PPP or SLIP connections to the Internet, the Proto column always reads TCP, which specifies a TCP/IP connection.

**Local Address**   Indicates the identity of your PC on the network.

**Foreign Address**   Shows the address of each distant computer to which a connection is currently active.

**State**   Shows the condition of each connection.

## Remote File Copy (RCP)

If you've ever wanted to copy a file from one directory or drive to another on a remote computer without having the file go through your modem twice (as a normal copy or xcopy would), you understand the purpose of the RCP program. You can also use RCP to copy files from one remote computer to another remote computer without being copied to your computer first. Not all systems permit you to use this command, and if they do, of course you are limited to the directory areas for which you have access rights. Type **-?** for specific usage and option information. To use RCP, open a command prompt, and type **rcp**.

## Remote Program Execution (REXEC)

The REXEC program is just as powerful as Remote Shell/Script (RSH; discussed in the next section), if not more so, and likewise, it is quite restricted by most system administrators. It functions just like RSH, except that it starts binary programs rather than scripts on the remote host. Windows XP Professional stations *do* permit remote execution of programs, provided the system administrator has enabled this and has given you the necessary access rights. To run REXEC, type **rexec** at a command prompt.

## Remote Shell/Script (RSH)

Another potentially powerful utility, RSH is used to start a script program on a remote host. Again, some host computers do not support this, and of those that do, your access rights may preclude or severely limit what you can do. To use RSH, type **rsh** at a command prompt.

## Remote Terminal (Telnet)

Telnet is one of the utilities you are somewhat more likely to use, particularly in university settings or when data you need to access without using HTML is stored on a remote host (a less and less common scenario, thankfully). When you connect through a Telnet connection, your PC becomes a terminal on the distant system. In most cases, a Telnet login requires an account on the host (remote) machine, but many systems accept logins from anybody who wants to connect. Among the most common public Telnet sites are online library catalogs. Other public Telnet sites let you use certain character-based Internet services that may not be available on your computer.

To set up a Telnet connection, type `Telnet hostname` at a command prompt (using the domain name or IP address of the computer to which you want to connect in place of *hostname*). Telnet connects your computer to the host whose name you supplied and displays messages from that host in the Telnet window.

Most Telnet hosts display a series of login prompts as soon as you connect. If you're connecting to a public Telnet host, it will probably tell you how to log in.

**NOTE**   Telnet is also used to configure some routers, although many are configured through a web (http) interface.

## The *route* Command

You can use `route` to view, add to, or modify a routing table on a Windows XP Professional computer with more than one network interface. If you have a *multihomed* computer (one with multiple network cards) and have enabled IP forwarding in the TCP/IP Properties dialog box, you can use the `route` command to view and modify the table of information that tells Windows XP Professional where to direct TCP/IP data from one interface to another. Using this command on a computer with one network interface will also display basic routing information. To use `route`, type **route** at a command prompt.

## Trace Route (*tracert*)

In most cases, when you set up a connection to a distant computer through the Internet, your signal path passes through several routers along the way. Because this is all happening in a fraction of a second, these intermediate routers are usually invisible. But when you're having trouble making a connection, the trace route command (`tracert`) can help isolate the source of the problem.

To run a trace route test, type `tracert target` at a command prompt. In place of *target*, type the address of the distant system. A trace route report appears in the prompt window.

In many cases, your connection will pass through one or more backbone networks between your connection to the Internet and your ultimate destination.

CHAPTER 13

`tracert` steps through the connection route, one step at a time. For each step, it shows the amount of time needed to reach that router, in milliseconds. If an intermediate router or a connection between two intermediate routers fails, `tracert` will not display any steps beyond that point in the route. If that happens, you can assume that the failed site is the reason that you are unable to connect to your intended destination.

## Summary

Within the space of a very few years, many of us have come to consider access to the Internet an essential component of daily life. It is now the first place I turn when I want information about almost anything, and it's rare that I don't find what I'm looking for.

Internet Explorer is far from the only tool available for communicating on the Internet. In the next chapter, you'll learn about Messenger, NetMeeting, and Remote Desktop Connection; then in Chapter 15 you'll learn about e-mail with Outlook Express.

# Chapter 14

# Using the Communications Programs

You may never have an occasion to use the programs I'm going to discuss in this chapter, but I'm including information about them so that you'll know they exist, what each is best suited for, and how to access them when the need arises. They're alternatives to the ubiquitous web browser interface for working with data between PCs on a network or the Internet.

◆ Connecting with HyperTerminal

◆ Using Windows Messenger

◆ Using Remote Desktop Connection

## Connecting with HyperTerminal

HyperTerminal is a utility program you can use to connect to another computer (perhaps one that uses a different operating system such as UNIX), to an information service such as the book catalog at your local library, or to a bulletin board. You can use this type of connection to download or transfer files.

**TIP**   HyperTerminal is a class of program known as *terminal emulation software*. In other words, it pretends to be a terminal attached to the remote computer. HyperTerminal is not a web browser and cannot access websites on the Internet. For that particular task, see the description of how to use Internet Explorer in Chapter 13.

### Creating a New HyperTerminal Connection

To create the phone numbers and specifics for initiating a HyperTerminal connection, follow these steps:

1. Choose Start ➢ All Programs ➢ Accessories ➢ Communications ➢ HyperTerminal to open the Connection Description dialog box in the foreground and the HyperTerminal window in the background.

2. The first time you run HyperTerminal, you might see a dialog box asking if you want to make HyperTerminal your default Telnet application. Click Yes or No as appropriate.

3. In the Name box, enter the descriptive name you want to assign to this connection, and then choose one of the icons from the selection displayed at the bottom of the dialog box. Click OK to open the Connect To dialog box.

4.  Verify the country and area code, type the telephone number you want to use with this connection, and confirm your modem type. Click OK to open the Connect dialog box.

5.  Check the phone number for this connection, and if it is incorrect, click Modify to change it. To look at or change any of the settings associated with the phone line or with dialing, click Dialing Properties to open the Phone and Modem Options dialog box. (See Chapter 12 for information about this dialog box.)

6.  When you are ready to make the connection, click Call. You will be connected to the other computer, and a named window for the connection will open. If you do not want to call now, click Cancel, and the named window for the connection will be displayed, as shown in Figure 14.1.

**FIGURE 14.1**

The HyperTerminal main window

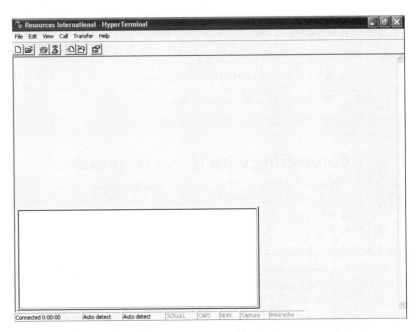

The next thing that you see in the window will depend on the service or computer you have connected to; you may be asked to select a terminal type, to enter a password, or to make a selection from a menu. When you are finished, use the appropriate command to log off the remote computer before you close the HyperTerminal window.

## Sending and Receiving Files

While using HyperTerminal, you can send and receive files and capture what you see on your screen to your printer. To send a file, follow these steps:

1.  Choose Transfer ➢ Send File to open the Send File dialog box.

2.  Enter the name of the file in the Filename box, or click Browse to locate it.

3.  In the Protocol box, accept the protocol that HyperTerminal suggests, or click the down arrow to select another protocol from the list.

**NOTE**    If you know the specific protocol for the system to which you are connected, select that protocol. If you don't know the protocol, stick with Zmodem, which is a generic, commonly used protocol.

**4.** Click Send.

To receive a file, follow these steps:

**1.** Choose Transfer ➢ Receive File to open the Receive File dialog box.

**2.** Indicate where the received file should be stored, and specify the protocol if necessary.

**3.** Click Receive.

To capture what you see on your screen to the printer, choose Transfer ➢ Capture to Printer.

# Using Windows Messenger

Windows Messenger is a real-time chat program, similar to its competitors Yahoo! Messenger and AOL Instant Messenger. You can type back and forth in real time with others, but you can also do a variety of other collaborative activities with your chatmates, including transferring files, chatting via voice (with microphones), sharing applications, and displaying one another's webcams. In this chapter, I'll refer to Windows Messenger as just plain old Messenger, for simplicity, but keep in mind that it is far from the only messenger service in town. It just happens to be the one you get for free with Windows XP.

Windows Messenger might look suspiciously similar to an earlier Windows product called Net-Meeting that shipped with Windows 2000. The two applications are indeed similar, and Microsoft has lately been trying to deemphasize NetMeeting and emphasize Windows Messenger instead. Nearly all NetMeeting features have been incorporated into Windows Messenger, so there is little reason to prefer NetMeeting anymore.

Microsoft periodically updates Windows Messenger, so the version you have might not look or work exactly the same as described here. When you start Messenger, it might prompt you to download the most recent version; if not, you can use Windows Update to retrieve it.

**TIP**    If you need to use NetMeeting instead of Windows Messenger for some reason, you might find this site helpful: www.microsoft.com/windows/netmeeting. It doesn't get updated very often since it's an "old technology" site, but from here, you can download a free copy of NetMeeting and learn about configuring it.

## Starting Messenger

To start Messenger, choose Start ➢ All Programs ➢ Windows Messenger. Alternatively, if Messenger is displaying an icon in the notification area, double-click it.

If you haven't added a .NET Passport to your Windows XP user account, Messenger displays a Click Here to Sign In link in its window. Clicking this link starts the .NET Passport Wizard, which guides you through the process of adding an existing .NET Passport to Windows XP or getting a new .NET Passport and adding that to Windows. Once you've done that, Messenger signs you in.

Once you've started Messenger, it displays an icon in your notification area. Click this icon to display a menu of actions you can take with Messenger.

When Messenger appears on your screen, chances are that it tells you that you don't have anyone in your contacts list and suggests you click the Add button to start adding contacts. (If you've just set Messenger up, your lack of contacts should be no surprise.) Figure 14.2 shows Messenger with one contact added.

**FIGURE 14.2**
Messenger with one
contact added

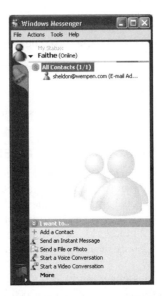

You're probably itching to add some contacts and get on with messaging. But before you do that, configure Messenger by choosing options as described in the next section.

## Configuring Messenger

Messenger comes with a raft of configuration options. You don't need to set all of them at once—this section covers them all in case you want to—but you should know about them before using Messenger. At the very least, you should edit your public profile so that you know what information other people can access about you.

Choose Tools ➢ Options to display the Options dialog box, and then configure your choice of the options described in the following sections.

### Personal Tab Options

The Personal tab of the Options dialog box (shown in Figure 14.3) contains a couple important settings and a couple of trivial ones.

**My .NET Messenger Service Display Name text box**   Enter the name you want Messenger to display for you.

**Change Font button**   Use this button and the resulting Set My Message Font dialog box to specify the font you want to use in instant messaging windows.

**FIGURE 14.3**
In the Personal tab of the Options dialog box, set your display name and edit your Passport public profile.

**Show Graphics (Emoticons) in Instant Messages check box**   Clear this check box (which is selected by default) if you want to prevent Messenger from displaying emoticons (for example, ☺).

**Quality**   Mark the check box in this section if you want to send information to Microsoft about your usage to help them improve the product.

## Phone Tab Options

The Phone tab of the Options dialog box (shown in Figure 14.4) lets you specify your country or region code and your home, work, and mobile phone numbers. Don't put any numbers here that you don't want to be public knowledge—or least viewable by everyone you chat with.

**FIGURE 14.4**
In the Phone tab of the Options dialog box, specify your country or region code and enter the phone numbers you want Messenger to know.

## Preferences Tab Options

The Preferences tab of the Options dialog box (shown in Figure 14.5) contains a slew of options that affect Messenger's behavior:

**Run Windows Messenger When Windows Starts check box**   Leave this check box selected (as it is by default) if you want Windows to launch Messenger every time you log on to Windows. Clear this check box if you prefer to run Messenger manually when you need it.

**Allow Windows Messenger to Run in the Background check box**   Leave this check box selected (as it is by default) if you want Messenger to be able to run in the background and lurk in your notification area when you're not actively using it. Keeping Messenger running in the background lets you know instantly when one of your contacts comes online or sends you a message, but it also means that you need to keep your Internet connection open all the time. If you don't want Messenger to run in the background, clear this check box, and Messenger will exit when you close its window.

**Show Me As "Away" When I'm Inactive for *NN* Minutes check box and text box**   Leave this check box selected (as it is by default) if you want Messenger to change your status to Away after the specified period of inactivity. (Adjust the number of minutes in the text box as necessary. The default setting is 10 minutes, which is too short for many busy people.) Clear this check box if you don't want Messenger to monitor you in this way.

**Allow Windows Messenger to Receive Ink check box**   When this is selected, people can use the Pen feature when chatting to chat with "ink" which is like a drawing tool. It's a feature of Windows XP Tablet PC edition but some regular programs can use it too. What you send with it is sent as a graphic of sorts. The Pen tool will not be available to people you chat with if you have this turned off.

**Display Alerts When Contacts Come Online check box**   Leave this check box selected (as it is by default) if you want Messenger to pop up an alert above the notification area when one of your contacts comes online.

**Display Alerts When an Instant Message Is Received check box**   Leave this check box selected (as it is by default) if you want Messenger to pop up an alert above the notification area when you receive an instant message.

**Block Alerts and Set Status to "Busy" When Running Full-Screen Programs**   Mark this to prevent people from trying to chat with you while you are running an application that is full-screen, like a game.

**Play Sound When Contacts Sign In or Send a Message check box**   Leave this check box selected (as it is by default) if you want Messenger to play a sound when contacts of yours sign in or send you a message. This audio alert is especially useful if you turn off the two visual alerts. If you use this option, you can click the Sounds button to customize the sounds displayed. Windows displays the Sound and Audio Devices Properties dialog box. In the Program Events list box on the Sounds page, scroll down to the Windows Messenger category. There you can assign sounds that you like to these events: the Contact Online event (when a contact signs in), the New Alert event (when Messenger displays an alert), the New Mail event, and the New Message event. Then click the OK button. Windows closes the Sound and Audio Devices Properties dialog box.

**File Transfer text box**   Specify the folder in which you want Messenger to put files that you receive from your contacts. The default setting is in your `My Documents\My Received Files` folder.

**FIGURE 14.5**
In the Preferences tab of the Options dialog box, customize Messenger's behavior.

## Privacy Tab Options

The Privacy tab of the Options dialog box (shown in Figure 14.6) is where you maintain your Allow List (people who can see your online status and can send you messages) and your Block List (people who can do neither).

**FIGURE 14.6**
Use the Privacy tab of the Options dialog box to keep your Allow List and your Block List up-to-date.

To move a contact from one list to another, select them in the appropriate list box and click the Allow button or the Block button.

**TIP**     By default, Messenger allows all other users to contact you and view your status until you block them. If you want to use Messenger privately, consider blocking all other users until you decide to allow them. To do so, select the All Other Users item in the My Allow List and click the Block button to move it to the My Block List.

To see which users have added you to their contacts lists, click the View button. Messenger displays the Which Users Have Added You? dialog box, which provides an unadorned list of names. You can right-click a name and choose Add to Contacts from the shortcut menu to add the person to your list of contacts, or you can choose Properties from the shortcut menu to display a Properties dialog box giving information about the person.

## Connection Tab Options

In the Connection tab of the Options dialog box, you can specify proxy server settings if you connect to the Internet through a proxy server (for example, through a company network). If not, leave these settings alone.

## Running the Audio and Video Tuning Wizard

If you have speakers (or headphones) and a microphone, you can use them to make voice calls via Messenger. If you have a webcam or another live video camera, you can make video calls as well. To set Messenger up for making voice and video calls, make sure your sound and video hardware is plugged in and working, and then run the Audio and Video Tuning Wizard by taking the following steps:

1. Choose Tools ➢ Audio Tuning Wizard. Messenger starts the Audio and Video Tuning Wizard, which displays its first screen. This instructs you to make sure that your camera, speakers, and microphone are plugged in and turned on, and to close any other programs that might be using them.

2. Click the Next button. The wizard displays its second screen (shown in Figure 14.7).

**FIGURE 14.7**
On the second screen of the Audio and Video Tuning Wizard, choose the video camera to use for video calls.

3. In the Camera drop-down list, select the video camera to use.

4. Click the Next button. The wizard grabs the video feed from the camera and displays it on its third screen (shown in Figure 14.8).

5. Adjust the picture until it shows what you want it to.

6. Click the Next button. The wizard displays its fourth screen with tips on positioning your microphone and speakers.

**FIGURE 14.8**
On the third screen of the Audio and Video Tuning Wizard, adjust your video camera to show the image you want.

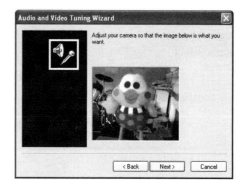

7. Move your microphone or your speakers if necessary.

8. Click the Next button. The wizard displays its fifth screen (shown in Figure 14.9).

**FIGURE 14.9**
On the fifth screen of the Audio and Video Tuning Wizard, choose which microphone and speakers to use.

9. In the Microphone drop-down list, select the microphone to use.

10. In the Speakers drop-down list, select the output device (for example, a sound card) connected to the speakers.

11. If you're using headphones, select the I Am Using Headphones check box, which tells the wizard to turn off echo cancellation. (With headphones, you don't need this because the echoes should be confined to your head.)

12. Click the Next button. The wizard displays its sixth screen (shown in Figure 14.10).

13. Click the Click to Test Speakers button to play a sound for a volume check. Drag the Speaker Volume slider to adjust the volume as necessary. Click the Stop button (which replaces the Click to Test Speakers button) to stop the sound.

14. Click the Next button. The wizard displays its seventh screen (shown in Figure 14.11).

CHAPTER 14

**FIGURE 14.10**
On the sixth screen of the Audio and Video Tuning Wizard, test your speakers or headphones.

**FIGURE 14.11**
On the seventh screen of the Audio and Video Tuning Wizard, set your microphone volume.

15. Speak into your microphone for 20 to 30 seconds at normal volume. (If you want, read the sample text shown, but it's instructive rather than magical, so declaim poetry or curse fluently if you prefer.) The Audio and Video Tuning Wizard adjusts the Microphone Volume slider to an appropriate level.

16. Click the Next button. You should see the eighth and final screen, telling you that you've completed the wizard. (If you had a microphone problem, you'll see instead a dialog box telling you that instead. Fix the problem and try setting the microphone volume again.)

17. Click the Finish button. The wizard closes and applies the settings it helped you choose.

## Signing Out and Signing Back In

Messenger automatically signs you in when you start it. But you can sign out manually, leaving Messenger running, by choosing File ➢ Sign Out.

**NOTE** The first time you sign out, if you have things going on, Messenger displays a dialog box explaining that signing out will close all your conversations and stop any file transfers. Click the OK button to proceed. After that, Messenger doesn't give you any warning when you sign out.

To sign back in as the same user, click the Click Here to Sign In As Username link in the Windows Messenger window. Messenger signs you in. To sign in using a different Passport, click the Or, Click Here to Sign In As Someone Else link, or choose File ➢ Sign In, or click the Messenger icon in the notification area and choose Sign In from the menu it displays. Messenger displays the .NET Messenger Service dialog box (shown in Figure 14.12). Enter your sign-in name and password, and then click the OK button.

**FIGURE 14.12**

Signing back in to Messenger Service

## Adding a Contact

You can add a contact to your list of contacts in several ways: by using their e-mail address or Passport sign-in name; by searching for them in a directory; by adding them when they contact you; or by reciprocating when they add you as a contact.

### Adding a Contact by E-mail Address or Passport Sign-In

If you know a contact's e-mail address or Passport sign-in name, you can add them to your contacts list as follows:

1. Click the Add a Contact hyperlink in the Messenger window (or choose Tools ➢ Add a Contact). Messenger displays the How Do You Want to Add a Contact? screen of the Add a Contact Wizard (shown in Figure 14.13).

2. Leave the By E-mail Address or Sign-In Name option button selected, as it is by default.

3. Click the Next button. Messenger displays the Please Type Your Contact's Complete E-mail Address screen.

4. Enter the e-mail address and click the Next button. Messenger searches for a matching user. If it finds one, it displays a Success screen telling you that it has added the contact to your list. If Messenger doesn't find a match, it offers to send a message to the user inviting them to try Messenger. Take up this request if you like.

**FIGURE 14.13**
On the How Do You Want to Add a Contact? screen of the Add a Contact Wizard, specify whether to add a contact by e-mail address or by Passport sign-in name or whether you want to search for them.

## Adding a Contact by Searching for Them

You can also add a contact to your contacts list by searching for them:

1. Click the Add a Contact hyperlink in the Messenger window (or choose Tools ➤ Add a Contact). Messenger displays the How Do You Want to Add a Contact? screen of the Add a Contact Wizard.

2. Select the Search for a Contact option button.

3. Click the Next button. Messenger displays a screen where you can enter information about a contact (shown in Figure 14.14).

**FIGURE 14.14**
To add a contact to your list in Messenger, you can search for them by name.

4. Enter the person's first name and last name. If you're sure of their country or region, specify that in the Country/Region drop-down list. Enter any other known information as well, like City and State, if the country you chose allows it.

   ◆ By default, Messenger searches in the Hotmail Member Directory. You may be able to choose another search location, such as your Address Book, in the Search for This Person At drop-down list.

5. Click the Next button. Messenger displays a Search Results screen showing possible matches.

6. Select the right person and click the Next button. Messenger then walks you through the process of having the .NET service send an e-mail to the person and tell them how to install Messenger and contact you. You can add your own message to this e-mail, but Messenger won't give you the person's e-mail address so that you can contact them directly.

### Adding a Contact When Someone Adds You to Their Contacts List

You can also add a contact quickly by adding a person who adds you to *their* contacts list (unless you've configured Messenger not to notify you when this happens).

When someone adds you to their contacts list, Messenger displays the Windows Messenger dialog box shown in Figure 14.15, asking whether you want to allow this person or block them. Select the Allow This Person to See When You Are Online and Contact You option button or the Block This Person from Seeing When You Are Online and Contacting You option button as appropriate. If you want to add the person to your contacts list, leave the Add This Person to My Contact List check box selected. If not, clear it. Then click the OK button. Messenger closes the dialog box and takes the actions you specified.

**FIGURE 14.15**
Messenger displays this Windows Messenger dialog box when someone adds you to their contacts list. Specify whether to allow the contact or block them.

## Removing a Contact from Your Contacts List

To remove a contact from your contacts list, select their entry and press the Delete key. Alternatively, right-click the contact and choose Delete Contact from the shortcut menu. Messenger deletes the contact without confirmation.

## Chatting

To chat with a Messenger user, double-click the user's entry in the Online list, or right-click the user's entry in the Online list and choose Send an Instant Message from the shortcut menu.

Messenger opens a Conversation window with the user. Figure 14.16 shows an example. Type a message into the text box and press the Enter key (or click the Send button) to send it.

**FIGURE 14.16**
Starting a conversation in Messenger

The other user receives a screen pop-up (of which Figure 14.17 shows an example) telling them that you've sent them a message and a minimized Conversation window. The user can display the Conversation window by clicking the screen pop-up (if they're quick enough to catch it before it disappears) or by clicking the Conversation window's button on the Taskbar.

**FIGURE 14.17**
Messenger displays a screen pop-up like this when someone sends you a message.

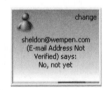

Figure 14.18 shows a chat getting started in a Conversation window. Note the readout at the bottom that tells you that the other protagonist in the chat is typing a message. This alert helps you avoid sending overlapping messages and having the conversations spiral off into multiple threads.

## Adding More People to a Conversation

To add a third or fourth person to your current conversation, choose Actions ➤ Invite Someone to This Conversation, or click the Invite Someone to This Conversation hyperlink on the right side of the conversation window. Then choose one of your other contacts from the dialog box that appears.

## Setting Font, Style, and Color for Text You Send

If you want to be distinctive, you can change the font, style, and color for text you send to others and that you see on your screen. For the text you see in the Messenger windows, you can change the size as well. (You can't change the size of the text that others see, and they can't change the size that you see.)

To set the font, style, color, and size, choose Edit ➢ Change Font. Messenger displays the Change My Message Font dialog box. Choose settings you like and click the OK button to apply them.

**FIGURE 14.18**

Chatting in a Conversation window. The readout at the bottom warns the user that the other participant is typing a message.

## Adding Voice to a Conversation

If both participants have functioning audio hardware, you can add voice to a Messenger conversation between two people. (You can't use voice in a conversation that has three or four people.)

As usual for Internet telephony, the audio that's transmitted is converted from its (spoken) analog form to a digitized version, transmitted digitally, and then converted back to analog output at the sound card, headphones, or speakers on the other end. As a result, the quality tends to suffer compared to a regular phone call, in which the audio stays analog the whole way. That said, you can get intelligible audio quality over a connection as slow as 21.6Kbps, acceptable quality in the 40–53Kbps range, and good quality over faster connections.

**NOTE**   If you haven't run the Audio and Video Tuning Wizard, Messenger runs it the first time you click the Talk button.

To add voice to your current conversation, click the Start Talking heading in the right pane of the Conversation window. Messenger displays a Speakers volume control (shown in Figure 14.19) and notifies the person you're chatting with that you want to have a voice conversation. They get to accept this or decline it. If they accept, Messenger establishes the connection.

To hang up the voice portion of the call, click the Stop Talking heading.

CHAPTER 14

**FIGURE 14.19**
When you add voice to a Messenger conversation, the Conversation window displays a Speakers volume control .

## Adding Video to a Conversation

If one or both participants have video hardware installed, you can add video to a Messenger conversation between two people. (As with voice, you can't use video in a conversation that has three or four people.)

To add video to a conversation, click the Start Camera heading. Messenger displays a camera panel on your computer with a picture-in-picture picture of the video you're sending, and invites your victim to take part in the video conversation. If they accept, they receive a larger version of the picture. Figure 14.20 shows a conversation with incoming video.

**FIGURE 14.20**
You can also add video to a Messenger conversation.

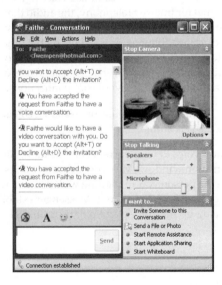

To toggle your picture-in-picture picture on and off, click the Options button and choose Show My Video As Picture-in-Picture from the menu.

To stop transmitting or receiving video, click the Stop Camera heading.

## Blocking and Unblocking Users

To block somebody from chatting with you, take one of the following actions:

◆ In a Conversation window with the person you want to block, click the Block button or choose Actions ➢ Block.

◆ In a Conversation window with multiple people, click the Block button and choose the person from the pop-up menu, or choose Actions ➢ Block and choose the person to block.

◆ From the Windows Messenger window, right-click the person and choose Block from the shortcut menu.

When you block a user from a Conversation window, Messenger displays the Windows Messenger dialog box shown in Figure 14.21 telling you that the blocked user will not be able to contact you or see your online status. When you unblock a user, Messenger displays a similar dialog box telling you that the other user *will* be able to do these things. In either case, you get an OK button to proceed with the blocking or unblocking, a Cancel button to cancel it, and a Don't Show Me This Message Again check box that you can select to prevent Messenger from telling you what you already know.

**FIGURE 14.21**

When you block a user, Messenger displays a dialog box to make sure you understand the consequences of your action. Select the Don't Show Me This Message Again check box to prevent Messenger from displaying this dialog box again.

To unblock a user, take one of the following actions:

◆ In a Conversation window, choose Actions ➢ Unblock.

◆ In a Conversation window with multiple participants, choose Actions ➢ Block and select the blocked user from the submenu.

◆ In the Windows Messenger window, right-click the blocked user and choose Unblock from the shortcut menu.

## Changing Your Status

To let people know what you're up to, you can change the status that Messenger displays for you. To do so, click the down arrow next to your name at the top of the Windows Messenger window and choose Online, Busy, Be Right Back, Away, On the Phone, Out to Lunch, or Appear Offline from the pop-up menu. You can also set your status by choosing File ➤ My Status and selecting the status from the submenu.

## Transferring Files

Messenger provides an easy way to transfer files quickly to other Messenger users who are currently online.

### Sending a File

To send a file to someone via Messenger, follow these steps:

1. During a conversation, choose File ➤ Send a File or Photo. Or, from the Messenger window, choose File ➤ Send a File or Photo and then choose a recipient from the dialog box and click OK.

   Messenger displays the Send a File To dialog box, which is an Open dialog box in disguise (see Figure 14.22).

**FIGURE 14.22**
Use the Send a File To dialog box to send a file to a Messenger user who isn't one of your contacts.

2. Navigate to the file, select it, and click the Open button. Messenger contacts the user, asking them if they want to accept or decline the file.

**TIP**   You can cancel the transfer by pressing Alt+Q or clicking the Cancel link.

3. If the user accepts the file, Messenger displays a progress readout in the Conversation window. When the file transfer is complete, Messenger lets you know that too.

**NOTE**   If the user does not accept the transfer, or if it fails, Messenger tells you that the user declined the file or the file could not be sent.

## Receiving a File

Receiving a file via Messenger is even easier than sending one. Here's what happens:

1. If you're using pop-ups, Messenger displays a pop-up telling you that someone is trying to send you a file. (Messenger identifies the user and the file by name.)

2. Click the pop-up to display the Conversation window. (If you're already in a messaging session with this user, you'll go directly to this step.)

3. To accept the file, click the Accept link (or press Alt+T). To decline the file, click the Decline link (or press Alt+D).

4. If you choose to accept the file, Messenger displays a Windows Messenger dialog box warning you that files may contain harmful viruses or scripts and advising you to make sure that the file you're receiving is from a trustworthy source. Click the OK button to dismiss this dialog box. You can select the Don't Show Me This Message Again check box before dismissing the dialog box if you're fully aware of malware tricks and you carefully check every file you receive before running it.

5. Messenger transfers the file, stores it in the folder specified in the Preferences tab of the Options dialog box, and displays a link that you can click to open the file. Figure 14.23 shows the anatomy of a successful file-transfer session from the recipient's point of view.

**FIGURE 14.23**
Messenger keeps you well informed when you're receiving a file.

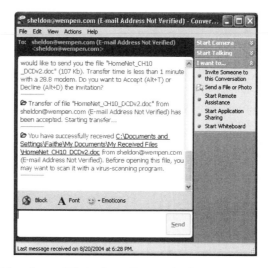

To access your received files folder, choose File ➢ Open Received Files.

## Sharing Applications

While you are in a conversation, in addition to sending files, you can share documents and applications. To do so, open the program you want to share, and then click the Start Application Sharing hyperlink. This sends a request to the other person to start application sharing. Provided you both agree to it, a Sharing window opens.

CHAPTER 14

If the PC has SP2 installed, the first time you use application sharing, a box appears asking if you want to unblock NetMeeting. (See, NetMeeting still exists! It's just hidden in the cloak of Windows Messenger.) Click Unblock to allow it continue.

**NOTE**    To share the Whiteboard, click the Whiteboard button in the main NetMeeting window.

In the Sharing window, choose the application you want to share with the other user, and then click Share (see Figure 14.24). The program appears in a window on the remote user's system.

**FIGURE 14.24**
Share an application.

When you switch away from the shared application on your own system, the display on the remote user's PC turns to an empty patterned window. Only when the shared application is in the foreground can he or she see it.

To unshare an application, go back to the Sharing window and click Unshare.

You can also share a Whiteboard in Windows Messenger. It's somewhat like Paint, but you can use it collaboratively with another person. To do this, choose Start Whiteboard from a conversation window, and the board appears as in Figure 14.25.

**FIGURE 14.25**
Share a whiteboard.

# Using Remote Desktop Connection

Remote Desktop Connection lets you connect via a dial-up connection, a local area network (LAN) connection, or across the Internet and take control of somebody's computer (or your own).

Remote Desktop Connection is designed to let you access and control one computer (say, your work computer) from another computer (say, your home computer or your laptop). It's great for catching up with the office when you're at home, or for grabbing the files that you forgot to load on your laptop before you dived into the taxi for the airport.

## Remote Desktop Connection Terminology and Basics

Remote Desktop Connection terminology is a little confusing. Here are the terms:

◆ The *home computer* is the computer on which you're working. The home computer needs to have Remote Desktop Connection installed. Remote Desktop Connection is installed by default in Windows XP Professional.

◆ The *remote computer* is the computer that you're accessing from the home computer. The remote computer needs to have Remote Desktop installed. Remote Desktop is separate from Remote Desktop Connection and is included in Windows XP Professional and Windows 2003 Server. Remote Desktop is not included in Windows XP Home.

So the typical scenario is for the home computer to be running Windows XP Home and the remote computer to be running Windows XP Professional. You can also access one Windows XP Professional computer from another.

**NOTE**   You can access more than one remote computer at a time from the same home computer. However, unless you have impressive bandwidth, this results in slow sessions.

In order for you to connect to another computer via Remote Desktop Connection, any active session (whether local or connected via Remote Desktop Connection) on that computer needs to be disconnected. You get a warning about this, but the other user doesn't. If you choose to proceed, the remote computer displays the Welcome screen while your Remote Desktop Connection session is going on. There's no easy way for anyone looking at that computer to tell that you're remotely connected to it.

If a user comes back and starts using the remote computer while your Remote Desktop Connection session is going on, your session will be terminated—with a warning on their side, this time, but not on yours. Frankly, this could be more elegant.

In lay terms, Remote Desktop Connection works as follows:

◆ Keystrokes and mouse clicks are transmitted from the home computer to the remote computer via the display protocol. The remote computer registers these keystrokes and clicks as if they came from the keyboard attached to it.

◆ Programs run on the remote computer as usual. (Programs aren't run across the wire—that would be desperately slow.)

◆ Screen display information is passed to the home computer, again via the display protocol. This information appears on the display as if it came from the video adapter (only rather more slowly, and usually in a window).

CHAPTER 14

Sound can be passed to the home computer as well, so that you can hear what's happening at the remote computer. Transferring sound like this enhances the impression of controlling the remote computer, but sound takes so much bandwidth that transferring it isn't a good idea on slow connections. The default Remote Desktop Connection setting is to transfer sound, but you may well want to switch it off.

## Setting the Remote Computer to Accept Incoming Connections

The first step in getting Remote Desktop Connection to work is setting the remote computer to accept incoming connections. Remember that this is the computer that's remote from you and that's running Windows XP Professional (or .NET Server).

To set your computer to accept incoming connections, follow these steps:

1. Click the Start button, right-click My Computer, and choose Properties from the shortcut menu to open the System Properties dialog box.

2. Click the Remote tab, which is shown in Figure 14.26.

**FIGURE 14.26**
The Remote tab of the System Properties dialog box

3. To allow users to connect to your computer, select the Allow Users to Connect Remotely to This Computer check box.

4. To specify which users can connect via Remote Desktop Connection, click the Select Remote Users button to open the Remote Desktop Users dialog box (shown in Figure 14.27). The list box shows any users currently allowed to connect to the computer. Below the list box is a note indicating that you (identified by your username) already have access—as you should have.

5. To add users, click the Add button. Windows displays the Select Users dialog box.

**FIGURE 14.27**

The Remote Desktop
Users dialog box

6. Select a user or group, and then click the OK button. Windows adds them to the list in the Remote Desktop Users dialog box.

7. Add further users or groups as necessary.

8. To remove a user or a group, select them in the list box and click the Remove button.

9. Click the OK button to close the Remote Desktop Users dialog box.

10. Click the OK button in the System Properties dialog box. Windows closes the dialog box and applies your changes.

That's the remote computer all set. Leave it up and running and return to the home computer.

## Choosing Settings for Remote Desktop Connection

Next, choose settings for Remote Desktop Connection on the home computer. Remote Desktop Connection has a modestly large number of settings, but many of them are set-and-forget. Even better, you can save sets of settings so that you can quickly apply them for accessing different remote computers (or the same remote computer under different circumstances, such as when the cable modem is working and when it's flaked out on you).

To choose settings for Remote Desktop Connection, follow these steps:

1. Choose Start ➢ All Programs ➢ Accessories ➢ Communications ➢ Remote Desktop Connection. Windows starts Remote Desktop Connection and displays the Remote Desktop Connection window in its reduced state (shown in Figure 14.28).

2. Click the Options button. Windows displays the rest of the Remote Desktop Connection window.

**FIGURE 14.28**

The Remote Desktop
Connection window
appears first in its
reduced state.

**3.** The General tab of the Remote Desktop Connection window (shown in Figure 14.29) offers these options:

**Computer drop-down list**   Enter the name or the IP address of the computer to which you want to connect; or select it from the drop-down list; or click the Browse for More item from the drop-down list to display the Browse for Computers dialog box, and then select the computer in that.

**User Name text box**   Enter the username under which you want to connect to the remote computer. Windows enters your username by default.

**Password text box**   If you want to store your password (for the remote computer) for the connection, enter it in this text box and select the Save My Password check box. If you don't enter your password here, you get to enter it when logging on to the remote computer.

**Domain text box**   If the remote computer is part of a domain, enter the domain name here. If the computer is part of a workgroup, you can leave this text box blank.

**Save My Password check box**   Select this check box if you want to save your password with the rest of the Remote Desktop Connection information. This can save you time and effort, but it compromises your security a bit.

**Connection Settings section**   Once you've chosen settings for a connection, you can save the connection information by clicking the Save As button and specifying a name for the connection in the Save As dialog box that Windows displays. Remote Desktop Connection connections are saved as files of the file type Remote Desktop File, which by default is linked to the RDP extension, in the My Documents\Remote Desktops folder. You can open saved connections by clicking the Open button and using the resulting Open dialog box.

**NOTE**   You'll see a file named DEFAULT.RDP in the My Documents\Remote Desktops folder. Windows automatically saves your latest Remote Desktop Connection configuration under this name when you click the Connect button. But by explicitly saving your settings under a name of your choice, you can easily maintain different configurations for different Remote Desktop Connection settings.

**FIGURE 14.29**

The General tab of the expanded Remote Desktop Connection window

**4.** The Display tab of the Remote Desktop Connection window (shown in Figure 14.30) offers three display options:

**Remote Desktop Size section**   Drag the slider to specify the screen size you want to use for the remote Desktop. The default setting is Full Screen, but you may want to use a smaller size so that you can more easily access your Desktop on the home computer. When you display the remote Desktop full screen, it takes over the whole of the local Desktop so that you can't see your local Desktop. (To get to your local Desktop, you use the connection bar, discussed in a moment or two.)

**Colors section**   In the drop-down list, select the color depth to use for the connection. Choose a low color depth (for example, 256 colors) if you're connecting over a low-speed connection. This choice will be overridden by the display setting on the remote computer if you ask for more colors than the remote computer is using.

**Display the Connection Bar When in Full Screen Mode check box**   Leave this check box selected (as it is by default) if you want Windows to display the connection bar when the remote Desktop is displayed full screen. The connection bar provides Minimize, Restore/Maximize, and Close buttons for the remote Desktop. (When the remote Desktop is displayed in a window, that window has the control buttons, so the connection bar isn't necessary.)

**FIGURE 14.30**

Choose display settings in the Display tab of the Remote Desktop Connection window.

**5.** The Local Resources tab of the Remote Desktop Connection window (shown in Figure 14.31) offers the following options:

**Remote Computer Sound section**   In the drop-down list, specify what you want Windows to do with sounds that would normally be generated at the remote Desktop. The default setting is Bring to This Computer, which transfers the sounds to the home computer and plays them there. This setting helps sustain the illusion that you're working directly on the remote Desktop, but it's heavy on bandwidth, so don't use it over low-speed connections. Instead, choose the Do Not Play setting or the Leave at Remote Computer setting. The Leave at Remote

CHAPTER 14

Computer setting plays the sounds at the remote computer and is best reserved for occasions when you need to frighten somebody remotely or pretend to be in your office.

**Keyboard section** In the drop-down list, specify how you want Windows to handle Windows key combinations that you press (for example, Alt+Tab or Ctrl+Alt+Delete). Select the On the Local Computer item, the On the Remote Computer item, or the In Full Screen Mode Only item (the default) as suits your needs.

**Local Devices section** Leave the Disk Drives, Printers, and Serial Ports check boxes selected (as they are by default) if you want these devices on your home computer to be available from the remote computer. This means that you can save documents from the remote computer to local drives, print them on your local printer, or transfer them via devices attached to serial ports (for example, a PDA). Local disk drives appear in the Other category in Explorer windows, named *Driveletter on COMPUTERNAME*. Local printers appear with *from COMPUTERNAME* in parentheses after them.

**FIGURE 14.31**

In the Local Resources tab of the Remote Desktop Connection window, specify how Windows should handle sound, keyboard shortcuts, and devices on the home computer.

6. The Programs tab of the Remote Desktop Connection window (shown in Figure 14.32) lets you specify that Windows run a designated program when you connect via Remote Desktop Connection. Select the Start the Following Program on Connection check box, then enter the program path and name in the Program Path and File Name text box. If you need to specify the folder in which the program should start, enter that in the Start in the Following Folder text box.

7. The Experience tab of the Remote Desktop Connection window (shown in Figure 14.33) contains the following options:

**Choose Your Connection Speed to Optimize Performance drop-down list** In this drop-down list, select one of the four listed speeds to apply a preselected set of settings to the five check boxes on this page. The choices in the drop-down list are Modem (28.8Kbps), Modem (56Kbps), Broadband (128Kbps–1.5Mbps), LAN (10Mbps or Higher), and Custom.

**FIGURE 14.32**

If you need to have a program run on the remote Desktop when you connect, specify it in the Programs tab of the Remote Desktop Connection window.

**Desktop Background check box** This check box controls whether Remote Desktop Connection transmits the Desktop background. Because Desktop backgrounds are graphical, transmitting them is sensible only at LAN speeds. (If you clear this check box, Remote Desktop Connection uses a blank Desktop background.)

**Show Contents of Window While Dragging check box** This check box controls whether Remote Desktop Connection transmits the contents of a window while you're dragging it or only the window frame. Don't use this option over a modem connection, because the performance penalty outweighs any benefit you may derive from it.

**Menu and Window Animation check box** This check box controls whether Remote Desktop Connection transmits menu and window animations (for example, zooming a window you're maximizing or minimizing). Don't use this option over a modem connection—it's a waste of bandwidth.

**Themes check box** This check box controls whether Remote Desktop Connection transmits theme information or uses "classic" Windows-style windows and controls. Transmitting theme information takes a little bandwidth, so you can improve performance over a very slow connection by clearing the Themes check box. But bear in mind that Windows will look different enough to unsettle some inexperienced users.

**Bitmap Caching check box** This check box controls whether Remote Desktop Connection uses bitmap caching to improve performance by reducing the amount of data that needs to be sent across the network in order to display the screen remotely. Caching could prove a security threat, so you *might* want to turn it off for security reasons. But in most cases, you're better off using it.

**8.** If you want to save the settings you've chosen under a particular name so that you can reload them at will, click the Save As button in the General tab of the Remote Desktop Connection window.

**CHAPTER 14**

**FIGURE 14.33**

In the Experience tab of the Remote Desktop Connection window, you can customize which graphical information Remote Desktop Connection transmits in order to balance performance against looks.

## Connecting via Remote Desktop Connection

Once you've chosen settings as outlined in the previous section, you're ready to connect. If you're connecting via the Internet (rather than a local network) and you have a dial-up connection, make sure it's up and running.

Click the Connect button in the General tab of the Remote Desktop Connection window. Windows attempts to establish a connection to the computer you specified.

If Windows is able to connect to the computer, and you didn't specify your username or password in the Remote Desktop Connection window, it displays the Log On to Windows dialog box (shown in Figure 14.34). Enter your username and password and click the OK button to log in. Windows then displays the remote Desktop. (If you chose to provide your password in the General tab of the Remote Desktop Connection window, you shouldn't need to enter it again.)

**FIGURE 14.34**

Windows displays the Log On to Windows dialog box for the remote computer.

If you left a user session active on the computer, Remote Desktop Connection drops you straight into it—likewise if you left a user session disconnected and no other user session is active. But if another user *is* active on the remote computer when you submit a successful logon and password, Windows displays the Logon Message dialog box shown in Figure 14.35 to warn you that logging on will disconnect the user's session. Click the Yes button if you want to proceed. Click the No button to withdraw stealthily.

**FIGURE 14.35**
Windows displays the
Logon Message dialog
box when you're about to
bump a user off the re-
mote computer by log-
ging on.

If you click the Yes button, the active user gets a Request for Connection dialog box such as that shown in Figure 14.36. This tells them that you (it specifies your name) are trying to connect to the computer, warns them that they'll be disconnected if you do connect, and asks if they want to allow the connection.

**FIGURE 14.36**
Windows displays the
Request for Connection
dialog box to tell the active user of your incom-
ing session.

The active user then gets to click the Yes button or the No button as appropriate to their needs and inclinations. If Windows doesn't get an answer within 30 seconds or so, it figures they're not there, disconnects their session, and lets you in.

If the active user clicks the Yes button in the Request for Connection dialog box, Windows logs them off immediately and logs you on. But if the active user clicks the No button, you get a Logon Message dialog box such as that shown in Figure 14.37, telling you that they didn't allow you to connect. Windows displays this Logon Message dialog box for a few seconds, and then closes it automatically, returning you to the Remote Desktop Connection window.

**FIGURE 14.37**
Windows displays this
Logon Message dialog
box when the active user
decides not to let you interrupt their session on
the computer.

If Windows is unable to establish the connection with the remote computer, it displays one of its Remote Desktop Disconnected dialog boxes to make you aware of the problem. Figure 14.38 shows two examples of the Remote Desktop Disconnected dialog box.

The first example of the Remote Desktop Disconnected dialog box tells you that the client couldn't connect to the remote computer and suggests that you try again later. The second example tells you that the remote computer couldn't be found and suggests checking that the computer name or IP address are correct. This should indeed be your first move—but if that doesn't work, that's about all you can do. If the remote computer has been shut down (or has crashed), or if its network or Internet connection has gone south, or if someone has reconfigured the computer not to accept Remote Desktop Connection connections or has revoked your permission to connect, then you're straight out of luck. No amount of retyping the computer name or IP address will make an iota of difference.

CHAPTER 14

**FIGURE 14.38**
If Windows is unable to connect, you'll see a Remote Desktop Disconnected dialog box.

## Working via Remote Desktop Connection

Once you've reached the remote Desktop, you can work more or less as if you were sitting at the computer. The few differences worth mentioning are discussed briefly in this section.

### USING CUT, COPY, AND PASTE BETWEEN THE LOCAL AND REMOTE COMPUTERS

You can use Cut, Copy, and Paste commands to transfer information between the local computer and the remote computer. For example, you could copy some text from a program on the local computer and paste it into a program on the remote computer.

### COPYING FROM REMOTE DRIVES TO LOCAL DRIVES

You can copy from remote drives to local drives by working in Explorer. The drives on your local computer appear in Explorer windows on the remote computer marked as *Driveletter on COMPUTERNAME*. The drives on the remote computer appear as regular drives. You can copy and move files from one drive to another as you would with local drives.

### PRINTING TO A LOCAL PRINTER

You can print to a local printer from the remote Desktop by selecting the local printer in the Print dialog box just as you would any other printer.

Printer settings are communicated to the remote Desktop when you access it. If you add a local printer during the remote session, the remote Desktop won't be able to see it. To make the printer show up on the remote Desktop, log off the remote session and log back on.

## Returning to Your Local Desktop

If you chose to display the connection bar, it hovers briefly at the top of the screen and then slides upward to vanish like a docked toolbar with its Auto-Hide property enabled. To pin the connection bar in position, click the pin icon at its left end. (To unpin it, click the pin icon again.) To display the connection bar when it has hidden itself, move the mouse pointer to the top edge of the screen, just as you would do to display a docked toolbar hidden there.

The connection bar provides a Minimize button, a Restore/Maximize button, and a Close button. Use the Minimize button and the Restore button to reduce the remote Desktop from full screen to an icon or a partial screen so that you can access your local Desktop. Maximize the remote Desktop window to return to full-screen mode when you want to work with it again. Use the Close button as discussed in the next section to disconnect your remote session.

## Disconnecting the Remote Session

You can disconnect the remote session in either of the two following ways:

♦ On the remote Desktop, choose Start ➤ Disconnect. Windows displays the Disconnect Windows dialog box (shown in Figure 14.39). Click the Disconnect button.

**FIGURE 14.39**
You can disconnect the remote session by issuing a Start ➤ Disconnect command and clicking the Disconnect button in the Disconnect Windows dialog box.

♦ Click the Close button on the connection bar (if the remote Desktop is displayed full screen) or on the Remote Desktop window (if the remote Desktop is not displayed full screen). Windows displays the Disconnect Windows Session dialog box (shown in Figure 14.40). Click the OK button.

**FIGURE 14.40**
The Disconnect Windows Session dialog box appears when you click the Close button on the connection bar. Click the OK button to end your remote session while leaving the programs running.

Windows disconnects the remote session but leaves the programs running for the time being. You can then log on again and pick up where you left off.

## Logging Off the Remote Session

To log off and end your user session, click the Start button on the remote Desktop and choose Log Off from the Start menu. Windows displays the Log Off Windows dialog box (shown in Figure 14.41). Click the Log Off button.

**FIGURE 14.41**
To log off from the remote computer, choose Start ➤ Log Off and click the Log Off button in the Log Off Windows dialog box.

CHAPTER 14

When someone else bumps you off the remote Desktop (by logging on locally or remotely), Windows displays the Remote Desktop Disconnected dialog box shown in Figure 14.42, telling you that the remote session "was ended by means of an administration tool."

**FIGURE 14.42**

This Remote Desktop Disconnected dialog box appears when you log off and when someone logs you off the remote computer.

If the network connection between the home computer and the remote computer is broken, the home computer displays a Remote Desktop Disconnected dialog box such as that shown in Figure 14.43.

**FIGURE 14.43**

This Remote Desktop Disconnected dialog box indicates that the network connection between the home computer and the remote computer was broken.

## Summary

In this chapter, we've taken a quick look at some of the communications programs included with Windows XP Professional: HyperTerminal, Windows Messenger, and Remote Desktop Connection. As I said at the outset, you may never have occasion to use any of these applications, or you may need only one of them from time to time. All are easy to learn and use, and if you frequently use any of them, you'll be up to speed with it in no time.

Now let's turn our attention to something you'll probably use every day—Outlook Express.

# Chapter 15

# Using Outlook Express for E-mail and News

Of all the features of the Internet, intranets, and local area networks (LANs), e-mail is, without question, the most used. Instead of playing phone tag with colleagues at work, you send them e-mail. Millions of extended families stay in touch via e-mail, and an e-mail address has become an expected component of a business card.

Outlook Express is an Internet standards e-mail reader you can use to access an Internet e-mail account. An Internet e-mail account is not the same thing as an account with an online information service. The difference is that an Internet account provides services such as Point-to-Point Protocol (PPP) Internet access and e-mail but does not include services such as chat rooms, access to databases, conferences, and so on. Consequently, you cannot use Outlook Express to access an e-mail account with Hotmail, MS Mail, cc:Mail, CompuServe, America Online, or versions of Microsoft Exchange Server prior to version 5.

In addition to being an e-mail reader, Outlook Express is also a news reader. In the first part of this chapter, I'll explain its e-mail features, and in the second part, I'll show you how to access newsgroups and post to them.

- ◆ Starting Outlook Express

- ◆ Touring Outlook Express

- ◆ Using Outlook Express to read, compose, and send e-mail

- ◆ Using Outlook Express to read news and post to newsgroups

- ◆ Customizing Outlook Express

## Using Outlook Express as Your Mail Reader

To start Outlook Express, choose Start ➢ E-mail Outlook Express or, from within Internet Explorer, click the Mail icon and then select an item from the submenu. In addition, if Outlook Express is set as the default e-mail application, you can select it directly from the top of the first-level Start menu.

If Outlook Express does not appear there but you would like it to, right-click the Taskbar and choose Properties, and then click the Start Menu tab and click Customize. In the Customize Start Menu dialog box that appears, choose Outlook Express from the E-mail drop-down list.

**NOTE**   Before you can open and use Outlook Express to send and receive e-mail, you need to configure your Internet connection. You'll find information on how to do this in Chapter 12.

## A Quick Tour

When you first open Outlook Express, you'll see a screen similar to that shown in Figure 15.1.

**FIGURE 15.1**

The opening screen in Outlook Express

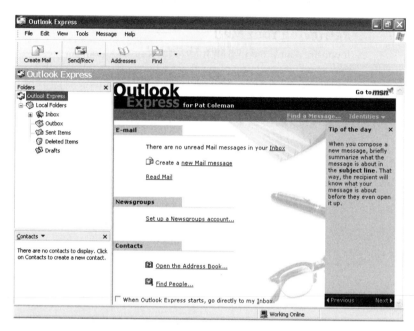

To read your mail, click Read Mail, or click Inbox in the Folders list. Initially the Preview pane is split horizontally; header information is displayed in the upper pane, and the message is displayed in the lower pane.

**TIP**   To change the arrangement of the Preview pane, choose View ➢ Layout to open the Window Layout Properties dialog box, and select options to show or hide certain parts.

### THE FOLDERS LIST

The Folders list is a tool for organizing messages. Initially, it contains the following folders, although you can create additional folders, as you'll see shortly:

**Inbox**   Contains newly received messages and messages that you have not yet disposed of in some way.

**Outbox**   Contains messages that are ready to be sent.

**Sent Items**   Contains copies of messages that you have sent (a handy device if you send lots of e-mail).

**Deleted Items**   Contains copies of messages that you have deleted.

**Drafts**   Contains messages that you are working on but which are not yet ready to be sent.

CHAPTER 15

### THE CONTACTS PANE

The Contacts pane contains the names of people in your Address Book. To compose a message to anyone on this list, simply double-click the name.

## Retrieving Your Mail

If you are connected to your Internet account, Outlook Express will automatically check the server for new messages and download them when you open Outlook Express. By default, Outlook Express will also check for new mail every 30 minutes, as long as you are connected. To adjust this time interval, follow these steps:

1. Choose Tools ➢ Options to open the Options dialog box:

2. In the General tab, click the up or down arrow to change the Check for New Messages Every *x* Minutes option.

3. Click OK.

You can also check for new mail by choosing Tools ➢ Send and Receive ➢ Receive All or by clicking the Send/Recv button on the toolbar in the main window.

## Reading and Processing Messages

If you are working in the split Preview pane view, simply click a message header to display the message in a separate window. Otherwise, simply double-click a header to view the message.

### PRINTING MESSAGES

For various reasons, it's often handy to have a paper copy of e-mail messages. You can print in a couple of ways:

◆ To print a message without opening it, select its header and click the Print icon on the toolbar in the main window.

◆ To print an open message, click the Print icon on the toolbar in the message window.

### MARKING MESSAGES

If you're like me, you don't always handle each message as you receive it or immediately after you read it, and it's easy to forget that you need to take some action or follow up on a message unless it stands out from the others in the header list. One trick that I use is to mark a message as unread even though I have read it (select the header and choose Edit ≻ Mark As Unread). You can also select the header and choose Message ≻ Flag Message to display a red flag to the left of the message header. To remove the flag, choose Message ≻ Flag Message again.

In addition, you can mark a message as read, and you can mark all messages as read.

### MOVING MESSAGES

You can easily move a message from one folder to another by dragging and dropping it. For example, if you receive a message that you want to modify and send to someone else, select the message header and then drag it to the Drafts folder. Open it, revise it, and then send it on its way.

### SAVING MESSAGES

You can save messages in folders you created in Windows Explorer, and you can save messages in Outlook Express folders. You can also save attachments as files.

#### *Saving Messages in Windows Explorer Folders*

To save messages in a folder in Windows Explorer, follow these steps:

1. Open the message or select its header.

2. Choose File ≻ Save As to open the Save Message As dialog box:

3. Select a folder in which to save the message. Outlook Express places the subject line in the File Name box. You can use this name or type another name.

4. Select a file type in which to save the message, and then click Save.

### Saving Messages in Outlook Express Mail Folders

As I've mentioned, you can create your own Outlook Express folders. For example, you might want to create folders for people with whom you regularly correspond, or you might want to create folders for current projects. To create a new folder, follow these steps:

1. In the main Outlook Express window, choose File ➢ New ➢ Folder to open the Create Folder dialog box:

2. In the Folder Name box, type a name for your folder.

3. Select a folder in which to place the new folder, and click OK.

You now have a new folder in your folders list, and you can drag any message to it. You have, however, an even easier and more efficient way to save messages in Outlook Express folders, and I'll look at that in the "Applying Message Rules" section, later in this chapter.

### Saving Attachments

An attachment is a file that is appended to an e-mail message. You'll know that a message has an attachment if the header is preceded by the paper clip icon. When you open the message, you'll see the filename of the attachment in the Attach line in the header. To open an attachment, double-click its filename.

To save an attachment, follow these steps:

1. Open the message, and choose File ➢ Save Attachments to open the Save Attachments dialog box:

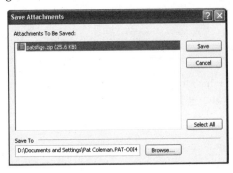

**2.** Select a folder in which to save the file, and click Save.

I'll discuss how to attach a file to a message later in this chapter.

### Blocking Unsafe Attachments

Under SP2, Outlook Express gains the ability to block unsafe attachments—that is, attachments that could potentially carry viruses. This includes executable files and scripts. Most of the time this is a good thing, especially for newbie users who are prone to blindly taking every attachment at face value.

However, advanced users might find that it blocks file attachments that they genuinely need to receive. You can get around this in a couple of ways. One is to ask the sender to zip the file before sending it. Another is to turn off the blocking option in Outlook Express, either temporarily or permanently.

To change the blocking setting:

**1.** Choose Tools ➢ Options.

**2.** Click the Security Tab.

**3.** Mark or clear the Do Not Allow Attachments to be Saved or Opened That Could Potentially Be a Virus. check box.

**4.** Click OK.

### REPLYING TO A MESSAGE

To reply to a message, click the Reply button on the toolbar in the message window. If the message is addressed to multiple recipients and you want to reply to all of them, click the Reply All button.

**TIP**    This is a quick and easy way to note the person's e-mail address. By default, Outlook Express automatically places the names of the people you reply to in your Address Book.

By default, Outlook Express includes the text of the original message in your reply. According to Internet tradition, this squanders bandwidth, and it's better not to include the original message unless it's really necessary. When is it necessary?

♦ When you want to be sure that the recipient understands the nature of your reply and the topic to which it is related

♦ When your message is part of a series of messages that involve some sort of question-and-answer sequence

♦ When it's important to keep track of who said what when

An alternative is to include only the relevant portions of the original message in your reply. To do so, follow these steps:

1. Open the message and click the Reply button.

2. The message is now addressed to the original sender, and the original subject line is preceded by Re:.

3. In the body of the message, edit the contents so that the portions you want are retained, and then enter your response.

4. Click the Send button.

If you don't want to include the original message in your reply, you can simply open the message, click the Reply button, place the insertion point in the body of the message, choose Edit ➤ Select All, and press Delete. If you're sure that you don't want to include the original message, choose Tools ➤ Options, and in the Options dialog box, click the Send tab. Clear the Include Message in Reply check box. If once in a while you need the message included, simply recheck the option.

### FORWARDING A MESSAGE

Forwarding an e-mail message is much easier than forwarding a letter through the U.S. mail, and it actually works. To forward a message, follow these steps:

1. Open the message.

2. Click the Forward button on the toolbar in the message window.

3. Enter an address in the To field.

4. Add your own comments if you want.

5. Click Send.

### DELETING MESSAGES

To delete a message, you can select its header and click Delete, or you can open it and then click Delete. The message is not yet really deleted, however; Outlook Express has placed it in the Deleted Items folder. And that is where the message stays until you empty the Deleted Items folder or tell Outlook Express to empty it when you close Outlook Express.

If you want to delete items from the Deleted Items folder yourself, follow these steps:

1. Select the Deleted Items folder.

2. Choose Edit ➢ Empty "Deleted Items" Folder.

3. When Outlook Express asks if you are sure you want to delete these items, click Yes.

To set up automatic deletion of the items in the Deleted Items folder, follow these steps:

1. Choose Tools ➢ Options to open the Options dialog box.

2. Click the Maintenance tab.

3. In the Cleaning Up Messages section, click the Empty Messages from the "Deleted Items" Folder on Exit check box, and then click OK.

## Creating and Sending Messages

In this section, I'll walk you through the steps to create a simple message and send it. You can also create messages in HTML (Hypertext Markup Language) and include hyperlinks, pictures, colorful formatting, sounds, and so on. We'll look at that in the next section.

Create Mail

**NOTE**  To begin a new message, you can click the Create Mail button in the main window to open the New Message window, as shown in Figure 15.2. Or, if the intended recipient is in your Address Book, you can double-click that person's name in the Contacts pane to open the New Message window; the To line will display the recipient's name.

**FIGURE 15.2**
You create a new message in the New Message window.

If your New Message window includes a Formatting toolbar, the message you compose will be formatted as HTML. For my purposes here, I want only plain text. If this is what you want as well, choose Format ➤ Plain Text before you begin composing your message. Now, follow these steps:

1. If necessary, enter the address of the primary recipient in the To field. If you are sending a message to multiple primary recipients, separate their addresses with semicolons. If you choose multiple recipients from your Address Book, they are automatically separated by semicolons.

2. Optionally, enter e-mail addresses in the Cc (carbon copy) and Bcc (blind carbon copy) fields. To enter a Bcc recipient, click the Cc icon, enter the name in the Select Recipients dialog box, and click Bcc.

3. Enter a subject line for your message.

**NOTE**   If you don't enter a subject line, Outlook Express will ask if you're sure you don't want a subject line. Unless you have a good reason not to do so, enter some text in the subject line. Your recipient will see this text in the header information for the message and will then have a clue as to the nature of your message.

4. Enter the text of your message.

5. If appropriate, establish a priority for your message. Choose Message ➤ Set Priority, and then choose High, Normal, or Low. The default is Normal.

6. Click Send to start your message on its way.

You can send your message immediately by clicking the Send button, or you can save it in your Outbox to send later by choosing File ➤ Send Later. The message will be sent when you choose Send and Receive All or when you choose Send All.

**TIP**   You can use Copy and Paste in Outlook Express just as you use those commands in other Windows programs. For example, to include a portion of a Word document in a message, open the document, select the text, and press Ctrl+C to copy it to the Clipboard. In Outlook Express, open the New Message window, place the insertion point where you want to copy the text, and press Ctrl+V. Use this same process to copy portions of e-mail messages to other messages or to documents in other applications.

## Creating E-mail Messages with HTML

In the previous section, I told you how to create a plain text message, but as I mentioned, you can also compose messages in HTML and include all sorts of neat effects. Before you send a formatted message, be sure that your recipient's e-mail program can display it effectively. When you open the New Message window and choose Format ➤ Rich Text (HTML), the message you compose is essentially a web page. Newer e-mail programs such as Netscape Messenger and the commercial version of Eudora, Eudora Pro, can read, compose, and send HTML messages, but others cannot. An easy way to find out if your recipient's e-mail program can handle HTML is to send a simple plain text message and ask.

That said, let's look at some bells and whistles you can include in Outlook Express e-mail messages. Click the Create Mail icon to open the New Message window, and be sure that the Rich Text (HTML) option is selected. You'll see the screen shown in Figure 15.3. Notice the Formatting toolbar, which contains many of the same tools you see and use in your Windows word processor. You'll also see the Font and Font Size drop-down list boxes that are present in your word processor.

As you create your message, just pretend that you're using a word processor, and use the Formatting tools to apply emphasis to your message. All the usual design rules apply, including the following:

◆ Don't use a lot of different fonts.

◆ Remember, typing in all capital letters in e-mail is tantamount to shouting.

◆ Don't place a lot of text in italics. It's hard to read on the screen.

◆ Save boldface for what's really important.

To insert a horizontal line that spans the message window, click the Insert Horizontal Line button on the Formatting toolbar.

**FIGURE 15.3**
You can use the Formatting toolbar when creating a message in HTML.

To apply HTML styles such as Definition Term or Definition, click the Paragraph Style button on the Formatting toolbar.

### ADDING A PICTURE TO YOUR MESSAGES

You can insert a picture in a message in two ways:

◆ As a piece of art

◆ As a background over which you can type text

### USING STATIONERY

In addition to formatting, you can add some class or some comedy to your e-mail messages in another way: stationery. In the New Message window, choose Message ➤ New Using, and then choose a predesigned format from the list in the submenu, or click Select Stationery to open the Select Stationery dialog box and select from a larger list. Here's one example of what you'll find:

To customize stationery, click Create New in the Select Stationery dialog box to start the Stationery Setup Wizard. Follow the on-screen instructions.

To insert a picture as a piece of art that you can size and move, follow these steps:

1. In the New Message window, click the Insert Picture button on the Formatting toolbar to open the Picture dialog box.

2. Enter the filename of the picture in the Picture Source text box, or click the Browse button to locate it.

3. Optionally, in the Alternate Text box, enter some text that will display if the recipient's e-mail program cannot display the picture, and specify layout and spacing options if you want. (You can also size and move the picture with the mouse once you place it in the message.)

4. Click OK.

To insert a picture as background, follow these steps:

1. In the New Message window, choose Format ➤ Background ➤ Picture to open the Background Picture dialog box.

2. Enter the filename of the picture, or click Browse to select a predesigned stationery background or locate another file.

3. Click Open, and then click OK to insert the background.

### ADDING A BACKGROUND COLOR OR SOUND TO YOUR MESSAGE

To apply a color to the background of your message, choose Format ➢ Background ➢ Color and select a color from the drop-down list. Now type something. Can you see it on the screen? If not, you have probably chosen a dark background and your font is also a dark color—most likely black if you haven't changed it from the default.

To make your text visible, click the Font Color button, and select a lighter color from the drop-down list.

To add a background sound, follow these steps:

1. In the New Message window, choose Format ➢ Background ➢ Sound to open the Background Sound dialog box.

2. Enter the filename of the sound, or click Browse to locate a sound file.

3. Specify the number of times you want the sound to play or whether you want it to play continuously. (In my opinion, a sound that plays continuously while the recipient is reading the message is far more likely to annoy than to entertain.)

4. Click OK.

### INCLUDING HYPERLINKS IN YOUR MESSAGE

When you insert a hyperlink in a message, the recipient can go directly to the resource simply by clicking the hyperlink. You can insert a hyperlink in three ways:

- ◆ Simply type it in the message body. Be sure to include the entire URL.

- ◆ In the New Message window, choose Insert ➢ Hyperlink to open the Hyperlink dialog box, and then enter the URL in the text box.

- ◆ In Internet Explorer, choose Tools ➢ Mail and News ➢ Send a Link to open the New Message window. The URL of the current page is automatically inserted in the message body.

### ADDING A SIGNATURE TO YOUR MESSAGES

I know people who never sign their e-mail messages. After all, their name is in the From line in the message header. I also know people who append elaborate signatures, touting their accomplishments or advertising their businesses. I usually just sign my first name at the bottom of messages, but what you do depends on your personal style or whether you're sending business or personal correspondence.

To create a signature that's automatically added to all your outgoing messages, follow these steps:

1. Choose Tools ➢ Options to open the Options dialog box.

2. Click the Signatures tab.

3. Click New.

4. To create a text signature, in the Edit Signature section, enter the content in the box next to the Text option button.

5. If you want to use a file you've already created as your signature, click the File option button and enter the filename, or click Browse to locate it.

6. If you have multiple e-mail accounts, click the Advanced button to open the Advanced Signature Settings dialog box, and specify which accounts should use this signature.

7. Click the Add Signatures to All Outgoing Messages check box, and click OK.

If you don't want the signature automatically appended to all outgoing messages, leave the Add Signatures to All Outgoing Messages check box unselected. Then, to add this signature to a message, choose Insert ➢ Signature in the New Message window.

## Attaching Files to Your Messages

In Outlook Express, sending a file or multiple files along with your message is painless and simple. Follow these steps:

1. In the New Message window, choose Insert ➢ File Attachment to open the Insert Attachment dialog box:

**2.** Select a file and click Attach.

Your message now contains the name of the file in the Attach line.

If the file is large or if you know that the recipient has a slow connection, you'll want to compress it. To do so, in the Insert Attachment dialog box, right-click the file, click Send To on the shortcut menu, and then click Compressed Folder. You'll now see a compressed folder for the file in the current folder (the folder displays a zipper). Windows XP Professional uses the WinZip program to compress files and folders, and WinZip is compatible with any compression utility your recipient may have. All the recipient needs to do to uncompress the file or folder is double-click it.

**TIP**   Digital picture files can be quite large, so if your recipient has a compression utility, be sure to compress them before you attach them.

## Applying Message Rules

Using the Rules Editor, you can specify where messages go after they are downloaded, block unwanted messages, and, in general, manage incoming messages more efficiently—especially if you deal with a lot of e-mail. In this section, I'll give you a couple of examples that illustrate the possibilities, but, as you will see, there are lots of possibilities, and you'll need to apply the options that make the most sense for your situation.

Let's start by establishing a rule that sends all mail from a particular person to that person's Outlook Express folder. Follow these steps:

**1.** In the main Outlook Express window, choose Tools ➤ Message Rules ➤ Mail to open the New Mail Rule dialog box:

**2.** In the Select the Conditions for Your Rule section, click the Where the From Line Contains People check box.

**3.** In the Select the Actions for Your Rule section, click the Move It to the Specified Folder check box.

4. In the Rule Description section, click the Contains People link to open the Select People dialog box:

5. Enter a name and click Add or select a name from your Address Book, and click OK.

6. Click Specified to open the Move dialog box.

7. Select the folder where you want this person's messages to go, and click OK. If you need to create a folder, click New Folder.

8. Accept the name of the rule that Outlook Express proposes, or type a new name.

9. Click OK.

Now, when messages arrive from that person, you'll find them in their folder rather than in your Inbox.

**TIP**    To delete a rule, select it and click Remove in the Message Rules dialog box. To modify a rule, select it and click Modify.

To establish a rule that blocks unwanted messages, follow these steps:

1. In the main Outlook Express window, choose Tools ➤ Message Rules ➤ Blocked Senders List to open the Message Rules dialog box at the Blocked Senders tab.

2. Click Add to open the Add Sender dialog box:

3. Enter the e-mail address that you want to block, specify whether you want to block mail, news, or both from this person, and click OK.

4. Click OK again in the Message Rules dialog box.

Now, mail from that address will go immediately to the Deleted Items folder. News from that person will simply not be displayed. (More on news in the last part of this chapter.) To change or delete this rule, open the Message Rules box, select the address, and click Modify or click Remove.

## Adding and Managing Identities

If several people use the same computer either at home, at the office, or elsewhere, and thus also use Outlook Express, you'll probably want to take advantage of the Identities feature, which lets each person view their own mail and have individualized settings and contacts. Once you set up Identities, you can switch between them without shutting down the computer or disconnecting from and reconnecting to the Internet.

When you install Windows XP Professional, you are set up in Outlook Express as the Main Identity. To set up other identities in Outlook Express, follow these steps:

1.  In the main Outlook Express window, choose File ➢ Identities ➢ Add New Identity to open the New Identity dialog box:

2.  Enter the name of the identity you want to establish.

3.  If you want to password protect this identity, click the Require a Password check box. Enter the password twice—once in the New Password box, and again in the Confirm New Password box. Click OK twice.

4.  Outlook Express asks if you want to switch to this new identify now. If you do, click Yes; otherwise, click No.

5.  In the Manage Identities dialog box, click New if you want to set up another identity; otherwise, click Close.

**NOTE**   You can also create an identity in Address Book if you open it by choosing Start ➢ All Programs ➢ Accessories ➢ Address Book. In Address Book, choose File ➢ Switch Identity to open the Switch Identities dialog box, and then click Manage Identities to open the Manage Identities dialog box. Now click New to open the New Identity dialog box and follow steps 2 through 5 just shown.

The first time you log on as a new identity, you will be asked for some information about your Internet connection. To switch from one identity to another, choose File ➢ Switch Identity to open the Switch Identities dialog box. Select the identity, and click OK. To log off from an identity, choose File ➢ Identities ➢ Logoff Identity.

To delete an identity, select the identity in the Manage Identities dialog box, and click Remove.

CHAPTER 15

## Using Outlook Express as Your Newsreader

A newsgroup is a collection of articles about a particular subject. A newsgroup is similar to e-mail in that you can reply to what someone else has written (the newsgroup term for this is *posting*), and you can send a question or a response either to the whole group or to individuals.

The primary (but not sole) source of newsgroups is Usenet, which is a worldwide distributed discussion system consisting of newsgroups with names that are classified hierarchically by subject. For example, `rec.crafts.metalworking` is a recreational group devoted to the craft of metalworking. The leftmost portion represents the largest hierarchical category, and the name gets more specific from left to right. Table 15.1 lists the major top-level newsgroup categories and explains what topics each discusses. Currently, there are thousands and thousands of newsgroups on every conceivable topic. For an extensive listing of them, go to `www.ibiblio.org/usenet-i/hier-s/master.html`.

**TABLE 15.1:**   The Major Newsgroups

| NEWSGROUP | WHAT IT DISCUSSES |
| --- | --- |
| alt | Newsgroups outside the main structure outlined in this table |
| biz | Business products, services, reviews, and so on |
| comp | Computer science and related topics, including operating systems, hardware, artificial intelligence, and graphics |
| humanities | Fine art, literature, philosophy, and the like |
| misc | Anything that does not fit into one of the other categories |
| news | Information on Usenet and newsgroups |
| rec | Recreational activities such as hobbies, the arts, movies, and books |
| sci | Scientific topics such as math, physics, and biology |
| soc | Social issues and cultures |
| talk | Controversial subjects such as gun control, abortion, religion, and politics |

You access newsgroups by accessing the server on which they are stored. Not all servers store the same newsgroups. The network administrator or the owner of the site determines what to store, but if you request a particular newsgroup from your ISP, the ISP can forward that request to another server that does provide the newsgroup. Almost all news servers "expire" articles after a few days or, at most, a few weeks because of the tremendous volume. Although they might be archived at the site, these articles are no longer available to be viewed by users.

**NOTE**    Newsgroups are uncensored. You can find just about anything at any time anywhere. Nobody has authority over newsgroups as a whole. If you find certain groups, certain articles, or certain people offensive, don't go there, or use the Rules Editor that I talked about earlier to prevent certain articles from even being displayed. But remember, anarchy reigns in newsgroups, and you never know what you might stumble upon in the least likely places.

## Setting Up a Newsgroup Account

Before you can read newsgroups, you must set up a newsgroups account. Before you start, get the name of your news server from your ISP, and then follow these steps:

1. In the main Outlook Express window, select the Outlook Express folder, and in the pane on the right, click Set Up a Newsgroups Account to start the Internet Connection Wizard.

2. Supply the information that the wizard requests and click Finish when you are done.

You'll now see a folder in the Folders list for your news server.

## Connecting to Newsgroups

The next task is to download the list of newsgroups from your server. When Outlook Express asks if you want to do this, click Yes. This may take a while if you have a slow connection, but notice the incrementing number of newsgroups in the Downloading Newsgroups dialog box. The number available depends on what the server has subscribed to (somewhere around 30,000 for the server I use).

**TIP**    Only the names of the newsgroups are downloaded to your computer; their contents remain on the news server. Periodically, you can update this list by clicking Reset List.

When the list has finished downloading, you'll see the Newsgroup Subscriptions dialog box, as shown in Figure 15.4.

**FIGURE 15.4**
Use this dialog box to
search for and subscribe
to newsgroups.

## Finding a Newsgroup of Interest

You can select a newsgroup to read in two ways:

◆ You can scroll through the list (this will take a lot of time).

◆ You can search on a term.

Just for the sake of doing it, scroll down the list a bit. As you can see, it's in alphabetic order by hierarchical categories. If you don't see anything right away that strikes your fancy, you can perform a search. Enter a term in the Display Newsgroups Which Contain text box, and then don't do anything! In a second, you'll see a list of newsgroups that contain articles about your topic.

## Subscribing to a Newsgroup

Subscribing to a newsgroup doesn't involve a fee or any other transaction. Subscribing means simply creating a subfolder for a particular newsgroup in your news folder. Then, instead of selecting it from the Newsgroup Subscriptions dialog box, you can simply click the newsgroup's folder to see the list of articles in it.

Once you've located a newsgroup you want to read, you can select it, click Subscribe, and then click Go To to open it, or you can simply click Go To. To unsubscribe to a newsgroup, right-click its folder, and choose Unsubscribe.

## Reading a Newsgroup

To read an article, simply click its header to display the message in the lower pane.

Outlook Express is a threaded newsreader in that it groups messages that respond to a subject line. If you see a plus sign (+) to the left of a newsgroup header, you can click it to display a list of related messages. The more up-to-date term for threads is *conversation*. Newsgroup articles are grouped by conversations by default.

**TIP**   You can also organize mail messages by conversations. With your Inbox selected, choose View ➢ Current View ➢ Group Messages by Conversation.

To read the articles from another newsgroup or to search for another newsgroup, double-click your main news folder, and then click Newsgroups to open the Newsgroup Subscriptions dialog box.

## Posting to a Newsgroup

Replying to a newsgroup article or sending a message to a newsgroup is known as posting. You post to a newsgroup in much the same way that you compose and send e-mail. To send an original message to a newsgroup, open the newsgroup and click the New Post button. The New Message window will open with the group's name in the To line.

To reply to an individual article, click the Reply button, and to reply to the entire newsgroup, click the Reply Group button.

**TIP**   You can also access newsgroups on the Internet at `http://groups.google.com/google-groups/deja_announcement.html`, and doing so is much easier than using Outlook Express.

# Customizing Outlook Express

Throughout this chapter, I've mentioned from time to time ways that you can specify how Outlook Express handles certain features, such as signatures. In most cases, you do this through the Options dialog box (shown in Figure 15.5), which you open by choosing Tools ➤ Options. Here's a quick run-down of what to use each tab for in the Options dialog box:

**General**   Use this tab to specify settings for how Outlook Express starts and for sending and receiving messages.

**Read**   Use this tab to set options for reading news and mail. For example, you can specify a maximum number of news article headers to download at one time.

**Receipts**   Use this tab if you want to verify that your message has been read by the recipient.

**Send**   Use this tab to set, among other things, the format (HTML or Plain Text) in which you will send all messages and the format you'll use to reply to messages. You can also specify whether copies of sent messages will be stored and whether you want Outlook Express to put the names and addresses of people you reply to in your Address Book.

**Compose**   Use this tab to specify the font and font size for mail messages and news articles that you create and to select stationery fonts for HTML messages.

**Signatures**   Use to create a signature, as discussed earlier in this chapter.

**Security**   Use this tab to specify your desired Internet Security zone and to get a digital ID.

**Connection**   Use this tab to specify how Outlook Express handles your dial-up connection.

**Maintenance**   Use this tab to specify what Outlook Express does with deleted items and to clean up downloaded messages, as well as to specify that all server commands are stored for trouble-shooting purposes.

**NOTE**   If you have installed any of the Microsoft Office applications that include a spell checker, you will also see a Spelling tab in the Options dialog box.

**FIGURE 15.5**
You use the Options dialog box to customize Outlook Express for the way you work.

## Summary

An e-mail program is arguably the most-used program in most businesses today. Though Outlook Express lacks the major features of its more robust sibling, Outlook, it contains everything you need to communicate over the Internet. And as you have seen in this chapter, it is extremely easy to use.

# Part 5

# Home Networking

**In this section you will learn how to**

- ◆ Understand Different Options for Networks
- ◆ Configure a Small Network
- ◆ Set up a Wireless Network
- ◆ Use Windows XP Security to Your Advantage

## Chapter 16

# Windows XP Professional Networking and Network Design Primer

You're at home, wondering if you should go through the trouble of connecting your computer with those of your spouse and children. Or maybe at work, your frugal boss says, "Hey, you seem to know a lot about computers. How about you take care of our network along with your other job." (Does that come with a pay raise too?) Before embarking on your journey, whether it's at home or for work, you need to understand the basics of networking.

This chapter is designed to give you the background you need to understand what happens on a network. Networks can do a lot of really cool things, such as allow multiple people to share one printer (so you don't need to spend the money on one for everyone) and exchange files quickly. And if you are into computer gaming, then you definitely need to understand the inner workings of networking, just in case something goes wrong when your friends are over and you're racing or blowing each other up.

If you've set up networks in the past, this chapter might just be review to you. But if you've never set one up, the information in this chapter will (hopefully) demystify some of the jargon of computer networking. This chapter covers the following topics:

- ◆ Overview of networking
- ◆ Networking vocabulary
- ◆ Theoretical networking concepts
- ◆ Types of networks
- ◆ Basic network connectivity
- ◆ Building your own network

## Defining a Network

Simply enough, a network is just two or more computers that communicate with each other. Many businesses commonly connect their networks together in a process known as *internetworking*. The largest internetwork is the Internet.

In most cases, when you connect your computer to the Internet, your computer joins a network that is set up by your Internet Service Provider (ISP). Your ISP is then connected to the Internet. In Chapter 12, you learned about some of the settings you need to connect to the Internet. In this chapter, you'll see what you need to set up a local area network (LAN).

## Early Networking: Sneakernet

The oldest form of the computer network is commonly referred to as the *sneakernet*, an official-sounding name for a very unofficial way of sharing information. In this popular networking arrangement, a user copied information to a floppy disk, put on a good pair of sneakers, and carried the file over to another computer or user. Not a very efficient method of networking by today's standards, but it got the job done. For some purposes, it may still be the best way to get information from one place to another.

Health benefits from additional walking aside, sneakernet poses a few serious disadvantages. Losing data is a big risk with this system because if you misplace or accidentally reformat the data disk, you'll lose the information. In an office environment, making sure that everyone who's working on a document or worksheet has the same information is also cumbersome:

♦ What happens if you have a copy of the original disk and someone makes changes to the original without telling you?

♦ What happens if more than one person is working on a document and you need to incorporate everyone's changes into one copy?

♦ How do you keep people from leaving the building with disks full of sensitive information?

Obviously, if you want data integrity, security, and the best use of the creativity of all the people working on a document (and who doesn't?), sneakernet is not the way to go. What you need instead is some way of tying your network together other than having to rely on people's goodwill and comfortable shoes. What you need is a LAN.

**NOTE**    The last few years have seen a bit of a resurgence of sneakernet. Instead of using floppy disks, which don't hold much information, people will burn CD-ROMs or DVDs and walk them over to their coworkers.

## LAN: The Better Way

LANs vary greatly in size—you can make a LAN out of two computers sitting across from each other in the same room or out of several thousand computers in the same building. The key parts to the definition of a LAN are that all the computers on the network are *grouped together in some fashion and are connected.*

**NOTE**    A network that extends over a larger area, such as a city block or a country, is known as a *wide area network (WAN).* These networks generally consist of two or more internetworked LANs.

On most LANs, cables connect the LAN by linking the network cards that reside within each computer or printer on the network. Situations in which cable is *not* the means of connection will be touched on later in this chapter, as well as in Chapter 18.

The preceding definition is the strict, textbook definition. However, in the real world, LANs are generally defined less by their physical characteristics and more by their function. In this sense, a LAN is a system in which linked computers and peripheral devices can share common information, software applications, printers, scanners, and fax services. LANs also enable the use of groupware for scheduling, shared databases, and e-mail. The quick electronic dispersal of computer-generated information to people striving toward a common goal and existing in a single-user-per-computer environment truly defines a local area network.

Most of the functions of a LAN are based on using one or two computers as servers. With a LAN, you can do all the following:

◆ Share files through a file server

◆ Share applications from an application server

◆ Share printers through a print server

◆ Share schedules, transmit e-mail, and hold electronic meetings through a Groupware server such as Microsoft Exchange or IBM's Lotus Notes

◆ Share Internet connections

◆ Utilize a common security platform

Other things that you can do on a LAN include sharing backup media such as tape drives and recordable CD and DVDs, playing multiuser games, and video conferencing with multiple users in a process known as *multicasting*.

### FILE SHARING

One of the primary purposes of a LAN is to provide a common storage area so that several people can access the same files. File sharing can help ensure that anyone who uses that file is always working with the most recent version. Alternatively, if you don't want to share a file with the network but you need someone else to do some work on it, you can transfer the file to someone else—just move it from your folder to theirs or send it as an attachment to an e-mail message.

Note that the act of sharing a file with the network does *not* automatically give everyone on the network access to it. In many network operating systems, you can attach a password to your files so that only people who have the password can access them.

Alternatively, you can grant different levels of access to specific users or a specific group of users. Access can be at levels such as read-only, read and change, and full control. This capability can prevent unauthorized users from seeing your work or making changes to your work. More information on this process is available in Chapter 19.

Sharing, transferring, and securing information between computers on a network is generally known as *file management*. You can share entire drives and folders. If you use an NTFS formatted drive, you can also share individual files.

**NOTE** As with individual files, you can restrict access to your shared resources (printers, CD-ROMs, scanners, tape drives, and so on) with passwords. Chapter 19 describes how you can restrict access to specific users.

### CONCURRENT USE OF APPLICATIONS

Many, but not all, software packages will work fine if you install them onto an *application server* and let other users access them from their computers. Here are a few of the advantages to locating software centrally (that is, on an application server):

◆ It frees disk space on individual computers. The bulk of the application is stored on one or two servers and not at each user's computer.

- Multiple users can use an application simultaneously (almost a necessity in many database applications).

- Upgrading software is easier because the application that needs to be updated is the copy of the software that is installed on the server.

**NOTE**　When upgrading, some Windows applications have a certain number of files that need to be updated at each user's computer even though the major part of Windows is located on the application server. These files usually include configuration information that is specific to each computer system in your office.

**WARNING**　If you store applications on an application server and let users access them from their individual workstations, *you are still required to buy more than one license*. You should have proper software licensing for every user, even if you load only one copy of the software onto the server. Otherwise, you are committing software piracy—stealing from the developers of that software. Software piracy is a federal crime. One exception is software that uses one of the free licenses such as the Free Software Foundation's General Public License (www.fsf.org).

LAN-dependent applications, such as e-mail, are usually licensed for a specific number of users. When you access the program from the server, a full-blown copy of the program is transported from the hard drive of the server to the memory of your computer. As you interact with the program, you are interacting with the copy that is stored in the memory of your computer. If you activate another program, such as a spell-check feature taken from a word processing program, that feature is transported from the hard drive of the file server to the memory of your computer. You need a license for every program and every computer that will store part of each program in its memory.

**NOTE**　Application servers are also often inaccurately referred to as file servers. Since applications require CPU power, application servers require the fastest possible CPU(s). On the other hand, file servers work best with extra RAM. When a shared file is already available in RAM, file access speed is increased.

### PRINT SHARING

Printers are just one of a host of peripherals that you can share. A lot of people get confused about the nature of peripherals these days, but basically a peripheral device is anything that is external to the CPU and memory.

**NOTE**　The words *peripheral device* and *peripheral* are just tech-speak for "a device that attaches to your computer system." Printers, scanners, sound cards, DVD players, PDA cradles, and keyboards are all peripheral devices.

A LAN enables its users to share high-cost peripheral devices such as printers, and manage them so that multiple users do not attempt to use the devices simultaneously.

Print sharing saves you both time and money. Of course, even without a network, you don't have to buy printers for every computer you own. One device will work just fine—if you don't mind standing in line to use it. However, if you must wait for a device to be free, you are spending the money you saved (by not buying the extra printer) on wasted time.

**NOTE**  You don't even need an extra computer to share a printer. Network print servers that are about the size of my hand are available. They have two connections: one to the network, the other to the printer. Once configured, a print server looks just like any other computer to a network.

As with file management, a network administrator can restrict access to the peripheral devices on a network so that only those people authorized to use them can access them. For example, you may not want people to print out rough drafts of your kid's homework or family pictures on the $8,000 color printer you bought for your home business. To set up Windows XP Professional as a print server, see Chapter 8.

### GROUPWARE

Groupware is a type of application that supports group scheduling, e-mail, and possibly other functions such as database management and file sharing. In office environments, this could be one of your office manager's favorite network features. Organizing departmental meetings can be an administrator's nightmare, as they try to sort through everyone's schedules to find a time when everyone can meet. Groupware can make this nightmarish task much more manageable.

Groupware keeps track of all users' schedules, either separately or together as one large calendar. Each person on the network keeps track of his or her own appointments in the virtual day planner. This information is automatically stored in a central database.

Now, let's say that you want to call a meeting of all the marketing people in your company. All you have to do is list the names of the people who should attend this meeting and then choose a date. The computer can tell you of any scheduling conflicts and let you modify the meeting time accordingly. Some scheduling software packages let you tell the computer to choose the first time that everyone is available, to save you the trouble of having to guess. After you've settled on a time, you can use the scheduling program to send "invitations" and ask people to confirm their attendance.

Groupware also supports input from multiple users to other applications, such as databases. For example, sales input from different stores can be merged on a database using the right kind of groupware. Some groupware packages such as Microsoft Exchange also include e-mail servers.

### INTERNET CONNECTIONS

Another good reason to set up a network is to share Internet connections. We first looked at Internet Connection Sharing (ICS) in Chapter 12, in which one system acts as a "gateway" for all of the other computers, and only one computer from your network is seen on the Internet.

Alternatively, you can use a hardware firewall router to protect your network as well as connect you to the Internet. As discussed later in this chapter, specialized routers can share one Internet connection and act as a firewall. With the right commands, the router can even block the communication ports used for specialty programs such as instant messaging and networked games. The router becomes the "computer" at risk; since there is no data on the hardware router, your risks are small.

These types of configurations work well in a home network, and not enough people take advantage of them. You have to pay for only one connection, and all computers can access the Internet! Of course, at most businesses, people share Internet connections all the time.

### SECURITY CONSIDERATIONS

The Internet can be a dangerous place for a computer. Every computer that connects to the Internet needs some form of security to protect it from attack. This means purchasing filters and virus scanners for every computer and a firewall or proxy server for the whole network. Maintaining these systems can be a difficult and expensive enterprise. With the Windows Firewall, as described in Chapter 12, the computer running ICS is the only one at risk from Internet attacks.

Unfortunately, this does not protect you from risks inside your network. Malicious or poorly trained users can still download e-mail viruses or sabotage your data.

By using a network, you can tightly control security through one common platform as opposed to trying to configure security on each individual system. You will have fewer concerns about who is logging in and what they can access if and when they do get in.

## Networking Vocabulary

Like most other specialized fields, networking has its own jargon. This list is far from exhaustive—in the following chapters, more terms will be introduced—but it gives you a good starting place. Remember these definitions:

**Client**  Any computer with independent processing power (CPU and RAM) that can provide *input* to the network is a client. This definition includes personal computers, handheld scanners, PDAs, and so on.

**Server**  A server is a computer that processes common requests from the network. For example, a print server queues and processes print jobs for a group of computers. The most common server is a file server. A file server is a computer that holds, manages, and secures access to files and data. It provides centralized control for and to your data and acts as a common location for your files for the purpose of centralized backup.

**Workstation**  Any computer physically operated by a user is a workstation. Most workstations are clients. Some workstations, especially in peer-to-peer networks, may also be configured as servers.

**Terminal**  A terminal is a computer-like device from which you can provide input to the network. While a terminal may include graphical processors, it may or may not have a processor or hard drive. Terminals are also known as slave computers.

**Node**  Each client, workstation, terminal, and server has a unique IP address on a TCP/IP network. Specialized hardware items such as routers and print servers also have their own unique IP address on a network. Each of these items is a *node*. Each node associates its IP address with the network interface card.

**Packet**  A packet is the smallest unit of information that can be sent across a network. A packet contains the sending node's address, the receiving node's address, and the data being sent between the two nodes.

**Ethernet**  The trade name for the most common form of networking in use today, Ethernet is more formally known as IEEE standards 802.2 and 802.3. While there are several other types of networks available, current network equipment in most computer stores is based on some form of Ethernet. The basic Ethernet standards are listed in Table 16.1. Devices supporting each of these standards are commonly available in major computer stores, with 10-Gb Ethernet being the hardest to find.

**Hub**  A hub is a box that connects that the computers on a LAN. On an Ethernet network, messages are broadcast to all computers that are connected to that hub. This device can increase traffic on a LAN as a device (or node) broadcasts packets to all devices connected to the hub.

**TABLE 16.1:**    Ethernet Standards

| COMMON NAME | STANDARD | SPEED |
|---|---|---|
| Ethernet | IEEE 802.3 | 10Mbps |
| Wireless ("Wi-Fi") | IEEE 802.11b | 11Mbps |
| Wireless ("Wi-Fi") | IEEE 802.11g | 54Mbps |
| Fast Ethernet | IEEE 802.3u | 100Mbps |
| Gigabit Ethernet | IEEE 802.3z | 1000Mbps |
| 10-Gb Ethernet | IEEE 802.3ae | 10,000Mbps |

**NOTE**   You will occasionally hear people refer to networking cable (usually twisted pair, such as Cat 5) as *Ethernet*. This is wrong. Ethernet is a set of rules for network communication and is not dependent upon one specific type of cable (or lack thereof for wireless).

**Switch**   A switch is a box that connects some or all of the computers on a LAN. A switch can determine the destination node for a packet and can send the message directly to the node. Since other computers aren't bothered with that packet, a switch can reduce traffic on a LAN.

**Router**   A router connects a LAN to other networks such as another LAN or the Internet. If your router has enough connections, it can also connect all of the computers in your LAN. What routers do is called *routing*, which is the transmission of data between networks.

# A Little Theory

In order to understand networks, you need to understand some theory. We'll start with some basics about the OSI model, which can help you understand the functionality of different types of network hardware and software.

The OSI model provides the basis for organizing and classifying network protocols into protocol stacks. There are two major protocol stacks commonly used by Windows XP Professional for networking: IPX/SPX and TCP/IP. You might also see a third protocol stack, NetBEUI, if you work with older Windows-based networks.

## OSI Model

The Open Systems Interconnect (OSI) model of networking provides the theoretical basis for all network hardware and software. It provides all of the functionality needed to translate the Word file that you're accessing from the server to the 1s and 0s that are transmitted over computer cables. The seven layers, from top to bottom, are as follows:

- Application (7)
- Presentation (6)
- Session (5)

- ◆ Transport (4)
- ◆ Network (3)
- ◆ Data Link (2)
- ◆ Physical (1)

**NOTE**  Some network designers refer to the numeric name for a layer; for example, the application layer is also known as layer 7.

The following sections describe each of these layers in some detail. Perhaps the most important of these protocols form the basis for IP addressing, which is covered in some detail later in this chapter.

**NOTE**  One alternative to the seven-layer OSI model is the five-layer TCP/IP model of networking. The top three layers of the OSI model (5, 6, 7) approximately correspond to the top layer in the TCP/IP model. The bottom four layers in both models are, for our purposes, the same thing. While purists may object, OSI layers are often used to describe the functionality of specific TCP/IP protocols, without reference to the TCP/IP model.

### APPLICATION (7)

The OSI application layer includes the services and commands that users call to connect to a network. Common application layer protocols that you've seen earlier in this book include HTTP, FTP, and Telnet. One other important application layer protocol is the Domain Name System (DNS), which contains a database of domain names such as www.mommabears.com and corresponding IP addresses such as 10.12.213.54.

OSI application layer protocols are different from regular applications. In fact, they translate the programs that you use, such as Microsoft Word, to a format usable by the OSI presentation layer.

One example of application layer hardware is a computer that has direct connections to more than one kind of network. For example, a computer that is connected to a TCP/IP network on one end and an IPX/SPX network on the other end is a true application layer gateway. A more common example of a gateway is a computer configured for ICS/Windows Firewall, as discussed in Chapter 12.

### PRESENTATION (6)

The OSI presentation layer is a translator. It formats and encrypts data. For example, some presentation layer protocols can translate the words you type into computer codes such as ASCII.

### SESSION (5)

The OSI session layer manages your time and connections on a network. Computers exchange messages at the session layer to keep a connection open. If a user is not active, session layer messages may stop after a designated timeout period.

### TRANSPORT (4)

The OSI transport layer drives the effort used by the network to ensure that your message gets to the destination. Some transport layer protocols keep trying until the receiving computer confirms delivery. Others just use a *best effort*, which means the sending computer spits out the message and hopes that the receiving computer gets it.

### NETWORK (3)

The OSI network layer includes the protocols that actually move data, in packets, from computer to computer and from network to network. The most important network layer protocol is IP, which handles computer addressing.

Hardware routers work at the network layer. A router is installed as the interface between two or more networks. There are some hardware routers that are known as *router/gateways*, because they function at both layer 3 and layer 7.

### DATA LINK (2)

The OSI data link layer translates packets to bits (1s and 0s). The data link layer includes two sublayers:

**Logical Link Control (LLC)**: Supports synchronization and error checking.

**Media Access Control (MAC)**: Allows computers to access a network. MAC addresses are the hardware addresses associated with a network interface card.

Hardware components known as switches work at the data link layer. Normally, a switch divides a LAN into segments. One or more computers are located on each segment. A switch can regulate traffic in a LAN; messages within a segment are not sent to other segments, thereby reducing traffic on other parts of the LAN.

**NOTE**   Another name for a switch is a bridge. While *switch* is in more common use today, *switch* and *bridge* can be used interchangeably.

**NOTE**   There are a number of hybrid switches on the market. For example, network salespeople may refer to a *Layer 4 switch* or a *Layer 7 switch*. These hybrids have some functionality at multiple layers. Since there is no standard for hybrid equipment, there is no true standard for what they do on a network.

---

#### WHAT DO I REALLY NEED TO KNOW ABOUT OSI?

The descriptions provided of the OSI layers might appear to be watered down, since they certainly don't outline each layer's complete functionality, but I've done that for a reason. It's handy stuff to know if you're shopping for a device for your home network, and the salesperson tries to display brilliance by referring to some little black box as a "Layer 3 device" or the like. You can also try starting conversations at cocktail parties with this knowledge, but you're on your own there.

While setting up your own network, it's pretty unlikely that OSI knowledge will help you out a great deal, unless you are reading your router's manual. In fact, those of us who troubleshoot networks for a living don't often rely on OSI knowledge either. Problems usually boil down to something like, "The network cable is unplugged," or, "The router is dead." Sure, those problems correspond to layers 1 and 3, respectively, but the bottom line is, fix it!

If at some point in your life you want to get a Cisco or Microsoft networking certification, then you will need to know these layers inside and out. But for now, use them as a reference to understand how the networking puzzle fits together. Pretty much everything relating to network communications revolves around these seven layers.

### PHYSICAL (1)

The OSI physical layer defines how messages are to be sent through cables, radio waves, light pulses, and so on, in the 1s and 0s of computer communication. Think of it as the workhorse that does the actual job of getting data from point A to point B.

## Protocol Stacks

With seven layers in the OSI model, you can imagine that there are a substantial number of protocols. In fact, there are literally dozens of major groupings of protocols, organized in their own protocol stacks. These two stacks are pretty common and are supported in the Microsoft world:

**IPX/SPX**: Novell developed the Internetwork Packet Exchange/Sequenced Packet Exchange (IPX/SPX) protocol stack for use with the Novell network operating system (NOS). IPX and SPX are just two of the available protocols in this stack. Novell NOSes are still commonly used in larger corporations; however, IPX/SPX use is less common since Novell included TCP/IP as the preferred option in NetWare 5.0, released several years ago. Some network administrators set up IPX/SPX on a LAN for security. Because IPX/SPX is essentially a different language from TCP/IP, it is considerably more difficult for someone using the Internet to break into this type of network.

**TCP/IP**: The language of the Internet is named for two of its component protocols, Transport Control Protocol (TCP) and Internet Protocol (IP). TCP/IP is routable and scales to any sized network. Most modern networks use TCP/IP exclusively. Since TCP/IP was developed concurrently with Unix, TCP/IP is native to any related operating system (Linux, BSD, Solaris). Specific TCP/IP protocols will be addressed in the next section.

**NOTE**    There is another protocol that you might run across if you're networking with older Microsoft operating systems, such as Windows 98, called the NetBIOS Enhanced User Interface (NetBEUI). It's relatively fast but not scalable for large networks. Because of its limitations, Windows XP doesn't support it natively. If you need NetBEUI, the files needed to install it are available on the Windows XP CD-ROM. For more information, see the Microsoft Knowledge Base article 306059.

**TIP**    Microsoft Knowledge Base articles are readily available online. Navigate to `http://support.Microsoft.com`, and enter keywords or the article number as a search term. Alternatively, if you enter the article number in a comprehensive search engine such as Google (`www.google.com`), you'll probably find a direct link to the article.

## The TCP/IP Protocol Suite

As inferred in the previous section, TCP/IP and other protocol suites are a collection of interdependent protocols working together to allow computers to communicate with each other. While there are several dozen protocols in the suite, there are only a handful of TCP/IP protocols commonly used. Some of the common ones are covered here and are related to what you see in this book. They are listed with their associated OSI layer number.

**Hypertext Transfer Protocol (HTTP) (7)**: Supports transmission of web pages over the Internet. You can see how to set up an HTTP server in Chapter 32.

**File Transfer Protocol (FTP) (7)**: Provides for streamlined uploading and downloading of files. You can learn how to set up an FTP server in Chapter 32.

**Simple Mail Transfer Protocol (SMTP) (7)**: Allows users to send e-mail messages. You can see how to set up an SMTP server in Chapter 32.

**Post Office Protocol (POP) (7)**: Lets users receive e-mail messages. The most common POP in use today is known as POP3.

**Transmission Control Protocol (TCP) (4)**: Sets up a connection between two different computers, with guaranteed data delivery.

**User Datagram Protocol (UDP) (4)**: Sets up a connection between two different computers, with *best effort* (no guarantee) data delivery. Alternative to, and faster than, its cousin TCP—but less reliable.

**Internet Protocol (IP) (3)**: Allows for unique numeric addresses on a network. Discussed in more detail in the next section.

**Internet Protocol Secure (IPsec) (3)**: Allows for encrypted IP messages. Requires an encryption key. Supports virtual private networking (VPN), which is discussed in more detail in Chapter 29.

**Dynamic Host Configuration Protocol (DHCP) (3)**: Provides automatic allocation of IP addresses and network configuration information to client computers. After a certain period of inactivity, the IP address can be reassigned to a different computer.

**Point-to-Point Protocol (PPP) (2)**: Supports a connection to other networks such as the Internet. Most commonly used for dial-up connections through a telephone modem.

**Point-to-Point Protocol over Ethernet (PPPoE) (2)**: Lets you use broadband connections such as DSL and cable modems to connect your LAN to the Internet.

**Point-to-Point Tunneling Protocol (PPTP) (2)**: Supports virtual private networking (VPN). An option to IPsec.

## IP Addressing

In order to communicate on a TCP/IP network, each node needs its own unique IP address. An IP address consists of four numbers (called octets) between 0 and 255, such as 125.23.252.2. IP addresses can be divided into two portions: a network address and a host address. The network address is shared by all of the nodes on that network. The host address is unique to that node.

---

**IP VERSION 6**

The IP addressing described in this chapter is actually IP version 4 (IPv4). Because of inefficiencies in the way IPv4 was designed, and consequently how network addresses are assigned, all available IPv4 network addresses are taken. Many are taken by ISPs that can assign you one of these addresses when you connect to the Internet.

There is another type of IP addressing, known as IPv6. Instead of the 32 bits in an IPv4 address, an IPv6 address includes 128 bits. This corresponds to over $3.4 \times 10^{38}$ addresses, or about 54,000,000,000,000,000,000,000,000,000 addresses for every human on earth. That should last for a few years!

While IPv6 is already in use in some countries, it's taking a long time to take hold, so you must still configure your computer with IPv4 addresses. Every IPv4 address is automatically translated to a unique IPv6 address for these more advanced networks.

There are 32 bits in every IP address. This corresponds to a total of $2^{32}$ = 4,294,967,296 possible addresses. You might think that 4 billion IP addresses would be enough for a world of just over 6 billion people, but that's not the case. Although not all IP addresses are engaged at once, all available IP addresses are taken. See the "IP Version 6" sidebar for some details on the next generation of IP addressing.

There are five different categories of IP addresses available, as described in Table 16.2.

**TABLE 16.2:**     IP Address Classes

| CLASS | DESCRIPTION |
|-------|-------------|
| A | IP addresses between 1.0.0.0 and 126.255.255.255. Suitable for networks with millions of nodes. |
| B | IP addresses between 128.0.0.0 and 191.255.255.255. Suitable for networks with thousands of nodes. |
| C | IP addresses between 192.0.0.0 and 223.255.255.255. Suitable for networks of up to 254 computers. |
| D | IP addresses between 224.0.0.0 and 239.255.255.255 are reserved for multicast applications. |
| E | IP addresses between 240.0.0.0 and 255.255.255.254 are reserved for experimental use. |

### DEFINING A SUBNET

A *subnet* is a group of computers whose IP addresses define them as being on the same network. This is determined by your computer's IP address and a parameter called the *subnet mask*. When you set up TCP/IP on any computer, an IP address and a subnet mask are required.

Whether or not a destination computer is on the same subnet as the sending computer is a critical distinction for TCP/IP networking. If they're on the same network, then the message is sent directly to the recipient. If not, then the message is sent to the default gateway, which then has the responsibility of forwarding the message appropriately.

For example, if you are trying to connect to www.sybex.com, you're actually looking for the web server that contains the files for the Sybex website. This is a specific computer. But your Windows XP computer doesn't know where the Sybex website is located. It needs an IP address. Chances are that it gets the IP address from your ISP's DNS server.

Once the address is located, the next step is for your computer to determine if the IP address for the Sybex website is on your subnet. If it is, then the message can be sent and communication established. Odds are, though, that you are on a different network than the Sybex website.

All IP addresses that are not on the subnet are routed to outside networks. If your subnet is properly defined, a request for the Sybex website will be routed outside your LAN (unless you work for Sybex, of course).

### IP Addresses and Subnetting

IP addresses have two parts: the network address, which is the same for all computers on your subnet, and the host address, which must be unique. The entire IP address must be unique for each computer on a network. Unfortunately, you can't just look at an IP address and determine which portion is the network and which portion is the host.

For example, take a look at 155.102.16.47. The network portion could be 155.102, or maybe 155.102.16, but you can't tell by looking at it. (If the network address is 155.102, the host address would be 16.47, and if the network address is 155.102.16, the host address would be 47.) The length of the network address is determined by the subnet mask.

There are three classes of IP addresses available to be assigned to hosts on the network, and the classes are determined by the number in the first octet of the IP address. Each class has its own default subnet mask. Table 16.3 illustrates this.

**TABLE 16.3:** IP Addressing and Default Subnet Masks

| FIRST OCTET | CLASS | EXAMPLE | DEFAULT MASK | NETWORK ADDRESS |
|---|---|---|---|---|
| 1-126 | Class A | 118.202.61.147 | 255.0.0.0 | 118.0.0.0 |
| 128-191 | Class B | 155.188.166.199 | 255.255.0.0 | 155.188.0.0 |
| 192-223 | Class C | 201.106.87.1 | 255.255.255.0 | 201.106.87.0 |

By looking at an IP address and its subnet mask together, you can discern what the network address is and then determine which computers are on the same network.

### Using the IP Address and Subnet Mask

Here is a quick and dirty way to determine the network address. Look at the IP address and look at the subnet mask. For each octet in the subnet mask that has a 255 in it, the corresponding octet in the IP address is the network. If there's a 0 in the subnet mask, the corresponding octet in the IP address is part of the host address.

While this will work in a lot of instances, it's not always that easy. In fact, subnet masks can have other values besides 0 and 255, such as 224 or 240. That makes things a bit more complex. Also notice that in the last section, I said that there is a *default* subnet mask for each class of addresses. Do you have to use the default? Of course not.

**NOTE** Understand that all of the configurations available with subnet masks can be pretty complex. In this book, I want you to understand it well enough so that you can set up your own network and not have problems. If you want more information, see the book *TCP/IP JumpStart* by Andrew Blank from Sybex (2002).

Let's look at an example. In Table 16.3, we used the address of 118.202.61.147. If you use it with a mask of 255.255.0.0, the network address portion becomes 118.202. If you were to use a mask of 255.255.255.0, then the network address would be 118.202.61. You don't need to use the default, but each computer on a subnet needs to have the same subnet mask.

Okay, so let's cut to the chase. Why should you care? Because if you're setting up a network and the computers won't talk to each other, frustration can set in quickly. And improper configuration is the most common cause of problems.

Here is a list of tips to keep in mind when dealing with IP addressing:

◆ Each host (computer, printer, router, etc.) needs to have its own unique IP address.

- All hosts on a subnet need to have the same network address, unless you are setting up a more complex, routed network.

- Each host needs to have a subnet mask. The subnet mask determines the network address. Each host on a subnet should have the same subnet mask, or you will likely have communications problems.

Keeping these tips in mind will help reduce network communications problems. If you set up a network and the computers won't talk, check your connections and check your configurations!

### CONFIGURING THE SUBNET

Now that you know some IP addressing rules, you can define the IP addresses that you can use on a network. For example, take the first example from Table 16.3. That network address is 118.0.0.0. At first glance, you might think that you could assign all addresses between 118.0.0.0 and 118.255.255.255. But there are two more rules governing IP addresses:

- The first address in the subnet is the network address and cannot be assigned to any specific computer.

- The last address in the subnet is the broadcast address for that network and also cannot be assigned to any specific computer.

In other words, the assignable addresses on the 118.0.0.0 network start at 118.0.0.1, and end at 118.255.255.254. Some other examples are shown in Table 16.4.

**TABLE 16.4:** Assignable IP Addresses

| NETWORK ADDRESS | SUBNET MASK | ASSIGNABLE IP ADDRESSES |
|---|---|---|
| 12.0.0.0 | 255.0.0.0 | 12.0.0.1–12.255.255.254 |
| 135.52.0.0 | 255.255.0.0 | 135.52.0.1–135.52.255.254 |
| 206.35.153.0 | 255.255.255.0 | 206.35.153.1–206.35.153.254 |

Although you can assign any address within the range, it's good practice to start with 1 and work your way up. For example, the first computer could be 12.0.0.1, the second 12.0.0.2, and so forth. This makes it cleaner and easier to remember the numbers you used!

### SPECIAL IP ADDRESSES

You might have noticed that I left out a whole range of IP addresses. Some are reserved for special purposes; others are reserved for private IP networks. These addresses include:

**0.0.0.0**: Used by any computer on a TCP/IP network to refer to the local network.

**127.0.0.0**: Reserved for loopback purposes. Includes all addresses on this network, from 127.0.0.0 through 127.255.255.255. The loopback address, 127.0.0.1, is used for troubleshooting. We use it in Chapter 17.

**224.0.0.0–239.255.255.255**: Addresses in this range are Class D and are used for multicasting (sending messages to groups of computers). Some programs use these to communicate, and these addresses aren't available for host use.

**240.0.0.0 and up**: Addresses in this range are Class E and are reserved for future use.

**255.255.255.255**: Used as a broadcast address to all computers on the local network.

### PRIVATE IP ADDRESS RANGES

If you never connect your network to the Internet, you now have all the information that you need to assign an IP address to a specific computer. However, most people with networks do want to connect to the Internet. For your Internet connection, you need a unique IP address. But you don't need an Internet-unique IP address for every computer on your network. For the computers wholly inside your LAN, there are private IP addresses.

For example, when you set up ICS/Windows Firewall in Chapter 12, you assigned a unique public IP address to the NIC or telephone modem connection to the Internet. Now you can assign a private IP address on that computer's connection to your LAN.

There are a series of private IP addresses available for this purpose. These four blocks of private IP addresses cannot be used "live" on the Internet, because they are officially reserved for private networks.

**NOTE**   I say they cannot be used "live" on the Internet, but computers with these addresses often access the Internet. How? These addresses work only on a private network, and in order to get on the Internet, computers with one of these addresses must go through a translator, such as a system running ICS or a router. The ICS system or router will actually make the connection to the Internet-based computer and return the requested information to the client. This process is sometimes called Network Address Translation (NAT).

The official private IP address ranges are shown in Table 16.5.

**TABLE 16.5:**     Private IP Address Ranges

| CLASS | PRIVATE NETWORK ADDRESS | ADDRESS RANGE |
| --- | --- | --- |
| A | 10.0.0.0 | 10.0.0.1–10.255.255.254 |
| B | 169.254.0.0 | 169.254.0.1–169.254.255.254 |
| B | 172.16.0.0 | 172.16.0.1–172.31.255.254 |
| C | 192.168.0.0–192.168.255.0 | 192.168.x.1–192.168.x.254 |

*There are 254 available Class C private network addresses (1–254 in the third octet). With the default Class C subnet mask of 255.255.255.0, you have to pick one of these network addresses. To get the corresponding address range, substitute the number you choose for x.*

The 169.254.0.0 network address was originally assigned to Microsoft and has recently been adapted by the Internet Assigned Numbers Authority (IANA) as a private network address. If you have a network of computers where Windows 98 and later operating systems are installed, the Microsoft *Automatic Private IP Addressing* (APIPA) system automatically assigns an IP address from this range to the NIC.

### SETTING UP A PRIVATE NETWORK

When you want to set up a LAN that's connected to the Internet, pick a private network address. Select from the list in Table 16.5. There are three basic ways to assign an IP address to different computers:

**Static IP Addressing**: Allows you to select an IP address and assign it directly to your NIC. For a NIC connected to your internal network, select an IP address from the range on your chosen private IP network. You can often get a static IP address from your ISP for your Internet connection, but you may have to pay more. Static IP addresses are convenient for anyone who wants to connect to your computer from a remote location on the Internet, but they can also be an open invitation to hackers.

**DHCP Addressing**: Lets a DHCP server assign the address. Hardware routers that connect a network to the Internet often include DHCP servers. You can often set up a hardware router with a range of IP addresses from your selected subnet. You can then set up each computer on your LAN to take an IP address from that router.

**Automatic Private IP Addressing (APIPA)**: Assigns an IP address when no DHCP server is available. This is a Microsoft protocol, which uses the 169.254.0.0 network address.

To set up one of these addressing schemes for your NIC, go into its properties. Click Start ➢ Control Panel. In Control Panel, click the Network Connections applet. You should see the Network Connections window with a list of your NICs, similar to what is shown in Figure 16.1.

**FIGURE 16.1**
Windows XP Network
Connections

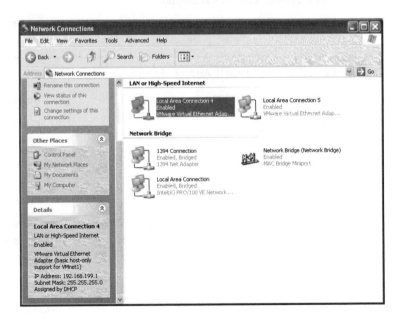

In Figure 16.1, Local Area Connection 4 is highlighted. The essential properties for this NIC are displayed in the lower left corner under the Details heading. This lists the currently assigned IP address, subnet mask, and the way the address is assigned. If you want to make a change, right-click the NIC. In the shortcut menu that appears, click Properties to get the properties window for that NIC, similar to Figure 16.2.

**FIGURE 16.2**

Properties for a network connection

The properties window for the NIC should include "Internet Protocol (TCP/IP)." Highlight it and click Properties to get the Internet Protocol (TCP/IP) Properties window shown in Figure 16.3.

**FIGURE 16.3**

TCP/IP Properties for a network connection

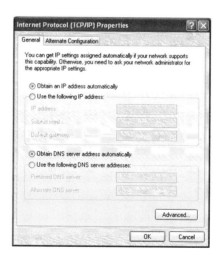

In this figure, the Obtain an IP Address Automatically option is selected. If you have a DHCP server on your network, this NIC gets its IP address from that server. Otherwise, the NIC gets its IP address through APIPA.

If you want to assign a static IP address, click Use the Following IP Address. Enter the IP address and subnet mask that you selected. For the Default gateway, enter the IP address of the router on your network (if you have one).

Having an assigned static IP address often means that you also have to set the DNS server address. DNS servers translate names like www.sybex.com to their corresponding IP address such as 63.99.198.12. Internet DNS servers have unique IP addresses, which should be available from your ISP.

**NOTE**    If you have a NIC that supports Universal Plug and Play (UPnP), you may not have to bother with any of this. The UPnP standard supports automatic configuration of the NIC, including IP addressing, on the attached LAN.

## Network Relationships

Now that you know a bit about network addressing, it's time to start thinking about your computers and their relationships to each other. There are three basic ways to set up relationships between computers on a LAN:

◆ Master/slave

◆ Client-server

◆ Peer-to-peer

Most networks depend on servers in some capacity, but not all networks require a server. In fact, in a truly pure sense, a peer-to-peer network has no servers at all.

### Master/Slave

In the early days of computing, processing power and memory were relatively expensive. Many users had to share the same computer. The computers were the servers or the masters of the network. Users were stuck with the slaves, also known as terminals. Servers were configured with separate storage areas for every user. In those days, terminals rarely had their own processor or memory.

Today, we may be coming full circle. With the development of the *network computer*, also known as the diskless workstation, it's possible to use Windows XP on a terminal in a master/slave network.

The Remote Desktop Connection discussed in Chapter 14 is one implementation of this kind of network. In that case, the *home computer* acts as a terminal, and the *remote computer* acts as the master. All signals, including keystrokes and mouse clicks, are transmitted from the slave to the master computer.

Even though this type of configuration is plausible, it's unlikely you will see many networks like this. Most of the time, you will see client-server networks in businesses and peer-to-peer networks in home environments.

### Client-Server

Client-server networks are similar in some ways to master/slave networks. In each, a central computer is in charge of the network and handles all requests. The main difference is that the client computers are able to compute on their own (assuming that they're PCs), unlike regular terminals. These networks are most commonly used in larger companies.

However, client-server networks are like their peer-to-peer (which is covered next) counterparts in a number of ways. Most important, each client can operate independently as a separate computer and can, by itself, function when the network stops.

Client-server networks are most commonly organized into logical structures called domains, which use centralized databases to store information about users and profiles, as well as security settings (rights and permissions) to specific files and folders.

**NOTE**    Chapter 20 covers the details of connecting Windows XP Professional through a network to a domain.

## Peer-to-Peer

Peer-to-peer networks represent an entirely different concept in networking. Rather than allocating every user on the network a central storage ground, peer-to-peer networking connects a group of totally independent computers. Each computer generally keeps its applications on its own hard disk so that if something happens to the network, the network simply breaks down into a group of individual yet functional computers. If one workstation goes down, life can go on for the rest of the network if all users keep their needed files at their own workstation. In other words, a peer-to-peer network enables every workstation to lead a double life: to be a client *and* a server.

**NOTE**    Chapter 17 goes into the details of using Windows XP Professional to connect a peer-to-peer network.

Peer-to-peer networks give their users many of the same capabilities that client-server networks do. Each user decides which files, applications, and peripheral devices they will share with the rest of the network and then shares them. You can attach passwords to your resources so that unauthorized people can't access them. Alternatively, you can share things selectively, saying, perhaps, "Accounting gets to use the C drive, and Personnel gets to use the printer." In that case, Accounting and Personnel would need their own accounts on your Windows XP Professional computer.

On the subject of sharing resources, remember that because important information on a peer-to-peer LAN is distributed throughout the network, you'll have to leave networked computers on and connected to the network as long as anyone is working who needs the information on those computers.

How does a peer-to-peer network work? On a stand-alone computer, when you ask your operating system to access the drive, it can do so directly. The application talks directly to the operating system, which sends the information to the computer's disk. The operating system needs no go-between to help it access information and peripherals on its own computer.

If you're working on a network, however, the situation is a little different. The operating system needs help accessing information on other computers on the network. Its helper is called the *redirector* (or the *shell*, if you're a Novell user).

## Servers

The keys to most large networks are servers. You might even want to set up a server at home, depending on your needs. Servers can be dedicated to certain purposes such as file storage and sharing in a client-server network. And workstations can be set up as nondedicated servers in a peer-to-peer network.

What truly defines a server is the role it plays on a network. Most often, servers have their own specific operating system. For example, Windows Server 2003 and Novell NetWare are operating systems specifically designed to be servers. Most Unix-based operating systems can function equally well as a client or a server. Windows XP is generally regarded as a client-side operating system, but that's not to say it can't function as a server on a network. It's just not as good at being a server when compared to NetWare or Server 2003.

Generally speaking, servers also have higher hardware requirements than client computers. This makes sense, because servers are used by almost everyone on the network, while clients are typically used by one person at a time.

A *dedicated server* is a separate computer whose only goal in life is to be a file or application server. By dedicating a computer as a server, you can configure its memory more efficiently. A *nondedicated server*, on the other hand, is a workstation that moonlights as a server—its memory is divided between its role as a workstation and as a server.

Why would you want a dedicated server? A dedicated server is faster, safer, and more efficient than one also being used as a workstation.

◆ It's faster because all of the server's memory and processing power are used to serve clients.

◆ It's safer because no one's using the computer as a workstation and possibly crashing it (everyone crashes *sometimes*). It's also safer because you can control security from one centralized location.

◆ It's more efficient because it does not have to divide its time between being a server (processing remote requests) and being a workstation (processing local requests).

In short, dedicating a computer as a server can greatly improve your network's performance. Of course, the downside is cost, because you must buy a computer just to hold and maintain the integrity and security of your information. Because your server will have a lot of demands on it, you're going to want something fast with as much RAM as possible and a big hard disk, and that type of computer isn't cheap.

The expense of a dedicated server gives nondedicated servers their place in life. A lower price tag is just about the only advantage you get from using your workstation as a server. Nondedicated servers tend to be slower because any time the server/workstation is in use, the other workstations have to wait to access the server. This wait time can slow down your entire network. If you have only a few computers on your network, though, this is definitely the way to go. You won't notice any major performance degradation unless you approach double-digit clients.

Also, nondedicated servers are much more likely to crash, increasing the risk of data loss all over your network. If you *must* use a server as a workstation, it's best to limit it to a less-risky capacity such as a print or fax server. If one of those servers crashes, it's a pain in the neck but probably won't stop other people from accessing Microsoft Word or getting to their e-mail.

## What Type of Network Is Best?

There is no "best" type of network. What's best for you depends on your needs and resources. If you're creating a network from scratch, some of the factors you should consider include:

**Number of computers**: If you have more than one computer, you don't want to have to purchase expensive peripherals for each system. All three types of networks permit you to connect a printer, for example, to one computer and share it on the network. Peer-to-peer networks of more than 10 or 15 computers are difficult to manage.

**Number of users**: If you have more than one user, you may have more than one person making changes to the files on your network. If you can afford it, a dedicated file server can ease the effort in maintaining a single copy of a file. Users who need access to client computers in different locations require a centralized database of users and passwords. Neither a dedicated file server nor a central database of users is possible in a peer-to-peer network.

**Shared applications**: If you have a substantial number of computers on your network, it can make sense to set up a dedicated application server. This is not an option in a standard peer-to-peer network.

**Independent needs**: If your users need the ability to work independently, even when the network is down, each user needs a separate computer. This is not possible in a master/slave network.

**Centralized control**: Domains in a client-server network provide a level of centralized control almost equal to that available with a master/slave network.

**Cost**: Dedicated file and application servers can be expensive, especially when applied to small numbers of users. An independent computer for every user creates a different kind of expense.

For home networks, the best choice is usually peer-to-peer. In businesses, client-server is generally the network of choice. However, the facts associated with your particular network may lead you to a different conclusion.

## The Look and Feel of a Network

The most common way to set up a LAN is with computers connected to a hub. The predominant choice for network technology is Ethernet. The nodes in most Ethernets are connected with twisted-pair cables. This type of cable contains eight wires and connects as easily as a telephone. This chapter covers the details later. Figure 16.4 gives you a feel for how a network is set up.

This is one LAN, organized into three different sets of computers. It could represent the setup of a LAN in a three-floor office. Assume that you install a hub in a wiring closet on each floor. You could then install cables between the hub and the computers on that floor. The cables between the hubs would run between floors.

**FIGURE 16.4**
A sample network

**NOTE** Of course, if you are setting up a home network, your diagram will look much simpler than this. You will probably have just one hub, with all devices and your Internet connection attached to it.

The cable that is used to connect one hub to another hub (or a switch or a router) is generally referred to as a backbone. You always want to make sure that the cable that you use for the backbone is rated for speeds that meet or exceed the speed of the cable that you are using throughout the network (from the hub to the nodes).

## Building Your Own Network

Now that you've selected the software configuration for a network and have a general idea of the physical layout, you're ready for the hardware. To build a network, you need a network interface card (NIC) for each computer. In most cases, you'll also need cables to connect to each NIC, and hardware such as hubs and routers to connect the NICs together.

All of the previously discussed network relationships—master/slave, client-server, peer-to-peer—work well with the various types of Ethernet networks. But before you can select a NIC, a cable, a hub, or a router, you need to know what type of Ethernet network you're going to build.

**TIP** Always plan out your network before purchasing anything!

### Selecting Ethernet Hardware

There are several types of Ethernet network equipment available at most larger computer stores. Before you go out and purchase equipment, you have to make some choices. At minimum, you need to select the speed of your network. If you want a wireless Ethernet, you need to accept the associated higher costs and limited speeds. Whatever choice you make, you can then make sure that your components are consistent with that type (e.g., speed, wired, or wireless) of network.

Ethernet networks can be built to capacities of 10Mbps, 100Mbps, or 1000Mbps. As illustrated in Table 16.1, these standards are sometimes known as regular Ethernet, Fast Ethernet, and Gigabit Ethernet. Full-duplex versions of each of these standards are available, with twice the speed. Wireless Ethernet offers speeds of 11Mbps and 54Mbps.

The hardware that you select in the following sections—NICs, cables, hubs, switches, routers, and so on—all need to support the characteristics that you select.

### Network Cards

The network interface card (NIC), or the adapter card, is a card that you use to connect your computer to servers or other computers. The NIC you select should be consistent with the rest of your network. NICs are available that vary in the following characteristics:

**Installation**: Internal or External or PC Card

   **Internal NIC**: PCI or ISA

   **External NIC**: USB or IEEE 1394

**Speed**: 10Mbps, 100Mbps, 1000Mbps, 10,000Mbps wired, and 11Mbps or 54Mbps wireless

**Duplex**: Full-duplex or half-duplex

**Connection**: Cabled or wireless

**SPEED**

Transmission speed is measured in millions of bits per second, or Mbps. A bit is short for a binary digit, the 1s and 0s associated with computers. NICs transmit bits of data through a network as a negative or positive electrical pulse.

### NIC Installation Options

A NIC can be internal or external to your computer. Internal NICs can fit into PCI or ISA expansion slots. Before you buy an internal NIC, make sure you have the right kind of slot free inside your computer. Some instructions for installing an internal NIC are available in Chapter 17.

Many internal NICs are older *legacy* components. For various reasons, legacy NICs don't always work with Windows Plug and Play. In those cases, you should note the I/O address, DMA channel, and IRQ ports used by your NIC. Some techniques for handling legacy NICs are available in Chapter 9.

NICs today are fairly inexpensive, unless you're setting up a Gigabit network (and it's unlikely that you *really* need that kind of speed at home, even if you are a gamer). If you have a NIC that can't be configured through the Windows XP Professional Plug and Play system, it is often more cost effective to purchase a Plug and Play NIC. If you have a lot of peripherals, you may not be able to use the techniques described in Chapter 9 to find a free IRQ and would otherwise have to uninstall a different component.

Windows XP Professional may not recognize all Plug and Play NICs. Other techniques to address this problem are described in Chapter 17.

**WARNING**   When installing any hardware inside your computer, be careful. Computers are sensitive to static electricity. Before touching any electronic components, touch a larger piece of metal, such as a computer case. While firm pressure can be required to install or remove a hardware card such as a NIC, never force a card into a slot. If it's the wrong slot, the crossed wires will likely destroy many of the circuits in your computer.

External NICs may connect to USB or IEEE 1394–enabled ports. Make sure your computer has the port that works with the network card you want. Be especially careful if you want to get a USB NIC. There are two standards: USB 1.0 and USB 2.0. Be sure to match the NIC to the USB standard port available on your computer.

**NOTE**   If you see a FireWire or iLink NIC in your computer store, you should be able to use either of them with an IEEE 1394 connection on your computer. FireWire and iLink are trade names for components that meet IEEE 1394 standards.

Credit card–sized NICs are also available, primarily for laptop computers, which conform to the PC Card standards discussed in Chapter 6. They often come with separate adapters to connect to a cable or exchange signals with a wireless network.

### NIC Speed

Ethernet, Fast Ethernet, and Gigabit Ethernet NICs are readily available. Many NICs work at both Ethernet and Fast Ethernet speeds, which allows you to upgrade your network without changing your NIC. Some NICs are full-duplex, which essentially doubles the maximum data transfer speed.

If you get a full-duplex NIC, make sure all of the other equipment that you get is also built for full-duplex data transmission.

### NIC CONNECTIONS

NICs are available for regular twisted-pair connections that look like oversized telephone cables. With the latest advances in wiring, even Gigabit NICs can use the same cables. Wireless NICs are also available. Whatever your choice, make sure that your cables and other hardware are compatible.

**NOTE**   The terms *NIC*, *network card*, and *network adapter* all refer to the same thing—the network interface card.

## Cables

Cables are the backbone of most computer networks, even though wireless networks have made huge inroads in recent years. All information runs through the cables, either in the form of electrical or light pulses through twisted-pair cable or fiber-optic cable. For your network to work well, information must pass through the cabling (or air) without electromagnetic or other interference. Interference generally won't corrupt the data, but it can slow down the network considerably. When you purchase a cable, you need to consider the following:

- Length
- Distance limits
- Interference
- Cable standards
- Connectors

### CABLE LENGTHS

When you calculate the distance between your computer and a hub, remember that you want to keep your cables out of the way. That probably means you'll be routing cables to walls, along baseboards, above ceilings, and more. For example, I use a 100-foot, Category 5 cable to connect two computers in adjacent rooms. This extra length allows me to route the cable along the far ends of walls and avoid doorways.

### DISTANCE LIMITS

The rated speed on an Ethernet cable is limited to 100 meters, which corresponds to about 328 feet. If the distance between a computer and a hub is greater than 100 meters, don't use a longer cable. You may not like the result. Instead, get a repeater to maintain the strength of the signal over the extra distance.

### INTERFERENCE

To avoid interference, keep your network cables away from anything that may create an electromagnetic field, including fluorescent lights, motors, and other cables or power lines.

Two alternate ways to avoid interference are by shielding your cable, such as with a metal conduit, or by running network cables at right angles to other cables or power lines. Another option is a fiber-optic based network, because light pulses are essentially impervious to electromagnetic interference.

Some judgment is required. For example, if you're using today's standard Ethernet cable for a 10Mbps Ethernet network, a little interference doesn't matter. The Category 5e (the *e* is for enhanced) and Category 6 cables available in most computer stores can handle Gigabit data transfer speeds. However, as your network speed requirements increase, you need to pay more attention to cabling and potential sources of interference.

### STANDARDS

The standard for wiring regular Ethernet is known as Cat 6 UTP. This is short for Category 6 standard unshielded twisted-pair cable, a standard of the Electronic Industries Association. While there are shielded cables, and lesser quality cables that support slower speeds, it is difficult to find these in most consumer computer stores today.

Cat 6 supports speeds up to Gigabit Ethernet levels without a problem and is backward compatible with older versions such as Cat 3, Cat 5, and Cat 5e. Cat 5e and Cat 6 cables should be readily available in any self-respecting computer store.

**NOTE**   There are regulations on the network cable that you can use in the workplace. If you install network cables in areas susceptible to fire such as ceilings, many governments require the use of *plenum* cables. These cables include special coatings that do not emit toxic fumes in a fire. Whatever you might think of government regulations, plenum cables are generally a good idea in any network installation.

**TIP**   Most networks can get by with Cat 5 cable, which supports transfer speeds of up to 100Mbps. Sometimes you will be able to find Cat 5 a lot cheaper than 5e or 6. Whatever you do, though, don't buy anything older than Cat 5!

### CONNECTORS

Most Category 6 UTP cable terminates using connectors that look like chunkier versions of the connectors used to plug your telephone into the wall, as shown in Figure 16.5. These are called RJ-45, whereas your telephone uses RJ-11 connectors. One end plugs into your computer's NIC, and the other plugs into a hub. Category 7 cables use different types of connectors than the older categories, but they plug into hubs and NICs in the same way.

Many cables are sold with the connectors already attached. For larger networks, it may make more sense to purchase long lengths of cable, cut the cables to fit the physical layout of your office, and then attach a connector. Crimping tools are available for this purpose.

**FIGURE 16.5**
RJ-45 connector

## Wireless Considerations

If you're going to create a wireless network, you don't need many cables. Wireless networks work through the air with radio signals, infrared, or even microwaves.

The most common wireless networks are based on the IEEE 802.11b and 802.11g standards, colloquially known as *Wi-Fi*. The 802.11b standard provides for an Ethernet-style network at up to 11Mbps, while 802.11g operates at up to 54Mbps. A number of other wireless networks are available, but most of them don't have the speed or the cost-effectiveness of a Wi-Fi network.

If you set up a wireless network, you need a wireless hub, switch, or router to send and receive the signals. These are radio-style signals. In the frequencies used by IEEE 802.11b/g, (2.4GHz), you may get interference from microwave ovens, wireless phones, and other wireless devices such as PDAs and BlackBerry handhelds. A wireless network on a different subnet can also cause interference. If you're operating a wireless network, keep these sources away from the *wireless access points*, where wireless devices send and receive signals. We will spend more time discussing wireless networks in Chapter 18.

## Hubs/Switches

Computers on a standard LAN connect to a hub. A hub includes multiple ports to which you can connect RJ-45 or other types of cables. If you have more than two computers on your network, you need a hub. Different hubs are available for different speeds. As described earlier, smart hubs may also include diagnostic functionality. When you purchase a hub, check for the following:

**Ports**: You need a port for each computer that you want to connect. If your network might grow in the future, you may want additional ports. If you're using a wireless hub, each antenna serves as a port.

**Uplink**: If you want to connect your network to any other network such as the Internet, you should get a hub with an uplink port. Some hubs use a toggle to change a regular port to an uplink port. You can connect two hubs together by connecting the uplink port on one hub to the regular port on the second hub using a regular patch cable. Alternatively, you can connect two hubs together via regular ports using a crossover cable. A crossover cable is wired slightly differently than a regular Ethernet cable and is used to connect some types of network devices in a daisy-chain fashion.

**Speed**: Ethernet hubs are available at all currently available speeds. But you need to make sure that the speed rating of your hub and NIC match. Some hubs can *autosense*, or automatically detect, the speed capabilities of a NIC, within limits.

**Power**: Remember, hubs are external and normally require a separate power supply.

**NOTE**  If you have a network of two computers, you can connect them with a crossover cable, which is a standard UTP cable with the send and receive wires flipped on one end. This simulates what happens to a signal when going through the hub and saves you the additional cost of purchasing a hub.

Switches are basically intelligent hubs. They work like hubs in that they connect multiple devices. However, switches are better at managing traffic and handling heavy data loads.

## Routers

Routers can serve the same function as a hub. With the right uplink port, a router can also serve as a junction between networks, such as a small business network and the Internet. In fact, specialized routers are available. Some have embedded telephone modems. Others connect to external ISDN, DSL, satellite, or cable modems.

**NOTE**   The only real "modem" is a telephone modem, because it can translate the 1s and 0s of computer talk to the sound waves transmitted through telephone wires. Broadband modems such as DSL, satellite, and cable modems are more closely related to Ethernet adapters. In fact, you can connect a NIC or the uplink port of a hub or router directly to most broadband modems. Consult your broadband modem manufacturer or ISP for more information.

The ICS/Windows Firewall setup discussed in Chapter 12 assumes that you have a computer that is connected to your LAN and to the Internet. This requires two separate NICs, or a NIC and a telephone modem. Each connection requires its own IP address. Since this computer has a direct connection to the Internet, the Windows Firewall may not always protect it from intruders. You can install a router in place of this computer. Since you don't store any data on the router (other than what's required to configure that router), this configuration is safer.

**TIP**   The IP address on an ICS/Windows Firewall computer that's directly connected to the LAN is important. To other computers on the LAN, that's the default gateway address.

---

### BUYING NETWORK EQUIPMENT

Purchasing the equipment for your first network does not need to be confusing or difficult. In fact, your choices for Ethernet networks are simple. They're based on speed and cabling, as required. The details are covered in previous sections. Here is a summary of your options:

**Speed**: 10Mbps, 100Mbps, 1000Mbps, 10,000Mbps.

**Duplex**: Full-duplex.

**Cabling**: Cat 5 UTP can handle speeds up to 100Mbps. Cat 5e and Cat 6 UTP can handle 1000Mbps networks. If you're going to create custom lengths of cable, you also need a crimping tool to attach the RJ-45–style connectors. If you're using a wireless network, you don't need a cable.

**Wireless Standard**: Wi-Fi (IEEE 802.11b/g) or some other standard.

**NIC**: Internal, External, or PC Card.

> **Internal NIC**: PCI or ISA

> **External NIC**: USB 1.0, USB 2.0, or IEEE 1394 (iLink/FireWire)

**Hub**: Requires enough ports for each node on your LAN, an uplink port, and any additional computers that you may add in the future.

**Switch**: Can substitute for a hub. If you have a lot of traffic between several computers on your network, a switch can reduce traffic.

**Router**: Substitutes for a computer with a NIC on your LAN and a NIC or telephone modem that connects to another network such as the Internet.

---

## Installation

If you use a cabled network, the biggest cost may be installation. Because bundles of network cables on the floor are often unsafe and unattractive, many people want the cables run through the walls, just like telephone wire. You can see why wireless has taken off!

If you're in the process of building, you may be able to set up the installation of network cables in the same conduits used for your telephone cables. You can then set up your network (RJ-45) and telephone (RJ-11) adapters in the same wall for every room that needs connections.

However, if you already have an existing structure, the time and expense associated with paying a contractor to set up your network can be daunting.

Speed becomes a major consideration now and in the future. If your old cable can't keep up with the transfer rate of your new network, you'll need to replace it when you upgrade parts of the network, and that upgrade could be expensive. Clearly, the need for upgrades is yet another reason to plan your network ahead of time.

## Summary

In this chapter, we looked at the basics of networking. LANs help users share files, applications, and more. We then covered some of the vocabulary and theory behind a network and discussed various network relationships: master/slave, client-server, and peer-to-peer. Finally, we walked through the network components that you might get at your local computer store. With all of this information behind you, it's time to start setting up your own network in the next chapter!

# Chapter 17

# Setting Up and Configuring Your Own Small Network

One of the most powerful features of Windows XP Professional is its capability to attach to and become part of a networking environment. In this chapter, we'll look at many of the decisions you will need to make in order to get the networking features to run reliably in that environment. You'll learn how to set up a simple Ethernet network, including what to do if Windows XP doesn't detect your network interface card, how to configure your Windows XP Professional machine using the Network Setup Wizard, and how to manually configure your own IP addresses. You'll also learn how to allow users to share documents and printers and how to create profiles for users and hardware. Finally, the chapter wraps up with a section on troubleshooting your network.

In this chapter:

◆ Setting up your network

◆ Physically connecting your network

◆ Configuring Windows XP Professional for a network

◆ Sharing resources

◆ Connecting to shared resources on the network

◆ Understanding and using profiles

◆ Troubleshooting

## Planning a Network

The whole idea of a network is to share things: space on a large disk drive, a particular file on that disk drive, a printer, and so on. Networks provide two major benefits. One, they can increase user productivity and collaboration. Two, they can save you money on hardware and software. Imagine the cost difference of buying one color laser printer for every person in your family as opposed to buying one for everyone to share. As an example, let's consider a family that needs to do some sharing.

In our happy family, Jennifer has more storage capacity on her machine than Joe does on his, but the laser printer that he convinced her he needed is attached to Joe's PC. Jennifer and Joe work on stuff like their finances and writing letters to family members together, so they need to share some files—or they'll have to pass floppies back and forth via sneakernet. Because Jennifer has more disk space, they store the files on her machine. So, the network problems that we need to solve are as follows:

♦ Sharing Joe's printer with Jennifer

♦ Sharing Jennifer's disk with Joe

Let's solve their problem with a basic peer-to-peer network. Microsoft generally refers to peer-to-peer configurations as *workgroups* (as opposed to *domains*). With this type of network, Jennifer makes her hard disk available on the network, and Joe makes his printer available on the network. Assuming that both computers are running Windows XP Professional, here's how to get Joe onto Jennifer's disk and Jennifer onto Joe's printer:

1. Jennifer tells the Windows XP Professional networking software, "Offer the Files subfolder on my C drive to anyone who wants it. Call it JenFiles." In Microsoft enterprise networking terminology, JenFiles becomes the *share name* of that folder on Jennifer's machine (GTW09), and it's the name that others will use to access the resource over the network. In a few pages, I'll show you exactly how to share such a resource on the network so others can access it, but for now, remember this: a machine (named GTW09) is sharing a resource called JenFiles with anyone on that network who's able to use it. In this case, it's only Joe.

**NOTE** Here's an important concept in Microsoft networking: You must name each machine in the network, whether it is a server or a workstation. Often you will hear this name referred to as a NetBIOS name. You also must name each user (in our example, Joe and Jennifer). Because the PCs need names, we may as well name the PCs with their inventory numbers, which in this example are DELL05 and GTW09. Another common naming scheme, used within many companies, is to name the computer based on the physical location within the company. A computer in the east wing, row L, station 6 could be called EL06.

**WARNING** Naming machines after their users is generally a bad idea, even in a home network, because PCs may be reassigned to other users or given to other family members.

2. Joe then tells the networking software on his PC, "Attach me to the JenFiles resource on Jennifer's machine."

3. Joe, meanwhile, tells his computer to share the printer on his LPT1 port, giving it a name—again, a share name—of JOLASER. Joe's machine is called DELL05, so the UNC name of that printer will be \\DELL05\JOLASER.

**NOTE** UNC stands for Universal Naming Convention. In the printer's UNC name, \\DELL05 is the machine name and \JOLASER is the share name. UNCs are used all the time in networking and always follow a \\computername\sharename format.

4. Jennifer then tells her networking software to make a network connection to JOLASER on Joe's machine and to create it on her LPT1 port.

From now on, whenever Jennifer tells an application program to print to a laser printer on LPT1, the network software will intercept the printed output and will direct it over the network to Joe's machine. The networking software on Joe's machine will then print the information on Joe's printer. I've left out some of the "how do we do this?" information; it's coming right up.

**WAYS TO CONNECT A PEER-TO-PEER NETWORK**

In the next section of this chapter, I'll show you how to connect a network that uses an Ethernet hub, which I discussed in the previous chapter. You can, however, connect a peer-to-peer network in a couple of other ways:

◆ By using a special network cable called a crossover cable, which allows you to connect two machines' NICs directly to each other and bypassing a hub. This saves you the cost of buying a hub, but they're cheap nowadays anyway. The downside of this type of configuration is that you don't have easy expandability.

◆ By using a wireless connection, which we'll talk about extensively in Chapter 18.

For some detailed information about these types of connections, from the Start menu open Help and Support Center, click the Networking and the Web link, click the Home and Small Office Networking link, and then click the Hardware Requirements for Home and Small Office Networking link.

Windows XP Professional is designed to work in a variety of networking situations. XP makes the perfect network client for both home and office users. It doesn't matter if your entire network consists of Windows XP computers or if you have servers running NetWare, Unix, or some other platform; Windows XP Professional will play nicely with a variety of network operating systems. Windows XP Professional can also act as a server in a pinch—although you're better off going with a true server product for a long-term solution.

The real key to good networking is good planning. Always draw a basic diagram of what your network will look like, such as where the computers will be, where the hub or router will be, and where the cables will run. In addition, don't forget to put down logical (as opposed to physical) information such as IP addresses, which computer will be the print server, and which files are stored where.

Even Joe and Jennifer mentioned in the earlier example should draw things out. A drawing can eliminate problems before they begin. Let's say that neither Joe nor Jennifer knows a lot about networking, but they make a diagram and take it to a friend who knows computers well. That friend (or a trusted salesperson) might be able to tell them if their plan will work, before they purchase potentially expensive hardware. If Joe and Jennifer want to expand their network at a later time, they have a diagram ready and can see what their possibilities are.

For large and complex networks, planning is even more critical. Still, plan ahead before installing even the smallest network; it will save you troubleshooting headaches in the future.

## Connecting Your Ethernet Network

In this section, I'm going to show you how to set up a simple peer-to-peer Ethernet network that solves the problems of Joe and Jennifer that I just described. Using the information in the previous chapter, you first need to design your network, and then you probably need to go shopping—either on the Internet or at one of many computer centers that are springing up all over the place.

You need a network interface card (NIC) for each computer on the network, a hub, switch, or router, and some cables. Many computers that you buy these days come with NICs already installed. If you have an older computer, though, you'll probably need to purchase a NIC. You can even buy a starter kit that contains everything you need—NICs, cables, and a hub—probably for less than $50. With that and a couple of screwdrivers, you're ready to get started. Follow these steps:

1. Turn off and unplug each computer that will be part of your network.

2. At each computer, open the case, and insert a NIC in an empty slot, screwing the card in securely so it won't come loose.

3. Replace the case.

4. Insert one end of the cable into the RJ-45 socket on the card and insert the other end of the cable into the hub. The hub number is not important as long as you don't plug it into a port labeled "Uplink" or "Crossover"—avoid those.

**NOTE**   One way to avoid using a hub altogether is to buy a *crossover* cable. Plug one end of the crossover into one machine and the other end into your second machine. The major drawback with this is that you can have only two computers on your network. While hubs are pretty inexpensive, this is an alternative if money is really an issue.

5. Plug the hub into the power supply.

6. Turn on the hub and all connected computers. You'll see some lights start blinking on the hub. Most hubs will have a light for each port indicating whether it detects a connection, along with a power light and traffic indicators.

**TIP**   Here's a quick troubleshooting tip. When you have everything plugged in and turned on, look for connection lights on the connecting device. If a computer is plugged into port 2, then there should be a light indicating a connection for port 2. If it's not on, double-check your cables to make sure they're plugged in right. No light generally means no connection, which means no networking.

Because Windows XP Professional is Plug and Play, when you restart your computer after inserting the NICs, the system automatically loads the device drivers you need for the NICs. For the most part, Windows XP is very good about automatically detecting network cards after installing them and rebooting. In this respect, Windows XP is very user-friendly. However, you will occasionally run across a network adapter that doesn't have a Windows XP driver available, and the NIC may not be detected. What do you do?

First of all, don't panic. Windows XP can sometimes use Windows 98 or Windows 2000 drivers. If your NIC came with a disk or CD with drivers on it (it should have), try the 98 or 2000 driver by using the Add Hardware Wizard. In Control Panel, click Add Hardware, and follow the on-screen prompts. If those drivers don't work, then look on the manufacturer's website to see if they have anything, be it advice or drivers, available for people in your situation. The absolute worst-case scenario is that you'll have to take the NIC back and get a different brand, but this is unlikely. Stick with name-brand parts, and you should never run into a problem that serious. Now you're ready to configure your network.

**TIP**   Always check to make sure that the hardware you're purchasing is in the Windows Catalog (also known as the hardware compatibility list [HCL] for older operating systems). You can find it at www.microsoft.com/whdc/hcl/default.mspx.

## Configuring Your Network

After successfully installing your network adapters, there are some common steps you need to take to get the network running properly. Among those steps are to name your computer and workgroup, add protocols necessary for communication (TCP/IP is installed by default; you generally do not need to add more), and configure protocol parameters, such as IP addresses. Using the Network Setup Wizard can help you simplify these configuration processes.

## Using the Network Setup Wizard

Setting up a peer-to-peer network has never been easier than it is with Windows XP Professional. You simply follow the steps in the Network Setup Wizard, and in a very few minutes you're finished. The only catch is that the other computers on your network must be running one of the following operating systems:

◆ Windows 98

◆ Windows Millennium Edition

◆ Windows XP Professional

◆ Windows XP Home

If the other computers on your network are running some other operating system, you'll need to manually configure the network. This is because the Network Setup Wizard is provided for only the four operating systems listed above. Running the Network Setup Wizard not only will connect your computers to each other, but the wizard will also configure all computers to access the Internet through one host computer.

**WARNING**   If you've already configured networking on your computer, the Network Setup Wizard overrides your current settings. In that case, look for the sections later in this chapter on manual configuration.

I'll show you how to manually configure the network in the next section.

If your network hardware is installed and working properly, you're ready to begin. Log on as a user with administrative rights on the host machine (the one that will share its Internet connection). (If you're not sure how to log on as an administrator, find out how in the beginning of Chapter 3.) Once you're logged in, connect to the Internet, and then follow these steps:

1. Click Start ➢ All Programs ➢ Accessories ➢ Communications ➢ Network Setup Wizard to start the wizard.

**NOTE** If you see a "Cannot Complete the Network Setup Wizard" message, your computer already belongs to a domain. Instructions for setting up your computer on a domain, or converting it back to a workgroup member, are included in Chapter 20.

2. At the Welcome screen, click Next.

3. At the Before You Continue screen, look at the checklist, make sure you have completed your preparations, and then click Next to open the Select a Connection Method screen.

**NOTE** If you do not have two connections (one for the Internet and one for your local network), you will not be able to make this computer a router/gateway.

4. Select the statement that best describes the setup of your system, and then click Next. What you do next depends on the configuration of your network. In this example, we've specified that this computer will connect directly to the Internet. For many small or home offices, where computers are connecting through a modem, DSL line, or cable modem, this is the appropriate choice. If you are participating in a larger network or otherwise have a proxy server, firewall, or hardware router/gateway between your computer and the Internet, you will need to choose the second option listed. If you're still not sure which option is right for you, select Other, and then click Next. There are three other options that can be configured through the Network Setup Wizard, as shown in Figure 17.1.

Now you need to configure the other computers on your network. Running the Network Setup Wizard on the other computers will make them look for a host computer with a shared Internet connection. Therefore, your host computer will need to be up and running and connected to the Internet. Follow these steps at each computer:

1. Insert the Windows XP Professional CD in the CD-ROM drive.

2. At the opening screen, click Perform Additional Tasks.

3. At the next screen, click Set Up a Home or Small Office Network, and click Yes to continue.

4. The wizard will give you some information on what it can do. Click Next on the next two screens to continue.

**FIGURE 17.1**
The Network Setup
Wizard is versatile.

5. Select the network connection you wish to use. If your NIC is installed properly, it should be listed in the Connections box. Click Next to continue.

6. Since you have already set up your host computer, choose the option This Computer Connects to the Internet through Another Computer on My Network or through a Residential Gateway, and click Next.

7. Provide a description and name for this computer, and click Next.

8. Enter your workgroup name. Make sure that all computers on your network have the same workgroup name. Click Next to continue.

9. Click Next a few more times, and finally click Finish. The wizard will end and offer to reboot your machine for you.

**NOTE**   To run the Network Setup Wizard on a Windows 98, Windows Me, or Windows 2000 computer, you will need to have a Windows XP CD-ROM.

## Configuring Older Windows Client Machines

When being used on a Windows XP–based network, Windows 95 and Windows NT Workstation computers need to be configured manually. Windows 98/Me/2000 computers can also be configured manually in nearly the same fashion, if you choose not to use the Network Setup Wizard. To manually configure a down-level network client, follow these steps:

1. Right-click Network Neighborhood and choose Properties from the shortcut menu to open the Network dialog box.

2. In The Following Network Components Are Installed list in the Configuration tab, you need to see at least the following (you may see more, and that's okay):

   ◆ TCP/IP

   ◆ Identification

   ◆ File and Printer Sharing for Microsoft Networks

**NOTE** For the remainder of this discussion, we are going to assume that this is a new installation and none of the required protocols are installed. We will begin by adding TCP/IP.

3. Click Add to open the Select Network Component Type dialog box. Select Protocol and click Add again. Under Manufacturers, select Microsoft. In the right pane, scroll down and click TCP/IP. Click OK twice.

4. Insert the CD-ROM disk for your appropriate operating system. Click OK. At this point, you may have to provide the path to the operating system files. For Windows 95 it should be x:\Win95; for Windows 98, x:\Win98; for Windows 98 Second Edition, x:\Win98_SE; and for Windows NT/2000, x:\i386. Replace x: with your CD-ROM drive letter; for example, if your CD-ROM drive is D, replace x: with **d:**.

5. Right-click Network Neighborhood and choose Properties from the shortcut menu to open the Network dialog box.

   In The Following Network Components Are Installed list in the Configuration tab, select TCP/IP *Your network adapter*. Click Properties.

   You will see two choices: Obtain an IP Address Automatically or Specify an IP Address. Select one, depending on the criteria in the "Configuring IP Addresses on a Network" sidebar:

## Identification

If you are going to connect your computers to share information, you must configure the Network Neighborhood (or My Network Places, depending on your OS) properties' Identification tab. This tab sets the computer name for the computer and configures your computer in a workgroup (a group of computers that can share information). Follow these steps:

1. Select the Identification tab.

2. In the Computer Name text box, enter a name. This name can be up to 15 characters long and must be unique within your network.

3. In the Workgroup text box, enter a workgroup name. This name *must be the same* for each computer in the network. If you're at a loss for a name, use WORKGROUP or MSHOME.

**NOTE** Capitalization of the workgroup name does not matter; *computers* is identical to *Computers*, which is identical to COMPUTERS. Also, do not give a machine the same name as any other machine in your environment. This can cause communication problems.

**TIP** Don't just accept the defaults. The default workgroup name for Windows XP, MSHOME, differs from the default workgroup name for other Microsoft operating systems, WORKGROUP.

4. Click OK.

5. Reboot the computer if prompted.

## CONFIGURING IP ADDRESSES ON A NETWORK

There are two basic ways to set up IP addresses for your peer-to-peer network. You can automate the process through DHCP or APIPA, or you can select and assign the IP addresses yourself. These techniques apply equally well to all older Windows operating systems (Windows 98 and above); you don't need the Network Setup Wizard.

### OBTAIN AN IP ADDRESS AUTOMATICALLY

Use this setting if you have a Dynamic Host Configuration Protocol (DHCP) server (a server that automatically assigns IP addresses to client machines) or if this machine is connected to an Internet Connection Sharing host.

### SPECIFY AN IP ADDRESS

Enter your IP address and subnet mask. If you are designing a network that is not connected to the Internet, you can choose any IP address you want. For example,

```
IP Address:      131.107.0.102

Subnet Mask:     255.255.0. 0
```

The numbers above the 255s in the subnet mask determine the network number. In this example, 131.107 is the network number. The network number *must* be the same for all the computers in the network. The number above the zero in the subnet mask is the host number, which must be *different* on each computer in the network.

On the other hand, if your network will be connected to the Internet, use one of the private network addresses described in Chapter 16. For example:

```
IP Address:   10. X. Y. Z

Subnet Mask: 255.0.0. 0
```

or

```
IP Address:   172. 16. Y. Z

Subnet Mask: 255.255.0. 0
```

or

```
IP Address:   192. 168. 56. Z

Subnet Mask: 255.255.255. 0
```

Of course, X, Y, and Z are not numbers. Substitute any number between 1 and 254 for X, Y, and Z, as long as each computer gets a unique number. Duplicate addresses on a network can cause a variety of communication problems. After you have made your selection and specified an IP address and subnet mask, click OK.

## File and Printer Sharing for Microsoft Networks

File and Printer Sharing for Microsoft Networks does not need to be installed on Windows 95/98/Me machines for them to participate on a network. Without it, Windows 95/98/Me machines can still be clients on a network; that is, they can retrieve files from and use printers on remote machines. However, they will not be able to host their own resources.

Windows NT machines also have the ability to share resources. However, Windows NT calls its server service "Server" and its client service "Workstation." These services are installed and configured by default on Windows NT machines.

Windows XP machines have the ability to share resources by default and do not require additional configuration of File and Printer Sharing for Microsoft Networks.

## Configuring Windows XP Manually

If you are running networked computers with an operating system older than Windows XP, manual configuration is probably warranted. Fortunately, if your network contains just Windows XP machines, there is no need to configure the networking parameters yourself. Simply use the Network Setup Wizard and have it take care of everything for you.

However, some people don't like all of the features installed automatically with automated computer and network setups. Although at times this might be obsessive, there's really nothing wrong with it. If you're one of those people who want to know everything that's going on in their machine, and therefore want to configure things manually in XP, here is some advice.

**TIP**  Double-checking your IP parameters and manually setting up your networking options are useful troubleshooting techniques if you are having communication problems on your network.

### IP CONFIGURATION

Windows XP also has two options for configuring IP addresses, much like previous versions of Windows operating systems. The first option is to obtain an IP address automatically (through a DHCP server or APIPA), and the second option is to configure addresses manually. If you want to configure addresses manually, then the sidebar on IP addressing in the "Configuring Older Windows Client Machines" section in this chapter will help you in XP.

Automatically obtaining an IP address can happen in one of two ways. First, if your network has a DHCP server, you will obtain an address from it. I'm guessing that if you have just a small office in your home, you don't have a DHCP server. That's okay. Let's say that you set your Windows XP machine to obtain an IP address automatically, but Windows XP cannot locate a DHCP server (which makes sense, because you don't have one). Windows XP will automatically assign an IP address and subnet mask to your machine. The address will be in the 169.254.X.X range, with a subnet mask of 255.255.0.0. This feature is called Automatic Private IP Addressing (APIPA).

**NOTE**  Windows 98, 2000, Me, XP, and 2003 support APIPA.

You should be careful of one thing when using APIPA, though. Let's say that you have manually configured one computer with an address of 131.107.2.102 and a mask of 255.255.255.0. Another computer on the same network gets an APIPA-assigned address of 169.254.225.128, along with a mask of 255.255.0.0. Those two computers will not be able to talk to each other using TCP/IP. The reason for this is they have different network addresses, so they each think the other is physically somewhere else, when they're really on the same physical network. The computers will be confused and won't talk.

To manually configure IP addresses on your Windows XP Professional computer, right-click My Network Places, and choose Properties. In the new window that opens, right-click Local Area Connection, and click Properties again. Highlight TCP/IP, and choose Properties. Select the Use the Following IP Address radio button, and enter your IP address, subnet mask, and default gateway (if necessary). You can specify an address for a DNS server as well or obtain that server's address automatically.

**TIP**    If you're configuring your network for an Internet connection and assigning IP addresses yourself, ask your ISP for their DNS server addresses. Enter these numbers in each of the computers on your network.

CHAPTER 17

### IDENTIFICATION

Windows XP Professional does not have an Identification tab as Windows 95/98/Me and NT did. Instead, right-click My Computer, choose Properties, and then choose Computer Name. Here you will see your computer name, as well as the workgroup or domain name. You can also change that information here.

## Network Bridging

If you have multiple NICs, you could set up a separate IP address for each NIC. Windows XP Professional looks at an IEEE 1394 adapter as a NIC. If you work with any virtual machine technology such as VMWare, that software also installs separate "virtual" NICs on your computer. Without Microsoft Windows XP Network Bridging technology, I would have to maintain four different NICs on just one computer. And managing a network can be difficult enough.

With a network bridge, I can easily manage four different NICs on the same computer, as shown in Figure 17.2.

**FIGURE 17.2**
You can manage multiple NICs with one Network Bridge.

Without the network bridge, I would need four different IP addresses. I would have to configure four sets of DNS addresses, reconfigure WINS as required, and so on. In addition, since the NICs could be connected to different networks, the computer could become a router, and if I wanted to do that I would then have to configure IP forwarding to get the NICs to talk to each other. Traffic from any one of these NICs could cause a traffic jam on the network.

With the network bridge, I need only one IP address. All of the NICs plug into my computer in the same way as they plug into a hub. But as a bridge (which is another name for a switch), it regulates traffic on the network. In other words, if I'm downloading a digital video through my IEEE 1394 port, that doesn't stop traffic that goes through my computer to a virtual machine or a USB device.

Sometimes you need separate IP addresses. For example, if you want two separate networks connected to your computer, it's easy to detach one of your NICs from the bridge. From the example shown in Figure 17.2, right-click the Network Bridge icon, and then click Properties in the pop-up menu. In the Network Bridge properties window shown in Figure 17.3, the Adapters area includes the connections that are connected to the bridge. Deselect the connection of your choice and click OK.

**FIGURE 17.3**

Just deselect any connection that you want to detach from the properties of the Network Bridge.

Now the Network Connections window is split between regular LAN connections and connections that are part of the Network Bridge, as shown in Figure 17.4. You can now configure the properties of the connections that you just decoupled from the bridge.

**FIGURE 17.4**

If you want to manage a NIC separately, just detach it from the Network Bridge.

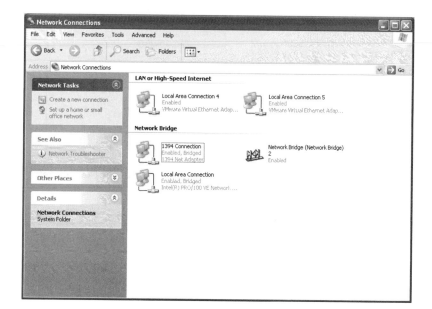

## Creating Shares

When you configure your network using the Network Setup Wizard, the Shared Documents folder and printers directly connected to your computer are shared automatically. Before users on your network can get to other resources on your computer, though, you must share those resources. To do this, you must be logged on as an administrator or have a user account with local administrator privileges. You can create shares using Windows Explorer or Computer Management. Using Windows Explorer is simple and direct, so in this section that's what I'll use.

**NOTE**  To open Computer Management, in Control Panel click Administrative Tools and then click Computer Management. Alternatively, click Start ➤ All Programs ➤ Administrative Tools ➤ Computer Management.

A share can be a folder, a drive, a program, or a file—any resource on your computer that you want other people to be able to use over the network. Most of the time, shares are either folders or drives; sharing files at the file level can get cumbersome in a hurry. For this example, I'm going to share a folder. Here are the steps:

1.  In Windows Explorer, right-click the folder, and choose Sharing and Security from the shortcut menu to open the Properties dialog box for that folder at the Sharing tab:

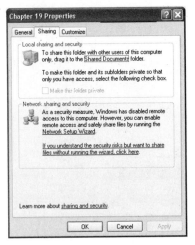

**TIP**  If you've already shared files without using the Network Setup Wizard, you're taken immediately to step 3.

2.  Before you can share the folder, you have to enable sharing. To do so, you can run the Network Setup Wizard by clicking that link in the Network Sharing and Security section, or you can click the If You Understand the Security Risks but Want to Share Files without Running the Wizard, Click Here link. Clicking this second link opens the Enable File Sharing dialog box:

Click the Just Enable File Sharing option, and then click OK.

**3.** Back in the Sharing tab, you'll see the following after you click the Share This Folder on the Network check box:

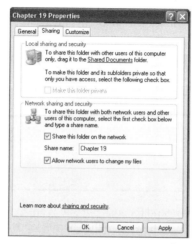

**4.** In the Share Name box, you can accept the name that Windows XP Professional suggests or enter another name.

**5.** If you want others on your network to be able to read the contents of the folder but not change them, clear the Allow Network Users to Change My Files check box.

**6.** Click OK.

**7.** Back in Windows Explorer you'll see that the folder now has a hand under it to indicate that it is a shared folder.

---

## FILE SYSTEMS AND NETWORK SHARING

A common question that I often hear is, "Can my Windows 98 computer access files on my Windows XP computer using NTFS?" To be sure, Windows 98 does not support NTFS, meaning that it has no way of being able to read NTFS volumes. Over a network, this is not a problem. Your Windows 98 computer can get files off your XP-mounted NTFS hard drive just fine.

Here's why: When you make a request to retrieve a file, Windows (regardless of version) first checks to determine where that file is located. If it's on the local hard disk, the request gets passed to a file system driver, which knows how to read a specific file system (FAT or NTFS). The file system driver gets the file and returns it to Windows. Windows 98 doesn't have an NTFS file system driver.

When the requested file is somewhere else on a network, the request is passed to the network *redirector*, which, if networking is installed, Windows 98 has. (Nice name, huh? It redirects network requests.) The network redirector figures out that the file is on your Windows XP computer and asks that computer for the file. It's then up to the Windows XP file system driver to get the file and return it to the network redirector for a safe journey back to the Windows 98 computer.

Another thing to keep in mind about all of this file transferring: when data is being transmitted on a network, NTFS and FAT are irrelevant. Data is just data: 1s and 0s. NTFS and FAT are merely methods of storing those 1s and 0s on a hard disk and have nothing to do with data on the network.

Although Microsoft does not recommend sharing a drive, you can still do so. Follow these steps:

1. Choose Start ➤ My Computer to open the My Computer window.

2. Right-click the drive you want to share, and then select Sharing and Security from the shortcut menu to open the Properties dialog box for that drive at the Sharing tab:

3. Click the If You Understand the Risk but Still Want to Share the Root of the Drive, Click Here link. You'll then see the following in the Sharing tab when you click the Share This Folder on the Network check box:

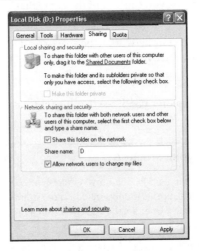

4. If you want others on your network to be able to read the contents of the drive but not change them, clear the Allow Network Users to Change My Files check box.

5. Click OK. The Setting Folder Permission dialog box will show the progress of sharing the drive.

6. Back in the My Computer window, you'll see that the drive now has a hand under it to indicate that it is shared.

**NOTE** Microsoft doesn't recommend sharing drives because they believe it allows too broad of access and a possible security hole. In reality, it's done all the time (especially for sharing CD/DVD drives). If someone else needs to access several folders on your computer, it's more efficient to put all the needed folders on one drive and share the drive. You can then set security at the drive level as opposed to the folder level, and it's easier to manage.

# Attaching to Network Resources

After your network is configured for sharing, one of the easiest ways to test your network connections is to attach to network resources. You can do so in the following ways:

◆ By browsing My Network Places

◆ By mapping a network drive

◆ By using UNCs to connect directly

## Browsing My Network Places

To access My Network Places, click My Computer on the Start menu. Under Other Places, click My Network Places to open a window that displays the options on your network. Click View Workgroup Computers under Network Tasks to display other computers on your network. Then, double-click a computer to view and connect to its shared resources.

## Mapping a Network Drive

Mapping a network drive involves assigning a drive letter to a network location. For example, if you frequently connect to someone else's shared folder, you might assign it an unused drive letter on your computer.

When you frequently access particular network resources, mapping a drive to the network share is a great way to ensure that they're easily available. When you map a drive, you're telling your computer, "make the `docs` shared folder on `computer1` my drive letter L." Drive L then appears in My Computer under Network Drives, and all you need to do to access it is to double-click it. Remember that the information is still physically stored on the other machine. All you've done is make a logical pointer on your machine pointing to the physical resource. It's purely for the sake of convenience.

One of the benefits to networking is being able to back up your files and folders on another computer. You'll find that some applications won't recognize other network drives unless they are mapped—so that's another reason you need to know how to map network drives.

To map a drive, follow these steps:

1. On the Start menu, click My Computer. Under Other Places, right-click My Network Places, and choose Map Network Drive to open the Map Network Drive dialog box:

2. From the Drive drop-down list, select an unused drive letter.

CHAPTER 17

**3.** From the Folder drop-down list, select the folder you want to map to, or click Browse to find the folder on your network.

**4.** If you want to use this mapping every time you log on, leave the Reconnect at Logon check box selected.

**NOTE**   Clicking the Connect Using a Different User Name link opens the Connect As dialog box. I'll discuss that option later in this chapter.

**5.** Click Finish. The drive now appears in My Computer under Network Drives along with your local drives.

To disconnect a mapped drive, follow these steps:

**1.** In My Computer, choose Tools ➢ Disconnect Network Drive to open the Disconnect Network Drive dialog box.

**2.** Select the network drive you want to disconnect, and click OK.

**TIP**   If this process isn't working for some reason, the next section provides an alternative method for mapping network drives that is more reliable.

**WARNING**   Here's a situation to avoid: don't disconnect a mapped drive and then map another drive using the same drive letter, telling it to automatically reconnect at login. If the original drive you disconnected is set to reconnect automatically as well, it can cause your system to become confused when remapping the drives.

## Making a Direct Connection via a UNC

At the beginning of this chapter, I mentioned UNC names. Using UNC names is yet another way to attach to network resources. You do this in one of two ways. One way is to click the Start menu and choose Run. The other way is by executing net use statements at the command prompt. But before you can attach to resources on the network, you need to know which resources are available.

If you are using the Run command from the Start menu, type \\*computername* and it will show you the resources available on that machine. For example, if I knew that Joe had shared his printer but I could not remember its name, I could type in \\**DELL05** and press Enter, and I would see what he has shared. To attach to a network resource using the Run command, use the full UNC name, like \\**GTW09\Shared**.

We already looked at how to use My Network Places and the Run command to locate network resources, but you can also do so at the command prompt using the net view command.

**NOTE**   So far in this chapter, I've been talking primarily about how to set up and configure a Windows XP Professional peer-to-peer network, although some of the information, such as mapping network drives, applies equally to a client-server network and domains. This section, however, contains information that sometimes applies to workgroups and sometimes applies to domains. You know which kind of network you have, so you'll know which instructions apply to your situation.

**NOTE**   In environments with lots of shared resources, complex group and permission issues can arise. For information on groups and permissions, see Chapter 19.

Here's how to use the `net view` command:

1. To display a list of the machines on your network, type **net view** at the command prompt.

2. To display a list of the resources on a particular machine, append the name of the machine. For example, if the machine name was spiritwolf, you'd enter **net view \\spiritwolf**.

3. To view the resources of a machine in another domain, for example, the server spiritwolf in the domain hq, you'd enter the following:

   **net view \\spiritwolf /domain:hq**

4. To display a list of all the domains on the network, simply enter **net view /domain**.

### USING NET USE: CONNECTING TO OTHER DRIVES AND PRINTERS

After you've browsed the network with the `net view` command, you can connect to all the available goodies (or disconnect from those you don't want) with the `net use` command. Use this command to connect to network resources as drives D through Z and printer ports LPT1 through LPT9.

**WARNING**   Drive letters can be used only once. So if your CD-ROM is drive D, you will have only drive letters E through Z available.

To display information about the workstation's current connections, type **net use** without options, and you'll see something like this:

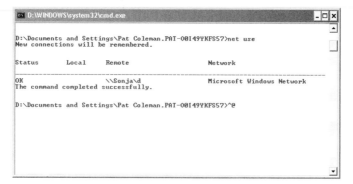

### USING LONG FILENAMES IN UNCS

If you wanted to connect to a folder called `Wpfiles` on the spiritwolf server and make that your E drive, your command would be **net use E: \\spiritwolf\wpfiles**. You get to specify the port name or drive letter that you want to connect a resource to, but again, you're restricted to drive letters D through Z and ports LPT1 through LPT9. To connect to a printer instead of a folder, you would use a port—such as **lpt1:**—instead of a drive letter and the printer name instead of the folder name. Your command may read **net use lpt1: \\spiritwolf\printer1**.

If the computer you're getting the resource from has a blank character in its name (that is, the computer name has two words in it), you must put the name in quotation marks, like this:

```
"\\eisa server"
```

CHAPTER 17

If a password (let's say it's "artuser") is attached to the resource that you're trying to connect to, you need to include that in your connection command, like this:

```
net use lpt1: \\ted\hp4m artuser
```

Or, if you want the computer to prompt you for the password so that it isn't displayed on the screen, append an asterisk:

```
net use lpt1: \\ted\hp4m *
```

#### USING OTHER SWITCHES

No matter what kind of connection you make, you can make it persistent (that is, have it reconnect automatically every time you reboot your machine) by adding the switch /persistent:yes to the end of the command. If you don't want it to be persistent, use /persistent:no instead.

If you don't specify one or the other, the default is whatever you chose last. If you want to make all future connections persistent, type the following (or type :no if you want all future connections to be temporary):

```
net use /persistent:yes
```

Typing /persistent by itself at the end of the line won't do anything.

To disconnect from a resource, type the following:

```
net use devicename /delete
```

where *devicename* is the connection (such as D or LPT1). You don't have to provide a password or say anything about persistency to disconnect from a resource.

## Using Profiles

Windows XP Professional uses two types of profiles: user and hardware. Although they're used for distinctly different purposes, both types of profiles are used to customize the computing environment. In this section, we'll look at how to create and manage them.

### Creating Hardware Profiles

If you use a laptop for business, you likely have encountered the following problem. When you bring your laptop into the office, you would like your computer to recognize the NIC and maybe an external monitor and keyboard. But when you take your laptop on the road, you want it to know that you do not currently have any of the "office" devices attached. Most laptops get their information by timing out on each device, which adds five minutes to the boot process and wastes time, not to mention wasting valuable battery life.

A feature of Windows XP Professional that is designed to alleviate this problem is a hardware profile. You can create a profile of the hardware that is attached to your machine when you are in the office and specify a different hardware profile for when you are on the road. And the fun doesn't stop there. You can create profiles for all the places in which you use your computer.

To create a hardware profile, follow these steps:

1. On the Start menu, right-click My Computer, and choose Properties from the shortcut menu to open the System Properties dialog box.

**2.** Select the Hardware tab, and click Hardware Profiles to open the Hardware Profiles dialog box:

**3.** To create a new hardware profile, choose a configuration from the Available Hardware Profiles list, and then click Copy to open the Copy Profile dialog box.

**4.** Give the hardware profile a new name, and click OK. (I'll show you how to configure a profile a bit later in this section.)

**TIP** When naming hardware profiles, use an intuitive naming pattern. As an example, "Office" and "On the Road" are much better alternatives than "Profile 1" and "Profile 2."

**5.** To play with the docking properties of this profile, click Properties to open the Properties dialog box for the profile you are creating:

You can specify whether the system is going to be attached to a docking station when it is using this profile. A docking station is a box on your desk (usually in your office) that you plug your laptop into. You use docking stations because you can attach peripherals to them, such as a larger monitor, full-sized keyboard, and mouse. Then, when you come into the office, you simply plug your laptop into the dock, and you can use the larger monitor, keyboard, and mouse instead of the smaller ones on the laptop. However, when you do this, your laptop needs to know that sometimes it's using the laptop screen, whereas other times it's using the larger monitor. You tell the laptop this by configuring the docking properties.

If Windows XP Professional is not able to automatically detect the docking status of your laptop when in this profile, The Docking State Is Unknown option is selected. You can also strictly specify the state if it is always docked when using this profile or if it is *not* always docked when using this profile.

If this computer is a desktop, uncheck This Is a Portable Computer. When you've set your options, click OK to close the Properties dialog box, and then click OK twice more.

## Managing Hardware Profiles

Now that you have created your hardware profile, you can begin to enable the services and devices that will be available through it. When you reboot your computer, choose a hardware profile. To enable or disable devices or services in this profile, follow these steps:

1. Click Start ➢ All Programs ➢ Administrative Tools ➢ Computer Management to open the Computer Management window.

2. Expand System Tools, and then select Device Manager to display the list of devices in the pane on the right.

3. Expand the device type you're interested in. Double-click the device that you want to enable or disable to open its Properties dialog box.

4. In the General tab, use the Device Usage drop-down list to enable or disable a device in the current hardware profile or in any (or all) hardware profiles, and then click OK.

5. To enable or disable services, expand Services and Applications, and then select Services to display the list of services in the pane on the right:

6. Double-click the service that you want to manage to open its Properties dialog box, and then click the Log On tab:

7. Select the specific hardware profile, click Enable or Disable, and then click OK.

**NOTE**  Services and the Service console are covered in detail in Chapter 31.

Hardware profiles are included in Windows XP for convenience. They are intended to be a useful option for those who travel with laptops, not a security measure. In other words, if you want to prohibit someone from using the modem, a hardware profile is not the answer. You will find that outside the laptop realm, hardware profiles are rarely used.

## Managing User Profiles

In Windows XP Professional, a user profile is a collection of environment settings that customize a user's interface. It can include display settings, network settings, printer settings, and so on. User profiles are of three types:

◆  Local

◆  Roaming

◆  Mandatory

User profiles are particularly useful when you have multiple people using the same computer. As examples, you and your significant other might share a computer, and some companies don't have assigned desk locations for their employees. If you and I use the same machine (you work days and I work the swing shift), you want to be able to have your settings (wallpaper, icons, printer, and network connections) every time you log in. So do I. User profiles is the answer.

The first time you log on to a computer, whether it's yours or that of someone else on your network, Windows XP Professional creates a *local user profile* for you that is specific to that machine. Since this is the first time you are logging on to this machine, Windows XP gives you what is called the *default user profile*. When you log off, any changes you've made to the environment during the sessions are saved in your local user profile. Local user profiles apply only to a local machine, hence their name.

**NOTE**  The *roaming user profile* and *mandatory user profile* configurations require a domain and will be covered in Chapter 20.

To customize the default user profile so that each new user of the machine gets the same settings, follow these steps:

1. Log on to the computer as a new user.

2. Establish the desired settings, such as Start menu options, network connections, and so on, and then log off the computer.

3. Log back on to the computer as Administrator.

4. Right-click My Computer, and choose Properties from the shortcut menu to open the System Properties dialog box.

5. Click the Advanced tab, and then click Settings in the User Profiles section to open the User Profiles dialog box:

6. Highlight the profile that you want each new user to use, and then click Copy To to open the Copy To dialog box:

**7.** In the Copy Profile To field, enter the following path:

```
%SYSTEMROOT%\Documents and Settings\Default User
```

**8.** Click OK, and then click OK again.

If you should happen to delete a profile folder in the Documents and Settings folder, Windows XP Professional will react as if the user has never logged on to the system before. When the user logs on again, Windows will create a new profile folder for the user. This feature can be useful if the user has placed icons and information all over the Desktop and is now complaining that it keeps coming up as a mess. You can simply delete the profile folder, and a new one will be created the next time that user logs on. It will be the default environment as created in the Default User folder.

# Troubleshooting Windows XP Professional Networking

Because Windows XP Professional is a network operating system, it makes sense that you will probably encounter issues with your network from time to time. In most documentation you find today, the troubleshooting text tells you to perform "standard network troubleshooting" without ever telling you what that is. This section lets you in on that secret. Troubleshooting networking is one area in particular where my basic methodology will help you.

First, you start with any error message that Windows XP Professional gives you. This is always the first step in troubleshooting Windows XP Professional: Use whatever information it provides. Write the error message exactly as it appears because you can later use that to query the Knowledge Base in Help and Support Center. Next, you want to see what the Event Viewer can tell you. Event Viewer is probably the best friend you have in troubleshooting Windows XP Professional. It's not always clear and concise, but it will often tell you exactly what the problem is. It's always worth checking.

These things are true for any type of troubleshooting in Windows XP Professional. But basic network troubleshooting goes beyond Windows XP Professional's systems to encompass any network operating system. That's what we need to focus on in this section.

## Is It Plugged In?

What do you need in order to have a conversation? You must have some kind of medium to carry the information from one person to another. You must also have some rules to determine how that conversation will take place. Imagine what happens when you meet someone on the street and strike up a conversation. You probably start by making eye contact, then smiling and speaking. If you both happen to speak at least one language in common, you can communicate easily. There may be a few failed attempts before you both find a language you can use, but eventually you will succeed.

A network is just like that. In its simplest form, a network can be two computers connected by a wire. When one wants to talk to the other, the first computer needs some kind of attention signal; then they both need to negotiate a common language and follow the rules of that language to communicate.

Networks can be simple systems or they can be complex. But however complicated they get, they all have certain things in common. They all have something connecting the nodes, and they all have at least one language. On most networks, the nodes are individual computers as well as intermediary systems such as routers, bridges, switches, and gateways. The language of a network is the protocol.

When troubleshooting any network system, keep these fundamental concepts in mind. Start with the communications medium. Is a proper cable plugged into the computer? Is the other end of the cable plugged into a hub or wall drop? If you are using coax cable, do you have a T-connector and possibly a terminator? Are the drivers for the network card installed and working? Do you have at least one protocol in common with the other computer?

**TIP** If a network cable is unplugged, or becomes unplugged when it's generally connected, Windows XP will generally notify you. Look in your system tray for an icon that looks like two small computer monitors. If there is a red X on the icon, that connection has a problem.

These sound like simple questions, and they are, really. You might be surprised how often these simple questions will resolve your networking issues.

## Configuration Testing

You will want to test your configuration if you can't connect to machines you think you should be able to connect to. Keep the following principles in mind when troubleshooting networks:

- Isolate the problem before fixing it.
- Be familiar with the tools you have available.
- Always check the obvious things (i.e., connections) first, no matter how silly it may seem.

When the system starts, you will know if Windows XP Professional can see the network during the logon procedure. You may see error messages, for example, if your TCP/IP address went awry or if the domain controller refuses to validate you into the domain. Even if no errors are immediately apparent, take a look in Event Viewer for potential conflicts. Event Viewer is a great tool for helping track down problems. To open Event Viewer, follow these steps:

1. Click Start ➤ All Programs ➤ Administrative Tools ➤ Computer Management to open the Computer Management window.

2. In the Computer Management pane, expand System Tools, and then expand Event Viewer.

3. Click System to display events in the pane on the right.

4. Look for red stop signs or yellow exclamation points. If you see one of these symbols, double-click it to open the Event Properties dialog box for that event, which will look similar to the following:

5. If the information in the Event Properties dialog box isn't sufficient to solve the problem, check the configuration of the component. In some cases, you may need to remove and reinstall it.

6. Click the Close button to close the Computer Management window.

**TIP** When using Event Viewer to troubleshoot network problems, start at the top of the list and work down until you find event ID number 6005 with a source of eventlog. This represents the last time you booted the computer. The most likely source of your problems will be the event immediately above or immediately below the 6005 event. You should focus most of your efforts on resolving these events before moving on to the others.

## Is Anybody Out There?

Most of the troubleshooting I've talked about so far has dealt with working on one computer at a time. Network troubleshooting often involves the connecting systems between the computers as much or more than the computers themselves. I've shown you many ways to work with problems on computers, but how do you see what's wrong with a whole network? That's what this section is about. Here I introduce you to some of the tools included in Windows XP Professional to troubleshoot the network.

The ultimate test of your configuration is being able to attach to all the resources you need. In Windows Explorer, look in My Network Places and click Entire Network; from there, clicking Microsoft Windows Network can give you insight into which parts of the network you can and cannot communicate with.

**TIP** If you get an error message when viewing the Microsoft Windows Network or a workgroup, try viewing your computers and shares from the command line based on the "Making a Direct Connection via a UNC" section earlier in this chapter.

### TROUBLESHOOTING TCP/IP

The single most common network protocol today is TCP/IP. Its popularity is most likely due to the Internet, but it's also because TCP/IP is an industry standard suite of protocols. It is not just one protocol but rather a group of them designed to perform specific tasks. The part that most people like is the industry standard part. That means that if you have Macs and NetWare and Unix computers on your network, your Windows XP Professional computer can communicate with all of them using TCP/IP. TCP/IP is also popular with support people because it has so many troubleshooting tools built into it.

### Ping

The packet Internet groper (ping) is the most basic test of network communication over TCP/IP. What ping does for you is bounce a series of packets off a remote host. You're essentially just saying "Hello?" over and over and (you hope) getting a response each time. The basic syntax is `ping www.host.com` or `ping 10.1.0.44`.

So what does this tell you? Getting a response when pinging by IP address means that your network card is installed correctly, the driver is working, the TCP/IP protocol is working, Windows Sockets is working, the other computer is working, and everything in between is working. That's quite a lot of information for just one small command! When you ping by hostname, you get all the previous information, plus you know that your hostname resolution is working.

You can also ping the address 127.0.0.1. This address is reserved for the local host (the local computer) and is a loopback diagnostic test of your installed TCP/IP software. Successfully pinging the local host verifies that TCP/IP is successfully installed on the local computer.

With this in mind, follow this procedure to test your IP configuration and network connection:

**NOTE**  Some of these tests assume that your LAN is connected to the Internet.

1.  Test that you've installed the IP software by pinging the built-in IP loopback address. Type **ping 127.0.0.1**. If that fails, you know that you've done something wrong in the initial installation, so check that the software is installed on your system. This test does not put any messages out on the network; it just checks that the software is installed. By the way, the same thing happens if you ping your IP address, except that pinging your address also tests the network card.

    If that fails, your TCP/IP stack probably isn't installed correctly, or perhaps you mistyped the IP number (if it failed on your specific IP address but not on the loopback), or perhaps you gave the *same* IP number to another workstation.

2.  Ping your default gateway to see that you can get to it, because it should be on your local subnet. For example, if your gateway were at 199.34.57.2, you would type **ping 199.34.57.2**, and you should get a response.

3.  If you can't get to the gateway, check that the gateway is up and that your network connection is all right. Nothing is more embarrassing than calling in outside help, only to find that your LAN cable fell out of the back of your computer.

4.  Ping something on the other side of your gateway, such as an external DNS server. (Ping me, Mark Minasi, if you like: 199.34.57.1. I ought to be up just about all the time.) If you can't get there, it's likely that your gateway isn't working properly.

5.  Next, test the name resolution on your system. Ping yourself *by name*. Instead of typing something such as **ping 199.34.57.35**, you'd type **ping test** (the machine you're on at the moment). That tests your DNS server, or your HOSTS file if you are using one instead of DNS.

6.  Then, ping someone else on your subnet. Again, try using a fully qualified domain name on your local network, such as mizar.Ursamajor.Edu, rather than an IP address. If that doesn't work, use the IP address. If the IP address works but the hostname doesn't, you've got a problem with the Hosts file or DNS.

7.  Finally, ping someone outside your domain, such as house.gov (the U.S. House of Representatives), www.yahoo.com, or orion01.Mmco.Com. If that doesn't work but all the pings inside your network work, you've probably got a problem with your Internet provider.

**WARNING**  While pinging websites can help test connectivity, some websites do not allow pings into their network. They block pings off as a security measure. So, the site may be up, but you won't get a response from a ping. Microsoft.com is a good example of this.

If you're successful on all these tests, your TCP/IP connection should be set up properly.

### Hostname

The hostname utility returns the hostname of the local computer. This can be helpful when you aren't exactly sure what it is.

### IPConfig

IPConfig is right up there with ping when it comes to valuable TCP/IP utilities. This tool enables you to view some or all of your TCP/IP configuration (as the name might imply). To use it, type **ipconfig** at the command prompt to receive your IP address, subnet mask, and default gateway. If you type **ipconfig /all**, you will see a list of every TCP/IP configuration for every interface on your computer. To give you some idea of the scope of information, Figure 17.5 shows the output of the **ipconfig /all** command.

**FIGURE 17.5**

Output of the ipconfig / all command

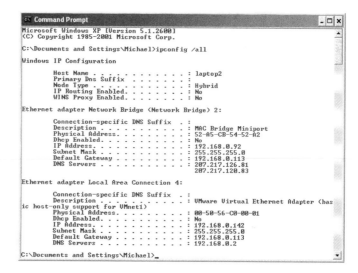

If IPConfig reports an address that is unfamiliar to you, or reports no information at all, then you may have found your problem. IPConfig can also be used to release and renew IP addresses acquired through DHCP. The process for this is **ipconfig /release** and then **ipconfig /renew**.

### ARP

The ARP command views and modifies the Address Resolution Protocol (ARP) cache. ARP is used by TCP/IP to resolve an IP address such as 10.1.0.1 to a unique hardware address or MAC address.

The process that TCP/IP uses to communicate between two computers that are on the same subnet as the host server is shown in Figure 17.6. At the application layer, the user types in a Uniform Resource Locator (URL) to browse a favorite website. The user's computer is configured to use a certain Domain Name System (DNS) server that is responsible for resolving the name in the URL to an IP address. Then TCP/IP uses ARP to resolve that IP address to a unique physical address. Every network card has a unique hexadecimal number assigned to it when it is manufactured. That's the physical address, or MAC address, of the card.

**FIGURE 17.6**

Resolving a hostname to a MAC address in TCP/IP networking

When ARP resolves an IP address to a unique hardware address, it stores the resolution in its cache. One thing you can do to improve the connection speed to a server that you use frequently is to make a static entry in the ARP cache. The command string below will add a static entry for a computer:

```
ARP -s 10.1.0.1 00-40-05-16-DA-8A
```

The −s switch tells the ARP command to make the entry permanent. You should be aware that *permanent* in this case means only until the computer is rebooted. If you want this entry to really be permanent, you must use the ARP command in a logon script or batch file in your Startup group.

### TraceRT

The Trace Route (TraceRT) command is very much like ping in that it bounces several packets of information off a remote computer. But TraceRT does more than that. It also shows a response from every router that the packets go through on their way to the remote computer.

This can be especially useful when dealing with communications issues with a remote host that is very far away (as in many routers away). TCP/IP uses a mechanism called a time to live (TTL) to determine how long a packet of data should be allowed on the network. If it didn't drop packets after a set period of time, packets would still be roaming the Internet from 20 years ago or more. The TTL is decremented automatically by at least one at each and every router it passes through (also called a *hop*). If a packet is forced to wait in a router because of network congestion, its TTL may be decremented by more than one.

TraceRT can reveal when the default TTL isn't high enough to allow for network congestion on the way to the remote host. The TTL setting can be adjusted in Windows XP Professional through the Registry at this location:

```
HKEY_LOCAL_MACHINE\System\CurrentControlSet\Services
\Tcpip\Parameters

Value name: DefaultTTL
```

The maximum setting for this value is 255.

The following troubleshooting scenario is a common support call in most networks. This time, imagine that you are the support person for a group of users on your company network and are attempting to correct a problem with network connectivity.

**NOTE** There are some very cool graphical route tracing programs available commercially. One such program is NeoTrace, available at www.neotrace.com.

### Scenario: Unable to "See" My Server

You have just received a call from a coworker, Mary, who is having trouble retrieving e-mail from her server. (She knows you know a lot about computers, and the help desk never seems to answer their phone.) When you talk with her at her office, you learn that she is unable to open her e-mail application without receiving an error that the server could not be found. She is using TCP/IP as the only network protocol.

**Has it ever worked before?**   Mary tells you that she was able to get e-mail until yesterday when someone installed the latest version of the e-mail client. Ever since then, no luck.

**Track possible approaches.**   The problem could be the e-mail client but is more likely a simple configuration problem. You decide to do the following:

1. Verify the IP address and configuration.

2. Test communication with the server.

3. Test communication with another computer other than the server.

The first thing to do is run `ipconfig /all` to verify the computer's current settings. You do this and find that the computer's IP address, subnet mask, and default gateway are all correct.

Next, you try pinging the server and get no response. You now try using ping in a methodical process to determine where the failure is. You try pinging the default gateway (router) and you do receive a response. You don't know if there is another router between your default gateway and the e-mail server, but you can find out by using TraceRT. TraceRT returns success messages from three routers but fails to find the e-mail server.

You now know that the local computer's configuration is fine and that the default gateway is up and running. You know that at least three routers between the local computer and the e-mail server are functional. What you need to know is whether the last router is passing the information directly to the e-mail server and the e-mail server is down, or whether there is another router beyond the third router that may be down.

When you pinged the e-mail server earlier, you did it by IP address. Now you try pinging by hostname. The attempt fails, but it does resolve the name to an IP address, so you can tell that name resolution is happening correctly. Looking at the address of the e-mail server, you try another address that should be another server on that same section of the network. The ping attempt to that address does respond.

**NOTE** Many network designers assign IP addresses in a set, predictable pattern. One common pattern is to assign all routers to the first 5 addresses on a subnet and servers to the last 20 addresses.

What you know now is that the network is working correctly all the way to the remote subnet where the server is located, but the server itself is still not responding. This would be a great time to call the administrator of that server to see if the server is running. Another possible solution is that the server may have an incorrect TCP/IP configuration. If the server *is* running, you should verify the configuration on the server to see if it can communicate with any other computer.

---

### TROUBLESHOOTING IPX/SPX

IPX/SPX used to be the protocol of choice on Novell networks, and it still is in many. It's a fine, routable protocol, relatively fast and easy to configure. So why is it being mentioned in a troubleshooting section? Because there are settings that are frequently misconfigured. The problems with the IPX/SPX protocol stem from those options for configuration that must be set correctly for two computers to hold a conversation. Most notable is the setting for frame type.

*Frame type* refers to the manner in which data is packaged when placed on the physical wire. It describes the header and addressing fields, the error correction, and the overall size of the data that can be sent at one time. IPX/SPX supports five frame types: 802.2, 802.3, Ethernet II, Ethernet SNAP, and Token Ring. The most common are 802.2 and 802.3. Windows XP Professional (like most operating systems) uses only one frame type at a time. Frame types are important because you must have the same frame type as the computer you are trying to communicate with. Mismatched frame types are probably the most common reason for failed communication over IPX/SPX.

In Microsoft networking, NWLink is called the IPX/SPX-compatible protocol even though it is fully compliant with all IPX/SPX standards. It is different only in that it provides a NetBIOS layer to facilitate name services on Microsoft network operating systems. For troubleshooting, that may or may not be important to know. What is important to know is that it is fully compliant with everyone else's IPX/SPX protocol.

Unlike TCP/IP in Windows XP Professional, NWLink doesn't ship with a bunch of troubleshooting utilities. That's usually not a problem because most issues will be resolved in the configuration. The primary tool for checking your NWLink configuration will be either the Network Connections applet in Control Panel or `ipxroute.exe`. Using `ipxroute.exe` enables you to view the current configuration of NWLink for each network adapter in the computer and to modify the IPX/SPX routing table if the computer has more than one network interface. Entering the command **ipxroute config** at the command prompt will display the current configuration of NWLink.

The properties dialog box for NWLink on Windows XP Professional covers the essentials—the adapter, the frame type, and the network number. The default setting for the frame type is Auto Detect. Microsoft tells us that this setting enables Windows XP Professional to scan the frame types being transmitted across the wire and then pick the most prevalent type. In fact, what appears to happen is that Windows XP Professional uses the very first frame type it comes across. Usually this will be correct. But on a network that utilizes multiple frame types, your Windows XP Professional computer may choose the wrong frame type when it starts up, causing you to be cut off from the servers you need.

The other important setting on this page is the network number. IPX/SPX handles routing of information by using these network numbers to identify each unique section of a network. Every segment (the section of network between two routers) must be assigned a unique network number. The default setting in Windows XP Professional takes care of that for you. When you are using Auto Detect for the frame type, it will also detect the local network number. If you change from Auto Detect to a specific frame type, you will need to enter a valid network number. Contact your network administrator if necessary.

## How Do You Troubleshoot Windows XP Professional Network Architecture?

Although it's true that a good troubleshooting method can work you through almost any problem, at times you need to know more. In fact, I believe that the more you know about how something's put together, the easier it is to find what's wrong. That's certainly true of a complex system such as Windows XP Professional.

Troubleshooting is the process of going from a big-picture view of things to a small-detail view. Asking questions is the primary tool for accomplishing this, but knowledge is also a valuable tool. Figure 17.7 shows the overall network architecture of Windows XP Professional.

### USER MODE COMPONENTS

The following are components of the user mode.

### Application Layer

The Application layer is where your program is accepting your network requests. For example, when you type in the URL of your favorite Web site, you are interacting with the Application layer.

**NOTE**   This application layer is completely different from the OSI or TCP/IP application layer.

**FIGURE 17.7**
The network architecture of Windows XP Professional

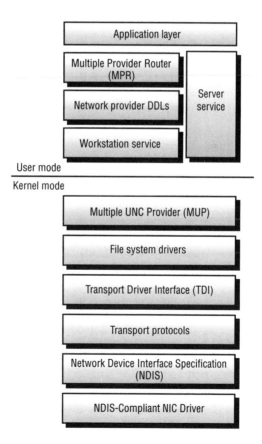

### Multiple Provider Router

The Multiple Provider Router (MPR) is kind of like a traffic cop in that its job is to direct the flow of communication. Windows XP Professional uses the MPR only when you are mapping a network drive. Its task is to decide which of the installed network clients will do the best job in making the drive mapping.

The MPR is contained in the file `mpr.dll`.

### Network Provider DLL

A DLL is a dynamic link library, which is basically a file that contains support functions for a program. In this case, the library of functions is part of a network client that is installed in Windows XP Professional.

There will be one provider DLL for each installed network client. The file for the native Windows XP Professional client, LanmanWorkstation, for example, is `ntlanman.dll`.

### Workstation Service and Server Service

These are the user mode components of the Workstation and Server services. Essentially, these are "stubs" that provide user mode applications with access to the kernel mode Workstation and Server services of Windows XP Professional.

### KERNEL MODE COMPONENTS

The following are components of the kernel mode.

### Multiple UNC Provider

The Multiple UNC Provider (MUP) is a traffic cop like the MPR, except that instead of directing traffic when mapping drives, the MUP directs traffic when you are using a Universal Naming Convention (UNC) path.

You will be using the MUP's services whenever you click Start ➢ Run and type a path such as `\\Server5\Public`, or when your application connects to a server resource without mapping a drive letter first. An example is your e-mail program, which is configured to talk with one particular server to retrieve mail but doesn't require that you first map a drive to the share on the server.

When the MUP receives a request for service, its job is to decide which file system driver (which network client) can best answer the request and then send the request to that driver.

The MUP is contained in the file `mup.sys`.

### File System Drivers

File system drivers are the network redirectors and servers. When you install network support in Windows XP Professional, you always get two of these drivers by default. The first, `rdr.sys`, is the kernel mode component of the Workstation service, your native Windows XP Professional client. The second, `srv.sys`, is the kernel mode portion of the Server service.

There may be other file system drivers installed for other network clients. One common example is the `nwrdr.sys` driver for the Client Services for NetWare in Windows XP Professional.

### Transport Driver Interface

Transport Driver Interface (TDI) doesn't actually exist as a file. It is what its name implies, an interface between the file system drivers and the transport protocols. The TDI is *exposed* by the two layers—that is to say that any file system driver for Windows XP Professional networking must support the functions used by TDI, and the same for the transport protocols.

This layered approach allows for portability and extensibility. Because of the TDI boundary layer, you can (in theory) install as many network clients and servers or as many protocols as you want on Windows XP Professional.

### Transport Protocols

These are the protocols used to communicate on your network. The files for each should be easy to identify because they are usually just the name of the protocol with a `.sys` extension.

In theory, you can install an unlimited number of protocols in Windows XP Professional so long as they conform to the two boundaries in the network stack. Transport protocols must expose the TDI boundary on top and the NDIS layer on the bottom.

### Network Device Interface Specification

Network Device Interface Specification (NDIS) is a boundary layer between the protocols and the adapter driver. But it has a more important job than that.

Years ago, when you wanted to develop a new driver for a network adapter card, you needed to think about details and settings such as the media access scheme, error detection and correction, frame types, and so on before you ever got to the part of the driver that just ran the card. NDIS was an effort by Microsoft, Intel, 3Com, and other companies to solve this problem. By conforming to a known standard, they could remove the common functions from the driver and load them into a library of functions that every network needs. Essentially, they wanted to stop reinventing the wheel every time they brought out another card.

NDIS, as it is implemented in Windows XP Professional, is an interesting component. It is both a file and a boundary layer. As a file, `ndis.sys` is a driver file that acts like a DLL in that it loads into memory and anybody who knows how to talk to it can ask NDIS for support. As a boundary, it defines a standard form of communication between the transport protocols and the network adapter card.

### NDIS-Compliant Network Adapter Driver

At the bottom of the stack but certainly very important, the network interface card (NIC) driver is responsible for error-free transmission and reception of data on the physical network medium.

Using the NDIS standard enables you to install as many NICs as you want in a computer (of course, you have only so many slots in your computer). As long as the drivers comply with the NDIS standard, you can bind multiple cards to one protocol or multiple protocols to one NIC.

The file containing the driver is named according to the naming convention of the manufacturer, but they all end with a `.sys` extension.

## Quick Advice

As with many skills, troubleshooting is best learned by doing. There really is no good substitute for experience. To make things easier, though, there are some quick tips you can always keep in mind when troubleshooting a network:

◆ Always check your connections. Try another network cable if possible.

◆ Check and double-check your IP configuration, including IP address, subnet mask, default gateway, and DNS server addresses.

◆ Run `ipconfig` and `ping`. Make sure you're set up properly, and see what, if anything, you *can* connect to.

◆ Look in Event Viewer for any errors.

◆ Use your help and online resources.

◆ Delete and reinstall the network adapter if necessary.

Also, the Windows Help and Support center has a lot of good information, including wizards, to assist in your troubleshooting. Take one step at a time, and if you make configuration changes, change one thing, test, and then change another if necessary. Don't change a bunch of stuff all at once, because you'll never know which change was the right one. One last thing—if you see someone troubleshooting a problem, and they say something like, "Huh, that's not supposed to happen," or "That's weird...," think about how silly a statement that *really* is. (I catch myself saying it, too!) If everything is working as advertised, then why are they troubleshooting in the first place?

## Summary

In this chapter, we've looked at how to set up and configure a network, create shares, attach to network resources, use user profiles and hardware profiles, and troubleshoot your network when things go awry. In the next chapter, we'll dive into a very popular topic these days—wireless networking.

# Chapter 18

# Wireless Networking

Let's face it, cables are so yesterday. We live in a society that demands instant communication gratification. If you doubt that, look around at the number of cell phones and PDAs out there. Ten years ago if you had access to the Internet, you were cutting edge. Now, if you don't have your cell phone browser going during your taxi trip to the airport, you feel as though you're somewhat technically inadequate.

There's a lot of fuss about wireless everything these days. Is it all hype? Not really. Cables are bulky and ugly (even if you bought cool neon colors) and a pain to string. And if you ever decide to move your office from one room to another, guess what? Yep, time to rerun the cable.

In the last five years or so, wireless networking has gone from a luxury that only a few could afford (mostly businesses and then only for special needs) to a mainstream form of communication for both home and business. Wireless networking is what this chapter is all about. Here are the specifics:

- ◆ Current wireless standards
- ◆ Required hardware
- ◆ Additional security considerations
- ◆ Setting up Windows XP on a wireless network

## Wireless Standards and Hardware

If you're unfamiliar with wireless networking, the idea of setting up this type of network might seem a bit daunting. You probably have a lot of questions. Are there extra security concerns? Yes. Do I need different hardware than for my old wired network? Yes. Is it as fast as my old wired network? No, but that probably won't matter much. Will the signals bother my goldfish? Not likely, unless their laptop doesn't have the right NIC.

Although desktop computers can and often do participate in wireless networks, this chapter will focus mainly on laptops. That is, after all, where the benefits of wireless networking truly shine. Before you dive into wireless, though, make sure you know what you're getting into by understanding the current standards and the hardware you'll need.

### Wireless Standards

In your quest to set up a wireless network, you will undoubtedly come across the term *Wi-Fi* very quickly. It's short for *wireless fidelity*, pronounced "why-fy" (think "why fry," and get rid of the *r*), and it's the most common wireless standard you will see today. More specifically, Wi-Fi refers to the collection of IEEE 802.11x standards; the name has been perpetuated by the Wi-Fi Alliance, a group of over 200 wireless hardware manufacturers and software providers established in 1999. Their goal was to ensure interoperability between wireless devices. They figured (correctly) that by getting together and branding the name Wi-Fi, they could have greater control over the development of the wireless networking business segment, as well as the associated profits.

All of this collaboration has been good for standardization within the wireless industry. Past computer history has shown us that superior technologies can easily lose out to inferior ones if the acceptance isn't there. Today, if a hardware or software product is "Wi-Fi Certified," you are assured that it will work with your existing Wi-Fi setup.

### IEEE 802.11x

The Institute of Electrical and Electronics Engineers has been around since 1963, setting standards for the computer and electronics industries. The original 802.11 specification was approved in 1997. There are three 802.11 standards floating around today:

- 802.11a
- 802.11b
- 802.11g

The most common one you will see is 802.11b. This standard transmits at a frequency of 2.4GHz and provides data speeds of 11Mbps. The 802.11g standard is a newer version of 11b; it uses the same frequency but can provide data speeds of up to 54Mbps (although roughly 20Mbps is more common).

The "oddball" standard is 802.11a. It transmits at 5GHz and allows data speeds of 54Mbps. There's one key thing to note, and it's that 11a uses a different frequency than either 11b or 11g, meaning that it's not interoperable with the other two.

Just in case I didn't hammer that last point home well enough, let me say it again: 802.11a is *not* compatible with either 802.11b or 802.11g. However, because they run on the same frequency and use similar transmission methods, 11b and 11g will work together. This means that if you have a NIC that supports only 11b but have a router that supports 11g, you won't have any problems. Of course, the NIC running 11b will still be slower than an 11g NIC, but it will still work.

#### BLUETOOTH

The most popular competing standard to Wi-Fi is Bluetooth. Like Wi-Fi, Bluetooth also has a supporting group, called the Bluetooth Special Interest Group. This group includes Microsoft, Intel, IBM, Apple, and Toshiba, as well as cell phone powers Ericsson, Nokia, and Motorola. Although most commonly referred to by the catchy Bluetooth name, it's also occasionally referred to as IEEE 802.15.1.

So far, Bluetooth hasn't achieved quite as much widespread popularity in networking as Wi-Fi. However, Bluetooth technology is not to be discounted. It's being used with a lot of laptops, peripheral devices (keyboards, mice, printers), PDAs, and cell phones, as well as with wireless automobile communications packages. Toyota and BMW are among the auto manufacturers that offer Bluetooth-enabled hands-free phone options.

Bluetooth operates in the 2.4GHz frequency, but because of differing transmission standards, it is not interoperable with Wi-Fi. In fact, if you have Bluetooth devices and Wi-Fi devices operating in the same space, it's possible you will experience some communication problems from time to time. It used to be worse, but in recent times, makers of both types of devices have worked on ways to eliminate interference.

---

**WI-FI OR BLUETOOTH: WHICH ONE SHOULD YOU CHOOSE?**

The makers of Bluetooth devices will tell you that their standard is not in direct competition with Wi-Fi, and it's for good reason. Although they transmit at the same frequency, Bluetooth's speed (about 700Kbps) is considerably slower than Wi-Fi's. That might make you wonder why anyone would use Bluetooth.

The two technologies really are best used in different applications. Wi-Fi is intended to be used as a wireless local area network (WLAN) technology, whereas Bluetooth is better suited for a wireless personal area network (WPAN). What's the difference? Distance, power, and devices. Wi-Fi signals are pretty reliable for a couple of hundred feet, but Bluetooth signals typically have a strength of about 30 feet. Since Bluetooth isn't designed to transmit as far, Bluetooth devices use significantly less power than Wi-Fi devices. This, in turn, makes them cheaper as well.

Here's the bottom line: for a network, go with Wi-Fi, unless you have found a compelling reason not to. Bluetooth will serve you better with devices such as cell phones, PDAs, and wireless peripherals such as keyboards, mice, and printers.

---

## Hardware

After reading Chapter 16 and Chapter 17, you should be pretty familiar with the types of devices needed for networking. With wireless networking, only a few things change. One, no more talk of Cat 6. Two, the devices have to be wireless enabled, which means they'll be slightly more expensive than their wired counterparts.

### NETWORK ADAPTERS

The key to selecting a NIC for your wireless network is to make sure it supports the right standard. For example, if your network is going to run 802.11g, be sure you don't buy an 11a card. It won't work. However, keep in mind that 11b and 11g are compatible, so you won't have problems with those two standards. In fact, a lot of cards are marked 11b/g, just as years ago wired NICs were labeled 10/100.

If you are setting up a desktop computer for a wireless network, make sure you have a free PCI slot available for your wireless NIC. Don't worry if your computer is under a desk; neither Wi-Fi nor Bluetooth requires a line of sight to communicate. That being said, thick obstructions such as steel or concrete walls can hinder wireless signals.

For laptops, you have a lot more wireless NIC options. Many computer manufacturers give you the option to have a wireless NIC built into your case. If you can get it, do it. In these situations, the antenna for the NIC is generally built into the case as well, so you usually get good reception. At the same time, this option frees up your PCMCIA slots and USB ports for other peripherals.

If you don't want to or can't go with a built-in NIC, then your choices are PCMCIA and USB. Both work equally well, so the most important consideration when buying a PCMCIA or a USB wireless NIC is convenience. Most laptops' USB ports are on the side of the computer, but the location of their USB port(s) varies. For example, one of my laptops has only one USB port, and it's located on the back of the system. It's not very convenient to get to, and if I had to push my system up against the back wall of a desk, that would cause problems. Figure 18.1 shows you a USB NIC.

USB NICs are smaller and fit easily into your pocket when you're on the move, but it's not like PCMCIA NICs are huge and bulky either. In the end, your purchase decision will probably boil down to brand and price.

**FIGURE 18.1**
USB wireless NIC

### CENTRINO

In the last section, I mentioned that many laptops come with built-in wireless NICs. If your laptop has the Intel Centrino chipset in it, then you are included in this group.

Centrino is Intel's product name for its Pentium M processor, packaged with an Intel 855 chipset for memory management and an Intel PRO/Wireless network card. As of this writing, there are three Intel PRO/Wireless options, summarized in Table 18.1.

**TABLE 18.1:**   Intel PRO/Wireless Network Adapters

| VERSION | SUPPORTED STANDARDS |
| --- | --- |
| PRO/Wireless 2100 | 802.11b |
| PRO/Wireless 2100A | 802.11a and 802.11b |
| PRO/Wireless 2100BG | 802.11b and 802.11g |

Each of these adapters has Intel's Wireless Coexistence System built in to help reduce interference between itself and Bluetooth devices. In addition, because they're packaged with the power-saving Pentium M, these adapters take less power than a PCMCIA NIC, saving precious battery life.

### CONNECTIVITY DEVICES

Once again, wireless networks parallel their wired counterparts. Just as with a wired network, you will need a device to connect the computers together. For wired networks, that choice is usually a hub or a switch, and if you have a larger network (or need segmentation), you connect the hubs and switches to a router. Wireless terminology is pretty similar, but you have slightly different options.

When you go to the computer store, you'll be stunned by the number of devices you can choose from. And for the most part, they each look the same. Which one do you choose?

The two main types of devices you will see are wireless access points (WAPs) and wireless routers. A WAP is basically a wireless hub. Wireless routers do the same thing that wired routers do. On wireless networks, though, instead of "plugging" all of your computers into a WAP and then connecting the WAP to a router, all you need is a router, and the computers can communicate directly with it. Price points for WAPs and wireless routers are usually similar, so the deciding factor will be functionality. If you're setting up a home network and have a few computers that need Internet access through your cable modem or DSL, then the router is the way to go. If you don't want anything to do with the Internet, or if your Internet access is already managed by another router, then a WAP will be just fine.

**NOTE** The majority of wireless routers have a few wired ports on them as well. This allows you to plug in computers that don't have a wireless card. In addition, there will usually be a wired port for your cable modem or DSL connection.

The prices of wireless routers have come down considerably in recent years, which has probably helped their popularity. If you shop the big electronics retailers, you can find 802.11b devices for around $40–$50, whereas the 11g ones will cost closer to $80–$100. Of course, if you want to, you can probably spend a lot more than that. If you don't have a NIC, and you need that as well as the router, you can find wireless kits for around $30 more than just the router.

### Faster Technologies

It seems that we're constantly striving for faster speeds, more storage space, and the like when it comes to computers. Once the latest and greatest fastest technology comes out, it's no longer fast enough. We want more.

To that end, wireless router manufacturers have released products designed to go above and beyond 802.11g speeds. These new technologies promise data transfer speeds of up to108Mbps while maintaining compatibility with 11Mbps 11b and 54Mbps 11g. The caveat is that you have to purchase a more expensive router (of course), along with their special, more expensive NIC that supports those speeds (of course).

There's no official name for this technology yet. D-Link calls theirs "Xtreme G," and Netgear refers to theirs as "Super G." Once again, it just goes to prove that if you want to spend the money, someone is sure to have a product to fit your needs.

### Security Concerns

Security on a wireless network is a much, much bigger issue than it is on a wired network. That's not to say that wired security isn't important, either. But when you look at how signals are transmitted— through the air—you really have to stop and think about how much easier it is to intercept those signals as opposed to the ones transmitted over a cable.

When you get your wireless router home and plug it in, one of the first things you will need to do is configure it. The outside port of your router (the one that gets the IP address from your ISP) will have a public IP address, and the inside ports should all have private IP addresses. This is the first step to securing your network, because private IP addresses are not "available" to computers on the Internet. The other thing that you need to take care of immediately is to change the defaults on the domain name used by the router and the password required to gain access to that router. Generally, there are two separate passwords. The first is required to gain administrative access to the router. Obviously, this is a good one to change. The second is the one needed to use the wireless signal. Change that as well. Your router's documentation should have step-by-step instructions on how to do this.

It might not sound like a big deal, but it really is. At the very least, someone sitting in their car on the street outside your house (or in your apartment building) could browse the Internet on your dime. More important, that same person is *on* your network, meaning that with just a little handiwork, they could be accessing files on your system (bank account information, anyone?), reading your e-mail, sending e-mail for you, and performing a variety of other nefarious activities.

CHAPTER 18

Recently, one of my local TV station's news teams went on a security-themed scavenger hunt. They found a local security consultant and, armed with a Wi-Fi–enabled PDA, traipsed through several neighborhoods. The consultant found plenty of signals. That was no surprise. What was surprising was that over half of the networks he located did *not* have the default domain name or password changed. The owner had basically just plugged the router in and let it go. Now, if you're a hacker, this will make you salivate uncontrollably. If you're not, please, please remember that if you're setting up a wireless network, take every security precaution you can, lest you get burned.

Any self-respecting wireless router will have a firewall option. Enable it. (Of course, enabling it and leaving the default password settings is still pointless. You might as well leave your front door open, put a sign in your front yard saying, "Take whatever you want from inside!" and go on vacation for two weeks.) Also, don't forget about enabling Windows Firewall, which we covered in Chapter 12.

## Wireless Windows XP Professional

Windows XP Professional supports wireless networking just as well as it supports wired networking. In this section, we will look at some of the specific Windows XP features related to wireless networking, as well as how to configure Windows XP to work on a wireless network.

### XP Wireless Support

One of the key wireless features Windows XP provides is its Zero Configuration Wireless (ZCW) service. This service is designed to help detect wireless networks visible to your network card as well as automatically configure your computer to participate on that network. Windows XP supports both Wi-Fi and Bluetooth networking.

---

**TO B OR NOT... TO G? THAT IS THE QUESTION.**

You're at the store. The salesperson is smiling at you. There are literally dozens of different models of wireless routers sitting in front of you. For some reason, the salesperson is recommending one of the more expensive models. What do you do?

Buying computer hardware is always a trade-off of wants versus needs. Sure, you want the quad flat-screen setup with a separate CD/DVD tower, but do you really need it? Probably not.

In wireless networking, your primary choices are 802.11b and 802.11g, with 11g being up to five times faster than 11b. One of the common reasons I hear for going with 11g is, "Well, I want to speed up my Internet." That's not a good reason. In fact, it's a bit silly. Even if you have great high-speed access, such as a cable modem or DSL, you will be lucky to get 1Mbps. Ever. Even if you run 11b, you will have 11Mbps internally. Boosting that to 54Mbps or even 108Mbps doesn't do anything to make your DSL line transmit or receive data to and from the phone company any faster.

On the other hand, if you do have a lot of internal networking going on, then the upgrade to 11g might well justify the costs. For example, if you transfer a lot of large graphics files internally, or if you are really into multiplayer action games, then 11g makes a lot of sense. Just make sure you get NICs that support 11g as well.

If cost isn't an issue, then there's absolutely no harm in going with 11g, even if you don't need it. Just don't get upset if you aren't able to download music files (legally, of course) any faster.

While Windows XP is generally very good about detecting available wireless signals, there might be an occasion where you want to look for one manually. Perhaps you're near an Internet café and want to look for a signal, or you're in a restaurant that has a hotspot. (Even McDonalds is granting wireless access in selected restaurants as part of its "I'm Lovin' It" program.) You can look for a signal by going to your Network properties (right-click on My Network Places and selecting Properties or double-clicking the Network Connections icon in Control Panel), right-clicking on your wireless connection, and choosing View Available Wireless Networks. This is shown in Figure 18.2.

As you can see in Figure 18.3, I'm not fortunate enough to detect any. But if I did, I could highlight it, click Connect, and the ZCW service would take over. If it doesn't work, you can click Advanced to work on the configuration yourself.

**FIGURE 18.2**
Looking for
wireless signals

**FIGURE 18.3**
No signals found

Many network adapters come with their own configuration utility. Windows XP does a good job of managing the card and all of its related services through the Network Connections Control Panel. In most cases, you won't ever need to use the NIC-specific wireless management tools.

Security should also be on your mind. Windows XP supports the Wi-Fi Protected Access (WPA) standard, as well as Wired Equivalent Privacy (WEP) encryption. If you use WPA, WEP is optional. WPA has two alternatives for encryption: Temporal Key Integrity Protocol (TKIP) and the Advanced Encryption Standard (AES). They're both newer and more secure than WEP. The wireless access point you connect to will likely support either WEP or WPA, and some will support both as more and more clients transition to WPA. This isn't something you'll probably actively think about when trying to get on a network, but you never know what problems will pop up.

**NOTE** WPA support is included with XP Service Pack 2. If you are not running SP2 or newer, then you need to download the WPA update from windowsupdate.microsoft.com (KB826942). It's not listed under Critical Updates and Service Packs but under Windows XP.

## Connecting Windows XP to a Wireless Network

The first thing you need to do is to install your wireless network adapter. If you have a desktop computer, follow these steps:

1. Turn off and unplug each computer that will be part of your network.

2. At each computer, open the case and insert a NIC in an empty slot, screwing the card in securely so it won't come loose.

3. Replace the case.

4. Make sure the wireless router (or access point) is turned on, and then turn on all connected computers.

Windows XP supports Plug and Play, so the network card driver should be installed automatically. In addition, the card will normally detect the network signal. If not, you will want to scan for networks, as mentioned in the previous section.

For laptop computers, the process is even easier:

1. Insert your network card into the appropriate (USB or PCMCIA) slot.

That's it. Plug and Play will detect the card and begin the installation process for you. You will see a pop-up notification in the notification area (next to the clock), and the drivers will be installed. When the Found New Hardware Wizard is finished, you should see a screen similar to the one shown in Figure 18.4.

You might need to reboot your computer after installing the card. Subsequently, when you plug in the network card, it will be automatically detected, and you will not need to reboot to use it.

### ACTIVELY MANAGING ZERO CONFIGURATION WIRELESS

One of the things that's very nice about Windows XP (SP2 and newer) is the ability to choose a preferred Service Set Identifier (SSID). An SSID is an identification broadcast by wireless access points; they're what ZCW uses to find networks. By setting a preferred SSID, you will always connect through that network when multiple signals are detected. With some network cards, though, multiple signals can cause problems. In cases like this, you will want to disable ZCW.

**FIGURE 18.4**
Successful installation

**WARNING**  Even with a preferred SSID set, you might run into a problem if the wireless network you want to use doesn't broadcast an SSID and your laptop is picking up a signal from an access point that is broadcasting. Regardless of your preferences, your laptop will try to use the broadcast SSID. The way around this is to disable the ZCW service and set your wireless configuration manually.

Here's how to manage your ZCW settings:

1. Open your Network Connections page (Control Panel ➢ Network Connections, or right-click My Network Places and choose Properties).

2. Right-click Wireless Network Connection and choose Properties.

3. Go to the Wireless Networking tab.

4. To enable ZCW, check the Use Windows to Configure My Wireless Network Settings check box. To disable ZCW, uncheck that box.

5. You can change the order of your preferred networks under Preferred Networks.

**NOTE**  If your network card does not support Zero Configuration Wireless, you will not have the Wireless Network Connection option.

### TROUBLESHOOTING WIRELESS CONNECTIONS

The first thing you should check when troubleshooting an issue that relates to hardware is whether or not your device is listed in the Windows Catalog (known as the Hardware Compatibility List for older Windows versions). It can be accessed at www.microsoft.com/windows/catalog. If it is not listed, then get a new NIC.

Provided that your NIC is compatible with Windows XP, check the drivers. It's always important to make sure these are installed properly. Find your NIC in Device Manager, as shown in Figure 18.5.

**FIGURE 18.5**
Network adapters in
Device Manager

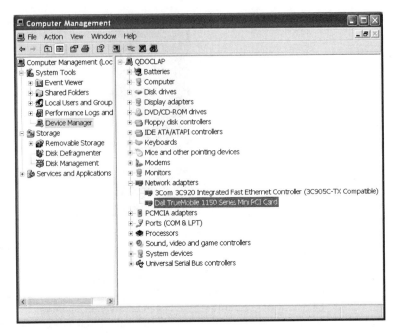

If there's a red X or an exclamation mark in a yellow circle over the icon for the adapter, there's a problem. Also, a NIC showing up under a category called Other Devices usually indicates a driver problem as well. Right-clicking the NIC and selecting Properties should tell you that the device is functioning properly, as in Figure 18.6.

**FIGURE 18.6**
A properly installed
network card

If it's not installed properly, right-click the card, select Properties, and go to the Drivers tab. There, click the Update Driver button, and follow the instructions.

The Zero Configuration Wireless service can be another source of problems. If you have multiple signals and the NIC is using the wrong one, you need to change the order of your preferred SSIDs. Higher SSIDs on the list will be used first. If the wireless network you use doesn't broadcast an SSID, but you're getting a signal from another network that does, then disable ZCW. It's the only way to get around that problem.

Finally, always be mindful of signal strength. By checking your connection's properties, you should be able to see it, as in Figure 18.7.

**FIGURE 18.7**

Excellent signal strength

Climate conditions, obstacles, and the mood of your network card can all affect signal strength. Poor signals (zero to two bars) can cause severe communications problems.

Other than the suggestions listed here, troubleshooting wireless networks is just like troubleshooting their wired cousins. For more network troubleshooting information, consult the "Troubleshooting Windows XP Professional Networking" section in Chapter 17.

## Summary

Wireless networking is the wave of the present and the future. Wireless installations are growing exponentially, and it's only a matter of time before there are more networks using wireless (at least partially) than completely wired networks.

This chapter examined the current wireless networking standards, as well as the hardware required to install a wireless network. Also covered were wireless considerations, such as extra security, and how to make your Windows XP Professional computer work on a wireless network.

I've mentioned security several times in this chapter and how security becomes more important on wireless networks. The next chapter will cover many more aspects of Windows XP security to help you ensure that your files and programs are as safe as they can be.

# Chapter 19

# Windows XP Security

In Chapter 17, I walked you through the steps for creating and configuring a network, but one big piece of the networking pie is still missing: securing the resources on your network. From its inception, the NT family of operating systems was designed with security as a primary feature, and, of course, this architectural element is omnipresent in Windows XP Professional.

One of the first things you will notice about Windows XP security is that XP requires you to create a user account for yourself right on your PC before you can do anything on that PC. Yes, the idea that you must create your own user account on your own PC before you can do anything with the PC is unusual; most other Windows-based operating systems don't have this requirement. If you are accustomed to working in a networked environment, you are probably used to needing individual domain-based user accounts, but not particular accounts on a workstation. But—as your father might say when you complain that something you don't like isn't fair—get used to it!

The user account is an integral part of Windows XP Professional and has some great benefits. For example, suppose you and Sue share a computer. You can set up the computer so that you own a folder on the hard disk and Sue owns another folder on the hard disk, and *it is completely impossible for Sue to access your data* (and vice versa) unless you give her permission.

In addition, you can restrict access to files and folders by setting permissions. As you may recall, in Windows XP Professional you can use the FAT, FAT32, or NTFS file system. If you use either FAT system, you can exercise only a limited amount of control over file and folder access, but if you use the NTFS system, you can exercise a great deal of control—whether the files are on your local computer or on your network.

In this chapter, we'll first look at how to set up user accounts, and then we'll look in detail at establishing permissions for shares, files, and folders. Finally, we'll examine a new feature available with Service Pack 2 (SP2), Security Center. You will learn about the following topics:

- ◆ Understanding and creating accounts in Windows XP Professional
- ◆ Setting permissions
- ◆ Understanding ownership
- ◆ Using Security Center

## Understanding User Accounts in Windows XP Professional

As you have just read, you must create separate user accounts on a Windows XP Professional machine before any user can log on to the workstation—and, unlike Windows 9x, Windows XP Professional won't let you get anywhere until you log on.

If your computer is part of a Windows XP Professional client-server network, two types of user accounts are available: domain accounts and local accounts. A domain account gives you access to the network and to the network resources for which you have permission. The manager of the server normally sets up domain accounts, which are stored in a directory on the server. The directory can be either Active Directory or a Windows NT domain directory.

A local user account is valid only on your local computer; local user accounts sit in a database called the *Security Accounts Manager*, or SAM. You create user accounts with the Users and Passwords applet, which you'll meet later in this chapter.

In this chapter, I'm going to talk about local user accounts only. If you happen to be working in a domain on a network and you need help creating domain user accounts, take a look at *Mastering Windows 2000 Server*, Fourth Edition (Sybex, 2002), or *Mastering Windows Server 2003* (Sybex, 2003), depending on the type of domain you have. I also talk about joining domains in Chapter 20.

Before I get into how you change or create an account, we need to look at the types of accounts in Windows XP Professional. The two broad categories are users and groups. A user account identifies a user on the basis of their user name and password. A group account contains other accounts, and these accounts share common privileges.

User accounts are of three types:

**Computer Administrator**    This account has full and complete rights to the computer and can do just about anything to the computer. The Computer Administrator account was created during installation and setup of Windows XP Professional. The Computer Administrator account cannot be deleted. You'll need to log on as Computer Administrator when you want to create new accounts, take ownership of files or other objects, install software that will be available to all users, and so on.

**Limited**    This account is intended for use by regular users, those who should not be allowed to install software or hardware or change their username. Someone with a Limited account can change their password and logon picture.

**Guest**    This built-in account allows a user to log on to the computer even though the user does not have an account. No password is associated with the Guest account. It is disabled by default, and you should leave it that way. If you want to give a visitor or an occasional user access to the system, create an account for that person, and then delete the account when it is no longer needed.

As I said earlier, a group is an account that contains other accounts, and a group is defined by function. People who want to log in to the computer will never log in as a group; everyone logs in as a user. However, when a user logs in, they receive the permissions and rights associated with any and all groups they belong to. Using groups allows the system administrator to easily create collections of users who all have identical privileges. By default, every Windows XP Professional system contains the following built-in groups:

**Administrators**    Can do just about anything to the computer. The things that they can do that no other type of user can do include loading and unloading device drivers, managing security audit functions, and taking ownership of files and other objects.

**Backup Operators**    Can log on to the computer and run backups or perform restores. You might put someone in this group if you want them to be able to get on your system and run backups but not to have complete administrative control. Backup operators can also shut down the system but cannot change security settings.

**Guests**    Have minimal access to network resources. As I mentioned earlier, creating user accounts for occasional users is a much safer bet than using Guest accounts.

**Network Configuration Operators**    Can manage network configuration with administrative-type access. Although they do not have administrative access to your system, these users can modify network and dial-up connections.

**Power Users**    Can create new printer and file shares, change the system time, force the system to shut down from another system, and change priorities of processes in the system. They can't run backups, load or unload device drivers, or take ownership.

**Remote Desktop Users**    Have the right to log on remotely.

**Replicator**    Enables your computer to receive replicated files from a server machine.

**Users**    Can run programs and access data on a computer, shut it down, and access data on the computer from over the network. Users cannot share folders or create local printers.

**HelpServicesGroup**    A group of users for the Help and Support Center.

**IIS_WPG**    The Internet Information Services Worker Process Group; this group is available only if you have installed IIS. A member of this group can manage the IIS Web server (not content, just service).

## Understanding User Rights

But what's this about shutting down the machine or loading and unloading drivers? Well, actually, the notion of a *user right* is an integral part of how Windows XP Professional security works. Basically, the difference between regular users and administrators lies in the kinds of actions that they can perform; for example, administrators can create new user accounts but regular users cannot. In Windows XP Professional terminology, the ability to perform a particular function is a user right. To take a look at the user rights in Windows XP Professional and the types of users to whom they are assigned, follow these steps:

1. In Control Panel, click Performance and Maintenance, click Administrative Tools, and then click Local Security Policy to open the Local Security Settings window.

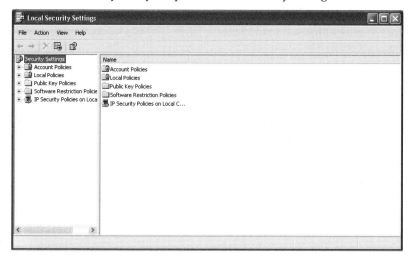

**2.** In the Security Settings pane, expand Local Policies, and then click User Rights Assignment to display a list of user rights in the pane on the right:

Most user rights are self-explanatory, but a few can use some clarification. Here's a list some of the rights and, where necessary, what they mean and what they're good for:

**Back Up Files and Directories**   Run backup utilities.

**Change the System Time**   Because the system time is important to the functioning of a network, not just anybody can change the system clock; it's a right. (Of course, you could always reboot the computer in DOS or go straight to the setup program in CMOS to reset the time, so it's not an airtight security feature.)

**Force Shutdown from a Remote System**   Some utilities let you select a Windows XP Professional machine and force it to shut down, even though you're not logged on to that machine. (One such utility comes with the Resource Kit.) Because you wouldn't want just anybody doing a forced shutdown, Microsoft made this a right.

**Load and Unload Device Drivers**   A device driver is not just a video driver or SCSI driver; a device driver may be part of a software application or operating system subsystem. Without this right, you'll often be unable to install new software, and you'll usually be unable to change drivers or add and remove parts of the operating system.

**Log On Locally**   Sit down at the computer and log on.

**Manage Auditing and Security Log**   You can optionally turn on a Windows XP Security Log, which will report every single action that woke up any part of the security subsystems in Windows XP Professional. In general, I don't recommend using the Security Log because the output is quite cryptic and can be *huge*; logging all security events can fill up your hard disk quickly, and the CPU overhead of keeping track of the log will slow down your computer. You can't enable any security logging unless you have this right.

**Restore Files and Directories**    As the name states.

**Take Ownership of Files or Other Objects**    If you have this right, you can seize control of any file, folder, or other object even if you're not *supposed* to have access to it. This right is obviously quite powerful, which is why only administrators have it.

**NOTE**    The user right to Take Ownership of Files or Other Objects is the secret to the administrator's power. You can do whatever you like to keep an administrator out of your data, but remember that the Computer Administrator can always take ownership of the file, and as the owner, do whatever they want to the file, including changing permissions. You cannot keep an administrator out; you can only make it slightly more time consuming to get in.

## Creating a User Account

Okay, now that you understand about the types of accounts and the concept of rights, let's create a new user account. You can do so in a couple of ways: using the Users and Passwords applet and using Computer Management. I'll start with the steps for creating a new user account with the Users Accounts applet:

1. Log on as Computer Administrator.

2. Choose Start ➢ Control Panel to open Control Panel, and then click User Accounts to open User Accounts.

3. Click the Create a New Account link to open the Name the New Account screen:

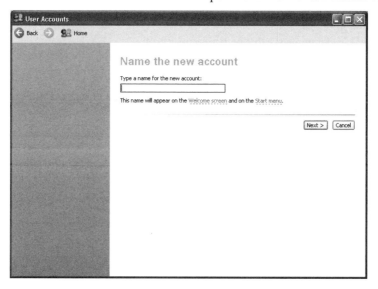

CHAPTER 19

**4.** Enter a user name for the person, and then click Next.

**NOTE** In Windows XP Professional, a user name can be a maximum of 20 characters and is not case-sensitive.

**5.** Specify the type of account that you want this user to have, and then click Create Account.

**6.** Back in User Accounts, click Change an Account, click the account that you just created, and then click Create Password to open the screen on which you can create a password for the account.

**NOTE** In Windows XP Professional, a password can be a maximum of 127 characters if you are in a pure Windows XP Professional environment. If you have Windows 9x machines on your network, keep the password to a maximum of 14 characters. Passwords *are* case-sensitive.

**7.** In the Type a New Password box, enter a password, and then enter it again in the Type the New Password Again to Confirm box. If you want, you can then type a hint (which can be seen by anyone using this computer) to trigger your remembrance of the password if you forget it.

**8.** Click Create Password to establish the password for the new user account.

To gain more control over the process of managing user accounts on Windows XP Professional, you will need to use the Local User Manager. In Control Panel, click Performance and Maintenance, click Administrative Tools, and then click Computer Management to open the Computer Management window. In the Computer Management (Local) pane, expand System Tools, expand Local Users and Groups, and then select Users to display a list of users in the right pane. Choose Action ➤ New User to open the New User dialog box, as shown in Figure 19.1.

Now follow these steps:

**1.** Enter a user name for this new account.

**2.** Enter the person's full name.

**FIGURE 19.1**
Use the New User dialog box to add a new user to your system.

3. Enter a description.

4. Enter and confirm a password.

5. Set the password options. The default option is User Must Change Password at Next Logon. This option means that only that user will know the password, which means better security. If you uncheck this option, the other two options become available. Select User Cannot Change Password if this account will be used for a service or for someone whom you do not want to give the ability to change their own password. Select Password Never Expires if this password should be considered "permanent" and not have an automatic expiration.

6. The final option is to specify whether the account should be disabled. This is often a good idea if you want to change other properties of the account before it can be used, such as setting permissions on files and folders that this user will use. If this is the case, check the Account Is Disabled box.

7. When all options are selected, click Create to complete the process of making the new user account.

**NOTE**   To enable a disabled account, in the Local Users and Groups window, right-click the account, and choose Properties from the shortcut menu to open the Properties dialog box for that account. Clear the Account Is Disabled check box.

## Creating a Group Account

The process of creating a new group account is similar to creating a new user account. Local groups are useful for assigning permissions to resources. To create a new group account, follow these steps:

1. In Control Panel, click Performance and Maintenance, click Administrative Tools, and then click Computer Management to open the Computer Management window.

2. Expand System Tools, expand Local Users and Groups, right-click Groups, and choose New Group from the shortcut menu to open the New Group dialog box:

CHAPTER 19

3. Type a name for the group in the space provided. The name can contain any numbers or letters and can be a maximum of 256 characters. The name must be unique in the local database.

4. Enter some text in the Description field that will describe the membership and purpose of this group.

5. Click the Add button to open the Select Users dialog box:

6. In the Enter the Object Name to Select box, enter the name of the user that you want to add to the group, and then click OK. Repeat step 5 and this step to add more users to the group.

7. Back in the New Group dialog box, click Close, and then close Computer Management.

## Setting Permissions

The capability to restrict access to data is a really great feature of NT and Windows XP Professional. Prior to NT, my experience with operating systems of all kinds was that if you could gain physical access to a computer, you could get to its data; before NT, the only way to secure data with any confidence was to put the data on a server and put the server behind a locked door.

But network security is only as good as you make it. If a person can gain physical access to your machine, they can remove your hard disk and have all your data. Data security includes educating users to protect passwords and to apply permissions responsibly.

In this section, I'm going to show you how to set permissions at the share level and at the file and folder level. Remember, however, that you can establish file and folder security only if you are using the NTFS file system.

**NOTE**    To set permissions on a shared resource, you need to disable simple file sharing, which is enabled by default. In an Explorer window, choose Tools ➢ Folder Options to open the Folder Options dialog box. Click the View tab, and then in the Advanced Settings list, clear the Use Simple File Sharing (Recommended) check box.

### Setting Share-Level Permissions

In Chapter 17, I showed you how to share resources on your computer with others on your network. Now we need to look at what kind of access you want to give those who use your shared resources. To do this, you set the permissions.

To set share permissions, follow these steps:

**NOTE**    This particular sequence of steps works only if you are part of a domain or have turned off the Use Simple File Sharing option. Following this list of steps, I will show you how to set share permissions using simple file sharing, which is the default if you're part of a workgroup.

1. In Explorer, right-click the shared resource, and choose Sharing and Security from the shortcut menu to open the Properties dialog box for the share at the Sharing tab.

2. Click the Permissions button to open the Permissions dialog box.

**NOTE** In older versions of Windows XP, the default shared permission was for the Everyone group to have Full Control. In a secure environment, be sure to remove this permission before assigning specific permissions to users and groups. With SP2, the default permission changed to Read for the Everyone group. It's still a good idea to remove this access, unless you do want everyone to be able to see the files.

**3.** Click Add to open the Select Users or Groups dialog box, in which you can select which groups will have access to a shared file or folder:

**4.** In the Enter the Object Names to Select box, enter the name of the user or group to whom you are granting permission, and click OK.

**5.** Back in the Permissions dialog box, you'll see that the user or group has been added to the Group or User Names list. In the Permissions section, click Allow or Deny to specify the type of permission that you want to grant this user or group. Table 19.1 explains the choices.

**6.** When you've granted the permissions, click OK.

**TABLE 19.1:**     File Permissions

| PERMISSION | DESCRIPTION |
| --- | --- |
| Full Control | The assigned group can perform any and all functions on all files and folders through the share. |
| Change | The assigned group can read and execute, as well as change and delete, files and folders through the share. |
| Read | The assigned group can read and execute files and folders but cannot modify or delete anything through the share. |

As I mentioned in the first note in this section, the steps I gave you to set share permissions are available only if you are part of a domain or have turned off the Use Simple File Sharing option. Here's where to find that setting. In Control Panel, select Appearance and Themes, and then choose Folder Options. On the View tab, look in the Advanced Settings box. The option is shown in Figure 19.2.

Let's see what happens when that setting is checked. In Explorer, right-click the shared resource, and choose Sharing and Security from the shortcut menu to open the Properties dialog box for the share in the Sharing tab, as shown in Figure 19.3. Notice that your Sharing tab looks a lot different now than when the option was unchecked.

If you share this computer with another person, you can make the folder visible only to you by putting a check mark in the Make This Folder Private box. If you don't select this box, other users on this computer will be able to see your folders; make sure you set up the proper NTFS permissions so they don't get into things they shouldn't!

**FIGURE 19.2**

Enabling and disabling simple file sharing

**FIGURE 19.3**
Simple file sharing is
enabled.

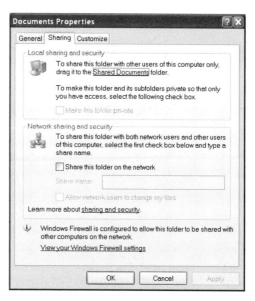

To allow others to see the folder across the network, put a check mark in the Share This Folder on the Network box. You'll have to provide a share name as well. By sharing the folder, you are giving the Everyone group Read permission. If you select the Allow Network Users to Change My Files box, you give the Everyone group Change permission. Although this setting might be convenient, it's not a good idea to use it. If you want to give people over a network the ability to modify files, then you must disable simple permissions and assign the permissions that you want to the appropriate groups of users—that is, unless you explicitly trust everyone who's on your network.

## Types of File and Folder Permissions

Share-level permissions determine who can access resources across the network and the type of access that they will have. However, you can still assign more detailed permissions to the folders and files that can be accessed through the share. In addition, by using file- and folder-level permissions, you can restrict access to resources even if someone logs on to the system and accesses those resources locally.

You've already seen that network shares have three types of permission levels: Read, Change, and Full Control. The permission types for files and folders are much more extensive, and each primary type includes still other types. Here are the primary types:

**Read**    Allows you to view the contents, permissions, and attributes associated with a resource. If the resource is a file, you can view the file. If the resource is an executable file, you can run it. If the resource is a folder, you can view the contents of the folder.

**Write**    Allows you to create a new file or subfolder within a folder if the resource is a folder. To change a file, you must also have Read permission, although you can append data to a file without opening the file if you have only Write permission.

**Read & Execute**    Allows you the permissions associated with Read and with Write and also allows you to traverse a folder, which means you can pass through a folder for which you have no access to get to a file or folder for which you do have access.

> ### MULTIPLE GROUPS ACCUMULATE PERMISSIONS
>
> Imagine running a small network for an auditing firm. You might have one group in your network called Accountants and another called Managers, and they might have different permission levels—for example, the Accountants might be able to only read the files, and the Managers might have Change access, which in NT was called Read and Write access. What about the manager of the Accounting department, who belongs to both the Managers and the Accountants groups—does he have Read access or does he have Change access?
>
> In general, your permissions to a network resource *add up*—so if you have Read access from one group and Change from another group, you end up with Read *and* Change access. However, because Change access *includes* all the things that you can do with Read access, there's no practical difference between having Read and Change and having only Change access.

**Modify**   Allows you the permissions associated with Read & Execute and with Write but also gives you Delete permission.

**Full Control**   Allows you the permissions associated with all the other permissions that I've listed so far and lets you change permissions and take ownership of resources. In addition, you can delete subfolders and files even if you don't specifically have permission to do so.

**List Folder Contents**   Allows you to view the contents of folders.

If these levels of access are a bit coarse for your needs, you can fine-tune someone's access with what Microsoft calls *special access*. To modify the special access permissions for a file or folder, follow these steps:

1. In Explorer, right-click the resource whose permissions you want to modify, and choose Properties from the shortcut menu to open the Properties dialog box for that resource.

2. Click the Security tab, and then click Advanced to open the Advanced Security Settings dialog box:

**NOTE**   If you don't see the Security tab in the Advanced Security Settings dialog box, in the Explorer view of My Computer, choose Tools ➤ Folder Options to open the Folder Options dialog box. Click the View tab, and in the Advanced Settings list, clear the Use Simple File Sharing (Recommended) check box, and click OK.

**3.** Click Edit to open the Permission Entry dialog box:

Here's a description of each of these permissions:

**Full Control**   As its name indicates and as discussed earlier in this chapter.

**Traverse Folder/Execute File**   You can change folders through this folder, and you can run this file.

**List Folder/Read Data**   You can display the contents of a folder and read the contents of a file.

**Read Attributes**   You can display the current attributes of a file or folder.

**Read Extended Attributes**   You can display the extended attributes of a file or folder, if there are any.

**Create Files/Write Data**   You can write data to a new file. When applied to a folder, this permission means you can write files into the folder, but you can't view what's already in the folder.

**Create Folders/Append Data**   You can create new folders in this location, and you can append data to existing files.

**Write Attributes**   You can modify the attributes of a file or folder.

**Write Extended Attributes**   You can create extended attributes for a file or folder.

**Delete Subfolders and Files**   You can remove folders contained within the folder you're working in, and you can remove the files contained in them.

**Delete**   You can delete files.

**Read Permissions**   You can display the current permissions list for the file or folder.

CHAPTER 19

**Change Permissions** You can modify the permissions for the file or folder. This permission is normally included only in Full Control.

**Take Ownership** You can claim ownership of a file or folder.

These levels of granularity make security considerations more difficult to grasp initially, but they give a skilled administrator much finer control over how files and folders can be accessed.

To prevent someone from accessing a file or folder, you have two choices. The first, and usually the best, is to simply not grant the person access to the file or folder. That means don't add their account to the list of permissions. The second method is to add the person's account to the permissions list, but check Deny for each permission. This creates an explicit No Access–type permission.

**NOTE** The special access items are all check boxes, not radio buttons, so you can mix and match them as you like.

## Assigning File and Folder Permissions

Now that you know something about the types of permissions that you can place on files and folders, let's walk though the steps to assign them:

1. In Explorer, right-click the file or folder for which you want to establish permissions, and choose Properties from the shortcut menu to open the Properties dialog box for that file or folder.

2. Click the Security tab:

3. Click Add to open the Select Users or Groups dialog box.

4. In the Enter the Object Name to Select box, enter the name of the user or group to whom you are granting permission, and click OK.

5. Back in the Properties dialog box, you'll see that those groups or users have been added to the Group or User Names list. Click OK.

## Auditing Files and Folders

In addition to assigning file and folder permissions, Windows XP Professional lets you keep track of who accessed a file and when. You can audit everyone or only specific users or groups. To enable, set up, and view auditing, you need to be logged on as an administrator. Enabling auditing is a bit of a pain, but you have to do it before you can set up auditing. Bear with me, and follow these steps:

1. At a command prompt, type **mmc /a** and press Enter to open the Microsoft Management Console.

2. Choose File ➢ Add/Remove Snap-in to open the Add/Remove Snap-in dialog box:

3. Click Add to open the Add Standalone Snap-in dialog box:

**4.** In the Snap-in list, select Group Policy, and then click Add to start the Group Policy Wizard:

**5.** If Local Computer is not selected in the Group Policy Object box, browse for it, and then click Finish.

**6.** Back in the Add Standalone Snap-in dialog box, click Close.

**7.** Back in the Add/Remove Snap-in dialog box, click OK.

**8.** Now, back in the MMC, expand Local Computer Policy, expand Computer Configuration, expand Windows Settings, expand Security Settings, expand Local Policies, and then click Audit Policy. You'll see the following:

**9.** In the pane on the right, right-click Audit Object Access, and choose Properties from the shortcut menu to open the Audit Object Access Properties dialog box:

**10.** Click the check boxes to audit for success and failure, and then click OK.

**11.** Close the MMC.

Whew! Now you're ready to set up auditing. Follow these steps:

**1.** In Explorer, right-click the share that you want to audit, and then choose Properties from the shortcut menu to open the Properties dialog box for that share.

**2.** Click the Security tab, click the Advanced button to open the Advanced Security Settings dialog box, and click the Auditing tab:

**3.** Click Add to open the Select User or Group dialog box.

4. In the Enter the Object Name to Select box, enter the name of a user or a group to audit, and then click OK to open the Auditing Entry dialog box:

5. Select the entries that you want to audit, and then click OK three times.

To take a look at the events that you've selected to audit, follow these steps:

1. In Control Panel, click Performance and Maintenance, click Administrative Tools, and then click Event Viewer to open the Event Viewer window.

2. In the pane on the left, select Security Log to display a list of audited events in the right pane.

# Understanding Ownership

Ownership—what a confusing concept. *Ownership* is a process by which you can take exclusive control over a file or a folder; and you can do all of this with a click of a button. But before you get power drunk with the possibilities, let's take a closer look at what being the owner of a file really means.

## Defining Ownership

Now, having worked with NT since its inception, I don't mind telling you that the whole idea of a folder or file's "owner" seemed a bit confusing until I finally figured out the definition. Here's a definition—and from this point on, let me shorten the term *file or folder* to *object*:

**Minasi's Definition of an Owner** An object's owner is a user who can *always* modify that object's permissions.

Ordinarily, only an administrator can control settings such as an object's permissions. But users need to be able to control objects in their own area, their own home folder, without having to involve an administrator at every turn. For example, suppose you want to give another user access to a folder in your home folder. Rather than having to seek out an administrator and ask the administrator to extend access permissions to another user, you as the owner can change the permissions directly. Ownership lets users become mini-administrators, rulers of their small fiefdoms.

To find out who owns an object, follow these steps:

1. In Explorer, right-click an object, and choose Properties from the shortcut menu to open the Properties dialog box for that object.

2. Select the Security tab, and then click Advanced to open the Advanced Security Settings dialog box.

3. Select the Owner tab.

## Taking Ownership

Users can't force themselves onto the permissions list for an object, but if they have the Take Ownership permission, they *can* become the owner, and once they are the owner, *then* they can add themselves to the permissions list.

If you highlight your name in the Change Owner To list and click OK, you can become the owner of the object, but you can't see what's in the object because you are still not on the permissions list.

**NOTE**    Owners of files can't necessarily access those files. All that the owners of files can do is change the permissions on those files.

Okay, then, how do you get to the object? Well, because you are an owner, you can change permissions. So you will add yourself to the permissions list and *then* gain access to the object.

Now, why were you able to do that? Because of a user right that all administrators have by default: Take Ownership. If you were logged on as someone other than an administrator, it wouldn't work. Try it! It's a necessary setting to keep the power in the administrator's hands.

Users can always shore up their security just a bit by taking control of their home folder from the administrators. Recall that users have Full Control of their home folder, and Full Control includes the ability to take ownership of an object.

And if you're concerned about an administrator being able to take control at any time—where's the security in that?—consider that an administrator must *take* ownership in order to add themselves to the object's permissions list. In doing that, they leave fingerprints behind; if you log on one day and find that you're no longer the owner of something that you owned yesterday, you'll know that an administrator has been snooping—and if file auditing is in place, you can even find out who snooped.

**NOTE**    You can't *give* ownership; you can only exercise the permission to take ownership. If an administrator were to take ownership of a file, they could not edit the file and then give ownership back to the original owner.

To summarize permissions and ownership:

◆ By default, new files and new subfolders inherit permissions from the folder in which they are created.

◆ A user who creates a file or a folder is the owner of that file or folder, and the owner can always control access to the file or folder by changing the permissions on it.

◆ When you change the permissions on an existing folder, you can choose whether those changes will apply to all files and subfolders within the folder.

◆ Users and groups can be denied access to a file or a folder simply by not granting the users or groups any permissions for it.

**WARNING**    It is possible to lock out everyone, including the operating system itself, if you do not apply permissions correctly.

## Security Center

By now you understand how important security is. Security management can take a lot of time, even if you just have two computers at home. Managing security on hundreds or thousands of computers is often a full-time job. In previous versions of Windows XP, security management tools were readily available, but they were scattered throughout Control Panel and various MMC applets. Now, with SP2, there is a Security Center applet right in Control Panel. It's shown in Figure 19.4.

While this applet doesn't allow you to specifically control user accounts or share, file, and folder permissions, it does give you an interface in which you can help manage overall system security. First, you can manage Windows Firewall, which is critical in the protection against hackers and viruses. Second, you can enable automatic updates. This ensures that you always have the latest software patches from Microsoft, just in case there might be a security hole. Third, Windows will check to see if you have an antivirus program and if it's up-to-date. If not, Windows will warn you. Windows XP can work with and help manage most antivirus applications. Clicking on any of the three sections will give you more details on how to manage your security. Happy securing!

## Summary

In this chapter, we looked at creating user and group accounts and at the rights that the various kinds of users and groups can have. We also walked through the steps involved in setting permissions for shares, files, and folders. Finally, we looked at a new feature of SP2, Security Center. Understanding and following these procedures is essential if you want the information on your Windows XP Professional system to be secure. And presumably, that's one of the main reasons you're working with Windows XP Professional anyway, right?

**FIGURE 19.4**
Windows Security
Center

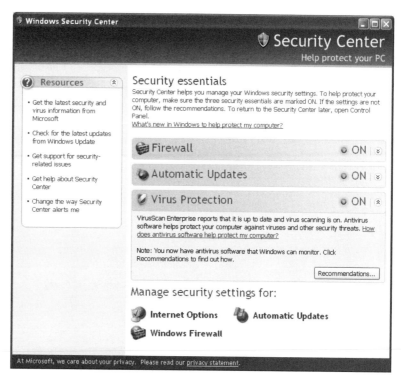

This chapter also ends our Home Networking section. In the next chapter, we'll dive into more technical networking concepts, such as joining domains and interoperating with non-Microsoft networks.

# Part 6

# Advanced Networking

In this section you will learn how to:

- ◆ Connect to Windows-Based Domains
- ◆ Work with Windows Server 2003
- ◆ Interoperate with Non-Microsoft Network Servers

# Chapter 20

# Connecting to Domains

Although peer-to-peer workgroups have beauty in their simplicity, there are some limitations. As an example, did you know that with Windows XP Professional, Microsoft has limited workgroups to 10 computers? For larger networks, you will need to create a domain.

A Microsoft Windows domain is a network with a single database of usernames, passwords, profiles, and more. Once you get an account on a domain, you can log on through any computer on the network and have access to your files and preferences. You can even log on to the domain remotely from halfway around the world. Except for the limits you might encounter in network speed, everything else would be the same.

In Chapters 16 and 17, you learned to configure and install networks in a peer-to-peer relationship. Chapter 16 also described the client-server relationships that are associated with larger computer networks. The lessons of these chapters apply equally well here. For smaller networks, the required network hardware isn't significantly different between a peer-to-peer and a client-server domain-based network.

Windows XP Professional is an excellent client on a network domain. In this chapter, we'll look at many of the decisions you will need to make in order to get the networking features to run reliably in that environment. You'll also learn how to connect documents and printers shared in the domain. To enable the consistent look and feel, you'll also create roving profiles for users and hardware. Finally, the chapter wraps up with a section on troubleshooting your domain.

In this chapter:

- ◆ Setting up a domain
- ◆ Requirements on the domain server
- ◆ Attaching to network resources
- ◆ Using profiles
- ◆ Troubleshooting

## Setting Up a Domain

The basic reasons for having a network are the same for peer-to-peer and client-server networks. A network allows you to share files, printers, applications, and more. However, a domain can let you do even more. With its centralized database of usernames, you can use the same username and password on any computer on the domain.

As with peer-to-peer networks, domains increase user productivity. With their dedicated servers, domains are better at supporting collaboration. The following is an example of how this can work.

In our offices, Leslie is one of several engineers. The engineering office is 50 miles away from the manufacturing plant, but the engineers often need to travel to the plant to check on the product. Sydney is the manufacturing supervisor, who is in constant need of engineering help. So, the network problems that we need to solve are as follows:

◆ Setting up workstations at the engineering and manufacturing facilities for all users

◆ Creating a common database for the engineers, accessible by manufacturing

Let's solve their problem with a client-server network on a Microsoft domain. With this type of network, Leslie can easily access her drawings from either facility, and Sydney can review the designs as they are developed. Assuming that both computers are running Windows XP Professional, here's how to get both users access to Leslie's files from any facility:

1. Using the user account, the computer account, and any folders that are set up for her on the domain controller, Leslie connects her Windows XP Professional workstation to the domain. She starts saving her engineering drawings on the domain server.

2. The network administrator sets up a roving profile on the server. Whenever Leslie logs on to the domain, she gets the same roving profile. It doesn't matter what workstation she uses.

3. The network administrator gives Sydney a different account on the domain controller. Sydney's username is included in a group with permissions to access Leslie's folder.

Now Leslie can access her drawings and files from either facility. Sydney can view Leslie's engineering drawings as required, so she can plan future manufacturing activity.

---

### MICROSOFT DOMAINS AND INTERNET DOMAINS

Microsoft domains and Internet domains are related but not identical concepts. A Microsoft domain includes a group of computers with a common database of users, groups, files, and so on. The Internet concept of a domain is based on a hierarchical organization of computers in a network, without any requirement for a common database of any sort. However, you can organize a Microsoft domain in the Internet hierarchical style.

For example, if you wanted to organize the Microsoft computers that belong to the mommabears.com network, you could give them the following names:

```
w95a.ms.mommabears.com

w98b.ms.mommabears.com

w2000c.ms.mommabears.com

wxpprod.ms.mommabears.com

wxpserver.ms.mommabears.com
```

All five computers (w95a, w98b, w2000c, wxpprod, wxpserver) would belong to the ms subdomain in the mommabears.com Internet domain. However, in a Microsoft domain, you don't have to follow Internet domain naming rules. Alternatively, you can follow the rules you used when you installed Windows XP Professional in Chapter 2, where the name of a computer is limited to 15 characters. This is also known as a NetBIOS name.

These actions apply on a server used as a domain controller. Domain controllers are by definition computers with one of the Windows Server operating systems that participate in managing domain security. (Servers can also be part of a domain but cannot control domain security. These are typically file, application, and print servers.) Therefore, many of these steps are for the administrator responsible for the domain and are beyond the scope of this book.

Windows XP Professional is designed to work in a variety of networking situations. XP makes the perfect network client for both home and office users. It doesn't matter if your network servers are running NetWare, Unix, or some other platform; Windows XP Professional will play nice with a variety of network operating systems. Windows XP Professional can also act as a server in a pinch—although you're better off going with a true server product for a long-term solution.

## Requirements on the Domain Server

As a Windows XP Professional power user, you'll sometimes need to know the basics of what an administrator does on a domain server. The details of this process are beyond the scope of this book. You wouldn't want to see detailed information about configuring Windows NT Server, Windows 2000 Server, or Windows Server 2003 in a book on XP Professional, anyway.

A domain controller includes the information that you need to connect to that domain from a workstation. There are four basic steps that an administrator has to take on a properly configured domain controller:

♦ Create a user account.

♦ Create a computer account.

♦ Set up appropriate profiles.

♦ Identify the new computer.

For more information on configuring domain controllers, refer to *Mastering Windows 2000 Server, Fourth Edition*, or *Mastering Windows Server 2003*, both from Sybex.

### User Accounts

You need a user account on a domain controller in order to connect to a domain. By default, that account has a standard set of rights and privileges to certain folders on the server, including a data folder for your everyday work files. In addition, the user account of anyone who needs access to your work should be made a member of a group with appropriate rights to your data folder.

User accounts on a domain controller are different from user accounts in Windows XP Professional. They are kept on separate databases. Once your computer is configured for a domain, you can log in to either system through your Windows XP Professional computer.

When you start your computer, a domain-enabled XP Workstation makes you use the Ctrl+Alt+Del key combination to get to the Log On to Windows login screen. At the login screen, you can select where you want to log in.

1. At the login screen, if you don't already see the Log On To: drop-down box, click Options.

2. Use the Log On To: drop-down box to select whether you want to log on to the local computer or a domain.

3. Enter the username and password for the database you selected.

CHAPTER 20

**4.** Click Start.

**NOTE** If your XP Workstation hasn't been configured for a domain yet, refer to the "Connecting to a Domain" section later in this chapter for instructions.

### Computer Accounts

If you want your Windows XP computer to participate in a Microsoft domain, your computer needs a computer account on the domain controller. Once your network administrator creates the account, you'll need to provide the computer account name and password to connect your XP Professional computer to that domain. You need to do this only once, and then you are part of the domain. Keep in mind that computer accounts are very different from user accounts. You will always log on as a user; the only time you will need your computer account name is when joining a domain.

Alternatively, your administrator might give you temporary access to an administrative username on the domain, which you could use to create a computer account when you connect your XP Professional computer. This doesn't happen very often, though. Administrators shouldn't give out administrative access to non-administrators, even on a temporary basis. It's just too much of a security risk.

### Profiles

In Chapter 17, I described the basics of user profiles on an XP Professional computer in a peer-to-peer network. There are two other profiles available: roaming and mandatory. Both require a domain and are discussed later in the chapter. However, to support access to your files and settings from any workstation on the domain, the domain administrator should set up a roaming or mandatory profile when creating your user account on the domain.

### Name of Domain

The final item you need to connect to a domain is the name. It could look like an Internet domain name such as mommabears.com, or it could be a NetBIOS-style name such as DOMAIN-COMPANY.

**NOTE** Ever since the introduction of Windows 2000, Microsoft has strongly encouraged administrators to name their domains in an Internet-style scheme. While this is good practice, you don't necessarily need to use an Internet-standard top-level domain name such as .com, .net, or .org. For example, you can call your domain froggy.pond, and it will work just fine (although others might find you strange).

## Connecting to a Domain

To summarize the previous sections, you need to get the following information from your system administrator to connect to a domain:

- Your domain username

- Your domain password

- The name of the domain that you will join

◆ Your computer name (you may have to provide the computer name to the administrator, especially if you configured it in a workgroup)

◆ IP configuration details for the domain

**NOTE** With the information shown above, you can set up your computer to join the domain during the Windows XP Professional installation process.

## Configuring Windows XP for a Domain

You may not be able to just connect. First, you need to check to see if your IP configuration parameters are compatible.

When you get the configuration parameters you need from the domain administrator, remember that the domain probably includes a substantial number of computers. There may even be multiple LANs on the same domain. This means you'll probably have a DNS, DHCP, and possibly a WINS server on the domain. If you don't, or if you recognize a DNS server from an outside network, be skeptical.

### IP CONFIGURATION

It's easier to configure your computer on a peer-to-peer network. As you read in Chapter 17, it's just a matter of selecting a group of IP addresses for your LAN and typing them in with associated subnet masks, gateway addresses, and possibly the DNS addresses from your ISP.

**TIP** Most domains include a DHCP server. If this applies to you, consult your network administrator. Depending on your domain's DHCP configuration, you may be able to skip some of the following steps.

There is more to configure when you're getting XP Professional ready to connect to a domain. To see what I mean, open up the properties for your network adapter. Click Start ➤ All Programs ➤ Accessories ➤ Communications ➤ Network Connections. Right-click the connection that you're using and then click Properties in the shortcut menu. For example, Figure 20.1 shows the properties for my computer's Network Bridge.

Now highlight Internet Protocol (TCP/IP), and then click Properties. You'll see where you may already have configured your IP and DNS addresses. Figure 20.2 illustrates this window with static IP addresses and DNS server IP addresses. Alternatively, you can select Obtain an IP Address Automatically. Your computer would first look to the DHCP server for an IP address assignment. If none were available, it would use the Automatic Private IP Addressing (APIPA) system. These systems are described in more detail in Chapter 17.

### Additional IP and Gateway Addresses

Click Advanced to open the Advanced TCP/IP Settings window. It includes four tabs. You should see the IP Settings tab by default, as shown in Figure 20.3. You can assign additional IP addresses to your NIC. If there is more than one way for messages to leave your network, you can also assign additional Default Gateways. Just click the appropriate Add button. Finally, the Automatic Metric setting is checked by default. It's designed to optimize network traffic through your gateway(s).

CHAPTER 20

**FIGURE 20.1**

Network Bridge
properties

**FIGURE 20.2**

IP address properties

**NOTE**   Multiple default gateways are more common in domains than in workgroups. While additional gateways can add to your security challenges, they also provide a backup if you need to ensure reliable connections to other networks and/or the Internet.

### Additional DNS Information

In a domain, your computers need a DNS server as an address book to figure out how to find other computers. Corporate domains include more than one DNS server. If one goes down or needs maintenance, backups keep a network going. If the domain is large, additional DNS servers help keep any one server from becoming overloaded.

**FIGURE 20.3**

You can add more IP addresses and gateways.

Click the DNS tab. As you can see in Figure 20.4, you can add as many DNS addresses as you might need. The other options in this tab are as follows:

**Append Primary and Connection Specific DNS Suffixes:** Adds the name of your domain to the end of any specified computer name. For example, if you have a computer on the `xp.mommabears.com` network and searched for the laptop2 computer, this option assumes that you're really looking for the computer at `laptop2.xp.mommabears.com`.

**Append Parent Suffixes of the Primary DNS Suffix:** Uses parent suffixes. For example, the parent suffix of `xp.mommabears.com` is `mommabears.com`. Thus, if your computer can't find a `laptop2.xp.mommabears.com` computer, it would then look for `laptop2.mommabears.com`.

**FIGURE 20.4**

You can set up DNS resolution in a number of ways.

**Append These DNS Suffixes (in Order):** Adds the suffixes in the text box shown below. For the example shown in Figure 20.4, if you searched for a computer named bigshot, it would automatically look for `bigshot.mommabears.com` and `bigshot.xp.mommabears.com`, in that order.

**DNS Suffix for This Connection:** Includes this suffix if all other options fail. Normally, you should enter the name of the local domain.

**Register This Connection's Addresses in DNS:** Requests that your DNS server include the name of your computer in its records.

**Use This Connection's DNS Suffix in DNS Registration:** Requests that your DNS server include the name of your domain in its database.

**WARNING** If you've specified DNS servers on the Internet, don't select either of the last two options under the DNS tab. At best, your ISP might get annoyed. It also provides an easy way for hackers to bypass your firewall. The exception is if you're using XP Professional as a server, with a "real" (not private) IP address on the Internet. But most ISPs charge more before they'll allow you to set up a server on their network.

### WINS

An alternative to DNS on Microsoft Windows networks is the Windows Internet Naming Service (WINS). Like DNS, WINS provides a database of computer names and IP addresses. The advantage is that WINS servers are automatically updated. However, Microsoft's relatively new Dynamic DNS service also provides for automatic updates. Therefore, you're more likely to use WINS on domains governed by older Microsoft servers such as NT 4.0. Click the WINS tab to review the information shown in Figure 20.5.

Because WINS will eventually become obsolete, I cover it in less detail. Under the WINS tab, you can include the IP addresses of WINS servers. Alternatively, LMHOSTS is a text file that you can substitute for a WINS server.

Generally on a Microsoft network, you want to enable NetBIOS over TCP/IP. However, this may already be set through your DHCP server. In any case, follow the instructions from your network administrator.

### Options

Click the Options tab. The only default option available in XP Professional is IP filtering, which allows you to block some of the ports and protocols used in TCP/IP communication. This is a form of a firewall, which regulates traffic to and from a network. Under the Options tab, click Properties to get to the TCP/IP Filtering window shown in Figure 20.6.

There are over 65,000 TCP/IP ports available. The first 1,024 ports are reserved for basic communication. For example, port 80 is reserved for HTTP, port 21 for FTP, and port 25 for sending mail (SMTP). It's common for a hacker to use one of these ports to get into a computer. The current list of TCP/IP port numbers is maintained by the Internet Assigned Numbers Authority at `www.iana.org/assignments/port-numbers`.

There are 255 IP protocol numbers available, which help define the purpose of each packet. For more information on IP protocol numbers, see `www.iana.org/assignments/port-numbers`.

**FIGURE 20.5**

You can also set up WINS to help find computer names.

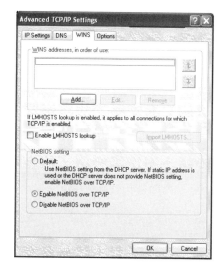

**FIGURE 20.6**

You can filter a number of TCP/IP ports.

Generally, you should limit port numbers and protocol numbers only on an Internet gateway. Creating these limits on a computer inside a LAN could limit what you can do on that network.

On most domains, Windows XP Professional computers are not used as gateways. If you want to set up an Internet gateway on an XP Professional computer, see Chapter 12. The ICS and Windows Firewall settings configured in that chapter are also an easier way to create a firewall.

### IDENTIFICATION

Now you're ready to change the identification of your computer from a workgroup to a domain. Windows XP Professional does not have an Identification tab as Windows 98 and NT did. Instead, that information is associated with the properties for My Computer. To access these properties, right-click My Computer, choose Properties, and then choose Computer Name. As shown in Figure 20.7, you will see your computer name, as well as the workgroup or domain name. You can also change that information here.

**FIGURE 20.7**

The Computer Name tab shows whether your computer is part of a workgroup or a domain.

## MAKING THE CONNECTION

Once you are armed with this information, you can join a domain using the Computer Name Changes dialog box in System Properties or the Network Identification Wizard. Since using the wizard is more descriptive, I'll walk through the process of using it next. If you want to use the Computer Name Changes dialog box, follow these steps to open it:

1. Click Start, right-click My Computer, and choose Properties from the shortcut menu to open the System Properties dialog box.

2. Click the Computer Name tab, and then click Change to open the Computer Name Changes dialog box.

3. In the Member Of section, click the Domain option, and then enter the name of the domain. Click OK to close the Computer Name Changes dialog box, and then click OK again to close the System Properties dialog box. If prompted, enter a username and password *on the domain* with the authority to add your computer.

Now, let's step through the wizard:

1. In the System Properties dialog box, click the Computer Name tab, and then click Network ID to start the Network Identification Wizard.

2. At the Welcome screen, click Next to open the Connecting to the Network screen.

3. Click the option that tells Windows XP Professional that this computer is part of a business network, and then click Next to open the next Connecting to the Network screen.

CHAPTER 20

**4.** Click the My Company Uses a Network with a Domain option, and then click Next.

**5.** Be sure that you have all the information listed on the Network Information screen, and then click Next.

**6.** On the User Account and Domain Information screen, enter your domain username, your domain password, and your domain name. Click Next. If you see confirmation that your computer already has an account on the domain, click Yes.

**7.** On the Computer Domain screen, enter the name of your computer and your new domain, and click Next.

8. You'll see the Domain User Name and Password dialog box. Enter a domain username and password for a user account in the domain with sufficient permissions to add this Windows XP Professional machine to the domain (the account must have Administrator rights in the domain), and then click OK. At this point, Windows XP Professional creates a machine name within the domain. Depending on your network, this could take a few minutes. When Windows XP Professional has created the machine name, it will return you to the User Account dialog box. Click Next.

9. On the Access Level Wizard, select the type of access that you want for the local computer. You can choose from three radio buttons: Standard User, Restricted User, and Other. Standard users can modify the computer and install applications but have no rights to read files that do not belong to them. Restricted users can save documents but have no rights to modify the computer or add applications. The Other option allows you to insert the user into a different group, such as Administrators, which would grant complete rights to the entire Windows XP Professional computer. Select a radio button, and then click Next.

10. The final dialog box, Completing the Network Identification Wizard, will appear. Click Finish and then click OK to reboot.

After the computer reboots, follow these steps to log on to the domain:

1. At the Windows logon prompt, press Ctrl+Alt+Del as you normally would to log on to Windows XP Professional.

2. Enter a username to log on to the domain (this is not always the same name as the local username), enter a password, and select the appropriate domain. You can either type in the domain name or select it from the drop-down list that Windows XP Professional automatically builds for you. If your domain name does not appear, click the Options button.

3. Click the OK button to complete the domain authentication process.

One thing to keep in mind is that these steps work only if the computer and user accounts already exist on the domain. In addition, only domain administrators are authorized to add your computer to the domain. It's not as though they want to give out the domain administrator password to everyone. If your user account does not have the necessary rights to join your computer to the domain, you may need some assistance from your network administrator.

**REJOINING A WORKGROUP**

It is easier to reconfigure your computer from a domain to a workgroup. First, make sure your IP address settings are consistent with other computers on your workgroup. For more information, see Chapter 17. Then return to the Computer Name tab shown in Figure 20.7. Click Change. Select the Workgroup option and then enter the name of your workgroup.

When you click OK, you'll be prompted for the username and password of an administrator on your computer (not on the domain). Once this information is entered, XP Professional joins the workgroup of your choice.

CHAPTER 20

## Attaching to Network Resources

After your network is configured for sharing, one of the easiest ways to test your network connections is to attach to network resources. The process is nearly identical to that for a peer-to-peer network. In fact, if you've read Chapter 17, a lot of the following sections will seem familiar; they're just repackaged for domains. You can test your connections in the following ways:

◆ By browsing My Network Places

◆ By mapping a network drive

◆ By using UNCs to connect directly

### Browsing My Network Places

Open Windows Explorer. Click My Network Places to open a window that displays the options on your network. Double-click a computer to view, and connect to its shared resources.

On a domain, this may not work if you didn't use the domain username and password. However, the other two methods can work, because they allow you to enter the domain username and password in order to make the connection.

### Mapping a Network Drive

The basic process for mapping a network drive is essentially identical to that described for a peer-to-peer network in Chapter 17. If you're not logged in with a domain username and password, there are two differences:

**Folder:** Specify the name of the domain server and the associated share name in the Folder text box. In Figure 20.8, that would be net-server and inetpub.

**User Name:** Select different username. In the Connect As window that appears, type in a domain username and password. An example is shown in Figure 20.9.

**FIGURE 20.8**
Just specify the name of the domain server and shared directory.

**FIGURE 20.9**
If you're an authorized
user on a domain, just
specify your domain
username and password.

---

**ALTERNATE DOMAIN ACCOUNTS**

But what if you are attaching to another server and you do not have an account on that server? This happens a lot to administrators.

If you have an administrator called Sheila Sanders, Sheila will have an account on her primary server that she logs on to. In addition, Sheila may need to attach to other servers that have resources she wants to use, even though she doesn't have an account on those servers. Another classic example would be that Sheila logs on to a Windows XP server as Sheila but has an account named SSanders on a NetWare server.

To resolve this issue, Sheila could log on to the Windows XP server as Sheila, but when she maps a drive to a Novell server, she could use the Connect As dialog box to connect to the NetWare server as SSanders. If Sheila's passwords on the Windows XP server and the SSanders account on NetWare are the same, Sheila gets direct access to the NetWare directory. If the passwords are different, Sheila will be prompted to enter a password for the NetWare server when she clicks OK to map the network drive.

---

## Making a Direct Connection via a UNC

Alternatively, you can use various forms of the net command at the command-line interface.
Here's how to use the net view command:

1. To display a list of the computers on your network, type **net view** at the command prompt.

2. To display a list of the resources on a particular server, append the name of the machine. For example, if the server name is spiritwolf, you'd enter **net view \\spiritwolf**. This works even if spiritwolf is the server for your domain.

3. To view the resources of a machine in another domain, for example, the server spiritwolf in the domain hq, you'd enter the following:

   ```
   net view \\spiritwolf /domain:hq
   ```

4. To display a list of all the domains on the network, simply enter **net view /domain**.

### USING NET USE: CONNECTING TO OTHER DRIVES AND PRINTERS

After you've browsed the network with the net view command, you can connect to all the available goodies (or disconnect from those you don't want) with the net use command. Use this command to connect to network resources as drives D through Z and printer ports LPT1 through LPT9.

**WARNING**   Drive letters can be used only once. So if your DVD player is drive D and your CD burner is drive E, you will have only drive letters F through Z available.

To display information about the workstation's current connections, type **net use** without options, and you'll see something like this:

### CONNECTING TO A RESOURCE IN THE LOCAL DOMAIN

To connect to a shared resource, such as a printer shared as lexmarko on server spiritwolf, type **net use lpt1: \\spiritwolf\lexmarko**. If you want to specify domain username jdoe and password, type **net use lpt1: \\spiritwolf\lexmarko * /USER:jdoe**, and then you'll be prompted for a password.

### USING LONG FILENAMES IN UNCS

If you wanted to connect to a folder called Wpfiles on the spiritwolf server and make that your E drive, you'd substitute E: for **lpt1:** and **Wpfiles** for **lexmarko** in the preceding example. Your command would be **net use E: \\spiritwolf\wpfiles**. You get to specify the port name or drive letter that you want to connect a resource to, but again, you're restricted to drive letters D through Z and ports LPT1 through LPT9.

If the computer you're getting the resource from has a blank character in its name (that is, the computer name has two words in it), you must put the name in quotation marks, like this:

```
"\\eisa server"
```

If a different username and password are attached to the resource that you're trying to connect to, such as on a domain server, you need to include that in your connection command, like this:

```
net use lpt1: \\ted\hp4m * USER:mjang
```

The asterisk tells the net command to prompt you for the password.

**TIP**   When you use the net command to connect to a share, don't use more than one domain username.

**CREATING A DRIVE MAPPING FOR YOUR HOME FOLDER**

To connect to your home folder (the folder on the server that has been assigned to you, assuming there is one), type the following:

```
net use /home
```

with the (optional) password and username on the end as just explained.

If you want to make the connection for another user, rather than for yourself, add the user's name (Frank) to the end of the line, like this:

```
net use lpt1: \\ted\hp4m * user:frank
```

The asterisk tells net to prompt you for a password. If the user for whom you are making the connection is in another domain, the user part of the statement looks like this:

```
user:domainname/frank
```

where *domainname* is the name of that user's home domain.

**CONNECTING TO A RESOURCE IN ANOTHER DOMAIN**

If you want to connect to a resource in a domain that is not your usual one, you must first log on to that domain. One way to do this is to have a user account for yourself in the second domain. Managing multiple accounts for one person can get extremely cumbersome, so it's not the best setup. When a password expires in one domain, and you have to change it, the password doesn't necessarily expire in the other domain. This can cause confusion, and profiles don't span domains either. Another way is to have a trust relationship between your domains. Trust relationships allow users in one domain the potential to access resources in the other domain. I say *potential* because we still have to deal with permissions.

Think of trust relationships in human terms. If I trust you, I may let you drive my car (my resource). However, you still can't drive my car until I give you the keys (permissions). But if I don't trust you, there's no way I am handing you my keys! After you've logged on to the proper domain, the process of connecting to resources is the same as described previously.

**NOTE**   Trust relationships are set up between domains, not specific computers. Generally, the setting of trust relationships is a domain administrator's responsibility and not something you will do from Windows XP Professional; however, it's important to talk about, since you may be part of a domain and need to access resources in another domain.

# Using Profiles

Windows XP Professional uses two types of profiles: user and hardware. Although each serves a specific purpose, both types of profiles are used to customize the computing environment. In this section, we'll look at how to create and manage them.

## Creating Hardware Profiles

Basic hardware profiles are addressed in Chapter 17. It makes no difference whether you're connecting a computer to a workgroup or a domain; the way you create and manage a different hardware profile remains the same.

## User Profiles

In Windows XP Professional, a user profile is a collection of environment settings that customize a user's interface. It can include display settings, network settings, printer settings, and so on. User profiles are of three types:

- ◆ Local
- ◆ Roaming
- ◆ Mandatory

Local user profiles apply only to a local machine, hence their name. Since local user profiles apply to the local computer, they are covered in more detail in Chapter 17.

A *roaming user profile* can be created by only your system administrator and is stored on the server. A roaming user profile contains settings that are specific to you and is loaded whenever you log on to any computer on the network. Local user profiles and roaming user profiles contain the same types of information. The only differences are that a roaming profile is stored on a server (as opposed to the local machine), and roaming profiles follow you no matter where you log in. You must have a domain to use roaming user profiles.

**TIP**   If your network uses roaming user profiles, do not store large files on your desktop, which is part of your profile. Every time you log on, the profile needs to be copied from the server it's stored on to the local machine. If there are large files as part of that profile, logging on to the network could take an excruciatingly long time.

A *mandatory user profile* specifies settings for an individual or a group of users and can be created or modified only by your system administrator. There is a major philosophical difference between mandatory user profiles and the other two we have discussed. With local and roaming profiles, users are allowed to customize their settings any way they choose. While this allows for freedom and personalization, people are known to abuse these types of privileges. With a mandatory user profile, the user gets a specified environment every time they log on. They are allowed to make changes, but every time they log off and back on, their settings go back to the defaults. Most of the time, when users realize that their changes are not being kept, they will simply stop making changes at all.

**NOTE**   Mandatory user profiles will work only if you are implementing them across a network. They will not work locally.

Please note that mandatory profiles do *not* keep users from making changes to their desktop settings. Mandatory profiles just don't save those changes that the user does make. If you want to keep people from changing desktop settings at all, you need to use either Local Security Policy (which affects only your computer) or Group Policies (which can affect an entire network).

## Attaching to Network Resources Using Login Scripts

A very common way in which you will attach to network resources is through network drive mappings that the network administrator created in a login script. Often drive letters such as H and M are pointing to files on a file server on the network. The good news is that login scripts run automatically every time you log in (hence their name); therefore, they require no thinking on the part of the user.

You will be able to distinguish between network drives and local hard drives by the icon associated with the drive. Network drives have the little T connector and cable beneath the icon. From time to time, you may see a drive with a red *X* across it. This symbol indicates that you formerly had a drive mapped to this drive letter, but the system cannot find the network location at this time. This situation happens most frequently if you are accessing the network remotely via a modem, but it could also be a sign of connectivity problems.

# Troubleshooting Domains

Entire books have been written on the topic of troubleshooting networks. It's such a voluminous topic that it requires a lot of attention. To that end, there is no way this chapter can teach you everything you need to know to troubleshoot network problems. The best training for troubleshooting is simply hands-on experience. That said, this section will give you some pointers to get you started.

## Receiving the Error Message "No Domain Server Was Available"

When logging on to the server, you may get an error message stating that no domain server was available to authorize you to log on to a domain. Often this error message will prevent you from seeing some resources in My Network Places and prevent you from accessing the network entirely.

**NOTE**  The title of this section is a good example of a specific error message. Whenever you receive specific error messages, write them down. They are invaluable to have when searching your resources for a solution. You're never going to know how to fix everything right away, but if you know where to look for help, you'll be a lot further ahead in the game.

**TIP**  A good place to get started is Microsoft's Knowledge Base. It has a lot of articles about known error messages and may be able to help you. Go either to Microsoft's web page (www.Microsoft.com) and click the Support link or to support.Microsoft.com. You will be able to type in your error message and search through all of Microsoft's products or choose the specific product you are interested in. The support page also provides a download area for patches, and newsgroups for you to post questions.

This message appears when the system is unable to contact a domain controller for the domain that you are logging on to. The obvious problem could be that the server is down. Another common cause of this error is that a switch, router, or gateway is malfunctioning in your environment, so check the hub and the bridges to make sure they are operating normally.

Easily the most common occurrence of this problem is when TCP/IP is the primary transport protocol in your environment. If the workstation is on one physical segment of the network and the domain controller is on another segment of the network, often the client machine is unable to see the server via NetBIOS. To test this situation, see if you can ping the server's address. If you can ping the server by using its IP address but are unable to contact the server for domain logon authentication, you have determined the cause of your dilemma.

One common solution is to install a Windows Internet Naming Service (WINS) server in your environment. It will handle the NetBIOS computer name to IP address name resolution (in much the same way that a DNS server handles IP hostname to IP address conversions). Once WINS is installed on a server, the Windows XP Professional computer must point to the WINS server. To point the client to the WINS server, follow these steps:

1. Click Start ➢ All Programs ➢ Accessories ➢ Communications ➢ Network Connections to open the Network Connections folder.

2. Right-click Local Area Connection (or Network Bridge if active) and select Properties to open the Properties dialog box for your connection.

3. Double-click Internet Protocol (TCP/IP) to open the Internet Protocol (TCP/IP) dialog box.

4. On the General tab, click the Advanced button to open the Advanced TCP/IP Settings dialog box. Select the WINS tab.

5. Click Add to open the TCP/IP WINS Server dialog box.

6. In the WINS Server box, enter the IP address of the WINS server, and click Add.

7. Click OK and then click OK twice more. Close Network Connections.

While installing WINS is a common solution to this problem, it has a few drawbacks. One, it means you must have an additional server available to run this service. Yes, WINS can be installed on a server that's already doing something else, such as a file or print server, but why pile more work on that machine? Two, Microsoft has moved away from using WINS and is using DNS for name resolution situations. The only time you really should need WINS is if you're running Windows NT or older domain controllers (and even then, they can use DNS).

That said, if your network has a DNS server (which it must if you are running a Windows 2000 or newer domain), configure your clients to use the DNS server. This should already be the case, and if the clients can find the DNS server, and the DNS server has the records it's supposed to have, you won't encounter this error message.

**TIP** If your client computers are getting their IP configuration information from a DHCP server, the addresses of WINS and DNS servers can be supplied along with the IP address, subnet mask, and other parameters.

### Identification

In a network with sufficient extra capacity, no extra work by the domain administrator should be required. However, if you have a problem connecting, have your administrator check the domain controller for the following issues:

**Services:** If the services related to networking such as DNS aren't running, they can't help your computer connect to the domain.

**DNS pointers:** If the DNS server on your domain doesn't know about your computer, it can't find you when you try to log on. This includes reverse lookup zones.

**DHCP scope:** If your domain uses DHCP to lease IP addresses, make sure you have enough available for the computers that are connected to your network.

**Subnet:** If you've manually assigned IP addresses, make sure each computer on the network belongs to the proper subnet. For examples of the range of IP addresses available on a subnet, see Chapter 17.

## Summary

In this chapter, we've looked at how to set up and configure an XP Workstation connection to a domain, attach to network resources, understand roaming and mandatory user profiles, and troubleshoot your network when things go awry. In the next chapter, we'll stick with the domains topic but focus our efforts on understanding Windows Server 2003.

# Chapter 21

# Working with Windows Server 2003

Any discussion of connecting to domains is incomplete without talking about Microsoft's most current offering in the server space, Windows Server 2003. As pointed out in Chapter 20, the true power of networking comes with being able to control resources and security from a centralized location. Windows 2000 introduced Active Directory, which allowed you centralized control while granting flexibility in your management structure as well as providing convenient management tools.

Windows Server 2003 still uses the basic core of Active Directory. But of course, because it's a newer product, there are updated features that didn't come with Windows 2000. Because the structure of Active Directory has not changed a great deal, this chapter won't focus on stuffing those types of details into your head. Rather, this chapter discusses new features of Windows Server 2003 and how they will impact your network.

Here are the topics included in this chapter:

- ◆ The Windows Server 2003 family tree
- ◆ Integration with Windows XP
- ◆ Two key server additions
- ◆ Networking improvements
- ◆ Active Directory improvements
- ◆ Security enhancements
- ◆ Other improvements
- ◆ Connecting Windows XP Professional to Windows Server 2003 domains

## The Five Flavors of Server 2003

Microsoft isn't quite Baskin-Robbins yet, but to some administrators, it seems like it's getting that way. In the good old days of Windows NT 3.5, there was only one version. Windows NT 4 also had an Enterprise Edition, which used an enhanced memory model and offered clustering. Because it was more expensive and didn't provide a lot of added value, few people used it.

Enter Windows Server 2003: Now there are five. Well, okay, if you include the 64-bit versions, the embedded versions, and so on, there are actually a lot more. But the main product grouping includes these five flavors:

- ◆ Windows Server 2003 Standard Edition

- ◆ Windows Server 2003 Enterprise Edition (32-bit and 64-bit)

- ◆ Windows Server 2003 Datacenter Edition (32-bit and 64-bit)

- ◆ Windows Server 2003 Web Edition

- ◆ Windows Small Business Server 2003

Which one is right for you? I'm glad you asked. Let's browse some of the features of each, and that might help you make up your mind.

## No More "Plain Old Server"

For the first time since 1983, the basic variety of server has a name; it is now Windows Server 2003 Standard Edition. In general, it has just about all of the features that it did back when it didn't have a name; it just takes twice as long to say.

Standard Edition comes with a bunch of new features that are new to all of 2003's editions, as you'd expect, but it also comes with a bit of quite welcome news: Standard Edition includes Network Load Balancing (NLB) (if you want clustering, you will still have to pony up for either Enterprise or Datacenter). NLB's not new, since it was included in Windows 2000 Advanced Server, the more expensive version of Windows 2000 Server. But where Microsoft once required you to buy the pricier version of 2000 Server to get this very useful feature, it's now included in all editions of Windows Server 2003. But that's not all that's new in Standard Edition—for instance, how does "You finally get a complete e-mail server free in the box" sound? Like sweet music in a field of daisies.

## Just for Web Servers

Windows Server 2003 Web Edition is the first Microsoft server offering specifically for web servers. The idea is that Microsoft really wants their web server, IIS, to completely crush, overtake, and over-whelm the competition: Apache and Sun web servers. So they ripped a bunch of things out of Server and offered it to hardware vendors as an OEM-only copy of Server 2003. It can address only 2GB of RAM (NT has always been able to access 4 or more GB) and supports only 2-way SMP, not 4-way.

- ◆ Be a domain controller, although it can join a domain

- ◆ Support Macintosh clients, save as a web server

- ◆ Be accessed remotely via Terminal Services, although it has Remote Desktop, like XP

- ◆ Provide Internet Connection Sharing or Net Bridging

- ◆ Be a DHCP or fax server

So it's unlikely that you'll actually see a copy of Web Edition, but if you do, then don't imagine that you'll be able to build a whole network around it. As its name suggests, it's pretty much intended as a platform for cheap web servers.

## Enterprise and Datacenter Features

Back in the NT 4 days, Microsoft introduced a more expensive version of Server called NT 4 Server, Enterprise Edition. It supported clusters and a larger memory model. When Windows 2000 Server came around, Microsoft renamed it Windows 2000 Advanced Server. With Server 2003, Microsoft still offers this higher-end version of Server but with yet another name change. Now it's called Windows

Server 2003 Enterprise Edition. Yes, you read that right: once it was Enterprise Edition, then it became Advanced Server, and now it's back to Enterprise Edition. Remember, people get paid big money to make naming decisions like these.

Enterprise Edition still does clusters—four-PC clusters now. It also lets you boot a server from a Storage Area Network (SAN), hot-install memory like Datacenter can, and run with four processors (eight if you have Enterprise). As of the writing of this book, only 32-bit versions of Server 2003 support these features (not the 64-bit versions). And of course, your hardware might limit you on some cool features, such as hot-installing memory.

With Server 2003, Microsoft has finally made me covetous of Datacenter. It has this incredibly cool tool called Windows System Resource Manager (also available in Enterprise) that basically lets you do the kind of system management that you could do on the mainframe years and years ago. How'd you like to say to your system, "Don't let SQL Server ever use more than 50 percent of the CPU power or 70 percent of the RAM?" WRM lets you do that, and it ships only with Datacenter. Datacenter also now supports eight-PC clusters as well as hot-installing RAM—yup, that's right, you just open the top of the server *while it is running* and insert a new memory module, wait a second or two, and the system now recognizes the new RAM, no reboot required. How cool is *that*?

### Small Business Server 2003

Based on the title alone, I can hear you thinking, "Gee, I bet this is for people who run small businesses." How absolutely correct you are. Microsoft's rationale behind offering a small business product is pretty simple. Small businesses, by nature, are strapped for resources. Instead of needing to hire an IT professional or worry about domain management issues that they don't have the time or expertise to deal with, why not make it easy? Make Server easy to install, manage, and use: that's the goal of Windows Small Business Server 2003.

Small Business Server 2003 comes in two varieties (see, I told you there were a ton): Standard Edition and Premium Edition. Premium Edition has three primary add-ons: ISA Server (Internet firewall), SQL Server (database), and FrontPage 2003 (design websites). All in all, Small Business Server 2003 has most of the same features as Windows Server 2003 Standard Edition (minus a few), but it's not nearly as stripped down as Web Edition.

Perhaps the biggest advantage to small businesses is that Small Business Server 2003 is cheaper than Standard Edition. Depending on where you buy it, you can generally find it for about 40 percent less than Standard Edition.

# XP Integration Is Here!

Windows 2000 Server came with a file named `adminpak.msi` that would let you install all of the administrative tools for a 2000 network on a 2000 Pro desktop. I *loved* that, since NT Workstation never really did a great job as an administrator's desktop and I always ended up running Server as my desktop OS. But 2000 Pro was a different story; get `adminpak.msi` on the Win2K Pro box and you could do all the server administration that you wanted.

When XP was first launched, there was outrage in the IT administration community. None of the server administration tools worked any more. The only ways to control your DNS server, AD domain controllers, DHCP server, and the like were either by keeping a Win2K machine around somewhere, walking over to the server to work on it, or just using Terminal Services to remotely control the server. It was irritating at best. Microsoft now has administrative tools that work on XP, but many administrators were left with a bitter taste in their mouth.

So it's good news that Microsoft did it right with Server 2003. There's a whole new set of administrative tools that run fine on XP.

To my mind, XP's two absolute best features from an administrator's point of view are its remote control/support and software-restriction capabilities. Both of those capabilities either absolutely require or considerably benefit from Group Policies, but Server 2000 knew nothing about them and so required some tweaking to support XP-specific policies on a Windows 2000–based Active Directory. That's all taken care of now, because Server 2003 supports XP Group Policies.

## Free E-mail Server and SQL Server "Lite"

Thank you, Microsoft.

Not too many people remember this, but back when Server first came out, it wasn't all that impressive in terms of performance. But over time, it took market share away from network OSes that were, in many ways, faster, more flexible, or more reliable. How'd they do it? Many ways, but I've always thought that there were two biggies. First, NT used the Windows interface, which meant that once you'd mastered Solitaire you were well on the way to administering an NT Server.

The second reason was that NT came with a lot of stuff free in the box. From the very beginning, NT contained software that most vendors charged for. At one time, most server OS vendors charged for the TCP/IP protocol, but NT always had it. Ditto remote access tools, or Macintosh support, or a web server, or FTP, or a dozen other things. In terms of features, Microsoft made NT an attractive proposition.

So I could never understand why they didn't include an e-mail server. Well, okay, I understood it—they wanted to sell you MS Mail (you in the back there, stop laughing) or Exchange and didn't want to offer a free alternative. But I've never understood that. Exchange is a mail server that, while powerful, is complex, difficult to set up, and expensive. Why not offer an e-mail server that is nothing more than an SMTP and POP3–based system? It would serve that five-person office well, and they're probably not about to buy Exchange. Nor would it keep the 100-person (or 100,000-person) enterprise from buying Exchange, because they're probably large enough that they want support for shared calendars, IMAP, mailbox forwarding, antivirus add-ons, and so on, and a super-basic POP3 service wouldn't do it.

I got my wish. All versions of Windows Server 2003 include a POP3 service. The other part, SMTP, has always existed, so between the two of them, you've got a complete low-end mail server. Again, there are no hooks for antivirus software, no way to set a mailbox to automatically forward to somewhere else, and no way to create an autoresponse message for a mailbox a la "Jack doesn't work here anymore; please don't send any more mail here to his address," but it may still do the job for you.

The next goodie wasn't on my wish list, but I'll bet it was on a lot of other people's: a free database engine. Even better, it's a free database engine that is a copy of SQL Server 2000, although with a "governor" and no administrative tools.

For years, Microsoft has offered a thing called Microsoft Database Engine, or MSDE. It was never generally available to NT users, but it was available to various groups of developers. The idea with MSDE was that Microsoft took SQL Server 2000—a fairly expensive piece of software—and crippled it in three ways:

◆   First, they limited the database size to 2GB. That may not sound like a big deal, but a "real" application of any size could grow beyond that very quickly. But it's a great size for testing and developing database-driven apps or for managing a database that will never get very big.

◆ Second, they put a "throttle" (Microsoft's word) on it so that if more than five people access it, it slows down. Again, it's a barrier to using this for member registration on a thousand-member website, but it's fine for testing and small networks.

◆ Finally, they do not ship any administrative tools for MSDE. If you want to do something as simple as changing the password on the default "sa" account, you'll have to do some scripting.

None of that is intended to sound negative, even though it's true the MSDE is a severely cut-down version of SQL Server 2000. The price is right and once you get past the basic lack of an admin interface—the hard part—then you'll find that it's a pretty nice add-on.

## Networking Enhancements

What good is a new server product if it doesn't include networking improvements? When Windows XP came out, it included some networking features that Windows 2000 Server didn't have. That made for an interesting paradox that the client system had more advanced networking features (in some cases) than the server. No longer is this the case, because Windows Server 2003 includes XP's networking functionality. New Windows Server 2003 networking features include

◆ NAT traversal (discussed in Chapter 12)

◆ IPSec NAT traversal (like NAT traversal, but secure)

◆ Routing and Remote Access Service (RRAS) NBT Proxy

◆ DNS conditional forwarding supporting multidomain AD-integrated networks

There are others as well, but these are some of the most useful upgrades.

## Active Directory Improvements

For a first try, Windows 2000's Active Directory was pretty good…not bad for a 1.0, Microsoft. (Of course, they *did* have Banyan and Novell's directory services to learn from, but let's ignore that for this discussion.) In Server 2003, Microsoft dishes up a 1.1 version of AD that solves several irritating problems, makes running branch offices easier, and expands AD's flexibility.

While I don't want this to sound negative, it's a fact that Active Directory still suffers most from its inflexibility—there is no simple way to rearrange the structure of an existing forest, to merge forests into one forest, or to break off a piece of a forest and make it a forest of its own. Don't think that those scenarios are marginal or unusual ones—they're not. The reorganizations that most organizations undergo every year or so often require rearranging a forest. Two firms merging need to be able to merge their forests as well. And a firm divesting itself of a subsidiary would want to be able to detach one or more domains or trees from a forest. But perhaps that will appear in a future version of Server; let's hope so.

Meanwhile, the 2003 edition of AD has, again, some very good news. Here's a look at its high points.

### Forest-to-Forest Trusts

Combining a bunch of AD domains into a forest offers two main benefits: first, those domains all automatically trust each other, and, second, the domains share a set of "super" domain controllers called global catalog (GC) servers, which are domain controllers that contain a subset of information not just about their own domains but about every single domain in the forest. Doing away with the unreliability of NT 4 trusts for the convenience and dependability of AD's automatic trusts is a big win for AD users.

But, as I suggested a few paragraphs back, AD forests were and are still pretty inflexible. So suppose you're an organization that finds itself with more than one forest, and you need to get those forests to share things? Well, there's always been the hard way—get a migration tool and copy all of the user accounts, machine accounts, and other objects from Forest 1 to Forest 2 and then just plain delete Forest 1. The problem with that solution is that while migration tools are pretty nice, they don't do the whole job and they're a lot of work to get working.

With a Server 2003–based forest, however, you have a new answer: forest root trusts. With these, you just build one new trust relationship between Forest 1 and Forest 2, and instantly every domain in Forest 1 trusts every domain in Forest 2 and vice versa. Cool; thank you, Redmond.

But I said that forests had two main features—complete trust and a centralized database of forest information called the global catalog. A forest-to-forest trust gives us back the first benefit of a single forest; what about the second? Unfortunately, two forests that trust each other do not share a global catalog. That means that forest trusts will not let applications that are GC-dependent see the trusting forests as one single overall directory. What apps are GC-dependent? Well, the most prominent one is Exchange 2000: it really wants to see your organization as one big forest. Forest trusts don't solve that problem.

I was surprised to learn of another limitation to forest trusts: they're not transitive. Interestingly enough, if Forest 1 trusts Forest 2 and Forest 2 trusts Forest 3, then Forest 1 does not trust Forest 3. Bummer. And *none* of this forest trust stuff works at all until you've upgraded every single DC in every single domain of both forests to Server 2003. So, overall the forest trusts are a good step forward…but not the whole story.

## Group Replication Problem Solved

It's always been ironic that while Active Directory can support a far larger user list than could NT 4 domains, AD couldn't support *groups* as large as NT 4 could. You can create literally millions of users in an AD, but because of a quirk in AD's method of keeping domain controllers' information consistent (AD replication) in combination with the way that group membership is stored in AD, you can't put more than about 5,000 users into a group.

In 2003's AD, Microsoft restructured the way they store group membership, and now the sky's the limit. It also solves another problem wherein it is possible in 2000's AD that you and I work in the same worldwide company and you change a group's membership while sitting in the Edenton office while I change that same group's membership while sitting in the Port Angeles office, and one of our changes overwrites the other person's changes. With 2003, that's fixed.

To get this benefit, you must upgrade all of the DCs in all of the domains in your forest to 2003.

## Domains Can Be Renamed

One of 2000's most annoying AD limitations was that it prevented you from renaming a domain; if Bell Atlantic had had an AD forest when it merged with GTE and was renamed Verizon, there would have been no way to rename an AD domain named bellatlantic.com to verizon.com. Now you can rename a domain, but it's not a simple matter, even now.

First, every DC in the domain to be renamed (not all DCs in the forest, just the ones in the domain) must be running Server 2003. And second, there are…well, I was going to write "… a few steps to perform in order to complete the domain renaming," but the truth is that Microsoft has a white paper online explaining how to do it.

The paper is *60 pages long*. So it's *possible*, just not easy, at least not yet.

## AD Can Selectively Replicate

Active Directory is a database, and domain controllers are database servers, just like systems running Access, Oracle, MySQL, or SQL Server and holding some other kind of database. (Well, not *just* like…DCs do not respond to SQL queries. Instead, their query language is LDAP.) While the AD database was originally designed for storing user accounts, machine accounts, and the like, there's no reason application designers can't take advantage of AD's built-in database engine to store other information.

Microsoft's own programmers did just that when designing 2000's DNS server. As you may know, 2000 introduced you to the option to create a DNS zone that was an Active Directory–integrated zone. A zone of that type stores the DNS info for your systems in the AD itself and replicates it along with the normal domain information from DC to DC. But *only* DCs get copies of the database, so if you choose AD-integrated DNS, all of your DNS servers must be DCs.

But now consider: what if you had a lot of DCs, but only a few of them were DNS servers? Wouldn't that be a bit wasteful? You'd use precious bandwidth to replicate DNS info to every DC, whether it used it or not. Server 2003 solves that problem with the notion of an *application directory partition*. Partitions are subsets of the AD that replicate only to a subset of DCs. Microsoft then applied that notion to their DNS servers, so in a network using AD-integrated zones only the DCs running DNS will get the DNS info. This feature doesn't require any preparation; you get its benefit on any DC running Server 2003.

# Better Security

Sometime in late 2001, two things occurred to Bill Gates: first, network security is important and, second, Microsoft software is buggy as heck when it comes to security (among other things), so a lot of Microsoft security is lacking a bit. So he derailed virtually all of Microsoft's coding efforts for two months as Microsoft trained nearly everyone about security.

In the end, this was a good thing. NT has always had a reputation of being an insecure operating system (the joke was that NT was a perfectly secure operating system until you installed the NIC), but it's an inaccurate reputation. NT (3.1–4, and Windows 2000) is an extremely secure OS in that it provides the option to lock many things; a properly tweaked NT server is a secure server indeed. NT's reputation comes, however, from the fact that a default installation leaves the vast majority of those locks unlocked. For Server 2003, that changes.

For example, NT 4 and Windows 2000 installed an unsecured web server by default on every server you ever installed. Not a good idea, as we learned in June 2001 when a worm called Code Red infected millions of servers—*through the web server*. With Server 2003, in contrast, you don't get IIS unless you ask for it. And even then, it's a pretty locked-down version of IIS.

To see another example, look at the NTFS permissions on the C drive of any Server 2003 computer. Where the default permission for every previous version of NT was Everyone/Full Control—"C'mon in, y'all, we're all friends here!"—Server 2003 gives Everyone only Read and Execute permission on the root of C. The Users group has more power because it can read files and create folders on C, but it cannot create new files on the root of C. You can change all of this, of course, but by default Server 2003 is a bit tighter security-wise than its predecessors.

That's a good thing. But it won't be an unmixed blessing. I'm sure that at least once in your life you will be sitting at the server trying to get something done but getting nowhere. You've got Help open, or a book at your side—this one, I hope!—clicking where the book says to click and dragging where the book says to drag, but it's not working. In that case, you may be doing the right thing but lack the permissions to do it. So Server 2003 offers us one more impediment to getting our jobs done: we'll have to wend a maze of security to do some things.

But don't take that as a negative comment. It is simply a fact of life in the twenty-first century that there are tons of dirt bags out there and the Internet has now given them the chance to come knock at our doors, so we have no choice but to install locks on our doors. Yes, it was nice back in the days when we didn't have to lock our doors or carry keys, but those days are gone forever. Operating systems are just changing with the times.

In addition, there are other security enhancements that dive deeper than the generalities I mentioned already.

## Profiles and Policies

When they first arrived, roaming profiles seemed like a great idea…but then we tried them. Slow, prone to breaking…auugh! But Windows 2000 made them more palatable, and so has Server 2003.

First of all, there's a new Group Policy that you can apply to a machine (or machines) that says, "ignore all roaming profiles." This is terrific—now I can ensure that just my laptop and desktop get my roaming profile, by setting up all of the public access/shared systems and the servers to "ignore roamers."

Another Group Policy makes roaming profiles better for laptop users. Sometimes I'll check into a hotel and find that it offers Ethernet connections to the Internet (yippee! I will sleep on a *stone floor* if it means I get high-speed Internet access), so I plug my laptop into the Ethernet and boot it up, only to realize that my stupid laptop is trying to suck my roaming profile over the Internet. A half hour later, it gives up.

Or at least that's what *used* to happen. Now I just set the Group Policy on my laptop that stops and asks, "Do you want to download your roaming profile?" I say no and log on in seconds. (Of course, the laptop must be running XP.)

Those are just two examples of the new things you can do to control profiles; there are many more.

## Software Restriction Group Policies

Every help and support desk person has a little list of things she'd like to see. One is almost always "I'd really like to keep users from running particular programs on the system." (If you're having trouble thinking of examples, then see if the names Morpheus and Kazaa ring any bells.) With XP desktops, you can do that.

XP and Server 2003 include a whole new set of Group Policies called software restriction policies. With them, you can tell a desktop, "Nothing runs except Word, Internet Explorer, Outlook, and the Palm Desktop." It's pretty neat and pretty powerful.

## The Group Policy Management Console (GPMC)

After reading the last section, you may be shaking your head saying, "Yeah, that's nice and all, but you're talking about Group Policies? Those guys are a nightmare." Yes, they can be, particularly when a Group Policy refuses to run—"Let's see, I just created this policy that keeps Access from running on Ronnie's desktop and he can *still* run Access!" Several things might keep your new policy from running—Ronnie's desktop might not have refreshed policies, or it might have refreshed policies but your policy might have been overridden by another policy. You look and see that there are only 24 other policies that apply to Ronnie and his desktop, so it's time to start sifting through policies…or not.

Microsoft has been working on a really terrific Group Policy troubleshooting tool called Group Policy Management Console. It *didn't* ship with Server 2003 originally, but it's available (for XP and Server 2003) and free at `www.microsoft.com/downloads`. Just search for Group Policy Management Console.

# Other Improvements

I could literally write an entire book talking about Windows Server 2003 features—wait, I *did!*—but that's obviously for a different book. By now, I hope your curiosity is piqued. Just in case it's not, I will leave you with three more enhancements that you might find useful: remote administration, reliability, and storage improvements.

## Remote Administration Upgrades

For years, remote administration and control of Microsoft operating systems drove me nuts. It seemed only Microsoft OSes required you to be physically sitting down at a computer in order to control the software running on it. Sure, there were third-party alternative tools such as PCAnywhere or VNC, but remote control/admin always seemed like something that really needed to be "in the box," integrated into the OS.

Windows 2000, then, was a great advance, incorporating remote Telnet sessions and a remote control tool called Terminal Services that was a cut-down version of a program from a company named Citrix. Terminal Services ran only on Server, though, so remote control of 2000 Pro boxes was dicey.

Windows XP Professional and Windows Server 2003 include Microsoft's adaptation of Citrix's remote control product. It and the server version of Terminal Services are built around a tool called the Remote Desktop Protocol (RDP). Microsoft has improved RDP to make it run on slower connections, and I'm not exaggerating when I say that remote control over a 40-kilobit dial-up connection works very well, almost as well as sitting at the computer.

RDP also matures in that it automatically gives your remote control session access to your local printers and drives, something that Terminal Services for Windows 2000 couldn't do. It supports colors beyond the simple 8-bit, 256 color of Windows 2000's RDP, and it transports sound as well.

Perhaps even better, XP and Server 2003 repackage RDP in two forms: *remote desktop support* and *remote assistance*. These are ways to provide remote control or offer remote assistance, but they are nothing more than new user interfaces placed atop Terminal Services. If you've not used them yet for XP, try them; they're great! If you want more information, look in Chapter 14.

Finally, Server 2003 offers a completely new set of remote control tools in the form of web pages. You can install a bunch of modules on your server that will let someone do approximately 80 percent of the administrative functions you'll ever need, all through a secure web connection. The bottom line is that we don't have to put up with those Unix guys kicking sand in our faces telling us that their OS is more manageable!

## Better Reliability

Windows 2000's System File Protection and Driver Verifier made great strides in making Windows 2000 far sturdier than its NT 4 predecessor; XP took that further with System Restore, Application Verifier, and

Driver Rollback. As with some other Server 2003 features, they're not exactly new, since they first appeared in XP, but they're new to Server.

Driver Verifier was—and is—a useful tool for checking up on new device drivers and other system-level programs. It was a great addition to 2000 and still is, with Server 2003; smoking out problems with kernel-mode programs is far easier with its help. It's covered in Chapter 27.

Application Verifier performs a similar service but for user-mode programs. Have a program that ran fine under NT 4 or Windows 9*x* but won't run under Server 2003? Then run it under Application Verifier. When it fails, Application Verifier will tell you what caused it to fail and, even better, it can add information to the application that lets it run under Windows Server 2003.

Another source of operating system instability can be new drivers. You've got the system running fine, but the vendor of one of your pieces of hardware comes out with a new driver. Since it looks like you're running smoothly, you're leery about chancing it with a new driver…there must be some subtle bug that someone found that this updated driver fixes, but this new driver could make your system unstable…what to do? Well, Driver Verifier is a great way to check out a new driver, as it was in Windows 2000. But now it's got a simple partner in Driver Rollback. You load a driver and decide that it's no good…now, where did you put the old driver? Just go to Device Manager, find the device with the new driver, right-click it, and choose Properties. You'll see a new button, Rollback Driver. Like XP, Server 2003 keeps the previous version of all drivers.

## Improved Storage

Windows XP Professional and Server 2003 brought some much-needed fixes to NTFS and one great new feature: volume shadowing.

In brief, volume shadowing lets you take snapshots of a file share. At predetermined times of the day, Server 2003 will record the status of whatever it's shadowing and let you roll back to that quickly and easily. For example, suppose you keep your important documents in share `\\serv01\documents`. You could tell 2003 Server to take snapshots—*shadow copies* is the Microsoft term—of the files in that share at 7 A.M., 10:30 A.M., noon, and 6 P.M.

A few days later, at 10:15 A.M., you realize that you've accidentally deleted an important document. But all's not lost; just fire up the shadow copy client software (included with Server 2003) and restore the 7 A.M. version of the document. A few hours' work lost, but that's all. And no need to go find the tape librarian and beg to get a tape with last night's backup mounted.

Volume shadowing lets you create a kind of imaginary copy of a file, with the state of that file frozen in time. That means that you can take shadow copies of open files and then back up the shadow copy! For example, suppose you have a SQL database that you need to back up every day, but there's never a good time to stop the database server. No problem: take a shadow copy at 3 A.M. That copy does not change on a second-by-second basis, unlike your real SQL database file, so you can back it up at your leisure.

I told you that NTFS got some other improvements; they include the following:

- ◆ NTFS clusters can be any size, unlike Windows 2000, where their cluster size could not exceed 4KB or the volume could not be defragmented.

- ◆ A server can now host as many Dfs (Distributed File System) roots as you like; Windows 2000 allowed each server to host just one root.

- ◆ Offline files can now cache encrypted files.

- ◆ You can set up encrypted files so that more than one person can view an encrypted file.

◆ You can now both compress and encrypt a file.

◆ EIDE drives can now run independently, meaning that you can run a small database server with two EIDE drives rather than SCSI drives—one drive for the database, the other for the transaction log. This was always possible in NT but never made sense, because EIDE drives were limited to run only one at a time—if your SQL software said to the hardware, "Save these bytes to the database file and those bytes to the transaction log," then in actuality the OS would make the EIDE drives take turns. It might first write the bytes to the drive holding the database file while the drive holding the transaction log cooled its heels, and then write to the transaction log while keeping the database idle. The techie term for this would be that EIDE drives are now *asynchronous*, at least when they are on different channels—for example, this works if one hard disk is on the primary EIDE channel and the other is on the secondary EIDE channel.

None of those are truly earth-shaking, but they're all quite welcome improvements.

# Connecting to a Windows Server 2003 Domain

Windows XP Professional is the ideal client for Windows Server 2003. The client and server operating system and user interface are the same, and XP supports all of the great Server 2003 features, including remote administration, remote installation services, and Group Policies. Universal Plug and Play makes installation of your supported network card driver virtually automatic. If your network card is present and detected when the OS is being installed, XP automatically loads the driver. If you accept the typical network settings during the installation of XP, setup will go ahead and install TCP/IP Protocol and the Client for Microsoft Networks. If you install the NIC later, XP automatically detects the new hardware and loads a driver or prompts the user for the location of the correct driver. Either way, once the driver for the NIC is loaded, you're home free. If you need only the TCP/IP protocol and the Client for Microsoft Networks, there's not much for the admin to do except join a domain or specify a workgroup.

## Verify Your Network Configuration

First, log on to the system as a user with administrative rights. Before trying to join the domain, you should at least take a look at the Network Connections applet in Control Panel to ensure that the network card was detected and the appropriate software has been loaded. As shown in Figure 21.1, if the network software has loaded properly, you will see an icon named Local Area Connection (if you have more than one NIC installed, you will see more than one Local Area Connection icon). You should see that the connection is enabled, and if you highlight the connection and expand the details (as in the lower-left side of Figure 21.2), you should also see the IP address that was assigned by DHCP. If you do not see a Local Area Connection icon, your NIC may not have been properly detected. Use Device Manager to isolate the problem, or try to add the network adapter manually using the Add New Hardware Wizard in Control Panel and your OEM-provided disk or CD-ROM.

If everything looks correct, right-click the Local Area Connection icon and choose Properties to view your network configuration information. The Properties page, shown in Figure 21.3, lists installed components: network card type, protocol, and the client software. TCP/IP is automatically configured to use DHCP; to statically assign IP information, select TCP/IP and choose Properties. Figure 21.4 shows the Internet Protocol (TCP/IP) Properties page.

**FIGURE 21.1**

The Local Area Connection icon in Network Connections

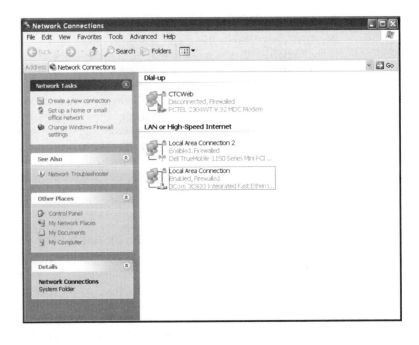

**FIGURE 21.2**

The Local Area Connection details

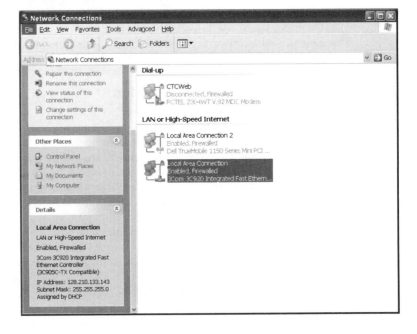

**FIGURE 21.3**

Local Area Connection
Properties page

**FIGURE 21.4**

Internet Protocol
Properties page

**NOTE**   To be absolutely certain that your network card and TCP/IP are working properly, open a command prompt, use IPCONFIG to verify your DHCP addressing, and then use Ping to test network connectivity. Ping your IP address, the IP of the router, and the IP of the server or another node on your network. While you are at it, ping a couple of systems by name to test your DNS resolution. See Chapter 17 for more information on troubleshooting network problems with TCP/IP.

## Joining a Domain

Now that you know your network card is working properly and you have successfully obtained configuration information from DHCP, it's time to join the domain. If your Windows XP Professional client will exist in an Active Directory environment, you need to create a machine account for it in the target domain. Members of the Administrators and Account Operators group on the domain can use the Active Directory Users and Computers tool to do this beforehand, and that is the recommended course of action. However, you can also create a machine account from the workstation during the network part of the setup program, or you can use the System Control Panel, if you know the username and password of an account with the ability to create machine accounts in the domain. I'll give you the steps to create the machine account from the workstation as you join the machine to the domain.

To join a domain, open the System applet. The System applet is in Control Panel, or you can right-click My Computer from the Start menu and choose Properties. I prefer this to wrangling with the XP Control Panel's Category View. Navigate to the Computer Name tab (see Figure 21.5). The XP Professional System, QDOCLAP, currently belongs to a workgroup named MSHOME (which is the default for Windows XP). Click Change to join a domain. As shown in Figure 21.6, change the radio button selection to Domain and type in your domain name, **SUSHIYUM.COM** in this case. Notice that you use the full Active Directory domain name here, not the NetBIOS name SUSHIYUM. Click OK. If an account for the system does not already exist on the domain, XP prompts you to supply a domain username and password with permission to create the account. If all goes well, you'll see a message welcoming you to the domain.

Restart the system for the changes to take effect. When the system restarts, you'll have the option to log on using a local account or using a domain user account. To access resources on the domain, users need to log on with a domain user account. Activate the drop-down list for Log On To and choose your domain name. From now on, the default choice will be to log on to the domain, not the local machine. When XP is finished logging you on and loading your personal settings, it's time to connect to network resources.

**FIGURE 21.5**
Computer Name tab in
System Properties

**FIGURE 21.6**

The Computer Name
Changes dialog box

**NOTE**  How is it possible to join the workstation to the domain and then log on using a domain account? How does the workstation identify you and assign you rights and permissions? Actually, when the workstation joins the domain, the domain's Domain Users group is added to the workstation's local Users group membership. In addition, the Domain Admins group is added to the Administrators group on the local workstation. By default, then, if a domain controller authenticates you as a member of the Domain Users group, the workstation will accept you as a local user. And if the domain controller recognizes you as a Domain Admin, the workstation will grant you local admin rights as well. This is the default behavior for all NT-based client operating systems: Windows Server 2003, Windows .NET, Windows XP, Windows 2000, and Windows NT.

## Connecting to Network Resources

The easiest way to connect to network resources is to use the My Network Places icon on your desktop. You can also get to it through My Computer, by opening My Computer from the Start menu and choosing My Network Places from the list of Other Places (see Figure 21.7).

My Network Places, shown in Figure 21.8, offers several different options for finding and connecting to network resources. Here are three of the most common methods:

◆ Click on Add a Network Place to use the Add Network Place Wizard to create a shortcut to a network resource. The wizard can locate the resource using a UNC name (\\***SERVER**\***SHARE***), which you provide, or you can open a browse list from within the wizard.

◆ Use Search Active Directory for shared folders or printers. This works only for shares and printers that have actually been published in Active Directory, though.

◆ Browse the network by choosing Entire Network from Other Places. This is the Network Neighborhood–style browse list that you've been familiar with since Windows 95.

**FIGURE 21.7**
Open My Network Places
from My Computer.

**FIGURE 21.8**
Finding resources from
My Network Places

Remember, of course, that to connect to a resource, you must have the proper permissions to access that resource.

### Changing Domain Passwords

It is good security practice for users to change their password the first time they log on to the network. It's also a default parameter set when the admin first creates a new user account. So if a user is logging on to the network for the first time, they will see a message informing them that they must change their password. The Change Password dialog box then opens and the user types the old password and the new one (twice for confirmation). If the old password is correct and the new password meets the password criteria and both new entries match each other, the user sees a confirmation of the password change and the logon process continues.

After the initial logon and password change, administrators can use Active Directory Users and Computers (from Windows Server 2003) to reset a user's password or to expire a password so that the user must change it the next time they log on. Users can change their own domain passwords after logging on by using Ctrl+Alt+Del and the Change Password button. The Ctrl+Alt+Del sequence is the same one used to lock the computer or shut it down, so it's important that everyone knows about it.

## Summary

This chapter covered some basics of Windows 2003, to help you understand how the operating system works, as well as how to join your Windows XP Professional computer to a Windows Server 2003 domain.

First, we discussed the different varieties of Server 2003. Then, we moved into some of the more notable features of Server 2003, including better e-mail server and database server functionality, networking improvements, Active Directory enhancements, and a few other nifty additions. Finally, this chapter ended with a discussion of how to join an XP computer to a Windows 2003 domain.

Of course, this book focuses on Windows XP Professional and does not provide a complete discussion of Windows Server 2003. For that, you will want to get *Mastering Windows Server 2003*.

Now that we've talked a lot about Microsoft-based networks, it's time to turn our attention to the competitors. Not that everyone doesn't love Microsoft, but there are other server products out there, and you need to be able to make your Windows XP Professional computer communicate with those products as well. The next chapter puts you on the path of cross-platform cooperation.

# Chapter 22

# Connecting to Non-Microsoft Networks

Thinking that Microsoft-based operating systems are the only ones in existence on networks is short-sighted. Although it's an oversight that Microsoft would surely allow you to maintain, now is a good time to discuss connecting to non-Microsoft operating systems and networks. This section specifically looks at connecting to Novell NetWare, Unix, and Macintosh networks.

Novell's NetWare retains its popularity mainly because of its Novell Directory Services (NDS). NDS is a redundant, scalable, mature distributed directory service that eases administrative tasks and provides unified authentication. Microsoft provides a NetWare client to connect Windows XP Professional to NetWare servers—albeit a very basic client. In this chapter, I'll discuss the capabilities of Microsoft's Client Service for NetWare (CSNW) and show you how to install it.

Unix has been around practically since the dawn of time. Well, the dawn of computer time, anyway. Although it's a gross generalization to treat all Unix-based operating systems the same, it's the appropriate thing to do in this book. Microsoft provides a client service to attach to Unix-based servers, and we'll look at that.

Finally, contrary to popular belief, Macintosh networks do exist. We'll look at how to make your Windows XP computer play nice with Macs on a network as well.

**TIP**  When working with multiple platforms, try to keep uniform usernames for all of your users. In other words, Sheila Sanders may have an easier time accessing resources if her account name is SSanders on all platforms, instead of Sheila on one and SSanders on another.

This chapter specifically covers:

◆  Understanding the difference between NDS and bindery-based services

◆  Using Novell administration utilities

◆  Running NetWare and Windows XP Professional together

◆  Printing to Novell printers

◆  Enabling long filename support on the Novell server

◆  Choosing a Novell client solution

◆  Installing the Novell client

◆  Configuring the Novell client

◆ Understanding interoperation with Unix-based computers

◆ Working with Macintosh computers on your network

## CSNW Features

CSNW provides the following features:

**Novell script processing** CSNW processes the system and individual login scripts created by the network administrator of the Novell network.

**Seamless File and Print Services** Drive letters can be mapped to NetWare volumes either through login scripts or by using any of the mapping utilities in Windows XP Professional. These volumes appear just like a local drive, and you can continue using long filenames on NetWare mapped drives since NetWare supports long filenames. You can print to NetWare print queues using conventional UNC naming, or you can capture a queue to an LPT port using standard Windows XP Professional tools. NetWare servers are *browsable* via the Network Explorer views, which makes it even easier to find NetWare resources, map network drives, or use printer resources.

**Bindery and/or NDS authentication** Versions of NetWare prior to 4.x used a server-centric database, called the *bindery*, for authentication. NetWare versions 4.x and later still provide bindery emulation; however, the preferred method is to authenticate with NDS. CSNW can use either of these methods to connect to a NetWare file server.

**WARNING** As mentioned earlier, CSNW is a very basic client for connections to NetWare servers. Microsoft has not made a strong effort to update CSNW since it was first released for Windows NT 4. A major drawback of CSNW is its lack of IP support. NetWare administrators will be forced to load the IPX protocol on servers that contain replicas or partitions of the NDS database and any other server providing services to a Windows XP Professional using CSNW. In addition, Windows XP for 64-bit processors will not support the Client Service for NetWare because of its dependency on the IPX protocol. If you must use IP as the protocol or if you need a feature-rich client to connect to NetWare, Novell will provide a 32/64-bit client. As of this writing, the most current version of the Novell Client is 4.90 SP2. Its filename is 49SP1aCLTe.exe and you can download it from download.novell.com .

Before we look at the procedure for installing the Client Service for NetWare, let's look at the versions of NetWare to which you may have to connect—NetWare 3, 4, and 5. Much of our focus will be on version 4 and beyond since Netware 3.x is no longer a mainstream network operating system and was discontinued by Novell in October 2000. I'll also discuss how you can use printer resources on NetWare servers, and then I'll talk about utilizing login scripts and mapping drives to NetWare servers.

## Novell Directory Services versus Bindery-Based Servers

NDS and bindery services are both directory services. All network operating systems contain a directory that stores user IDs, passwords, and rights to folders at a minimum. The NDS directory is much more complicated than the bindery directory and will be the subject of most of this section, which will serve as only a primer. Having an overview of NDS will help you understand the parameters you'll need to enter to connect to NDS later when you install CSNW or a Novell-supplied client.

The hierarchy of NDS is similar to that introduced with Windows 2000 Server's Active Directory (AD). The NDS hierarchy or directory tree consists of network resources known as NDS *objects*. NDS can be compared to the directory structure on your PC's hard disk. On your PC, you organize your data by creating folders off the root directory, and you insert data files into folders. NDS is organized similarly into *containers* and *leaf* objects, respectively. NDS containers can contain other container objects, or they can contain leaf objects that represent network resources, such as servers, printers, users, and groups. All objects within NDS contain attributes or properties. The combination of all of these attributes within the directory tree is called the *schema*. The schema can be extended, so third-party application developers can extend object attributes and create completely new objects. Therefore, NDS can be more than just a directory for authentication and permissions. It can also be used to provide applications and network services. For example, it can be used to distribute applications, control hardware inventory, and monitor applications that require tight security such as a VPN (virtual private network) and e-commerce applications.

NDS containers are organizational folders that are frequently designed to look like company locations and business units. At the top is the root object. Typically the root contains only a few organizational objects called the Country (C) or Organization (O) objects. The Country object is optional, but every tree must contain an Organization object, which is typically the company name. Beneath the Organization object are containers known as organizational units (OUs). An OU can contain other OUs or it can contain leaf objects. A leaf object is often referred to by its *common name* (CN). It is important to know these objects and their abbreviations when you configure CSNW and the Novell client.

Copies of the NDS database, called replicas, are usually distributed among multiple file servers to load balance and for redundancy purposes. Replicas are synchronized so that every server contains an up-to-date version of the same informational database. Furthermore, NDS can be partitioned at various layers of the tree, so a server might contain only a portion of the database or a part of the tree. This capability is important for file servers in remote locations across wide area networks that need to conserve bandwidth and preserve CPU usage. In organizations that have many servers, some are usually dedicated to NDS. NDS can burn quite a number of processing cycles since it provides authentication services and runs a number of processes, including replication.

When you install the first Netware NDS server, you need to think through the NDS design and implementation carefully. Scrutinize all logistics, including standards-based naming conventions for all objects and the placement of OUs within the directory. A directory that has not been thought out often contains random authentication problems, and replication performance will suffer. Fortunately, Novell provides plenty of tools to resolve these issues.

A NetWare 3 server holds its security information in a security database called the *bindery*. The bindery method of security views each server as an individual entity, and the security that you assign to various directories is kept independently on each server. The bindery is a flat database, meaning it has no hierarchy and is not graphically viewed.

To illustrate the difference, assume that you have to build 100 user accounts on 5 NetWare servers and that each of the 100 users needs access to the 5 NetWare servers. In a NetWare 3 environment, you have to build 500 user accounts—one for each of the 100 users on each of the 5 servers. In a NetWare 4, 5, or 6 environment, you have to build only 100 user accounts because all 5 servers are part of the same NDS tree; you have to log on to an NDS tree only once.

This difference is important to you at the Windows XP Professional level because the information you'll provide to configure CSNW is different for bindery servers than it is for NDS. You'll need this information for troubleshooting purposes, and you will need to understand what it is you are configuring!

# Using Novell Administration Utilities

NetWare 3.*x* used various DOS-based utilities for administration. The primary utilities are called SYSCON and Pconsole. SYSCON, short for system configuration utility, is a DOS-based menu-driven program for creating users, groups, and login scripts and for managing accounting, setting directory permissions, and setting user restrictions. Pconsole, short for printer console, is also a DOS-based menu-driven program that allows you to create print queues and printers. You can also use a handful of other administrative utilities and many powerful command-line tools instead of these menu-driven applications. The following list shows them in simple alphabetical order:

| | | | |
|---|---|---|---|
| Chkvol | Help | rconsole | settts |
| Colorpal | listdir | remove | slist |
| Dspace | Map | revoke | SYSCON |
| Fconsole | Ncopy | rights | tlist |
| Filer | Ndir | security | userlist |
| Flag | Pconsole | send | volinfo |
| Flagdir | Psc | session | whoami |
| Grant | Pstat | setpass | |

You must map a drive to the NetWare volume where these utilities are located in order to run them. Windows XP Professional will not run them correctly from a UNC path.

Most administrative tasks in NDS require just one tool, the NetWare Administrator (NWADMIN). NWADMIN is a graphical view of NDS that allows you to create organizational units; create users, printers, and groups; modify login scripts; and more. NWADMIN is similar to Windows XP's Microsoft Management Console (MMC) in that you can extend the capabilities of NWADMIN by "snapping-in" new administration tools. For example, you can snap-in Symantec's Norton AntiVirus (NAV) to administrate NAV on all your NetWare servers. You can launch NWADMIN only from a workstation (running Windows 9*x*, Windows NT, Windows 2000 Professional, or Windows XP Professional) attached to a NetWare server. However, Novell has released a new administration utility called ConsoleOne (see Figure 22.1) that has many of the same features of NWADMIN and more.

ConsoleOne is a graphical tool for administering network resources, including NDS objects, schema, partitions, replicas, and NetWare servers. The real beauty of ConsoleOne is that it can be launched on the console of a Netware 5.*x* server or from a workstation. In the past, NetWare servers always required a workstation to begin administrative tasks. Now, you can walk right up to a server and begin adding users and setting permissions. This is particularly helpful in first-time installations and smaller networks.

Another cool feature of ConsoleOne is its web portal to NetWare servers that allows you to use some utilities and view the status of your NetWare file server, as shown in Figure 22.2. ConsoleOne is not fully baked, especially when running from a NetWare server. This means that not all of the utilities have been blended into ConsoleOne and you must use legacy tools, but it is Novell's intent that ConsoleOne be the complete tool for all administrative tasks, and it does show a lot of promise.

**FIGURE 22.1**
ConsoleOne will be the one-stop administration tool for Netware 5 servers and beyond.

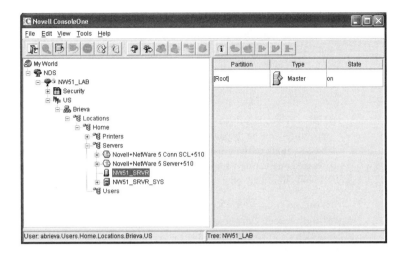

**FIGURE 22.2**
The NetWare Management Portal accessible through ConsoleOne

The bad news for people who want to use Windows XP Professional to manage their NetWare 5 network is that NWADMIN and ConsoleOne will not work with CSNW. NWADMIN and ConsoleOne require several Novell dynamic link libraries (DLLs) that are installed only when using Novell's client software. If you are serious about managing your NetWare environment from within Windows XP Professional, you should strongly consider downloading Novell's Client version 4.90 SP2 for Windows 2000 and Windows NT. Later in this chapter, I'll get into the special installation for this client that is required for Windows XP.

## Accessing a NetWare Server

After you install the Client Service for NetWare (discussed in the "Configuring Windows XP Professional to Run in Parallel with NetWare" section of this chapter), you can access the resources of a NetWare 3 server as well as a NetWare 4, 5, or 6 server, as long as you have a valid login ID and password. The login scripts that reside on the Novell server will run even on your Windows XP Professional workstation, mapping your drives and capturing your printer ports.

**NOTE**   When Windows XP Professional starts up and the CSNW is installed, you will first be prompted for the standard Windows login ID and password. The user ID and password you enter are passed along to the CSNW. Therefore, the user ID that you enter must match the ID that has been created on the NetWare file server. This is another weakness of the CSNW and a reason for using the Novell client instead of CSNW.

You can browse for NetWare servers, map network drives, and browse for network resources within the tree. Mapping a network drive is an easy way to use the same drive letter for common applications or to access shared data every time you log in to the network. You can map drives using the Map a Network Drive command that's available in every Explorer window, or you can browse through the list of server volumes on any given server. To map a network drive, follow these steps:

1. Choose Start ➢ My Network Places to open the My Network Places window.

2. Choose Tools ➢ Map Network Drive to open the Map Network Drive dialog box:

3. Click Browse to open the Browse For Folder dialog box and view a list of network resources:

4. Double-click NetWare or Compatible Network to view all NetWare servers and NDS trees.

5. Double-click a server to which you want to map a network drive.

6. You can map a drive directly to a volume or you can expand a volume to map directly to a folder on the server. Select a folder and then click OK.

7. To make this a permanent mapped drive, click the Reconnect at Logon check box, and then click Finish.

# Running NetWare and Windows Networking Together

The idea here is simple: Your office contains both a Windows server or servers (Windows NT, Windows 2000, Windows .NET, or Windows Server 2003) and a NetWare server or servers. Many NetWare servers are still using the IPX/SPX protocol, and in most cases, Windows servers will be using TCP/IP. Windows XP Professional can easily resolve this problem because it can handle network clients and run multiple protocol stacks at the same time.

**NOTE**   A common belief in the networking world is that Microsoft operating systems use only NetBEUI and that NetWare uses only IPX/SPX. Today you will typically find that both are coexisting quite well using TCP/IP to communicate. To communicate, matching protocols must be running on the server and on your Windows XP Professional client configurations.

**WARNING**   Although both operating systems can use TCP/IP to communicate over the network, the Microsoft Client Service for NetWare will work *only with the NWLink IPX/SPX protocol installed.* Here again, Microsoft is fostering the belief that NetWare uses only IPX/SPX for network communication.

## Configuring Windows XP Professional to Run in Parallel with NetWare

Running Windows XP Professional in parallel with NetWare requires that the Client Service for NetWare be installed on the Windows XP Professional machine. Installing the Client Service for NetWare is a straightforward procedure. Follow these steps:

1. Choose Start, right-click My Network Places, and choose Properties from the shortcut menu to open the Network Connections window.

2. Select Local Area Connection, and then in the Network Tasks bar, click the Change Settings of This Connection link to open the Local Area Connection Properties dialog box.

3. Click the Install button to open the Select Network Component Type dialog box.

4. Select Client from the list, and click Add to open the Select Network Client dialog box.

5. Double-click Client Service for NetWare to open the Local Area Connection Properties dialog box.

6. Click Install. Windows XP Professional copies the appropriate drivers to your system and makes changes to your Registry that enable the Client Service for NetWare to load the next time you start your system.

If you are loading the Client Service for NetWare and have not previously loaded the NWLink IPX/SPX–Compatible Transport protocol, this protocol will load automatically as you install the service. The Client Service for NetWare will not work at all without NWLink installed. If you disable NWLink, Windows XP Professional will automatically disable the Client Service for NetWare.

Normally, you do not need to modify the properties of NWLink. However, if there are multiple frame types on the same network, you may need to adjust the properties of NWLink. To change the properties of NWLink, follow these steps:

1. Select NWLINK IPX/SPX/NetBIOS Compatible Transport, and click the Properties button to open the Properties dialog box for this protocol:

2. Select your preferred frame type from the Frame Type drop-down list.

3. Click OK to save your settings.

**WARNING**   It is highly recommended that you not alter any other settings in the NWLink Properties dialog box. These refer to prior releases of Windows that were capable of emulating NetWare servers. Microsoft removed this capability in Windows 2000 and has not updated CSNW in quite some time.

After you reboot the system, Windows XP Professional attempts to log on to Novell for the first time, as shown in Figure 22.3.

With the client software provided by Microsoft, you can either log on to a Novell 3 bindery by clicking the Preferred Server button or log on to an NDS tree by clicking the Default Tree and Context button. If you are going to log on to an NDS tree, you need to provide the context of your user object within the directory tree. Your context is a path to where your user login ID resides in the tree. You need to enter the path, beginning from where the user ID resides in the tree, all the way up the tree. The path is a series of container objects separated by periods. You should not provide the parameter codes before each option (that is, omit the O= and the CN=). This is where it becomes helpful to understand NDS as explained in the previous section, " Novell Directory Services versus Bindery-Based Servers."

**FIGURE 22.3**
CSNW will prompt you to provide information the first time you attempt to log in to NetWare.

An example of entering context into CSNW is supplied in Figure 22.4. In this case, the user ID Abrieva is a user object that resides in the organizational unit called users. Working your way up the tree, you can see that the OU=users is a child of OU=home, which is a child of OU=locations, which is a child of OU=Brieva, which is a child of OU=US.

**FIGURE 22.4**
Configuring the Client Service for NetWare

Figure 22.5 displays the NetWare NDS administration tool, NWADMIN, and shows where the user object resides within the tree for this example. If you enter the context information incorrectly, you will get a dialog box telling you that you've entered the context wrong or it can't find a server. If you receive this message, you have not entered the correct context or the protocols on your Windows XP Professional do not match the protocols on the server. You can try to either reenter the correct context or abandon the NDS authentication and continue logging in to Windows XP Professional.

The nature of being a client in a networked environment is that you can log on to one server one day and log on to another server on another day. If you are an administrator, you can switch between servers more frequently. You can change the NetWare server that you log on to with great ease. In Control Panel, you will notice the CSNW icon. By clicking this icon, you can adjust your settings and the NetWare servers or tree that you log on to. The dialog box is identical to that shown earlier in Figure 22.4.

From the Configuring the Client Service for NetWare dialog box, you can specify or change the server, or you can log on to a NetWare NDS tree. In addition, you can set the print settings. The three options are as follows:

**Add Form Feed**   Adds a form feed to the end of each print job

**Notify When Printed**   Displays a screen message when your print job finishes printing

**Print Banner**   Adds a cover page to the beginning of each print job, specifying who printed the job and the date and time

Any settings that you make here will apply to any Novell print queue that this Windows XP Professional computer accesses.

The final option in CSNW determines whether the system login script that resides on the NetWare server will run. This feature will run either a NetWare 3.*x* login script or an NDS login script.

## Printing to Novell Printers

You can connect to Novell printers in Windows XP Professional in a number of ways. I'll go over the two most common.

This first option may be necessary if you want to print directly to the printer. That is, this option does not perform a redirect to an LPT port and uses UNC conventions to find printer resources.

To connect to a NetWare print queue, follow these steps:

1. Choose Start ➤ Printers and Faxes to open the Printers and Faxes folder.

2. In the Printer Tasks bar, click the Add a Printer link to start the Add Printer Wizard.

3. At the Welcome screen, click Next to open the Local or Network Printer screen.

4. Click the A Network Printer or a Printer Attached to Another Computer option, and then click Next to open the Specify a Printer screen.

5. Click the Browse for a Printer option, and then click Next to open the Browse for Printer screen:

6. Double-click NetWare or Compatible Network to view a list of servers and NDS trees. Queues that reside in NDS require that you browse the NDS tree and know the location of the queue object within the tree. Bindery queues require you to know which server the queues reside on. In either case, work your way down the server or the NDS tree to locate the queue, and then click Next to open the Printer Selection screen.

7. Select the printer manufacturer and printer model.

8. Have the appropriate driver CD or disk ready, or know the location where the driver is stored. At the Printer Driver screen, insert the disk that contains the driver when prompted, and click OK.

9. Click Finish to complete the printer installation.

Alternatively, you can capture or redirect output that is destined for an LPT to a network printer. This option is easier, but it's not for everyone. Here's what you need to do:

1. Install your printer drivers as if they were being installed to your LPT1 port. Follow the instructions above to install the printer locally. Be sure that in the Local or Network Printer screen you choose the Local Printer Attached to This Computer option, and check the Automatically Detect and Install My Plug and Play check box.

2. Choose Start ➢ My Network Places to open the My Network Places folder.

3. From the Network Tasks bar, choose View Network Connections.

4. Double-click Netware or Compatible Network to display Netware Servers and NDS Trees.

5. Double-click the Server icon to display a list of server resources, including print queues and server volumes.

6. Right-click the print queue, and select Capture Printer Port from the shortcut menu. Choose an LPT port to connect to, for example LPT1.

## Enabling Long Filename Support on the Novell Server

NetWare requires you to enable long filename support on the NetWare servers prior to revision 5. NetWare 5 and 6 file servers have long filename support enabled by default. Different revisions of NetWare require slightly different commands. It is not necessary to restart the server after entering these commands; however, this process will slow your NetWare server down dramatically. Make sure you perform these tasks after hours.

For versions of NetWare earlier than 4.10, follow these steps:

1. At the NetWare server prompt, type the following:

   Load os2
   add name space os2 to volume sys

   (and to every volume where you want long filename support)

2. Add the following to the startup.ncf file:

   load os2

For versions of NetWare 4.11 and later, follow these steps:

1. At the NetWare server prompt, type the following:

   Load long
   add name space long to volume sys

   (and to every volume where you want long filename support)

2. Add the following to the startup.ncf file:

   load long

## Choosing a Novell Client Solution

I've already mentioned that the Novell 32-bit client solution has more features than CSNW and that it will resolve problems with TCP/IP connectivity and using NDS administration tools. Novell's client is a true 32-bit client, and eventually we may see a 64-bit version of the client.

Novell has a package of network tools called Zero Effort Networking, or *ZENworks*. ZEN.works gives you complete control over desktop and user management from the NetWare 4 and newer environments. It's actually similar in many ways to Microsoft's Zero Administration Windows (ZAW) initiative in that it uses policies and login scripts to manage users and computers. But in the case of ZENworks, the policies are being applied based on NDS objects across all client platforms, not just one version of Windows.

The full version of ZENworks provides several useful help desk functions as well, including a ticketing system for reporting problems and remote control ability. The version that is supplied with NetWare 5 and newer is the "light" version, which includes everything except the help desk tools and is supported by all the current Novell client platforms.

## Installing the Novell Client

Before you even think about installing the Novell Client, make sure that CSNW is not already installed on your Windows XP Professional system. Such an installation causes horrible instability in Windows XP and should be avoided at all costs. If CSNW is installed, remove it and reboot your computer.

**NOTE** Always look for the latest Novell client available. Windows clients are available on Novell's website at download.novell.com.

Here's how to install the Novell client:

1. After downloading the client, double-click the executable and extract the contents to a subdirectory on your computer.

2. In the directory where you unzipped the files, navigate to the /WINNT/i386 directory (we all know that WINNT is old, but hey, this *is* a Novell product).

3. Click setupnw.exe. Accept the licensing agreement.

4. Choose between Typical Installation and Custom Installation. For the most part, the typical installation should work just fine.

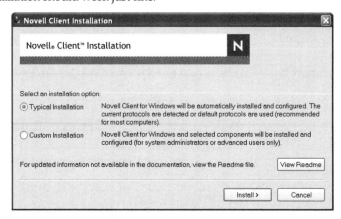

5. When the files have finished copying, click Reboot to restart your computer.

6. After you reboot, the login screen you get will be for the Novell client, as opposed to the Windows XP splash screen you're used to seeing. If you have a user account on a NetWare server, enter the appropriate username and password. If you want to log on to this local machine only, check the Workstation Only check box in the lower-left corner, and enter the proper credentials to log on to the computer.

If you are using Novell in a pure IP environment, you have completed the installation. If you require the IPX protocol, do not reboot. Add the NWLink IPX/SPX protocol. Follow these steps:

1. In the Local Area Connection Properties dialog box, click Install to open the Select Network Component Type dialog box.

2. Select Protocol, and then click Add to open the Select Network Protocol dialog box.

3. Choose Microsoft from the list of manufacturers in the left pane, and then select NWLink IPX/SPX NetBIOS Compatible Transport Protocol from the list of available protocols. Click OK.

4. When this installation of the protocol is complete, you'll return to the Local Area Connection Properties dialog box. Click Close, and then reboot your computer.

## Configuring the Novell Client

Once the Novell client is installed, it integrates very well with Windows XP Professional, offering multiple logins that can be configured between the NetWare and Windows XP Professional environments with a single click.

When you reboot the workstation, you'll notice immediately that the Novell client has been installed. The Microsoft login has now been replaced with a Novell dialog box requesting you to enter your username and password. There's also a Workstation Only check box. When this check box is selected, the Novell client will bypass a Novell login and log in to the local workstation or the domain of your choice.

Clicking the Advanced button extends the view of the Novell login client to display the NDS, Script, Dial-up, and NMAS tabs, as shown in Figure 22.5. The Novell client allows you to log in to servers after you've logged in to Windows XP, and this is the dialog box being shown. On the NDS tab, you can select to browse for NDS trees, browse NDS to easily insert the correct context, and browse to find a preferred server. These options alone are a world of difference in comparison with CSNW, in which you had to know exactly where your login object was created within the tree. While you still need to have an idea of where your object is, a well-designed tree will help you find your user ID quickly.

**FIGURE 22.5**

Novell login screen, with advanced options

The Scripts tab allows you to run NetWare scripts and/or run your own login scripts. You use the Dial-up tab to dial in to any connections you have already preconfigured.

Once you are logged in, you will notice a couple of other changes, too. First, you will have more options when you right-click My Network Places, as shown in Figure 22.6.

In addition, you will be able to configure your Novell Client properties (all 13 tabs' worth) by going to the properties of your network connection, selecting Novell Client, and choosing Properties. This is shown in Figure 22.7.

# Entering the Dark World of Unix

Right now, you may be thinking, "But I don't know much about Unix, much less how it networks!" That's okay. By now, you have some knowledge of general networking principles, and the principles do not change from platform to platform. You still need to find a way to make the machines talk, and you still need to make resources available across the network.

Probably the biggest difference if you're using a Unix-based machine is the interface. Although there are some graphical interfaces for Unix (such as KDE and GNOME), most of the time Unix is run from a command prompt. Don't be scared of the dark place; just be able to type and you'll make it through. The good news is that accessing Unix-based resources from a Microsoft Windows XP Professional machine is incredibly similar to accessing Windows-based resources.

**FIGURE 22.6**
Novell options

**FIGURE 22.7**
Novell Client properties

Microsoft offers two Unix interoperability products: Services for Unix 2.0 and Interix 2.2. The one you will be dealing with most is Services for Unix, which allows you to integrate your Windows XP Professional machine into a Unix environment. If you want to run Unix-based applications or logon scripts on your Windows XP Professional machine, you will need Interix.

**NOTE**  For purposes of this discussion, Unix, Solaris, and Linux support require the same configurations.

The first thing you need to look at when trying to connect to a Unix-based machine is the network protocol. Unix uses TCP/IP by default, and so does Windows XP Professional. First problem solved. Just make sure the machines are configured properly.

**NOTE**    One of the great things about the TCP/IP protocol is that it's universal. Whether you're using Windows, Unix, or any other operating system, the rules for configuring addresses don't change. Therefore, if you're trying to communicate with a Unix machine, just make sure that all computers have the same network address but a unique host address. If you've forgotten how this works, take a look at the "Configuring IP Addresses on a Network" sidebar in Chapter 17.

The next thing to look at is how the computers make requests. Windows XP Professional uses a protocol called Common Internet File System (CIFS) to make requests of the server. Unix uses the Network File System (NFS) protocol. Since the two are incompatible, we need to figure out a way to make the two platforms talk. Enter Services for Unix.

**NOTE**    Services for Unix is an umbrella term for four separate products: File Services for Unix, Client for NFS, Server for NFS, and Print Services for Unix. Only Print Services for Unix is automatically included with Windows XP Professional.

Services for Unix contains many components—more than are necessary to cover here. Probably the most important ones are Client for NFS and Server for NFS. When you install Services for Unix on your Windows XP machine, these services allow you to not only request stuff from an NFS server but to host resources for NFS clients as well. Specifically, Services for Unix allows you to access files and printers on a Unix server, as well as have Unix machines access your files and printers. Services for Unix is a separate product that can be installed from its CD-ROM.

**NOTE**    Services for Unix is an optional add-on product that must be purchased from Microsoft.

**TIP**    If you're planning to install Services for Unix 2.0, be aware of the telnet vulnerability described in Microsoft Knowledge Base article 286043.

Printing in Unix is also slightly different from Microsoft printing. Installing Services for Unix installs two critical printing components: Line Printer (lpr) and Line Printer Daemon (lpd). You can install Print Services for Unix from the Windows XP CD:

1. In Control Panel, click Network Connections.

2. Select the Advanced menu, and then choose Optional Networking Components.

3. Place a check next to Other Network File and Print Services, and click Next.

4. Windows XP will copy the necessary files to your hard drive and close the dialog box.

The lpr utility is what is used to send print jobs to the print service, which is lpd. Daemon, in Unix terms, simply refers to a service. If you wanted to, you could use lpr from a command prompt to send print jobs through lpd. It's easier to map to the printer, though. Here's how to add an LPT port:

1. Click Start, and choose Printers and Faxes.

2. Under Printer Tasks, select Add a Printer, which opens the Add Printer Wizard. Click Next.

3. Choose Local Printer Attached to This Computer, and clear the Automatically Detect check box.

**4.** Click Create a New Port, and for the Type of Port, choose LPR Port. Click Next.

**5.** In the Name or Address of Server Providing lpd box, enter the DNS name or IP address of the host providing the lpd service (the Unix printer). You will also need to provide the name of the printer or print queue. Click Next.

**6.** The wizard will finish the installation for you.

**TIP**   Services for Unix is not required for Unix and Windows to communicate. Samba is the Unix implementation of the Server Message Block format, which is the foundation of the NetBIOS protocol. If you install Samba on Unix (or Linux or Solaris), you don't need to make any changes to Windows XP. With Samba, shared Unix directories and printers work in a standard Microsoft Network Neighborhood or domain.

## Macintosh Networks

Networking professionals will tell you that the words *Macintosh* and *network* should never be used in the same sentence. Native Macintosh networking is horribly slow by today's standards, and creating Macintosh-accessible volumes on NT servers could cause crashes and headaches. Because of these issues, Macs don't have a good name in the PC-networking arena.

But for all the flak Macs get regarding networking, they make excellent graphics and design machines. Besides, most of the Macintosh networking components, including the NIC, are built in.

Macintosh computers use the AppleTalk networking protocol by default. Fortunately, however, Macs also support TCP/IP. It's recommended that if you want to network with Macs, you should use the TCP/IP protocol. Windows XP Professional does not support the AppleTalk protocol.

Windows XP Professional does not come with any products or services to support Macs on a network. Windows 2000 Server comes with Services for Macintosh, which allows Mac users to save files on

Windows 2000 servers. If you absolutely must get Windows XP Professional and Macs talking to each other, you will need a third-party solution. One such solution is PC MACLAN, by Miramar Systems.

**NOTE**  For more information about PC MACLAN, visit www.miramar.com/

## Summary

Many networks run pure Microsoft operating systems. That's fine, but you need to be aware of other possibilities that exist, in case you must network with other vendors' products. In this chapter, we took a long look at connecting to an existing NetWare network with Windows XP Professional, including how to connect to a NetWare printer and how to log on to a NetWare system. We also discussed Unix and Macintosh networking.

This chapter ends Part 6: "Advanced Networking." In the next chapter, we begin a new section dedicated to network administration topics.

# Part 7

# Network Administration

**In this section you will learn how to**

- ◆ Manage Administrative and Diagnostic Tools
- ◆ Manage Active Directory
- ◆ Understand and Use the Registry
- ◆ Use Scripts to Automate Tasks
- ◆ Prevent Disasters and Recover from Them
- ◆ Audit Security

# Chapter 23

# Administrative and Diagnostic Tools

Windows XP Professional comes with administrative tools for you to use when you add new disk volumes and check on existing ones, track system events, watch system performance, and run general diagnostics. Let's take a look at these tools and how they can help you keep your system running smoothly.

◆ Managing hard disks through Disk Management

◆ Tracking down problems using Event Viewer

◆ Monitoring system performance

◆ Managing resources and applications with Task Manager

## Using Disk Management

In Windows XP Professional, Disk Management is part of the Computer Management console in Administrative Tools. To open Disk Management, follow these steps:

1. Choose Start ➤ Control Panel to open Control Panel.

2. Click the Performance and Maintenance link, and then click Administrative Tools to open the Administrative Tools folder.

3. Click Computer Management to open the Computer Management window.

4. In the Computer Management pane, expand Storage, and then click Disk Management. You'll see something similar to the following.

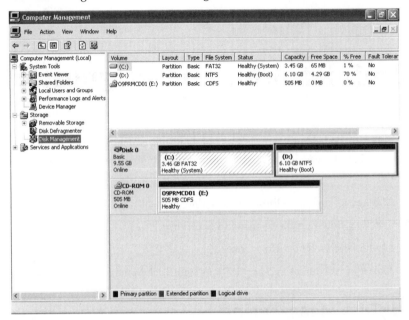

The Disk Management tool, which is displayed in the upper right-hand pane of the Computer Management window, gives you a graphical representation of the hard disks and CD-ROM devices in your computer. You can, however, customize the way information is presented in a variety of ways.

The Disk Management window is in three parts. On the left is the Computer Management pane of the Computer Management console. The lower-right pane contains the information for all the physical disks installed in the computer, excluding floppy drives. The upper-right pane contains descriptions of those disks, including data on the amount of space used and free, the type of file system, and the health of that system.

To use Disk Management to create or delete partitions, format drives, and create stripe or volume sets, simply click the disk that you want to modify, and select the change that you want to make from the Action menu. Or you can right-click the drive that you want to modify, and then select the appropriate action from the shortcut menu.

## Deciding Which File System Is Best

Windows XP Professional can use the File Allocation Table (FAT) file system supported by DOS and all versions of Windows, the File Allocation Table 32 (FAT32) file system supported by Windows 9*x* and Windows 2000, and the New Technology File System (NTFS) supported by Windows NT/2000/ XP/2003. Each file system has its respective upsides and downsides. Here's a quick rundown.

FAT's main advantage is its backward compatibility with DOS and with Windows $9x$ systems using FAT. FAT's main disadvantage is that it's a 16-bit file system with a minimum cluster size of 32KB. The result is that FAT can address partitions only up to 2GB. If your drive is larger than this, you'll have to create two or more partitions to use FAT. (And how many hard drives these days are this small?) Also, FAT has no security features, which is a huge problem. As a positive note, under Windows NT/2000/XP/2003, the FAT file system has a maximum file and partition size of 4GB. Still, it's not a good file system to use anymore.

The FAT32 file system evolved from the traditional FAT file system used by DOS and Windows. Windows XP can format FAT32 partitions up to 32GB and can access FAT32 partitions up to the maximum size (although this is not recommended for partitions larger than 32GB). One downside to FAT32 is that, like FAT, it does not provide any local security.

In contrast, NTFS is a robust, 32-bit file system with many security features, including password protection for specific files, the capability to limit access to specific files, file compression, file recovery, and the capability to address very large partitions. Although a system using NTFS in some cases run a bit slower than one using FAT, NTFS is your best bet if you want the additional features of Windows XP Professional. The speed issue isn't usually significant enough for you to even notice.

To add another twist, Windows XP Professional provides support for usage quotas on NTFS partitions.

**NOTE**   Remember, Windows 98 can still access files on an NTFS volume across a network, but it cannot read an NTFS volume locally.

### USING COMPRESSION IN NTFS

In Chapter 7, we looked at how to compress files and folders, but Windows XP Professional can also compress entire volumes. The compression ratio usually winds up being about 1.5:1, or 33 percent.

---

### DUAL-BOOTING CONSIDERATIONS

Let's say you want to run Windows XP Professional and Windows 98 on the same computer. Why you would want to do this is beyond me, but let's just say that you do. Which do you install first, and what file systems can you use?

Install Windows 98 first and then XP. When you install Windows XP, it will create a boot menu so you can choose the operating system you want when you boot up. If you install 98 second, it won't do this for you. Also, it's best to install them onto separate partitions. For this example, Windows 98 will be installed on the C drive (it has to be), and Windows XP Pro will be on D.

More important, which file systems do you use? For Windows 98, you will have to use FAT32. So, C will be FAT32. The D drive can be FAT32 or NTFS. For security reasons, it's better to go with NTFS.

Now, when you boot into Windows 98, it will *not* be able to see the D drive, because Windows 98 *cannot* read NTFS. Windows XP Pro will be able to see both C and D without any problems. If you made D FAT32 as well, then 98 would be able to read it just fine.

To compress an NTFS hard-disk volume, follow these steps:

1. Click Start, and then click My Computer.

2. Right-click the volume you want to compress, and choose Properties from the shortcut menu to open the Properties dialog box for that drive:

3. On the General tab, click the Compress Drive to Save Disk Space check box, and then click OK.

### USING NTFS FILE SECURITY FEATURES

NTFS file security lets you change settings for disk drives, folders, and even files. These features can be useful if your machine stores many files that you share with other users on your network, as well as your private files.

For information on how to set permissions for NTFS drives, folders, and files, see Chapter 19.

## Setting Up a New Disk Drive in Windows XP Professional

If you've added a new disk drive to your system, Disk Management will be able to see it, but you'll need to create a partition and a volume on it before Windows XP Professional can use it.

**NOTE**   After you create a partition on a new disk and format it, you can use it in Windows XP Professional without rebooting. You can even change the size of a partition or extend it across several hard drives without rebooting.

Let's step through adding a new partition and creating a volume on a new disk:

1. In the Disk Management window, right-click the drive, and choose Initialize Disk from the shortcut menu to open the Initialize Disk dialog box:

2. Click OK to initialize the disk. When the initialization is complete, you'll see the Disk Management window again.

3. In the Disk Management window, select the new disk, and choose Action ➤ All Tasks ➤ New Partition to start the New Partition Wizard.

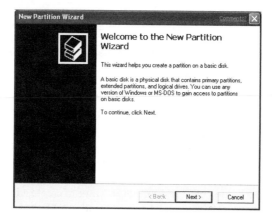

4. Click Next to open the Select Partition Type screen:

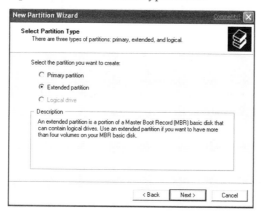

**NOTE**   Windows XP Professional supports a maximum of four primary partitions per hard drive or three primary partitions and one extended partition.

**5.** Select the type of partition you want to create, either primary or extended, and click Next to open the Specify Partition Size screen:

**6.** In the Partition Size in MB spin box, indicate the size of the partition, and then click Next to open the Completing the New Partition Wizard screen. Click Finish to close the wizard and create the partition.

### CREATING EXTENDED PARTITIONS AND LOGICAL DRIVES

The main difference between a primary partition and an extended partition is that you can create multiple logical drives only on an extended partition. So what's a logical drive? Simply put, a logical drive is a designated portion of a physical drive. Windows XP Professional is aware of two kinds of drives, physical and logical. A physical drive is the actual drive itself; you can touch it and Windows XP Professional can create partitions on it and format it. You can create a logical drive on an extended partition that may be only part of a physical disk, but Windows XP Professional will see that logical drive as a separate unit, and you can map a drive letter to it.

**NOTE**   Operating systems should be installed on and boot from primary partitions.

**NOTE**   Only extended partitions can contain logical disk volumes.

To create a logical drive on an extended partition, follow these steps:

**1.** In the Disk Management window, right-click the partition, and choose New Logical Drive to open the New Partition Wizard.

**2.** At the Welcome screen, click Next to open the Select Partition Type screen, select the Logical Drive option, and click Next to open the Assign Drive Letter or Path screen:

**3.** Click the Assign the Following Drive Letter option, use the spin box to select a drive letter, and then click Next to open the Format Partition screen:

**4.** If necessary, click the Format This Partition with the Following Settings option, specify the file system you want to use and how to allocate the disk, and then give the volume a label. Tell the wizard whether you want to perform a quick format or to enable file and folder compression, and click Next.

**NOTE**    Remember, FAT will give you somewhat better speed performance but with limited volume size. NTFS enables you to use Windows XP Professional file compression, security features, and file recovery.

> **NOTE** Disabling QuickFormat tells Windows XP Professional to first scan the partition for bad sectors. If you know the disk is free of bad sectors, go ahead and QuickFormat it. If you're not sure, it's better to have Windows XP Professional scan for bad sectors. It will take considerably longer than a QuickFormat but could save you trouble up the road.

**5.** In the final screen of the wizard, click Finish to format the drive.

#### USING DYNAMIC VOLUMES

Traditional partition types stored their information in a *partition table* that was located in the first physical sector of the hard disk. It was this location and its limited storage space for partition information that limited us to four partitions per physical disk. The partition table stores information for the size and location of each partition and is used to find the bootable partition during the startup procedure.

*Dynamic volumes* store their partition information in the data portion of the drive, and thus they are not limited in the amount of information they can store. To convert a basic disk to a dynamic disk, right-click the disk in the Disk Management tool, and select Dynamic from the shortcut menu. You will have to reboot to perform the conversion. After the restart, you will be able to create or modify dynamic volumes on the disk, including expanding the volume across multiple disks.

Dynamic volumes come in various flavors:

**Simple** A simple dynamic volume is similar to a traditional partition in that it exists on a single drive. It can be resized by extending the volume if it is on a dynamic disk that was created as a dynamic disk and not upgraded from a basic disk.

**Spanned** This dynamic volume spans two or more disks to create one logical volume, as its name implies, but it can be extended. Spanned volumes are the same as volume sets in NT 4, but in Windows XP Professional they are available only on dynamic disks.

**Mirrored** This volume type is available only on server operating systems. Mirrored volumes provide fault tolerance by keeping an exact mirror image of all data in the volume on a separate hard disk. If you lose one disk, you still have an exact copy of all the data.

**Striped** Striped volumes are the fastest type of dynamic volume and yield great benefits in performance. They are not fault tolerant, however. If you lose one disk, you lose all the data in the volume. In that sense, they are actually *less* fault tolerant than a single volume. They are the same as the traditional stripe sets available in NT, but stripe volumes are available in Windows XP Professional only on dynamic disks.

**RAID 5** This type of dynamic volume is available only in Windows Server operating systems. RAID 5 is also known as striping with parity. RAID 5 allows the volume to lose one hard disk without failing. It does this by combining the remaining data with the parity information to re-create the data on-the-fly.

> **NOTE** Dynamic volumes are not supported on portable computers, removable disks, detachable disks using Universal Serial Bus (USB) or IEEE 1394 (also called FireWire) interfaces, or on disks connected to shared SCSI buses.

# Using Event Viewer

One of Windows XP Professional's more handy tools is the Event Viewer, which can be helpful for troubleshooting a misbehaving PC or for getting a better handle on what Windows XP Professional is doing behind the scenes. To open Event Viewer, follow these steps:

1. Choose Start ➢ Control Panel to open Control Panel.

2. Click Performance and Maintenance, click Administrative Tools, and then click Event Viewer.

3. In the pane on the left, select Application, Security, or System. If you select System, you'll see something similar to the following:

System events are logged by Windows XP Professional's system components, including hardware drivers. For example, if a driver fails to load, it will write a system event to the System log. Or if a Windows XP Professional service fails to initialize, the service reports its failure in the System log. There are three types of System log events:

**Information**   Logged when a driver or service starts successfully and indicated by the blue letter *i*. For example, each time you boot up Windows XP Professional, a system event is logged, indicating that the event log service was started.

**Warning**   Logged when a condition occurs that could mean future trouble, for example, a nearly full hard drive. Indicated by an exclamation point in a yellow triangle.

**Error**   Logged when a service or a driver fails to start or load and indicated by an *X* in a red circle. For example, if your network card driver fails, that error is logged, as is an error indicating that any network protocols communicating with that network card have failed.

Security events occur if you've enabled auditing on a shared disk, subfolder, or file. Audited events are written to the Security log when someone accesses your shared area and logs in. An administrator can specify which events are logged into the Security log. There are two types of Security log events:

**Success**  Logged when a user successfully logs on to one of your shared areas: a disk, a subfolder, or a file.

**Failure**  Logged when a user fails to log on to one of your shared areas.

Windows XP Professional applications write status and error messages in the Application log. If an application is crashing or behaving oddly, it's usually a good idea to check the Application log for error messages. The Application log uses the same three event types as the System log: Information, Warning, and Error. Application developers specify which events to log.

With Event Viewer, you can look at only one event log at a time. To change views, select the log you want to see.

**TIP**  When opening old log files, be careful not to confuse them with your system's actual logs. The system log files live in the Winnt\System32\Config subfolder. If you open a log other than one of your system's three primary logs, its name will be displayed in the title bar of the Event Viewer window. Each time you open Event Viewer, it loads the system's three event logs.

For any of your three logs, Event Viewer supports two viewing modes: All Records and Filter. The default view is the All Records view. In this view, you see all the events currently stored in a log. To view only specific events, follow these steps:

**1.** Choose View ➢ Filter to open the Properties dialog box for the log you are viewing.

**2.** Click the Filter tab:

**3.** Select the types of events, their source, category, and so on, and then click OK.

If a hardware device isn't loading or is behaving oddly, one of the first places to look for the cause is the Event Viewer because a misbehaving device will likely document its problems in the System log. And even though Warning and Error events are sometimes short on specifics, they can often be good indicators of where to begin looking. Here's what a troubleshooting session might look like.

On startup, the driver for a Sound Blaster card fails to initialize; the result is a lack of wave audio in Windows XP Professional. The first indicator you get is a message informing you that at least one Windows XP Professional service failed to start.

Upon opening Event Viewer, you'd see an Error event in the System log reported by Windows XP Professional's Service Control Manager. After clicking it, you'd see the message "The following boot-start or system-start driver(s) failed to load: sndblst." Although this somewhat terse message doesn't provide any specifics from Event Viewer, you could then check your Sound Blaster driver's status by following these steps:

1. Click Start, right-click My Computer, and choose Properties from the shortcut menu to open the System Properties dialog box.

2. Click the Hardware tab, and then click the Device Manager button to open Device Manager.

3. Expand Sound, Video and Game Controllers, right-click Sound Blaster, choose Properties from the shortcut menu to open the Properties dialog box, and check the settings.

Event Viewer has a few other handy features to check out. From the Action menu, you can clear all events from all three logs. Be careful here, however. Although Windows XP Professional will issue a warning, there's no Undo for clearing the logs. If you think you might want to access event information contained in the logs, save them as backups in a different subfolder so that you can access them later if need be.

To change the size of a log or overwrite its settings, right-click the log, and choose Properties from the shortcut menu to open the log's Properties dialog box. Figure 23.1 shows the General tab for the System log's Properties dialog box.

**FIGURE 23.1**

You can change log settings in the log's Properties dialog box.

Log size can be anywhere from 64KB on up (the default is 512KB). Windows XP Professional defaults to overwriting events more than seven days old; so if your network administrator wants to back up your event logs weekly, all events will be cataloged. This can pose a problem only if your system is generating an unusually large number of log events—for example, an application or device isn't working properly or a network protocol stack is continuously issuing warning events.

If you're getting event log information about other computers (or they're getting event log information about your computer) on your network and if you are connected to that network via a modem, click the Using a Low-Speed Connection check box.

**NOTE**   If you've set event overwriting to be cleared manually or have specified to overwrite events of a certain age, the Windows XP Professional System log can fill up and can no longer be updated until you make more room in the log. If your system is having problems and can't update the System log, diagnosing a problem may be more difficult. If your log file has filled, you can't re-enable event logging by increasing the logs' file sizes. You'll have to back up your logs, clear all events from them, and then increase the files' sizes.

**WARNING**   Be careful to watch the size of logs as they grow. If you have set the logs to never overwrite and they fill up, Windows XP Professional may hang. If you are auditing for security events, the recommended setting is to never overwrite because security events should be documented over long periods of time. Clearing and archiving the log should be a part of routine maintenance.

Using the View menu in Event Viewer, you can sort events chronologically, listing either the oldest or the newest events first. To find a specific event, choose View ➢ Find to open the Find in Local System dialog box:

This feature essentially duplicates the Filter function, except that Event Viewer's Find displays, one by one, events that fit a certain description rather than listing them all at once.

To modify the display in Event Viewer, choose View ➤ Customize to open the Customize View dialog box:

Click or clear a check box to show or hide an item.

# Monitoring Performance

Windows XP Professional is designed to "self-tune" for optimal performance but also provides several tools for detecting possible performance bottlenecks. You can use the Windows XP Professional Performance console to monitor and log the performance of hundreds of variables, including some very esoteric ones intended to be used by developers and network administrators when tracking application and system behavior. In addition to tracking performance on your system, you can track performance counters on other Windows XP Professional machines on your network. We'll take a look at the Performance console and some of its components. Rather than cover every variable counter you can assign in Performance, we'll look at about a dozen or so key counters that deliver the most relevant system information.

**NOTE**  If you want only a quick read on Windows XP Professional "vitals," right-click the Taskbar and select Task Manager from the shortcut menu. Task Manager has a Performance tab that reports CPU usage and memory statistics. Task Manager also lists applications you have open, as well as processes that are running (those created by programs and Windows XP Professional services). Task Manager is discussed in detail at the end of this chapter.

To open the Performance console, in Control Panel click the Performance and Maintenance link, click Administrative Tools, and then click Performance. Figure 23.2 shows the Performance console.

Performance provides three views of real-time data in System Monitor. To access one of these views, click the corresponding button on the toolbar. (To display a button's label, simply place the cursor over it.) The three views are simply different displays of the data that Performance can report. Here's a quick rundown:

**View Graph**  Displays counters graphically. This is the view shown in Figure 23.2. You can add as many counters as you like, although more than about a half-dozen makes for a rather cluttered graph.

**FIGURE 23.2**

The System Monitor in the Performance console delivers constantly updated information about the performance of subsystems, and it can update its display dozens of times a second.

**View Histogram**   Displays bar graphs that dynamically update as the data changes.

**View Report**   Displays counters in real time (as Chart view does). Selected counters are listed and their values are updated at a specified rate.

Before getting into detail about each of these views, let's look at some counters you're most likely to monitor.

Windows XP Professional classifies its subsystem components into objects, and each object has anywhere from two to more than a dozen counters that you can monitor. In addition, certain objects—such as processors, physical disks, and logical disks—also have instances because your Windows XP Professional system may have more than one of these types of hardware.

To display an explanation of what any counter monitors, follow these steps:

**1.** Click the Add button on the toolbar (it has a plus sign) to open the Add Counters dialog box:

2. Select an object from the Performance Object drop-down list.

3. Select a counter from the Select Counters from List drop-down list.

4. Click the Explain button.

Obviously, you also use the Add Counters dialog box to specify which counters you want to monitor, and we'll look at how to do that shortly.

So without further ado, let's take a look at several objects and some of their counters. Tables 23.1 through 23.4 show you the counters, the functions, and the importance of four objects: the Paging File object, the Processor object, the PhysicalDisk object, and the Server object.

**TABLE 23.1:**    The Paging File (Swap File) Object

| COUNTER | IMPORTANCE |
|---------|------------|
| % Usage | A value that stays persistently high is one indicator that additional RAM would noticeably improve system performance, given the type of work you're doing. |

**TABLE 23.2:**    The Processor Object

| COUNTER | IMPORTANCE |
|---------|------------|
| % Processor Time | May indicate that an application or a service is using the CPU excessively, cutting into overall system performance. |
| % Interrupt Time | Interrupts execute in Windows XP Professional's kernel mode; applications execute in user mode. Excessive hardware interrupts can hamper overall system performance. |
| % Privileged Time | Similar to % Interrupt Time; if your system is spending excessive amounts of time in privileged mode, applications, which all run in user mode, have to wait for the CPU to return to user mode to access the CPU. |
| % User Time | An indicator of how much CPU time applications have available to them. |

**TABLE 23.3:**    The PhysicalDisk Object

| COUNTER | IMPORTANCE |
|---------|------------|
| Disk Read Bytes/sec | Gives a general indication of a disk's read performance. |
| Disk Write Bytes/sec | Gives a general indication of a disk's write performance. |

CHAPTER 23

**TABLE 23.4:** The Server Object

| COUNTER | IMPORTANCE |
|---|---|
| Bytes Total/sec | Excessive network access of your system by other users can drag down your overall performance. |
| Errors Logon | Repeated failed logon attempts may mean a password-guessing program is trying to crack into your system. |
| Sessions Timed Out | Useful for setting idle time-out values. Each active peer connection to your system slightly diminishes overall system performance. |

## Adding a Counter in Graph View

Performance defaults to Graph view, which graphically displays any selected counters. Let's go through the steps to add the Processor object and % Processor Time counter and the Paging File object and % Usage counter:

1. In the Performance console, select System Monitor, and click the Add button to open the Add Counters dialog box.

2. In the Performance Object drop-down list, select Processor.

3. In the Select Counter from List drop-down list, select %Processor Time, and then click Add.

4. In the Performance Object drop-down list, select Paging File.

5. In the Select Counter from List drop-down list, select %Usage, and then click Add.

6. Click Close.

Back in the Performance console, you'll see something similar to the following:

To save this view at any point in time, right-click the chart, choose Save As from the shortcut menu to open the Save As dialog box, give the file a name, and click Save. You can save the view as a web page or as a report.

**TIP**  To highlight a counter, select it at the bottom of the window and press Ctrl+H.

To customize the chart's colors, fonts, and other graphical elements, follow these steps:

1. Right-click the chart, and choose Properties from the shortcut menu to open the System Monitor Properties dialog box:

2. Click one of the five tabs, and then specify your options.

3. When you've finished, click OK.

## Using Alerts

Alerts can be very useful when monitoring the computer system over a long period of time or when you have several computers to monitor. An alert is triggered when a condition you have selected occurs. For example, if you wanted to find out how often your CPU was being stressed by the normal level of activity throughout the day, you could make an alert that would trigger whenever the System object Processor Queue Length counter exceeded a count of two.

To set Alert counters, follow these steps:

1. In the Performance window, expand the Performance Logs and Alerts entry in the Console Root pane, and then click Alerts.

2. Right-click in the right pane, and choose New Alert Settings from the shortcut menu to open the New Alert Settings dialog box:

3. In the Name box, enter a name for this group of Alert settings, and then click OK to open the Properties dialog box for the new Alert group.

4. Enter a comment that describes the settings, and then click the Add button to open the Add Counters dialog box:

5. Select Use Local Computer Counters.

6. In the Performance Object drop-down list box, select an object.

7. In the Select Counters from List drop-down list box, select a counter, and then click Add.

8. When you've finished, click Close.

9. Back in the Properties dialog box, you can set a trigger using the Alert When the Value Is drop-down list box. Set a limit by entering a percentage in the Limit box.

10. Specify the frequency at which data is sampled using the Interval spin box and the Units drop-down list box.

11. Click OK.

To save this view of the Alert log, choose File ➢ Save As.

**NOTE**   You cannot set an alert for both over and under conditions on the same counter.

## Using Counter Log View

Performance lets you track hundreds of counters in real time (as they happen), but often you may want to review system events one by one. To do this, you set Counter Logs to capture objects' counters to a file for later review. Let's step through logging Processor and Memory counters.

1. In the Console Root pane of the Performance console, expand Performance Logs and Alerts.

2. Select Counter Logs, right-click in the right pane, and choose New Log Settings from the shortcut menu to open the New Log Settings dialog box.

3. Enter a name that will describe this log, and click OK to open the Properties dialog box for this log.

4. Click the Add Counters button to open the Add Counters dialog box.

5. Click Use Local Computer Counters, and then select the Processor Performance object.

6. Click the All Counters button to add all the counters for this object.

7. Click the Add button.

8. Now repeat steps 5 through 7 using the Memory object.

9. Click the Close button.

10. Click OK to close the Properties dialog box and return to Performance.

11. Right-click the icon for the log settings you just created, and select Start from the shortcut menu to start the log. When you want to stop the log, right-click the icon again and select Stop from the shortcut menu.

**WARNING**    Carefully watch the size of the log file as it grows. It is easy to gather enough data to fill a hard drive if left unattended for too long. When monitoring performance over a long period of time, it is more common to set the time interval to several minutes to avoid gathering too much data.

Viewing specific data points is a little tricky here because the timeframe "slider" controller works differently in each of the three views. Let's take a look at it. Follow these steps:

1. In the Performance console, select System Monitor, right-click in the right pane, and choose Properties from the shortcut menu to open the System Monitor Properties dialog box.

2. Click the Source tab.

3. Click the Time Range button, and then set the beginning and ending time to view using the end handles on the slider bar.

4. Click OK.

Because Log view shows only one data point at a time, you can change the data point by using the Time Range slider to change the start point. After you click OK, you'll see a data point for that time value. This view is useful for zeroing in on data at an exact time, but it isn't very useful for looking at multiple data points.

## Using Report View

Similar to Graph view, Report view shows up-to-the minute statistics on object counters but displays them numerically rather than graphically. If you want to watch many counters simultaneously, Report view is your best bet because Graph view gets to be a cluttered mess when you try to display too many counters simultaneously. To display counters in Report view, click the View Report button. You'll see something similar to the following:

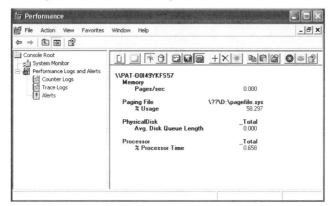

## Running System Information

When everything on your system works, new devices install painlessly, and services work right the first time, life is good. If only it were always so. Alas, the general headaches of new hardware installation follow—cracking the box open, finding an available I/O slot, dealing with the mysterious force that makes your system's box much easier to rip open than it is to put back together. Then, after you restart the system, there may be I/O resource conflicts or services may fail for whatever reason. The fun never ends.

Fortunately, Windows XP Professional provides some tools to ease system troubleshooting. Chief among them is System Information, which you can use to display system information ranging from detailed display driver data to the services that are installed and the other services or devices on which they depend. To open System Information, click Start ➢ All Programs ➢ Accessories ➢ System Tools ➢ System Information.

The pane on the right displays the version and build of Windows XP Professional you're running, your CPU type, a serial number, and registration information, as well as information ranging from the manufacturer on your system and its model number to the amount of memory free or the amount of paging file in use. Figure 23.3 shows information about my system.

**FIGURE 23.3**

The System Summary screen displays local configuration details.

To view information on the hardware installed in your computer, expand Hardware Resources. For information about display hardware and drivers, expand Components, and then select Display. You'll see something similar to the following:

For information about the drives on your system, expand Storage under Components, and then select Drives. You'll see something similar to the following:

The Drives screen gives detailed information about local floppy, hard, and CD-ROM drives. Although there isn't really any diagnostic information available here per se, the Drives screen can indicate trouble with a drive simply by showing you that Windows XP Professional cannot see the drive. For example, say you have a second hard drive that is *not* displayed on this list. The drive's absence may indicate either a faulty data or power cable connection to the unit. If the drive is a SCSI device, the SCSI chain may be incorrectly terminated. If it's a second EIDE hard drive, there may be an incorrect master-slave configuration on the second drive. Before looking at more complicated problems, always check your physical connections. Often, the solution is simpler than you think.

**TIP**    You cannot get information about floppy, removable disk, or CD-ROM drives unless a disk is in the drive. With a disk present, you'll get information about that specific disk.

For information about services, expand Software Environment, and click Services. You'll see something similar to the following:

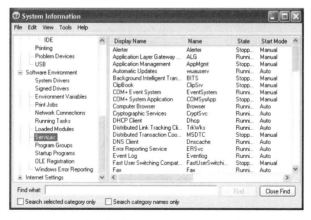

**NOTE**    You can't use the Services folder to start and stop services. For that, you use Services under Services and Applications in Computer Management.

For information about system resources, expand Hardware Resources and select one of the subfolders. Figure 23.4 shows the IRQs in use on my system, which I displayed by selecting the IRQs folder.

**FIGURE 23.4**
The IRQs in use on my system

**NOTE**   Windows XP Professional supports interrupt sharing by hardware devices to try to alleviate IRQ conflict problems. But older hardware devices that aren't aware of this feature frequently expect to be the sole possessors of a given IRQ and won't do very well sharing it with another device. The best plan of action is for each hardware device to have its own dedicated IRQ(s).

Since Windows XP Professional is a Plug and Play operating system, the values contained in the System Information screen should be correct. But sometimes, a device won't be displayed here because its resources are in conflict with another device. In this case, the two devices in question should be displayed when you click Conflicts/Sharing. It's a good idea to check here before you install a new device so that you can figure out which resources are allocated and which are available. Be sure to check all three resource types: IRQs, DMA, and I/O.

For Registry information, expand Software Environment, and click Environment Variables. You'll see something similar to the following:

The Environment Variables folder is another view-only portion of the System Information screen; it displays Registry information about CPUs and system paths. You can't edit this information, but it may be valuable to a technical support engineer trying to troubleshoot your system. Windows applications, in addition to using the system's paging file, will often write temporary files for storing less-frequently-used data rather than using system memory. It's a method of "cheating" on the amount of memory the application allocates or using allocated memory for more immediate or more frequently used tasks.

To create and print a report from any of the System Information screen items, select the item and choose File ➢ Print. Because so much information is generated, you might want to save the information in a file rather than printing it. To save the file, choose File ➢ Save to open the Save As dialog box.

# Using Task Manager

Task Manager (see Figure 23.5) is a tool that lets you quickly monitor and troubleshoot Windows XP Professional, particularly in terms of the programs you are running.

**NOTE**    If multiple users are logged on to your computer, you will also see a Users tab in Task Manager.

**FIGURE 23.5**
Use Task Manager to easily monitor programs you are running.

To run Task Manager, do one of the following:

◆ Right-click your Taskbar, and choose Task Manager from the shortcut menu.

◆ Choose Start ➢ Run, type **taskmgr** in the Open box, and click OK.

**TIP**    If your system is causing some difficulty that makes the above methods unavailable, press Ctrl+Alt+Del to open Task Manager. Go ahead—try it.

Figure 23.5 shows Task Manager open at the Performance tab. Regardless of which tab you are looking at, though, the bottom of Task Manager displays the number of processes being run, the percentage of CPU usage, and the amount of memory being used, including any virtual memory you may be using. This quick reference tells you everything you need to know in order to immediately understand the operating condition of your system.

## Task Manager Applications

Task Manager's Applications tab lists all running applications and their current status (see Figure 23.6). An application's status will be either Running, if the program is behaving properly, or Not Responding, if the program is having problems.

**FIGURE 23.6**

The Applications tab of Task Manager

To close a running application, select it, and click End Task. To switch to a running application, select it, and click Switch To. To start a new application, follow these steps:

**1.** Click the New Task button to open the Create New Task dialog box:

**2.** Type the name of the application in the Open box, and click OK.

## Task Manager Processes

You can use the list on the Processes tab (see Figure 23.7) to monitor and halt any processes that are running on your computer. Processes are measured in all the separate executables that Windows XP Professional runs concurrently. This includes any applications you are running and all the background executables that Windows XP Professional runs automatically, including services. To terminate a running process, select it, and click the End Process button.

**WARNING**    Don't end a process unless it is marked as being errant. Ending a process that is running may crash other programs that are running correctly if they depend on that process.

**FIGURE 23.7**

Task Manager lets you monitor running processes.

## Task Manager Performance

You use the Performance tab to monitor your computer's usage of memory, processor time, and other resources. The two central graphs on the page measure the amount of memory used and the amount of processor time used. For multiple processors, you can choose to show one graph for each CPU or one graph for combined CPUs. The Performance tab also contains information on how much physical memory is being used and how much memory the Windows XP Professional kernel is using.

**TIP**    When you run Task Manager, a small green square appears on your Taskbar next to your clock. This is a CPU usage meter. Point to the usage meter to display the percentage of CPU usage at the current moment.

## Task Manager Networking

You use the Networking tab (shown in Figure 23.8) to monitor Internet and local area network usage. At the bottom of this tab is information about the link speed and the number of bytes transferred for each adapter.

By default, Task Manager is always on top when you have multiple windows open on the Desktop. If you don't prefer this arrangement, choose Options ➢ Always on Top to clear the check mark. You can also use Task Manager to put your computer in hibernation, turn it off, restart it, log off, or switch users. Choose the appropriate item from the Shut Down menu.

**FIGURE 23.8**
The Networking tab in
Task Manager

# Summary

Windows XP Professional's suite of administrative tools covers the gamut of system functions, ranging from providing networking settings to detailed information about the operating system's main "plumbing."

Most of the tools are intended to help troubleshoot system problems; using them in concert, you can gather sufficient information to remedy most system hiccups and even avert larger ones by catching them early. Although no set of tools is a panacea for all problems, those in Windows XP Professional will do a good job of helping you keep your system up and running.

In the next chapter, we will cover a topic that, although relatively new in Microsoft networking terms (it's been around only since 2000), is critical to understanding the Microsoft domain structure: Active Directory.

# Chapter 24

# Active Directory Essentials

If you're using Windows XP Professional in a corporate environment, chances are good that your XP box is networked and that the network is based on servers running either Windows NT 4, Windows 2000 Server, Windows .NET Server, or Windows Server 2003. Even if you have a home network, you might want to install a server for security purposes or to manage your home business files (tax write-offs are a beautiful thing).

If that's true and if you're networked with Windows NT 4, you have what is (not surprisingly) called an "NT 4 domain." (For details about an NT 4 domain, see my book *Mastering NT Server 4*, Seventh Edition, published by Sybex.) But if your networks are based on Windows 2000 Server or newer, you probably have what is called an "Active Directory" domain. Although I can't make you an Active Directory (AD) expert in one day, I'll introduce you to the basics of AD here.

Not that long ago, networks were small (remember when the only "networks" you cared about were CBS, NBC, and ABC?), and so were their problems. But nowadays it's not unusual to see worldwide networks connecting hundreds of thousands of PCs and users. Managing that kind of complexity brings up big problems—oops, we're supposed to call them challenges; I always forget. One of the answers to the obvious question "Why bother with Windows 2000 Server, .NET Server, or Server 2003, anyway?" is that they were designed with some of those challenges in mind. That's important because NT 4 *didn't* address many of those problems.

You'll notice that, for most of this chapter, I'll be talking about Windows 2000 Server. And, yes, I realize that this book is about Windows XP Professional and that there are newer Windows Server products out there. I'll stick with Windows 2000 simply because it was the first Microsoft operating system to use Active Directory. Although some new features have been added over the years, the basic concepts remain the same.

If you're using Windows XP Professional on a standalone computer or a small peer-to-peer network that connects Windows XP Professional, Windows 2000, NT, and Windows 9x machines, you don't need to know anything about Active Directory. But if you're part of a large client-server network, and your Windows XP Professional workstation is connected to a server version that incorporates Active Directory, you do need to understand Active Directory, and the information in this chapter is important to you. After I explain what the hoopla is all about, I'll give you step-by-step instructions for connecting to an AD domain.

**NOTE**  Throughout this chapter, I will refer to "Windows Server" quite a bit. When I use that designation, I am referring to all Windows-based server products that support AD: Windows 2000 Server, Windows .NET Server, and Windows Server 2003.

- ◆  Keeping track of who can use the network
- ◆  Finding stuff on the network

- ◆ Creating new types of subadministrators

- ◆ Subdividing control over a domain

- ◆ Dealing with connectivity and replication issues

- ◆ Building big networks

## Security: Keeping Track of Who's Allowed to Use the Network and Who Isn't

A network's first job is

- ◆ To provide central places to store simple things such as files or more complex things such as databases, shared printing, or fax services

- ◆ To make it possible for people to communicate by means of e-mail, videoconferencing, or whatever technology comes up in the future

- ◆ More recently, to make it easier for people to buy things

Fast on the heels of that first job, however, is the second job of every network: to provide security. Once, most computer networks were unsecured or lightly secured, but human nature has forced a change, and there's no going back. Just as businesses have locks on their doors, file cabinets, and cash registers to protect their physical assets, so also do most modern firms protect their information assets. And no matter which vendor's network software you're using, computer security typically boils down to two parts: authentication and authorization. To see why, consider the following example.

Acme Industries sells pest control devices. They've got a sales manager named Wilma Wolf; Wilma wants to see how the sales of a new product, Instant Hole, is doing. Acme's got it set up so that Wilma can review sales information through her web browser—she just surfs over to a particular location on one of the company's internal web servers, and the report appears on her screen.

Of course, Acme management wouldn't be happy about just *anybody* getting to these sales report pages, so the pages are secured. Between the time that Wilma asked for the pages and the time that she got them, two things happened:

**Authentication**   The web server containing the sales reports asked her workstation, "Who's asking for this data?" The workstation replied, "Wilma." The server then said, "Prove it." So the workstation popped up a dialog box on Wilma's screen asking for her username and password. She typed in her name and password, and assuming that she typed them in correctly, the server then checked that name and password against a list of known users and passwords and found that she is indeed Wilma.

**Authorization**   The mere fact that she's proven that she's Wilma may not be sufficient reason for the web server to give her access to the sales pages. The web server then looked at another list sometimes known as the access control list, a list of people and access levels—"Joe can look at this page but can't change it," "Sue can look at this page and can change it," "Larry can't look at this page at all." Presuming Wilma was on the "can look" list, the server sent the requested pages to her browser.

Now, the foregoing example may not seem to contain any deep insights—after all, everyone's logged into a system, tried to access something, and either been successful or rejected—but understanding how Windows 2000/.NET/2003 Server and in particular AD work together requires examining these everyday things a bit. Here's a closer look at some of the administrative mechanics of logins.

## Maintaining a "Directory" of Users and Other Network Objects

Every secure system has a file or files that make up a database of known user accounts. NT 4 used only a single file named SAM, short for the less-than-illuminating Security Accounts Manager. It contained a user's username (the logon name), the user's full name, password, allowed logon hours, account expiration date, description, primary group name, and profile information. Of course, the file was encrypted; copy a SAM from an existing NT 4 system and pull it up in Notepad, and you'll see only garbage.

Server versions using AD store most of their user information in a file called `ntds.dit` (think of it as standing for NT directory services directory information table), but `ntds.dit` is different from SAM in a couple of ways:

◆ First, `ntds.dit` is a modified Access database, and Windows 2000 Server, Windows .NET Server, and Windows Server 2003 actually contain a variant of Access's database engine in their machinery. (Microsoft used to call the Access database engine JET, which stood for Joint Engine Technology—no, the meaning isn't obvious to me either, I think they just liked the acronym—but now it's called ESE, pronounced "easy," which stands for the equally useful name Extensible Storage Engine.)

◆ Second, as you'll see demonstrated over and over again, `ntds.dit` stores a much wider variety of information about users than SAM ever did.

The information in `ntds.dit` and the program that manages `ntds.dit` are together called the *directory service* (DS). (As a matter of fact, most folks will never say "`ntds.dit`"; they'll say "directory service.") Which leads to a question: What exactly is a "directory"?

It would seem (to me, anyway) that what we've got here is a database of users and user information. So why not call it a database? No compelling reasons, mostly convention, but there *is* one interesting insight. According to some, databases of users tend to get *read* far more often than they get *written*. That allows a certain amount of database engine tweaking for higher performance. This subset of the class of databases gets a name—*directories*. I guess it makes sense, since we're used to using lists of people called office directories or phone directories. I just wish the folks in power had come up with some other name; ask most PC users what a directory is, and they start thinking of hard disk structures: `C:\Windows`—isn't that a directory?

## Centralizing the Directory and Directories: A "Logon Server"

"Please, can't we set things up so I need to remember only *one* password?"

Consider for a moment when Windows 2000 Server, Windows .NET Server, or Windows Server 2003 will use that user information located in AD. When you try to access a file share or print share, AD will validate you. But there's more at work here. When fully implemented, AD can save you a fair amount of administrative work in other network functions as well.

For example, suppose your network requires SQL database services. You'll then run a database product such as SQL Server or Oracle on the network. But adding another server-based program to your network can introduce more administrative headaches because, like the file and print servers, a database server needs authentication and authorization support. That's because you usually don't want to just plunk some valuable database on the network and then let the world in general at it—you want to control who gets access.

So the database program needs a method for authentication and authorization. And *here's* where it gets ugly: in the past, many database programs required their administrators to keep and maintain a list of users and passwords. The database programs required you to duplicate all that work of typing in names and passwords, to redo the work you'd already done to get your Novell, Banyan, NT, or whatever type LAN up and running. Yuk. But it gets worse. Consider what you'd have to do if you ran both NT as a network operating system *and* Novell NetWare as a network operating system: yup, you're typing in names and passwords yet again. Now add Lotus Notes for your e-mail and groupware stuff, another list of users, and hey, how about a mainframe or an AS/400? More accounts.

Let's see—with a network incorporating NT, Oracle, NetWare, and Notes, you've got each user owning *four* user accounts. Which means each user has *four* passwords to remember. And, every few months, four passwords to remember to change.

This seems dumb; why can't you just type those names and passwords once into your Windows Server and then tell Oracle, NetWare, and Notes to just ask the local Windows Server machine to check that you are indeed who you say you are rather than making Oracle, NetWare, and Notes duplicate all that security stuff? Put another way, you have a centralized computer that acts as a database server, another that acts as a centralized e-mail server, another as a print server—why not have a centralized "logon" server, a centralized "authentication" server? Then your users would have to remember (and change) only one password and account name rather than four.

Centralized logons would be a great benefit, but there's a problem with it: how would Notes actually *ask* the Windows Server to authenticate? What programming commands would an Oracle database server use to ask a Microsoft "logon server" (the actual term is *domain controller*, as you'll learn later) if a particular user should be able to access a particular piece of data?

Well, if that domain controller were running NT 4, the programming interface wouldn't have been a particularly well-documented one. And third parties such as Oracle, Lotus, and Novell would have been reluctant to write programs depending on that barely documented security interface because they'd be justifiably concerned that when the *next* version of NT appeared (Windows 2000 Server, and then Windows .NET Server, followed closely by Windows Server 2003), Microsoft would have changed the programming interface, leaving Lotus, Novell, and Oracle scrambling to learn and implement this new interface. And some of the more cynical among us would even suggest that Lotus and Oracle might fear that Microsoft's Exchange and SQL Server would be able to come out in Windows Server–friendly versions nearly immediately after a new Windows Server's release.

Instead, Microsoft opted to put an industry standard interface on its AD, an interface called the Lightweight Directory Access Protocol (LDAP). Now, LDAP may initially sound like just another geeky acronym, but it's more than that—what Microsoft's done by putting an LDAP interface on Active Directory is to open a doorway for outside developers. And here's how important it is: yes, LDAP will make Oracle's or Lotus's job easier should they decide to integrate their products' security with Windows Server's built-in security. But LDAP also means that it's (theoretically, at least) possible to build tools that create Active Directory structures—domains, trees, forests, organizational units, user accounts, all of the components. It means that if Windows Server gets popular but Microsoft's Active Directory control programs turn out to be hard to work with, some clever third party can just swoop in and offer a complete replacement, built atop LDAP commands.

Which, after you spend a bit of time with the Microsoft Management Console (MMC), may not seem like a bad idea—but I'll leave you to make your own judgment about that.

# Searching: Finding Things on the Network

Thus far, I've been talking about the directory service as if it contains only user accounts. But that's not true—the DS not only includes directory entries for people, it also contains directory entries describing servers and workstations. And that turns out to be essential, for a few reasons.

## Finding Servers: "Client-Server Rendezvous"

Client-server computing is how work gets done nowadays. You check your e-mail with Outlook (the client), which gets that mail from the Exchange machine down the hall (the server). You're at your PC (the client) accessing files on a file server (the server). You buy a shirt at L.L. Bean's web server (the server) from your PC using Internet Explorer (the client).

In those three cases, the copy of Outlook on your desktop had to somehow know where to find your local Exchange server, you couldn't get files from your file server until you knew which file server to look in, and you couldn't order that shirt until you'd found the address of the L.L. Bean web server, www.11bean.com.

In every case, client-server doesn't work unless you can help the client find the server, hence the phrase "client-server rendezvous." In the Outlook case, your mail client knows where your mail server is probably because someone (perhaps you) in your networking group set it up, feeding the name of the Exchange server into some setup screen in Outlook. You may have found the correct file server for the desired files by poking around in Network Neighborhood in Windows 9*x* or in My Network Places if your workstation is running Windows XP Professional, or perhaps someone told you where to find the files. You might have guessed L.L. Bean's address, seen it in a magazine ad, or used a search engine such as Yahoo! or Google.

Those are three examples of client-server rendezvous; many more happen in the process of daily network use. When your workstation seeks to log you in, the workstation must find a domain controller, or to put it differently, your "logon client" seeks a "logon server." Want to print something in color and wonder which networked color printers are nearby? More client-server rendezvous.

In every case, AD can simplify the process. Your workstation will be able to ask AD for the names of nearby domain controllers. You can search the AD for keywords relevant to particular file shares and printers.

## Name Resolution and DNS

But merely getting the name of a particular mail, web, print, or file server (or domain controller) isn't the whole story. From the network software's point of view, www.11bean.com isn't much help. To get you connected to the Bean web server, the network software needs to know the *IP address* of that server, a four-number combination looking something like 208.7.129.82. That's the second part of client-server rendezvous.

In the case of a public website such as Bean's, your computer can look up a web server by querying a huge network of publicly available Internet servers called the Domain Name System, or DNS. The public DNS contains the names of many machines you'll need to access, but chances are good that your company's internal network doesn't advertise many of its machines' names on the Internet; rather, your internal network probably runs a set of private DNS servers.

After its inception in 1984, DNS didn't change much. But RFC 2052 (introduced in October 1996) and RFC 2136 (introduced in April 1997) transformed DNS into a naming system that's good not only for the worldwide Internet but also for internal intranets. Many of the pieces of DNS software out in the corporate world don't yet support 2052 and 2136, so it's a great convenience that all Windows Server DNS server versions support those features.

**NOTE** RFC stands for Request for Comments, which is a document or a set of documents in which proposed Internet standards are described or defined.

## Creating New Types of Subadministrators

The next network challenge becomes apparent after a network has grown a bit. When a network is small or new, a small group of people does everything, from running the cables and installing the LAN adapter boards to creating the user accounts and backing up the system. As time goes on and the network gets larger and more important to the organization, two things happen:

♦ First, the organization hires more people—*has* to hire more people, because there are more servers to tend and user accounts to look after—to handle all the different parts of keeping a network running.

♦ Second, networks get political: all of a sudden, some of the higher-ups get clued to the fact that *what those network geeks do affects our ability to retain our power in this organization.*

Both of those things mean that your firm will soon start hiring more network helpers. In some organizations, these newly created positions get to do much of the scut work of network administration, stuff that is (a) pretty simple to train people to do and (b) of no interest to the old-timer network types. Examples of the I-don't-want-it-you-can-have-it jobs in a network include

**Resetting passwords** For security's sake, network administrators usually require users to change their passwords every couple months or so. Administrators also inveigh against the evils of writing those passwords down, so it's common for users to forget what they set their most recent passwords to. Resetting passwords to some innocuous value is something that really needs to be done quickly—the natives get restless when it takes a week to get them back on the network—and it's a relatively simple task, so it's perfect for the newly hired, minimum-wage network assistant.

**Tending the backups** For tediousness, nothing matches the sheer irritation of backups. Most people who manage large networks are forced to use tape drives for backups, and, well, some days it seems like tape drives were invented by someone who was abused by network administrators as a small child. They're balky and prone to taking vacations at random times, and you never can predict exactly how much data you can get on 'em—eight gigs one day, three the next, and as a result, *someone's* got to be around ready to feed in another blank tape. And somebody's got to label them and keep track of them; ask most network admin types what job they'd most like to give someone else to worry about, and backups are likely to be at the top of their wish list.

Hiring a few low-wage backup watchers and password fixers also gives a firm a sort of a "farm team," a place to try out folks to see if they're capable of learning to eventually become network analysts with more responsibilities (and, they hope, more salary).

But regular users can't do things such as resetting passwords and running backups—you need at least some administrative powers to do those things. Recall that we'd like to hire this "network scut work" person or persons at a pretty low hourly rate, and that's troublesome from a security point of view. If they can leave this job and go off to one with the same pay level whose main challenge is in remembering to say, "Would you like fries with that, sir?" it might not be the brightest idea to give them full administrative control over the network. Is there a way to create a sort of partial administrator?

NT 4 gave us *some* of that, since there was a prebuilt group called Backup Operators, but there wasn't a Reset Password Operators group, and besides, all NT 4 offered was a small set of prebuilt groups of types of administrators—the groups were called Server Operators, Account Operators, and Backup Operators—with different levels. There wasn't a way to create a new type of group with a tailor-made set of powers. Windows 2000 Server, Windows .NET Server, and Windows Server 2003 change that, offering a sometimes bewildering array of security options.

# Delegation: Subdividing Control over a Domain

In the last section, I offered two examples of things that might motivate changing how the network works—a growing set of network duties that require some division of labor (which I covered in that section) and growing attention from upper management as it becomes increasingly aware of the importance of the network in the organization. That second force in network evolution is perhaps better known as "politics." Despite the fact that it's something of a bad word, we can't ignore politics—so how does Windows Server address an organization's political needs?

To see how, consider the following scenario. Some fictitious part of the U.S. Navy is spread across naval facilities around the world, but perhaps (to keep the example simple) its biggest offices are in Washington, DC; San Diego, CA; and Norfolk, VA. There are servers in DC, San Diego, and Norfolk, all tended by different groups. For all the usual reasons, the officers in charge of the Norfolk facility don't want administrators from DC or San Diego messing with the Norfolk servers; the DC folks and the San Diego folks have similar feelings, with the result that the Navy technology brass wants to be able to say, "Here's a group of servers we'll call Norfolk and a group of users we'll call Norfolk Admins. We want to be able to say that only the users in Norfolk Admins can control the servers in Norfolk." They want to do similar things for San Diego and DC. How to do this?

Well, under NT 4, they could do it only by creating three separate security entities called *domains*. Creating three different domains would solve the problem because separate domains are like separate *universes*—they're not aware of each other at all. With a DC domain, a Norfolk domain, and a San Diego domain, they could separate their admins into three groups that couldn't meddle with one another. It's a perfectly acceptable answer and indeed many organizations around the world use NT 4 in that manner—but it's a solution with a few problems.

For one thing, enterprises usually want *some* level of communication between domains, and to accomplish that, the enterprises must put in place connections between domains called *trust relationships*. Unfortunately, trust relationships are a quirky and unreliable necessity of any multidomain enterprise using NT 4. With Windows Server, in contrast, the Navy need only create *one* domain and then divide it using a new-to-NT notion called *organizational units*, usually abbreviated *OUs*.

More specifically, the Navy would solve their problem in this way:

- They'd create one domain named (for example) NAVY.

- Inside NAVY, they'd create an organizational unit named Norfolk, another called DC, and a third named San Diego. They would set up their servers and then place each server into the proper OU.

- Also inside NAVY, they'd create a user group named Norfolk Admins and two others named San Diego Admins and DC Admins. They'd create accounts for their users and place any administrators into their proper group, depending on whether they were based in DC, San Diego, or Norfolk.

At this point, understand that the San Diego Admins (kinda sounds like a baseball team, doesn't it?) don't yet have any power: there's no magic in Windows Server that says, "Well, there's an OU named San Diego and a group named San Diego Admins, I guess that must mean I should let these Admin guys have total control over the servers in the San Diego OU." You have to create that link by *delegating control* of the San Diego OU to the user group San Diego Admins. (Windows Server has a wizard that assists in doing this.) OUs are an excellent tool for building large and useful domains.

## Satisfying Political Needs

"That's *my* data, so I want it on *my* servers!" As information has become the most important asset of many firms—for example, I once heard someone comment that the majority of Microsoft's assets resided in the crania of their employees—some firms have been reluctant to yield control of that information to a central IT group. Nor is that an irrational perspective: if you were the person in charge of maintaining a five-million-person mailing list, and if that list generated one half of your firm's sales leads, you might well want to see that data housed on a machine or machines run by people who report directly to you.

Of course, on the other side of the story there is the IT director who wants Total Control of all servers in the building, and her reasoning is just as valid. You see, if a badly run server goes down and that failure affects the rest of the network, it's *her* head on the chopping block.

So on the one hand, the department head or VP wants to control the iron and silicon that happen to be where his data lives, and on the other hand, the IT director who's concerned with making sure that all data is safe and that everything on the network plays well with others wants to control said data and network pieces. Who wins? It depends—and that's the "politics" part.

What do Windows Servers do to ameliorate the political problems? Well, not as much as would be nice—there is no "make the vice presidents get along well" wizard—but Windows Server's variety of options for domain design gives the network designers the flexibility to build whatever kind of network structure they want.

Got a relatively small organization that would fit nicely into a single domain but one VP with server ownership lust? No problem, give the VP an OU of their own within the domain. Got a firm with two moderately large offices separated by a few hundred miles? Under NT 4, two domains and a trust relationship would be the answer, and you could choose to do that under Windows Server, but that's not the only answer. Since Windows Server is extremely parsimonious with WAN bandwidth in comparison with NT 4, you might find that a single domain makes sense because it's easier to administer than two domains but not impossible from a network bandwidth point of view. And bandwidth utilization is our next topic.

## Connectivity and Replication Issues

More and more companies don't live in only one place. They've purchased another firm across the country, and what once were two separate *local* area networks are now one firm with a wide area network need. If that WAN link is fast, there's no network design headache at all: hook the two offices up with a T1 link, and you can essentially treat them as one office.

That's beneficial because each site will usually contain a domain controller—one of those servers that hosts the AD database and that acts as a machine to accomplish logins. But those domain controllers must communicate whenever something changes, such as when a user's password changes or when an administrator creates a new user account. This is called *AD replication*. The same thing happened with NT 4, because NT 4 also allowed you to put multiple domain controllers in an enterprise.

In NT 4, suppose you've got two offices connected by a slow WAN link. Suppose further that you've got a domain controller in each of these offices. They need to replicate their SAM database between domain controllers (recall that NT 4 used a user database named SAM; the Windows Server database is called AD). NT 4's domain controller updates happened every five minutes. That means that a domain controller might try to replicate changes to another domain controller every five minutes, even if they're connected with only a very slow link. All that chatter could well choke a WAN link and keep other, more important traffic from getting through.

Windows Server improves upon that by allowing you to tell domain controllers about how well they're connected. The idea is that you describe your enterprise in terms of *sites*, which are just groups of servers with fast connections—groups of servers living on the same local area network, basically. You can then define how fast (or probably, slow) the connections *between* those sites are, and Windows 2000 Server will then be a bit smarter about using those connections.

In particular, Windows Server AD servers compress data before sending it over slow WAN links. Taking the time to compress data requires a certain amount of CPU power, but it's well worth it, since AD is capable of a 10 percent compression ratio!

Not only do you often face slow links, you often must live with *unreliable* links, ones that are up and down or perhaps up for only a short period of time every day. Windows 2000 Server lets you define not only a WAN link's speed but also the times that it is up.

NT 4's directory replications require a real-time connection called a Remote Procedure Call (RPC). RPCs are like telephone calls—the domain controller programs on each side must be up and running and actively communicating simultaneously. Inasmuch as domain controllers can be more or less busy as the day wears on, requiring this kind of shared concentration in order to get a simple directory replication accomplished is a bit demanding. It might be nicer if replications could work less like a telephone call and more like a mailing—and to a certain extent, Windows 2000 Server allows this, or rather points to a day in the future when it'll be possible.

It's possible for one domain controller to simply *mail* part of its replication data to another domain controller. Then, even if the receiving domain controller is not currently online, the mail message is still waiting for it, ready to be read when the receiving domain controller is again awake.

Site control will make life considerably easier for those managing multilocation networks.

## Scalability: Building Big Networks

Large enterprise networks found NT 4 lacking in the number of users that its SAM database could accommodate. Although you could theoretically create millions of user accounts on an NT domain, it's not practical to create more than about 5,000 to perhaps 10,000 user accounts in a domain. (If you took the MCSE exam for NT Server and are looking at that number oddly, it's because they made you memorize 40,000 as the answer to the question "How many user accounts can you put on an NT domain?" In my experience, that's just not realistic, hence my 5,000 to 10,000 number.)

Five thousand user accounts are more than most companies would ever need. But some large firms need to incorporate more user accounts into their enterprise, forcing them to divide their company's network into multiple domains—and multiple domains were to be avoided at all costs under NT 4 because of the extra trouble in maintaining them.

AD can accommodate many more user accounts than NT's SAM. Furthermore, AD allows you to build larger networks by making the process of building and maintaining multidomain networks easier. Whereas once an administrator of a multidomain network had to build and maintain a complex system of interdomain security relationships—the *trust relationships* I've already referred to—now Windows Server will let you build a system of domains called a *forest*. A forest's main strength is that once a group of domains has been built into a forest, the trusts are automatically created and maintained. There are also smaller multidomain structures called trees that also feature automatic trusts.

## Simplifying Computer Names or Unifying the Namespace

Devices on a network mainly identify themselves by some long and unique number. On an intranet or the Internet, it's a unique 32-bit number called an *IP address*. Networks also commonly exploit a 48-bit address burned into each network interface card called a *MAC* (Media Access Control) *address*. Any Ethernet, Token Ring, ATM (asynchronous transfer mode), or other network interface has one of these addresses, and some conventions that network manufacturers have agreed upon have ensured that no matter whom you buy a NIC (network interface card) from, the NIC will have a 48-bit address that no other NIC has. Some parts of NT identify PCs by their IP address (or addresses—a machine with multiple NICs will have an IP address and MAC address for each NIC), others by the PC's MAC address or addresses.

But people don't relate well to long strings of numbers—telling you that you can send me mail at mark@11001110111101101111110111001000 is technically accurate (presuming that you can find a mail client that will accept network addresses in binary) but not very helpful. It's far more preferable to be able to instead tell your mail program to send mail to mark@minasi.com, which you can do. Somehow, however, your mail client must be able to look up minasi.com and from there find out where to send mail for minasi.com. In the same way, pointing your web browser to www.microsoft.com forces the browser to convert www.microsoft.com into the particular IP address or addresses that constitute Microsoft's website. This process of converting from human-friendly names such as minasi.com to computer-friendly addresses such as 11001110111101101111110111001000 is called *name resolution*. It's something every network must do.

So why is name resolution a problem with NT? Because most of the networking world uses *one* approach to name resolution, and up through version 4, NT used a different one.

Most every firm is on the Internet, has an internal intranet, or both. Intranets and the Internet use the DNS form of name resolution. DNS names are the familiar Internet names such as www.microsoft.com. PCs resolve DNS names by consulting a group of servers around the world called, not surprisingly, DNS servers. Your company or Internet Service Provider operates one or more DNS servers, and your Internet software uses these nearby DNS servers to resolve (for example) www.minasi.com to the Internet address 206.246.253.200.

NT-based networks using Internet software don't use DNS for much of their work. Instead, Microsoft invented its own name servers somewhat like DNS but using NetBIOS names; they called these name servers Windows Internet Name Service, or WINS, servers. The NetBIOS naming system is incompatible with DNS; NetBIOS names are simpler—no more than 15 characters, no periods.

That leads to this problem: nearly every firm is on the Internet—*has* to be on the Internet—and so every firm must give DNS names to their computers. But if they're also using NT, they need to give their systems NetBIOS names. That in and of itself is not a great burden; what *is* a burden is that these names are important to the programs that use them, and programs typically can need one of the two names and can't use the other of the two.

Let's take an example. Suppose someone wants to log on to an NT 4 domain at Acme Technologies. To accomplish that, this person's workstation must find a domain controller for that domain. The workstation does that by searching for a machine with a particular NetBIOS name. Let's say that Acme does indeed have a domain controller around named LOGMEIN (its NetBIOS name), which *also* acts as a web server with the DNS name reptiles.pictures.animalworld.com, because it hosts pages of pictures of local reptiles. Let's also suppose that for some reason ACME has no WINS servers but has a great network of DNS servers.

DNS names are of no value to the workstation looking for a logon. You could have the finest set of DNS servers in the world, but it would make no difference—without a functioning WINS server, that workstation would probably be unable to locate a domain controller to log you in. On the other hand, if someone sitting at that very same workstation sought to view the reptile pictures on `http:/` `/www.reptiles.pictures.animalworld.com`, they'd just fire up Internet Explorer and point it at that URL. Internet Explorer is, of course, uninterested in NetBIOS names, relying mainly on DNS names. The workstation would quickly locate the web server and browse its pages, even as that same workstation was unable to detect that the very same server could perform logins.

Windows Server solves this problem by largely doing away with WINS, using DNS for all its name resolution needs. Unfortunately, however, Windows Server uses DNS for all *its* name resolution needs—older Windows 9*x* and Windows NT 4 systems still rely on WINS. So while WINS' role is diminished, it'll still be around until you've pulled the plug on the last Windows 9*x* and NT machines.

## Satisfying the Lust for Power and Control

Well, okay, maybe it's not *lust*, but it's certainly *need*. Put simply, there just plain aren't enough support people around, and there is no shortage of users to support. In 1987, many firms retained one support person for every 100 users; in many companies nowadays, that ratio is more like one support person for every 2,000 users.

Although it was once possible for a support person to physically visit every user's PC to perform support tasks, it's just not reasonable to expect that anymore. Support people need tools that allow them to get their work done from a central location as much as possible. And, although not every user is all that happy about it, one way to simplify a support person's job is to standardize each PC's desktop. In some cases, support staffs need software tools to allow them to *enforce* that standard desktop. (As you can imagine, it's a very political issue for many firms.)

In NT 4, Microsoft started helping support staffs centralize their desktop control with something called *system policies*. But system policies were lacking in a few ways. AD improves upon system policies with a kind of "system policies version 2" called *group policies*.

Better security, more flexible administration options, wiser use of bandwidth, and providing god-like control to administrators: that's basically what AD is trying to accomplish.

## Connecting a Windows XP Professional Machine to an AD Domain

So now that you know all about Active Directory and what it's for, let's take a look at how you can connect your Windows XP Professional workstation to an Active Directory domain. The steps are actually quite easy, and if you work along with the examples that follow, you should be connected to an Active Directory domain in no time.

### Checklist

First, there are a number of things that you should make sure you know in advance before trying to connect to an Active Directory domain. Specifically, be sure you have the following information available before starting:

◆   The name of the AD domain you will be joining.

CHAPTER 24

♦ Your username and password, as they are defined in the AD.

♦ Whether an account has already been added to the AD for your machine (each machine has an account, as does each user).

♦ If an account has not been added for your machine, you will need a login name and password in Active Directory with the rights to create an account for your machine.

## Connecting to AD

Once you have verified all of the items on the checklist, you've got what it takes to add your machine to an Active Directory domain. The next step is to verify that the correct components are installed on your Windows XP Professional computer (and to install them if they're not) and then to add your machine to the Active Directory domain.

### VERIFY OPERATING SYSTEM PREREQUISITES

In order to connect to an Active Directory domain, two networking components must be in place on your system:

♦ Client for Microsoft Networks

♦ An appropriate communications protocol (NWLink IPX/SPX or TCP/IP)

Both components are necessary for any Microsoft operating systems to talk to each other, so it is important to make sure they are properly installed before trying to join an Active Directory domain. To verify that both components are installed, follow these steps:

1. Choose Start ➢ Connect To ➢ Show All Connections to open the Network Connections folder.

2. Right-click the icon that represents your network (Local Area Connection), and choose Properties from the shortcut menu to open the Properties dialog box for your network.

3. In the list of configured components you should see the Client for Microsoft Networks and Internet Protocol (TCP/IP). Make sure that both items are enabled (the check box next to the item is selected).

You now have everything you need to connect to a domain. You just need to tell Windows XP Professional to do it.

### CHANGE YOUR COMPUTER NAME

To tell Windows XP Professional to join an Active Directory domain, you change the network identification information on your system. However, the configuration for doing so is a bit hidden. Instead of being with the other networking items, the Active Directory domain items are configuration parameters in My Computer. To change network identification, follow these steps:

1. Click Start, right-click My Computer, and choose Properties from the shortcut menu to open the System Properties dialog box.

2. Click the Computer Name tab, and you will see the current identification of your system consisting of a machine name and the current domain or workgroup your system is configured to use. On this tab, you have two choices for joining a domain. By clicking the Network ID button,

you begin the Network Identification Wizard. Selecting Change will get the same job done, but manually.

**3.** To change this configuration, click the Change button to open the Computer Name Changes dialog box:

As you can see, the name of my machine is QDOCLAP, and it was originally a member of a workgroup called MSHOME. I've told Windows XP Professional to join an Active Directory domain called SUSHIYUM by clicking the Domain radio button and entering the name of the domain that my system should join. After you make the necessary changes to your system, click OK. Either one of two things will happen.

First, you might see a dialog box welcoming you to the domain you specified. What that means is that someone—an administrator or someone else—has already set up an account for the name of your computer within Active Directory. If this is the case, all you will need to do is reboot to complete your changes. You can now proceed to the "Logging In to Active Directory" section of this chapter.

However, more often than not there won't be an account for your computer within Active Directory, so you'll need to add one. You'll know this is the case if you get prompted for a username and password.

Active Directory doesn't let just anyone add machine accounts to its database; you need an Active Directory user account that has the right to do so. The Administrator account will work for these purposes, but depending on your circumstances, you may not have been provided with the administrative password to Active Directory. There are also ways to create special accounts for one purpose—to add machines to domains—but ultimately if you don't know of an account to use at this point, you will need to contact an administrator for Active Directory in order to complete this process (that's why this information was listed in the prerequisites).

Assuming you have the correct username and password to use (or that someone has entered it for you), the next thing you should see is a dialog box welcoming you to the domain you've joined. Your machine will need to be rebooted for the changes to take effect, so go ahead and reboot your system.

### LOGGING IN TO ACTIVE DIRECTORY

The next time your computer boots up, it probably won't look much different. You'll be presented with the same login box that you've always seen. However, if you click the Options button on the main login screen, you will see a drop-down list of domains to choose from. By default, your system will continue to use its own local accounts database for logging in, so you will need to click the drop-down list and choose the domain you just joined. Select the appropriate domain, and then enter your Active Directory username and password in the appropriate fields. If everything is configured correctly, you should end up logging in to the Active Directory domain. Congratulations!

## Summary

The purpose of this chapter was to introduce you to AD. As you can tell from even these few pages, AD is a complicated topic. If you're interested in learning more, I recommend that you take a look at *Mastering Windows 2000 Server,* Fourth Edition (Minasi, Anderson, Smith, Toombs; Sybex, 2002), and *Active Directory Best Practices 24seven: Migrating, Designing, and Troubleshooting* by Brad Price (Sybex, 2004), or *Mastering Windows Server 2003* (Minasi, Anderson, Beveridge, Callahan, Justice; Sybex, 2003).

Active Directory can be a somewhat nebulous topic; until you get in to it, it might not make a lot of sense. The same can be said for the topic of our next chapter: the Registry.

# Chapter 25

# Understanding and Using the Registry

This chapter covers how to work with one of the most mentioned but least understood components of Windows—the Registry, the giant repository of Windows' knowledge and wisdom about your computer. The chapter starts by discussing what the Registry is, what it does, why you might want to mess with it, and what the dangers are of doing so. It then details the step you *must* take before you make any changes to the Registry: backing up the Registry so that you can restore it if something goes wrong. After that, the chapter shows you how to use the Registry Editor to examine the contents of the Registry, find what you're looking for, and make changes.

In this chapter:

- ◆ Understanding the Registry and what it does
- ◆ Running Registry Editor
- ◆ Backing up your Registry
- ◆ Restoring the Registry from backup
- ◆ Registry subtrees and data types
- ◆ Finding and changing information in the Registry

## What Is the Registry and What Does It Do?

Put simply, the Registry is a hierarchical database of all the settings required by your installation of Windows and the programs you've installed. These settings include information on the hardware installed on your computer and how it's configured; all the programs and their file associations; profiles for each user and group; and property settings for folders and files.

The Registry stores the information needed to keep your computer running. Windows itself stores a huge amount of information in the Registry, and each program you install stores information there too. You can store information in the Registry yourself if you want to, though unless you're creating programs, there's not much reason to do so.

The number of entries in the Registry depends on the number of users of the computer and the software installed, but between 50,000 and 100,000 entries is normal. This multitude of entries makes browsing through the Registry practical only for those with serious amounts of time weighing on their hands. Even searching through the Registry can be a slow process, because many of the entries contain similar information.

The Registry was introduced in Windows 95, and all 32-bit desktop versions of Windows have used it. In Windows 3.*x*, information was stored in initialization files—INI files for short. For example, Windows configuration information was stored in files such as WIN.INI and SYSTEM.INI. Most programs typically created configuration files of their own.

Centralizing all the information in the Registry has two main advantages. First, all the information is in one location. (Actually, it's in a couple of locations. More on this a little later in the chapter.) And second, you can back up the Registry (though most users forget or fail to do so) and restore it.

Not surprisingly, this centralization has the concomitant disadvantage that damage to the Registry can cripple Windows completely.

## Why Work with the Registry?

Paradoxically enough, you *don't* work with the Registry—most of the time. In theory, you should never need to mess with the Registry.

That's why Windows provides no direct way from the user interface to view the Registry and change its contents. If you want to explore and change the Registry, you need to deliberately run the Registry Editor program, which is tucked away in a safe place where no casual user should stumble across it.

Most of the information that's stored in the Registry you'll never need to change. Those relatively few pieces of information that Windows is happy for you to change are accessible through the Windows user interface, which provides you with an easier—if more restrictive—way of changing them than working in the Registry. For example, the settings in Control Panel applets store most of their information in the Registry, so you *could* edit the Registry and change the information there. But for all conventional purposes, you'll do better to work through those Control Panel applets and let them set the values in the Registry for you. Control Panel is designed to be easy to use, while the Registry isn't. Control Panel shows you your options in (mostly) intelligible ways; the information in the Registry is arcane when not incomprehensible. And Control Panel seldom screws up in translating your choices into hex and binary, whereas the Registry will happily accept input that will instruct Windows how to disable itself.

That said, sometimes you may need to access the Registry to change a vital piece of information that you cannot change through the user interface. Sometimes you'll need to access the Registry because something has gone wrong, and you need to change an entry manually. But more often, you'll hear about a cool tweak that you can perform by entering a new value in the Registry or by changing an existing value.

You can also use the Registry to store information of your own that you want to have available to Windows or to the programs you use. You might want to do this if you write your own programs or if you use a macro language to create automated procedures in a program—for example, if you use VBA to automate tasks in Word, Excel, or Outlook. (You *could* also use the Registry to store odd information, such as names and addresses—but there are far better ways of spending your life.)

## Preparing to Access the Registry

Before you do anything to the Registry, you need to understand this:

*If you mess up the Registry, you may disable parts of Windows' functionality. You may even disable Windows itself so that it cannot boot.*

So before you do *anything* to the Registry, back it up by exporting it as discussed later in this chapter. In fact, even if you don't make any changes to the Registry, it's a good idea to keep a backup of your Registry in case a program, Windows itself, or (more likely) a piece of malware makes a change for the worse.

# Running Registry Editor

To work with the Registry, you use Registry Editor. Windows provides no Start menu item for Registry Editor, though you can of course create your own Start menu item if you want.

Unless you create a Start menu item or shortcut, the easiest way to run Registry Editor is to choose Start ➤ Run (or press Winkey+R), enter **regedit** in the Run dialog box, and click the OK button. Windows starts Registry Editor (shown in Figure 25.1).

**FIGURE 25.1**

Launch Registry Editor by choosing Start ➤ Run and entering regedit in the Run dialog box.

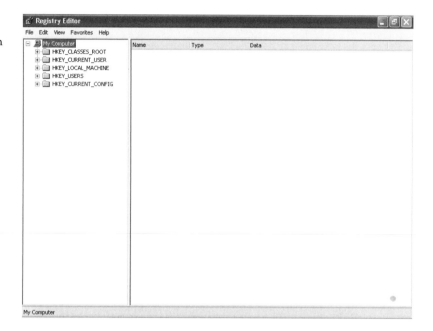

**NOTE**    If you've worked with the Registry in Windows 2000 or in Windows NT, you'll recall that those OSes included *two* Registry Editors—REGEDIT.EXE and REGEDT32.EXE. Both were functional but offered slightly different features from each other. Windows XP includes just one Registry Editor (with full functionality), REGEDIT.EXE, but there's a stub for REGEDT32.EXE so you can start the same Registry Editor by using either name.

## Backing Up Your Registry

Before you do anything else with Registry Editor—and that includes exploring the subtrees and keys of the Registry, let alone changing any values—back up your Registry.

To back up the Registry, export it by taking the following steps from Registry Editor:

**1.** Select the My Computer item in Registry Editor.

**TIP**    If you want to back up only a subtree of the Registry, select the subtree instead of the My Computer item.

2. Choose File ➤ Export. Registry Editor displays the Export Registry File dialog box. As you can see in the graphic below, this dialog box is a common Save As dialog box with an extra section tacked on at the bottom to house the Export Range box.

3. In the Export Range section, make sure the All option button is selected. If you chose a subtree in step 1, the Export Registry File dialog box appears with the Selected Branch option button selected and the subtree's name entered in the Selected Branch text box.

4. Specify the filename and location for the file as usual.

**TIP**  Registry files tend to be large—on the order of 20–30MB—so don't try to save yours to a floppy. If you have a CD recorder, save the Registry file to disk, and then burn it to CD.

5. Click the Save button. Windows saves the Registry file.

## Restoring Your Registry

To restore your Registry (or part of it) from a Registry file you've exported, follow these steps:

1. From Registry Editor, choose File ➤ Import. Windows displays the Import Registry File dialog box, which is a renamed Open dialog box.

2. In the Files of Type drop-down list, select the Registration Files item or the Registry Hive Files item as appropriate.

3. Select the Registry file to import.

4. Click the Open button. Registry Editor imports the Registry file and adds it to the Registry.

# Working in the Registry

Now that your Registry is safely backed up, it's time to examine how the Registry works and how you can change it.

As mentioned earlier in this chapter, the Registry is a hierarchical database. It's hierarchical in that its contents are arranged into a hierarchy of folders organized into five main areas called *subtrees* or *root keys*. You'll also sometimes hear them called *predefined keys*, though the term tends to be confusing because the Registry contains thousands of keys that are predefined. As you can see in Figure 25.1, the name of each subtree begins with the letters HKEY.

## The Five Subtrees of the Registry

These are the five subtrees and the types of information they contain:

**HKEY_CLASSES_ROOT**   This subtree contains an exhaustive list of the file types that Windows recognizes, the programs associated with them, and more.

**HKEY_CURRENT_USER**   This subtree contains information on the current user and their setup. For example, when you're logged on, all your Desktop preferences are listed in this subtree.

**HKEY_LOCAL_MACHINE**   This subtree contains information on the hardware and software setup of the computer.

**HKEY_USERS**   This subtree contains information on the users who are set up to use the computer, together with a DEFAULT profile that's used when no user is logged on to the computer.

**HKEY_CURRENT_CONFIG**   This subtree contains information on the current configuration of the computer—the hardware with which the computer booted.

## Keys, Subkeys, and Value Entries

In Registry Editor, expand the HKEY_CURRENT_USER subtree by clicking the plus (+) sign next to it or by double-clicking its name. Registry Editor displays the items contained within the subtree—an apparently endless list of folder-like objects, many of them containing further objects. Figure 25.2 shows the HKEY_CURRENT_USER subtree and some of its subkeys expanded.

Within each subtree, there are keys, subkeys, and value entries. A *key* is one of the folders within the subtree. Just as a subfolder is a folder within a folder, a *subkey* is a key within a key. Also as with "folder" and "subfolder," many people say "key" rather than "subkey" except when they need to be specific; this chapter does the same.

Each key or subkey can contain subkeys and value entries. The term *value entry* sounds like a management-consultant way of saying "value," but in fact it's not: a value entry is the current definition of a key and consists of a name, a data type, and the value assigned to the key.

For example, consider the MinAnimate key and value entry that you can see in Figure 25.2 in the HKEY_CURRENT_USER\Control Panel\Desktop\WindowMetrics subkey. As you can see in the Data column, the value of MinAnimate is 1. This value entry controls whether Windows animates windows when you minimize, maximize, or restore them. (The animation zooms the window from its displayed size and position down to its button on the Taskbar, and vice versa, instead of popping it off or back on the screen instantly.) A value of 0 indicates that the animation is off, a value of 1 that the animation is on.

**FIGURE 25.2**

Each subtree contains keys, subkeys, and value entries.

MinAnimate is interesting in that it's an example of a key added to the Registry in Windows XP in order to implement functionality already in Windows. In earlier versions of Windows, including Windows NT and Windows 2000, this key wasn't included in the Registry, though its functionality was implemented in Windows. These versions of Windows automatically animated windows that you minimized, maximized, or restored.

This animation was (and remains) pure eye candy—and like much eye candy, this animation didn't appeal to everyone. On a slow computer, or one with an underpowered graphics card, it was particularly irritating, because Windows seemed to be running arthritically. To switch off this animation, you needed to create the MinAnimate value entry in the Registry, assign it the value 0, and then restart Windows. (You could also implement this change by using a utility such as TweakUI, which created and adjusted the MinAnimate value entry transparently for you.)

Windows XP lets you control this setting via the Animate Windows When Minimizing and Maximizing check box on the Visual Effects tab of the Performance Options dialog box. When this check box is selected, MinAnimate has the value 1; when the check box is cleared, MinAnimate has the value 0.

## Registry Data Types

As you can see in Figure 25.2, the MinAnimate value entry is of type REG_SZ. REG means Registry, as you'd guess; SZ means string, indicating that the value entry contains a string of text (text characters, as opposed to, say, binary data). The WindowMetrics key also contains value entries of another data type, REG_BINARY. You get no prize for guessing that these are binary data.

Strings and binary data are the most widely used of the data types in the Registry. Next comes REG_DWORD, a double-word value entry. Figure 25.3 shows the HKEY_CURRENT_USER\Control Panel\

`Desktop` key, which contains some double-word value entries as well as string and binary value entries.

The other two most widely used data types are REG_MULTI_SZ, multi-string entries, and REG_EXPAND_SZ, expandable strings. Table 25.1 provides a roundup of the five most widely used data types.

You can create and edit value entries with any of these data types. We'll get to that a bit later in the chapter, after discussing where the Registry is stored and how to find information in it.

**FIGURE 25.3**
The HKEY_CURRENT_USER\Control Panel\Desktop key contains a variety of data types.

**TABLE 25.1:** The Five Most Widely Used Registry Data Types

| TYPE | TYPE DISPLAYED | EXPLANATION |
| --- | --- | --- |
| String | REG_SZ | Text. |
| Multi-string | REG_MULTI_SZ | Text, but with multiple text values. |
| Expandable string | REG_EXPAND_SZ | Text, but expandable. |
| Binary | REG_BINARY | A binary value, displayed as hexadecimal. |
| DWORD | REG_DWORD | Double-word: A 32-bit binary value displayed as an 8-digit hexadecimal value. |

**NOTE** Beyond these five widely used data types, the Registry can contain many different data types, such as REG_DWORD_BIG_ENDIAN (a value stored in reverse order of double-word value), REG_DWORD_LITTLE_ENDIAN (another type of double-word value), REG_FULL_RESOURCE_DESCRIPTOR (a hardware-resource list), REG_QWORD (a quadruple-word value), and REG_FILE_NAME (three guesses). You shouldn't need to mess with any of these unless you get into programming Windows—in which case, you'll need a book more specialized than this one.

## Where the Registry Is Stored

Most of the Registry is stored in several files on your hard drive. (Part of the Registry is created automatically when Windows boots and discovers which devices are attached to your computer.) These files are called *hives* (think bees, not allergies) or *hive files*. The hives are binary, but (as you'll see in the next section), if you're feeling curious, you can open them in a text editor and peek inside them.

Hive files containing computer-related information are stored in the *Windows*\system32\config folder, where *Windows* is your Windows folder. Hive files containing user-specific information are stored in the Documents and Settings\*Username* folder for each user.

These are the main hive files:

**SYSTEM** This file contains information about the computer's hardware and about Windows. This information goes into the HKEY_LOCAL_MACHINE\SYSTEM key.

**NTUSER.DAT** This file contains information about the user's preferences. Windows XP keeps an NTUSER.DAT file for each user in the \Documents and Settings\*Username* folder. This information goes into the HKEY_CURRENT_USER subtree.

**SAM** This file contains the user database. This information goes into the HKEY_LOCAL_MACHINE\SAM key.

**SECURITY** This file contains information on security settings. This information goes into the HKEY_LOCALMACHINE\SECURITY key.

**SOFTWARE** This file contains information on the software installed on the computer. This information goes into the HKEY_LOCAL_MACHINE\SOFTWARE key.

**DEFAULT** This file contains information about the default user setup. This information goes into the HKEY_USERS\DEFAULT key.

Each of the hive files has a log file named after it: DEFAULT.LOG, SOFTWARE.LOG, NTUSER.DAT.LOG, and so on. These log files note the changes to the hive files so that, if a change is applied that crashes the system, Windows can read the log, identify the problem change, and undo it.

Having read this, you're probably longing to lift the lid off a hive so you can see what's inside it. Perhaps if you use Notepad or another text editor, you can get a peek inside…

Don't.

Taking a text editor to a hive file would be like taking one of those old-fashioned can openers (you know, the ones that leave those nice jagged edges) to your favorite black box of electronic wizardry: clumsy, messy, and ultimately fruitless. In any case, Windows keeps the hive files open the whole time it's running so that it can write information to them and retrieve information from them whenever it needs, so they're locked. All you'll get for your pains is a message box telling you something like "The process cannot access the file because it is being used by another process." Translation: Windows needs this file. Hands off.

Let's look at what you *can* profitably do with the Registry: find keys and value entries or information in it, change values, and create (and delete) keys and value entries of your own.

## Finding Information in the Registry

You can find information in the Registry in two ways: by digging through the Registry looking for it or by using the Find function.

Digging through the Registry takes minimal explanation, because it's very similar to browsing in Explorer in Explore mode. You can expand and collapse keys as you would drives and folders in Explorer, and you can use type-down addressing to reach the next key or entry matching the letters you type. But because of the number of keys and value entries the Registry contains, you'll usually do better by searching through it than browsing.

If you know the name of a key, the name of a value entry, or the data contained in a value entry, you can search for it. For example, if you wanted to find where FTP sites were listed, you might search for FTP Sites. If you wanted to find out what the entry for the AutoCorrect file was called, you might search for .ACL, the extension of the AutoCorrect file. You can restrict the search by selecting only the check boxes for the items you're looking at—Keys, Values, or Data—in the Look At group section of the Find dialog box (shown in Figure 25.4). (Choose Edit ➤ Find to open the Find dialog box.) And you can search for only the entire string by selecting the Match Whole String Only check box. Selecting this check box prevents Find from finding the string you're looking for inside other strings—it makes Find find only whole strings that match the string in the Find What text box.

**FIGURE 25.4**

Use the Find dialog box in Registry Editor to find the keys, values, or data you want to manipulate.

Because of the volume of information that Windows stores in the Registry, the first match you find may not be the key (or value entry, or value) you need. For example, if you use your company's name as the Find item when looking for the `RegisteredOrganization` key for Windows, you may find another key, such as the registered organization for Internet Explorer. Close examination of the key will usually tell you whether you've found the key you were looking for. If not, press the F3 key or choose Edit ➤ Find Next to find the next instance.

## Editing a Value Entry

To edit a value entry in the Registry, navigate to it and double-click it. (Alternatively, select it and choose Edit ➤ Modify.) Windows displays an Edit dialog box appropriate to the type of data the value entry contains.

String values and expandable string values are the easiest values to edit. In the Edit String dialog box (shown in Figure 25.5), enter the text of the string in the Value Data text box, and then click the OK button.

**FIGURE 25.5**

You can edit both string values and expandable string values in the Edit String dialog box.

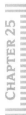

Multi-string values are relatively simple to edit. In the Edit Multi-String dialog box (shown in Figure 25.6), enter all the data for the value entry on separate lines, and then click the OK button.

**FIGURE 25.6**
Editing a multi-string value in the Edit Multi-String dialog box

Double-word values are the next-easiest values to edit. In the Edit DWORD Value dialog box (shown in Figure 25.7), enter the data in the Value Data text box, and then choose the Hexadecimal option button or the Decimal option button as appropriate in the Base section. (When you're editing a built-in double-word value, you shouldn't need to change the existing Base setting.) Click the OK button.

**FIGURE 25.7**
Editing a double-word value in the Edit DWORD Value dialog box

Binary values are brutes to change, and you probably won't want to mess with them for fun. In the Edit Binary Value dialog box (shown in Figure 25.8), edit the data in the Value Data text box with great care, and then click the OK button.

**FIGURE 25.8**
Editing a binary value in the Edit Binary Value dialog box is hard work.

## Adding a Key or a Value Entry

You can add a key or a value entry to the Registry either automatically or manually.

To add a key or value entry to the Registry automatically, double-click a REG file that you've received. For example, some programs sold via download use Registry keys to implement a license: you pay for the program and download it. The company then e-mails you a license and a REG file. To add the registration data to your Registry, double-click the REG file. Windows adds the necessary keys and value entries to the Registry.

To add a key or a value entry to the Registry manually, follow these steps:

1. Right-click the key in which you want to create the new key or value entry, choose New from the shortcut menu, and choose the appropriate item from the submenu: Key, String Value, Binary Value, DWORD Value, Multi-String Value, or Expandable String Value. Registry Editor creates a new key named `New Key #1` or `New Value #1` (or the next available number) and displays an edit box around it.

2. Type the name for the key or value entry.

3. Press the Enter key or click elsewhere in the Registry Editor window. Registry Editor assigns to the key or value entry the name you specified.

If you created a value entry, double-click it. Registry Editor displays the Edit dialog box appropriate to its type. Enter the data for the value entry as described in the previous section.

## Deleting a Key or a Value Entry

Just as you can create keys and value entries, you can delete them. Generally speaking, it's a bad idea to delete any keys other than those you've created. Windows itself and Windows programs protect some keys in the Registry, but you'll find a surprising number that aren't deleted and that you can therefore delete freely.

To delete a value entry, right-click it and choose Delete from the shortcut menu. Registry Editor displays the Confirm Value Delete dialog box or the Confirm Key Delete check box (shown in Figure 25.9). Click the Yes button to confirm the deletion.

**FIGURE 25.9**
Confirm a deletion in the Confirm Key Delete dialog box (shown here) or the Confirm Value Delete dialog box.

If the key or value entry is locked against deletion, Registry Editor displays an error message box.

## Copying a Key Name

If you're describing to someone how to find particular information in the Registry, you'll need to get the key name right. But you don't need to type it painstakingly—you can copy it instead.

To copy a Registry key name, select it in the left-hand pane in Registry Editor and choose Edit ➤ Copy Key Name. You can then paste it from the Clipboard into a program.

## An Example: Changing Your Windows Name and Organization

As mentioned at the beginning of the chapter, Microsoft reckons you should seldom (or preferably never) need to make changes to the Registry directly. But you'll probably run into tips and tweaks, online or in magazines, that promise to improve Windows' performance, compatibility, or behavior with a judicious change or two.

For example, say you misspelled your name or your organization's name during setup. Or perhaps you've bought a computer loaded with Windows from someone else. Either way, when you display the General tab of the System Properties dialog box, there's the misspelling or the wrong name laughing at you.

You'll want to change the name or organization name so that they're correct. There's no way to do so through the Windows user interface, but by navigating to the HKEY_LOCAL_MACHINE\ SOFTWARE\Microsoft\WindowsNT\CurrentVersion key and changing the RegisteredOwner and RegisteredOrganization value entries as appropriate, you can fix the problem in a minute or two.

## Using Registry Favorites to Quickly Access Keys

If you find yourself using the Registry a lot, there's another feature you should know about: Registry favorites. To access the keys you need to work with frequently, you can create favorites in Registry Editor much as you can in Explorer and Internet Explorer.

To create a favorite, follow these steps:

1. Select the key to which you want the favorite to refer.

2. Choose Favorites ➢ Add to Favorites. Registry Editor displays the Add to Favorites dialog box:

3. In the Favorite Name text box, enter the name for the favorite. (By default, Registry Editor suggests the key name, but you may well want to change this to more descriptive text.)

4. Click the OK button. Registry Editor adds the favorite to your Favorites menu.

To access a favorite, display the Favorites menu and choose the favorite from the list.

To remove a favorite from the Favorites menu, choose Favorites ➢ Remove Favorite. Windows displays the Remove Favorites dialog box. Choose the favorite in the Select Favorite list box and click the OK button.

## Summary

This chapter has discussed what the Registry is, what it does, why you *must* back it up before messing with it, how to mess with it, and why you shouldn't mess with it most of the time.

The next chapter will dive into a concept that can make administration easier if you have a large network: scripting. Scripting allows you to automate common repetitive tasks in order to ease your administrative burden.

# Chapter 26

# Scripts for Automation

Virtually every administrative task we've performed so far has, in one way or another, involved utilizing Windows' many GUI tools such as the MMC, System Applet, Network Applet, and the like. Microsoft has gone to great pains to ensure that we have a variety of tools at our disposal for performing administrative functions. However, certain tasks—particularly common, repetitive tasks—can become quite tedious when executed one at a time using the GUI tools. It is in these instances that leveraging scripts can be advantageous. Not only does scripting save time, it can also allow you to accomplish certain tasks that are difficult, or even impossible, with the standard GUI tools. This chapter covers the following topics:

◆ Brief overview of scripting

◆ Writing shell scripts

◆ The Windows Script Host

◆ Advanced scripting concepts

◆ Sample scripts for common tasks

## What Is Scripting?

Quite simply, *scripting* is the process of arranging individual commands such that they follow a logical course and produce a desired result. These commands can be DOS commands (shell scripting) or commands specific to a particular scripting engine (Windows Script Host [WSH] scripting). Scripting is a form of computer programming. Notice that I didn't say "simple form" or "small form" of programming. Indeed, while most scripts are comparatively small and designed to perform quite specific, limited tasks, the differences between scripts and fully functioning computer programs have more to do with how they are deployed than what they do. Here's a brief comparison.

**Scripts are interpreted.** In the XP world, scripts must be interpreted by a script engine during execution. Computer programs are generally precompiled into the bytecode of the target platform.

**Scripts provide limited functionality.** Most of the available scripting engines are subsets of larger programming languages. VBScript, for example, is based on Microsoft's more powerful Visual Basic language. While there are some things that it simply cannot do, there are ways to give your scripts power that rivals "professional" development languages. We'll discuss these techniques in the "Advanced Concepts" section.

**Scripts are "clear text."** Once a computer program is compiled to bytecode, it is very difficult (but not impossible) to view the original code. Scripts are stored as ANSI text so the script engine can parse the file and translate each command into the appropriate operation. For security reasons, scripts should be kept in a secure location on an NTFS partition with limited access. The script files themselves can also be encoded to make deciphering contents somewhat more troublesome.

Even with these limitations, scripting can be a powerful weapon in your administrative arsenal. The rest of this chapter will cover some of the basic concepts of scripting and will include sample scripts to help you apply this knowledge.

# Shell Scripting with BAT and CMD Files

Many people look at shell scripting as a basic entry point into scripting—something to use to get their feet wet until they graduate to the more advanced scripting available with the Windows Script Host. While it is true that the WSH does provide a more powerful scripting environment, I tend to view the differences between the two based on the task I am trying to accomplish at the time. I believe it was Confucius who said, "Don't use a cannon to kill a mosquito." If the task at hand can be completed with a batch script, then there's no reason not to use one.

**NOTE**  It doesn't matter whether you use the extension .bat or .cmd—there's no difference. I use the .cmd extension for the scripts in this section.

A *shell script* (also known as a *batch file*) is essentially a group of shell commands encapsulated into a file and executed in sequence. Shell commands are those commands that are typed directly at the Windows XP command prompt. These can include standard DOS commands such as copy, dir, mkdir, etc., as well as any executable applications that are capable of receiving command-line arguments, such as cacls and net.

In addition to OS commands and programs, shell scripts can contain additional code to aid in executing the script, including commands to perform script logic such as comparisons, loops, etc. Shell scripts have the extension of either .bat or .cmd and can be executed simply by typing the name of the script (with or without the extension) on the command line.

## Tools for Scripting

Before you can begin creating scripts, you'll need an editor to get your code into the computer. The perennial favorite for creating batch scripts (and scripts for the Windows Script Host, for that matter) is Notepad. Veteran scripters refer to this simple text editor as "Visual Notepad," as in *Visual* Basic or *Visual* Studio—Microsoft's integrated development environment. While this sarcasm may be justified (Notepad does not perform any syntax checking, error handling, or even simple text formatting), virtually every scripter I've met relies on Notepad almost exclusively.

There are many third-party script editors available, as well. Feel free to experiment with them. Some are shareware and some are "professional" products. Each has its own distinct advantages and disadvantages. I'm sure you'll find one that suits you just fine.

**WARNING**  Notepad always tries to save a new script as a TXT file. You have to remember to Save As ➢ Save As Type ➢ All Files (*.*), and then type the filename along with proper extension.

For creating XML-based WSH scripts, an XML editor comes in handy. I like to use FrontPage, because it came with my Office XP software. I don't much fancy buying software when a tool I already have will work just fine. We'll discuss this in further detail in "XML-based Scripts" later in this chapter.

## Your First Shell Script

There is an unwritten law of computer programming that states that your first application in any environment must be "Hello World!" Let's write a batch script to print "Hello World!" on the screen. (See Figure 26.1.)

```
rem HelloWorld.cmd
rem Displays "Hello World!" on the command line
echo off
echo Hello World!
```

**FIGURE 26.1**
Output from
HelloWorld.cmd

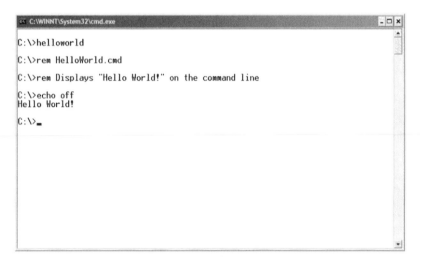

This simple script shows us some very important features of shell scripting. First, we can include remarks to help us understand what the script does. The rem keyword causes the rest of the line to be ignored, allowing you to comment your code.

Text is displayed using the echo function. Echo is also used to turn automatic echoing on or off. By default, the command interpreter automatically echoes each command to the screen, thus allowing you to follow the execution of the script. Sometimes this is advantageous, but it can quickly get out of hand. Turning this feature off allows you to limit output to only the text that you specify, so that important information doesn't get lost in a sea of echoes.

## Adding Logic to Shell Scripts

While printing "Hello World!" on the screen can provide endless hours of entertainment for the whole family, let's see if perhaps we can write a batch script to do something a bit more productive. At the same time, we'll learn some of the advanced logic available to batch scripts.

Since batch scripts can include any shell command, the possibilities are limitless. Don't believe me? Go to a command prompt and, after the C:\, simply type **help**. Quite a list, no? And that's just the tip of the iceberg. The Windows XP Resource Kit contains a wealth of utilities that can be used in batch scripts (as well as sample VBScripts, too.)

Any and all of these commands can be placed in a batch file to be invoked whenever necessary. That alone is worth the price of admission, in my opinion! May I enthrall you with a personal example? I have a batch file called Connect.cmd that stays on my Desktop. Although small (it contains only two lines), it really comes in handy:

```
nbtstat -R
ping myinternalserver
```

I use this script every time I travel and need to tunnel into my private network over the Internet. The first line purges and reloads my remote cache name table (causing my LMHOSTS file to be parsed, which contains the IP addresses of computers in my internal network). The second line attempts to make a connection based on an internal name (invoking my firewall-security login screen). It sure is a lot easier to simply double-click this file on my Desktop than to open a command-prompt window and type both lines.

The real power of scripting, however, is its ability to perform repetitive operations. In order to do this effectively, you need to be able to pass arguments to the script, store data in variables, perform comparisons and loops on this data, and control the flow of the script. Actually, there's quite a bit more involved in order to fully realize the capabilities of shell scripts, but the following list should get you off to a good start.

### ARGUMENTS

Command-line arguments are automatically passed to your script when you run it. All that is required is that you include the code to capture these arguments. These arguments are stored, in the order entered, in the numbered variables *%1*, *%2*, *%3*, etc. The arguments on the command line are separated by a space. Here's an example:

```
C:\ShowArgs arg1 arg2 arg3
```

If you need to include more than one word as an argument, enclose the whole thing in quotes (just remember that the quotes themselves become part of the argument). You can strip out the quotes by referring to the variable as *%~x*:

```
C:\ShowArgs2 arg1 arg2 "This is argument 3"
```

Figure 26.2 shows these arguments being displayed in a script, both with and without the quotation marks removed.

### VARIABLES (THE *SET* COMMAND)

Quite often the need arises to create variables to store additional data. This can be accomplished by using the set command to create an environment variable. Just remember to reset the variable back to empty before the script terminates.

```
rem The following line creates an environment variable
rem named 'var1' and assigns it the value of 'MyData'
set var1=MyData
rem the following line resets the environment variable to nothing
set var1=
```

**FIGURE 26.2**

Passing arguments to batch scripts

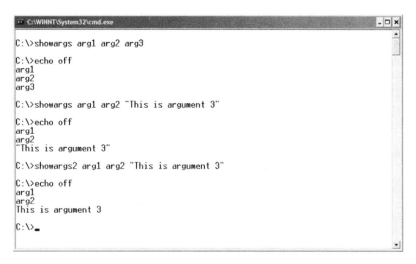

The set command can also solve numerical expressions and assign the data to a variable. The expression can include both real numbers and/or other variables. This is accomplished using the /A flag:

```
echo off
rem The following line adds the two command-line
rem arguments together and multiplies them by 10
set /A var1=10*(%1 + %2)
echo %var1%
Set var1=
```

When I run this script as C:\ShowSet 5 4, the script echoes 90 to the screen, just as it should. In addition to "standard" math, these numerical expressions can include logical shift; bitwise AND, OR, and XOR; and more.

You can even use the set command to take user input from the command line. The /P flag allows you to prompt the user for input:

```
echo off
rem The following line prompts the user to enter their name
set /P var1=Enter your first name:
echo %var1%
Set var1=
```

Figure 26.3 shows the output from both of the previous scripts.

### COMPARISONS AND LOOPS (THE *IF* AND *FOR* COMMANDS)

The real "logic" of a script is found in the ability to perform operations selectively. The if and for commands allow you to perform two very important logical operations:

◆ Ensure that a particular criterion has been met prior to executing a section of the script (if)

◆ Execute the same operation over and over using different criteria (for)

**FIGURE 26.3**

Output from the set command

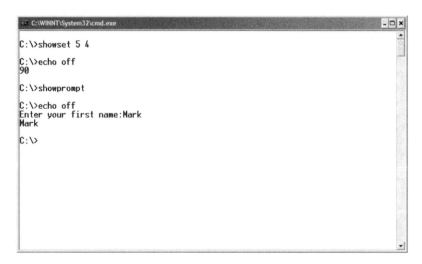

```
C:\>showset 5 4

C:\>echo off
90

C:\>showprompt

C:\>echo off
Enter your first name:Mark
Mark

C:\>
```

The if command allows you to check for the existence of a file, compare the values of two strings or sets of numbers, and more. This is particularly useful when you have several subroutines set up to perform different operations. Depending upon the result of the if comparison, a particular subroutine can be called. When checking for files, the process is simple:

```
If exist file.tmp del file.tmp
```

Or you can use variables:

```
If exist %1 del %1
```

If necessary, you can specify the path, drive, etc. The if command also evaluates a variable and determines script flow:

```
If %1==delete goto :DeleteFiles
```

The for command enables you to perform operations on each file in a set of files:

```
For %%i in (*.txt) do copy /a All.txt+%%i All.txt
```

I said earlier in this chapter that scripts allow you to do some things that are impossible to do using GUI tools; this is one of those times. The above code takes every TXT file in the current directory and copies them all into one big file called All.txt. You can't do that in Explorer!

The /R option allows you to specify a root directory and perform the specified operation on every file in that directory and all subdirectories.

The /D option performs the command specified on all directories (rather than files) in the current directory.

Finally, as with the set command, you can strip the quotes out of the variable (%%~i), expand it to a path only (%%~pi), and expand it to a file extension (%%~xi).

### FLOW CONTROL (THE *CALL* AND *GOTO* COMMANDS)

As your scripts become more complex, you need to maintain control over script execution. Remember, doing the same things over and over are what scripts do best. If you find yourself using the same code again and again, you can use `call` and/or `goto` to save a *lot* of typing. The `goto` command is pretty straightforward. It simply causes the script to jump to the specified label:

```
rem Just a hop, skip, and a goto
echo Hello There!
goto :goodbye
echo How are you?
:goodbye
echo Goodbye
```

In this script, `Hello There!` and Goodbye are the only things echoed to the screen. The `goto` statement caused us to skip over the line to echo `How are you?` When using `goto`, each jump is final. If you want to get back to where you were, you have to use another `goto` (and another label).

The `call` command allows you to either run another script (complete with arguments) or jump to a label in the current script and execute it as if it were a separate script. Once the code has executed to the end of the script (or the command `goto :EOF` has been executed), control is passed back to the line directly following the initial `call` command. Figure 26.4 shows the output from using `call...goto` for flow control.

**NOTE** EOF is programming shorthand for End of File. You might also see BOF on occasion. If you guessed that it means Beginning of File, you are correct.

```
echo off
rem The following "calls" several subroutines
echo Hello!
call :labl1
call :labl2
echo Nice seeing you!
goto :EOF
:labl1
echo How are you?
goto :EOF
:labl2
echo Goodbye
goto :EOF
```

Using `call...goto :EOF` in this manner is very similar to using subs and functions in VBScript, which we discuss a bit later. It allows you to create procedures you can call over and over. To ensure proper execution, you merely need to place these subroutines at the end of your script and place a `goto :EOF` on the line just prior to the first routine.

**FIGURE 26.4**

Using `call...goto` for flow control

```
C:\WINNT\System32\cmd.exe

C:\>type showcall.cmd
echo off
rem The following "calls" two subroutines
echo Hello!
call :labl1
call :labl2
echo Nice seeing you!
goto :EOF
:labl1
echo How are you?
goto :EOF
:labl2
echo Goodbye
goto :EOF

C:\>showcall

C:\>echo off
Hello!
How are you?
Goodbye
Nice seeing you!

C:\>_
```

# Introduction to the Windows Script Host

While batch scripts can be very effective, there's no substitute for the power and flexibility of the Windows Script Host (WSH). The WSH is a COM-aware scripting environment (COM is Microsoft's Component Object Model) that not only allows you to create scripts in various languages, such as VBScript or JScript, it also enables you to extend the functionality of your scripts by directly accessing external COM components. (More on this topic in the "Advanced Concepts" section.)

## The WScript and CScript Executables

A significant difference between shell scripts and WSH scripts is that the latter must be executed by passing the script as an argument to one of two engines: CScript.exe or WScript.exe. CScript.exe executes at the command line. The output of the script is similar to that of shell scripts (although the underlying code is quite different). WScript.exe executes the script within the Windows XP GUI. As such, all output is window-based, in the form of a message box.

**NOTE**   Because the WScript.exe engine displays all text in the form of a message box, you are required to click OK or press Enter every single time text is displayed before script execution will continue. For this reason alone, we will be using CScript to run the scripts we write for the rest of this chapter.

You pass the desired script to the engine as an argument on the command line, along with any other required information such as flags or arguments required by your script: **cscript helloworld.wsf**

Scripts can also be started directly, either by typing their names at the command prompt or by double-clicking the script file from Windows Explorer.

**WARNING**   Directly executing scripts causes them to run under WScript.exe (i.e., in the GUI). The only way to invoke scripts with CScript is to explicitly specify it when running the script.

## Script File Languages

A key advantage to writing scripts for use in the WSH is the choice of scripting languages available. Windows XP includes scripting engines (not to be confused with the script host engines `WScript.exe` and `CScript.exe`) for the VBScript and JScript languages. Additional ActiveX scripting engines, created by third-party vendors, are available for other languages. For the purpose of consistency, we'll stick to VBScript for the scripts we feature here.

### VBSCRIPT

As I've mentioned, VBScript is a subset of Visual Basic. While it derives its functionality from a full-featured development language, there are quite a few limitations. Rather than discuss them here, I'll highlight them as they become apparent in our scripts. However, I try to follow these rules religiously when writing scripts in VBScript:

**Option Explicit**: This command should be placed at the beginning of the `<script>` section of every script you write. It forces you to declare variables before you use them. Variables are declared using the `dim` statement. This helps immensely when debugging. You'd be surprised how many times I've spent hours trying to figure out why a script isn't working properly, only to find that I misspelled a variable name at a critical stage.

**Hungarian Notation**: When you declare a variable, it is customary to have the variable name include a prefix that indicates the type of data it will hold. While VBScript does not allow you to specify the data type of variables, using Hungarian Notation will help keep your scripts more readable and less confusing.

> **strMyVariable**: Indicates that the variable will hold a string of text.
>
> **intMyVariable or iMyVariable**: Indicates an integer (whole number) value.
>
> **bMyVariable**: Indicates a Boolean (True/False or Yes/No) value.
>
> **objMyVariable**: Indicates that the variable will contain an object. We discuss objects in the "Advanced Concepts" section.

There are others, but these will pretty much cover the variables we will be using in our scripts.

## XML-based Scripts

WSH 2.0 introduced the capability to write scripts in XML format. Prior to this, all scripts were single-language, with the script's file extension indicating the language: `.vbs` for VBScript, `.js` for JScript, etc. By contrast, all WSH 2.0 scripts have the extension `.wsf`; they can contain multiple scripts, with each script having the capability of being in a different language. WSH 2.0 scripts offer some rather unique features not found in their WSH 1.0 counterparts.

**Multiple jobs**: WSH 2.0 scripts can contain several jobs, each identified by a particular job ID. When a job is specified at runtime, only that job executes. If no job is specified, the first job is executed and the script terminates.

**Multiple scripts**: Each job can contain multiple scripts, specified by the `<script>` tag. The language of the script is also determined by this tag, allowing a single script job to utilize scripts in any (or all) of the supported languages.

**Objects**: A significant XML tag is `<object>`. It allows you to specify an object that will be used by the entire job. This allows you (among other things) to persist data between several scripts.

**Runtime tags**: These XML tags allow you to specify the usage requirements of a script. They also allow you to name your command-line arguments, enabling you to enter them in random order when running the script. As your scripts become more complex, the ability to ask the script what it does and what data it is expecting becomes invaluable.

**Editing**: Since the scripts are in XML format, you can use a standard XML editor to create and edit them. Most editors of this type perform basic text formatting and color coding to make the scripts easier to debug. Microsoft's FrontPage has an HTML view that you can use for this purpose.

## Your First WSH 2.0 Script

In Listing 26.1, we have modified the `HelloWorld` script for use in the WSH. Figure 26.5 shows the output from this script when each job is executed individually.

**LISTING 26.1:** *HelloWorld.wsf*

```
<?xml version="1.0" ?>
<package>
  <comment>
  Hello World.wsf
  This script contains two jobs:
  Hello and Goodbye
  </comment>
  <job id="hello">
    <script language="VBScript">
    <![CDATA[
    'This script prints "Hello World!"
    WScript.Echo "Hello World!"
    ]]>
    </script>
  </job>
  <job id="goodbye">
    <script language="VBScript">
    <![CDATA[
    'This script prints "Goodbye World!"
    WScript.Echo "Goodbye World!"
    ]]>
    </script>
  </job>
</package>
```

**FIGURE 26.5**

Output from
HelloWorld.wsf

```
C:\>cscript helloworld.wsf
Microsoft (R) Windows Script Host Version 5.6
Copyright (C) Microsoft Corporation 1996-2001. All rights reserved.

Hello World!

C:\>cscript helloworld.wsf //job:hello
Microsoft (R) Windows Script Host Version 5.6
Copyright (C) Microsoft Corporation 1996-2001. All rights reserved.

Hello World!

C:\>cscript helloworld.wsf //job:goodbye
Microsoft (R) Windows Script Host Version 5.6
Copyright (C) Microsoft Corporation 1996-2001. All rights reserved.

Goodbye World!

C:\>
```

Listing 26.1 shows us quite a bit about XML-based scripts:

**XML version**: The <?xml?> tag tells the script parser that this file needs to be strictly parsed (i.e., attribute names are case-sensitive, values are enclosed in quotes, etc.) By contrast, HTML files are loosely parsed. This tag is not required but may be necessary for your scripts to be displayed properly, depending upon which XML editor you are using.

**Package**: The <package> tag tells WSH that one or more jobs follows. It is optional if your script only has one job.

**Comments (XML)**: The <comment> tag allows you to include comments that pertain to the entire script. You can still comment individual lines of code, which we will see next.

**Job IDs**: The <job id="xxx"> tag specifies the name of each job in the script. The ID is optional if the script contains only one job. Figure 26.5 shows how this job is specified on the command line. If no job is specified, the first job in the script is executed.

**CDATA**: This tag causes the data contained within it to become opaque to the XML parser. It is necessary only when combined with the <?xml?> tag. Without this tag, logic from your script might "confuse" the XML parser. It might, for instance, read this script code, If intA < intB, and think that the "is less than" comparator is actually the beginning of an XML tag.

**Comments (inline)**: You can add comments inline with your script code, as well. The keyword is the same as for shell scripts: rem. However, VBScript provides a shortcut—a single quote mark ( ' ).

## Adding Logic to Your Scripts

The XML tags I just listed notwithstanding, the real meat of the script is what resides inside the <script> tag. This is where you *get stuff done*. One of the best ways to get that stuff done in a structured, logical manner is through the use of procedures: subs and functions. The difference between the two is that a function may return a value, but a sub does not. These are similar to the call...goto :end subroutines we used in our batch scripts, except that they are quite a bit more robust. For one thing, they don't execute unless they are called. You can place them anywhere in your script and rest assured they won't get in the way until you need them. Listing 26.2 uses both types of procedures to take a filename from the command line and display that file's properties. I've left out the "standard" XML in the interest of space. To use it in a .wsf file, simply place it between the <script>...</ script> tags. It can also be saved as is to a .vbs file and used directly. Figure 26.6 shows the message box output by this script.

---

**LISTING 26.2:**     *GetFileInfo.vbs*

```
'Use Subs and Functions to display file info
Option Explicit
Dim strArg, objFSO, objFile, strTxt
Set objFSO=CreateObject("Scripting.FileSystemObject")

strArg=GetArgs()
Display
Set objFSO=Nothing
WScript.Quit

Function GetArgs()
  If Wscript.Arguments.Count < 1 Then Wscript.Quit
  GetArgs=objFSO.GetAbsolutePathName (Wscript.Arguments(0))
End Function

Sub Display()
  'Display file information
  Set objFile = objFSO.GetFile(strArg)
  strTxt="Drive:" & objFile.Drive & vbCRLF
  strTxt=strTxt & "File name:" & objFile.Name & vbCRLF
  strTxt=strTxt & "Path:" & objFile.Path & vbCRLF
  strTxt=strTxt & "Size:" & objFile.Size & vbCRLF
  strTxt=strTxt & "Date created:" & objFile.DateCreated & vbCRLF
  strTxt=strTxt & "Date last modified:" & objFile.DateLastModified
  msgbox strTxt
End Sub
```

---

I threw a curve ball at you, did you notice? I used the FileSystemObject (FSO) to access information about the file specified on the command line. We discuss the FSO in more detail in the "Advanced Concepts" section. I included it in this script to give you a practical demonstration of subs and functions and, at the same time, show you how to perform a very useful task.

**TIP**    Indenting your code is important. Without it, tracing your logic can be a real pain! The general rule is to indent the code inside procedures, If...Then statements, and loops (For...Next, Do...Loop, etc.).

**FIGURE 26.6**
Detailed file information using the FileSystemObject

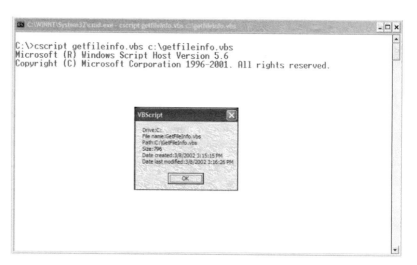

I also used another common technique designed to keep my code readable. You'll notice in both the GetArgs function and the Display sub that I have some long lines of code. When viewed in Notepad (with Word Wrap off, of course), the line can be as long as you want (but it can make it hard to follow the logic.) On a page in a book, there is limited width to work with. In either case, when you want to break a long line of code, simply type a space followed by an underscore ( _) and a carriage return. This tells the VBScript parser that the following line of code is a continuation of the previous line. It's also customary to indent the following line so you know it is part of the previous line.

Structuring your code into subs and functions not only keeps things organized, it also aids in debugging your code (something we all have to deal with, no matter how long we've been scripting!)

## Advanced Concepts

As discussed earlier, the WSH is a COM-aware scripting environment; COM provides a mechanism that allows for interoperability. It is the foundation of such things as object linking and embedding (OLE), a magic feature that allows you to drag a spreadsheet from Excel and drop it into a Word document. I could go into a bunch of boring details about the inner workings of COM, but space is limited and I'm sure you'd rather get to the good stuff. Suffice to say, COM allows us to access COM-enabled components (aka, objects) from our scripts. This section also discusses scheduling your scripts to run at a specified time.

### Objects

Objects are COM-enabled components that can be accessed from within scripts. Components are a special kind of binary file. They are not executable on their own but can provide their functionality to COM environments via exposed interfaces. There are two main interface types that pertain to scripting:

**Properties**: Properties hold data. This data can be as simple as a value that determines how the object works. A property may also store (persist) user data when necessary. Let's assume you have a component that allows you to perform symmetrical encryption on a file. This component would require a property, likely named "key," that specifies the key used to encrypt the file.

**Methods**: Methods perform a function. In the encryption example I just used, the component would likely have a method called *EncryptFile* that, when executed, uses the key specified in the "key" property to encrypt the file. There is an example of both properties and methods in the "Callable Objects" section later in this section.

### INTRINSIC OBJECTS

Intrinsic objects are built in to the Windows Script Host. Every time you execute a script, these objects are created and sit waiting for you to use them. They can be referenced directly, without ever having to be assigned to variables or created. There are two intrinsic objects that you will likely use quite often:

**The WScript object**: This object is used to print information on the screen (WScript.Echo) and to access command-line arguments (WScript.Arguments). Other methods include Quit and Sleep. Properties include Name, ScriptName, and Version. This object also contains several child objects that are not intrinsic but can be called to perform other functions such as editing the Registry or mapping network drives.

**The Err object**: This object allows you to trap errors in your scripts. Its main properties are Number and Description, which return the error number and a description of the error. It also has two methods: Clear and Raise. Clear resets the Err object. Raise actually allows you to cause an error to occur. This is invaluable when debugging your scripts. You want to make sure your error handling code works, don't you?

### CALLABLE OBJECTS

In addition to intrinsic components, you can access external components, as well. To call a component, you simply create a variable to house it and execute the CreateObject method. Once this is done, the object is referenced via the assigned variable. Properties and methods are specified using a dot (.). For example, to call the EncryptFile method of the previously discussed encryption component, I would simply execute the following code:

```
Dim objMyObject
Set objMyObject=CreateObject("MyEncrypt.Encryption")
objMyObject.File="C:\MyConfidentialData.mdb"
objMyObject.Key="secret"
objMyObject.EncryptFile
```

Many callable objects come built in to Windows XP. One such object that you are likely to use extensively is the FileSystemObject. The FSO actually consists of a parent object and several child objects. Once you have created the "main" component, additional components are called by executing specific methods. This is demonstrated in Listing 26.2. Once I created the FileSystemObject, I simply executed the GetFile method Set objFile=objFSO.GetFile(strArg) to create an instance of the File object (a child object of the FSO).

Another useful built-in object is the Active Directory Services Interface. ADSI enables you to perform a gazillion useful tasks. Listing 26.3 in the next section demonstrates how to perform one very useful task with ADSI.

**AUTOMATION**

There are certain applications that can be utilized in the same manner as components. Indeed, the entire Office XP suite can be automated from within a script. In order to support automation, the application must have an exposed object model. This object model must be represented in a file called a *Type Library*. Type Libraries usually have the file extension of .tlb (the Office XP Type Libraries use .olb as their extension).

Utilizing the Type Library, you can, for example, start Word, create a new document, enter text, and save it. Or you can launch Internet Explorer and load a specified web page! Or you can read information from an Excel spreadsheet and process it with your script! Or...well, you get the point.

## Scheduling Scripts

A key advantage to using scripts is the ability to schedule them to run at any time. With the XP Task Scheduler, you can schedule a script to run every night, on a specific day every week, or on the next occurrence of a day and time. Scripts are scheduled using the AT command. You must remember to include all of the command-line arguments required by your script when scheduling it.

# Scripts for Common Administrative Chores

No discussion of scripting would be complete without including a nice selection of sample scripts for you to use and learn from. The scripts included in this section cover different administrative tasks you are likely to perform quite frequently. Following each script, I've highlighted the salient code sections.

## AddUser.wsf

This script (see Listing 26.3) uses the Active Directory Services Interface to automate adding users to your computer. It illustrates how useful ADSI can be even if you aren't part of a domain. You specify the username and password via the command-line arguments.

---

**LISTING 26.3:**  *AddUser.wsf*

```
<?xml version="1.0" ?>
<package>
<comment>
AddUser.wsf
This script adds a user to the local computer
Using the ADSI interface
</comment>
  <job>
  <runtime>
    <description>
    Add a user to the local computer
    and place it in a group
    </description>

    <example>
```

```
        C:\cscript AddUser.wsf /uname:[username] /group:[group]
      </example>

      <named
        name="uname"
        helpstring="The username of the new user"
        type="string"
        required="true"
      />
      <named
        name="group"
        helpstring="The group in which to place the user"
        type="string"
        required="true"
      />
    </runtime>
    <script language="VBScript">
    <![CDATA[
    ' Add a user and place him/her into a group
    dim objADSI, objGroup, objUser, strUser, strGroup
    strGroup=WScript.Arguments.Named.Item("group")
    strUser=WScript.Arguments.Named.Item("uname")
    Set objADSI=GetObject("WinNT://mycomp,computer")
    Set objUser=objADSI.Create("User",strUser)
    objUser.SetInfo
    Set objGroup=GetObject("WinNT://mycomp/" & strGroup & ",group")
    objGroup.Add(objUser.ADsPath)
    objGroup.SetInfo
    ]]>
    </script>
    </job>
  </package>
```

The only "hard-coded" parameter in this script is mycomp, the name of the local computer. The script could be easily expanded to accept this information as an argument as well, making it capable of adding a user to an NT domain. The usage of the <runtime> tags is explained following the next script.

You'll notice that once I create the user, I still have to execute the objUser.SetInfo method. This finalizes the deal. Once that's done, I can pass that user information to the objGroup.Add method to place the user into the group. Lots of possibilities exist using this script as a starting point. You could even use the application automation we discussed earlier to add a list of users from a spreadsheet.

### ChangeRole.wsf

This script (see Listing 26.4) uses the WScript.Shell object to make a change to the Registry—specifically, the Win32PrioritySeparation value. When you use the System applet to change your computer's performance option to adjust for Programs or Background Services, it utilizes this Registry entry. It is this value that determines the role of your computer: Server or Workstation. No, it can't convert Windows XP Professional to Windows 2002 Server. What it does is determine how XP handles background processes in relation to foreground processes. If you are using XP Pro as, say, an intranet server in your organization, specifying a Server role will increase its performance in this capacity.

**LISTING 26.4:**    *ChangeRole.wsf*

```
<?xml version="1.0" ?>
<package>
<comment>
ChangeRole.wsf
This script updates the Win32PrioritySeparation
key in the registry to change the performance
of applications running in the foreground
</comment>
  <job>
  <runtime>
    <description>
    This script allows you to change the
    performance role of your computer
    </description>

    <example>
    C:\CScript ChangeFGPerf.wsf /Role:[W/S]
    </example>

    <named
    name="Role"
    helpstring="The role for the computer"
    type="string"
    required="true"
    />
  </runtime>

  <object id="objShell" progid="WScript.Shell"/>

  <script language="VBScript">
  <![CDATA[
  'Change foreground performance
  Option Explicit
  On Error Resume Next

  Dim strRole, strKey, strDataType
  strKey= _
    "HKLM\System\CurrentControlSet\Control\PriorityControl\Win32PrioritySeparation"
```

```
    strDataType="REG_DWORD"
    strRole=UCase(WScript.Arguments.Named.Item("Role"))

  Select Case strRole
    Case "W"
    objShell.RegWrite strKey, 38, strDataType
    WScript.Echo "Priority Control has been set to optimize foreground
applications."
    WScript.Quit

    Case "S"
    objShell.RegWrite strKey, 24, strDataType
    WScript.Echo "Priority Control has been set to optimize background services."
    WScript.Quit
  End Select

  WScript.Arguments.ShowUsage()
  WScript.Quit
  ]]>
  </script>
  </job>
</package>
```

This script uses the <object> tag to create an instance of the WScript.Shell object. The computer's role is specified via a <named> argument. It also includes the <runtime> tags <description> and <example>. These tags specify the information that is displayed whenever the script is run using incorrect (or no) arguments or when it is run using the /? argument. Figure 26.7 shows this output.

**FIGURE 26.7**
WSF scripts can display usage information describing how to run the script.

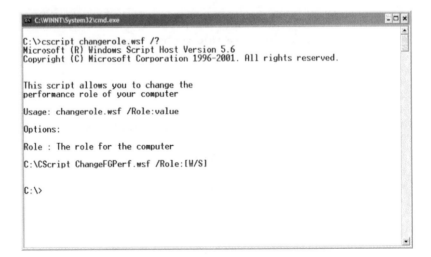

```
C:\WINNT\System32\cmd.exe

C:\>cscript changerole.wsf /?
Microsoft (R) Windows Script Host Version 5.6
Copyright (C) Microsoft Corporation 1996-2001. All rights reserved.


This script allows you to change the
performance role of your computer

Usage: changerole.wsf /Role:value

Options:

Role : The role for the computer

C:\CScript ChangeFGPerf.wsf /Role:[W/S]


C:\>
```

### LogEvent.vbs

This script (see Listing 26.5) allows you to log an event to Windows XP's Application Event Log. While not terribly useful on its own, it can be invaluable when added to an existing script. As we discussed in the "Advanced Concepts" section, one of the joys of scripting is that you can schedule a script to run whenever you want it to. An event log entry noting whether or not the script completed successfully may be your only indication of potential trouble. Since you will likely add this code to an existing script, I have put the script in the .vbs file format.

**LISTING 26.5:**    *LogEvent.vbs*

```
'Logs an event to the XP application log
Option Explicit
Dim objShell
Set objShell=CreateObject("WScript.Shell")
objShell.LogEvent 0, "Script: " & WScript.ScriptName & " Completed Successfully."
```

We use the WSHShell object to write the log entry. The LogEvent method requires two arguments, with a third optional argument:

**Event type**: In this script, we logged an event type of 0, which is a "Success." Other types include Error, Warning, Information, Audit_Success, and Audit_Failure.

**Message**: This is the text that is entered into the event log. If a script error happened to trigger the LogEvent method, you would want this text to include that error information.

**Target (optional)**: This allows you to log an event to another computer. This is useful for aggregating all of the logged events on every computer in your organization to one central location.

Figure 26.8 shows this event viewed in the application log of the Event Viewer.

**FIGURE 26.8**

Log events to the application log.

## Summary

We've crammed quite a bit into this chapter. I hope it's given you a good foundation of knowledge to build upon, as well as provided some useful code that you can put to work right away.

Shell and WSH scripts allow you to automate some (or all!) of the redundant and not-so-redundant tasks that you face each day. Repetitive tasks can be accomplished much faster than is possible using the GUI tools. Scripts can be scheduled to run during off-hours and, through the use of COM objects, can perform some very powerful operations. For more information about WSH scripting, go to `msdn.microsoft.com/scripting`. It is my scripting home-away-from-home. You'll find downloads for the scripting engines, tutorials, a VBScript reference, and much more.

The next chapter will change gears and focus on yet another critical administrative responsibility: disaster prevention and recovery. Make sure to pay close attention, because even the most reliable networks can fail from time to time.

# Chapter 27

# Disaster Prevention and Recovery

Despite Windows XP Professional's resilient nature, it still sometimes crashes. Some crashes are caused by random events: it really *is* possible for a cosmic ray to hit a critical part of a chip and freeze up a PC (and in that case there's not much to do other than to turn the machine off and then back on). But if you find Windows XP Professional crashing *regularly*, you have to do something about it, because it's not supposed to. Of course, to do something effective about system crashes, you'll need a method, and that's what this chapter offers.

I'll avoid trotting out all the old an-ounce-of-prevention bromides (though there *is* a lot of truth to those old saws). I start off with a discussion of preventing trouble in the first place and then look at techniques you can use to gather the information needed to ascertain, attack, and fix problems that may sooner or later arise.

- Avoiding Windows XP Professional crashes
- Defragmenting files, cleaning up disks, and checking disks
- Restoring a configuration
- Installing and using the Recovery Console
- Using the Driver Verifier
- Using System File Checker
- Forcing a core dump
- Backing up and restoring

## Avoiding Windows XP Professional Crashes

You can keep Windows XP Professional trouble at bay in a few basic ways:

- Buy reliable hardware, preferably hardware that is on the Windows XP Windows Catalog.
- Protect the machine from environmental hazards, most notably substandard electric power.
- Install Windows XP Professional properly, or, in some cases, *re*install Windows XP Professional properly.
- Obtain the latest Microsoft-certified drivers for your hardware.
- Always shut down Windows XP Professional properly.

◆ Back up your hard disk.

◆ Be sure you have the proper security level for whatever function you're performing.

Let's look quickly at each of these.

## Buy Reliable Hardware

One of the things that causes instability for *any* PC operating system is the hardware that the operating system must sit atop. PCs made by IBM were once the standard and, right or wrong, "PC-compatible" meant that they "did the same thing that the IBM machines did, including the bugs." Nowadays, there *is* no standard, and so no two brands of computers work exactly the same way.

A major point of difference between makes and models of computers is the expansion bus, the slots on a PC motherboard into which you plug expansion cards such as video boards, sound cards, and network boards. Because these slots must accommodate the connectors on the bottom of the expansion cards, the person who designs the motherboard and the person who designs the expansion card must agree on how that interface should work; the interface must be *standard*.

That's where the problem arises. A common PC interface standard is called the Industry Standard Architecture, or ISA, board. The *problem* with the ISA standard is that it's not really a standard; there is no carved-in-stone specification for it, just an informal industry consensus. The result is that if you take a "standard" ISA board and plug it into a "standard" ISA slot, it may not work perfectly 100 percent of the time. It'll probably work most of the time, but some small percentage of the time, data may get lost passing between the expansion card and the motherboard. If that data is crucial, the PC may lock up.

What can Windows XP Professional do about that? In other words, how can an operating system that wants to be stable work around an inherently unstable hardware platform? To a certain extent, there's nothing that the operating system can do, and some crashes are unavoidable. But some ISA boards are designed better than others, and only experimentation will separate the good from the bad. Further, the operating system can incorporate drivers for the hardware that are a bit more "forgiving." By forgiving, I mean that the driver is built to *anticipate* a certain number of hardware errors and to simply step around them.

"Aha!" you cry. "If they can make drivers 'forgiving,' why don't they *always* do that?" Well, for one thing, it's harder to write such drivers. For another, most driver authors resent writing drivers to support hardware that isn't really standard. Talk to them for a bit, and they start muttering about hitting moving targets and the like. Finally, and most important, adding forgiveness to a driver *slows it down*, and as all PC speed freaks know, slow is bad.

Again, what can you do about it? For one thing, stay as far away from ISA boards as you can. Yes, they're the most common and the cheapest boards, but there's usually a reason why cheap things are cheap.

**TIP** Buy systems that have PCI slots (at least three slots), and use only PCI boards. Some of these systems also have ISA, but don't use them. Multiprocessor systems usually have a combination of PCI and EISA slots; both of those are fine to use because both are truly standard interfaces.

The Peripheral Component Interconnect (PCI), Extended Industry Standard Architecture (EISA), MicroChannel Architecture (MCA), and Accelerated Graphics Port (AGP) buses were all designed by a central authority that published specifications, which, if followed, yield an expansion board that works predictably. That's why I strongly recommend staying with those expansion slot types. In reality, however, you won't find many of today's systems with the MCA bus; it's ancient history. Again, you'll find EISA slots on many multiprocessor systems, but not many EISA expansion boards are on the market. PCI has been the de facto standard for several years. AGP is a very common standard for video adapters, and FireWire (IEEE 1328) and USB are fast and readily available.

## Guard against Environmental Hazards

A decent number of PCs die each year because they get bad power. It's not something you can easily detect; it just happens. But you can prevent it.

PC power problems fall into three categories:

◆ Incorrect voltage—usually too low. Low voltage is called a voltage sag or brownout.

◆ Loss of power altogether.

◆ Extremely brief (under one 1/100 of a second) increases in voltage and power, called surges or spikes.

Low voltage causes your PC's power supply to try to compensate by drawing more current, which heats up the PC components and shortens their lives. You change voltage on an electrical circuit with a device called a transformer. A transformer that's smart enough to know whether to move the voltage up or down is called a *voltage regulator*, and for most PC applications, the name of the device that contains a voltage regulator is a *power conditioner*.

Loss of power altogether requires a battery of some kind. The two kinds of battery backup are *standby power supply* (*SPS*) and *uninterruptible power supply* (*UPS*). An SPS has a battery that "wakes up," so to speak, when power to the PC is interrupted. Because an SPS doesn't always wake up fast enough, you need an SPS with a switching time (wake-up time) of 4 milliseconds or less. A UPS, in contrast, is always supplying power from the battery (while refilling it, of course) and so has no switching time. Clever marketers call their SPSs "UPSs." If in doubt, ask about the switching time.

Surges and spikes can be brushed aside by a power conditioner. Do *not* buy a surge protector, a cheap device that does little to protect you from power problems. A surge protector is based on a device called a Metal Oxide Varistor (MOV), which is a "kamikaze" device: After you get a little surge, the MOV stops the surge but dies in the process. The *next* surge goes through without trouble.

**NOTE**   To read more about PC power problems and solutions, pick up the latest edition of my book *The Complete PC Upgrade and Maintenance Guide*, 2005 Edition (Sybex, Inc.).

## Install Windows XP Professional Properly

A look back at Chapter 2 will remind you that you've got a lot of choices to make when you install Windows XP Professional. If you end up with a bad installation, reinstall Windows XP Professional or your Windows XP Professional applications. If you reinstall a piece of software, however, don't install it on top of an existing installation; that often doesn't wipe the old installation clean. Before reinstalling any software, remove it completely and check the Registry for any leftover pieces.

In Chapter 2, I tell you how to upgrade from an earlier version of Windows or NT, but the truth is, the most stable and reliable installations are built from the ground up. This usually means installing on a freshly formatted hard drive and then installing applications. If you simply must perform an upgrade, be sure to disable all third-party services. Heck, disable all the services you can easily live without for a while. The less that Setup has to worry about, the fewer things that can go wrong.

## Obtain Tested, Certified Drivers for Your Hardware

Although Windows XP Professional was a solidly built system, it does have one fairly large Achilles' heel (or maybe a whole Achilles' foot): drivers. During the development of Windows XP Professional, Microsoft took a hard line with hardware vendors, insisting that they write "good" drivers that would pass Microsoft certification. In some cases, you may even see a warning message if you attempt to install new hardware or software with drivers that are not certified. Take this message to heart. A poorly functioning driver can be difficult to track down and can crash your system.

## Always Shut Down Windows XP Professional Properly

Most people seem to know this by now, but it's worth repeating that you should *shut down Windows XP Professional properly*. Don't just turn off the computer; choose Start and then Turn Off Computer.

If you don't do that, not only do you stand to lose data from your applications, but you may damage the operating system. If you are using only NTFS-formatted disks, the damage will be less than it would be with a FAT disk (NTFS incorporates fault-tolerant features), but you could lose data nevertheless.

## Back Up Your Disk Regularly

I shouldn't have to say this, but...

The hard disks in most people's PCs aren't backed up. And there are as many excuses for this as there are PCs. But there's no reason for it, at least not anymore. Iomega's Zip drives are a terrific way to quickly and easily save 100MB of data onto a thing that *looks* like a floppy but that stores much more data. Tape drives get cheaper all the time. And I just can't say enough about the value of CD-ROM and DVD burners for backups.

Windows XP Professional even comes with its own backup program, Backup, that I'll discuss later in this chapter. So there's no excuse *not* to back your stuff up.

## Be Sure You're Authorized to Do Something Before Doing It

As you've read elsewhere in this book, living with Windows XP Professional means thinking differently because you're now living in a more secure world. That means that you may run into a kind of trouble fairly new to PC users—the inability to do a particular function on your system.

For example, imagine that when someone logs on to your network, they run a logon batch script that synchronizes their PC's clock with the time on the server; the command is `net time\\` `servername`/set/yes. When you log on to a Windows XP Professional workstation as a simple domain user, you get an error indicating that you don't have the right to set the PC's clock.

Now, if you are a network techie, you would likely understand this error message and where it comes from—again, the account you used to log on is too low on the network's totem pole, so to speak. But for a regular, less-technical user, it could be somewhat disconcerting.

In general, remember that a Windows XP Professional computer runs different kinds of user accounts—administrators, users, power users, and so on. You'll make your life easiest if you remember to log on as an administrator for that particular workstation before trying to change permissions on files or do anything with the Administrative Tools.

# An Ounce of Prevention

Before I get into what you can do to fix Windows XP Professional before it breaks, I want to point you toward some tools you can use from time to time that might well prevent some common, everyday problems: Disk Defragmenter, Disk Cleanup, and Check Disk.

## Defragmenting Files

As files on your computer grow, they will not fit back into their original locations on your hard disk, so Windows XP Professional divides the files into pieces and spreads the files over several different disk locations. This is how Windows is designed to work and how the system juggles constantly changing file sizes. An unfortunate side effect is that as a file is divided into more and more pieces, it takes longer and longer for your system to find and retrieve the whole file when you open it. A disk defragmenter keeps your hard disk performance at its peak by finding fragmented files on your system and rewriting them into contiguous, continuous areas of your hard disk.

Disk Defragmenter works behind the scenes; although the files on your hard disk have actually been moved, you will still find them in the same folders. Follow these steps to use the Disk Defragmenter:

1. Choose Start ➢ All Programs ➢ Accessories ➢ System Tools ➢ Disk Defragmenter.

2. Choose the disk you want to defragment, and click the Analyze button. Disk Defragmenter looks at the drive and prepares a display and reports on the condition of the files on that drive; the analysis display box shows fragmented files, contiguous files, system files, and hard disk free space as stripes of different colors, as seen in Figure 27.1. Once the analysis is complete, Disk Defragmenter will display a message box that tells you whether you should defragment this disk. Click View Report to open the Analysis Report dialog box. At the top of the Analysis Report dialog box, you will see volume information, including the amount of fragmentation, free space, and file fragmentation. In the lower part of this dialog box, you will see detailed information on specific files. Click the heading at the top of the columns to sort the data in that column.

3. Click Defragment to continue, or click Close to return to the main window.

4. Once Disk Defragmenter starts working, you can click either the Pause or Stop button to pause or stop the process.

You can certainly perform other work on the computer while Disk Defragmenter is running, but the response time will be much slower, and Disk Defragmenter will start over each time you write a file to your hard disk. The best time to run Disk Defragmenter is while you are out for lunch or after you've finished your work for the day.

## Cleaning Up Disks

Have you ever wished there was some way you could just wave a magic wand and get rid of all the unused or temporary files that take up space on your hard disk? Well, there is such a tool, and it is called Disk Cleanup. Choose Start ➢ All Programs ➢ Accessories ➢ System Tools ➢ Disk Cleanup to open the Select Drive dialog box. Choose the drive you want to work with, and click OK to open the Disk Cleanup dialog box shown in Figure 27.2.

**FIGURE 27.1**
Disk Defragmenter analysis display for a badly fragmented drive

**FIGURE 27.2**
The Disk Cleanup dialog box

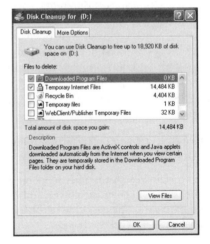

The Disk Cleanup dialog box has these tabs:

**Disk Cleanup**  Displays the amount of free space that could be recovered by deleting temporary files in certain categories or by emptying the Recycle Bin on your Desktop. As you check the boxes to delete files, a running counter tells you how much disk space will be recovered.

**More Options**  Lets you remove applications or Windows components that you don't use. In the Windows Components section, click the Clean Up button to start the Windows Components Wizard, which you can use to add or remove components. In the Installed Programs section, click the

Clean Up button to open the Add or Remove Programs dialog box and change or remove a program. In the System Restore section, click the Clean Up button to remove all but the most recent restore point. I'll talk about System Restore later in this chapter.

### Checking Disks for Errors

Another disk-management task you might have to perform from time to time is to check a hard disk for errors, and Windows XP Professional includes a tool for checking FAT32 volumes. All NTFS volumes log file transactions and replace bad clusters automatically. To check out a hard disk, open Explorer or My Computer, right-click the disk you want to work with, and then choose Properties from the shortcut menu. In the Tools tab, click the Check Now button to open the Check Disk dialog box, which contains these two options:

- Automatically Fix File System Errors

- Scan For and Attempt Recovery of Bad Sectors

Check the appropriate boxes, and then click Start to begin scanning the disk. A status bar across the bottom of the Check Disk dialog box indicates the progress of the tests, and you will see a message when the disk check is complete.

## Restoring a Configuration

Sometimes, no matter how vigilant you've been, mistakes happen or something just goes wrong, and you need to fix your system. These fixes range from easy to horrific.

One thing that you *could* do is reinstall Windows XP Professional, a time-consuming process. But not only do you have to do the installation process itself, you have to set up all services and user accounts again, and this gets very boring and/or frustrating very quickly. Fortunately, there are other ways to fix your setup when something's gone wrong.

### Using the Last Known Good Configuration

If you've changed your system so that it can't boot Windows XP Professional, one of these better solutions can be seen while you're rebooting. If you watch while your machine's booting up, you'll see a message on a black screen that says "For troubleshooting and advanced startup options for Windows XP Professional, press F8." If you press the F8 key, you'll see a menu with the following choices:

- Safe Mode

- Safe Mode with Networking

- Safe Mode with Command Prompt

- Enable Boot Logging

- Enable VGA Mode

- Last Known Good Configuration (Your Most Recent Settings That Worked)

- Directory Services Restore Mode (Windows Domain Controllers Only)

- Debugging Mode

◆  Start Windows Normally

◆  Reboot

◆  Return to OS Choices Menu

**NOTE**  You'll see this last choice only if you dual-boot Windows XP Professional and some other operating system.

These options cover most of the possible troubleshooting scenarios involving the boot process. If your machine won't boot, you probably don't want to use the current configuration; so choose the Last Known Good Configuration. This should make your machine bootable.

### WHEN DOES (AND DOESN'T) IT WORK?

What are the criteria for a configuration being the Last Known Good one? To qualify, a configuration must not have produced any critical errors involving a driver or a system file, and a user must have been able to log on to the system at least once.

The Last Known Good Configuration can't always help you. If any of the following are true, you'll have to use another solution:

◆  You made a change more than one successful boot ago and want to restore things as they were before the change.

◆  The information that you want to change is not related to control-set information—user profiles and file permissions fall into the category of information that can't be changed with the Last Known Good Configuration item.

◆  The system boots, a user logs on, and then the system hangs.

◆  You change your video driver to an incompatible driver, restart the system, and then log on with the bad driver (you can still type, even if you can't see).

**NOTE**  The key to getting Last Known Good to work is knowing what constitutes a *successful logon*. A successful logon occurs when you have entered your username and password and *have been authenticated*. Ever seen the message that a domain controller could not be found but you have been logged on with cached credentials? Windows XP Professional considers that a successful logon. If you suspect even for a moment that the change you made might not work, don't log on. Let the computer sit at the Ctrl+Alt+Del prompt for a couple of minutes. If you do not receive any messages about failed services, then log on.

## Using System Restore

If Windows XP Professional has been working correctly but you suddenly, inexplicably can't boot into Windows, you can use a feature that is new in Windows XP—System Restore. In a nutshell, System Restore creates restore points, such as the following:

◆  System checkpoints, which are scheduled and created by your computer

◆  Manual restore points, which you create

◆  Installation restore points, which are automatically created when you install certain programs

You use these restore points to revert to a system configuration that was working properly. (System Restore does not recover changes to personal data files.) You can change some System Restore settings, and we'll look at how to do that next. First, though, let's walk through a typical scenario.

You turn on your computer, Windows XP Professional starts to boot, but then just sits at the opening screen, doing nothing. You turn off your computer and turn it back on, and the same thing happens again. Turn your computer off again, turn it back on, and this time boot into Safe Mode, as described in the previous section.

After Safe Mode loads, you'll see a dialog box that gives you the choice of working in Safe Mode or using System Restore. Click No to use System Restore and to open System Restore at the Welcome screen. Click Next.

**TIP**  Sometimes all you need to do to get your system back in shape is to boot into Safe Mode and then restart the system. Safe Mode loads only a minimal number of drivers, thus simplifying the boot process.

In the Select a Restore Point screen, if no restore points have been created for the current day, click a boldface date on the calendar, and then, from the list on the right, select a time. Click Next to open the Confirm Restore Point Selection screen.

If you are ready to restore, click Next. When the restoration is complete, you'll see a message to that effect. Windows XP Professional will restart, using the settings in the restore point you selected. With a bit of luck, everything will be working properly.

**NOTE**  During the restoration process, don't fiddle with your computer. Let Windows do its thing.

### CREATING YOUR OWN RESTORE POINTS

You can also run System Restore from a working Windows XP Professional system and use System Restore to create your own restore point. To open System Restore, choose Start ➢ All Programs ➢ Accessories ➢ System Tools ➢ System Restore. You'll see the Welcome to System Restore screen:

If you want to restore your computer to an earlier time, click that option. To create a restore point, click that option and then click Next to open the Create a Restore Point screen:

Enter a description for your restore point in the Restore Point Description box, and click Create. Windows creates the restore point and adds the current date and time to the description.

### CHANGING SYSTEM RESTORE SETTINGS

To change the amount of disk space allotted to restore points or to disable System Restore, you use the System Restore tab in the System Properties dialog box (shown in Figure 27.3).

You can open this dialog box in the following ways:

◆ On the first System Restore screen, click the System Restore Settings link.

◆ Click Start, right-click My Computer, and then choose Properties from the shortcut menu.

◆ In Control Panel, click the Performance and Maintenance category, and then click System.

To disable System Restore (which is enabled by default), click the Turn Off System Restore on All Drives check box. (If you have multiple drives on your system, you can't turn off System Restore for only a single drive. All drives have System Restore disabled or enabled.) Unless you have a good reason for doing so, I suggest that you leave System Restore enabled.

**FIGURE 27.3**

You can disable System Restore by clicking the Turn Off System Restore on All Drives check box, but it's best to leave System Restore enabled, as it is by default.

To change the disk space allotted to restore points, click the Settings button to open the Settings dialog box:

Move the slider bar to change the amount of disk space.

## Creating and Using the Automated System Recovery Disk

Every time you successfully edit your system's configuration, you should back up the configuration against the time when you unsuccessfully edit the settings. This backup is called the Automated System Recovery (ASR) disk.

**TIP**  Re-create the ASR after you have successfully booted with the new configuration information. This way, you'll know that the configuration you're backing up works.

Versions of Windows NT and 2000 Professional used an Emergency Repair Disk (ERD) as a boot disk to run the repair tools on the CD. In Windows XP Professional, you create the Automated System Recovery Backup disk instead. It then contains only the files needed to start your system. You use the Automated System Recovery Backup disk and a backup of your system on some other medium to restore your system after a disk failure.

To create the Automated System Recovery Backup, follow these steps:

1. Choose Start ≻ All Programs ≻ Accessories ≻ System Tools ≻ Backup to start the Backup or Restore Wizard.

2. On the initial screen, click the Advanced Mode link to open the Backup Utility at the Welcome tab:

3. Click Automated System Recovery Wizard to start the Automated System Recovery Preparation Wizard:

**4.** Click Next to open the Backup Destination screen:

**5.** The wizard assumes you are backing up to a floppy disk and gives it the name of `Backup.bkf`. Place a floppy in the drive, and click Next to open the last screen of the wizard. Click Finish, and the wizard copies to the floppy disk the system files that you'll need to restart after a failure.

To use the ASR disk and the backup of your system on another medium to recover from a system failure, have those two items and your Windows XP Professional CD available, and then follow these steps:

**1.** Place your installation CD in the drive.

**2.** Restart your computer. If you are asked to press a key to start the computer from the CD, do so.

**3.** During the text mode of Setup, press F2 when prompted.

**4.** Insert the ASR disk when prompted, and then follow the onscreen instructions.

# The Recovery Console

Recovery Console is a command-line tool that you can use to start and stop services, format drives, and repair your system. To use Recovery Console, you really should be a power user, and you must be logged on as an administrator. This tool is not installed by default when you install Windows XP Professional, so the first order of business in this section is telling you how to install it.

## Installing the Recovery Console

You install the Recovery Console from the Windows XP Professional installation CD. Insert your CD in the drive, and then click Exit when the installation options are displayed. Now, follow these steps:

**1.** At a command prompt, switch to your CD-ROM drive. If you have a 32-bit computer, type \ `i386\winnt32.exe /cmdcons`, and press Enter. (Yes, there's a space between `exe` and the following slash.) If you have a 64-bit computer, type `\ia64\winnt32.exe /cmdcons`, and press Enter.

2. Windows now displays the Windows Setup dialog box, asking if you want to install the Recovery Console. Click Yes, and follow the on-screen instructions.

3. Windows XP Professional Setup will copy some files from the installation CD and then tell you that to use Recovery Console you'll need to restart the computer.

4. After you restart, the Recovery Console will be in the Startup menu (the text menu you see when you start up the computer), listed as Microsoft Windows XP Professional Command Console. To start it, just choose that option before the timeout to your default startup option expires.

## Using the Recovery Console

When you choose to run the Recovery Console, select it from the list of available operating systems at startup. You can also run Recovery Console from your installation CD.

If the term "console" led you to expect some kind of GUI, you'll be surprised to see a simple command-line interface. Although it looks like an ordinary command prompt, the Recovery Console is not the command prompt that you can open from the Accessories menu. First, it supports only a few commands and only locally—this is not a network tool. Second, those commands are specialized for this interface and perform only a limited set of functions. The wildcard options in the copy command don't work in the console; you can copy files only from removable media to the system partition (but not the other way around—you can't use the console to back up files to other media); and although you can move to other logical drives on the hard disk, you can't read files on any partition other than the system partition—or even perform a dir function on them. If you try, you'll get an Access Denied error. The Recovery Console is not a command-line version of Windows XP Professional, cool as that would be.

**NOTE**   I'd expected that the Recovery Console would include a command-line version of RegEdit, as Windows 9x *does*. Sadly, it does not.

You can't back up files. You can't read the contents of any folder not in the system root. You can't use wildcards. You can't edit security information. What *can* you do with the Recovery Console?

Mostly, you can fix your system partition to make it usable again. As you can see in Table 27.1, the Recovery Console is a set of commands that you can use to manipulate the files and structure of the system partition. There are a lot of functions with duplicate commands that use the same syntax; unless I specify otherwise, there's no difference between the two commands.

**TABLE 27.1:**   Supported Recovery Console Commands

| COMMAND NAME | FUNCTION |
| --- | --- |
| attrib | Changes the attributes of a selected file or folder. |
| batch | Runs the commands specified in a text file so that you can complete many tasks in a single step. |
| cd or chdir | Displays the name of the current directory or changes directories. Typing **cd**.. closes the current directory and moves you up one in the tree. |

**TABLE 27.1:**     Supported Recovery Console Commands *(CONTINUED)*

| COMMAND NAME | FUNCTION |
| --- | --- |
| chkdsk | Runs CheckDisk. |
| cls | Wipes the screen of any previous output, so you can see better. |
| copy | Copies files from removable media to the system folders on the hard disk (does not accept wildcards). |
| del or delete | Deletes one or more files (does not accept wildcards). |
| dir | Lists the contents of the current or selected directory. |
| disable | Disables the named service or driver. |
| enable | Enables the named service or driver. |
| diskpart | Replaces the FDISK tool you're probably familiar with. Creates or deletes disk partitions. |
| extract | Extracts a compressed installation file (one with a .cab extension) to the local fixed disk. Works only if you're running the Recovery Console from the installation disk. |
| fixboot | Writes a new partition boot sector on the system partition. |
| fixmbr | Writes a new Master Boot Record (MBR) for the partition boot sector. |
| format | Formats the selected disk. |
| help | Display a list of Recovery Console commands. |
| listsvc | Lists all the services and drivers running on the Windows XP Professional installation. |
| logon | Logs on to a Windows XP Professional installation. |
| map | Displays the drive letter mappings currently in place. Handy for getting the information you need to use diskpart. |
| md or mkdir | Creates a directory. |
| more, type | Displays the contents of the chosen text file. |
| rd or rmdir | Deletes a directory. |
| rename or ren | Renames a single file. |
| systemroot | Makes the current directory the system root of the drive you're logged into. |

CHAPTER 27

**WARNING**   If you thought the Registry Editor was potentially dangerous, the Recovery Console is worse. You can really screw up your system here, to the point that the only thing to do is reinstall and reload your backups. There's no Undo feature, not all the commands ask for confirmation, and there's no Read-Only setting like the one in regedt32. If you're not used to working from the command line, review what you want to do and the tools you need to do it before you open the console. And, unlike Regedit, there's no way to make a backup before playing around. Just be careful!

Some of the commands shown in Table 27.1 will look familiar to old DOS hands, but many of them work a little differently from the way they did under DOS, using a slightly different syntax or working only under specific circumstances. Let's take a look at how you can use these commands to get things back up and running.

### ENABLING AND DISABLING SERVICES

Why would you need to enable or disable services from the command line? Therein lies a tale.

Several years ago, I bought a new PC. Installed everything; ran the installation program for the 3Com network card in the server. Life was good.

Until I rebooted the computer.

You see, a diagnostic program was part of the setup for the NIC—an unavoidable part that you could not choose to not install. (Trust me: I tried, on several computers with the same set of hardware.) Whenever I started up the computer, this diagnostic program would scan the system and display a message that a newer version of my NIC's driver was available—did I want to use the new driver? Click OK or Cancel, and the message box would close for a second and then reopen, with the same message. Add to this that the searching and displaying was using up 100 percent of CPU time for a 350MHz Pentium II doing *nothing else but running the diagnostic*. Running the Task Manager (when I could get a spare cycle here or there to open it) didn't help, because the program wouldn't shut down even when I killed the process.

Okay, I figured—the problem is a runaway service, so if I can shut down the service I will resolve the problem. But shutting down the service is hard when you're clicking OK in a repeatedly reappearing dialog box and then frantically grabbing CPU cycles to open Control Panel and then Services before the dialog box opens and the CPU usage starts running at 100 percent again.

In this case, I was finally able to get to the Services applet, find the service (named 3Com Diagnostics, or some such, so identifying the problem child wasn't hard), and then stop and disable it. Problem solved. But it took a lot of time and mouse-clicking to get to that point. A tool that would enable me to boot to the command prompt and disable that service without having to work around the CPU-eating message box would have been nice. And that's where the services-related tools in the Recovery Console come in.

The first step to fixing a problem like this is running the listsvc utility from the Recovery Console. There are no arguments to this—just type **listsvc** at the command prompt, and Windows XP Professional will display a list of all the services and drivers currently installed for that installation of Windows XP Professional, a short description of what they are, and their start type (boot, automatic, manual, system, or disabled). Seeing all the services will probably take a few screens, but the services are listed alphabetically, so you can find the one you want fairly easily. Write down its name.

**TIP**   The names of services and drivers are not case sensitive.

Once you've found the suspected problem child, it's time for the disable command. The syntax is simple: disable *servicename*. Windows XP Professional will then notify you that it found the

Registry entry for this service (or tell you that it can't find an entry for this service, in which case you need to check your spelling and try again). It will also display the current start type and new start type for the service. Write down the current start type for the service in case you want to start it again.

To make the change take effect, type **exit** to leave the Recovery Console and restart the computer. See if disabling that service fixed the problem. If it did, you're home free. (Not sure how you'd know? Depends on what the problem was. In the case of the runaway 3Com Diagnostics, the fix was pretty immediate. As soon as I turned off the service, the problem disappeared.) If it didn't, you can return to the console, reenable that service, and try something else.

You don't have to disable a service to keep it from running when Windows XP Professional starts, however. Instead, you could change its start type from automatic to manual. To do so, or to reenable a service you disabled, you'll need to use the enable command. Like disable, enable's syntax is simple: enable *servicename*. If run on a disabled service, this syntax will enable the service and restore it to whatever its start type was when it was disabled.

To change a service's start type without disabling it, add the new start type to the end of the enable command, like this:

```
enable servicename start_type
```

where *start_type* is one of the options in Table 27.2.

**TABLE 27.2:**     Start Types

| START TYPE | MEANING |
| --- | --- |
| Service_boot_start | Boot |
| Service_system_start | System |
| Service_demand_start | Manual |
| Service_auto_start | Automatic |

So, for example, instead of disabling the 3Com diagnostic service, I could have changed its start type from automatic to manual. That way, I could have started it at any time during the Windows XP Professional session, but it wouldn't start automatically.

### REPLACING DAMAGED FILES

Perhaps the problem isn't a runaway driver or service but a corrupted part of the operating system, as in error messages that say Bad or Missing NTOSKRNL.EXE. In such a case, you may need to replace all or part of your operating system. The tools most likely to apply to this scenario are the ones to create and delete folders, rename files, change attributes, and copy or extract files from other media.

Creating folders is simple. The command syntax is as follows:

```
md [drive:]path
mkdir [drive:]path
```

where *drive:* is the drive letter of the drive on which you want to create the folder, if it's not the current one, and *path* is the name of the folder you want to create. Just make sure that if you don't spell out the location of the new folder, you're currently in the place where the new folder should be created.

The syntax for the rmdir and rd commands (for deleting folders) is the same as that for md. The only part of folder deletion that you have to watch is that you can't delete folders unless they're empty, with no subfolders. If you try, you'll get an error message telling you that the folder is not empty, and there's no switch to make rd act like deltree (an old DOS command that would delete subdirectories).

Before you delete a folder, run the dir command to check out its contents and make sure that you really do want to remove it. Conveniently, dir displays all files, hidden or not, and shows their attributes.

Rather than deleting entire folders, however, you're more likely to need to replace individual files. That's where copy and extract come in. The copy command is what it sounds like: a method for copying a file from one location to another, with the caveat I've mentioned before that you can only copy files *to* the system folder, not copy files *from* the system folder to removable media such as a Jaz drive. The syntax for copying files is simple:

```
copy source [destination]
```

where *source* is the name of the original file and *destination* is the folder where you're pasting the original (along with a new name, if you need it). If you don't specify a folder, the file will be copied to the folder from which you're running the command. The extract utility works the same way as copy and uses the same syntax, with one exception: you can use extract only if you started the Recovery Console from the Repair option in Setup. Neither copying utility supports wildcards (so you can't copy the entire contents of a folder very easily), but copy automatically decompresses compressed installation files for you. Both utilities will alert you if a file with the name of the one you're pasting already exists in that location.

If you're not sure that you want to replace an existing file, try renaming it and then copying the new file to the relevant location. The syntax for rename is as follows:

```
rename [drive:][path] filename1 filename2
```

This command works only on single files, and the renamed file must be in the same place as the original. That is, you can't use rename to move files. To do that, you'd need to use copy.

### Fixing Boot Sectors and Boot Records

Your computer uses a couple of pieces of information to navigate your hard disk. Those two pieces are the boot sector and the Master Boot Record (MBR). Most of the time, these pieces are pretty safe, but some things (such as some viruses) can target and infect them, or they can be lost. In such a case, you'll need a way to restore them.

First, a little background. The partition boot sector contains the information that the file system uses to access the volume. The Master Boot Record (discussed soon) examines the information in the boot sector to load the boot loader.

The Windows XP Professional boot sector contains the following information:

♦   A jump instruction

♦   The name and version of the operating system files (such as Windows XP Professional)

◆ A data structure called the BIOS Parameter Block, which describes the physical characteristics of the partition

◆ A data structure called the BIOS Extended Parameter Block, which describes the location of the Master File Table for NTFS volumes

◆ The bootstrap code

Most of the information in the boot sector describes the physical characteristics of the disk (for example, the number of sectors per track and clusters per sector), in addition to the location of the File Allocation Table (for FAT volumes) or the Master File Table (for NTFS volumes). The layout and exact information included in the boot sector depends on the disk format used.

Given that a disk may have more than one partition, how does the hard disk know where to find the different partitions? The first sector on every hard disk (whether the hard disk has an operating system on it or not) contains that disk's Master Boot Record (MBR). The MBR contains the partition table for that disk and a small amount of code used to read the partition table and find the system partition for that hard disk. Once it finds that partition, the MBR loads a copy of that partition's boot sector into memory. If the disk is not bootable (has no system partition), the code never gets used, and the boot sector is not loaded.

In short, a hard disk needs a functioning MBR to boot. The MBR is in the same place on every hard disk, so it's potentially an easy virus target.

Okay—all that said, to write a new boot sector to a drive, type **fixboot**. This will write a new boot sector to the current boot drive. To create a new MBR, type **fixmbr**.

### DELETING, CREATING, AND FORMATTING PARTITIONS

The Recovery Console includes tools not only for fixing Windows XP Professional but also for completely wiping things out and starting over. With these tools you can repartition and reformat your hard disk. Partitioning is setting up logical drives on the disk; formatting is placing a file system on those drives so you can store data on them.

**WARNING**  You probably already know this, but just in case you've forgotten, repartitioning and formatting are destructive. *Any data on the hard disk you've reformatted or repartitioned is history. Keep your backups.*

Before you start formatting or repartitioning, you might want to take a look at what you've already got in place. The Recovery Console's map command can help you do that. Type **map** at the command prompt, and you'll see output like the following:

```
?               0MB          Device\HardDisk0\Partition0
C:    FAT16     1028MB       Device\HardDisk0\Partition1
?               3310MB       Device\HardDisk0\Partition0
E:    NTFS      1028MB       Device\HardDisk0\Partition2
H:    NTFS      1028MB       Device\HardDisk0\Partition3
G:              1028MB       Device\HardDisk0\Partition4
?               227MB        Device\HardDisk0\Partition0
A:                           Device\Floppy0
D:                           Device\CDROM0
```

You can see from this that logical drive G on the hard disk hasn't been formatted, because it's not showing any file system. To format it, you would use the following syntax:

```
format g: [/q] [/fs:filesystem]
```

Here, /q tells format to do a quick format (not checking for bad sectors), and the /fs switch is for specifying the file system to use. You don't have to specify a file system (your options are NTFS, FAT32, and FAT), but if you don't, Windows XP Professional will format it to NTFS. When you run this command, Windows XP Professional will tell you that all data on that drive will be lost and ask you to confirm that the format should proceed. Do so, and a few seconds later you will have a newly formatted drive.

**TIP**   You can convert a FAT partition to NTFS, but you cannot convert an NTFS partition to FAT.

You can format the G drive safely, or at least without affecting any other logical drives. What you can't do, even before formatting, is repartition to make the G drive bigger, perhaps giving it some of that space that isn't used on the disk.

When you've finished with the Recovery Console, type **exit** and press Enter. The computer will reboot.

## The Driver Verifier—a Babysitter for Your Drivers

It goes without saying that reliable hardware is the number one most important consideration when building reliable Windows XP Professional systems. However, equally as important is making sure that reliable drivers are used.

A hardware device—as far as Windows XP Professional is concerned—is only as good as its associated driver.

If you've been lucky, all the hardware on your system has well-behaved drivers that don't cause any problems. But what if you wanted to add an old, slightly outdated card to your system? How would that impact your system's stability? Or what if you found a new driver on the Internet for some existing hardware you have? Will the new driver be as stable on your system as your current driver? How can you be sure that updating to a new driver won't compromise your system stability in some way?

The Driver Verifier, first released in Windows 2000 Professional and included with Windows XP Professional, is the answer to all these questions and more. In reality, what the Driver Verifier does is quite simple. During normal Windows operations, all the drivers on your system reside in the kernel of the Windows XP Professional operating system and are supposed to play nicely together and with the operating system. Windows XP Professional doesn't really look at what they are doing. It more or less assumes that the drivers will be on their best behavior as long as they respond appropriately when called on. As an analogy, imagine a bunch of children playing around unsupervised in a backyard. Now, as long as they respond when you call to them, would you assume that they aren't doing anything they shouldn't be doing? I should hope not!

As anyone who has children knows, just because you don't find out that your kids are misbehaving doesn't mean that they're not causing trouble. Kids need supervision. Well, sometimes the drivers in your system need supervision. That's basically what the Driver Verifier does—it acts as a babysitter for your drivers. It puts them under a microscope and scrutinizes every single thing they do. Using our children analogy, imagine taking one of the children, putting them in their own private sandbox, and standing over them watching every single thing they do.

In effect, this is what the Driver Verifier does. By keeping an eye on how the drivers on your system utilize and access memory, your system will display a blue screen if a driver misbehaves. So, what does Windows XP Professional consider misbehaving? Well, the list is rather long—and *extremely* technical—to the point where addressing those issues would take up far more pages than are allocated to this book. Therefore, let's just take a look at the common circumstances in which you would want to use the Driver Verifier and how to use it.

## Running the Driver Verifier

As I mentioned before, you will probably want to use the Driver Verifier if you want to add a new piece of hardware to your system or if you want to update an existing driver. In any case, if you are concerned about system stability, run the Driver Verifier in order to place the new (or updated) driver in its own private sandbox for the first few weeks.

**WARNING**  During the course of writing this chapter, I placed the driver for my network adapter in the Driver Verifier to make sure it was behaving appropriately. For whatever reason, when I took the driver back out, my system would no longer access the Internet without causing a blue screen. Eventually, I figured out that this was due to a conflict with some personal firewall software that I was using. The personal firewall software worked fine before I started testing the Driver Verifier, but after I took my network adapter in and out of the Driver Verifier, my personal firewall would no longer work consistently. I'm sure that this was an atypical symptom of using the Driver Verifier program—and more likely a problem with my personal firewall software—but it does warrant a bit of caution. Even though this is a great diagnostic utility, unless you have something specific that you want to troubleshoot, it may not be wise to play around with it. And just in case you do want to use it, you might want to back up your system first.

You can start the Driver Verifier in two ways:

◆ At the command prompt, type **verifier.**

◆ Choose Start ➢ Run to open the Run dialog box, and in the Open box, type **verifier**.

In either case, the Driver Verifier Manager opens, as shown in Figure 27.4.

On the first screen of the Driver Verifier Manager, you select the settings you want the program to use, create custom settings, delete existing settings, display existing settings, or display information about verified drivers. Unless you are the developer of a driver, click the Create Standard Settings option if you are ready to place a driver "in its sandbox," and click Next.

You can then select which driver or drivers you want to verify. Select an option to display a description of what that option will do at the bottom of the screen. If you select Automatically Select Unsigned Drivers, the Driver Verifier Manager will immediately search your system for any unsigned drivers and display a list of any it finds. Driver Verifier Manager will do the same if you select the Automatically Select Drivers Built for Older Versions of Windows option.

If you want to verify all drivers on your system, click that option, and then click Finish. If you just want to see a list of drivers, click Select Driver Names from a List. When you've made your choice, click Next, and Driver Verifier Manager will take care of the task.

**FIGURE 27.4**

The Driver Verifier
Manager program

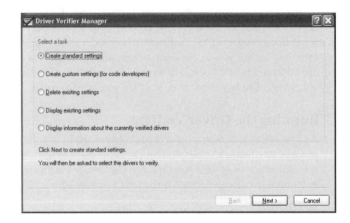

# System File Checker

One of the things that Microsoft has learned over the years is that more often than not, unreliable
behavior in Windows can be directly attributed to missing, corrupted, or conflicting versions of critical system components. In an effort to resolve this problem, Microsoft has included a utility in Windows XP Professional called the System File Checker (SFC).

The System File Checker is a command-line utility that will scan the critical system files on your
computer and replace any suspicious files with original copies either from your installation media or
a special folder on your system. If you suspect that a Windows file on your system might have been
damaged, run the System File Checker to find out for sure.

## Running the SFC

The SFC will check approximately 2,700 files on your system—namely most of the SYS, DLL, EXE,
TTF, FON, and OCX files that were originally installed. When you run the SFC, you are in effect telling the utility to compare all the files on your system against the original installation media. Therefore, the SFC will need a copy of the original files to work from. Make sure that you have your original
Windows XP Professional CD-ROM handy when you need to run this utility.

The SFC is a command-line utility, so you won't find it on any of the menus in your system. To
launch the SFC, type **SFC** at a command prompt. If everything is working correctly, you should see a
help screen giving you the available command options. The options are listed in Table 27.3.

**TABLE 27.3:** SFC Command-Line Options

| COMMAND-LINE OPTIONS | DESCRIPTION |
| --- | --- |
| /scannow | Forces an immediate scan of your system |
| /scanonce | Tells your system to scan all files on your system at the next bootup |
| /scanboot | Tells your system to scan all files on your system at every bootup |

**TABLE 27.3:**  SFC Command-Line Options *(CONTINUED)*

| COMMAND-LINE OPTIONS | DESCRIPTION |
| --- | --- |
| /purgecache | Purges the Dllcache folder and begins scanning all protected system files immediately |
| /revert | Returns the scan to its default setting |
| /cachesize=x | Sets the file cache size |

Since you're reading this chapter, you're most likely looking for troubleshooting information, either to repair a system that is currently experiencing problems or for future reference. For most troubleshooting purposes, a simple SFC /SCANNOW will suffice. This will begin checking each of the critical system files on your computer, comparing them against the original copies, and determining if any of the files have been corrupted.

As the tool is running, a status monitor will keep you informed as to how far the system has proceeded with its checking. If the SFC finds any files that are missing or corrupted (when compared with the Windows XP Professional source media), it will replace the file with the original version either from its cache on your hard drive or from the original media.

Just for giggles, I tested this capability on my system by overwriting one of the True-Type Font (TTF) files. Sure enough, once I ran the SFC, it saw that one of my files was corrupted and replaced it with an original copy of the file. I can definitely see where the SFC is useful in the case of corrupted files, virus infections, or just plain ol' human error. The SFC is a lifesaver!

# The Registry Entry That Lets You Force a Blue Screen (Core Dump)

Okay, so far in this chapter, I've been talking about ways to avoid blue screens or at least to minimize their impact. But what if you actually *want* to cause a blue screen?

Although unusual, on occasions you might want to force your system to crash via a blue screen. For example, you might want to test that Windows XP Professional will reboot itself properly and that all the necessary services on your system will start again. Or you might want to see how well an application that is running on your system will perform in the event of a critical failure. For whatever the reasons, if you want to force your system to blue screen, you can do it.

All you need is one simple Registry modification. To modify the Registry in Windows XP Professional, you use RegEdit. As always, before making *any* modifications to your Registry, back it up.

After you back up your Registry, you will need to navigate to the HKEY_LOCAL_MACHINE\SYSTEM\CurrentControlSet\Services\i8042prt\Parameters. In there, you will create a key called CrashOnCtrlScroll as a DWORD type. Enter a value of 1 for the Registry key, and then reboot your system.

So what does this do? Well, the i8042prt service is responsible for handling your keyboard input. So this Registry entry allows you to force the system to crash through the use of a special keystroke. Useful for both diagnostic testing purposes and practical joking! Once you have this Registry key in your system, a simple Ctrl+ScrollLock+ScrollLock will cause your system to immediately blue screen (you must use the Ctrl key on the right side of the keyboard and press the ScrollLock key twice).

# Backing Up and Restoring

A lot of what I've talked about in this chapter won't do you any good unless you've backed up your system. So, as I promised early on in this chapter, here are the steps for backing up and for restoring.

## Making a Backup

The next thing you can do to make life easier for yourself is to back up important files. Yes, we know you have heard all this before; everybody's heard about making backups, but why should *you* make a backup?

**To protect against hard disk failure**   A hard disk can fail at almost any time, but when it does, it is always at the most inconvenient moment.

**To protect against accidental deletion of a file**   If you work on many projects, your chances of accidentally deleting a file are far higher than if you work on only one at a time.

**To create an archive at the end of a project**   You can make a backup that contains all the files relating to a single project when the work is done; then if you need to refer to the files again, you know where to find them.

These are the main reasons to make a backup, but there are others. You might back up the files of a terminating employee in case the computer is reassigned within your department or is transferred to another department. In either case, the new user will likely clean up the hard disk—in other words, delete all the most important files. In addition, making a backup is one way to transfer a large number of files from one computer system to another. Finally, you should always back up before making a substantial change to your system such as installing new hardware, upgrading the operating system, or making a major configuration change to your application software.

Once you decide to make a backup, you need to plan your backup strategy and, most important, stick to it. With no plan, you will simply accumulate floppy disks or tapes haphazardly, you will waste tapes, and you will waste time looking for a file when you need to restore a file deleted by accident.

So how often should you make a backup? For an answer that fits the way you work, answer these questions:

- How often do your data files change? Every day? Every week? Every month?

- How important to your day-to-day operations are these files? Can you work without them? How long would it take you to re-create them?

- How much will it cost to replace lost files in terms of time spent and business lost?

In our computerized world, it takes hours to create an HTML page with just the right look or a budget spreadsheet that everyone agrees to, but either can be lost or destroyed in milliseconds. A hard-disk failure, a mistaken delete command, overwriting the file with an earlier version with the same name—these can destroy a file just as surely as fire, flood, or earthquake. You just have to lose one important file to become an instant convert for life to a program of regular, planned backups.

To start the Windows XP Professional backup program, choose Start ➢ All Programs ➢ Accessories ➢ System Tools ➢ Backup.

### USING THE BACKUP OR RESTORE WIZARD

Using the Backup or Restore Wizard is a quick and easy way to learn about backups; it gets you going quickly with the minimum of technical knowledge. Later in this section, I'll walk you through the steps to do a manual backup.

To back up using the wizard, follow these steps:

1. At the Welcome screen, click Next to open the Backup or Restore screen:

2. Click the Back Up Files and Settings option, and then click Next to open the What to Back Up screen:

CHAPTER 27

**3.** Select what you want to back up, and then click Next to open the Backup Type, Destination, and Name screen:

**4.** Select the type of medium to which you'll back up, give the backup a name, and then click Next to open the Completing the Backup or Restore Wizard screen.

**5.** Click Finish to start the backup.

**NOTE** To select additional backup options, click the Advanced button on the final screen of the wizard before you click Finish.

A time will come when you want a little more control over your backups, and that is when you stop using the wizard and take charge of the process yourself. At the Welcome dialog box, rather than invoking the wizard, click the Advanced Mode button. Using the Backup Utility program involves essentially the same tasks that the Backup or Restore Wizard does for you—selecting the files, deciding where to put them, and specifying how the backup should actually be made. Let's take a look.

**TIP** You must have the right permissions to make a backup or a restore. Make sure you are logged on as an administrator or as a backup operator if you are backing up files on a local computer. If you are not logged on as an administrator or backup operator, you must be the owner of the file or folders you want to back up, or you must have one or more of the following permissions: Read, Read and Execute, Modify, or Full Control.

### MAKING A MANUAL BACKUP

The Backup Utility dialog box opens at the Welcome tab, from which you can choose to use the wizards. To make a manual backup, click the Backup tab, which is shown in Figure 27.5. If you have previously specified and saved a backup job, you can select it for use again using Job ➢ Load Selections. That done, all you have to do is click the Start Backup button to begin the backup.

If you don't have a previously saved backup job or if you want to do things a little differently this time, the first task is to decide which files to back up. You can back up all the files and folders in the Backup tab, or you can back up only files that have changed, along with any new files never before backed up.

**FIGURE 27.5**

The Backup tab in the Backup Utility program

In the Backup tab, check the box next to the files and folders you want to back up. A blue check mark indicates that the folder or file is selected for backup; a gray check mark indicates that some of the files in the folder or on the drive have been selected for backup.

The next task is to select the destination device or drive for the backup and to name the backup file itself. Use the Backup Destination list below the main window to select the destination and the Backup Media or File Name box to specify a name for this backup.

The last part of the process is to review the backup configuration settings. Choose Tools ➢ Options to open the Options dialog box shown in Figure 27.6.

**FIGURE 27.6**

The Options dialog box

Across the top of the Options dialog box you will see the following tabs:

**General**   Lets you specify that the backed-up data are compared against the original files to ensure the data were properly backed up. You can also specify how data compression is performed and how you want the Backup program to respond if it finds that the medium (tape, disk, or CD) you are using already contains a backup.

**Restore**   Lets you specify what happens when duplicate files are found during a restore operation.

**Backup Type**   Lets you choose how the backup is made:

**Normal**   Backs up all the selected files and clears the archive bit.

**Copy**   Backs up all the selected files but does not clear the archive bit.

**Differential**   Backs up all the selected files that changed since the last Normal or Incremental backup. When the backup is complete, the archive bit for each file is left on.

**Incremental**   Backs up all the selected files that have changed since the last Incremental or Normal backup. When the backup is complete, the archive bit for each file is turned off.

**Daily**   Backs up all the files that have been modified today.

**Backup Log**   Lets you specify the elements you want to include in the backup log file.

**Exclude Files**   Lets you specify file types that you want to exclude from this backup; use the Add New and Remove buttons to select files for exclusion.

All that remains is to click the Start Backup button to begin the backup. Keep the backup in a safe place, preferably not next to your computer; if your computer is damaged by the sprinklers going off by accident, there is a very good chance that the backup will be destroyed at the same time.

**TIP**   Click the Schedule Jobs tab in the Backup Utility main window to specify the date for a backup.

## Restoring a Backup

Most of the time, making a backup is a simple precaution, and you put it on the shelf along with the other tapes or Zip disks. But there will come a time, after a hard-disk controller failure perhaps, when you will need to restore a backup. Again, as when making the backup, you can use a wizard, or you can do it manually.

### USING THE RESTORE WIZARD

Using the Backup or Restore Wizard is a quick and easy way to learn about restoring backups; it gets you going quickly with the minimum of technical knowledge. To access this feature, click Restore Wizard in the Welcome tab of the Backup Utility dialog box. (You can also use the Backup or Restore Wizard described earlier.) If you would rather not use the wizard, click the Restore and Manage Media tab, which is described in the next section.

The wizard walks you through a sequence of dialog boxes that specify the following:

**What to Restore**   You can restore all files and folders in the backup set, or you can restore selected files and folders.

**Restore From**   Specify the type and location of the backup you want to restore.

**Select Backup Sets**   Select a backup set for the restore.

**Where to Restore**   Specify the target of the restore; most of the time, selecting Original Location to put the file back where it came from makes the most sense.

**How to Restore**   Specify whether existing files on your hard disk should be overwritten during the restore.

### USING THE RESTORE AND MANAGE MEDIA TAB

Using the Restore and Manage Media tab in the Backup Utility dialog box involves essentially the same tasks that the Restore Wizard does for you—selecting the files, deciding where to put them, and specifying how the restore should actually be made. A check mark in a gray check box means that only some of the files in a folder have been selected. A check mark in a white box means that all files in a folder have been selected.

## Summary

This chapter introduced you to some of the vital skills needed for troubleshooting Windows XP Professional when things go wrong. I discussed how to avoid Windows XP Professional crashes, which is the best troubleshooting technique of all, and how to restore a configuration. We then looked at System Restore, a new feature in Windows XP Professional, and at Recovery Console. Following that, we took a look at the Driver Verifier, the System File Checker, and the Registry entry that lets you force a core dump. Fixing Windows is no fun, but at least now you have an idea of how to go about it. You also know why it's important to back up your files, you know how to back up, and you know how to restore.

In the next chapter, I'll show you how to perform a critical administrative task that is often overlooked—auditing security.

CHAPTER 27

# Chapter 28

# Auditing Security

Back in Chapter 19 we took a detailed look at how Windows XP security works. If securing your computer is a primary concern to you, then the obvious first step is to know how to apply security settings. However, you can't just assume that since you set up security on your machine all is well. There are many things you could have overlooked. Maybe you forgot to set security on a specific folder. Perhaps the security you set isn't as strict as it should be. Things like this happen because, after all, we are human.

This is where auditing comes into play. After you have established security measures, auditing can help you check to make sure that no one is getting access to resources that they shouldn't. Auditing can act as a watchdog, if you will. In this chapter, we'll look at the many benefits of auditing, a few inconveniences of auditing, and how to set up auditing. We'll also look at

- ◆ Reasons to use and not to use auditing
- ◆ Implementing auditing through policies
- ◆ Auditing folders, files, and printers
- ◆ Monitoring audited events

## Deciding What to Audit

Windows XP gives you a great deal of flexibility in auditing. You can decide to audit every time any user opens any file on your machine. You can also go to the other extreme and choose no auditing whatsoever. But if you're like most people, you will choose a position somewhere in the middle.

**NOTE**  Most home networks have no auditing enabled. It's mostly because people aren't worried about their home network. After all, who would want to break into it? Plenty of people would. In the workplace, a company that does not audit security is asking for serious problems. At the very least, unauthorized people could be poking around in sensitive areas. At the worst, there could be legal problems, thanks in part to the Sarbanes-Oxley Act of 2002. Information on Sarbanes-Oxley as it relates to IT can be found in a variety of places. A good one to start with is the Information Systems Audit and Control Association (ISACA) at www.isaca.org.

Although there could be many factors that play into your decision to enable auditing, the most important consideration is the security of your computer. If you don't care about security and could care less who sees your files or uses your printers, then auditing isn't for you. There's no sense in enabling it. However, if the files on your machine are confidential, then you'll likely want to know if someone is trying to get to them or, worse yet, has gotten to them.

## Benefits of Auditing

Auditing provides increased security for your computer. No, auditing won't actually keep someone out of your files. That's what permissions are for. Auditing is there to let you know about potential security breaches. For example, you can audit logon attempts to your computer. If someone has tried to log on to your machine a dozen times, using your username but the wrong password, auditing can track that. By reviewing your security logs, you will notice attempts to hack your machine. If you didn't have auditing, you might not know until it's too late.

You can use auditing to track almost everything that happens on your computer. You will know what happened (log on, file access, printer access), when it happened, and who did it. This way, if something bad does happen, you will have a culprit. In this way, auditing can be thought of as supplemental security. It won't keep a specific event from happening but will leave a detailed electronic paper trail.

A discussion of the benefits of auditing wouldn't be complete unless you knew what types of things were available to audit. After all, how do you know it's good for you if you don't know exactly what it does? There are nine different types of events that can be audited in Windows XP. These events are listed in Table 28.1.

**TABLE 28.1:**     Windows XP Audit Events

| EVENT | DESCRIPTION |
| --- | --- |
| Account logon events | Audits when a user logs on to or off of another computer from this computer. This typically happens only in domains, so you won't likely use this event in Windows XP Professional. |
| Account management | Audits when changes are made to a user or group. These changes can include creation, deletion, renaming, disabling or enabling, and password changes. |
| Directory service access | Audits whenever a user accesses a directory service object other than a file, folder, or printer. Used only in Windows 2000 and Windows .NET domains. |
| Logon events | Audits whenever a user logs on or logs off of this computer. Very helpful. |
| Object access | Audits a user's access to files, folders, and printers. Very helpful. |
| Policy change | Audits changes made to user rights policies, audit policies, and trust relationships. |
| Privilege use | Audits whenever a user executes a user right, other than logon, logoff, system shutdown, or network access events. |
| Process tracking | Tracks changes made by programs in Windows XP. Generally not very useful. |
| System events | Audits system shutdowns and restarts or any attempted changes to the system's Security log. Sometimes useful. |

Some of the events may seem redundant and can be confusing as to their purpose. Let's try to clarify them now:

**Account logon events vs. logon events**   Account logon events are useful if someone uses your machine to log on to a Windows 2000, Windows .NET, or Windows Server 2003 domain. If you don't have a domain, you won't need to use these events. Logon events will track who logs on to your individual machine.

**Directory service access vs. object access**   Directory service access tracks whenever someone accesses a specific object in the Windows 2000, Windows .NET, or Windows Server 2003 directory. Object types include, but are not limited to, shared folder objects, user objects, and group objects. Once again, this is not generally useful for Windows XP Professional because it implies that a domain is present. Object access tracks access to files, folders, and printer objects specifically. Implementing tracking on these three types objects is a two-step setup process, which we'll cover in the "Setting Up Auditing in Windows XP" section of this chapter.

The events listed in Table 28.1 can be quite a lot to absorb. The two most commonly used audit events are logon events and object access. Account management, privilege use, and policy change are common in environments where there are multiple users with administrative privileges. Account logon events and directory service access are used only when you have a domain. Process tracking and system events are rarely audited.

### The Dark Side of Auditing

When deciding what to audit on your Windows XP computer, there are two negative aspects you will want to be aware of. The first one is performance overhead, and the second one is the volume of audited information.

Auditing adds overhead to your computer. Auditing is a process, much like an application, in that it performs a task based on a specific event happening on your computer. So if you have enabled auditing on every file on your machine, your computer needs to make a note of *who*, *what*, and *when* every time someone opens a file. This extra work slows down the machine. The more you audit, the more overhead you will have. Overhead becomes a more extensive issue when you are auditing servers, because they generally have more people accessing them than do workstations. Even so, overhead is still something to keep in mind when deciding what to audit on your XP workstation. Too much auditing can cripple your system's performance.

The sheer volume of audit records that your computer may generate can become overwhelming. Once again, the more you audit, the more you will have to deal with. With so many audit events to sort through, it can be difficult to find the specific piece of information you're looking for. Fortunately, Windows XP allows you to restrict your display to specific types of events through filtering. We'll look at how to filter events in the "Monitoring Security" section later in this chapter.

All in all, the benefits of auditing far outweigh the drawbacks. As long as you apply your auditing judiciously, you should be able to enjoy the benefits without causing any serious performance problems.

## Setting Up Auditing in Windows XP

Auditing is enabled in Windows XP Professional through the Local Security Settings console. Local Security Settings is part of Administrative Tools located in Control Panel. Figure 28.1 shows where Audit Policy is located within the security console. You must have administrative privileges to enable auditing.

**NOTE** Windows XP Home Edition does not come with a Local Security Settings console. Consequently, you cannot set up auditing from a Windows XP Home Edition computer.

**FIGURE 28.1**

Local Security Settings

Notice in Figure 28.1 that we have enabled a few of the more common auditing events. Also, when you enable auditing, you have the choice of auditing successes or failures of each type of event. Auditing logon failures could warn you about a potential hacker, whereas logon successes may just show you that you've indeed logged on every day for the last month. Once again, you have to decide on an appropriate auditing level for your computer. To set up auditing of an event, double-click it in the right pane, and check the Success and/or Failure box. An example is shown in Figure 28.2.

**FIGURE 28.2**

Auditing object access

**WARNING** If you are part of a Windows 2000, Windows .NET, or Windows Server 2003 domain, domain-wide security policies set with Group Policy objects will override your local settings. Check with your domain administrator to see if this is going to be an issue.

For most audit events, all you need to do is open up Local Security Settings, find the event you want to audit, and select the Success and/or Failure boxes. It's a relatively painless procedure. However, for object access, specifically auditing folders, files, and printers, you will need to perform an additional step.

The first step to auditing objects is just like auditing anything else. Open Local Security Settings and check Success and/or Failure for the Audit object access event. For object access, it's recommended that you always check both the Success and Failure boxes. By performing this first step, you have set up your machine to allow the auditing of folders, files, and printers. Now you have to tell your computer *which* folders, files, and printers you want to monitor.

There is logic in Microsoft making this a two-step process. If all you needed to do were to check the boxes in Local Security Settings, you would automatically enable auditing on *all* folders, files, and printers. In most cases, this is completely unnecessary—definite overkill. This two-step process lets you fine-tune audit control over your machine.

**NOTE**   In order to audit folders and files, the folders and files must be on an NTFS partition. FAT partitions do not support auditing. If you don't have a Security tab on your folder's Properties, check to make sure your partition is NTFS.

For the second step, start by finding the folder, file, or printer you want to audit. Generally, it's best to audit folders rather than specific files, much like Microsoft recommends setting permissions at the folder level rather than the file level. Once you have found the folder that you want to audit, right-click it and choose Properties. In the Security tab, click the Advanced button and then the Auditing tab. You will see a screen similar to the one shown in Figure 28.3.

**FIGURE 28.3**
The Auditing tab for the Docs folder

Unless you have set up auditing before, it's likely that your text box will be blank, as opposed to having the Everyone group in it like Figure 28.3 does. To add a group of people to audit, click the Add button. You will get a screen similar to Figure 28.4. Select the group or user you want to watch in the Name box by clicking the Change button, and then check the boxes for which actions you would like to audit. Clicking the Full Control box will enable the whole column. If you want to be safe, choosing Full Control is the best option, but keep in mind that this increases the amount of overhead for the workstation. In order to audit multiple groups, click the Add button in the Auditing tab again, and add the additional group. You can specify separate auditing policies for different groups.

**FIGURE 28.4**

Enabling audit entries
for the Docs folder

You can further customize your auditing preferences with the drop-down menu shown in
Figure 28.5.

**FIGURE 28.5**

Fine-tuning audit
entries

Auditing printers is done much the same way as auditing a folder. Go to the printer's Properties,
click the Security tab, click the Advanced button, and then click the Auditing tab. Click the Add button to add a group, and you will get a display similar to Figure 28.6. Notice that printers give you
fewer things to audit than do folders. From the Apply Onto drop-down menu, you can choose to
audit the printer, documents sent to the printer, or both the printer and documents.

For the most part, setting up auditing in Windows XP Professional is pretty simple. It does get
more complex when you want to audit folders and printers, but if you remember to complete both
steps, your auditing setup will turn out fine.

**FIGURE 28.6**
Auditing printers

But now that you've enabled auditing, where do you go to see who has tripped audit events? Setting up auditing isn't enough. You need to periodically monitor your security logs to see if anything has gone awry.

## Monitoring Security

The Event Viewer utility is used to monitor your security audits. Event Viewer is located in Administrative Tools in Control Panel. There are three logs in Event Viewer; the one we are interested in for auditing purposes is the Security log. Event Viewer's Security log is shown in Figure 28.7.

**FIGURE 28.7**
The Security log in Event Viewer

**NOTE**   In order to view the Security log, you must have administrative privileges.

A quick look at the Security log will tell you whether the logged event was a success or failure, the date, time, category, event number, user performing the action, and computer that it was performed on. It's an electronic paper trail of what's happened on your computer—at least what's happened in regard to what you've been auditing. To find out more details about a specific event, double-click it. You will get a screen similar to Figure 28.8.

**FIGURE 28.8**
Event detail

As I mentioned earlier, your Security log can quickly acquire a large number of events. It can be difficult, if not impossible, to find the specific types of events you want to look at. Fortunately, Windows XP Professional Event Viewer comes with an ability to filter events based on almost any criteria you choose. As an example, if you wanted to find events that related to the user JSmith only, you could filter for the username JSmith. This is illustrated in Figure 28.9. To use filtering in Event Viewer, click View and then Filter.

**FIGURE 28.9**
Filtering for Jsmith

Because the Security log can get quite large, Microsoft recommends that you periodically clear out the log. You can choose to delete all old security records or save them for future reference. For details on how to do this, and more Event Viewer management topics, see Chapter 23.

## Summary

Auditing allows you to monitor various security-based aspects of your computer. You can see if someone logged on or off, made changes to security settings, created or modified users, or accessed system resources.

Perhaps the biggest benefit of auditing is how it affords you the ability to check for potential system abuses. By enabling auditing of logon and logoff events, you can see if someone has been trying to hack your account. By auditing your folders, you can see who has accessed critical files. You can even audit your printers to see if someone in the Accounting department has been printing high-quality glossy color photos of his family vacation on your printer at one o'clock in the morning.

Auditing is enabled through Local Security Settings in Administrative Tools in Control Panel. Once you have enabled auditing, you can check your Security log in Event Viewer to see if any events have happened. Although auditing itself will not keep people out of your resources—that's what permissions are for—auditing can tell you what actions were performed on your machine, allowing you to further control your security.

This chapter ends our section on network administration. Within these pages is a plethora of information that can help you effectively manage small and large networks alike. Keep in mind, though, that the best administrators are the "best" because of their experience. They've been there, done that, and seen it all. Well, maybe not "seen it all," but seen enough to have a good idea where to go when there's a problem. Practice and experience are the keys if you want to be a solid administrator.

In the next chapter, we begin a journey into additional advanced topics. These include things that you might or might not use Windows XP for, such as telecommuting and web services, as well as a few more management tools. We will begin with setting up secure telecommuting.

CHAPTER 28

# Part 8

# Advanced Topics

In this section you will learn how to:
- Configure Safe Telecommuting
- Use the Microsoft Management Console
- Manage Services within Windows XP
- Configure and Host Web and FTP Servers
- Troubleshoot Windows XP

# Chapter 29

# Secure Telecommuting

This chapter begins the final part of this book. Each topic in this part is one that you likely won't have to deal with on a daily basis. However, failure to understand how to deal with these issues when you need to can cause serious problems for your Windows XP computer and your network.

In this chapter, we'll take a look at a common scenario—a corporate user who wants (or needs) to telecommute a portion of the time and needs to do so as securely as possible. We'll look at some of the common threats that a telecommuting user must face, along with what Windows XP Professional can do to protect against those threats.

- ◆ Overview of telecommuting
- ◆ Protecting against data interception
- ◆ Protecting against user impersonation
- ◆ Protecting against data abduction

## Telecommuting Overview: Risks and Rewards

As telecommuting becomes more commonplace, the risks and rewards associated with it are becoming more apparent. The rewards are obvious: no dealing with traffic jams, being able to work in your bathrobe (if you want to), no office distractions, and so on. The risks, however, are a little less obvious. One of the biggest problems is the risk involved when corporate data is moved outside the corporation's walls.

The risks of telecommuting fall into three distinct areas:

- ◆ The interception of corporate data
- ◆ The impersonation of an authorized user
- ◆ The potential abduction of confidential data

It's interesting to look at the irony of the situation. Corporations are increasing their efforts to secure their data within their walls, but at the same time they are allowing more and more employees to telecommute. I can imagine that people who want to steal corporate data will eventually start to focus their efforts on telecommuting workers instead of the corporation's main systems, because most telecommuters make much easier targets.

The interception of data is an obvious threat: as data passes from your Windows XP Professional computer into your corporation's main systems, someone eavesdrops on the data transmission and reads the data. If your transmission is crossing the Internet, it will travel through many systems outside your company's control before it reaches its final destination. The same is true with dial-up modems, although the risks are slightly less because your traffic is being carried over the telephone network (a bit more secure). Still, risks do exist, and the main way to deal with the risk of data interception is through data encryption between the source and destination computers. I'll talk about some of the ways you can protect against data interception by encrypting transmissions leaving your Windows XP Professional computer.

The impersonation of a user is also a threat. If someone obtains your username and password, and if your account has dial-in access, that person can log in to your company's systems under your account, effectively impersonating you. Although the problem of account/password discovery happens within the corporation's walls as well (for example, users writing passwords on yellow sticky notes and attaching them to their monitors), it becomes more of a problem when a user's account is granted dial-in access. The pitfalls of this type of security breach are many—corruption of data, deletion of data, abduction of data, and the introduction of malicious viruses, just to name a few. You can take steps to prevent user impersonation. Some of them are built into Windows XP Professional, and others are security measures that your corporation must implement. We'll take a look at a number of possible solutions later in this chapter.

Finally, the risk of having data abducted is also a threat. Corporate espionage is a significant problem in many large organizations (although corporations usually keep silent about it since reporting it would have a negative impact on the company's stock price). Again, although corporations are taking significant steps to increase the security of their data within the company's walls, they are allowing users to keep copies of some data on their own home computers or laptops. Instead of targeting a corporate network, it will eventually be easier for someone to target a telecommuting user if they want to obtain a copy of sensitive corporate data. After all, which would be more difficult—breaking into a company and trying to steal a computer, or breaking into someone's home and stealing their computer or laptop? We'll take a look at some of the utilities provided in Windows XP Professional that will allow you to secure data on your system so that even in the worst-case scenario—your computer is completely stolen—your company's sensitive data won't fall into the wrong hands.

## Protecting against the Interception of Data

If you are telecommuting, odds are you are connected to your corporation's network in one of three ways: directly—through some sort of wide area network connection, indirectly—through an analog dial-up networking connection, or through a high-speed digital connection or possibly a virtual private network (VPN). No matter how you are connected, you can take steps to secure your communications.

### Securing RAS Dial-In Sessions

The dial-in scenario is probably familiar if you've been using computers for any length of time. You install a modem, you define a dial-up networking entry to call into a remote network, and then your computer initiates a connection over your phone line. This is a relatively secure means of communicating with a remote network, but it still could be compromised: someone could tap into your phone line and record the data conversations traveling back and forth between your computer and the remote computer. Therefore, the primary means to protect RAS (remote access server) dial-in sessions is via encryption. Windows XP Professional makes it easy to implement (and require) encryption on any dial-up networking connection.

**NOTE**   Encryption is the process of encoding information so that it is secure from unauthorized access. Decryption is the reverse of this process.

Assuming you have a working dial-up networking connection, setting up encryption is relatively easy. Follow these steps:

1. Choose Start ➢ Connect To ➢ Show All Connections to open the Network Connections folder.

2. Right-click the icon for your dial-up connection, and choose Properties from the shortcut menu to open the Properties dialog box for that connection.

3. Click the Security tab, click the Advanced (Custom Settings) option button, and then click the Settings button to open the Advanced Security Settings dialog box:

You'll notice that the very first item in the Advanced Security Settings dialog box is the Data Encryption drop-down list box. This option has four possible settings:

**No Encryption Allowed**   This setting will attempt to force your computer into a nonencrypted communication session. If the remote system that you are dialing into will allow any type of connection (encrypted or not), you will be able to connect. However, if the remote system will accept only encrypted connections, you will not be able to connect.

**Optional Encryption**   This setting will defer to whatever is required by the remote system you are calling into. If the remote system does not require encryption, this setting will let you connect. If the remote system does require encryption, this setting will also let you connect.

**Require Encryption**   Enabling this setting will implement a 40-bit encryption channel between your Windows XP Professional computer and the remote system. If the remote system cannot support encryption, your session will immediately disconnect, and you'll see a disconnection error message.

**Maximum Strength Encryption**   Enabling this setting will require a strong (128-bit) encryption channel between your Windows XP Professional computer and the remote system. You will see this option only if you purchased Windows XP Professional in the United States. If the remote system cannot support strong encryption, your session will immediately disconnect with an error message.

Enabling a data encryption option ensures that all your communications are kept private, even if someone is able to intercept them.

CHAPTER 29

To enable encryption on your dial-up connection, select one of the protocols in the Logon Security section of the Advanced Security Settings dialog box.

## Virtual Private Networking Connections

Virtual private networking (VPN) connections are, by definition, meant to be private. VPNs were originally developed as a means to route confidential, private data across untrusted networks. As a result of the reach and popularity of the Internet, VPNs have enjoyed a considerable amount of success in the current market.

One of the better analogies I've found for explaining the concepts of a virtual private network is to refer to them as "pipes." To conceptualize VPNs, think of two pipes, one large and one small. Now, imagine that the small pipe actually runs *inside* the large one. It starts and ends at the same places the large pipe does, and it can carry materials on its own completely independently of whatever is happening in the large pipe. As a matter of fact, the only thing the small pipe is dependent on the large pipe for is the determination of the start and end points. Beyond that, the small pipe can operate independently of the large pipe in terms of direction of travel, materials it carries, and so on.

To add another layer to this analogy, let's assume that the large pipe is made of a transparent material and that the small pipe is made of metal. Anyone taking a look at the pipe-within-a-pipe would easily be able to see whatever is moving through the outer (large) pipe. However, whatever is traveling through the inner pipe would remain a mystery.

Finishing off this analogy, think of the large pipe as representing the unsecured network (that is, the Internet) and the small pipe as representing the virtual private network. VPN is a way of tunneling data packets through a connection that already exists but that can't be used on its own for privacy reasons. Obviously, the Internet is a perfect example of a network that often can't be used on its own for privacy reasons.

To establish a VPN connection to your corporate network, your company must have set up a VPN server capable of receiving those connections. (More information on setting up a virtual private networking server is available in *Mastering Windows 2000 Server*, Fourth Edition, Sybex, 2002, and *Mastering Windows Server 2003*, Sybex, 2003.) If your company has set up a VPN server for you to dial in to, you will need to know the answers to the following questions:

◆ Which authentication type does it require?

◆ Which encryption strength does it require?

◆ What is the IP address or DNS (domain name service) name to connect to?

Once you know the answer to these questions, you can set up a VPN connection on your Windows XP Professional computer.

Since a VPN (typically) runs over the Internet, the first thing you must have on your system is a functional Internet connection. Whether your connection is a dial-up modem or a dedicated cable/xDSL connection is mostly irrelevant. Assuming you have an Internet connection in place, you can easily create a VPN connection. Follow these steps:

1. Choose Start ➤ Connect To ➤ Show All Connections to open the Network Connections folder.

2. In the Network Tasks bar, click the Create a New Connection link to start the New Connection Wizard.

**3.** Click Next to open the Network Connection Type screen:

**4.** Select the Connect to the Network at My Workplace option, and then click Next to open the Network Connection screen:

**5.** Click the Virtual Private Network Connection option, and then click Next to open the Connection Name screen:

**6.** Enter a name for your connection, and then click Next to open the Public Network screen:

As we discussed earlier, connecting to a VPN (over the Internet) requires that a functional Internet connection be in place before establishing the VPN connection. Now, your connection to the Internet will most likely be one of two types—either a dial-up connection (such as a modem or an ISDN [Integrated Services Digital Network] line) or a dedicated connection that you do not need to dial (that is, it's always there, always on). If you are using a dial-up connection to connect to the Internet, you can instruct Windows XP Professional to automatically establish that connection first before initiating your VPN connection by selecting the Automatically Dial This Initial Connection option. Select your Internet dial-up connection from the drop-down list, and then any time you launch your VPN connection, Windows XP Professional will automatically log you in to the Internet. If you have a direct connection to the Internet (cable, xDSL, other), simply skip this step by selecting the Do Not Dial the Initial Connection option. When you are finished with this step, click Next to open the VPN Server Selection screen:

Since virtual private networks function over the Internet, you will connect to a VPN either via an IP address or a DNS name (which resolves into an IP address). Enter the name of your target VPN server, or enter the IP address of the destination system, and then click Next to finish your VPN connection.

In the final screen of the wizard, specify whether you want a shortcut to this connection on your desktop, and click Finish. You have now successfully created a VPN connection.

Now, if your corporation has implemented their VPN server correctly, it should be set up so that you can't connect unless your connection is encrypted. Assuming that is the case, you may need to set the appropriate encryption level for your VPN connection the same way you would set one for a RAS connection (as discussed earlier in the chapter).

Once you've got everything correctly defined on your system, you should be able to double-click your VPN icon on your Windows XP Professional system and get connected—securely—to your corporate network. Once you're connected, you should be able to navigate throughout your company's corporate network just as if you were sitting in the office.

## VPN Performance Considerations

Our look at virtual private networking wouldn't be complete without taking a bit of time to discuss performance issues. Although virtual private networking is a neat technology, some performance drawbacks are associated with it.

In the right set of circumstances, virtual private networking can provide fast, reliable, and secure connections to your company's network from across the Internet (or another unsecured network). However, in the wrong set of circumstances, virtual private networking can make an already slow dial-up connection seem even slower.

So what are the right circumstances? In my professional opinion, high-speed connectivity on the corporate side of your VPN, and preferably high-speed connectivity on both the corporate side and your personal connection. On occasions when I have been able to implement VPN circuits at locations with a T1 or better available at both the company and client ends, performance has been wonderful and the connections reliable. However, due to the protocol overhead involved with PPTP (Point-to-Point Tunneling Protocol) and L2TP (Layer 2 Tunneling Protocol) and the inherent latency of the Internet, don't have high-performance expectations if you are planning to implement a VPN with a dial-up modem.

If you are using a dial-up modem, nothing will ever be faster than a direct dial-in connection. Period. Dial-in connections are simple. There's no encryption, and there's no VPN protocol overhead involved. Plus, your traffic does not have to cross through a countless number of routers before reaching its destination. Simply put, with a direct dial-in connection your packets go out of your computer, across the phone line, and directly into the corporate network.

If you are implementing a VPN connection over a dial-up modem, your packets must first be encrypted. They must then be bundled into a VPN protocol and then bundled again into another TCP/IP packet. After that, they are transmitted across the Internet, where they will probably pass through anywhere from 4 to 12 routers before reaching the VPN server at your corporation. Once the VPN server receives the packet, it must unpackage the entire payload and then decrypt it. Although computers can do this quickly, it does add overhead to the process.

How much overhead? Well, there are no official numbers to go by, but I'd say you can expect a decrease in your performance ranging anywhere from 10 to 50 percent. Now, without getting into all the technical details, it is worthwhile to note that this isn't entirely Microsoft's fault; after all, they can't be blamed for the fact that the Internet can be inherently slow at times (or can they?). However, even with the worst-case scenario of a 50 percent reduction in performance, if there is 1Mb worth of bandwidth available on each side of the VPN, the effective speeds of the network are still roughly in the 500Kbps range—a very respectable amount. However, if you're using a 56K modem on your Windows XP Professional workstation (which probably won't connect much faster than 48Kbps), you can easily see how a 50 percent performance penalty can make a connection go from "slow" to "unusable."

Everything in life is a trade-off, and it will be up to you to decide if this will work adequately enough for your needs. After all, what is adequate to one person might be great to another and unacceptable to yet another. In either case, expect a performance penalty when implementing virtual private networking and plan accordingly.

# Protecting against the Impersonation of a User

Compromising a valid user's account name and password is a network administrator's worst nightmare. An unauthorized user—posing as a valid one—can steal, compromise, or sabotage data from the company's network. If that user has remote dial-in access capabilities as well, the problem is even worse because someone can dial in from anywhere in the world and make trouble for the network. Therefore, it is important to prevent your user ID and password from falling into the wrong hands.

## Common Sense Guidelines

It still amazes me how many times I run into users who have written their usernames and passwords on a yellow sticky note and then stuck the note to their monitor. Talk about a security nightmare! Even if people don't stick their passwords on their monitors, users have a tendency to write them down on cards in their wallets or put them into an organizer such as their PDA. The first measure of good security is to never write down your username and password. If, for some reason, you must do so, at least write them on separate sheets of paper and store them in different places. Don't store them with each other.

Another common security problem is users who choose passwords that are easily guessed. For example, it's common for many people to use simple things for passwords, such as the type of car they drive, their favorite sport or a favorite athlete, their mother's maiden name, their middle name, other family names, pet names, and so on. All those types of passwords can be easily guessed if someone is determined enough.

Better types of passwords are complex combinations that have nothing whatsoever to do with you. Even better yet is complete gibberish. You can make your passwords a bit more complex—but still easily remembered—by substituting letters, numbers, or symbols in place of actual words. This is the same type of logic that people use to spell out phrases on custom license plates. For example, you could use the phrase "No soup for you today!" as a password (with all due respect to the *Seinfeld* "Soup Nazi" episode) by using "nosoup4u2day." Such a password is still easy to remember, but is much more difficult to guess. Other suggestions for substitutions are

- Instead of the word "to" or "too," use the number 2.

- Instead of the word "for," use the number 4.

- Instead of the word "at," use the @ symbol.

- Instead of the word "and," use the & symbol.

- Instead of the word "you," use the letter U.

- Instead of the word "are," use the letter R.

I'm sure you get the point. The object is to keep the password something that you can remember while making it difficult to compromise. I've had good success using this formula. At the very least, always use a combination of upper- and lowercase letters, numbers, and symbols if possible.

## Encrypted Authentication

If you are dialing into a remote network—either via a direct dial-in line or a VPN connection—Windows XP Professional must pass your user credentials (your username and password) to the remote system for authentication. The remote system will then check those credentials to determine if your account has been granted dial-in access. But how does Windows XP Professional send your credentials to the remote computer?

The answer can be found in the Advanced Security Settings dialog box. As you can see in that dialog box, Windows XP Professional can send your user credentials to the remote system in a number of ways, as long as the remote system is able to understand them. Some of these authentication methods are encrypted, and some are not.

**Extensible Authentication Protocol (EAP)**   Since security and authentication is a constantly changing field, embedding authentication schemes into an operating system is impractical at times. To solve this problem, Microsoft has included support for Extensible Authentication Protocol, which is simply a means of "plugging in" new authentication schemes as needed. Presumably, any type of extensible authentication would be encrypted, but that could vary from one case to the next.

**Unencrypted Password (PAP)**   Password Authentication Protocol (PAP) is one of the first options and is also one of the least secure. It is no more secure than a simple conversation from your server saying "What is your name and password?" to the client, and the client responding with "My name is Mark and my password is 'let-me-in.'" There is no encryption of authentication credentials whatsoever.

**Shiva Password Authentication Protocol (SPAP)**   SPAP is an encrypted password authentication method used by Shiva LAN Rover clients and servers. Windows XP Professional can provide SPAP authentication if needed.

**Challenge Handshake Authentication Protocol (CHAP)**   Defined in RFC (Request for Comments) 1334, and later revised in RFC 1994, CHAP is a means of encrypting authentication sessions between a client and server. Since this protocol is defined by an RFC, it enjoys a broad base of support among many operating systems and other devices.

**Microsoft CHAP (v1 and v2) (MS-CHAP)**   Microsoft's derivative of CHAP, or Challenge Handshake Authentication Protocol, is an encrypted authentication method that also allows you to encrypt an entire dial-up session, not just the original authentication, which is important when it comes to setting up virtual private networking sessions.

## Caller-ID/Callback Security

Although Caller-ID/callback security isn't an option for Windows XP Professional, it is worth discussing in terms of security. Simply put, let's assume that you have dial-in access to your corporate network, and the worst-case scenario comes true—someone obtains your user ID and password. Caller-ID and callback security can still provide your corporation with some level of protection. Both features work by verifying that you are actually calling from an authorized phone number—a phone number that has been predefined by the administrators of your corporate network.

CHAPTER 29

**Caller-ID security**    If the dial-in systems on your corporate network can support it, your account can be set up with a Caller-ID–based security option. In this scenario, when the computers on your corporate network receive your incoming call, they take note of the phone number. Once you provide a username and password authentication, your username is checked for an associated Caller-ID number. If the two numbers match, your call is granted. If the two numbers don't match, your call is denied. Therefore, even if someone has your username and password, this type of security can protect your corporation's computers. The drawback is that whenever you want to connect to your company's network, you must be calling in from the approved number.

**Callback security**    This functions in a similar manner to Caller-ID security but is a bit more secure (I've read that Caller-ID information can be spoofed with the correct equipment). With callback security enabled, your user account is associated with a callback number. When you initiate a dial-in session to your company's network, you will provide your username and password. The system that verifies your dial-in credentials will see that you have a callback number associated with your account and immediately disconnect you. After it disconnects you, it will then initiate a call to your system and establish the connection. This is a very secure method of verifying a dial-in user; however, it comes at the price of having to always log in from the same phone number.

If you are concerned that your account credentials might fall into the wrong hands, talk to your network administrators to see if either of these options is available for your dial-in system. Windows 2000 Server and Windows Server 2003 support both of them.

## Third-Party Products: SecurID, SafeWord

Although this is a book about Windows XP Professional, I want to mention two products that fall into the "extremely cool" category of security products: SecurID from RSA Security and SafeWord from Secure Computing.

The nature of these two products is similar—they are what's known as a "second factor" authentication method. What that means is that your "first factor" of authentication—your username and password—is not good enough to obtain access to a resource; you must authenticate yourself in another (second) manner before access is granted. You can think of a second factor authentication as being similar to having two different locks on a door—a regular one and a deadbolt. You won't be granted access until you can provide the correct authentication (a key) for both.

How they work—from a user perspective—is quite simple. When you start a dial-up networking session, you are prompted for your username and password. That is your first authentication. After successfully negotiating a dial-in connection to your corporation's network, you are then prompted for a second authentication—a second "password," if you will. What's unique about this second password is that it's a different password every time.

SecurID works through a small key fob that has a digital readout on it. Every 60 seconds, a new number appears on the readout. The key fob is given to a user and must be used to gain access to the company's network. Let's take a look at a typical example.

Let's assume that a user named Wendy is trying to dial in to her company's network. Now, Wendy has a password for her account—let's assume that it's "arlington." Wendy also has a SecurID key fob that has been assigned to her. At the moment she is trying to sign in, her key fob is displaying the six-digit number 378265. As an added measure, Wendy also has a four-digit "pin" number assigned to her. Let's assume that she used 1234 for her pin number.

When Wendy dials in, she'll type in her username and password (wendy/arlington) just as in a normal dial-up connection. Her Windows XP Professional system will dial in to the company's network and negotiate a connection. Once the connection is negotiated, Wendy will be prompted for her SecurID passcode. At the moment she is logging in, the correct passcode for her will be "1234378265". Her passcode is validated by a SecurID server within the company's network, and if the passcode is correct, she is granted access to the network. The SafeWord system also functions on a similar, one-time password concept.

As you can see, this is an *extremely* secure means of authenticating a user. If someone manages to obtain Wendy's username and password, they are useless without her SecurID key fob. And even if someone were to obtain the key fob itself, it would still be useless without knowing Wendy's individual pin number.

# Protecting against the Abduction of Data

Okay, I'll admit it, the word "abduction" sounds a bit too much like an *X-Files* episode, but the word just fits so well with the concept I am trying to get across. In any case, the abduction of data is simply someone without authorization copying corporate data off your system. You know, your typical corporate espionage stuff.

As I stated earlier in the chapter, I can imagine that this will become more and more of a problem as companies allow increasing amounts of data outside their corporate walls. After all, who is it more difficult to steal data from—the well-guarded and physically secured corporate network or Joe the account executive walking out of the building late at night with his laptop? A quick bop on Joe's head and a grab of the laptop would compromise all the data stored on the laptop.

Or would it? Windows XP Professional contains encryption technologies that specifically address this type of situation. The encrypting file system (EFS) can ensure that no one other than you will be able to read your encrypted files if your computer is ever stolen.

The encryption capabilities available in Windows XP Professional (right out of the box) are very good. And with a few additional precautions, you can make sure that they are absolutely secure—that no one will be able to ever read your encrypted files.

**NOTE**  It goes without saying that if someone gets hold of your username and password, all bets are off. As far as Windows XP Professional is concerned, if someone logs in with your username and password, it must be you! Windows XP Professional will gladly decrypt all your files in that scenario. So, it's critical to make sure that your password is not discovered.

## Encrypting Files with EFS

Encrypting data is merely a matter of a few clicks of the mouse, and an entire folder or folder structure can be protected from prying eyes. Having said that, you should try to follow a few "best practices" principles when working with EFS:

**Don't encrypt the Windows XP Professional folders.**  This would have a significant impact on your system—most likely it wouldn't boot. Fortunately, EFS will always try to prevent you from encrypting system files, but you probably shouldn't even try to in the first place.

**Don't encrypt your *My Documents* folder.**  This runs 100 percent contrary to Microsoft's suggested practices. The reason I recommend that you *don't* encrypt your My Documents folder is because there are almost no visual clues in the Windows interface that a file or folder has been encrypted. I've already read a few accounts of users who were "playing around" with EFS and followed Microsoft's suggestions to encrypt the My Documents folder, but months later they forgot that they had done it. Because of some sort of failure (in one instance, a simple HAL [hardware abstraction layer] upgrade), the users reloaded Windows XP Professional. Guess what? Since they hadn't taken the additional step to back up their recovery keys, all their documents were irrecoverable. Gone. Personally, I like to make a folder called `Encrypted Stuff`, which gives me an obvious visual reminder that anything within that folder is encrypted.

**Encrypt your *Temp* folder.**   Your temporary folder (which can usually be found by typing **SET** at a command prompt and looking for the TEMP= and TMP= folders) is often a repository for fragments of your data, documents, and so on. Sometimes programs don't properly clean up after themselves, and they leave fragments of your files in this folder. If this folder is encrypted, no leftover fragments can be used by anyone else.

**Encrypt entire folders, not just files.**   As I mentioned earlier, I like to make a special folder on my machine and call it `Encrypted Stuff`—then I just copy everything into it that I want protected.

Encrypting files and folders is really quite simple. Follow these steps:

1. Click Start, right-click My Computer, and choose Explore from the shortcut menu to open an Explorer-type window.

2. Right-click the file or folder, and choose Properties from the shortcut menu to open the Properties dialog box for that item.

3. Click the Advanced button to open the Advanced Attributes dialog box:

Notice the two check boxes at the bottom of this dialog box: Compress Contents to Save Disk Space and Encrypt Contents to Secure Data. These two items are mutually exclusive, meaning that if you compress a file you can't encrypt it, and if you encrypt a file, you can't compress it.

4. If necessary, uncompress the file, and check the Encrypt Contents to Secure Data check box.

5. Click OK, and then click OK again to encrypt the file.

It almost seems too easy, doesn't it? Well, don't take my word for it—try logging in as someone else and see if you can read the file. You can't. Even if you have full access to the file under another user account, you won't be able to open the file, copy it, or do anything else with it. Only the user account that encrypted the file can decrypt it, so use encryption carefully.

## Summary

In this chapter, we talked about the security of corporate data once it moves outside your corporation's walls. We covered how to encrypt the data as it is transferred to your computer and even how to encrypt the data once it is stored on your computer. We talked about how to protect your account credentials and proposed solutions that you can provide to your corporate network administrators if an additional level of security is necessary.

The next chapter will cover the Microsoft Management Console (MMC). This single tool is inherently powerful and can be complex. You should make yourself intimately familiar with it if you're managing a number of Windows XP computers.

# Chapter 30

# The Microsoft Management Console

This chapter addresses the Microsoft Management Console, the Swiss Army knife of administrative tools for Microsoft Windows XP Professional.

Starting with Windows 2000, individual administrative tools—such as User Manager, Server Manager, Event Viewer, and even Disk Administrator—were assimilated into the Microsoft Management Console (MMC). This all-in-one administrative tool can be set up to include everything that you need to administer Windows XP Professional, including Internet Information Server (IIS), which is covered in Chapter 32.

MMC is a framework for management applications, providing a unified interface for Microsoft and third-party management tools. MMC doesn't replace management applications; it integrates them into one single interface. (However, you can still access many tools through their original interfaces.) There are no inherent management functions in MMC at all. It uses component tools called snap-ins, which do all the work. MMC simply provides a user interface; it doesn't change how the snap-ins function.

To become a true power user, you must fully understand the MMC. This chapter covers the following topics:

- ◆ MMC structure
- ◆ MMC terminology
- ◆ Exploring MMC snap-ins
- ◆ Using the MMC
- ◆ The Computer Management Console

## The Basic Features of MMC

The following benefits are associated with MMC:

- ◆ You have to learn only one interface to drive a whole mess of tools.
- ◆ Microsoft is encouraging software vendors to use MMC snap-ins.
- ◆ You can build your own consoles, which is practical and fun. Administrators can even create shortcuts on the console to non-MMC tools such as executables, URLs, wizards, and scripts.
- ◆ By customizing MMC consoles, an administrator can delegate tasks to underlings without giving them access to all functions and without confusing them with a big, complicated tool.
- ◆ Help in MMC is context sensitive; it displays subjects for only the appropriate components. Okay, that's not really new, but it's still cool. Context-sensitive menus are available through the Action and View menus or by right-clicking the snap-in.

**WHY ONLY ONE TOOL?**

In the first years of Windows NT, administrators had to master multiple administration tools. A whole set of built-in tools, plus independent third-party tools, made administration sort of a mess. Although many administration tools functioned remotely, you had to install some of them separately (unless your desktop happened to include Windows NT Server), and with third-party tools, you often had to jump through hoops to get them to work remotely, if at all. Even worse, with menus, buttons, toolbars, wizards, tabs, HTML, Java (you get the picture), just learning how to navigate new software was a chore. Also, there was no simplified version of the User Manager that could be given to account operators and no way to hide menu items in administrative tools for those without full administrator rights.

So we complained. "As administrators, we need to be able to administer our networks from the comfort and luxury of our cubicles. And we don't want to waste time exploring all the windows, wizards, and tabs in every new tool. And we need more flexible tools," we said. Behold, Microsoft heard our cries, and their response was the MMC. It's even available for Windows NT 4 if you've installed some of the later service packs.

The MMC turned out to be so popular that Microsoft expanded the number of available tools. Third-party vendors also create tools that can be installed in the MMC as snap-ins.

## MMC Terms to Know

This section defines important terms you'll need to know when working with MMC.

A *console*, in MMC-speak, is one or more administrative tools in an MMC framework. The prebuilt admin tools, such as Active Directory Users and Computers, are console files. You can also make your own consoles without any programming tools—you needn't be a C++ or Visual Basic programmer, as I'll discuss a bit later. The saved console file is a *Microsoft saved console (MSC)* file and it carries the .MSC extension.

**NOTE** It's important to distinguish between Microsoft Management Console and console tools. MMC provides a framework to create customized console-based tools. MMC.EXE is a program that presents administrators (and others creating console tools) with a blank console to work with. It might help to think of a new instance of MMC.EXE as providing the raw material for a tool. In that case, Microsoft Management Console provides the rules and guidelines for building the tool, and the new console you create is the finished product.

*Snap-ins* are the name for administrative tools that are added to the console. (Other companies use a similar process: *plug-ins*. Of course, Microsoft couldn't use that term.) For example, the DHCP administration tool is a snap-in, and so is the Disk Defragmenter. Snap-ins can be made by Microsoft or by other software vendors. (You *do* need programming skills to make these, in other words.) A snap-in can contain components that allow us to manage various facets of our computer, such as hard drives, users, and security. Although you can load multiple snap-ins in a single console, most of the prebuilt administrative tools contain only a single snap-in (except the Computer Management tool).

**TIP** By default, all MMC consoles, including the ones you create, are accessible through the Start menu. Click Start ➤ All Programs ➤ Administrative Tools and select the console of your choice.

An *extension* is basically a snap-in that can't live by itself on the console but depends on a stand-alone snap-in. It adds some functionality to a snap-in. Some snap-ins work both ways. For example, the Event Viewer is a standalone snap-in, but it's also implemented as an extension to the Computer Management snap-in. The key point is that extensions are optional. You can choose not to load them. For example, Local Users and Groups is an extension to the Computer Management snap-in. If you remove the extension from the COMPMGMT.MSC file used by your support folk, or simply don't include it in a custom console that uses the snap-in, those who use the tool won't have the option to create or manage users and groups with the tool. They won't even see it. (Please note that this will not prevent them from creating users and groups by other means, if they have the correct administrative privileges.)

Administrators can create new MSC files by customizing an existing MSC file or by creating one from a blank console. MMC.EXE plus the defined snap-ins create the tool interface. Also, it's possible to open multiple tools simultaneously, but each console runs one instance of MMC. Open an MSC file and look in Task Manager while it's running—you see only the MMC.EXE process running, not the MSC file, just as would you see WINWORD.EXE running in Task Manager but not the Word document's name.

# The MMC Console

Microsoft Management Consoles (MMCs) can be configured and run in one of four different modes:

**Author mode**: Allows you to create your own consoles with the snap-ins of your choice.

**User mode–full access**: Allows you almost total control of installed snap-ins, except you can't install or remove a snap-in.

**User mode–limited access, multiple window**: Allows you to use MMC with multiple embedded windows. However, you can't open a new window or close any of the preconfigured windows.

**User mode–limited access, single window**: Allows you to use MMC with a single embedded window.

Author mode is where you create and customize a console. But you shouldn't manage your system from any MMC Author mode. Instead, you can save the console in one of the User modes. Different User modes are suitable for different types of users. The following sections describe the snap-ins and each mode in more detail.

## What Are Snap-ins?

Snap-ins include the essence of different Windows XP administrative utilities. You can add the snap-ins of your choice to the MMC. Some are already included with Windows XP Professional. More can be added through other applications such as Internet Information Server.

Many of the following snap-ins are the same as those used on Windows 2000. Some of these snap-ins can be used on local or remote computers. Successful remote access depends on configured rights and permissions on that computer. Available snap-ins include the following:

**ActiveX Control**: Allows control of the list of ActiveX objects that help Windows XP applications share information and more.

CHAPTER 30

**Certificates**: Permits browsing of your computer's collection of digital signatures associated with applications, drivers, websites, and more.

**Component Services**: Allows configuration of COM components based on Microsoft's Component Object Model and related COM+ applications.

**Computer Management**: Installs the standard Computer Management Console, which is described later in this chapter. It can also be installed as a snap-in in a customized console.

**Device Manager**: Configures the manager of hardware devices as an MMC snap-in. This tool is covered in Chapter 9.

**Disk Defragmenter**: Installs the Disk Defragmenter discussed in Chapter 27 as an MMC snap-in.

**Disk Management**: Sets up Disk Management, which can help you manage the file systems and partitions on your drives. This tool is discussed in Chapter 23.

**Event Viewer**: Installs the Event Viewer, which is one of the key troubleshooting tools for Windows XP Professional. This tool is described in Chapter 23.

**Folder**: Installs the Folder snap-in, which can help you organize your other snap-ins into different categories. Once it is installed, you can rename the Folder snap-in. When you add new snap-ins, you can select this folder before adding the new snap-in.

**FrontPage Server Extensions**: Sets up the snap-in that can help you administer FrontPage Server Extensions for web servers.

**Group Policy**: Installs the Group Policy manager, which can help you administer XP policies for computer and user accounts on local or remote computers.

**Indexing Service**: Includes the Microsoft Indexing Service, which collects information from documents on local or remote computers in a separate database for quicker searches.

**Internet Information Services (IIS)**: Add the management tool for IIS, which is the Microsoft server for web, FTP, and mail services. IIS is addressed in more detail in Chapter 32.

**IP Security Monitor**: Allows you to monitor traffic on local or remote computers based on various IP Security Policies. Associated with the IPSec protocols that require encryption keys and can support virtual private networking (VPN).

**IP Security Policies**: Allows you to set up specific policies for monitoring traffic on your network from a local or a remote computer.

**Link to Web Address**: Prompts you to enter a website or web file. This allows you to use MMC as a browser based on the given location. You can also use this as a link to a specific e-mail address. For example, if there is a remote administrator who needs information from your console, you can set up their e-mail address in the following format: `mailto:administrator@abc.cba`.

**Local Users and Groups**: Lets you view and manage the users and groups on a local computer. With the right permissions, you can also set up users and groups on remote computers.

**Performance Logs and Alerts**: Allows you to configure counters, traces, and alerts. This snap-in can be used to manage the Performance console discussed in Chapter 23.

**Removable Storage Management**: Allows you to manage the information from removable media such as CDs, tape drives, and more. Can be configured for a local or a remote computer.

**Resultant Set of Policy**: Allows you to check or test the effect of multiple policies on specific users or computers. On a domain, you can use this to check the effect on remote computers.

**Security Configuration and Analysis**: Includes configuration and analysis tools to let you configure and analyze the effect of your security policies. This snap-in is covered in more detail in Chapter 19.

**Security Templates**: Includes the Windows XP Professional security templates that you can use in your security configuration and analysis. You can also set up the import (and export) of custom templates for your workgroup or domain. This snap-in is covered in more detail in Chapter 19.

**Services**: Permits you to monitor and manage services on local or remote computers. This snap-in is covered in more detail in Chapter 31.

**Shared Folders**: Allows you to monitor and manage shared files and folders on local or remote computers. As an administrator, you can disconnect users who are connecting to a share over a network. For more information on setting up a shared folder, see Chapter 17.

**WMI Control**: Installs the control tools for the Windows Management Instrumentation service, which includes VBScript objects that can further help you manage the Windows XP Professional Environment. For the latest information on WMI objects, use an Internet search engine such as `www.google.com` and enter the following search phrase: "Managing Windows with WMI."

## Working in Author Mode and Adding Snap-Ins

When you open the MMC without snap-ins, Windows XP Professional takes you to MMC Author mode to allow you to customize the administrative tool that you need. To start MMC, type `MMC.EXE` at a command prompt. Figure 30.1 shows MMC in Author mode.

**FIGURE 30.1**
MMC in Author mode

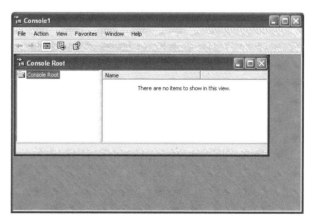

Start configuring your administrative tool. Add some of the available tools by following these steps:

1. Click File ➤ Add/Remove Snap-in to open the Add/Remove Snap-in window.

2. Click Add to open the Add Standalone Snap-in window.

3. Select a snap-in of your choice. Click Add. Repeat with as many available snap-ins as desired. Click Close when you're finished.

4. The snap-ins that you selected are then shown in the Standalone tab of the Add/Remove Snap-in window. If you want to delete a snap-in, highlight it and click Remove. When you're ready, click OK to add these snap-ins to your console.

   Some snap-ins, such as Shared Folders and Computer Management, include extensions that are usually other snap-ins that are normally grouped together. Click the Extensions tab to see if the option is available for the snap-ins that you selected.

5. Some of the available snap-ins allow you to easily access key utilities such as the Device Manager, although the format is slightly different than what you saw in Chapter 9.

**6.** Save the result under another name. Choose File ➢ Save As. In the Save As window, enter a descriptive name such as **Cert-Device**, and click Save. The console is saved with the .MSC extension by default.

Note that the title bar now reflects the filename that you used. You can now close this window, because it is also saved in your Start menu. Click Start ➢ All Programs ➢ Administrative Tools ➢ Cert-Device.MSC (or the name that you used to save your console). Windows XP Professional opens the console that you've set up.

Once you're happy with your new administrative tool, you'll want to save it in one of the User modes to prevent further changes. Choose File ➢ Options. The Console tab of the Options page opens, as shown in Figure 30.2.

**FIGURE 30.2**

Consoles can be saved in different modes.

You can select from the four previously mentioned modes in the Console Mode drop-down box. The different user modes are discussed in following sections. For each mode, you can choose whether to allow the user to customize the tool with the other check boxes in the Options page:

◆ Do Not Save Changes to This Console: If checked, this option prevents users from making any permanent changes to this console.

◆ Allow the User to Customize Views: If checked, this option allows users to access the Customize View window.

Once you've created the options of your choice, click OK to exit the Options window. Choose File ➢ Save As and enter the name of your choice.

## Customizing MMC Views

If you set up a console that allows users to customize views, they can modify the look and feel of that console. To access the Customize View window shown in Figure 30.3, choose View ➢ Customize. Each of the options is described below:

**Console Tree**: Displays a list of snap-ins that are included in the console.

**Standard Menus**: Includes the Action and View menus in the console toolbar. The Action menu allows you to see a context-sensitive list of options associated with the highlighted snap-in. Alternatively, you can just right-click the snap-in. The View menu allows you to customize the look and feel of the details associated with each tool.

**Standard Toolbar**: Activates typical toolbar icons for navigation, help, and other context-sensitive options.

**Status Bar**: Shows a message associated with the highlighted tool at the bottom of the console window.

**Description Bar**: Provides information about the selected snap-in option in the details pane of the console.

**Taskpad Navigation Tabs**: Allows the user to use context-specific commands associated with snap-ins. See the "Taskpad" section for more information.

**Snap-in Menus**: Displays menus associated with a particular snap-in. Some snap-ins don't have individual menus.

**Snap-in Toolbars**: Includes toolbars associated with a particular snap-in. Some snap-ins don't have individual toolbars.

**FIGURE 30.3**
You can customize the
look and feel of an MMC
console.

## User Mode–Full Access

By default, prebuilt console tools such as Computer Management open in *User mode - full access*. This is the best setup for junior system administrators or power users. Changes cannot be made to the console design. They can't add or remove snap-ins, for example. When a user is running a tool and not configuring it, it should be running in one of the User modes. The tool actually looks different in User mode than it does in Author mode.

The most prominent example of a prebuilt console tool is the Computer Management Console. To start it, click Start ➢ All Programs ➢ Administrative Tools ➢ Computer Management. Figure 30.4 shows the Computer Management Console in User mode - full access.

In User mode, File menu options are limited. You can't add or remove snap-ins or change the mode of the console. But full access allows you to add windows and/or change the format of the console, such as the columns of data associated with a specific snap-in.

**FIGURE 30.4**

Computer Management
in User mode

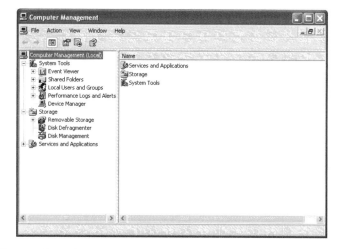

If you need to change a User mode tool, open MMC.EXE at the command line. Use the File menu to open the tool you want to change in Author mode. Console files are normally stored in either the \Documents and Settings\username\Start Menu\Programs\Administrative Tools\ or the \Windows\system32\ directory.

## User Mode–Limited Access, Multiple Window

In Author mode, you can restrict access further to different parts of the console. And you can set up limited access with multiple windows by default. This mode is known as *User mode - limited access, multiple window*. As you can see in Figure 30.5, multiple windows are open by default, and the close button (the *X* in the upper-right corner) in both windows is disabled. However, you can open additional windows. When you exit and return to this console, the changes are automatically saved.

**FIGURE 30.5**

Sample console in User
mode - limited access,
multiple window

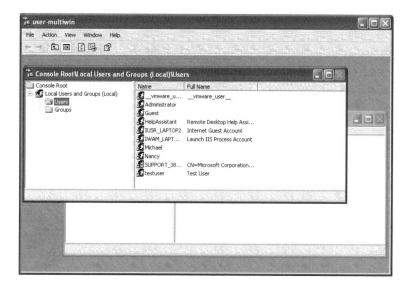

Limited access, multiple window mode is best for users with specific dedicated tasks such as monitoring various print servers.

### User Mode–Limited Access, Single Window

You can restrict console access to a single window. You can't open new windows in this type of console. The controls associated with multiple windows are disabled. Not surprisingly, this mode is known as *User mode - limited access, single window*. An example of this mode is shown in Figure 30.6.

**FIGURE 30.6**
Sample console in User mode - limited access, single window

Limited access, single window mode is best for less-experienced users. The limited flexibility associated with this type of console reduces the risk to your system.

## The Computer Management Console

The most important prebuilt MMC tool is the Computer Management Console. The console tree includes System Tools, Storage, and Services and Applications (see Figure 30.7). Notice that the focus is on the local machine by default; to connect to other computers on the network, right-click the Computer Management icon at the root of the tree (or click the Action menu) and choose Connect to Another Computer from the shortcut menu.

The Computer Management Console is *the* main tool for administering a single server, local or remote. If you have only one server on your network and you want to use only one admin tool, Computer Management fits the bill. To open the Computer Management Console, click Start ➤ All Programs ➤ Administrative Tools ➤ Computer Management.

Expand the nodes in the Computer Management Console tree to reveal the configuration tools and objects, as shown in Figure 30.8. Most of the core functions are under System Tools. Some functions even work remotely on NT 4 machines (you can view a remote machine's event logs, for example), but new features require the remote machine to be a Windows XP Professional box.

**FIGURE 30.7**
The Computer Management window

**FIGURE 30.8**
The expanded Computer Management window

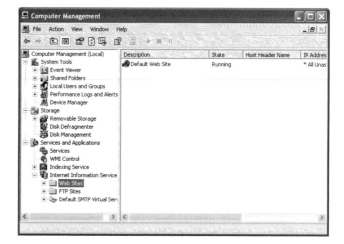

In the System Tools node, you can complete the following tasks:

♦ View events and manage the event logs. Basically, the Event Viewer tool is turned into an MMC snap-in.

♦ Manage shared folders. You can view, create, and manage shares; view sessions and open files; and disconnect sessions.

♦ Manage devices. Device Manager is a great place to track down information about your hardware, update drivers, and troubleshoot resource conflicts.

♦ Configure Performance Logs and Alerts. You can create, configure, and monitor various performance settings.

♦ Create and manage local users and groups.

The Storage node includes options for managing removable storage, along with the Disk Defragmenter tool and the Disk Management tool, which is the equivalent of the Disk Administrator in NT 4. There is also a component to view logical drives, including network drive mappings, and their properties. This is useful if you want to quickly view free space or set NTFS security at the root of a partition, for example. Too bad you can't browse folders as you can in Explorer. Oh well, I guess we don't need *another* desktop shell program, do we?

The Services and Applications node includes telephony settings, services configuration, Windows Management Instrumentation (WMI), indexing, and IIS management stuff, the last of which is also available in the Administrative Tools group by itself (the tool is called Internet Services Manager, while the extension in Computer Management is called Internet Information Services). The components available in the Services and Applications node depend on which services are installed on your system. For instance, if Internet Information Services is not installed (and it isn't by default), you won't see that component.

It's easy to connect the Computer Management Console to a remote computer. Highlight Computer Management (Local), then choose Action ➢ Connect to Another Computer. In the Select Computer window, enter the name of the other computer. The format depends on whether you've set up Windows XP Professional in a workgroup or a domain.

◆ Workgroup: Use the name of the workgroup and the computer in the format workgroupname\ computername.

◆ Domain: Use the fully qualified domain name for the computer, such as \\xpcomp.windows .mommabears.com.

What you can do on a remote computer depends on the applicable permissions and access rights associated with each tool. These concepts are explained in Chapter 19.

## Additional Customization Options

Author mode in MMC is quite flexible. You can even use it to modify prebuilt tools such as the Computer Management Console. To open up this tool in Author mode, start the MMC. Type **MMC.EXE** at a command prompt. Choose File ➢ Open and select compmgmt.msc from the \Windows\system32 directory.

Whenever you change a standard tool, it's a good practice to make a backup before you begin. To back up the Computer Management Console, choose File ➢ Save As and save it as another file such as compmgmt-rev.msc. Now you can experiment and still have the original Computer Management Console in reserve. The following sections address other available Author mode options, menu by menu from the toolbar. The exceptions are the Window and Help menus, which you already know because they work in the same way as the Window and Help menus in other Microsoft applications.

### File

The File menu should look familiar. You've already added snap-ins to other consoles and used the Options window to save customized consoles in one of the four different modes.

In any User mode, most File menu options are disabled. The File ➢ Options command opens the Options window. The Delete Files button in this window deletes the changes that you've made to other User mode consoles. For example, if you've opened new windows, they're normally saved. If you click Delete Files, the original console configuration is restored.

## Action

Action menus in MMC are partially context sensitive. For example, in the console tree, navigate to Local Users and Groups ➢ Users and then select the Action menu. As you can see in Figure 30.9, you can set up new users from this menu. The options that you'll see in every Action menu (except a User mode - limited access, single window console) are as follows:

**New Window from Here**: Opens a new window within the available console.

**Rename**: Allows you to rename the top-level folder in the console tree.

**Export List**: Creates a text file with a list of plug-ins. You can share this information with other users for more standard consoles.

**Help**: Opens help topics on MMC and any plug-ins that you've installed.

Only context-sensitive options are available in a User mode - limited access, single window console.

**FIGURE 30.9**
The Computer Management Action window

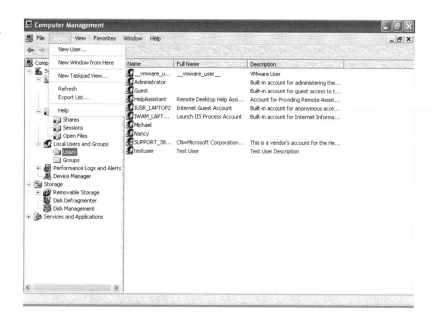

## Taskpad

A *taskpad* is a graphical HTML window customized for a specific MMC plug-in. Taskpad options are available only in Author mode. To open a new console in Author mode, type **MMC.EXE** at a command prompt. Use the File menu to open the console of your choice. Highlight the desired plug-in and then choose Action ➢ New Taskpad View. This starts the New Taskpad View Wizard. Click Next to start the wizard, and navigate to the Taskpad Display page shown in Figure 30.10.

CHAPTER 30

**FIGURE 30.10**
The New Taskpad View
Wizard

In the Taskpad Display page, you can set up the way the tasks are shown in the console. The options are divided into three categories:

**Style for the Details Pane**: Organizes the tasks and configured options for this snap-in. If you deselect Hide Standard Tab, you can easily switch from the taskpad display to the standard pane by clicking the appropriate tab near the bottom of the console window.

**Style for Task Descriptions**: Determines whether the descriptions are shown on the screen or in a pop-up window.

**List Size**: Sets up the columns associated with each task. The Small, Medium, and Large options are associated with the number of columns shown in the taskpad display.

Make your choices and click Next to continue. In the Taskpad Target page, you can set up whether this will apply to just the selected snap-in. Make your selection and click Next to continue.

In the Name and Description page, enter a name and description for the taskpad, and then click Next to continue. This completes the New Taskpad View Wizard, as shown in Figure 30.11. To continue, select the Start New Task Wizard and then click Finish.

**FIGURE 30.11**
Transition between
wizards

You're taken to the Welcome to the New Task Wizard page. Click Next to continue. As shown in Figure 30.12, there are three types of commands available:

**Menu Command**: Allows you to select a task from the Action menu associated with the snap-in.

**Shell Command**: Helps you configure a text command at the command-line interface based on what you might use at the MS-DOS–style prompt. This is appropriate if you've set up a script such as for automated monitoring of disk activity.

**Navigation**: Allows you to select from a list of favorite snap-ins. The associated list of Favorites is different from any that you may have saved in your web browser.

**FIGURE 30.12**

Select the right command type.

Click Next to continue. Depending on your selection, you'll need to choose a menu command, type in a shell command, or select a favorite.

Click Next to continue. Enter a task name and description. If the tool is not familiar to your users, the description can be quite important.

Click Next to continue. Select an icon appropriate to your task.

Click Next to continue. You're shown a list of tasks that you've selected. If you need additional tasks, select the Run This Wizard Again check box, as shown in Figure 30.13. Click Finish.

**FIGURE 30.13**

Selected tasks are shown before you complete the New Task Wizard.

CHAPTER 30

Now the tasks that you've selected are shown in the right-hand pane. As you can see in Figure 30.14, they do not have to be related to the task at hand. Now you can start the selected tasks by clicking them just like any link in a web browser. Alternatively, you can return to the original view by clicking the Standard tab near the bottom of the console.

**NOTE** If you don't see tabs at the bottom of the console, you selected Hide Standard Tab near the beginning of the New Taskpad Wizard, as shown in Figure 30.10.

**FIGURE 30.14**
A console with
some tasks

If you want to change the taskpad, click the Action menu. You can now select Edit Taskpad View or Delete Taskpad View to edit or delete the task of your choice.

## View

The View menu allows you to customize the look and feel of the options associated with each snap-in. The basic options (Large Icons, Small Icons, List, and Detail) work in the same way as from the Windows Explorer View menu. There are two other options unique to MMC:

◆ Add/Remove Columns: Allows you to customize the displayed columns for each snap-in.

◆ Customize View: See the "Customizing MMC Views" section earlier in this chapter.

In many cases, you can also open a View menu by right-clicking the snap-in of your choice.

## Favorites

You can set up Favorite tools in MMC the same way that you set up Favorite websites in Internet Explorer. (They are separate lists.) Select the snap-in of your choice and then choose Favorites ➢ Add to Favorites and follow the prompts in the windows that appear. You can then quickly navigate to Favorite snap-ins or add a Favorite through the taskpad.

# Summary

In this chapter, I've given you the basics of the Microsoft Management Console (MMC). It's a complex tool, so it's useful to recount the basic steps associated with creating or modifying a console:

- Open an existing console. Click Start ➢ All Programs ➢ Administrative Tools and select the console of your choice.

- Open a new console in Author mode. Type **MMC.EXE** at a command prompt.

- Add a snap-in in Author mode. Choose File ➢ Add/Remove Snap-in.

- Add Taskpad views with links to other tools. Choose Action ➢ New Taskpad View and follow the prompts.

- Set up a console in one of the four modes. Click File ➢ Options and select a Console mode with the settings of your choice.

- Save the console with the File ➢ Save As command. Saved consoles are accessible through the Start menu.

The next chapter dovetails quite nicely with the material presented here. It covers a lot of Windows XP services that you need to be familiar with to manage Windows XP. Most of the time, you won't need to manually tweak services, but there are times when something goes wrong and you have no other choice.

## Chapter 31

# Managing Windows XP Professional Services

A service is a program that runs in the background to support basic activities, everything from auto-mated updates through website connectivity. Everything important in Windows XP Professional depends on one or more services. As with many other critical systems, you can manage your services through the Microsoft Management Console, which was covered in Chapter 30. Properly managed, many services allow Windows XP Professional to continue operating without reboots. Properly con-figured, Windows XP turns on only the services that you need. This chapter covers the following topics:

- Why services exist
- Service management consoles
- Types of services
- Managing and configuring Windows XP Professional services
- Troubleshooting service issues

## The Purpose of a Service

Services run in the background. Most are started automatically when you start Windows XP Profes-sional. Among other things, services provide the interfaces that allow you to connect to the Internet, manage interfaces to an uninterruptible power supply (UPS), and more.

Windows XP Professional services are similar to *daemons* in the world of UNIX and Linux. In either case, these are programs that run in the background and provide the interfaces required to run pro-grams such as Internet connections and print servers.

It's practically unheard of to find a Windows XP computer that needs to run every service. Each service takes up space in RAM and places demands on your CPU. Even if you have the fastest com-puter and gigabytes of RAM, you generally do not want all services to run simultaneously. Some ser-vices have been known to conflict with each other.

In fact, if you have a relatively small amount of RAM (64MB–128MB), you'll want to disable as many services as possible. The following sections highlight several services that you may be able to disable if you're not using the associated applications.

Specialized programs come with their own services that may cause problems. For example, some database programs explicitly state that you should turn off all but a few services on Windows XP Professional before starting the installation process.

## The Service Management Console

Take a look at the installed services in Windows XP Professional. To open the Service Management Console shown in Figure 31.1, click Start ➤ All Programs ➤ Administrative Tools ➤ Services. By default, it opens this console in User mode - limited access, single window, which means you can use it just for your services. It also opens with a taskpad that can allow you to start, stop, pause, or restart different services with a single click.

**FIGURE 31.1**

The Service Management Console

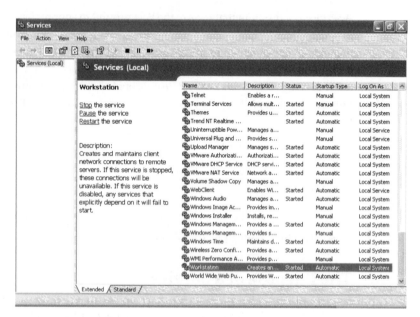

Note the two tabs at the bottom of Figure 31.1. The Extended tab is configured to allow you to manage the highlighted service. In contrast, the Standard tab includes no such feature.

**NOTE** This chapter assumes that you've read Chapter 30 and are comfortable with the basic operation of the Microsoft Management Console.

**TIP** The Services snap-in is also available as part of the Computer Management Console. Alternatively, click Start ➤ Run and type `services.msc` to start the Service Management Console.

Click the Extended tab if required, and then click a service. Note the options for what you can do with this service. Repeat this with other services. Figure 31.1 shows the Workstation service selected, which allows you to connect to other computers on a LAN. The links allow you to quickly Stop, Pause, or Restart that service.

# Windows XP Professional Services

There are a large number of services that are installed on Windows XP Professional. The following lists are based on a standard computer with IIS installed. I've divided these services into four categories:

◆ Services that are started automatically

◆ Services that you start manually

◆ Services that are disabled

◆ Services that you can add after installing Windows XP

Since required services vary with the hardware and software configuration of your computer, this may not be a complete list. Based on previous work on your computer, the service may be in a different category. Other services that you might see, such as VMware Authorization Service, are associated with a particular program, in this case, with VMware. New services are under constant development. If you don't see your service here, consult the developer of the associated application, or check the Microsoft Knowledge Base, available at http://support.Microsoft.com.

In the section "Configuring Services," you'll learn how to change the status of a service. Automatic services are started when you boot Windows XP. Specific programs often start manual services. Disabled services aren't available to support any programs that might need them. And other programs such as IIS and VMware add additional services that fall into one of the other three categories.

## Automatic Services

The following is a list of services that are started automatically when you boot Windows XP Professional. The list you see will vary by configuration.

While this is a long list, it can help you learn a lot about Windows XP Professional. If you're not using the applications associated with one of these services, you may be able to disable it and save resources for the programs that you need.

**Automatic Updates**: Permits automatic Windows XP updates. You can safely disable this service and still run Windows Update manually. Keep it if you're configuring Windows XP Professional for users who would not run Windows Update on their own.

**Computer Browser**: Allows Windows XP to keep a list of computers on the LAN. If there are Windows servers on your network, they generally take on this task. A Windows XP Professional computer can take on a backup role for this service.

**Cryptographic Services**: Manages the certificates that you need to verify the authenticity of critical files and programs.

**DHCP Client**: Lets your computer get an IP address from a DHCP server. See Chapter 20 for more information on DHCP, which is the Dynamic Host Configuration Protocol. Don't disable this service unless you have a fixed IP address.

**Distributed Link Tracking Client**: Allows your computer to maintain the links between files on your computer or network. One example of a link is an Excel spreadsheet embedded in a Word document. If you don't have an NTFS partition, you can disable this service.

**DNS Client**: Permits contact between your computer and Domain Name System (DNS) servers. This is almost always a requirement for computers on larger networks or with a connection to the Internet. For more information, see Chapter 17.

**Error Reporting Service**: Allows error logs from nonstandard applications. This service may not be necessary unless you need logs to help troubleshoot a specific application.

**Event Log**: Sends notification of major events and errors to the Event Viewer. This is a critical troubleshooting tool discussed in Chapter 30. It is also required to support IIS, which is covered in Chapter 32.

**Fax**: Allows you to send and receive faxes. If you have trouble sending a fax, this service might be disabled and need restarting.

**Help and Support**: Lets you run the Help and Support center discussed in Chapter 3.

**IPSEC Services**: Manages security on TCP/IP networks. It is required to support virtual private networks.

**Logical Disk Manager**: Manages the status of disk drives automatically. This allows Windows XP Professional to see removable drives when they're installed.

**Messenger**: Allows administrative alerts. Not related to Windows Messenger. This is useful if you need to warn remote users about problems such as an impending reboot. Change the setting to match the Alerter service, which is addressed in the next section.

**Net Logon**: Supports sending usernames and passwords to a domain controller on a network. If you're not on a domain as described in Chapter 20, you can disable this service.

**Plug and Play**: Supports most modern hardware on a Plug and Play operating system such as Windows XP.

**Portable Media Serial Number**: Retrieves the serial number of portable music players that are connected to your computer. If you're not using a portable digital music device such as a Rio player, deactivate this service.

**Print Spooler**: Loads files that are translated to your printer in memory. If you print, you need this service.

**Protected Storage**: Allows password protection for the files you specify.

**Remote Procedure Call (RPC)**: Supports communication between applications on a client-server network. Many other services depend on RPC. If you plan to be on a network, you should always enable this service.

**Remote Registry**: Allows users with appropriate rights to modify the local Registry from a remote computer. Disable this service unless you absolutely need to manage the Registry from a remote computer.

**Removable Storage**: Permits different applications to share access to removable storage devices such as tape drives. You can set this to Manual, activating it only as needed.

**Secondary Logon**: Allows users to log on more than once to the same system. This important security feature is described in more detail in Chapter 20.

**Security Accounts Manager**: Stores security information for local accounts. See Chapter 19 for more information.

**Server**: Permits access to the local computer as a server, typically for sharing files and printers.

**Shell Hardware Detection**: Allows the Autoplay feature to automatically run a CD that you've just inserted into a drive. Autoplay is described in Chapter 1.

**SNMP Service**: The Simple Network Management Protocol (SNMP) allows you to use services such as the Performance console discussed in Chapter 23 to monitor network activity. It also supports network monitoring from other computers, even through other operating systems such as Linux.

**System Event Notification**: Supports connectivity for mobile devices. For example, this service allows you to enter e-mail on a laptop computer. Your mail is sent when you connect to a network.

**System Restore Service**: Allows you to restore systems to a predetermined configuration. This service is discussed in more detail in Chapter 27.

**Task Scheduler**: Permits you to schedule a task to run automatically on a specific time and date.

**TCP/IP NetBIOS Helper**: Allows Windows computers to communicate on a TCP/IP network. For more information on NetBIOS and TCP/IP, see Chapter 17.

**Themes**: Supports the basic themes and desktop backgrounds shown in Windows XP.

**Upload Manager**: Manages file transfer between clients and servers on a network.

**Windows Audio**: Supports sound. If you want sound, you need this service.

**Windows Management Instrumentation**: Sets up a common model for administering local and remote systems.

**Windows Time**: Synchronizes the time between computers.

**Wireless Zero Configuration**: Configures compatible wireless network adapters automatically.

**Workstation**: Manages network connections from a client computer on a network.

## Manual Services

Manual services are not normally activated when you boot Windows XP Professional. However, associated programs and utilities can usually start these services on an "as needed" basis. The following list of services is usually set up for manual startup:

**Alerter**: Enables administrative alerts, such as a message from a system administrator that the server is about to go down. Closely related to the Messenger service described in the last section.

**Application Layer Gateway Service**: Allows you to use the Internet Connection Sharing (ICS) and Windows Firewall features on the local computer. Don't let the Service console's reference to third-party plug-ins confuse you; this is required for ICS/WF. For more information on ICS/WF, see Chapter 12.

**Application Management**: Allows for the installation and updating of certain types of applications. Required to support Windows XP fast booting through the `bootvis.exe` tool.

**TIP**  One tool that may reduce the time it takes for your system to start is `bootvis.exe`. You can download it as of this writing from `www.microsoft.com/hwdev/fastboot`. Instructions are available in the white paper associated with this utility, named `fastboot-winxp.doc`.

**Background Intelligent Transfer Service**: Manages network file transfers through unused bandwidth; allows for interrupted file transfers.

**Clipbook**: Permits sharing of clipboard data. For more information, see Chapter 5.

**COM+ Event System**: Supports the System Event Notification service discussed in the previous section. In this case, COM is the Component Object Model, required for ActiveX programs.

**COM+ System Application**: Manages the configuration and tracking of COM+-based components. Closely related to the COM+ Event System service.

**Distributed Transaction Coordinator**: Allows resource communication between programs that manage databases, even on non-Windows operating systems.

**Fast User Switching Compatibility**: Supports multiple users on a Windows XP computer. Others may log on to your computer remotely through Terminal Services, even while you're logged on.

**IMAPI CD-Burning COM Service**: Allows recording onto CDs through the Image Mastering Applications Programming Interface (IMAPI).

**Indexing Service**: Allows the organization of the contents of local and remote files into a database. Supports the organization of data in web searches. Required for the Fast Find feature associated with Microsoft Office. Since this uses a substantial amount of resources, do not use this feature unless your users need this level of access to data on your system.

**Windows Firewall (WF)/Internet Connection Sharing (ICS)**: Supports the secure sharing of an Internet connection. For more information see Chapter 12.

**Logical Disk Manager Administrative Service**: Configures disks. Works with the Logical Disk Manager service. You do not need to start this to configure a new disk.

**MS Software Shadow Copy Provider**: Manages a special type of dynamic backup known as a shadow copy. Closely related to the Volume Shadow Copy service.

**NetMeeting Remote Desktop Sharing**: Allows remote users access to your computer through the NetMeeting communication service described in Chapter 14. Unless you use NetMeeting, disable this service. Otherwise, this can be a security issue.

**Network Connections**: Supports network connectivity. Do not disable, unless your computer never connects to another network. Even Internet connections require this service.

**Network DDE**: Allows two applications to share the same data on a network. Supports Object Linking and Embedding (OLE) links, as discussed in Chapter 5.

**Network DDE DSDM**: Enables sharing over a network. A prerequisite for the Network DDE service.

**Network Location Awareness**: Maintains information on connected logical networks. Required for ICS/ICF.

**NT LM Security Support Provider**: Provides security for some forms of network communication. Should be set at least to manual if you use Message Queuing, Telnet, or IIS.

**Performance Logs and Alerts**: Allows collection of performance data. If preconfigured benchmarks are met, this service triggers an alarm. If you're troubleshooting through the Performance console, enable this service.

**QoS RSVP**: Allows configuration of messages to specific Quality of Service (QoS) parameters. In networking, messages are prioritized by a predetermined QoS.

**Remote Access Auto Connection Manager**: Supports network connections that require a search through a database of computer names based on a DNS server or NetBIOS names.

**Remote Access Connection Manager**: Supports Internet connections. Required for ICS.

**Remote Desktop Help Session Manager**: Allows the use of Remote Assistance. For more information on Remote Assistance, see Chapter 3.

**Remote Procedure Call (RPC) Locator**: Supports remote administration from the local computer.

**Smart Card**: Enables the use of smart card readers, which may become the standard for remote identification.

**Smart Card Helper**: Supports non–Plug and Play smart card readers.

**SNMP Trap Service**: Allows the receipt of messages through SNMP traps such as those associated with the Performance console.

**SSDP Discovery Service**: Allows the use of Universal Plug and Play (UPnP) devices such as those related to small business or home networks. As strange as it sounds, UPnP is not related to Plug and Play.

**TCP/IP Print Server**: Enables clients with Line Print Daemon (LPD) software to print to the local computer. LPD is common in UNIX/Linux systems as well as Windows NT computers that are connected through TCP/IP.

**Telephony**: Supports the Telephony Application Programming Interface (TAPI), which is required for communications programs such as Microsoft Fax and HyperTerminal. For more information on these programs, see Chapter 14.

**Telnet**: Allows remote access through Telnet clients on a TCP/IP network. For a description of the Remote Terminal (Telnet) service, see Chapter 13.

**Terminal Services**: Enables the use of Terminal Services Advanced Clients (TSAC) such as the Remote Desktop Connection discussed in Chapter 14.

**Uninterruptible Power Supply (UPS)**: Supports the management of a UPS that is connected to and controlled by your computer. For more information, see Chapter 9.

**Universal Plug and Play Device Host**: Supports many home and small business network devices. Depends on the SSDP Discovery Service. This service is not related to Plug and Play.

**Volume Shadow Copy**: Supports the dynamic backups associated with the Microsoft Backup utility. Closely related to the MS Software Shadow Copy Provider. For more information on backups, see Chapter 27.

**Windows Image Acquisition**: Enables communication with some image devices such as scanners and digital cameras. Associated with the Scanners and Cameras Wizard in Control Panel.

**Windows Installer**: Supports the installation and maintenance of any application that uses instructions configured in MSI files such as Microsoft Office.

**Windows Management Instrumentation Driver Extensions**: Provides system management information for drivers. Related to the Windows Management Instrumentation Service described in the previous section.

**WMI Performance Adapter**: Enables the high-performance (HiPerf) class of data associated with the Performance Monitor discussed in Chapter 23.

## Disabled Services

Disabled services are not activated when you boot Windows XP Professional. Unless you activate them in the Services console, associated programs and utilities cannot start these services. The following list of services is usually set up as disabled:

**Human Interface Device Access**: Associated with *hot buttons* on input devices such as keyboards and mice.

**Routing and Remote Access**: Enables configuration of the local computer as a router, which acts as the interface between your network and another network such as the Internet. If you're using ICS/ICF, you don't need this service.

## Additional Services

Additional services are added to the Services console when you install the associated application. They can fall into any of the above categories (Automatic, Manual, Disabled). In preparation for Chapter 32, the services described here are associated with Internet Information Server (IIS):

**FTP Publishing**: Supports the configuration of an FTP site for sharing files with others. Information on accessing FTP sites is available in Chapter 13.

**IIS Admin**: Enables administration of IIS through the Microsoft Management Console.

**Simple Mail Transfer Protocol**: Allows the setup of a mail server through IIS. Do not confuse this with SNMP.

**World Wide Web Publishing**: Permits the setup of local website files, accessible through the network with IIS.

# Configuring Services

You can modify how a service works on Windows XP Professional. The properties for each service include General Startup, Log On, and Recovery properties. The dependencies of each service are listed with the properties, as well. Finally, you can stop or start a service through the console or at the command line.

These are all tabs in the Properties window associated with each service. A few services such as SNMP include other tabs that support the special configuration requirements of that service.

## General Startup

In the Services console, highlight the service of your choice. Choose Action ≻ Properties to open a Properties window named for your service. The properties for the IIS Admin service are shown in Figure 31.2. If you don't have the IIS Admin service listed in your Services console, just select a different service. The basic information is consistent for all services.

**FIGURE 31.2**
Service properties

As you can see in Figure 31.2, this window opens to the General tab by default. It lists the basic parameters of the service: the name, description, and the location of the associated executable file.

**NOTE**  Note the actual file associated with the service. It will come in handy later in the "Service Commands" section.

The Startup Type can be set to Automatic, Manual, or Disabled. As described earlier in this chapter, Automatic startup means this service starts when you boot Windows XP Professional. Manual startup leaves the service available for other programs or applications to start on an as-needed basis. Disabled startup means that service is unavailable for such programs.

As shown in the Service Status section, you can Start, Stop, Pause, and Resume each service. When a service is stopped, you can specify Start parameters as you would at the command-line interface.

## Log On

Every running service needs to log on before it starts. In the Properties window for your service, click the Log On tab, which is shown in Figure 31.3. Most services have their own generic account, known as the Local System account. The options are listed here:

**Local System Account**: Allows most services to be set to log on to their own account, known generically as the Local System account. You won't find this account in the User Management list.

**Allow Service to Interact with Desktop**: Supports special configuration for services such as the Print Spooler service. Alternatively, may allow some services to send messages to your desktop.

**This Account**: Many services can be configured to use a different local or remote account. Some need special accounts, especially if network access to other computers is required. Two exceptions are the DNS and DHCP services.

**Hardware Profile**: Configured services can vary by the hardware profiles discussed in Chapter 17.

**FIGURE 31.3**
Log On properties

## Recovery

If you install just a few applications, you may have over 100 configured services on your computer. Many services fail for "ordinary" reasons, such as a broken network connection or a modified configuration file. You don't want to have to restart the computer every time a service fails.

Click the Recovery tab on the Properties window for a service. As you can see in Figure 31.4, you can set different actions for the first, second, and subsequent failures. You can set each service to take one of the following four actions in any of these cases:

**Take No Action**: Allows a noncritical service to fail. Unless you use this option, some services such as IIS will automatically restart after a failure. If you're having a problem with IIS, you may want it to stop to give you a chance to maintain the associated web or FTP server.

**Restart the Service**: Allows a service to be restarted, which is appropriate if the problem is temporary. For example, some network services fail if there is a temporary problem with the connections. Many of these services will work again if restarted.

**Run a Program**: Permits you to run the program of your choice, as shown in the Run Program box. For example, you can automate a logging program to document the problem or send a message to your users stating that a service is down.

**Restart the Computer**: Lets the failure of a service restart your computer. If you set this option, the configured service failure automatically restarts the computer based on the Restart Service After text box. Click the Restart Computer Options button. As you can see in Figure 31.5, the Restart

Computer Options window allows you to send a message to computers on the network. The message shown in the figure appears when you select the Before Restart, Send This Message to Computers on the Network check box. You can rewrite the message as desired.

**FIGURE 31.4**
Recovery properties

**FIGURE 31.5**
You can warn remote users that you're about to restart your computer.

## Dependencies

Many services depend on others. For example, you can't run a DNS Client service without TCP/IP. Click the Dependencies tab in the Properties window for your service. The Dependencies tab of the IIS Admin service is shown in Figure 31.6. The two text lists under this tab are described here:

**This Service Depends on the Following System Components**: Lists the services required by the current service. You'll see in Figure 31.6 that the IIS Admin service depends on the Remote Procedure Call and Security Accounts Manager services.

**The Following System Components Depend on This Service**: Lists the services supported by the current service. You'll see in Figure 31.6 that the FTP Publishing, Simple Mail Transfer Protocol, and World Wide Web Publishing services won't run without the IIS Admin service.

**FIGURE 31.6**
Dependencies of a
service

## Service Commands

You don't need the Services console to manage your services. In fact, you can use the net command at the command line to manage just about any Windows XP Professional service. The basic commands are fairly straightforward: net start *service* starts a service; other commands include net stop *service*, net pause *service*, and net continue *service*. The only twist is the net start command by itself, which lists currently running services.

As long as the Telnet service is started locally, you can even work from a remote computer. For example, open a Telnet session in HyperTerminal as described in Chapter 13. Enter the username and password that you use to administer the target Windows XP Professional computer, and Telnet takes you to a command prompt. Figure 31.7 shows this interface from a Windows 2000 HyperTerminal screen. The interface is nearly identical from just about any command line, including from a Windows 9*x* or a UNIX/Linux computer.

**TIP** Don't connect to Telnet through the Windows 2000/XP command-line interface. There are limitations on Telnet connections through the command line that do not apply to HyperTerminal or even a Windows 9*x* command-line interface. If security is a concern, find and install a *secure shell*. There are many good options available online. Then disable the Telnet service so nobody can get in through that channel.

Now try some of the net commands. If you want to see a list of open services, try net start | more. A partial list of open services is shown in the screen, similar to what you see in Figure 31.8. Press the spacebar to scroll through additional open services.

You can start, stop, pause, or resume any installed service. For example, if you wanted to stop the IIS Admin service, type **net stop "iis admin"**. The quotes apply if the name of the service is more than one word. As you can see in Figure 31.9, Windows XP Professional warns you about any dependent services that must also be stopped and gives you a chance to cancel the operation. If you continue, messages are shown indicating the progress of the operation.

**FIGURE 31.7**
You can use Hyper-Terminal to Telnet from a remote computer.

**FIGURE 31.8**
A Telnet view of open services

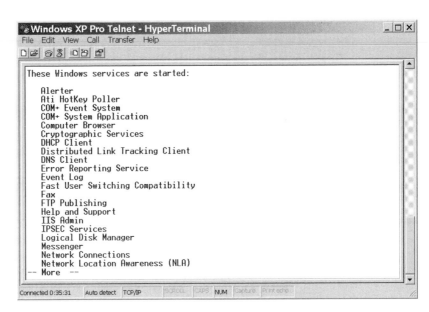

**FIGURE 31.9**
Remotely stopping a service through the command line

If you wanted to restart your web server, just restart the World Wide Web Publishing service. Any dependent service, in this case, IIS Admin, is also started automatically.

**TIP**    When maintaining a service, you can use the service name or the display name. For example, since the service name for the World Wide Web Publishing service is W3SVC, the net start w3svc command has the same effect as net start "world wide web publishing".

## Troubleshooting Service Issues

Managing services is like maintaining a network. If you have a problem with a service, you troubleshoot it. Based on the troubleshooting methodologies discussed in Chapter 33, it's best to check the simplest things first. On a network, you would check the connections between computers and power to the hubs, switches, and routers. Sometimes rebooting a computer or resetting a hub, switch, or router will address a problem on a network.

But if others are connected to your computer, they are depending on the connection. If your computer goes down, they can lose data. Therefore, you don't want to have to reboot it unless absolutely necessary.

This system applies equally well to services. For example, if you have a problem accessing web pages on your Intranet, you may not have to reboot. First, you'll want to make sure your IIS Admin and World Wide Web Publishing services are actually active. Then you might try resetting these services by setting them to stop and then start again. The next step would be to check your connections and network as discussed in Chapter 16. You should also check other network-related services. For example, if the computers on your network rely on DNS to find each other, you need to make sure that the DNS service is active.

Other applications may have the same solution. If you're having problems printing, you can try stopping and restarting the Print Spooler service. If you're having problems printing from a Linux computer to a printer that's connected to a Windows XP computer, try stopping and restarting the

TCP/IP Print Server service. If you can't connect from a remote computer via Telnet or Hyper-Terminal, try stopping and restarting the Telnet service.

## Summary

The basic low-level programs that form the backbone of Windows XP Professional are also known as services. There are many different kinds of services that help you manage the basic functions of the operating system, as well as the way it interacts with a network. Some are started automatically when you start Windows XP Professional. Others can be manually started by specific applications. Still others are disabled by default. You can manage Windows XP services through the preconfigured MMC Service console. Alternatively, services can be managed at a command-line interface, even from a remote computer.

One of the first steps in troubleshooting many problems is to check the associated service. Sometimes you just need to turn it on. Sometimes resetting the service by turning it off and back on is sufficient.

In the next chapter, I'll describe two specific services that are implemented all over the Internet: web (HTTP) and FTP.

# Chapter 32

# Hosting Web/FTP Servers

You can host a small website on your Windows XP Professional computer with Internet Information Services (IIS). While the number of connections is limited, IIS is easy to install and is highly configurable as a Microsoft Management Console snap-in. You can also use IIS to host a File Transfer Protocol (FTP) site for sharing files and even a Simple Mail Transfer Protocol (SMTP) site for e-mail servers.

All three services are highly configurable. You can use the IIS console to manage these services locally or remotely. This chapter addresses the following configuration options in some detail:

- ◆ Installing Internet Information Services
- ◆ Understanding the limits of Windows XP Professional on IIS
- ◆ Configuring IIS as a snap-in to the Microsoft Management Console
- ◆ Setting up a web server
- ◆ Setting up an FTP server
- ◆ Setting up a Mail Server
- ◆ Troubleshooting IIS

## Installing Internet Information Services

IIS is not installed by default. Unless you've upgraded from a Windows operating system with IIS or Personal Web Server, you need to install IIS to set up a web, FTP, or SMTP site on your computer. This is a fairly easy process. Just use the Windows Components Wizard described in Chapter 5. Have your Windows XP Professional CD available and then follow these steps to install IIS:

1. Click Start ➢ Control Panel to open Control Panel.

2. Click the Add or Remove Programs link. Windows displays the Add or Remove Programs window.

3. Click the Add/Remove Windows Components button, and Windows displays the Windows Components Wizard.

4. Click the Internet Information Services (IIS) check box. By default, the check box is gray, which means that not all of the optional components are installed.

5. Click Details to open the Internet Information Services (IIS) window shown in Figure 32.1. As discussed in Chapter 5, you need to select the desired components and click OK to continue. See the "IIS Components" sidebar for more information on the available choices.

**FIGURE 32.1**
There are many components available for IIS.

6. Click Next to continue. The Windows Components Wizard proceeds to install IIS on your computer.

7. When you see the Completing the Windows Components Wizard page, IIS is installed. Click Finish to complete the process.

---

### IIS COMPONENTS—TO INSTALL OR NOT TO INSTALL?

You don't have to install all of the features associated with IIS. In fact, you should install just what you need. The more services you install, the more doors you open for hackers to get into your computer. For example, if you install the FTP service, some hackers may be able to get into your computer through the associated TCP/IP port. If you install FTP and don't use it, you may not even be paying attention when a hacker uses your computer for malicious purposes. With that in mind, the IIS components shown in Figure 32.1 have the following purposes:

**Common Files:** Includes the basic files required by all of the other components of IIS. If you delete this component, the Windows Components Wizard automatically deselects all other IIS components for you.

**Documentation:** Adds about 7MB of IIS help files and guides on your computer, in the \%SystemRoot%\ Help\iisHelp directory, where %SystemRoot% is the directory with your basic operating system files, such as C:\Windows.

**File Transfer Protocol (FTP) Service:** Configures the FTP service for file transfers. If you need to set up an FTP server, check this box. By default, this is deselected because FTP has often been a security problem in the past.

**FrontPage 2000 Server Extensions:** Includes the programs that allow you to use the full capabilities of the Microsoft FrontPage application for creating websites. The associated tools are fully compatible with FrontPage 2000 or FrontPage 2002.

**Internet Information Services Snap-in:** Allows you to use an MMC console to administer FrontPage. It's more difficult to administer IIS without this snap-in.

**SMTP Service**: Adds outgoing mail service. The Simple Mail Transfer Protocol governs the TCP/IP service that allows you to set up an outgoing mail server. You probably already have SMTP service through your ISP, so this service shouldn't be necessary unless you want your e-mail to bypass your ISP's servers.

**World Wide Web Service**: Includes the Microsoft Web server service. Highlight this option and click Details. This service includes four subcomponents:

♦ **Printers Virtual Directory**: Allows remote users to access your web server to print on your computers. Don't activate this unless absolutely necessary, because this can be a security hole.

♦ **Remote Desktop Web Connection**: Permits you to control this computer from a remote location through Internet Explorer. The basic requirements for Remote Desktop Connections are discussed in Chapter 14. Don't activate this option unless absolutely necessary, because this can be a security hole.

♦ **Scripts Virtual Directory**: Sets up a directory with scripts for your website. If you have any complexity in your web pages, such as database access, you need this subcomponent.

♦ **World Wide Web Service**: Adds the web server. This service is required to support any other web service, to support the mail (SMTP) service, or to display IIS documentation.

If you want to remove one or more of these services, repeat the basic steps you used to install IIS. Just deselect the components you no longer need during the process.

Assuming that you've installed the World Wide Web service, IIS should now be installed and active on your computer. It's easy to verify a successful installation. Open up Internet Explorer and enter `localhost` in the Address text box. Assuming you don't already have a web page, you'll see the default shown in Figure 32.2. If you've installed the help files, you'll see those as well in a separate browser.

**FIGURE 32.2**
The IIS default web page is visible only on the local computer.

## Windows XP Professional Limits on IIS

The IIS that you just installed on Windows XP Professional is essentially the same software that you can install on Windows Server products, with one major exception: Windows XP Professional limits access to 10 simultaneous TCP connections. That includes all connections made to your web, FTP, and SMTP servers. Very few Internet web or FTP sites would be practical with this limit. Obviously, Windows XP Professional wasn't designed to be a full-fledged web server. It does fine for small sites (such as your family home page), however.

**NOTE**   In fact, some connections to a website open multiple pages that require more than one TCP connection. In other words, access to your website on a Windows XP Professional computer may be limited to fewer than 10 users.

However, Windows XP Professional with IIS is still useful in the following ways:

◆   As a test bed: You can load a website on Windows XP Professional and test its look and feel over your LAN. However, you won't be able to test the response of your website to any serious traffic. For that purpose, you need to test your website on an operating system such as Microsoft's .NET Web Server.

◆   With an intranet: IIS on Windows XP Professional can be great if you're communicating with a small number of users, especially within a LAN or a domain.

◆   For a small group: IIS on Windows XP Professional can be used to share information with a small group, such as for a project.

These are common uses on an intranet. You can also connect IIS on Windows XP Professional to the Internet. Before you do this, talk to your ISP. Many ISPs, especially those that provide broadband service, may not even allow you to set up an Internet web server on your home computer.

However, many ISPs do provide space for a small website with a limited amount of traffic with your ISP membership. If desired, you can pay your ISP (or another company) for more space and larger amounts of traffic.

## The Internet Information Services Console

If you included the Internet Information Services snap-in when installing IIS, you have access to the IIS console. Click Start ➢ All Programs ➢ Administrative Tools ➢ Internet Information Services to open a console like what you see in Figure 32.3.

As with other MMC snap-ins discussed in Chapter 30, the IIS console allows for detailed configuration of each service. Just highlight the desired service and use the Action menu. Much of this chapter is dedicated to the details of this configuration process.

### Connecting to Remote IIS Services

You can use the IIS console to administer remote computers that include IIS 4.0 and above. Highlight Internet Information Services, and then click Action ➢ Connect. In the Connect to Computer window shown in Figure 32.4, enter the name or IP address of the other computer. Assuming you want to administer the remote server, check Connect As. This allows you to enter the remote username and password you need to administer IIS on the remote computer.

**FIGURE 32.3**

The Internet Information Services console allows you to manage websites, FTP sites, and SMTP mail servers.

**FIGURE 32.4**

Connecting to a remote IIS server

You can disconnect the IIS console from a remote or even the local IIS server. Just highlight the server of your choice, choose Action ➤ Disconnect, and then confirm your selection.

## Basic Configuration Management

Frequent backups are a good practice when you administer any computer. It's easy to back up your configuration that you set up through the IIS console. Highlight the server of your choice, and then choose Action ➤ All Tasks ➤ Backup/Restore Configuration to open the Configuration Backup/Restore window shown in Figure 32.5.

The options are fairly self-explanatory. If you want to create a backup, just click Create Backup. If you want to restore a previously backed-up configuration, highlight the name of the backup and click Restore. The default location for an IIS configuration backup file is the %SystemRoot%\System32\inetsrv\MetaBack directory.

**NOTE** In IIS, the terms *directory* and *folder* are used interchangeably.

**FIGURE 32.5**
Backing up an IIS
configuration

# Configuring the Web Server

It isn't practical to run a "real" website on Windows XP Professional. If you're setting up a website, you're eventually going to move the files you create to one of the Microsoft Windows Server operating systems. IIS on Windows Server products allows you to configure multiple websites. Therefore, the following sections assume that there are multiple websites on the IIS web server.

By now, we all realize that you can configure only one website on IIS for Windows XP Professional. But to understand the configuration process, it's best to look at a situation where you can configure multiple websites on the same IIS web server. Then, the configuration process for an IIS console becomes a simple exercise in configuring properties. There are four basic configuration levels in any IIS web server:

**Web Sites**: Applies to all IIS websites configured on the local computer. The discussion throughout this section assumes that there are multiple websites.

**Individual Web Site**: Configures only one specific website. On Windows XP Professional, there is only one website. On Microsoft Server operating systems, it's possible to install multiple websites, each with a unique configuration.

**Folder**: Allows you to configure each individual folder associated with a website.

**Individual File**: The configurable properties for individual files are identical to those for a folder.

Configuration is based on the properties at each level. Highlight the desired level in the left-hand pane of the IIS console and then choose Action ➢ Properties.

Some of the Properties tabs in the following sections look identical. Since they affect only one configuration level, the choices that you make will vary. This chapter addresses configuration at the Web Sites and Default Web Site levels. After reading through the following sections, you will see that the configuration of folders and individual files in a web server follows the same pattern.

## Generic Website Configuration

You can configure a number of options associated with all of the websites on IIS. In the IIS console, highlight the Web Sites (not the Default Web Site) folder and choose Action ➢ Properties to open the Web Sites Properties window shown in Figure 32.6. The ISAPI Filters tab should be open by default. Other tabs are described in the sections that follow.

**FIGURE 32.6**
Configuring ISAPI filters
for all websites

## ISAPI FILTERS

An ISAPI filter is a Dynamic Link Library (DLL) in a DLL file that customizes the content of the web page that is sent to a specific user. For example, if a cookie on a user's computer locates that computer in West Virginia, an ISAPI filter could send a web page customized for that U.S. state.

The ISAPI filters shown in Figure 32.6 apply to all websites configured on the server. The listed filters are processed on individual web pages, based first on the priority (High or Low) and then on the order shown in the tab.

You can adjust the processing order by highlighting the filter you want to change and then clicking the up or down arrow on the left side of the ISAPI Filters tab. The first four of these default filters are located in the %SystemRoot%\System32\inetsrv\ directory:

**sspifilt**: Allows for the transmission of secure websites. These are the web pages associated with sensitive information such as bank accounts and credit card payments. Secure websites can be identified in a browser based on the letters in front of the address, https (which stands for secure HTTP).

**Compression**: Permits the compression of files such as pictures before sending them to the user.

**md5filt**: Lets IIS use digest authentication.

**pwsdata**: Supports the use of websites configured through Personal Web Server, which was included in older Microsoft operating systems for the home such as Windows 98.

**fpexedll.dll**: Allows the use of legacy web pages created with FrontPage 1.x. If you use Microsoft proxy servers, you may need to delete these files before your users can access your website, which are located in the \Program Files\Common Files\Microsoft Shared\Web Server Extensions\ 40\bin\ directory.

### HOME DIRECTORY

Click the Home Directory tab. This configures the home directory properties for all websites on this server. But since individual websites need their own home directories, you'll need to configure some details later, in the Home Directory section associated with a specific website. For this reason, details associated with a particular website are not available under the Web Site Properties window shown in Figure 32.7.

**FIGURE 32.7**
Websites can share only some Home Directory properties.

However, wherever the directory is located, you can choose to set the same permissions for all websites on your implementation of IIS. The options associated with directory access include the following:

**Script Source Access**: Permits users to access the source code of a web-based application, if Read or Write access is enabled.

**Read**: Allows users to read or download files from your websites.

**Write:** Lets users upload files to your websites' directories. Requires a browser that complies with the HTTP 1.1 standard, such as Internet Explorer 4.0 and above.

**Directory Browsing**: Allows users to read a list of files in the associated virtual directory. This option works only if there are no default documents or if that option is disabled under the Documents tab, as discussed in the next section.

**Log Visits**: Enables logging for each user's visit to your website. As you'll see in the later sections on logging, this can provide valuable data for anyone interested in the background of visitors to a specific site.

Applications can be associated with website home directories. In this case, an application is any executable file on a website. But since they are also associated with specific directory locations, the details are described in the "Home Directory" section associated with configuring a specific website.

### DOCUMENTS

Click the Documents tab. Default documents are what you see when you type in just the name of a website. Based on the documents shown in Figure 32.8, any website will search for a `default.htm`, a `default.asp`, and an `index.htm` file in the home directory for a specific website. The first available file from this list is returned to the browser that's trying to connect to your site.

**FIGURE 32.8**
Website default documents

Document footers are typically HTML-formatted files that are added to the end of every web page on a website.

### DIRECTORY SECURITY

Click the Directory Security tab. At this level, only one option is available, to edit the authentication methods required for access to your website. Click Edit and review the Authentication Methods window shown in Figure 32.9.

By default, websites are set up for anonymous access. Anyone with a browser and the address of your website can access it if you make it available on the network. However, you can also set up Authenticated Access, which requires a web directory on an NTFS partition with associated user-level security limits. For more information on NTFS-based limits, see Chapter 19. The drawback of setting up such security at this level is that access passwords are sent in clear text. Anyone with the right network equipment can read the passwords as your users send them over the network.

### HTTP HEADERS

Click the HTTP Headers tab. The options shown in the tab are generally associated with specific websites and are therefore covered in detail in the "HTTP Headers" section associated with configuring a specific website.

### CUSTOM ERRORS

Click the Custom Errors tab. Along with web pages, browsers and web servers exchange messages all of the time, based on HTTP. The Custom Errors tab is shown in Figure 32.10.

**FIGURE 32.9**
Authentication methods

**FIGURE 32.10**
There are many types of
HTTP errors.

There are five basic categories of HTTP messages:

**1xx**: Messages between 100 and 199 are intermediate responses; communication is continuing between the browser and the server.

**2xx**: Messages between 200 and 299 tell the browser that the access request for the web page and associated information was successful.

**3xx**: Messages between 300 and 399 are associated with redirection, such as a move to a different web address.

**4xx**: Messages between 400 and 499 are error messages based on a problem at the browser such as "file not found."

**5xx**: Messages between 500 and 599 are error messages based on a problem from the web server.

Microsoft provides standard error messages to send to users' browsers associated with each HTTP message. For example, Figure 32.11 shows a browser with the standard error page when a file is not found on the browser.

**FIGURE 32.11**

A standard file not found (404) error message

Alternatively, you could set up a different message. Under the Custom Errors tab, click 404 under the HTTP Error column, and then click Edit Properties. The Error Mapping Properties page that opens gives you a chance to change the HTML file used for a 404 error. For example, if you try to access a nonexistent page at www.minasi.com, you'll get the 404 error message shown in Figure 32.12, which provides additional helpful information for users.

**FIGURE 32.12**

A customized file not found (404) error message.

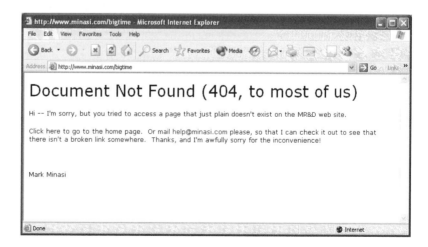

## Specific Website Configuration

Now that you have the basics, it's time to configure a specific website. In the IIS console, open the Web Sites folder and select a specific website. If you've just installed IIS, the Default Web Site is available for this purpose. Now choose Action ➢ Properties. This opens the Properties window associated with your website.

As you can see in Figure 32.13, the Properties window for the specific website includes two additional tabs, Web Site and Server Extensions. But all tabs will be covered in the following sections, because there are detailed items that you can configure for a specific site. In some cases, a comparison of properties can help you learn more about configuring IIS.

**FIGURE 32.13**

There are many things to configure for a specific website.

### WEB SITE

The Web Site tab as shown in Figure 32.13 should be open by default. As you can see, it includes three sections. The Web Site Identification section allows you to configure the following most basic parameters for the site:

**Description**: Identifies the website in the IIS console.

**IP Address**: Sets the IP address used to connect to this particular website. The Advanced button allows you to assign different TCP ports. For more information on TCP ports, see Chapter 17.

**TCP Port**: Fixes the default port for basic website communication. Port 80 is the default for HTTP.

**SSL Port**: Notes the default port for secure website communication. Port 443 is the default for HTTPS. You need a server certificate to allow IIS to serve web pages through a secure port. If you have one, assign it through the Directory Security tab. Once a certificate is assigned, the SSL Port text box will become active.

The Connections section allows you to regulate how connections are maintained with users. The Connection Timeout sets a limit on idle time. As shown in Figure 32.13, the default is 900 seconds. If there were no communication between the server and browser for that period of time, the user would have to reconnect to the website. HTTP Keep-Alives are required for "complex" web pages. Unless this check box is enabled, a browser may have to send new connection requests for each web page element from a different file, such as pictures and icons.

**NOTE** If you were configuring IIS on one of the Windows Server operating systems, you would also see options for regulating the number of simultaneous connections.

The Enable Logging section is important to any website. If you want to know anything about your users, you want to check Enable Logging. Try a format, and then try connecting to the server from the local computer and a remote computer on your LAN. You can then review the log file in the %SystemRoot%\System32\LogFiles directory. All formats provide a list of requests from the browser, which includes their IP address, username, time, requested file, and the amount of data transmitted. There are three log formats available for IIS:

**Microsoft IIS Log File Format**: Associated with a fixed ASCII format originally developed for older versions of IIS. Not in common use today.

**NCSA Common Log File Format**: Allows for log files in a format originally developed by the National Center for Supercomputing Applications (NCSA) in the 1980s. The NCSA developed the first viable web servers at the University of Illinois. One of the developers of this web server, Marc Andreeson, went on to develop the Netscape browser.

**W3C Extended Log File Format**: Configures the most current and flexible log file format, maintained by the World Wide Web Consortium, which is also the IIS default format.

The W3C format is in most common use today. In the Active Log Format drop-down box, switch to W3C Extended Log File Format if it isn't already selected, and then click Properties. You'll see the Extended Logging Properties window, as shown in Figure 32.14.

**NOTE** Log files grow quickly. If you use the default website, your users call a single web page. But since this calls up icons, banners, and more, it creates 19 log entries (based on the W3C Extended Log File Format). And this is a fairly simple website. Commercial websites are known to have daily log files in the hundreds of megabytes. If you're administering a larger website, watch the size of your log files carefully.

**FIGURE 32.14**
Setting up basic website logging

The General Properties tab should be open by default. There are a few options available, related to regulating the size of a log file:

**New Log Time Period**: New log files can be created on an hourly, daily, weekly, or monthly basis. Alternatively, you can set up a new log file after the current one reaches a specific size.

**Use Local Time for File Naming and Rollover**: If you deselect this option, IIS uses Greenwich Mean Time (GMT). Based on the settings shown in Figure 32.14, new daily log files would be created every day at midnight GMT.

**Log File Directory**: The location of your log files. If you have large log files, you may want to select a directory on a less-crowded drive.

**Log File Name**: The default shown indicates the subdirectory (W3SVC1) and a specific file format. The yymmdd part of the filename corresponds to the current date. For example, if this is a log file for December 25, 2002, the log filename will be ex021225.log.

> **TIP** Although you can set log files to start based on local time or GMT, each entry in a log file is based on GMT. For example, if you see a log file entry at 02:30:43 and identify the user as being from the east coast of the U.S., that user accessed your server at 9:30 P.M., Eastern Standard Time.

Click the Extended Properties tab. As shown in Figure 32.15, there is a substantial number of details you can get about every request to your website. See the "W3C Log Files" sidebar for more information on what you can configure. Log files can be useful for troubleshooting and are discussed in the "Log Files" section toward the end of this chapter.

**FIGURE 32.15**

There are a lot of W3C log file configuration options.

## ISAPI FILTERS

Click the ISAPI Filters tab. The format is identical to that from Figure 32.6. The filters you configured there apply to all the websites on this installation of IIS. The filters that you add here apply only to this specific website. If desired, click Add to start the process of adding a filter.

## W3C LOG FILES

There are numerous options for data that you can collect in a W3C log file. The options shown below are associated just with IIS for Windows XP Professional. More log options are available with the Windows XP Server packages, especially if you use some form of the Microsoft Commerce Server. Some of these options are shown in Figure 32.15. They include the following list:

**Date:** Indicates the date of the request. If you keep daily log files, this information isn't necessary.

**Time:** Notes the time of the request. If you weren't limited by the Windows XP Professional 10-connection limit, this could help you measure the busy times for your website.

**Extended Properties:** Allows you to change the following other extended logging options, when selected:

**Client IP Address:** Adds the IP address from the computer that the browser is using.

**User Name:** Includes the username, usually only from the LAN or local domain.

**Service Name:** Adds the name of the logging service, in this case, W3SVC1. This shouldn't change.

**Server Name:** Lists the computer name used to serve the web pages. Useful for websites where user requests could go to different web servers.

**Server IP Address:** Notes the IP address associated with the computer used to serve the web pages.

**Server Port:** Includes the port number of the connection. For regular web pages, the default TCP port is 80.

**Method:** Notes the command used by the browser (usually GET).

**URI Stem:** Lists the name of the file that is accessed, which can be the web page, an ActiveX control page, an icon, and more.

**URI Query:** Includes a search term, such as through a search engine.

**Protocol Status:** Notes the HTTP message associated with the request.

**Win32 Status:** Notes the Windows message associated with the request.

**Bytes Sent:** Includes the number of bytes sent by IIS to the client. Usually corresponds to the size of the requested file.

**Bytes Received:** Includes the number of bytes received by IIS.

**Time Taken:** Lists the amount of time on the server between when it gets the first packet of data from the client and when it gets the acknowledgment from the client that it received the requested data.

**Protocol Version:** Notes the protocol, usually FTP, HTTP 1.0, or HTTP 1.1.

**Host:** Includes the name or IP address of the computer with the web server.

**User Agent:** Notes the browser used on the client. Most browsers are compatible with some form of a protocol known as Mozilla or Gecko.

**Cookie:** Lists the content of a cookie sent to the client.

**Referer:** Notes the web page or site where the subject file is used.

### HOME DIRECTORY

Click the Home Directory tab. While the format is identical to that shown in Figure 32.7, there is more that you can configure for a specific website. As you can see in Figure 32.16, you can specify the location of this website's files. At the top of the tab, there is one implied question: When Connecting to This Resource, the Content Should Come From:

**FIGURE 32.16**
There is more to config-
ure for a specific web-
site's home directory.

**A Directory Located on This Computer**: Allows you to place the directory of your choice in the Local Path text box. This directory should contain the files you need for your website.

**TIP**   If you're going to set up a real website directory on a Windows Server computer, always set it up on an NTFS partition. Otherwise, if you configure Server Extensions to support the use of Microsoft FrontPage, it is possible for someone to upload malicious code to these less-protected folders. For more information, see the "Server Extensions" section later in this chapter.

**A Share Located on Another Computer**: Lets you use a directory on a remote computer. If you select this option, the Local Path text box changes to a Network Directory text box, where you can enter the path to the directory in the \\Server\Share format.

**A Redirection to a URL**: Permits you to send any browser that tries to connect to a website on your computer to a different network directory or a website such as www.mommabears.com. If you select this option, the Local Path text box changes to a Redirect To text box, where you can enter the name of the directory or website. Since you would no longer be responsible for local scripts or applications, all such references are deleted, as shown in Figure 32.17. There are three other options:

**The Exact URL Entered Above**: Redirects all requests to your home page or subdirectories to the specified URL.

**A Directory below This One**: Allows you to redirect requests to a child directory.

**A Permanent Redirection for This Resource**: Sends a message to the browser that the redirection is permanent, also known by its HTTP code, 301. Some browsers will use this code as a trigger to change associated bookmarks.

**FIGURE 32.17**
It's easy to redirect users
to a different website.

### DOCUMENTS

Click the Documents tab. The default settings appear identical to Figure 32.8, which identified default documents for all websites on the local IIS. You don't have to make any changes. However, unique default documents can help avoid confusion when you're running multiple websites on the same server. They can also improve security, if they are based on a name that a hacker wouldn't anticipate.

### DIRECTORY SECURITY

Click the Directory Security tab. The default settings appear identical to Figure 32.9, which identified authentication and other security limits for all websites on the local IIS. You don't have to make any changes. However, any access controls or certificates that you add at this stage apply only to this specific website. If a hacker acquires the security key for one of your websites, individual certificates would protect any other websites on your server.

### HTTP HEADERS

Click the HTTP Headers tab. This includes information related to the content of your website and is therefore normally customized differently for each site. As you can see in Figure 32.18, this tab can be divided into four different sections.

If you check Enable Content Expiration, the content on the current website is not updated after the expiration date and time that you set.

Custom HTTP Headers allow you to use special programming instructions. For example, it's possible to force client browsers to refresh periodically, which can be useful for time-sensitive data such as the price of stocks or mutual funds that you own. More information on this topic can be found in the Microsoft Knowledge Base, article 240774.

**FIGURE 32.18**
HTTP headers help you
classify the content of a
website.

**TIP**   Microsoft Knowledge Base articles are available online. Navigate to http://support.Microsoft
.com, and enter keywords or the article number as a search term. Alternatively, if you enter the article
number in a comprehensive search engine such as Google (www.google.com), you'll probably find a
direct link to the article.

Content ratings allow you to classify your website. General guidelines are available through the
Internet Content Rating Association of the Recreational Software Advisory Council (RSAC), available
online at www.rsac.org. The content that you configure for your website works with Internet Explorer's
Content Advisor, described in Chapter 13. To set up a rating for your website, click Edit Ratings. You'll
see the Content Ratings window in Figure 32.19.

By default, you should see the Rating Service tab, which allows you to view the RSAC website and
start a rating for your own website. Alternatively, you can set your own ratings for the level of Vio-
lence, Sex, Nudity, and Language associated with your website through the Ratings tab. Once you're
finished setting up ratings, click OK to return to the HTTP Headers tab.

IIS already configures all of the file types such as .htm, .jpg, and .asp that most users need for
their web servers. If you need an unusual file type for your website, click File Types and configure it
in the File Types window that appears.

### CUSTOM ERRORS

Click the Custom Errors tab. The default settings appear identical to Figure 32.10, which identified
HTTP error codes and associated web pages for all websites on the local IIS. Any special web pages
that you configure for an HTTP error under this tab apply only to this specific website. While you
don't have to make any changes, individualized error pages can help promote a unique look and feel
for your website.

**FIGURE 32.19**

You can configure RSAC Content Ratings for your website.

## SERVER EXTENSIONS

Click the Server Extensions tab. This is found only with specific websites, as the properties that allow you and other web page authors on your computer to use Microsoft FrontPage to edit your web pages. As you can see in Figure 32.20, the information on this tab can be divided into three sections.

**TIP**   If you don't see any information under this tab, you haven't yet configured Server Extensions. To do so, return to the IIS console, highlight the website, and then click Action ➤ All Tasks ➤ Configure Server Extensions. This opens the Server Extensions Configuration Wizard, which allows you to configure the e-mail contact points for the author and administrator of the website. If your web pages are not on an NTFS partition, the wizard warns you of potential security problems. You can change the location of your web pages through the Home Directory tab associated with your website.

**Enable Authoring**: Allows the use of FrontPage to edit local web pages. Version control allows you to have a historical record of changes. The Performance option and Settings button optimize caches based on the size of your website. And there are two available types of Client Scripting: JavaScript and VBScript.

**Options**: Lets you note how and where website-related e-mail, such as to the administrator, should be sent. If the Microsoft Office Web Server is installed, you can also set up workgroup discussions through your website.

**Don't Inherit Security Settings**: Permits you to override any security settings that you created earlier for IIS. This includes logging of authors who change the website, overriding of FrontPage security settings to allow you to manage permissions manually, and the use of SSL to verify author identities before allowing them to change a web page.

**FIGURE 32.20**

Server Extensions help you configure authoring and security options.

## NEW VIRTUAL DIRECTORIES

You can create virtual directories for your website. These directories can help hide the real location of sensitive files. To create a new virtual directory, highlight the website in the IIS console. Choose Action ➤ New ➤ Virtual Directory to start the Virtual Directory Creation Wizard. Click Next to go to the Virtual Directory Alias page shown in Figure 32.21.

**FIGURE 32.21**

You can use an alias that is different from the name of the directory you want to use.

Enter an Alias of your choice and click Next to continue. On the next page, specify the path to the actual directory you want to use. Click Next to continue. You'll see the Access Permissions page shown in Figure 32.22. The permissions shown are fairly standard:

**Read**: Allows users to read website documents through their browsers.

**Run Scripts**: Permits users to run the basic scripts associated with many web pages, such as Active Server Pages (ASP).

**Execute**: Lets users run applications through your web pages.

**FIGURE 32.22**
The default access permissions can help protect the files in your virtual directory.

**Write**: Allows users to upload new pages to your website.

**Browse**: Sets up the website to list files in the current directory, if the default documents shown under the website's Document tab have been disabled or do not exist.

Perhaps the most interesting of these options is Browse, which allows you to set up an FTP-style interface for sharing files. For example, Figure 32.23 shows some of the files that I used to write this book in a virtual directory named `Secret Directory`. Anyone with access to this page can download these files. But take care with the directories that you use; the wrong virtual directory settings could also help a malicious user find the vulnerabilities in your system.

**FIGURE 32.23**
You can share files with a browser through your website.

CHAPTER 32

## Configuring the FTP Server

When the first pre-Internet networks were developed in the 1970s, there was a lot of trust in the computer world. There was little need for computer security; few people made money from computer data. Most of the people working on this network were university researchers; they just wanted to exchange information. Anonymous connections allowed for the quickest possible exchange of data. The File Transfer Protocol was developed to help make this possible.

It's easy to configure an FTP server. Since multiple FTP sites on a single server are uncommon, you'll be configuring just the default FTP site. Return to the IIS console and highlight Default FTP Site. Choose Action ➢ Properties. This opens the Default FTP Site Properties window, as shown in Figure 32.24.

**FIGURE 32.24**
It's easy to set up an FTP site.

As you can see, there are four tabs shown in Figure 32.24 that address basic configuration (FTP Site), security (Security Accounts), messages to users (Messages), and the configuration of the FTP server home directory (Home Directory).

### FTP Site

You have already seen the information associated with the FTP Site tab. As shown in Figure 32.24, the information appears quite similar to the Web Site tab that you configured earlier in this chapter for the default website. There are four sections that you can configure:

**Identification**: Describes the name of the FTP site, the IP address used to connect, and the TCP port. (The default TCP port for FTP communication is 21.)

**Connection**: Allows you to regulate the number of connections, as well as the amount of time the connection can be inactive before it's disconnected. Remember, for Windows XP Professional, the total number of connections is limited to 10. If you've configured a website as well, you may want to reduce this number further so your website is accessible by at least one user.

**Enable Logging**: Permits logging per W3C Extended Log File Format or the Microsoft IIS Log File Format, based on the general criteria described earlier in this chapter. The default directory with the actual FTP log files is slightly different from that for other servers.

**Current Sessions**: Lets you monitor currently connected users. Click this button, and you can disconnect currently logged on users in the FTP User Sessions window that appears.

## Security Accounts

Click the Security Accounts tab. You see the options normally associated with FTP security, as shown in Figure 32.25. The default is Allow Anonymous Connections. While people who log on to FTP anonymously get a generic username, passwords aren't even required.

**FIGURE 32.25**
IIS uses standard FTP
security requirements.

If you deselect Allow Anonymous Connections, only people who have a username and password on your system can log on to your FTP server. Even if they're administrative users, they don't automatically have Write access through your FTP server.

**NOTE**    The FTP Site Operators section of the Security Accounts tab is not active and cannot be changed when you're configuring FTP on IIS on Windows XP Professional.

## Messages

You can set up various messages for your FTP users. Click the Messages tab. The message boxes shown in Figure 32.26 are fairly self-explanatory.

**Banner**: Lists the message you see when you connect to the FTP server, before you log in.

**Welcome**: Sends a message to a user after a successful login.

**Exit**: Sends a message to a user after exiting from the server.

**Maximum Connections:** Sends a message to the user if there are already too many other connections to the server.

Figure 32.27 illustrates the effect of these messages on an FTP session: the banner upon connection, the welcome message after the password is accepted, an exit message after terminating the session, and the maximum connections message when the server is too busy.

**FIGURE 32.26**
Creating messages for
your FTP users

**FIGURE 32.27**
The effect of FTP
messages

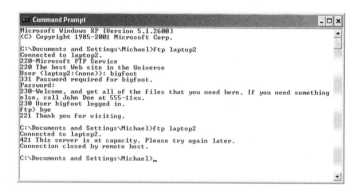

## Home Directory

There are a number of options available for the home directory for your FTP server. Click the Home
Directory tab, and you'll see that the options shown in Figure 32.28 are fairly straightforward.

The first option is whether the files on your FTP server should come from the local or a remote
computer. If you keep A Directory Located on This Computer selected, the FTP Site Directory section
allows you to type a path in the Local Path text box. If you select A Share Located on Another Computer, the Local Path text box turns into a Network Share text box, where you can enter the share in
the \\Servername\sharename format. In that case, you'll also see a Connect As button, which you
can use to let IIS log in to the remote computer.

In either case, there are three options associated with configuring a specific FTP site directory:

**Read**: Gives you Read access to the home directory. Allows you to use various directory commands such as dir and ls to list the files in that directory. Read access is required at least on the
home directory; otherwise, your users won't be able to log in to your FTP server.

**FIGURE 32.28**
Setting up the FTP home
directory

**Write**: Permits you to upload files to the FTP server. Since users with Write access can overwrite the files on your FTP server, this would create a security issue.

**Log Visits**: Data from visitors is collected in log files, as described earlier with the FTP Site tab and in related information discussed in configuring a web server.

There are two different Directory Listing Style options, UNIX and MS-DOS. The style you select determines the FTP server response to the `ls` command, which is an FTP command from UNIX used to list the contents of directories. If UNIX style is selected, the `ls` (and `dir`) command gives you a file list with permissions, ownership, file size, file type, and creation date. If your users are more comfortable with a UNIX-type operating system such as Linux, BSD, or Solaris, consider using a UNIX directory listing style. It does not change anything else related to your FTP site. For more information on FTP as a client, see Chapter 14.

## Virtual Directories

If you want to share files in a specific directory, you don't have to copy them to the FTP server home directory. You can set it up as a virtual directory. You won't have to move your files. To create a virtual directory in the IIS console, highlight your default FTP site. Choose Action ➤ New ➤ Virtual Directory to start the Virtual Directory Creation Wizard, and then click Next to continue. This takes you to the Virtual Directory Alias page shown in Figure 32.29, where you can enter the virtual directory name of your choice. Just remember the name that you use.

Click Next to continue. Enter the path to the directory containing the files you want to put on the FTP server, and then click Next to continue. This takes you to the Access Permissions page shown in Figure 32.30, where you can set Read and Write permissions on your new virtual directory.

While you need to select Read permissions to let FTP users read the contents of your new virtual directory, remember that Write permissions may be a security risk. Click Next to continue, and then click Finish to complete the Virtual Directory Creation Wizard.

**FIGURE 32.29**
Setting up a virtual
directory alias

**FIGURE 32.30**
Setting up permissions
on a virtual directory

Before you can use your new virtual directory, you need to create a "mirror" as a subdirectory of your FTP home directory. The default FTP home directory as shown in Figure 32.28 is `C:\Inetpub\ftproot`. Navigate to this directory in Explorer and create a new folder with the same name as your virtual directory alias. Don't add any files to this folder. The FTP server automatically mirrors the files through your virtual directory.

Now you're ready to use the new virtual directory. Figure 32.31 illustrates an FTP session using the virtual directory shown in Figure 32.29 (`Important Project Files`).

## Configuring the SMTP Server

Outgoing e-mail uses the Simple Mail Transfer Protocol (SMTP). Most home users send e-mail through the SMTP facilities provided by their ISP. However, the ISP's SMTP server may not always be available. The standard Microsoft application for large organizations that need an outgoing e-mail server is known as Microsoft Exchange.

However, with the SMTP server included with IIS, you may not need Microsoft Exchange to handle outgoing e-mail. This service already provides what you need for small-scale systems. Of course, if you're satisfied with the outgoing e-mail service provided by your ISP, you should uninstall or deactivate this service instead.

**FIGURE 32.31**

Accessing a virtual directory

If you want to set up SMTP on your IIS console, highlight Default SMTP Virtual Server. Choose Action ➤ Properties to open the Default SMTP Virtual Server Properties window shown in Figure 32.32.

**FIGURE 32.32**

Setting up an SMTP virtual server

**NOTE**  Although it does support the SMTP Server service, Windows XP Professional is *not* designed to be a fully functional e-mail server. Use another product, such as Microsoft Exchange Server, for proper handling of e-mail.

## Basic SMTP Configuration

Examine the information associated with the General tab of the Default SMTP Virtual Server Properties window. If you've studied the properties associated with configuring a web or FTP server, these settings should look familiar by now. Otherwise, here is a brief description of the settings associated with the General tab:

   **IP Address**: Allows you to specify the IP address associated with the SMTP server. If you need to set a TCP port other than the default of 25, click Advanced.

**Limit Number of Connections To**: Permits you to limit the number of users who connect simultaneously to this SMTP server. Remember, this is also subject to the 10-connection limit associated with Windows XP Professional.

**Connection Time-out (Minutes)**: Closes a connection after the specified period of inactivity.

**Enable Logging**: Begins the logging process, based on the same log formats described earlier when configuring an IIS web server. The Properties button allows you to configure the details of what is actually logged.

## Access

There are a number of ways to limit access to an SMTP server on IIS. Click the Access tab to view the four basic categories of controlling access, as shown in Figure 32.33. The only item that you must configure to get SMTP to work for you is based on the Relay Restrictions.

**FIGURE 32.33**

Controlling access to an SMTP virtual server

**Access Control**: Allows you to set up different forms of authentication for users who want access to your SMTP server. These include anonymous access, basic authentication with clear-text passwords, and access with some forms of encryption.

**Secure Communication**: Lets you add a server certificate to your SMTP server. If you click Certificate, you start the Web Server Certificate Wizard.

**Connection Control**: Permits you to set up a list of allowed (or prohibited) computers by their fully qualified domain names or IP addresses.

**Relay Restrictions**: Allows you to identify computers that are allowed to use this SMTP server. This is the only item under Access that you must reconfigure to let users on your network use this server. Click Relay to open the Relay Restrictions window. Select the Only the List Below option, and then click Add. This opens the Computer window shown in Figure 32.34. Click Single Computer and add the IP address of your computer. Alternatively, click Group of Computers and add the Subnet Address and Subnet Mask for your computer. Click OK. The result should be shown in the Relay Restrictions window, similar to what you see in Figure 32.35. For more information on IP addressing, see Chapter 17.

**FIGURE 32.34**
Adding computers to an SMTP server

**FIGURE 32.35**
The list of computers allowed to use your SMTP server

## Messages

There are a number of ways to regulate messages on an SMTP server on IIS. Click the Messages tab to view the message control options, as shown in Figure 32.36. These options include the following:

**Limit Message Size to (KB)**: Specifies the maximum allowed message size. The minimum limit is 1KB. If your users send HTML-enabled e-mail or attachments of any size, you'll need much larger limits.

**Limit Session Size to (KB)**: Notes the maximum amount of data that a user is allowed to send through the SMTP server during each connection.

**Limit Number of Messages per Connection To**: Creates a limit on the number of e-mail messages that can be sent per connection.

**Limit Number of Recipients per Message To**: Sets a maximum number of e-mail addresses for each message.

**FIGURE 32.36**
Controlling message
information

**Send Copy of Non-Delivery Report To**: Specifies an additional e-mail address for undeliverable
e-mail messages, such as those sent to an unavailable e-mail address.

**Badmail Directory:** Notes the directory with undeliverable e-mail, based on the limits shown
under the Delivery tab.

## Delivery

There are a number of ways to manage the delivery of messages on an SMTP server on IIS. Click the
Delivery tab to view Outbound and Local options, as shown in Figure 32.37. These options are
required because not all attempts to deliver e-mail actually work:

**FIGURE 32.37**
Controlling delivery
methods

**Outbound**: Applies to e-mail addresses on external servers. If your SMTP server has trouble delivering a message, it will try again several times. By default, if a message is not delivered the first time, the server tries again in 15 minutes. If the message isn't delivered the second time, it tries again 30 minutes later, and so on, until the time specified as the Expiration Timeout. The Delay Notification specifies the wait time before the SMTP server tells the sender that there is a problem.

**Local**: Applies to e-mail addresses on a local server. The Delay Notification and Expiration Timeout settings work in the same way as for Outbound settings.

**Outbound Security**: Specifies authentication that is sent to external servers.

**Outbound Connections**: Limits the number of simultaneous external connections.

**Advanced**: Details the routing options for external messages.

## LDAP Routing

The Lightweight Directory Assistance Protocol (LDAP) allows you to use a specific type of server to help identify e-mail recipients. Normally, LDAP isn't required to find an e-mail address, and therefore it isn't enabled by default. Click the LDAP Routing tab to view relevant options, as shown in Figure 32.38.

**FIGURE 32.38**

Controlling message information

If you select Enable LDAP Routing, you can specify more information about the LDAP server:

**Server**: Notes the name of the server with the LDAP database.

**Schema**: Lists the type of directory service, which may be associated with an Active Directory domain, a Site Server/Commerce Server directory, or an Exchange mailbox service.

**Binding**: Specifies the authentication method.

**Domain**: Lists the domain, if account and password information has to be sent to access the database.

**User Name**: Notes the name required to log in to the database.

**Password**: Adds the authentication password for the database.

**Base**: Specifies a naming context.

### Security

This is the simplest property associated with the SMTP virtual server. It establishes the list of users allowed to act as SMTP virtual server operators. By default, the Administrators group is part of this list. If you need to add additional users, click the Security tab and then click Add to add users.

# Troubleshooting IIS

Troubleshooting is an exercise in checking the simplest causes first. You've read about the three services associated with IIS. If you have a problem with any of these services, the simplest causes relate to

**Installation**: Make sure that the service in question is actually installed.

**Activity**: Check the service to make sure that it's actually started.

**Implementation**: Stop and start a service. That is often all that is required to implement any recent configuration changes to a particular service.

You can even go so far as to uninstall and reinstall a service. Assuming that you've backed up a good configuration, you can safely uninstall and reinstall a service. Then you can test the original setup, make any necessary changes, and restore the service. Restoring an existing configuration is fairly easy. In the IIS console, highlight the name of the server, and then choose Action ➢ All Tasks ➢ Backup/Restore Configuration.

**NOTE**  For more information on backing up an IIS console configuration, see the section earlier in this chapter titled "Basic Configuration Management."

### Log Files

If a service is working, you can get more information on what is happening from the log file that you've set up for the service. Log files are available and are easily configurable for all of the IIS services.

For example, assume you're looking at a lot of activity on your network interfaces, and you know that nobody on your LAN is accessing your Intranet site. If you're collecting the right kind of data, log files can help you diagnose the problem. For example, look at the following excerpt from a web log file:

```
00:29:12 10.39.52.112 - W3SVC1 MainServer GET /private.htm
```

This tells you that at 12:29 A.M., someone using IP address 10.39.52.112 and no defined username accessed the server named MainServer and accessed the `private.htm` file from your website home directory. Assume that you don't expect users to access the `private.htm` file outside of regular work hours.

But remember, the entries in a log file are based on GMT. If the IP address is assigned to one of your offices on the west coast of the U.S., the access attempt was made at 4:29 P.M. PST, which is probably just the end of their workday. In this case, your troubleshooting through your log files explained the problem.

Remember, you can configure the IIS web server to collect a lot of different kinds of information that can help you diagnose other problems.

## Summary

This chapter addressed the three basic services that you can set up and configure with Internet Information Server (IIS): web service, FTP service, and SMTP service. IIS and associated services are easy to install through the Add or Remove Programs link in Control Panel. Windows XP Professional limits the number of connections to your IIS services to 10, which makes it impractical for a full-scale business web sites but perhaps adequate for your own personal sites.

It's easy to configure IIS through its own MMC snap-in, the IIS console. You can use it to monitor local or remote services. Once set, the configuration can be readily backed up and restored.

Website configuration is a complex enterprise; the properties for the service affect the properties for the website. Configurable settings include ISAPI filters, directory locations, default documents, security, HTTP headers, custom HTTP error messages, logging, and server extensions.

FTP site configuration is a bit less complex. Configurable settings include connection control, logging, security, status messages, and directory settings. You can even customize the site for UNIX users.

You can also configure a mail server on Windows XP Professional, known as an SMTP server. As with FTP, you can configure connection control, logging, security, and directory settings. You can also manage the size of information sent by your users, manage delivery issues, and use LDAP access to identify some types of e-mail recipients.

Despite the complexity of IIS, troubleshooting is easy. Whenever you make a change, just restart the applicable server. Make sure all the components are there. And you can use the log files that you configured for each service to diagnose most problems.

In the next chapter, we'll wrap things up by hitting the topic everyone loves to hate: troubleshooting.

CHAPTER 32

# Chapter 33

# Advanced Troubleshooting Methodology

Ever have one of those days? A day when nothing seems to go right with your computer? Unfortunately, an operating system such as Windows XP Professional is extremely complex, and any complex system will inevitably have those days. Just remember this quote from a favorite Scottish engineer: "The more they over-tink the plumbing, the easier it is to stop up the drains." With a system such as Windows XP Professional, things can go wrong in so many places that it's often difficult to find a place to start.

Troubleshooting always seems to get pushed to the back of every technical book. It's almost as if we authors say, "If they make it this far, *then* we'll finally give them the Holy Grail." Just because troubleshooting seems to be hidden away in the cobwebs of a book, don't assume it lacks importance. In fact, it's just the opposite. Someone with good troubleshooting skills is a valuable person indeed. It's here at the back of the book because so much of troubleshooting depends on understanding what you're dealing with (in our case, Windows XP Professional). Once you have an understanding of your product, *then* you can dive in and try to fix it.

In this chapter, we take a look at the "how" of troubleshooting Windows XP Professional. I want to give you a workable method for finding your way through the maze. You will learn about the following:

- ◆ Troubleshooting principles and procedures
- ◆ Troubleshooting printing
- ◆ Troubleshooting Windows XP Professional Setup
- ◆ Dealing with SCSI problems during setup
- ◆ Troubleshooting Stop errors

## The Tao of Troubleshooting

At first it seems that troubleshooting mostly involves memorizing a lot of details about everything. When working with an experienced troubleshooter, you've probably even found yourself thinking, "How do they know that?" Truth is, most people never do well by simply trying to memorize everything. Human beings succeed best when working from their strengths; we all have problems when working from our weaknesses. To make troubleshooting a strength, you need to find the pattern in the chaos.

**NOTE**    The process of troubleshooting is the process of moving from the big picture to the small details. Asking questions is the tool for breaking the big picture into small details.

Consider this scenario: A friend tells you he is having trouble getting a vending machine to accept a dollar bill. If you happen to be a vending machine expert, you might know everything about how the dollar bill is drawn into the machine, every detail of the mechanisms that control the entire process. But you probably aren't a vending machine expert. Instead, being a good troubleshooter, you consider the directions on the machine. Then you start asking questions: "Has it ever worked before?" "Did you put the dollar in facing the right direction?" "Is the dollar bill folded?"

With this last question, your friend admits that the corners of the bill are a bit folded. So you try straightening them out. Then you test your solution by reinserting the bill. It works, and you are a hero. Of course, solving a problem like this has a low glory quotient, but it serves to illustrate the basics.

## Define the Problem: "It's Broken."

The first step to successful troubleshooting is to define the problem accurately. Many times people will define a problem in very simple terms and expect you to know what they are talking about. Your job as a troubleshooter is to define the details of the problem: "So, what *exactly* is broken?" This is a good question to start the conversation. (Incidentally, this may be a conversation with yourself if you are trying to solve your own problem.) Start by getting a clear description of what the person who is reporting the problem feels is the issue. It is often a good technique to take the time to write these points out on paper.

Try to get all the details that describe the problem as the user sees it. Ask such questions as "Has it ever worked before?" or "When did you notice that it stopped working?"

## Explore the Boundaries

This can be a painful lesson to learn. Often the person you are working with to solve a problem (yes, this can even be yourself) leaves out important details. This is almost never because they want you to fail, but rather because they don't think a particular detail is relevant. This is a painful lesson because you may spend a great deal of time pursuing irrelevant issues when the real problem is very simple. Consider the following illustration.

You are talking with a friend about their computer problem. The issue, as reported, is that their new modem isn't working. So right away you dig into the settings and configuration for the modem. You eventually discover that the friend has disabled the COM port in Device Manager because they didn't think they needed it!

Exploring the boundaries means finding out everything that may be wrong with the system. The extra information you get here *may* be unrelated to the problem, but it may be exactly the piece you need to solve the puzzle.

## Brainstorm and Document

Now that you have a clue about where the problem lies, it's time to come up with some ideas to help focus on the real issue. While you are gathering your thoughts, write them down. It's a good idea to have at least three things to try before proceeding.

Writing down your ideas is important. You will be trying each possible approach, and this may take time. It may be difficult to remember each idea when you're in the heat of battle (figuratively speaking). Don't be afraid to add to this list as you go. Often you will discover the best approach while trying one of your initial ideas.

---

**DOCUMENT EVERYTHING!**

One piece of advice I give to anyone who is new to troubleshooting (or anyone who will listen, for that matter) is to keep a notebook handy. It can be a simple 3×5 notebook or a full-sized one. That's up to you. But in your notebook, write down any problems, what you did, and what fixed the problem. Later, if you run into a similar problem, you'll have a record of what worked last time. Eventually you might become less and less reliant upon the notebook, but it will pay dividends almost immediately if you do a lot of troubleshooting.

---

## Test Your Ideas

This is a critical point: Test each approach—one at a time.

It is impossible to overemphasize this point. Many troubleshooters will try the "shotgun" approach, meaning they test every idea they can muster all at once. Most likely one of the ideas will work, but which one?

During the course of troubleshooting an operating system, you will frequently be disabling certain functionalities. If you try every idea at the same time, you may fix the problem, but you'll be left with an operating system that has been crippled by your actions. Worse yet, you won't know which areas to reenable and which one to repair. So, test your ideas one at a time, and if the idea doesn't work, change your setting back to the way it was before trying your next fix. You don't want to cause more problems for yourself!

Testing each idea one at a time enables you to discover clearly what's broken and to easily find your way back through the maze of settings that have been changed.

## Repair the Problem

This is the easy part—usually. Finding the problem can often be a time-consuming process, but repairing the broken portion of the system can be as simple as replacing a corrupt file. Perhaps the issue arises from bad hardware. This is easy to fix; just replace the hardware. (The hard part here is to find the money for the replacement.)

## Clean Up after Yourself

Remember how I said earlier to test each possible solution individually? This is the phase where you undo some of the ideas that were unsuccessful, if you haven't already done so. Never leave the system worse than you found it. There are few support issues worse than a customer who is upset that the previous support person made their problems worse or caused new ones.

Again, it's helpful to have documented the approaches you tried—especially if you kept notes about what you did during the troubleshooting phase. If you did, it is simple to backtrack and turn features back on.

## Provide Closure

If you are dealing with other people in your troubleshooting process, providing closure means informing them of what the problem was and what you did to resolve it. If you are going through this process to solve your own problem, it means reviewing what you did and understanding how to avoid this problem in the future.

CHAPTER 33

Nearly every person you work with when supporting an operating system will want to know what the problem was and how to fix it. We all like to feel that we have been included in finding a solution, that we are part of a team effort. A word of advice here: If you are supporting people on Windows XP Professional as part of your job, always try to include the customer in the troubleshooting process. It helps them to feel better about the incident and about your presence. That, in turn, helps them to participate by giving you good information. And that makes everyone's day go better.

Now a moment for the darker side of support. If the problem was caused by the user's ignorance, getting closure is your opportunity to educate. If you do this with some sensitivity, you can turn this into a positive experience. If you give in to the temptation to tell the person that they're an idiot, you will be burning bridges that will be difficult to rebuild later. Your choice. If *you* are the customer, this is where you can ask advice or discover an opportunity for education.

### Document the Situation

The problem is fixed, and the customer is happy. You have explained to them what went wrong, and they promised to never touch that button again. You're finished, right? Not quite.

The last step, and one that most people often forget, is to document the situation. What was the problem? How did you fix it? It may even be helpful to leave brief notes about what you tried that didn't work. The question is, where do you document all of this? It really depends on your work situation. Some companies require server and workstation maintenance logs. They are generally stored in an easily accessible area so the network administrators can find them in a hurry.

If you work for a company that has multiple administrators (or network troubleshooters), keeping notes on a fixed problem is critical. If the problem happens again, you don't want to be the person who spends three hours trying stuff that someone else already tried to no avail. Nor do you want to be the person who has to look at your coworker who just spent three hours doing what didn't work for you last time either. Common logs are a great way to keep track of issues and expedite troubleshooting.

If you are the only troubleshooter, or if it's otherwise possible, keep your own logbook of your activities, especially if you are new to troubleshooting. No one can possibly know or remember everything. The book can help your memory. Eventually, you may rely on it less and less, but when you need it, it's an invaluable tool.

No matter what your situation, the documentation rule is simple. Document what you do, and do what you document. It will save everyone time and headaches in the long run.

# Troubleshooting Printing

Printing is one of those areas that are most important to users of computer systems. Remember the promise of the "paperless office"? Anyone ever seen one? Printing is one of the highest causes of support calls, and it's one of the hardest areas in which to get good support. This area in particular is one in which you need to think simple. Don't forget to ask yourself the easy questions such as "Is it plugged in?" "Is it turned on?" and "Is the correct driver properly installed?" If they are answered up front, these three questions can save you a lot of time troubleshooting printing issues. Just remember to ask diplomatically when troubleshooting someone else's printing problem. No one likes to feel dumb.

Let's work through a scenario to get a feel for how to apply the methodology to printing issues in Windows XP Professional. Here is your trouble ticket:

| | |
|---|---|
| **User:** | Bob |
| **Telephone:** | 12345 |
| **Problem:** | Can't print |
| **Description:** | Nothing comes out when I try to print. |
| **Priority:** | URGENT! |

As you can see, your user Bob is having trouble trying to print a document and feels it is urgent that this be resolved quickly. The first step is to define the problem, so you contact Bob at his cubicle. Bob informs you that the job he is trying to print is a monthly profit-and-loss report for The Boss. Sounds pretty important, so you get right to work on the problem.

## Troubleshooting Scenario 1: Printer Is Unplugged

**Simple questions first.** Has it ever worked? Bob tells you that the printer worked fine the last time he tried to print, which was yesterday. What happened when he tried to print this time? He clicked Print in Word and got a message that the printer was offline or out of paper.

**Test the approach.** You look at the print device that is on Bob's desk, and you see that the lights are on. This indicates that the printer is plugged in and can access electricity. Next, you try toggling the online/offline switch and find that the print device is online. Still thinking simple, you next check the back of Bob's print device to make sure the parallel cable is firmly attached. It is. Bob's computer is a tower and is located under his desk. You crawl under the desk to check the parallel cable and find that it has fallen off the back of the computer. You reconnect the cable and try to print a test page. It works!

**Provide closure.** The closure comes with the determination that Bob may have accidentally kicked loose the cable when he stretched his feet out under his desk. One possible solution to avoid this is to be sure that the retaining clips of the parallel cable are correctly fastened on the computer's parallel port. Providing an explanation of the cause along with a solution gives the customer some closure on the issue.

This sounds ridiculously easy, right? You might be surprised to find out that this ticket, or a slight variation thereof, is a very common answer for help desks. Don't forget to document!

## Troubleshooting Scenario 2: Nothing in the Print Queue Will Print

**Explore the boundaries.** When you contact Bob regarding his printing issue, he tells you that he has been trying to print for the last two hours but nothing is coming out of the printer. Bob tells you that there were no messages when he tried to print other than the pop-up message that the job was successfully printed. Windows XP Professional is accepting the print jobs when he submits them, but nothing is coming out.

**Ask the simple questions.** You investigate the simple issues first. The print device is connected and plugged in. It does display indicator lights, so you know that it is turned on and getting power. The cables are connected. Bob tells you that it printed fine yesterday, but it hasn't printed at all this morning. He insists that nothing has been changed on his computer, no software added, no hardware changed.

**Track the possible approaches.**　You decide that some of the possibilities are that he might be printing to a different printer and doesn't realize it or that something is wrong with the print queue.

**Test the approaches.**　You check the Printers and Faxes folder on Bob's computer and verify the setting for his locally attached printer. Next, you verify that this printer is set as the default and that he has not redirected the output to another network printer. Opening the printer icon, you discover a long list of jobs that Bob submitted earlier today. Every job he has tried to print is listed, and the job on top of the list is a report from Excel.

You try checking to make sure that the printer has not been paused. Everything looks fine, but no print jobs will process. You determine that the queue itself has become either corrupted or jammed.

**Repair the problem.**　After closing the Printers and Faxes folder, you open the Administrative Tools folder and double-click the Services icon. You scroll down the list to find the Print Spooler service and highlight it. You stop the service, wait a few seconds, and then start it again.

**TIP**　When the Print Spooler service becomes corrupt, or a job gets jammed in the queue, stopping and restarting the service may be enough to resolve the issue with no further effort.

After restarting the Print Spooler service, you examine the queue and find that the jobs are unchanged. At this point, the most likely cause is a corrupted document stuck at the top of the queue. Make a note as to the document size and timestamp. Stop the Print Spooler again, and then open Explorer.

Using Explorer, open the WINNT folder and find the system32\Spool\Printers folder. Find the files with the approximate timestamp of the print job that was stuck at the top of the queue. There will be two files, one with the extension .spl, the other with the extension .shd. If you have trouble deleting the SPL file, you may still be able to fix the problem by renaming the SHD file and restarting the Print Spooler service.

**NOTE**　Windows XP Professional uses two files for each print job submitted. The first is the actual spool file (*.spl), which contains the formatted data to be printed. The second is the shadow file (*.shd), which is basically a transaction file for the print job.

After successfully deleting the two files, you restart the Print Spooler and immediately the print jobs begin to print.

**Provide closure.**　Talking with Bob, you describe the issue as a corrupted print job that acted like a cork in a bottle, plugging up the queue. This could have been caused by a problem with the printer settings, the queue itself being corrupt, or most likely the document being corrupt. In the last case, Bob could open the document in the original program and select Save As from the File menu to save a new copy of the document without the corruption. Once again, don't forget to document.

## Other Print Troubleshooting Steps

There are several standard troubleshooting steps that you can add to your support toolbox. We have already discussed one of the most important—asking simple questions. Believe it or not, verifying that the print device is plugged in and turned on can solve many problems. This is no reflection on either the intelligence of the user or their knowledge of computing. Some *very* experienced people have called support with printing issues that were solved by either plugging in the print device or turning it on. We've all done it at some time.

Assuming that the print device is plugged in and turned on and that you have verified the parallel cable as well, you need to test the print subsystem directly. To do so, follow these steps:

1. Choose Start ➤ Control Panel ➤ Printers and Faxes to open the Printers and Faxes folder (if you are using the Classic view of Control Panel, and as a system administrator or power user, you surely are).

2. Right-click the icon for your printer, and choose Properties from the shortcut menu to open the Properties dialog box for your printer.

3. In the General tab, click Print Test Page.

If you are troubleshooting a non-PostScript print device that has been redirected to LPT1, you can try the following command at a command prompt:

    Type dir > lpt1:

This copies the output of a dir command directly to the print device and bypasses the spooling provided by Windows XP Professional. If this fails or if the output is garbled, the issue may be a bad cable, faulty parallel port, or other hardware problem. If it works, you know the problem exists in Windows XP Professional or in the program.

**NOTE** Redirecting the output of a command to the port will not work if you are testing a PostScript device.

If any devices are connected to the computer's parallel port between the computer and the print device, you should remove them and try printing again. Windows XP Professional is often not very forgiving about sharing ports with multiple devices.

Try a generic driver for the print device. If you are using a PostScript device, try installing the Apple LaserWriter driver. This is a very basic PostScript driver. If it works, you have identified the problem as a bad *.ppd driver for the PostScript print device. If it is a non-PostScript device, try the Generic-Text Only driver.

**NOTE** PostScript printers don't really have a printer driver. Instead they use a PostScript Printer Description file (*.ppd), which is essentially a text file that describes how to send print jobs to the print device.

An issue that is often overlooked is the amount of space available for the spool file. Check to make sure that plenty of free space remains on the partition where Windows XP Professional is installed. If you run out of room for the spool file, one of two things will happen: Either the jobs won't print, giving you an error message about being out of memory; or the jobs will print, but the printing process will be incredibly slow. If you have multiple partitions on your hard drive, or multiple hard drives in your machine, you can move your print spooler to a location with more free space. To do this, open

CHAPTER 33

the Printers and Faxes window, and choose File ➤ Server Properties. In the Advanced tab, you will see a location for the spool folder. Type in an alternate folder location (on a different drive), and then click OK.

Another thing to try is printing from another operating system on the same computer if there is a dual-boot configuration. Or you could even try printing from the same application on a different computer.

One last possibility is that there is a problem with your document. It is possible that you will be able to print a less-complex document from the same application. If this is the case, the problem is probably within the application.

# Troubleshooting Windows XP Professional Setup

Many people encounter problems during the installation of Windows XP Professional, though most of the problems are minor and can be easily avoided. This section helps with troubleshooting the more difficult Setup issues.

In this section, we talk about troubleshooting Setup on the Intel and compatible platforms. The techniques work well for machines that are on the Hardware Compatibility List (HCL) and also for most machines that aren't on the list. Why would you want to install Windows XP Professional on a "noncompatible" system? Ever build your own computer? It wouldn't likely be on the HCL unless you want to pay Microsoft to test your computer and certify it for Windows XP Professional.

I've broken this section into parts that address problems you might encounter when planning for or during the text mode portion of Setup, during the transition to GUI mode, and during the final phase of rebooting.

## Planning and Text Mode Setup

If you can restrain yourself from simply tearing the shrink-wrap from the box and whipping the CD-ROM out to start Setup, you should think about some things before you begin. Does your computer meet or exceed all the requirements? You may want to take the time to consult Chapter 2 again for setup guidance and hardware requirements. Assuming that you have done this and your computer meets all the requirements, there are some additional points you will want to document before starting.

What cards are installed in your computer? Do you have a network card? A sound card? What about a 3D accelerator card? Do you have the settings for all these devices written down? Remember that Windows XP Professional is a Plug and Play operating system; it can find the settings for most of your hardware on its own, but you should still know what those settings are in case it can't find them. Do you have the latest, certified drivers for Windows XP Professional? Are the drivers on floppy disk or CD-ROM where you can get to them easily? Or are they on a network share? By the way, it won't do you any good to have your network card drivers out on a network server somewhere if you don't already have a functioning network card. Keep these handy on a floppy disk. Use Table 33.1 as a guide for the information you should have on hand prior to running Setup.

Now let's look at another troubleshooting scenario involving Setup issues. In this situation, imagine you are the person responsible for installing Windows XP Professional and for providing general technical support to a group of users.

**TABLE 33.1:** Useful Information for Setup

| DEVICE | INFORMATION TO GATHER |
| --- | --- |
| Video display | Adapter brand and model, chip set |
| Network adapter | IRQ, I/O address, DMA, transceiver type |
| SCSI adapter | Manufacturer and model, chip set, IRQ, bus type |
| Mouse (pointing device) | Manufacturer and model, bus type, port |
| I/O ports | Serial, parallel, IRQ, I/O addresses |
| Internal modem | Port, IRQ, I/O address |
| Sound card | Manufacturer and model (or compatible model), IRQ, I/O address, DMA |
| Other devices | Hardware resources, device type, drivers |

## Troubleshooting Scenario 3: Drives Not Found

You are responsible for installing Windows XP Professional on a computer for one of the users in your department. You insert the installation CD and begin Setup. When Setup reaches the point where it displays your current disk and partition information, Setup displays the following error message:

```
Setup did not find any hard drives on your computer.
```

You know there are two hard disk drives in this computer and you can hear them spinning, so you know that they are receiving power. The first step in your troubleshooting methodology is to explore the boundaries of the problem.

You open the case of the computer to find out exactly what kind of hard disk drives are installed (after turning off the power, of course). You find that the drives are SCSI-2 2.1GB and that they are attached to an Adaptec 2940 controller. No other SCSI devices are installed in this computer. When you investigate, you find that the computer had IDE drives and has recently been updated with a new SCSI controller and SCSI disks.

What you know and don't know at this point:

◆ The computer has never worked before in this configuration.

◆ The drives are SCSI, which require electronic termination and unique ID numbers on each bus.

◆ You do not know the state of the termination.

◆ You do not know the SCSI ID numbers for each drive.

Based on this information, you should already be suspecting that something is wrong with the hardware configuration. You reach into the case to ensure that the cables are tightly attached and find that they are. On these hard disks drives, the SCSI IDs are set by jumpers on the rear of the drive (you will probably have to remove the drives to get at them).

CHAPTER 33

Your plan of attack:

1. Verify the SCSI ID numbers of the drives and controller.

2. Verify the termination of the drive chain.

3. Check the BIOS settings of the controller.

Before you go through the work to remove the hard disk drives to check their ID numbers, you boot the computer to run the SCSI BIOS program. This program enables you to view and modify the configuration of the devices, as well as run diagnostics and other utilities. This utility tells you that it sees both hard disk drives, one as SCSI ID #0, the other as SCSI ID #1. This means the ID numbers are not the issue. SCSI ID #0 and #1 are usually reserved for hard drives.

**NOTE**   SCSI ID numbers are important. Having a conflict between two or more devices on the same SCSI bus can cause Setup to fail to recognize installed hard disk drives. It can also cause the system to fail when booting or to hang after booting.

The BIOS utility on the Adaptec controller also provides the capability to enable or disable termination on the controller card itself. You check and find that it is enabled correctly. Now you have verified the SCSI ID numbers, the controller settings, and half of the termination. The only thing left on your list is termination. To do this on older hardware, you have to pull out the last hard disk drive on the ribbon cable and check its termination. Newer drives are self-terminating, and normally the termination is on the ribbon cables.

Checking the last drive on the chain, you find that its terminator packs (resistors) are not set. This means that the SCSI bus is not terminated at one end. This may or may not be the problem, but it certainly needs to be fixed. You correct the termination and are ready to test the setup again. You start Setup, and this time everything runs fine.

Today, many SCSI drives are self-terminating, and you can also terminate on the ribbon cable instead of the drive. Today's SCSI is usually terminated on the SCSI controller and on the ribbon cable if building internal (to the PC) SCSI chains.

When you are troubleshooting problems on a SCSI-based system, always remember to check the termination. With SCSI, both ends of each drive chain must be terminated. Windows XP Professional is so sensitive about the stability of the hardware components that improper termination can be fatal to Setup. Even if you succeed with Setup, termination issues can result in hanging or even a blue-screen error. Even mismatched termination levels can cause this situation. If your controller has active termination and your hard disk has passive termination, you may have problems. Upgrading your SCSI chain to active termination or even forced-perfect termination at both ends can relieve the problem.

## SCSI Troubleshooting

In the previous scenario, we looked at the possible importance of SCSI termination. In my experience, nearly 90 percent of the troubleshooting issues of Windows XP Professional Setup on SCSI-based computers involve termination problems. But there are other issues to be aware of as well. For instance, is the BIOS of the SCSI controller activated? This is another problem that would cause the preceding scenario.

A low-level format that is incorrect for the current drive geometry could cause file corruption, drives not being recognized by Setup, and system crashes. If you are installing a new SCSI drive or changing to a new make or model of SCSI controller, you should perform a low-level format of the drive to assure that the drive geometry will line up correctly.

In simpler terms, the drive controller performs a format of the disks within the drive so that the operating system will be able to write data to the individual sectors on the drive. In a way, sectors are like tiny boxes that are meant to contain information. Imagine trying to drop golf balls into small boxes. If you are lining them up correctly, it's easy. The balls simply drop right into place every time. But imagine now that you're slightly off your aim. The balls usually go in the boxes, but sometimes they bounce off the edges and roll away. That's what's happening when your drive isn't low-level formatted correctly for the specific controller. Each SCSI controller has its own geometry, its way of laying out those little boxes.

If multiple SCSI controllers are in the computer, does more than one of them have an active BIOS? If so, they may be competing for Int13 calls. This means that the "wrong" controller may be trying to boot the computer and therefore prevents the "right" controller from doing its job.

It's common today for people to try to mix SCSI device types—that is, to add 50-pin SCSI-2 devices to the same chain as SCSI-3 devices with 68 pins. That means that the cable has to change sizes from 68 wires to 50 wires. If you mix these devices, be certain that you buy the proper cable to make the conversion. If you don't, or if you try to convert from 68 to 50 wires and then back to 68, you will have wires that are not being terminated correctly. It is better by far to have only "wide" devices with 68 pins on one chain and "narrow" devices with 50 pins on a separate chain.

One other major factor with SCSI disks involves the controller. If the SCSI controller to which your drives are attached is not on the Windows XP HCL, you could run into major problems during installation. It's difficult, if not impossible, to install any operating system on a drive it refuses to acknowledge. To work around this, Windows XP will prompt you to press the F6 key early in Setup (look at the messages at the bottom of the screen) to install third-party SCSI drivers. If you are having problems getting Setup to recognize your SCSI controller, pressing F6 and providing a driver is certainly worth a shot.

## Troubleshooting Text Mode to GUI Mode

The transition from the character-based portion of Setup to the graphical portion is the number one point where problems occur. This is a delicate time when Windows XP Professional (albeit a limited version of Windows XP Professional) is being booted for the first time. During this phase, Windows XP Professional is loading the kernel for the first time and initializing hardware and drivers. Some of the Setup specialists at Microsoft say that this is the toughest test of your computer hardware configuration that Windows XP Professional will ever make.

During this transition, Windows XP Professional is switching your CPU to a flat memory model and initiating multithreading. Windows XP Professional is also loading the hardware abstraction layer (HAL) at this time. If your computer requires a customized HAL, you may have severe problems here. Normally, it's only the top-of-the-line computer brands that take advantage of custom HALs. If you don't know, consult the manual for your system or contact the manufacturer.

This is the most likely point for blue screens, also called *Stop errors* because of the text at the top of the screen. Even though this may be the most likely point in which you'll encounter Stop errors, these errors can happen in other places, too. Because of their importance, I've set aside an entire section for Stop errors later in this chapter.

There is one critical error to talk about here:

```
Setup has encountered a fatal error that prevents it from continuing. Contact your
software representative for help. Status code (0x4, 0, 0, 0)
```

This error message is displayed on a blue screen but is not actually considered a blue screen because it does not display the typical Stop message. This indicates a problem with the Master Boot Record (MBR). Either the MBR has become corrupted or it's infected with a boot-sector virus. This usually happens only on dual-boot systems that use FAT as their primary boot partition, but it can also happen if you boot the computer with an infected floppy disk. Even though NTFS can become infected with viruses, NTFS is resistant to viruses in that Windows XP Professional doesn't allow any program to access the hardware directly. In theory, this should prevent any boot-sector virus.

Another possible MBR-related error message is this one:

```
Missing operating system. Insert a system diskette and restart the system.
```

It is possible to repair the MBR if you have a bootable floppy that you know is clean of any virus infection. (That's the hard part in getting rid of a virus.) An emergency boot disk from Windows 9x is especially helpful for this because you need fdisk.exe. After booting the infected computer with the boot floppy (you did write-protect the floppy, didn't you?), run mem.exe at the command prompt. The total bytes of memory (before anything is subtracted) should equal 640K. Next, run chkdsk.exe and look at the line for Total Bytes Memory (it's near the bottom), which should read 655,360. If either amount of memory is off, and especially if only *one* of them is off, you probably have a boot-sector virus loaded in memory. If both of these programs correctly report the amount of conventional memory, you can be reasonably certain that the virus is not in memory. If that's the case, you can type **FDISK/MBR** at the command prompt to rebuild the MBR. This command won't do anything else, provided the virus is not in memory. If the virus is in memory, this command may be fatal to your data.

**WARNING**    The FDISK/MBR command is dangerous and should never be used without being absolutely positive that the boot-sector virus is not loaded in memory. *The result could be total data loss.* Most boot-sector viruses work by moving the MBR elsewhere on the disk and then replacing it with their own code. Anything that tries to scan the MBR is first infected by the virus and then redirected out to the real MBR in its new location.

**NOTE**    It's interesting to note that the Master Boot Record is operating system–independent. It's quite possible to rebuild the MBR for a Windows XP Professional computer using an emergency boot disk from Windows 98.

### MISCELLANEOUS SETUP ISSUES

If your computer hangs during the final reboot of Windows XP Setup, try removing the CD-ROM from the drive. Windows XP Professional supports the "El Torito" standard of bootable CD-ROMs using the No Emulation mode. If the BIOS of your computer supports bootable CD-ROMs but not the No Emulation mode, your system may hang. It may also give this error message:

```
BOOT: Couldn't find NTLDR
Please insert another disk.
```

This is fixed the same way—just remove the CD-ROM from the drive and reboot the computer. Setup should continue normally after booting.

**NOTE**    If there are no CD-ROMs or floppy disks in your drives, and you are still getting the BOOT: Couldn't find NTLDR error message, you will need to boot to either a Windows XP boot disk or CD-ROM to continue. For more information on this, see the "Boot Process Troubleshooting" section later in this chapter.

**NOTE** *El Torito* is the official name for a bootable CD-ROM technology and is derived from the place of its creation—a restaurant where the engineers were having a few drinks.

### Addressing GUI Mode and Initial Boot Issues

During this phase of Setup, Windows XP Professional installs drivers and configures the system. Problems in this portion of Setup are typically fewer and generally related to configuration rather than failing hardware or drivers. This is also where Windows XP Professional will try to load the network for the first time in a full configuration.

It is possible to encounter video problems at this phase of Setup. On some computers the display will not reset correctly during a warm boot under Windows XP Professional. If this occurs, your display will be black or very distorted. Try turning off the power to the computer (yes, this is one of those rare cases where you power down without shutting down first) and then restarting it. If this resolves the issue, you will have to power down the computer every time you reboot. This is a hardware issue related to the video and system BIOS and not a Windows XP Professional problem. If you've tried this and the display is still distorted, you will need to boot Windows XP Professional with the VGA option and change your display properties (and possibly the driver) to one that does work with your hardware.

## Troubleshooting Stop Errors

As I mentioned earlier, Windows XP is an incredibly complex operating system. And with anything this complex, problems are bound to occasionally occur. The good news is that Windows XP is very stable. Problems are generally kept to a minimum, and the operating system itself should rarely crash. The bad news is, because of its stability, when a problem *is* serious enough to make it crash, Windows XP crashes hard.

Some people call Stop errors the "Blue Screen of Death," or BSOD, though you should be aware that there may be hundreds of possible blue-screen errors in Windows XP Professional. None of us will likely ever see them all; at least we can hope that we never see them all.

When you first see a Stop error, you may be overwhelmed with the information in front of you. Most of the time, the ominous blue background is a placemat for a horde of binary and hexadecimal information that is indecipherable to mere mortals. This information is provided for developers and debuggers. The first thing you want to look for is near the top of the message: the word STOP followed by a message. Depending on the Stop error, you may also find the name of the offending driver or application on the screen as well.

Stop errors can occur at almost any stage of Windows XP installation or operation. The errors can be broken into three categories, based on when they occur:

**During Windows XP installation**   If a Stop error happens here, it may indicate a BIOS incompatibility issue, failing hardware, or a faulty device driver. Make sure that all of your hardware is on the HCL.

**During Windows XP startup**   If Windows XP has been installed and working for some time, but an error occurs during startup, it could mean a couple of things. Generally, the culprit is a device driver or system service. If you just installed a new service, application, or driver and you get a BSOD upon reboot, the new software could be your problem.

**During Windows XP operation**   This is the most ambiguous time an error can happen. The error could be practically anything. A Stop error during operation can be caused by failing hardware (particularly memory and processor), system services, device drivers, and applications. The text of the Stop message will give you valuable information as to the cause of the problem.

## Common Stop Errors

The title of this section, "Common Stop Errors," does not mean to imply in any way that Stop errors are common. In fact, it's quite the opposite. However, if you are one of the unlucky souls to encounter a Stop error, these are some of the more common ones that appear. They are listed in hexadecimal order for convenience.

```
STOP: 0x0000000A
IRQL_NOT_LESS_OR_EQUAL
```

This Stop message can appear at almost any time. Most of the time, this error points to a problem device driver, service, or application. On the Stop screen, it will usually tell you the name of the offending driver, service, or application. Be sure to write down the name of the offender, because this can be invaluable for troubleshooting.

```
STOP: 0x0000001E
KMODE_EXCEPTION_NOT_HANDLED
```

This Stop message occurs when the processor receives an instruction that it doesn't understand. Many times this is caused by invalid memory access violations. This Stop error often lists the name of the offending device driver.

```
STOP: 0x00000023
FAT32_FILE_SYSTEM
```

A problem has occurred with the FAT32 file system driver. This could indicate a hard disk connectivity problem or a hard disk failure.

```
STOP: 0x00000024
NTFS_FILE_SYSTEM
```

This is the same as the 0x23 error, except it's for the NTFS file system.

```
STOP: 0x0000002E
DATA_BUS_ERROR
```

This is most often caused by failing physical memory (including video memory) but could also indicate a physical problem with the motherboard.

```
STOP: 0x00000077
KERNEL_STACK_INPAGE_ERROR
```

If Windows XP tries to read information from the page file and does not locate the information it expects, you will receive this error message. Failing physical memory, failing hard disks, corrupted data, and viruses can cause this error message. A very similar error message is the STOP: 0x7A KERNEL_DATA_INPAGE_ERROR message.

```
STOP: 0x0000007B
INACCESSIBLE_BOOT_DEVICE
```

This error almost speaks common English. Your computer can't find the boot device. Check your physical connections. This could also indicate a failing hard disk or disk controller.

One of the most interesting causes of the STOP: 0x7B message is adding an IDE drive to a SCSI-based system. IDE controllers are enumerated before the SCSI controllers, meaning that the BIOS of the computer looks for them first. If you add an IDE drive to a computer that is already working fine with SCSI hard disks, you may very well see this blue screen. That situation can be fixed in the computer's BIOS. If your BIOS supports the option, set the boot order to go to the SCSI drives first and then to the IDE.

```
STOP: 0x0000007F
UNEXPECTED_KERNEL_MODE_TRAP
```

Hardware failure generally causes this error message. If you are running an over-clocked processor, you can expect to see this Stop error at some point.

```
STOP: 0x000000D1
DRIVER_IRQL_NOT_LESS_OR_EQUAL
```

This cryptic message is actually one of the more common Stop errors. It happens when a device driver tries to access a memory address that it's not supposed to. Poorly written drivers are generally the culprit, although software applications (particularly antivirus programs or backup programs) can cause this error as well.

```
STOP: 0x000000D8
DRIVER_USED_EXCESSIVE_PTES
```

Once again, this is caused by a faulty driver. We can gather that from the error message, even if we have no idea what a PTE is. PTEs are page table entries, which Windows XP uses to keep track of memory information. Poorly written or corrupt drivers can cause this error. Another related error is STOP: 0x3F NO_MORE_SYSTEM_PTES.

```
STOP: 0xC000021A
STATUS_SYSTEM_PROCESS_TERMINATED
```

This error message usually indicates that a Windows XP user-mode subsystem has been compromised in some way. This is a serious problem. You may also see this error message if a backup has been only partially restored or if permissions have been modified so that the System account no longer has access to required system files and folders.

```
STOP 0xC0000221
STATUS_IMAGE_CHECKSUM_MISMATCH
```

This error message usually points to a corrupted file or hard disk. You will usually see the name of the offending file on this blue screen.

This list is by no means intended to be complete. It's here to give you a general idea of what types of problems may cause your Windows XP machine to blue screen. As you can see, most Stop errors are caused by failing hardware, device drivers, services, or applications. If you encounter an error message not listed, or just want more information on blue screens, you can go to Microsoft's support site at www.microsoft.com/support and search for your specific error message.

One more thing to mention about blue screens applies more to upgrading Windows XP Professional from an earlier version than to a fresh installation. During an upgrade, Setup will notify you with a blue-screen error that you must remove an application before you can continue. As soon as the application is removed, Setup will proceed normally.

CHAPTER 33

## Responding to Stop Errors

You can configure Windows XP Professional to respond in a variety of ways once it encounters a Stop error. To do this, you need to go to System Properties (either open the System icon in Control Panel or right-click the My Computer icon in your Start menu and choose Properties). Then in the Advanced tab, choose Startup and Recovery ➤Settings. You should see a screen similar to Figure 33.1.

**FIGURE 33.1**

Customizing Stop error response

In Figure 33.1, take a look at the System Failure section. In the event of a system failure, you can configure Windows XP to do any of the following three tasks: Write an Event to the System Log, Send an Administrative Alert, and Automatically Restart.

Writing an event to the System log will create an event for you to look at in Event Viewer, System log. While this event may not tell you everything you want to know, it will list the Stop error code so you have a point from which to start troubleshooting. Sending an administrative alert will do just that: send a pop-up alert to the administrator account. Automatically restarting is self-evident. If you do not choose this option, you will have to restart your computer manually after a Stop error occurs.

**TIP**  If you choose to have your system automatically restart, make sure to have Windows XP log an event in the System log as well. Otherwise, you may never know what went wrong, other than the fact that your computer just rebooted itself.

Within the System Failure section, you also have the opportunity to customize the debugging information Windows XP writes when a Stop error happens. The debugging information is basically the contents of physical memory when the system crashed. Although the information may not be incredibly relevant for most of us, it can be useful to programmers or to the technicians at Microsoft's help desk.

## Fixing Stop Errors

Fixing a Stop error is no different than troubleshooting any other problem with your computer. First and foremost, don't forget about your list of good troubleshooting procedures: define the problem, explore the boundaries, brainstorm, test your ideas, repair the problem, provide closure, clean up after yourself, and document the situation. Here are some general guidelines for fixing Stop errors:

◆ After you write down the message, reboot your computer. If the error doesn't come back, it's not a problem. This may sound cynical, but it's true. Sometimes the computer will "hiccup" and produce an error. Things happen. If the error keeps happening, then you have a problem.

◆ Suspect recent changes. If you just added hardware (including drivers) or software, it could be causing the problem. Try removing the hardware or application or trying an alternate device driver.

◆ Check your system BIOS. Sometimes incorrect BIOS settings, especially with an ACPI-compliant BIOS, can cause blue screens. If possible, reset the settings to BIOS defaults.

◆ Search Microsoft's Knowledge Base. This site often has specific fixes for the problem you've just encountered. Remember, good troubleshooters don't necessarily know everything. They just know where to look to find answers.

Most of the time you can find a fix for your Stop error. The fix may be replacing hardware or installing different drivers or software. In more extreme cases, you may need to restore from a backup. In a worst-case scenario, you can always reinstall the operating system.

# Boot Process Troubleshooting

The boot process is a common area where things can go wrong on your computer. There is a list of specific files that must be in a certain location on your hard disk and loaded in a certain order. If any of these files are missing or corrupt, your Windows XP machine will not boot.

Your system partition (generally your C drive) contains three required files and two optional files for booting Windows XP. The required files are `ntldr`, `boot.ini`, and `ntdetect.com`. The optional files are `ntbootdd.sys` and `bootsect.dos`.

Here's a quick overview of the boot process. After the BIOS has completed its check, it looks for the `ntldr` file on your system partition. `Ntldr` loads the `boot.ini` file, which has two responsibilities: to point to the location on your hard disk(s) where your operating system files are located and to provide you with a boot menu if you have multiple operating systems installed (or, in other words, you are dual-booting). If you boot into Windows XP, the `ntdetect.com` file performs a hardware detection and hands over to a file called `ntoskrnl.exe`, which is the executable to officially load Windows XP.

Let's say you are dual-booting Windows XP Professional and Windows 98. If you choose to load Windows 98 from your boot menu, the `bootsect.dos` file takes over instead of the `ntdetect.com` file. If the ARC paths in your `boot.ini` file use the SCSI option, you will need the `ntbootdd.sys` file. (Look in your `boot.ini`, and if you see the word SCSI followed by a bracketed number, you need the `ntbootdd.sys` file.)

If you receive an error message about any of these boot files, or a missing or corrupt `ntoskrnl.exe` file, there are two good ways to proceed. One is to boot to the Windows XP CD, which will start the Setup program. When prompted, press R to begin the Recovery Console. Details on how to use the Recovery Console are located in Chapter 24.

The second method is to create a Windows XP boot disk. To do this, format a floppy disk in Windows XP, and then copy the `ntldr`, `boot.ini`, and `ntdetect.com` files to it (and the `bootsect.dos` and `ntbootdd.sys` files if you need them). This disk is quite useful if you don't have your Windows XP

CHAPTER 33

Professional CD nearby. It doesn't start a fancy troubleshooting process like the Recovery Console, but it may get your computer up and running if one of your boot files is missing or corrupt.

The key to boot-process troubleshooting is to figure out how far the boot process gets and then determine what you need to do to get your computer booted the rest of the way. In other words, if the ntldr file is working but it's the boot.ini causing the problem, how do you fix it? Just like troubleshooting anything else, narrow down the possibilities until you isolate the problem. Once the problem is isolated, it's a great deal easier to fix.

## Summary

No matter what your interest is in Windows XP Professional, there will be times when understanding the process of troubleshooting will be helpful to you. Even if troubleshooting is never going to be part of your responsibility, things may go wrong. If you have even a basic understanding of the process, you will convey much more meaningful information to the person who *is* responsible for the troubleshooting.

Use the methods listed in this chapter when troubleshooting your own computer. Follow the guidelines for documenting the steps taken and the possible approaches to use. Always remember to think simple at first, and then move on to the more exotic as you eliminate basic possibilities.

# Index

**Note to the Reader:** Throughout this index **boldfaced** page numbers indicate primary discussions of a topic. *Italicized* page numbers indicate illustrations.

# Master These Fundamentals